The Challenge of Community Mental Health and Erich Lindemann

These volumes make new contributions to the history of psychiatry and society in three ways. First, they propose a theory of values and ideology influencing the evolution of psychiatry and society in recurring cycles and survey the history of psychiatry in recent centuries in light of this theory. Second, they review the waxing, prominence, and waning of community mental health as an example of a segment of this cyclical history of psychiatry. Third, they provide the first biography of Erich Lindemann, one of the founders of social and community psychiatry, and explore the interaction of the prominent contributor with the historical environment and the influence this has on both. We return to the issue of values and ideologies as influences on psychiatry, whether or not it is accepted as professionally proper. This is intended to stimulate self-reflection and the acceptance of the values sources of ideology, their effect on professional practice, and the effect of values-based ideology on the community in which psychiatry practices. The books will be of interest to psychiatric teachers and practitioners, health planners, and socially responsible citizens.

David G. Satin is a board-certified psychiatrist who has trained at the Massachusetts General and McLean Hospitals; has been an assistant professor of psychiatry at Harvard Medical School, where he also obtained his MD and taught gerontology and the history of psychiatry; and has had a clinical practice in adult and geriatric psychiatry.

The Challenge of Community Mental Health and Erich Lindemann

Community Mental Health, Erich Lindemann, and Social Conscience in American Psychiatry, Volume 2

David G. Satin

Routledge
Taylor & Francis Group

NEW YORK AND LONDON

First published 2021
by Routledge
52 Vanderbilt Avenue, New York, NY 10017

and by Routledge
2 Park Square, Milton Park, Abingdon, Oxon, OX14 4RN

Routledge is an imprint of the Taylor & Francis Group, an informa business

Library of Congress Cataloging-in-Publication Data
Names: Satin, David G., author.
Title: Community mental health, Erich Lindemann, and social
    conscience in American psychiatry / David G. Satin.
Description: New York, NY : Routledge, 2021. | Includes
    bibliographical references and indexes.
Identifiers: LCCN 2020026022 (print) | LCCN 2020026023 (ebook) |
    ISBN 9780429331350 (v. 1 ; ebook) | ISBN 9781000169805
    (v. 1 ; adobe pdf) | ISBN 9781000169812 (v. 1 ; mobi) | ISBN
    9781000169829 (v. 1 ; epub) | ISBN 9780429331374 (v. 2 ; ebook) |
    ISBN 9781000169867 (v. 2 ; adobe pdf) | ISBN 9781000169881
    (v. 2 ; mobi) | ISBN 9781000169904 (v. 2 ; epub) | ISBN
    9780429331367 (v. 3 ; ebook) | ISBN 9781000171280 (v. 3 ;
    adobe pdf) | ISBN 9781000171273 (v. 3 ; mobi) | ISBN
    9781000171297 (v. 3 ; epub) | ISBN 9780367354336 (v. 1 ;
    hardcover) | ISBN 9780367354374 (v. 2 ; hardcover) | ISBN
    9780367354350 (v. 3 ; hardcover)
Subjects: LCSH: Social psychiatry. | Community psychiatry. | Mental
    health services.
Classification: LCC RC455 (ebook) | LCC RC455 .S197 2021 (print) |
    DDC 362.2—dc23
LC record available at https://lccn.loc.gov/2020026022

ISBN: 978-0-367-35437-4 (hbk)
ISBN: 978-0-429-33137-4 (ebk)

Typeset in Sabon
by Apex CoVantage, LLC

This history is dedicated to those who created it: the people who raised and struggled with issues of social influences on mental health, the place of social responsibility in mental health professional practice, and the social conscience of society. Committed and thoughtful people took different approaches to these questions but confronted them seriously. Sometimes this brought fulfillment, sometimes despair. Often it took courage; sometimes this resulted in professional and personal injury. Such is the fate of committed people in the historical clash of values. This record and its interpretation are especially dedicated to those who unearthed for the record their experiences, memories, and insights—sometimes with pain—to teach their successors about this endeavor. We trust it has been worth their efforts:

"All of us bear witness to the dissolution of our piece of creation. Only the novelist can restore to us, in the miracle of ink that pours itself like blood onto paper, the lineaments of our lost worlds, alive."[1]

Figure 0.1 Frontispiece: Erich Lindemann lecturing, Suicide Prevention Center, 1963.
Source: [Courtesy Lindemann Estate]

Contents

Figures

Preface for All Three Volumes

One of the pitfalls of the celebration of history is presentism: the self-centered belief that current values and perspectives are the only or highest in history. As Oliver Wendell Holmes tartly observed, "Much, therefore, which is now very commonly considered to be the result of experience, will be recognized in the next, or in some succeeding generation, as no such result at all, but as a foregone conclusion, based on some prevalent belief or fashion of the time."[2] And, further, that perspectives change: "One has to remember there's a kind of cyclical rhythm in American public affairs, cycles of intense activism succeeded by a time of exhaustion and acquiescence".[3]

The era of fullest flowering of Community Mental Health is, importantly, a lesson in social change, and social change is painful:

> The painfulness of new ideas and our habitual resistance to them can also be seen in this context. The more far-reaching a new idea the more disorganization of existing theoretical systems has to be tolerated before a new and better synthesis of old and new can be achieved.[4]

Those who work for change face struggle and discouragement:

> Let us, then, be up and doing,
> With a heart for any fate;
> Still achieving, still pursuing,
> Learn to labor and to wait.[5]

Ideals need to be transformed into performance: "La Théorie c'est bon mais ça n'empêche pas d'exister". [Theory is nice, but it does not take the place of reality.]"[6]

And the champion of change may struggle with feelings of overwhelming rejection:

> Ja, was man so erkennen heisst!
> Wer darf das Kind beim rechten Namen nennen?
> Die wenigen, die was davon erkannt,

Die töricht gnug ihr volles Herz nicht wahrten,
Dem Pöbel ihr gefühl, ihr Shauen offenbarten,
hat man von je gekreuzigt und verbrannt.[7]
[Yes, the things people claim to know!
Who dares call the child by its true name?
The few who know something about it,
And foolishly do not guard their overflowing hearts,
But open their feelings, their responses to the mob,
Have always been crucified and burned.]

Social history has a tradition of tracing historical movements through outstanding figures, the individuals exemplifying as much as determining the movements.[8] "Psychohistory" goes further, seeking to understand group movements as the cumulative effect of the psychodynamics of individuals: "Methodological individualism is the principle that group processes may be entirely explained by . . . psychological laws governing the motivations and behavior of individuals".[9] Erich Lindemann's life—1900 to 1974—was contemporaneous with the origins of and developments in the community mental health (CMH) movement. He was involved in many important CMH activities and with important participants, and he contributed to and influenced CMH in important ways, both as a leader of its admirers and as a target of its critics. His personal development, the social movements and academic developments around him, the education to which he was exposed and which he chose, the sequence of his professional development, and the responses—positive and negative—that he received, paralleled at least the health promotion and illness prevention branch of CMH. We see in his person the development of the values and ideology that were mirrored in that branch and its conflict with other psychiatric ideologies. For these reasons, he is a useful microcosm of the history of CMH. In addition, there has never been a comprehensive biography of this important contributor to CMH and psychiatry, such that people develop their opinions of him based on only reports or fragments of his thinking and activities. A more complete understanding of the man will make him and his place in psychiatry more comprehensible.

Most emphatically, this is not a work of hagiography. We subscribe to Iago Galdston's dual cautions:[10]

> Medical history as it has been written during the past 100 years manifestly suffers from two corrupting biases, *progressivism* and *hero worship*. Medical history is represented as a pageant of progressive enlightenment, celebrating the labors and achievements of its medical heroes.

On the contrary, we take the social history stance of seeing people and events as the manifestations of social conditions and forces from which they arise. In this sense, Lindemann was molded by the values and ideas of the personal and public times through which he lived and contributed his values and ideas to the ideologies and movements in which he participated. Here we seek to understand the interaction of the man and the social (and mental health) environment. We try to understand the special contributions of these ideologies and ideas, resisting the temptation to see some as more ideal than others, heeding Sigerest's admonition: "Nothing could be more foolish in comparing ancient theories with ours than to call progressive what corresponds to our views, and primitive what is different".[11]

This book contributes to the understanding of the roots, germination, flowering, response, overthrow, and successors of CMH. Norman Bell had proposed a similar study of the origins of social psychiatry:[12]

> It is characteristic of the United States as a nation that it pays little attention to its past. Our eyes are usually on the future. . . . This is particularly true of psychiatry and of the social sciences. Only major figures are preserved in the memories of the present generation and even these memories tend to fade. . . . In the field of social psychiatry, this fall-out of information works a special hardship. Although the term "social psychiatry" has been in use for half a century, it is treated as if it were a recent development. Insights which were gained decades ago are repeatedly discovered anew. The long history of engagement, uneasy marriage, annulment or divorce and remarriage between psychiatry and social science is unknown or disregarded. Thus, the lessons which the past has to offer are not available to the present generation. . . . In the last ten years the phrase, social psychiatry, has been institutionalized in the titles of journals, professorships and institutes. There is little current disagreement that social factors are involved in the etiology, treatment and effects of mental illness. . . . The investigators believe that the field of social psychiatry has reached the stage of maturity where it can and should examine its origins and assess its present standing.

That the neglect of important aspects of the past continues to be true of CMH at present is attested to by a comment of a reviewer who persisted in rejecting this study for publication to correct that neglect:[13]

2. Is the article/book/monograph a significant contribution to knowledge?
A. What is its relation to other works in the field? Does it offer new concepts?

> I'm not actually sure how much of a field there is, since I'm unaware that there is much current writing about topics such as prevention and social psychiatry. The basic concepts it explores are old but by

no means irrelevant. The field of mental health prevention essentially has been abandoned over the past 25 years.

People often speak of organizations or institutions as influencing or leading society. While society is heterogeneous and there is ongoing dissonance and rivalry for influence among the subcultures and ideologies, they are all substantially creatures of the society in which they developed. As such, they reflect the manifold needs and values of the host society, rather than being external influences on it. The life cycle of the CMH movement illustrates the contest of values in psychiatry, and we argue that this reflects the contest of values in the society. Thus, this exploration of the CMH movement contributes to an understanding of the shifting of societal values and ideologies during that era.

A "movement" is defined as "a series of actions and events taking place over a period of time and working to foster a principle or policy . . . an organized effort by supporters of a common goal".[14] Few movements are so homogeneous that all actions are focused toward a single goal. Usually there are shifting and evolving ideas among people who have varying intensity, duration, and motivations for participation. It is after the fact—in historical perspective—that the commonality of ideas and character of results become apparent.

From this, a movement is an accumulation of activities, people, concepts, and, above all, intentions. These intentions are the action implications of the ideologies and ideas through which participants understand the participants and goals of the movement. Further, ideas and ideologies are related to values—beliefs and feelings of esteem, worth, and priority that weight these ideas and ideologies. Thus, it follows that the values that shape the ideas and ideologies that, in turn, form the intentions of those participating in a movement all, in some sense, become embodied in the actions and programs that result from that movement. In other words, movements, even those believed to be "objective" and "scientific", are not independent of the ideas, values, and ideologies of those who participate in them. As Oliver Wendell Holmes the elder recognized,[15]

> The truth is, that medicine, professedly founded on observation, is as sensitive to outside influences, political, religious, philosophical, imaginative, as is the barometer to the changes of atmospheric density. Theoretically it ought to go on its own straightforward inductive path, without regard to changes of government or to fluctuations of public opinion. But look a moment . . . and see . . . a closer relation between the Medical Sciences and the condition of Society and the general thought of the time, than would at first be suspected. Observe the coincidences between certain great political and intellectual periods and the appearance of illustrious medical reformers and teachers.

Murray Levine and Adeline Levine applied much the same observations to more-recent mental health theory and practice:[16]

> As social scientists, and as practitioners in the mental health field, we pride ourselves on our objectivity, and upon the empirical base of our theories, our generalizations, and our practices. Let me suggest, on the contrary, that we are all creatures of our times; that our theories and practices are shaped as much, or more, by broad social forces as they are by inference from hard data . . . the set of variables which have been included in the theories is too limited. . . . The forms of practice are said to be determined by whatever conceptions of personality and of psychopathology are dominant . . . vital details of practice in the mental health fields are determined by potent social forces which are reflected in the organization and delivery of services, in the forms of service which are delivered, and in conceptions of the nature of the mental health problem.

The relationship between ideology and values applies also to psychiatry. In Erich Lindemann's talk at Stanford Medical Center, he hearkened back to the sociology and psychology of psychiatry:

> Karl Mannheim, in the sociology of knowledge, began to talk about ideologies. He pointed out that theories represent values which for some reason are important to an individual, and for which he feels he must fight. And about ten years ago, Melvin Sabshin together with Anselm Strauss came around to the notion that most of the convictions in psychiatry are really ideologies for which you fight; and that some of the information which you gather is collected . . . because they want to get to a particular goal.[17]

These issues certainly apply to the community mental health movement. The overriding commonality is attending to populations of functionally interrelated people ("community") in addition to individuals, problems, or techniques. There have been many studies of this movement focusing on chronology of events, personages, politics, economics, and technical theories.[18] The present history is unique in its focus on the ideas and ideologies that participants brought to the movement, that motivated their participation, that they understood CMH through, and that became actualized in their plans and actions.

The CMH movement embodied several ideologies reflected in their respective definitions of CMH. One was making traditional psychiatric treatment available to a larger population. A second was developing new strategies and facilities for the treatment of mental illnesses and for bringing these treatments to mentally ill populations, with special emphasis on the severely and chronically mentally ill. A third was an interest in the prevention of mental illness; a professional role in "mental health" and human fulfillment; and often the association of these with a democratic, participatory approach to caregiving and care programs in the context of cultural settings. And a fourth was the shift of attention and effort to change and improve society as the source of mental illness and mental health. These all imply values that contended with one another in professional technical debate, in competition for material resources and programmatic control, and in battles for public and official recognition. These considerations will lead us to a consideration of the social values implied in the various psychiatric ideologies—biological, psychological, and social—and the mental health goals and programs that are the consequences of these values.

Three overarching issues are highlighted by this study and will be followed throughout:

1. Cycles of psychiatric ideology repeat through history, contrasting and contesting with one another. Biological, psychological, and social perspectives and priorities predominate sequentially. CMH represents a social psychiatry phase.[19]
2. These ideologies reflect differing societal values, which, in turn, appear in their theories and are essential constituents of their goals and programs. The interrelationship of societal values, psychiatric ideology and movements, and Lindemann's professional and personal life are mutually illuminating.
3. Any new ideology confronts attitudes toward change vs. those toward conservation. These can be expressed through growth vs. tradition or, more aggressively, overthrow vs. suppression. The character and strategy of change affects its reception by the host system. In addition, the character of leadership reflects and colors the program led and the reaction of its environment. This leadership may be nurturing and convincing or threatening and attacking, and it may take the role of the guru or the wielder of power.

Resources on which this study is based include the following: The author has the advantage of having participated in and observed firsthand some of these events and people and thus has a technical and personal understanding of them. Important literature on social and psychiatric ideologies have been reviewed as the lens through which to understand the CMH movement. We explored the social and psychiatric climate and movements just before the movement (the late 19th and early 20th centuries), during the movement (roughly the middle third of the 20th century), and just after the CMH movement (the late 20th century). We have reviewed other studies of CMH. Primary sources[20] include 105 interviews (by the author or others) of people who have worked in CMH and psychiatry, in the United States and Germany (Erich Lindemann's country of origin), participants in CMH programs, and authorities in contemporary psychiatry and society. We used interviews of Lindemann himself, members of his family, and those who knew him. We also reviewed all of Erich Lindemann's papers and selected documents from other CMH programs and institutions. The author is solely responsible for the selection of materials and for the interpretations and conclusions drawn from them.

CMH touched on major social issues, such as the causes and cures of mental and social pathology, the responsibilities of private agencies and government in dealing with these problems, and priorities in the allocation of social resources—"what we can afford". It also raised considerations of professionalism: identity, scope of practice, financial support, power, and interrelationships—all sensitive issues. Therefore, it caused much debate and not a little hostility and conflict. We expect that revisiting events, persons, issues, and interpretations in this book will stimulate reaction. We hope for debate and the surfacing of further information. We expect also the resumption of old hurts and prejudices: In the past, people accepted only information and interpretations that validated their prejudices about community mental health. For example, Dr. Lindemann's professional files were relegated to a flooded basement in an outhouse of the Massachusetts General Hospital, and successors in the Department of Psychiatry resisted releasing them to safety and study because of their resentment of Lindemann and rejection of the legitimacy of CMH.[21] We intend light and expect heat from this endeavor.

Historical writing can be memoir, advocacy, or observation without conclusion. Memoir offers the most authentic anecdotes. Advocacy is always present, whether overt, covert, or unconscious. Observation without conclusions has limited usefulness. This study brings some information not heretofore published. It is a further attempt at assembling it in a coherent narrative regarding ideas and ideologies—a perspective not previously attempted. It suggests patterns and draws conclusions about values, motivations, and their effects. It is in this manner that this study contributes to a new, useful perspective on CMH, with implications for the history of its social context. We offer it as a further product of the community mental health movement.

In sum, this work offers the following:

- a theory of values and their elaboration to ideologies as motivators of history with historical documentation
- this theory, demonstrated in the historical cycle of ideologies in society, medicine, and psychiatry
- a history of the CMH movement and its historical context as one manifestation of social ideology
- a biography of Erich Lindemann as an outstanding figure in social and community psychiatry
- Lindemann and CMH as examples of the interaction of personality and historical context.

This work is presented in three volumes:

The Sources and Development of Social and Community Psychiatry: Community Mental Health, Erich Lindemann, and Social Conscience in American Psychiatry, Volume 1

The Challenge of Community Mental Health and Erich Lindemann: Community Mental Health, Erich Lindemann, and Social Conscience in American Psychiatry, Volume 2

The Eclipse of Community Mental Health and Erich Lindeman: Community Mental Health, Erich Lindemann, and Social Conscience in American Psychiatry, Volume 3

Acknowledgments for All Three Volumes

Elizabeth Brainerd Lindemann contributed invaluable acute observations about Erich Lindemann and his activities and associates and facilitated in granting access to other valuable sources. However, she maintained a realistic perspective, balancing keeping faith with Lindemann and his works with having this history honest, even-handed, and constructive. She also lent the gentle impetus to bring to fruition the review of community mental health that Dr. Lindemann could not bring himself to complete.

Special appreciation is due to Richard J. Wolfe, former Joseph Garland librarian at the Boston Medical Library and Rare Books librarian at the Francis A. Countway Library of Medicine, Harvard Medical School. His idea of archiving was to support all areas of scholarship and researchers, and in this service, he was most generous with advice, space, resources, and encouragement. His mentorship helped turn an idea into a completed work. The resources and support that he offered were sorely missed after his departure.

The late Francis O. Schmitt, PhD, chairperson of the Department of Biology and institute professor at the Massachusetts Institute of Technology, chairperson of the Neurosciences Research Program, and trustee and chairperson of the Committee on Research of the Massachusetts General Hospital, was crucial in obtaining Erich Lindemann's papers and transferring them to the Countway Library of Medicine for safekeeping and study.

Appreciation is due the 105 people interviewed for their insights into community mental health (CMH), Erich Lindemann, the development of psychiatry, and the influence of contemporary society. They made themselves available and took time to discuss their experiences and ideas. These often rearoused difficult and sometimes painful memories. We are grateful for their honesty and unique contributions.

The American Philosophical Society provided financial support via Grant No. 8224 from the Penrose Fund. Its interest in this exploration extended to the publication of a preliminary monograph, which helped structure this research. Similarly, the *Deutscher Akademischer Austausch-dienst* (German Academic Exchange Service) awarded Grant Program Area II No. 315 to support a study trip through the Federal Republic of Germany. This allowed both exploration of community mental health and the social psychiatry tradition in Germany, as well as Dr. Lindemann's learning and teaching there at various times in his career.

The National Library of Medicine, through Publication Grant Award No. 42 USC 280–9 42 CFR 52, provided limited financial support for a period during the collection and organization of interviews and records, though it denied extension of funding with the prediction that the book would not be completed—now happily disproved.

The following photographs are included with permission:

> Photographs from the Lindemann family and Erich Lindemann papers retained by the Lindemann family are included with the permission of Brenda Lindemann, family executrix.
> Photographs by David G. Satin are included with his permission.

The author has the advantage of having lived through the latter part of the CMH movement, participated in and observed firsthand some of these events, and met some of those involved. He interviewed many principal contributors to CMH, those who knew Erich Lindemann, and participants in parallel programs. He also consulted others with experience of CMH and contemporary psychiatry and society and consulted written reports and reviews. He is solely responsible for the selection of materials to be included, their interpretation, and the conclusions drawn.

The Psychiatry Service of the Massachusetts General Hospital, which Lindemann had led, was not interested in or supportive of this review of his work and person. A successor chief of the service, Thomas Hackett, was reluctant to release his papers for adequate preservation and use until Francis O. Schmitt, a member of the MGH Board of Trustees, expressed his interest in the project. And a subsequent MGH chief of psychiatry, Edwin Cassem, thought community mental health and those interested in it did not represent good psychiatry and sought to eliminate them from the department. Also, while professional journals outside psychiatry (*the Proceedings of the American Philosophical Society*, and *the American Journal of Community Psychology*) found monographs on this topic worthy of publication, psychiatry journals (*The Archives of General Psychiatry, Hospital and Community Psychiatry, The Journal of Nervous and Mental Diseases*, and *Social Psychiatry*) did not. This all took place in an era of biological psychiatry ideology; perhaps it is another illustration of the difference in these value systems extending beyond the theory and practice of social psychiatry, even to its literature.

Notes

1. Rosen, Norma, "My Son, the Novelist", LIVES column, *The New York Times Magazine*, 8/3/1997, p. 60.
2. Holmes, Oliver Wendell, "Currents and Counter-Currents in Medical Science", an address delivered before the Massachusetts Medical Society Annual Meeting 5/30/1860, in *Medical Essays, 1842–1882 by Oliver Wendell Holmes* [Boston, MA: Houghton, Mifflin, 1883], pp. 175, 177).
3. Schlesinger, Arthur M., "Arthur Schlesinger Answers His Critics", *Boston Sunday Globe,* October 1, 1978.
4. Bowlby, John, "Processes of Mourning", *The International Journal of Psycho-Analysis XLII* Parts 4–5: 317–340 [p. 335, footnote 17]. Paper given in New York on 4/60, the second of two Sandor Radio Lectures; and in London in 10/60 to the Medical Section of the British Psychological Society.
5. Longfellow, Henry Wadsworth, "A Psalm of Life"; one of Lindemann's favorite poems. Lindemann, Elizabeth, letter to Rosenberg, Pearl, 6/12/1988: "[one] of Erich's favorite poems (you remember how he declaimed Longfellow". [older "HRS 40th anniversary 1988, box Human Relations Service via Elizabeth Lindemann, Erich Lindemann Collection, Center for the History of Medicine, Francis A. Countway Library of Medicine, Boston, MA]
6. Charcot, Jean-Martin.
7. Von Goethe, Johann Wolfgang, *Faust* (Garden City, New York: Avalon Books/Doubleday & Co., 1962), p. 108.
8. See, for example, Tuchman, B.W., *A Distant Mirror* (New York: Ballantine, 1978), Tuchman, B.W., *Stillwell and the American Experience in China* (New York: Ballantine, 1971), Caro, Robert A., *Robert Moses and the Fall of New York* (New York: Knopf, 1974).
9. DeMause, Lloyd, *Foundations of Psychohistory* (New York: Creative Roots, Inc., 1982). For instance,

   > Methodological individualism is the principle that group processes may be entirely explained by (1) psychological laws governing the motivation and behavior of individuals and (2) descriptions of their current physical historical situation, which itself is only the outcome of prior motivations acting on physical reality. . . . All group phenomena have psychological explanations; individuals in groups act differently than individuals alone only because they split their psychic conflicts differently, not because some 'social' force is acting on them. . . . With the disappearance of the deathless entity 'society' all group values are revealed as tentative and subject to change each generation; what now seems problematic is not change but constancy".
   >
   > (Chapter 4 The Psychogenic Theory of History . . . 1C., p. 134)

10. Galdston, Iago, "Preface: On Medial Historiography—By Way of Introduction" in Galdston, Iago (ed.), *Historic Derivations of Modern Psychiatry* (New York: McGraw Hill, 1967), p. 2.
11. Sigerist, Henry, *A History of Medicine* vol. I (London: Oxford University Press, 1951), p. 10.
12. "2/27/63 'The Origin of Social Psychiatry', grant application to PHS, DHEW", 2/27/1963, p. 7. [folder "BELL, NORMAN W., MD", Box IIIB1 e 2), A-E, Erich Lindemann Collection, Center for the History of Medicine, Francis A. Countway Library of Medicine, Boston, MA]
13. Reviewer 2 comment, American Philosophical Society, 11/6/18.
14. *The American Heritage Dictionary of the English Language, Third Edition* (Boston, MA: Houghton Mifflin, 1992), p. 1182.

15. Holmes, Oliver Wendell, "Currents and Counter-Currents in Medical Science", address before the Massachusetts Medical Society, Annual Meeting, 5/30/1960, pp. 173–208, in *Medical Essays 1842–1882* (Boston, MA: Houghton Mifflin, 1883), p. 177.

16. Levine, Murray and Levine, Adeline, "THE MORE THINGS CHANGE", Yale University-Psycho-Educational Clinic (manuscript, late 1960s). [folder "LEVINE: SOCIAL FORCES + M.H.", IIIB3 d, Erich Lindemann Collection, Rare Books Department, Countway Library of Medicine, Boston, MA]

17. Lindemann, Erich, "Talk Given by Erich Lindemann to Staff of Student Health Center at Stanford, November 12, 1971 (Lindemann Collection, Rare Books Department, Francis A. Countway Library of Medicine, Boston, MA), p. 13.

18. Musto, David, "Whatever Happened to Community Mental Health?", *The Public Interest* no. 39: 53–77 (Spring 1975); Greenblatt, Milton, *Psychopolitics* (New York: Grune & Stratton, 1978).

19. Almond and Astrachan identified these three competing ideological perspectives in the training of psychiatric residents, and named them "Directive-Organic", Analytic-Psychological (described in Hollingshead, A. and Redlich, F., *Social Class and Mental Illness* (New York: Wiley, 1958)), and "Sociotherapeutic" (as discussed by Sharaf, M. and Levinson, D., "The Quest for Omnipotence in Professional Training", *International Journal of Psychiatry* 4: 426–442 (1967)). The overlap of these ideologies was noted by Armor, D. and Klerman, G., "From Community Mental Health to Human Service Ideology", *Journal of Health and Social Behavior* 9: 243–255 (1968); and Brauer *et al*. Almond, R. and Astrachan, B., "Social System Training for Psychiatric Residents", *Psychiatry* 32: 277–291 (1969).

20. Primary sources are archived in the Erich Lindemann Collection, Center for the History of Medicine, Francis A. Countway Library of Medicine, Harvard Medical School, Boston, MA.

21. For instance, Francis O. Schmitt, who shared scientific values and mutual support with Lindemann, used his position as trustee and member of Scientific Advisory Committee of the Massachusetts General Hospital to have the papers released, using a mixture of diplomatic notice and warning:

> I was informed that you have been good enough to interest yourself protectively in the papers of the late Erich Lindemann. Erich, who was a very close friend of mine, was a great scholar and a great contributor to the development of social psychiatry. . . . It is a matter of great importance that his papers be preserved and it is my understanding that they now rest in the basement of the Mass General but that Countway Library has offered to take them into protective custody. Dr. Satin is working on the papers as a labor of love. . . . I believe that Mr. David Crocket [Special Assistant to the General Director of the Massachusetts General Hospital] is also acquainted with the facts on the case and is also very much interested in helping. . . . I intend to keep in touch with the progress of Dr. Satin and Mrs. Lindemann and to be helpful. . . . I look forward to seeing you again at the time of the visitation of the Scientific Advisory Committee. . . . With best personal greetings, I am.
>
> (letter from Francis O. Schmitt to Dr. Thomas Hackett, [chief] Psychiatry Department, Massachusetts General Hospital, 12/5/78; in Box XII 1 folder "Satin-Bio of E.L.", Erich Lindemann Collection, Center for the History of Medicine, Francis A. Countway Library of Medicine, Boston, MA

1 Perspectives and Ideologies

Variety of Perspectives on Community Mental Health

Among those involved in community mental health (CMH) were many perspectives reflecting the aspect being commented on (history, implementation, evaluation, etc.), medical vs. social model of psychiatry, primary vs. secondary vs. tertiary prevention goals, provider and recipient of benefit focused on, etc. All are apposite, making up the tapestry of ideas and participants in a complex social movement. We present an instructive sample.

Arthur Schmale put the shift from biological concepts to psychological concepts of illness in historical context:[1]

> In medicine during the eighteenth and nineteenth centuries, it was common to ascribe illness to grief, disappointment, bereavement, despair, and mental depression. With the development of "scientific" medicine, interest in the pathophysiology of disease took precedence. Then it was thought people died not of grief, but of heart disease, cancer, etc. Within recent medical times psychologic investigations have reawakened interest in the psychological settings in which illness develops . . . a group of psychologically trained internists has led to an increasing interest in the history of object loss and depressive-like reactions which have been reported by patients to have occurred prior to the onset of the disease.

A *politico-economic perspective* traced the shift from institutional to community treatment of mental illness from the accumulation of chronic organic brain disease and consequent overcrowded maintenance treatment to the institution of drug treatment, the rebellion of publicity about poor conditions and the advocacy of the civil rights of the downtrodden, and the financial support for non-institutional care:[2]

> From 1890 to 1950, the tide turned. State mental institutions became surrogate old-age homes, and more than half the admissions were of

people over 65, said [Gerald] Grob. "If they could define senility as a psychiatric problem, the localities could pass the care—and costs—to the states".

By the mid-20th century, 75% of patients were not only old but also had no relatives to care for them. Mental institutions became even more custodial until radical change arrived in the 1950s and 1960s.

The introduction of psychiatric drugs like chlorpromazine meant that some mental patients could be treated on an outpatient basis. The ascendancy of Freudian therapy, the experiences of conscientious objectors who worked in asylums during World War II, the beginnings of an antipsychiatry movement, and the promotion of community mental health centers steered the focus of mental health treatment away from the large mental hospitals after the war.

"But perhaps the most important cause was financial", said Grob.

The passage of Medicaid and Medicare redefined senility in psychiatric terms and sent patients to chronic care institutions . . . from mental hospitals to nursing homes, which were eligible for Medicaid funds. Other entitlement programs, passed in the 1970s, contributed even more to the movement out of mental hospitals.

Galdston, tracing the influence of "parochial and temporal" social influences on historical trends, saw productivity and common people's voice and vote as propelling community psychiatry and welfarism.[3] The power and successes of World War II came from one source.

Urofsky[4] finds legal empowerment in [the] incorporation of the Bill of Rights which [Louis D.] Brandeis helped to being in the 1920s . . . and before he left the [US Supreme Court] bench in 1939 had helped to lay the foundation for what became the postwar rights revolution [p. 626]. . . . what came to be known as the doctrine of incorporation by which the Due Process clause of the Fourteenth Amendment [to the US Constitution] applied the liberties protected by the Bill of Rights to the states. This doctrine . . . would be at the heart of the constitutional revolution that transformed American law after World War II [p. 633] . . . the great "rights revolution" of the 1950s and 1960s also grew out of the seed he had planted. [p. 641]

Education in the 1960s saw a neo-romantic revival. "High Romantics" wanted interplay between feeling (creativity) and reason. "Low Romantics", greater in number, "voiced a simple dissent from science and technology. Basically it was a no vote. . . . It was a repudiation of thinking". These forces were expressed through community mental health and other fields. In the *arts*, it was felt that liberals and moderates did not represent weighty constituencies and thus were politically unimportant, ignored, used, or attacked as symbols.[5]

> But the sentiments of nonjudgmental liberalism that characterized the movements of the period [the 1960s and early 1970s] had made it possible for every idiot with a Bic pen and a Big Chief pencil tablet to claim to be a poet, so long as he or she was a member of some oppressed group, imitated Orwell's use of pigs as the symbol of the oppressor and occasionally stapled together a rudimentary chapbook of poems that seemed unified only because they were repetitious.
>
> (p. 26)

Conservatives and extremists of either (any) persuasion represented and brought constituencies of weight, and therefor merited negotiation with respect, seriousness, and trust. Independents were autonomous and changeable and thus not trusted or depended on.

"*Radical lawyers*" who participated in the civil rights/institution-challenging era offer a parallel.[6] Their radical and grandiose activities were supported by the feeling that a large movement was behind them. Feelings of dissention were united in large causes; they believed that societal institutions were weak and vulnerable, attention-getting devices (such as demonstrations) were reacted to, funding was available; and they believed they could make large changes in society quickly. After the active 1960s, the large causes had devolved into many competing small causes; there was less fervor and ferment in society; institutions proved more durable than expected; attention-getting devices attracted less attention and sympathy; and funding proved short-lived (one to two years for new fads). The radical lawyers evolved into staid practices with more-established and better-paced social issues cases. They found that radical law was too exhausting, and they were more comfortable appealing to rather than browbeating the courts. They phased into incremental change in society, sometimes from within the government.

Henrik Blum saw the US social system as "open to experimentation and least open to significant change. . . . You have these grand experiments and they're all written up and then you write off the goddam thing and it becomes something in the library but you don't make any changes in the system". That's how you get it off your chest.[7] In an allied observation of failure of implementation, Powledge wryly comments on the half-heartedness of government programs:[8]

> Government had a tendency to start poverty programs with speeches and promises, estimate that X million dollars would be needed, appropriate one-half X, shortly grows disenchanted with the program generally, refunds it the following fiscal year for one-quarter

X, and then declare the program a failure but retain the bureaucracy that operated it.

Gerald Caplan saw the essence of CMH as a population approach to the social systems in the field of social forces in the community, community agencies, and medical institutions such as the hospital.[9] He observed that

> Opposition to the population ideology has long characterized the politically dominant groups in the psychiatric professions. These elites have been committed to an individual-patient ideology, whether their professional philosophy has been dominated by psychoanalytic and psychodynamic ideas, by a focus on individual, group, or family treatment, or by a primary interest in biological processes".

He outlined, step by step, a population-focused, primary prevention definition of CMH and its importance to the broader mental health of the community:[10]

> The prevention of mental disorders . . . demands a threefold focus. The traditional approach is to reduce the number of existing cases by early diagnosis and prompt treatment, known as *secondary prevention*. In addition . . . to reduce the level of residual defect. . . *tertiary prevention*. Most important, however, is *primary prevention*, which lowers the risk of new cases . . . by attenuating harmful forces in the community and increasing the capacity of the exposed population to cope with the stresses in healthy ways. . . . The basic model for prevention is no longer that of intervention early in a person's life history. This is superseded by intervention in crisis situations at any phase of life. . . . The opportunity to repair previous damage and the danger of new disorder recur repeatedly. . . . Preventive programs should therefore utilize the leverage of crises at all ages. . . . The target of a preventive program is the whole population. . . . The majority of disturbed people must inevitably be dealt with by the other professional caregivers of the community—the nurses, teachers, clergymen, doctors, welfare workers, and the like . . . their families and friends and by their administrative superiors at work. . . . Mental health consultation and collaboration on cases, as well as participation in professional and inservice education, must play a large part in a preventive program . . . the widespread impact of sociocultural forces on the mental health situation of individuals . . . is highly significant. Mental health specialists must study these forces and must seek to influence them by social action . . . participating in community organization and community planning activities . . . a special interest group of mental health specialists might

profitably focus social action efforts on behalf of . . . age, class, or diagnostic category.

. . .

we must look to the universities for leadership . . . not by an ivory-tower condemnation of the community mental health movement as ill-advised and unscientific, but by a scholarly participation in the new programs . . . assess pioneering demonstration, training, and research institutions . . . to develop new methods and approaches and . . . appraise these for efficiency and effectiveness. . . . they will educate a cadre of mental health leaders who will spread this scientific approach throughout the country and promote further solid developments . . . it must beware of setting up too precious a program which is out of touch with the major problem of keeping abreast of community demands . . . work out . . . participation with other community agencies . . . a systematic transfer to them of the knowledge and skills it pioneers.

In many cases, programs for the eradication of social problems, economic improvement, and community mental health were stymied, and their proponents perplexed by hostility and attempts at dispossession by the disadvantaged groups they sought to help and collaborate with. Slate sees this as a reaction against distant powers: "When we create bureaucratic mechanisms to avoid conflict with our neighbors, we just find ourselves beleaguered by some impersonal far-off agency".[11] When the sources of identity, relationship, and problem-solving are far off, it leads to frustration, irritation, and feelings of helplessness and exploitation and thence to the displaced hostility of a penchant for impersonal violence against alien people.

Bernard Bandler traced the community mental health movement from President Lyndon B. Johnson's great vision for redressing social problems and including community participation, which, he thought, might have succeeded but for the political divisiveness and material drain of the Vietnam War.[12]

He focused on the mental health profession's understanding of and relationship with the community. He was another psychoanalyst who became dedicated to social and community psychiatry. He graduated from Harvard College, and earned a master's degree in philosophy, and taught at Harvard.[13] He obtained his medical education at the Columbia University College of Physicians and Surgeons, was a neurologist at the Boston City Hospital 1939–40, and then was a psychiatry resident and staff member at the Massachusetts General Hospital (MGH). In 1947, he was appointed chairperson of the Division of Psychiatry at the Boston University School of Medicine (BUSM), founded the Boston University/Solomon Carter Fuller Community Mental Health Center (CMHC), and served a term as acting director of the Division of Manpower

Development and Training of the National Institute of Mental Health (NIMH). He died March 9, 1993.

In a comprehensive review of the roles of psychiatry, the university, and the community, Bandler saw community psychiatry as the most significant change in psychiatry at the time—spectacular and therefore controversial:[14] "It overcomes the alienation of psychiatry from those in need of services and brings psychiatry into relationship to the revolution of our time [the community effort toward identity, autonomy, and democracy]".[15]

> By "community psychiatry", I mean in part the knowledge and skills necessary for the planning, organization and delivery of comprehensive mental health services to a discrete population. . . . The novelty in community psychiatry is that the health of the total population is our goal and that services should be continuous, comprehensive and coordinated. . . . Mental health care, as a result, is neither episodic nor focused exclusively on the individual patient.[16]

He conceived of four models of mental health:

1. Medical: diagnosis, treatment, life history, current precipitants, family and social setting, the soma. Attacked by psychology and social work in order to gain participation in psychotherapy. Community mental health centers directed at secondary and tertiary prevention.
2. Developmental: biological, standards of growth and function, services to individuals and groups. Directed at primary and secondary prevention.
3. Organizational: structure, participation, decision-making, leadership, milieu, interrelationship of participants. Incorporates elements of community psychiatry especially if it considers extrainstitutional influences on patients, though the individual has more control over institutions than the community resident has over social institutions (such as "the establishment").
4. Ecological: health as the result of the interaction and balance of all elements of the social system, including mental health. The community evaluates and criticizes community mental health in terms of respect, including domination over and exploitation of the community. Community mental health centers belong to the community.

He gives thought to the power and control relationships and struggles between the medical (and CMH) center and the community as part of an educational process, bringing the authoritarian medical system into a more respectful and egalitarian relationship with the community. He saw the need for change in the service delivery system and the training of psychiatrists to integrate all four models of mental health and to become broad and creative. He saw the mental health consultant as a facilitator of this responsiveness, integration, broadening, and change, based on core professional and clinical skills and not militant social activism. He saw the need for creative interaction among all levels of participants.

Taking a broad look on the US mental health system as acting director of the NIMH Division of Manpower and Training after his experience directing a community mental health center wrestling with a fractious academic center, community, and governmental entities, Bandler tried to paint a multidimensional picture of community psychiatry that compared with medical psychiatry:[17]

> [T]he present health and human service delivery systems are failures. They do not provide comprehensive care to our population . . . the concept of community mental health centers . . . hold certain assumptions in common. . . . The first is the assumption of responsibility for the mental health of a distinct population. . . . The second is the importance of demographic and epidemiologic data. . . . The third is the concept of mental health as optimal psychosocial functioning . . . not simply [to] be defined in terms of symptoms. . . . The fourth is the importance of prevention. . . . The skeptics are employing a medical diagnostic treatment disease model. The community psychiatrist is using additional models: the developmental, organizational and ecological models. . . . The fifth is the importance of consultation and education. . . . Health is indivisible from the conditions in which people live . . . health, education, housing, employment, human dignity, degradation, poverty and racism. . . . The sixth is the importance of indirect services. . . . The seventh is the importance of continuity of care. . . . The eighth is the enlargement of the knowledge and skills of the psychiatrist . . . in addition [to traditional skills], competence in group and family therapy, and understanding and skill in group processes with groups far removed from his traditional ritualized settings. . . . The ninth is an awareness of . . . community organization. . . . The tenth is community participation . . . when from the beginning there is planning with the community rather than for it, when power is explicitly shared, then the community and the Center will . . . share a common identity and a common destiny. Then the community will fight for the Center rather than with it, will organize to defend the Center rather than to destroy it. The eleventh is the experience with new careerists. Mental health professionals . . . have as much . . . to learn from the neighbors of minority groups as to teach them. . . . The minority community has developed an extraordinary new teaching device—confrontation. Confrontation is an educational process over time. . . . Training in community psychiatry, I believe, should be an integral part of basic

> residency training. . . . There is so much to learn about basic psychia-
> try, it is said, that the inclusion of community psychiatry will dilute
> training and leave the resident both superficial and confused. . . . The
> educational continuum . . . include the years of college and medical
> school . . . the training take place in a community-based comprehen-
> sive health service delivery system.

Later, he thought the "war on poverty" raised unrealistic popular expectations with nonrational discourse and urgent need. Inadequate resources
were focused on the highest priority needs, including mental health funds
directed to a social model (including political action) rather than a medical model. Thus, CMHCs differed from the medical concept embodied in
the Joint Commission on Mental Illness and Health's recommendations:
"Action for Community Mental Health". Bandler's experience led him to
believe that to be effective and viable, CMHCs must develop close partnerships with diverse elements of the community. Mental health authorities must understand psychiatry, and community oversight boards must
be accountable; otherwise, they just act out fantasies and arbitrary power.
He found no mechanisms or regulations for enforcing accountability to
the total community as opposed to acting for narrower personal, agency,
or advocacy group interests.

John A. Talbott, MD, represents a medical psychiatric point of view.
As former president of the American Psychiatric Association (APA), editor of the American Psychiatric Association's journal for community and
clinical psychiatry *Psychiatric Services*, and the professor and chair of the
Department of Psychiatry at the University of Maryland, he concluded
that buildings and models, with their attendant money and materials,
are more important and enduring than philosophy and values.[18] Utilizing these resources, the focus of service can shift, such as from drugs to
deinstitutionalization, from information systems to managed care. He
observed that people with mental illness will always need care except
when ejected from society (e.g., to institutions or to the street). All
approaches have benefits and problems. Managing care is a permanent
task—big, comprehensive systems; effective and efficient treatment; monitoring; and outcomes assessment. "What Do Public Psychiatrists Do
Then? Hang on; keep learning, innovating, and reengineering; stick to
basics; don't get complacent or stuck on one practice, model, or building;
and never even think of going back".[19]

Talbott interpreted CMH as meaning the provision of mental health
treatment more broadly to the community—secondary prevention, in
public health terms. He encouraged government mental health programs
to expand and encouraged academic training programs to collaborate
with them and encourage graduates to work in the public sector:[20]
"according to APA President John Talbott, MD, . . . The time is long
overdue to begin work toward increasing the participation of top-quality

psychiatrists in public mental health settings and to put an end to the two-tiered mental health care system in this country".

Warren T. Vaughan, Jr., represents the use of public health perspective and techniques. He was a psychiatrist who came to Boston to spend time in many of Lindemann's projects, including the Harvard School of Public Health [HSPH]. Later, he directed the Division of Mental Hygiene, the arm of the Massachusetts Department of Mental Health (DMH) that worked to evolve outpatient treatment facilities into a CMH orientation and CMH goals. He brought his public health perspective to these endeavors and later to the Department of Psychiatry at the Peninsula Hospital in California.[21] He worked on the Joint Commission on Mental Illness and Health, whose bent was much more toward the treatment of established mental illness. His views on mental health foundations and approaches were recorded as part of a conference with Lindemann:[22] For these purposes, people are the results of economic and sociocultural forces that they cannot control. Some mental health workers endorse a "shallow optimism" about simple manipulation of social forces to control destructive effects. A utopian goal is useful, including raising the morale of mental health workers, but is inconsistent with reality.

Mental health problems and solutions differ by place: New England has tradition and individualism; San Francisco has new people and community and implements new programs. Approaches include treatment of illness or preventive (as in fluoridation for dental health). He found the trend in the mental health world to be toward increased intensiveness, specialization, and cost of treatment and toward a decrease in the number of people served. The designation of psychiatrists to make policy and supervise other mental health professionals in treatment encounters and provokes resistance from professional vested interests by those who have had a hard time establishing themselves (such as clinical psychologists).

Labeling people as "sick" and "patient" is a social judgment provoking rejection of service leading to pauperism that leads to sinfulness that in turn leads to hospitalization and dumping problems, social control, and profit from professional services. A distinction must be made between normal reactions to external pathological situations and internal pathological conditions. General hospitals select admissions on the basis of rare and profitable diseases, leaving mental patients to state institutions—evidence of social and medical processes resulting in social exclusion. Private money (corporations) is not interested in mental health. Professions and philanthropists encouraging social health programs may be naïve and avoid dealing with the complex and unforeseen social consequences to the complex field of social forces.

Vaughan sought social solutions to social problems. Sigmund Freud pointed out the continuity between everyday life problems and illness. Maxwell Jones incorporated patients into treatment planning in his Northfield experiment and milieu therapy. Stanley Cobb and psychosomatics saw a fusion of psychology and biophysiology. CMH and community psychiatry incorporate social science and community methods. Psychiatrists lead community processes to medically help troubled people (sick people, mentally ill people, criminals, etc.); mental health centers, health maintenance groups, and psychosocial planning groups bring resources to troubled people at critical points in their and their communities' lives.

Vaughan proposed a comprehensive plan built on broad community mental health programming, including community analysis, epidemiology, situational analysis, and preventive resources and excluding clinics and psychotherapy. The object would be to identify life predicaments and then change situations rather than patients so that they were able to cope and to develop nonprofessional supportive people (such as Dr. Querido had in Amsterdam). He recognized, however, that biological strengthening via medications would be less expensive in dealing with large groups.

Planning and management would seek sites alternative to mental hospitals with their damaging effects. Small community units based on state departments of mental health program experiences would address mentally ill people, criminals, etc. and provide services to the healthy community. They would include open hospitals, general hospital psychiatry wards, and small state hospitals (about 800 patients) close to the community. Open hospitals would transform the hospitals' character and relationship to the community. New and high technology and treatment in human relations would take less time than psychotherapy would. Also, decentralized treatment would be advantageous to mental health consultation with community caregivers and psychiatrist consultation with medical doctors (e.g., Hunterton County, New Jersey).

Resources would comprise a hierarchy of competence, including psychologists, social workers, nurses, and semi-professionals under the supervision of highly skilled psychiatrists. A consensus would be developed regarding basic philosophy and curriculum. Psychiatrists as a group are not good at administration, so lay administrators should be included. Policy could be determined by a committee led by a psychiatrist, with other mental health professionals involved in implementation. They would explore the roles of medicine, religion, social services, and economics. Social scientists are needed to lend their expertise in community dynamics, though it is uncertain whether they would be involved in clinical action. Local voluntary agencies are program innovators with the state implementing proven programs, though the present Massachusetts government is encouraging and initiating programs of basic change in government function. Community organizers would develop groups and talents of community cadres. Patients and their families would be involved in hospital treatment as patients retain their community roles through such programs as day and night hospitals. The treatment emphasis would be on job placement, rehabilitation, occupational therapy, community facilities for people with disabilities, and industry.

There would be resistance to this approach from societal structures, traditional practices, and differences in class values and prejudices. In addition, a community approach was not valued professionally by psychiatrists, who were not trained in CMH but rather oriented toward personalities and individual treatment. CMH training would be done best in their third and fourth years of training, after they had gained professional competence with patients.

William Ryan is an example of the mental health professionals who joined a radical interpretation of the change in ideology toward social psychiatry. He took the discipline of psychology to task for overlooking the social responsibility of social psychology.[23] The "American dream", he states, implies individual effort with success to the worth and failure to most. It was being doubted and was in conflict with experience with unfairness and the need to demand social support. He found psychology to be preoccupied with the myth of individual and internal dynamics and isolated from the social environment. It was making weak efforts at understanding the relationship of the individual to the group: cognitive dissonance, prosocial behavior, attribution theory, etc. It should see real individuals in the social and historical setting and emphasize cooperation and concern in collectivities. He advocated partisanship and action to advance equality and social justice:

> Now this is easy to say but not easy to do. Which of us, for example, wishes to be held up before the world bearing the shame of bias, of preference, of visible values, even, God help us, of moral commitment? If we were to take such a position, we would stand exposed and trembling, waiting to be stripped of our scientific buttons and of having our sword of statistical significance broken before our faces. A terrible fate, perhaps. Or perhaps simply a narrow, exaggerated fear".[24]

Alexander Leighton articulated the ideology opposing social activism:[25] In the Stirling County Study, he studied the relationship between the sociocultural environment and mental illness[26] but criticized CMH for putting scientific formulation, observation, and testing in danger from antiscientific, antiestablishment social activists and counterculturists: "The counterculture of the 1960s . . . manifests a strong antiscientific bias as part of the condemnation of 'the establishment'. Instead, the emphasis is on quick solutions to human problems by adversary and advocacy procedures". These pose social and psychological threats to science in mental health: The conviction of already knowing the truth and therefore having no need to test these convictions leads to disillusionment and opposite convictions without proof. Relying on metaphysical concepts—self-contained logic not needing proof—leads to dogmatic and warring schools. The Lord Ronald Syndrome (ride madly off in all directions) would apply psychiatry to all fields and act on this conviction rather than test it. In the mental health field, this results in Balkan wars among schools and disciplines, including attacks from within and without on the concept of mental illness and on practitioners.

Leighton gives us a more moderate position in social psychiatry:[27]

> Clearly one is dealing here with an interplay between the structure and function of an institution as a social system and psychiatric disorder in people. This means that advancement of understanding calls for the skills and orientation of such disciplines as sociology, social psychology, and anthropology, as well as psychiatry.[28]

Prevalence of psychiatric disorder is influenced by social disintegration or the social breakdown syndrome. Therefore, prevention requires knowing social systems. Psychiatric high-risk situations include poverty, amorphic suburban culture, migration, and rapid social and cultural change. Psychiatry properly addresses social disintegration and not, for instance, poverty.

Frederick Redlich and Max Pepper address definitions of focus and terminology in the social psychiatry ideology.[29] According to them, social psychiatry is theoretical and scientific, whereas community psychiatry is practical and therapeutic. They find some definitions of social psychiatry vague, overly inclusive, idealistic, and missionary (see Thomas Rennie) and include the application issues proper to community psychiatry (see Alexander Leighton). They recommend focusing on etiology, diagnosis, and the treatment of mental illness and on interdisciplinary in participation. Unlike those coming from a public health and social science approach, Redlich and Pepper concluded that social psychiatry's approaches are not different enough from individual psychiatry to be considered a separate subspecialty of psychiatry.

Robert Bragg, director of HRS, noted that psychiatry was not best prepared to deal with certain types of psychosocial disorders, such as drug addiction and criminal behavior, which might best be addressed by other mental health disciplines.[30] He found community psychiatry a heterogeneous collection of techniques applicable and adapted to specific sites and times. Pinel's casting off of chains, Freud's discovery of the unconscious, and community psychiatry are not revolutions but evolutions—the achievements of each remains present in later times. New ideas from community psychiatry include social and cultural influences on mental health and the location of services in social agencies and not just in mental hospitals, professional offices, and academia. It is associated with shorter hospital stays, treatment closer to the community, integration into social agencies, and greater association with case finding and rehabilitation. Psychiatrists consult other professions. Treatment is brought to lower classes and ignored populations, such as the elderly, people with addictions, people with intellectual disabilities, and justice-involved youth. Different methods are used: group, family, milieu, and vocation. It addresses pathogenic conditions in groups and institutions. It works with groups. The introduction of social ("mass") psychiatry into academic departments that were used to individual psychiatry challenges old beliefs and causes upset. It requires attention from all, not just those devoted to it.

John Seeley, community-oriented sociologist, saw community mental health growing out of an increasingly humane viewpoint.[31] Pragmatically, he recognized that a mental health practice cannot be imposed on a population without tailoring it to that ethos. The champions of CMH wanted to develop a national program embodying these ideas, but that would necessarily become a mass product with bureaucratic and thus inhumane implementation—a contradiction to its founding ideals.

Franco Basaglia led a psychiatric reform movement in Italy that saw social rebellion mislabeled as mental illness, thus representing a sociopolitical rather than a medical problem.[32] This joined other social activist movements of the time. He campaigned for mental health treatment outside institutions, culminating in Law 180, which closed almost all mental hospitals in Italy (see Chapter 10).

John G. Glidewell of the Washington University Social Science Institute saw CMH as amorphous and without boundaries, but he supported it:[33]

> Community mental health is sometimes seen as a professional practice based upon rigorous scientific discipline; it is often defined and discussed in quite impressionistic terms; it has no clear boundaries; it has no body of organized knowledge specifically applicable to its problems; it has no professional consensus of good practice amenable to inculcation by a professional school. It includes an incredible variety of roles: consultant, group therapist, social diagnostician, counselor, advisor, scientist, researcher, collaborator, social change agent, public health officer, educator, trainer, and, yes, reformer. In spite of its vague boundaries and its diverse functions, I and many others are undertaking to train psychologists to function in at least a few of the roles included in this amorphous field of work.

Erich Lindemann started from a social concept of mental health that developed into a social concept of psychiatric intervention:[34]

> the reasons why I think the mental health movement has evolved in juxtaposition and sometimes in contrast to clinical psychiatry [is that] . . . the term mental health is of practical usefulness in delineating a broad program far beyond the confines of clinical psychiatry dealing with rehabilitation, prevention, with the control of disease in the population and with the promotion of positive mental health.

the term mental health operates as a value much as religious values do bringing forth dedicated loyalties. By reference to mental health certain types of child rearing practices are sanctioned and promoted when there is little more basis for these practices than pious beliefs. Value terms have a tendency to become global and diffuse. They are useful for promotional purposes but not conducive to better understanding.

As a scientific concept, the term mental health is useful only in so far as it permits one to define subregions of interest in which evidence can be collected to prove assertions and in which methods can be developed for practices based on scientific insight. Two large sub-regions immediately present themselves—the control of disease, the promotion of positive health. Both areas are by no means free from controversy.

one might say mental health deals with problems raised by the community because of deviant behavior on the part of its members and deals with problems raised by individuals who feel distressed by the social order in which they have to live.

Thus, social relations define mental illness. Definitions of mental disease are vague, varied, and overlapping.

The other approach to mental health disorders regards deviant behavior as occurring in a continuum leading from small deviations to large deviations and trying to define the degrees of severity of maladjustment.[35] The disordered behavior is viewed as a type of reaction to a situation setting up a disturbance in equilibrium in the organism and leading to a series of responses designed to restore equilibrium.

Pathological defenses are regression to infantile behaviors. Mental health problems are familiar adjustment problems with the struggle to readjust and adapt, rather than a separate category of people and problems:

This leads us to the "why" of the mental health program. It is of course true that public servants and administrators responsible for general welfare are struck with the very high cost of care for mental disease which in number of beds, length of care and public expense exceeds most other medical problems. It is also clear why persons interested in the preservation of manpower in industry and in the Armed Forces will wish to avoid the very considerable loss due to absenteeism and to psychoneurotic and psychotic breakdown and the large segment of the population which is disqualified for Service in the Armed Forces and in industry. However, among psychiatrists themselves it is not very common to find persons who are willing to discontinue preoccupation with clinical problems and with the fascination of therapy in favor of a new orientation dealing with the whole population, the healthy as well as the sick.

[Someone might have] asked me what I would do in a mental health program if I had all the resources I wanted at my disposal. My first priority would be the opportunity of training future workers. The second would be the establishment of a number of mental health agencies . . . to study populations in different communities . . . with respect to the mastery of crises. The third would be that teams of anthropologists, public health men and mental health workers. . . [would explore] in a variety of different cultures to see in what way the way of life of various societies is related to the patterns of occurrence of mental ill health and the patterns of successful adjustment.

In many places, he advocated for a social adaptation rather than a disease treatment concept of mental health practice:[36]

[Current mental health professional] concerns are essentially clinical . . . relating to . . . care of the ill and handicapped. They might be . . . core concerns of mental health work. But I, for one, believe that mental health concerns within a community are much broader . . . extended to . . . prevention of ill mental health . . . issues which are not . . . mental diseases but are related to . . . modifying human behavior and at anticipating and preventing illness . . . a psychiatrist. . . [would] arrange different . . . behavior on a continuum with respect to the degree of abnormality. . . [This would] not mean always more or less severe 'disease', but . . . more or less deviant patterns of adaptive behavior, of reaction types . . . attempts to master a specific life situation. The psychiatrist then becomes a student of behavioral science. . . [considering] matters of physiology . . . but also the social context . . . Much of what we used to consider as . . . personal disposition is now recognized as typical for . . . social groupings.

We have learned to describe social systems . . . All of this has had much complication for understanding . . . creating <u>stressful</u> situations or facilitating productive and cooperative [collaboration].

The World Health Organization gives the following definition of "health": "Health is a state of complete physical, mental and social well-being and not merely the absence of disease or infirmity".[37]

Ideologies of Psychiatrists

To focus down from a broad range of ideas and attitudes to those of a specific profession, it is useful to learn how the interests, attitudes, and plans of psychiatrists relate to the psychiatric ideologies that they are attracted to and adopt. The National Conference on Mental Health Teaching in Schools of Public Health observed[38]

> the development of professional sub-groups [within psychiatry] with different skills, different value orientations, and a certain degree of mutual incompatibility. Some of these are: (1) the biological psychiatrists with almost exclusive interests in central nervous system functions and pharmacological or surgical approaches, perhaps with some side interests in hereditary factors; these are found more commonly in mental hospitals and in laboratories; (2) the psychoanalytic psychiatrists with orientation towards prolonged study and therapy with a small number of patients, mostly concerned with the neuroses and psychosomatic disorders; (3) the child psychiatrists who are concerned principally with developmental issues, with some affinity for teamwork with other professions in guidance programs; and (4) a few psychiatrists who explicitly are dealing with issues of social organization and community studies, such as A. Leighton, John Spiegel, James Tyhurst, and the late Thomas Rennie.

In Hollingshead and Redlich's 1950s study of social class and mental illness, they contrasted those psychologically analytically (PA) oriented with those directively organically (DO) oriented.[39] The PA psychiatrists tended to be more introverted, charged higher fees, kept regular office hours, made no home visits, and were attached to analytic institutes or societies. The DO psychiatrists charged lower fees, made home visits, responded to emergencies, kept irregular hours, and were attached to medical, neurological, or general medicine societies. PAs were concerned with understanding behavior; DOs were concerned with understanding with helping people, administrative tasks, and economic barriers to treatment. These were largely exclusive groups with hostile relations. The PAs were more likely to be recent immigrants from the lower classes and Jewish; the DOs were more likely Christian and less involved in organizations and community affairs.

Strauss and Schatzman took a social science view of somatotherapeutic (biological), psychotherapeutic, and sociotherapeutic (environmental milieu) psychiatric ideologies in CMH:[40] They found that these ideologies constantly fade, emerge, and coalesce over time (though we argue that they cycle in dominance). As a result of working with those with other ideologies and professional specialties, they observed the following: "As social scientists, we are most impressed by the potential of hospital settings for the generation of influential psychiatric ideologies". Psychotherapeutic and somatotherapeutic ideologies emphasize specific treatment for specific illnesses and treatment through single expertise. Sociotherapeutic ideology emphasizes multifaceted treatment influences as conducive to recovery, blurring professional distinctions and encouraging new roles.

Ehrlich and Sabshin further studied the concept of sociotherapeutic orientation, which they added to psychotherapeutic and somatotherapeutic orientations in psychiatric training and practice.[41] It was stimulated by a shortage of state mental hospital psychiatrists, the development of pharmacotherapy to maintain psychiatric patients in non-restricted settings, increased interest in social therapies, an increased study of social factors in mental illness and health, British social psychiatry (Maxwell Jones, Main), and the report of the Joint Commission on Mental Illness and Health's demonstration of the need to supplement the traditional psychiatric treatment system. In a sample of psychiatrists, 70% self-identified with psychotherapy, 23% with somatotherapy, and 7% with sociotherapy. Questionnaire scores on sociotherapy showed a mild positive correlation with psychotherapy and a significant negative correlation with somatotherapy. However, sociotherapists identified themselves as having only a low correlation with psychotherapy and a higher correlation with somatotherapy—perhaps demonstrating a rebellion against the most popular of psychiatric ideologies. The sociotherapeutic orientation involved the therapeutic use of interpersonal and situational factors, the involvement of all hospital personnel and of other disciplines in treatment, seeing social factors as the etiology of mental illness, the encouragement of change in the social and physical environment, criticism of institutional restrictions, and a disapproval of traditional authority and current hospital practice. These psychiatrists were not exclusively committed to their ideological choice and were more likely to be involved in administration, research, and teaching (including interdisciplinary teaching). They were associated with higher-status medical schools, had public health internships, were second-generation or more US citizens, had professional parents, and were Protestant in religious affiliation. The impression was that these people were exploring an intellectual interest in social psychiatry.

Sharaf and Levinson studied ideologies among psychiatric residents in the Boston area, where a psychoanalytic/psychodynamic approach outweighed a biological approach; they were interested in how this psychological approach was interpreted.[42] They found that in the course of the many adaptive and professional tasks of residents, they endorsed psychotherapeutic, somatotherapeutic, and milieu or sociotherapeutic ideologies. Those with a psychotherapeutic orientation focused on a depth, dyadic relationship and sought fundamental change in patients. They were more hostile to milieu therapy (which they saw as a waste that interfered with and diluting the therapeutic relationship) than toward somatic therapy (which they saw as barbaric and of limited use). Those with a sociotherapeutic orientation had less-clear role models and a less-clear ideology; were more varied; saw a larger context as therapeutic; were more flexible regarding types and degrees of therapeutic change; had broader concepts of tasks, therapeutic contributors, and treatment approaches; were open to the participation of more disciplines; blurred professional roles and status; and were more interested in administration. While psychotherapeutically oriented residents tended toward more traditional professional roles and therapeutic structures and planned individual clinical practice careers, those with a sociotherapeutic orientation planned to work in hospitals and allied medical fields were interested in social problems, were interested in reaching more patients, had broader work experience and interests, and did not accept modal professional stereotypes or authority.

Notes

1. Schmale, Arthur H., jr, MD, Departments of Psychiatry and Medicine, University of Rochester School of Medicine and Dentistry, Strong Memorial and Rochester Municipal Hospitals, Rochester, NY: "The Relationship of Separation and Depression to Disease: I. A Report on a Hospitalized Medical Population", manuscript. [folder "CMH—Clinical Practice", David G. Satin files, Newton, MA]
2. *Psychiatric News* (9/2/1905).
3. Galdston, Iago, "Preface: On Mendical HIstorigraphy—By Way of Introduction" in Galdston, Iago (ed.), *Historic Derivations of Modern Psychiatry* (New York: McGraw, 1967), p. 7.
4. Urofsky, Melvin I., *Louis D. Brandeis: A Life* (New York: Pantheon Books, 2009).
5. Bradley, David and Walker, Alice, "Telling the Black Woman's Story", *The New York Times Magazine* 1/8/1984.
6. Kellogg, Mary Alice, "The Radical Change in the Radical Lawyers" in *Parade, The Boston Sunday Globe* 8/27/1978, p. 21.
7. Blum, Henrik, interview by telephone by David G. Satin, 3/23/1979. [caddy 1, Box 4, X, Lindemann Collection, Center for the History of Medicine, Francis A. Countway Library of Medicine, Boston, MA]
8. Powledge, Fred, *Model City: A Test of American Liberalism: One Town's Efforts to Reuil Itself* (New York: Simon & Shuster, 1970), p. 219.
9. Caplan, Gerald, MD [Professor of Child Psychiatry and chairperson, Department of Child Psychiatry, Hadassah University Hospital, Ein Karem, Jerusalem], Epilogue: "Personal Reflections by Gerald Caplan" in Schulberg, Herbert C., Killilea, Marie (eds.), *The Modern Practice of Community Mental Health: A Volume in Honor of Gerald Caplan* (San Francisco: Jossey Bass, 1982), pp. 540–564.
10. Caplan, Gerald, MD, D.P.H., "Beyond the Child Guidance Clinic", in *Working Papers in Community Mental Health* 2 no. 2: 6–12 (Boston, MA: Laboratory of Community Psychiatry, Department of Psychiatry, Harvard Medical School, Summer 1964. [found also in folder "CMH—Policy, Politics, Administration, Institutions", David G. Satin files, Newton, MA]
11. Slate, Philip, *The Pursuit of Loneliness: American Culture at the Breaking Point* (Boston, MA: Beacon Press, 1976).
12. Bandler, Bernard, interview by David G. Satin at Bandler's summer home in Swampscott, Massachusetts, 8/11/1978. [Erich Lindemann Collection, David G. Satin files]
13. Bandler, Bernard, interviewed by David G. Satin at his office on 11/16/1978. [Box 4, X, Lindemann Collection, Center for this History of Psychiatry, Francis A. Countway Library of Medicine, Boston, MA]

14. Bandler, Bernard, "Current Trends in Psychiatry from the Academic Point of View", at the Third Annual Seminar for Continuing Education for Psychiatrists, sponsored by the American College of Psychiatrists, Atlanta, Georgia, 1/12–15/1970.
15. Bandler, Bernard, 1970, *ibid.*, p. 15.
16. Bandler, Bernard, 1970, *ibid.*, pp. 6–7.
17. Bandler, Bernard, Acting Dr., Division of Manpower and Training Prog.s, NIMH, "Psychiatric Training and the Role of Psychiatry in Comprehensive Health and Human Services" in *Selected Papers on Mental Health Manpower and Training*, David C. Wilson Lecture, Univ. of VA, 4/23/1971, Charlottesville, VA (Rockville, MD: U.S. Department of Health, Education, and Welfare, Pub Hlth Svc, Hlth Svcs and Mental Health Admini.), pp. 1–5; to be published in Proceedings of the Inter-University Forum for Educators in Community Psychiatry. [folder "Bandler, Bernard", Lindemann Collection, Center for the History of Medicine, Francis A. Countway Library of Medicine, Boston, MA]
18. Talbot, John A., "From No Care to Managed Care: Lessons for the Next Century", *Psychiatric News, XXXIV* no.17, 9/3/1999, p. 10. [Erich Lindemann Collection, files of David G. Satin, Newton, MA]
19. Talbot, John, 1999, *ibid.*
20. Hausman, Kenneth, "Cooperation Needed Between Universities, State Institutions", *Psychiatric News, 19* no 1: 26 (7/6/84, p. 1). [also found in folder "CMH—Policy, Politics, Administration, Institutions", David G. Satin files, Newton, MA]
21. "Warren Taylor Vaughan, Jr., class of 1943B", *Harvard Medical Alumni Bulletin,* Autumn, 2002; p. 61. [also found in folder "Harvard School of Public Health", David G. Satin files, Newton, MA]:

    Died January 29, 2002, at the age of 81, in Portola Valley, California, of pulmonary fibrosis complicated by long-standing coronary artery disease . . . a psychiatrist and community mental health pioneer. In the early 1950s he was director of the Massachusetts Division of Mental Hygiene (in Department of Mental Health) . . . and assistant professor of mental health at the Harvard School of Public Health. He also was associate director of a task force for the Joint Commission on Mental Illness and Health [vs. co-author of monograph *New Perspectives on Mental Patient Care*; not listed as member of Advisory Committee on Patterns of Patient Care] . . . and held appointments at Harvard, the University of Colorado, and Stanford.

22. Vaughan, Warren T., Jr., "Conference with Dr. Erich Lindemann, Saturday, July 27, 1957". [folder "Joint Commission (1956–1961), box IIIA6, Erich Lindemann Collection, Center for the History of Medicine, Francis A. Countway Library of Medicine, Boston, MA]
23. Ryan, William, "Waking from the American Dream", presented as part of the Symposium on Reflections of Social Change in Social Psychological Research, at the Annual Meeting of the American Psychological Association, Anaheim, California, 8/1983.
24. Ryan, William, 1983, *ibid.*, p. 10.
25. Leighton, Alexander H., "The Compass and the Troubled Sea", *Psychiatric Annals 8*: 43–54 (1978).
26. Dohrenwend, Bruce P., social analyst, Cornell University, Social Science Research Center, Department of Sociology and Anthropology, College of Arts and Sciences, "The Stirling County Study: A Research Program on Relations Between Sociocultural Factors and Mental Illness", *The American*

Psychologist 12 no. 2: 78–85 (2/1957). [found in folder "CMH—Clinical Practice", David G. Satin files, Newton, MA]

27. Leighton, Alexander H., "Social Psychiatry: Socioeconomic Factors in Mental Health and Disease", Ch. 8 in Galdston, Iago (ed.), *Historic Derivations of Modern Psychiatry* (New York: McGraw Hill, 1967).

28. Leighton, Alexander, 1967, *ibid.*, pp. 223–224.

29. Redlich, Frederick C. and Pepper, Max, "Are Social Psychiatry and Community Psychiatry Subspecialties of Psychiatry?", *American Journal of Psychiatry 124*: 1343–1350 (1968).

30. Bragg, Robert, interview by David G. Satin at the Wellesley Human Relations Service, 7/13/1979. [Erich Lindemann Colleciton, David G. Satin, Newton, MA]

31. Seeley, John, interview by David G. Satin by phone, 4/12/1979. [caddy 5, box 5X, Erich Lindemann Collection, David G. Satin, Newton, MA]

32. Bergstresser, Sara, NIMH Postgraduate Fellow in the Department of Health Care Policy, HMS. She was an antropologist who tudied mental helth policy in Italy. Informal discussion, Colloquium on the History of Psychiatry and Medicine, Harvard Medical School, Boston, MA, 10/21/2004.

33. Glidewell, John G., Social Science Institute, Washington University: "Graduate Training in Community Mental Health", in *Community Mental Health: Individual Adjustment or Social Planning; A Symposium, Ninth Interamerican Congress of Psychology, 1964* (Adelphi, MD: Mental Health Study Center, National Institute of Mental Health, 1965). [found also in folder "CMH—Policy, Politics, Administration, Institutions", David G. Satin files, Newton, MA]

34. Lindemann, Erich, "The What, Why and How of Mental Health", 11/1956. [folder "Joseph Macy Jr. Foundation 11/56". [Box IIIA7 1955–9 1 of 3, Erich Lindemann Collection, Center for the History of Medicine, Francis A. Countway Library of Medicine, Boston, MA]

35. This concept of a spectrum between "health" and "disease" was enunciated by the HSPH epidemiologist John Gordon:

> Gordon defines the biological gradient as follows: "Health and disease are not absolute and opposite conditions, but relative states, and they tend to shade one into the other . . . Sometimes described as the spectrum of disease, the term <u>biologic gradient of disease</u> is believed to express more appropriately the series of variations which together form the composite of [morbid] process. Conditions in nature present . . . a shifting relationship, qualitatively and quantitatively changing as the biologic forces which give rise to it also change. Through quantitating the factors active in one form of the disease, and comparing them with those of another, information regarding the causes that act in the total process may be obtained.
>
> "PROGRAMS IN MENTAL HEALTH FOR DISCUSSION BY INTERFACULTY COMMITTEE ON THE BEHAVIORAL SCIENCES JULY 18, 1955", p. 1, referring to Gordon, John E. The Newer Epidemiology in "Tomorrow's Horizons in Public Health", Transactions of the 1950 Conference of the Public Health Association of New York City. New York, 1950. [folder "Interfaculty Committee on the Behavioral Sciences July 1955 (H.U. Faculty Committee)", IIIC1 c, Erich Lindemann Collection, Center for the History of Medicine, Francis A. Countway Library of Medicine, Boston, MA]

36. Lindemann, Erich, "The Nature of Community Mental Health Education", Keynote Address presented to the National Assembly on Mental Health Education; Ithaca, New York; 9/11/1958, pp. 10–12. [file #56; "Lindemann—The Mental Health Educator + The Community 1958", Box XII #3, Lindemann Collection, Center for the History of Medicine, Francis A. Countway Library of Medicine, Harvard Medical School, Boston, MA]

37. "Constitution of the World Health Organization", *Basic Documents*, Forty-fifth edition, Supplement, October 2006; The Constitution was adopted by the International Health Conference held in New York from June 19 to July 22, 1946, signed on July 22, 1946, by the representatives of 61 States (Official Records of the World Health Organization, 2100), and entered into force on April 7, 1948. [copy in file "J.H. Knowles—Medical Center + Community M.H. Center", Box XII #3, Lindemann Collection, Center for the History of Medicine, Francis A. Countway Library of Medicine, Harvard Medical School, Boston, MA]

38. Committee I, National Conference on Mental Health Teaching in Schools of Public Health, Columbia University, "Development of Scientific Psychiatry and of the Role of the Psychiatrist During the Last Half Century", p. 16. [folder "Mimeo material for Committee I-Nat'l Conf. on Mental Health Teaching in Schools of Public Health, April 23, 1959", Box IIIA7 1955–9 box1 of 3, Erich Lindemann Collection, Center for the History of Medicine, Francis A. Countway Library of Medicine, Boston, MA]

39. Hollingshead, August B. and Redlich, Frederick C., *Social Class and Mental Illness* (New York: John Wiley and Sons, 1958).

40. Strauss, Anselm, Schatzman, Leonard, Bucher, Rue, Ehrlich, Danuta, and Sabshin, Melvin, *Psychiatric Ideologies and Institutions* (New York: The Free Press of Glencoe, 1964).

41. Ehrlich, Danuta and Sabshin, Melvin, "A Study of Sociotherapeutically Oriented Psychiatrists", *American Journal of Orthopsychiatry 34*: 469–480 (1964).

42. Sharaf, Myron and Levinson, Daniel J., "Patterns of Ideology and Role Definition Among Psychiatric Residents", in Greenblatt, Milton, Levinson, Daniel, and Williams, Richard (eds.), *The Patient and the Mental Hospital* (Glencoe, IL: The Free Press, 1957), pp. 263–285.

2 National Interest

Community Mental Health and Community Mental Health Centers

The community mental health center (CMHC) program was a concrete manifestation of the CMH perspective with all its varying and conflicting definitions, contributions, and consequences.

In the post–World War II era, there was disquiet in the field of medicine:[1]

> doctors working in rural or inner-city areas or state institutions. . . [were] lowest in prestige . . . the most professionally isolated of physicians, though some worked almost in the shadows of the great medical centers . . . a reflection of contrasts in the medical care system. Gleaming palaces of modern science, replete with the most advanced specialty services, now stood next to neighborhoods that had been medically abandoned, that had no doctors for everyday needs, and where the most elementary public health and preventive care was frequently unavailable. In the 1960s many began to observe that abundance and scarcity in medicine were side by side. After World War II, medicine had been a metaphor for progress, but to many it was now becoming a symbol of the continuing inequities and irrationalities of American life (p. 363). . . . The emerging view among liberals in health policy was that federal policy overemphasized hospital construction, while ambulatory care was neglected. . . [This] took the same course as contemporary criticism of the bricks-and- (p. 364) mortar approach of urban renewal. Indeed, the same words recurred. "community", "coordination", "comprehensive services" critics attacked. . . [the] fragmented approach and lack of understanding of broader "community needs".
>
> (p. 365)

The field of medicine where the "rediscovery of community" found an immediately welcome reception was mental health services. . . .

The national census of mental hospitals declined from a peak of 634,000 in 1954 to 579,000 by 1963. The predominant . . . explanation for the drop is that the . . . introduction of the major tranquilizers . . . was the decisive event. Patients . . . could now be safely treated . . . on an outpatient basis. Another interpretation points to the adoption by Congress in 1956 of amendments to Social Security that provided greater aid to states to support the aged in nursing homes . . . states could transfer part of the cost of upkeep to the federal government. . . . [It was to] receive strong encouragement from advocates of "community psychiatry", who argued that . . . local services . . . could help return the mentally ill to normal roles in society. . . . In 1960 a national commission [the Joint Commission on Mental Illness and Health] . . . called for a major new commitment of federal funds . . . more money for community clinics, but . . . more hospital aid, too. The Kennedy administration chose to emphasize community services alone, along with . . . research and training . . . the president . . . told Congress, "reliance on the cold mercy of custodial isolation will be supplanted by the open warmth of community concern and capability"[2] (365). . . . There was no permanent federal funding: the program was meant to be a demonstration project . . . other sources were supposed to sustain the effort, if evaluations showed it to be effective . . . the tax cut . . . in 1964. . . propelled the economy into expansion and . . . higher revenues. . . . The economy expanded by one fourth between 1961 and 1965. . . Democrats . . . in 1964. . . gain a margin. . . . For liberals, it was a rare moment of political opportunity . . . made possible. . . [by] Kennedy's initiatives . . . an antipoverty program. . . . The civil rights movement was also increasingly emphatic about economic issues. . . . The summer of 1963 saw the start of the ghetto riots.

(p. 366)

In the mental health field in the late 1950s and in the 1960s, a variety of social, political, and economic forces put pressure on mental health institutions to change.[3] In terms of treatment, there was movement toward relationships with host communities, the employment of community residents, the education of employees, and the modification of care. Indirect services (consultation, education, access to the social welfare system) competed with traditional tasks (treatment, education, research). Social politics included the demand by new population groups for the redistribution of power and of economic and political relations. Advocacy for a children's or developmental institute in the National Institutes of Health, interest in aging, and the search for a market for consultation by the behavioral scientists stimulated general interest in the behavioral sciences.[4]

This in turn stimulated reaction from established groups, whether in the form of creative accommodation or political, economic, and/or professional counterreaction. The former is represented by the Action for Mental Health in Massachusetts via Minutes of Committee of the Massachusetts Association for Mental Health (MAMH). (Although Lindemann declined to join the Association's Professional Advisory Committee,[5] he did contribute to its work.)[6] The Committee's recommendations to the MAMH Board of Directors[7] included the following:

> emphasize the need for improved care and treatment of the mentally ill through an integrated system oriented toward community-based services and including hospitals, clinics, and other modern mental health facilities. These services should include psychiatric beds in general hospitals and facilities for the prevention and treatment of childhood mental illnesses, as well as community extensions of mental health out-patient services. . . . The use of non-medical mental health workers in the treatment programs [is encouraged] . . . this recommendation is a challenge to the system of doctor control. . . . The professions of psychology and social work were strongly in favor of these recommendations.
>
> (pp. 2, 4)

An interesting observation was that the building trades supported the CMH program as a source of construction jobs and abandoned it when the building boom ended.[8]

An example of professional counterreaction was a newly formed association of general hospital psychiatrists. Harry C. Solomon reported that[9]

> They are opposed to community-based psychiatric services which are not part of a hospital service. The question of community psychiatric services being "socialized medicine" has been raised by this group (p. 1). . . . By and large psychiatrists are in agreement with the JCR [Joint Commission on Mental Illness and Health Report]. As the medical schools move in the field of mental health, so will the doctors who seem to have little interest in the whole field of mental health activity. . . . The resistance to the JCR recommendations are coming mainly from the psychiatric professionals connected with state hospitals for: The recommendation that no hospital be larger than 1,000 population in contrast to the present size of state hospitals and the development of clinics and other out-patient facilities may result in these institutions being left with the chronic, untreatable populations.
>
> (p. 2)

Philip Hallen, the director of the Maurice Falk Fund, reminisced on the place of community mental health in the US mental health scene.[10] He believed that Lindemann's ideas in the late 1940s contributed to the federal expenditure of millions of dollars 15 years later during a period of intense national idealism, concern with populations whose mental health needs were unserved, and involvement in poverty and other social issues. Lindemann was recruited as a resource person on family living as part of a review of the US social security administration's expenditures.[11] CMHCs were the foci of politics, health concerns, conflicting philosophies, and the contest between the "medical" and "social" models of mental health. Community mental health was a flashpoint in addressing social needs as well as individual pathology, psychiatry's involvement with other human services, and the involvement of federal and state bureaucracies. It was implicated in federal involvement in social problems and their solution, in citizen participation, and their extension in political and social radicalism. The Joint Commission (1955–1960) recommended major federal support for mental health.

Gerald Klerman lived through the transitions from psychological to social and eventually to biological ideology. He saw the linkage between values, therapeutic experimentation, and social policy:[12]

> Goffman's concept of total institution[13] . . . [was] a moral critique of those institutions. . . . [It] synthesized a large body of research on the social and psychological characteristics of mental hospitals. . . . Stimulated by these [ideas] . . . major efforts at therapeutic reform were widely initiated . . . during the 1950s and 1960s. The British "open hospital" in 1946–47. . . . led to halfway houses and crisis intervention centers. . . . [It was] crystalized in the ideal of the therapeutic community enunciated by Maxwell Jones.[14] . . . Some community mental health programs already were operating when the first new drug was discovered in France in 1952. In the mid-1950s the United States began to import the new drugs. . . . [B]ecause the new drugs made therapeutic community and community care practices easier, some assumed that all subsequent changes in treatment and outcome had been caused by the drugs. . . . [However, t]he introduction of widespread community mental health practices reduced the number of occupied hospital beds by about 50 percent in 10 years.
>
> (p. 620–2)

There has been much attention paid to this issue of the relative contributions of biological vs. social psychiatry to the shift in mental illness treatment from mental hospital settings. In addition to medications and social treatments, it is argued that nonpsychiatric (economic) factors rather than biological science were decisive in driving psychiatric policy and supporting a (social psychiatry) ideology. While this change has been termed "deinstitutionalization", in some part it is a shift of institutions from state-funded state hospital institutions to federally funded general hospital and nursing home institutions:[15]

- In his annual message to the New York State Legislature, Governor [William Averell] Harriman underlined, in 1958, apart from the human benefits, the economic savings stemming from the decrease of patients in mental hospitals. In his words,

   In addition to the incalculable human benefits which this reversal of the prior trend [toward increased hospital populations] represents, it has also meant that the state has been saved a very large amount of additional cost. Had the earlier rising trend continued, we would have been faced by 1959 with increased construction needs of some $170,000,000 and increased maintenance costs of nearly $10,000,000 annually.[16]

- In 1956, Congress adopted amendments to Social Security to help states support elderly in nursing homes. In the transfer of patients from mental hospitals to nursing homes, states were able to transfer a part of the cost of upkeep to the Federal government . . . the continued reduction of the resident patient load coincides with increases in mental hospital personnel, improved social treatment of patients, and more liberal parole and discharge policies, as well as other factors that complicate the simple explanation: patients plus drugs equal more discharges. Increased use of psychiatric beds and other beds in general hospitals, outpatient psychiatric clinics, nursing homes, halfway houses, and sheltered workshops may also have been factors in the shift of population out of, rather than into, state hospitals".[17]

- The shift (in mental hospitalization) also began to receive strong encouragement from advocates of "community psychiatry", who argued that the state hospitals reinforced disability and isolation, while local services and halfway houses could help return people with mental illness to normal roles in society.[18]
- Some community mental health programs were already operating when the first new drug was discovered in France in 1952. In the mid 1950s the United States began to import the new drugs from France and new psychosocial techniques from Britain because the new drugs made therapeutic community and community care practices easier, some assumed that all subsequent changes in treatment and outcome had been caused by the drugs (p. 5).[19]

- Deinstitutionalization, observes [Gerald] Klerman,

  became possible due to introduction of tranquilizers. . . . The deinstitutionalization policy of the 1960s originates . . . apart from introduction of tranquilizing agents, from social psychiatric reform and
  "concomitant changes in public attitudes in the 1950s".[20]

-
  These [tranquilizing] drugs have revolutionized the management
  of psychotic patients in American mental hospitals, and probably
  deserve primary credit for reversal of the upward spiral of the State
  hospital inpatient load in the last four years. . . . Unquestionably, the
  drugs have delivered the greatest blow for patient freedom, in terms
  of nonrestraint [vs. labeling these "chemical restraint"], since Pinel
  struck off the chains of the lunatics in the Paris asylum 168 years ago.
  The most noticeable effect of the drugs is to reduce the hospital ward
  noise level. Bedlam has been laid to rest.

  (p. 23)

  The great virtue of the tranquilizer seems to be that they make
  the patient a more appealing person to all those who must work
  with him.

  (p. 53)

  Above all, we have good evidence that the tranquilizing drugs make
  mental hospital patients easier to work with and live with.

  (p. 88)

  The drugs have made it possible to change the institutional atmosphere . . . to one of therapeutic enthusiasm and constructive activity . . . and results in an increased return to the community.

  (p. 57)

  they render persons hitherto out of contact with their surroundings
  accessible to psychotherapy, re-education, and rehabilitation. Thus,
  they actually increase the need for trained therapists (p. 159).[21]

- The increasing trend toward higher and higher concentrations in
  these institutions (mental hospitals) has been reversed—by the use of
  new drugs, by the increasing public awareness of the nature of mental illness, and by a trend toward the provision of community facilities, including psychiatric beds in general hospitals, daycare centers
  and outpatient psychiatric clinics (p. 6).[22]

The reduction in state hospital populations was another result of CMH. The adoption of short-term treatment and community placement occurred before the introduction of mass use of tranquilizing medications: After 1955, state hospital populations began a continuous decline (Worcester State Hospital in Massachusetts reduced its population by half), though only Boston Psychopathic Hospital had access to tranquilizers through the French and the pharmaceutical corporation Smith Kline and French, and mass use did not start until 1958.[23]

These philosophies, forces, and findings (such as those of the Mental Health Planning Committee) encouraged action on the state level before the launch of the federal government's CMH program. Private child guidance clinics (in Boston: the Douglas Thom Clinic, James Jackson Putnam Children's Center, Judge Baker Guidance Center, etc.), which had been developed out of an ideology of psychology and philanthropy, were now attacked as elitist because they were selective and more available to more-affluent populations.[24] State mental health services were delivered mainly through state child guidance clinics until states began to address the mental health needs of communities as a whole:[25]

> The first comprehensive community mental health legislation was passed by New York State in 1954, with California following in 1957. . . . By 1959 Minnesota, New Jersey, Indiana and Vermont also had state aid programs . . . counties in Iowa, Kansas, and South Dakota. . . . By January 1962, there was a total of fourteen such state-local mental health programs.

Harry Solomon had developed as a neuropsychiatrist, studying neurosyphilis, and was appointed visiting neurologist to several Boston hospitals. However, as an administrator, he recognized the need to expand psychiatric services to broader practices and populations.[26] As commissioner of the DMH, he wrote of an expansion of state child guidance clinics into more comprehensive CMHCs, presaging future federal guidelines:[27]

> [T]he Commonwealth's existing outpatient mental health services fall far short of meeting the needs of the communities where this Department's mental health centers are now located and with the fact that in more than half of the State there are no such centers.

For these reasons, the Division of Mental Hygiene has organized a project to explore the advisability and feasibility of outlining by means of a new statute a comprehensive all-purpose community outpatient psychiatric program for the entire state. This would involve the consideration of a plan that would formalize our present program for children plus the following additional types of services: outpatient services for adults, daycare services for adults, daycare services for children, and special services in cooperation with the Department of Education for mentally ill children.

William J. Curran, the director of the Law-Medicine Research Institute of Boston University, was engaged to draft a legal petition and departmental regulations for this. This was to include relative collaboration with local communities; appropriations by the state legislature; and responsibilities shared between communities, the DMH, and vital relationships with the local medical community. A special advisory committee received travel expenses and secretarial assistance for the recording of meetings and interim and final reports.[28]

President John F. Kennedy's special message to the Congress on Mental Illness and Mental Retardation on February 5, 1963, included expectations that CMHCs would decrease social problems leading to a decrease in mental illness; mental health involvement in community organization, structure, and politics; the development of Indigenous workers; and the "deinstitutionalization" of mental patients, and it would highlight the necessity of these views (this message will be further discussed later on).[29] Note that here too arose the competition between addressing social factors in the precipitation and prevention of mental illness vs. meeting the needs of the already mentally ill, as well as treatment vs. prevention:

> There are now about 800,000 such patients in this Nation's institutions—600,000 for mental illness and over 200,000 for mental retardation. Every year nearly 1,500,000 people receive treatment in institutions for the mentally ill and mentally retarded. . . . The average amount expended on their care is only $4 a day. . . . In some states the average is less than $2 a day.
>
> The total cost to the taxpayers is over $2.4 billion a year . . . about $1.8 billion for mental illness and $600 million for mental retardation. Indirect public outlays—in welfare miscosts and in the waste of human resources—are even higher.
>
> (p. 127)

> New medical, scientific, and social tools and insights are now available. . . . First, we must seek out the causes of mental illness and of mental retardation and eradicate them. Here, more than in any other area, "an ounce of prevention is worth more than a pound of cure". For prevention is far more desirable for all concerned. It is far more economical and it is far more likely to be successful. Prevention will require both selected specific programs directed especially at known causes, and the general strengthening of our fundamental community, social welfare, and educational programs which can do much to

eliminate or correct the harsh environmental conditions which often are associated with mental retardation and mental illness.

(p. 127)

reliance on the cold mercy of custodial isolation will be supplanted by the open warmth of community concern and capability. Emphasis on prevention, treatment and rehabilitation will be substituted for a desultory interest in confining patients in an institution.

(p. 128)

I. Comprehensive community mental health centers (129) Consultative services to other community agencies, and mental health information and education. These centers will focus community resources. . . . Prevention as well as treatment will be a major activity.

(p. 130)

Socioeconomic and medical evidence . . . shows a major causative role for adverse social, economic, and cultural factors. Families who are deprived of the basic necessities of life, opportunity and motivation have a high proportion of the Nation's retarded children. . . . the only feasible program with a hope for success must not only aim at the specific causes and the control of mental retardation but seek solutions to the broader problems of our society with which mental retardation is so intimately related . . . research must go ahead . . . calling upon . . . many types of scientists, from the geneticist to the sociologist. . . . Prevention should be given the highest priority . . . health, education, welfare and urban renewal programs will make a major contribution in overcoming adverse social and economic conditions.

(pp. 132–3)

We must act—to bestow the full benefits of our society on those who suffer from mental disabilities; to prevent the occurrence of mental illness and mental retardation wherever and whenever possible; to provide for early diagnosis and continuous and comprehensive care, in the community, of those suffering from these disorders. . . . We must promote—to the best of our ability and by all possible and appropriate means—the mental and physical health of all our citizens . . . reorient these programs to a community-centered approach . . . to reinforce the will and capacity of our communities to meet these problems, in order that the communities, in turn, can reinforce the will and capacity of individuals and individual families.

(p. 137)

If we launch a broad new mental health program now, it will be possible . . . to reduce the number of patients now under custodial care by 50% or more. More . . . can be helped to remain in their own homes. . . . Those who are hospitalized. . . [a]ll but a small proportion can be restored to useful life. We can spare them and their families much of the misery which mental illness now entails. . . . With respect to mental illness, our chief aim is to get people out of State custodial institutions and back into their communities and homes."

(p. 137)

Proponents of CMH saw the president's support as marking an inflection point in the adoption of this ideology. For instance, James Kelly expected it to result in social action and social change:[30]

the ecological relationships between the mental health center, the local population groups, and the social organization of the community can contribute along with other community resources to planning and managing emerging social problems. A community mental health program can function as an additional planning resource to assist communities to clarify objectives and to identify alternative approaches for the solution of problems. . . . the community mental health center . . . can also contribute to the planning of specific action programs . . . a community mental health program is pivotal for the active, systematic development of a community rather than solely as a passive resource for helping the troubled. If the proposed community mental health center becomes an active component for community planning, there may be less need in the future for a continued accelerated expansion of services.

Kennedy's address was part of a movement in the US federal government of support for the planning, building, and staffing of CMHCs:[31]

In 1962, Congress appropriated funds to assist states in studying their needs and resources as a basis for developing comprehensive plans for mental health programs. Subsequently, in 1963, it authorized a substantial Federal contribution toward the cost of constructing community mental health centers proposed within the framework of state mental health plans. It appropriated $35,000,000 for use during fiscal year 1965. The authorization for 1966 is $50,000,000 and for 1967 $65,000,000. Recently, in 1965, it passed legislation to pay part of the cost of staffing the centers for an initial period of 5 years. In the meantime, 50 states and 3 territories have been drafting programs to meet the challenge of this imaginative sequence of Federal legislation.

(p. 499)

As regards financing this program, Sharfstein[32] noted that

> At the time of its inception in 1963. . . it was assumed that after a
> 51-month period of declining federal financial support, the [com-
> munity mental health] centers would generate alternative sources of
> funding and become self-sufficient. After the first 51 months, when
> significant nonfederal sources did not materialize, the period of fed-
> eral support was extended to 8 years.

As regards program development, Greenblatt observed the expansion of
the CMHC program, though less comprehensive than expected:[33]

> During the 13 years in which the comprehensive community men-
> tal health center program has been in operation, approximately 570
> centers have been funded by the NIMH. This is considerably fewer
> than the 2,000 centers originally estimated as necessary to blanket
> the nation. . . . Staff in these centers has more than doubled between
> 1970 and 1975, from 21,500 to 52,600. . . increase in the average
> number of staff per center, from 83 full-time equivalents in 1971 to
> 94 full-time equivalents in 1975. . . . the *average* number of psychia-
> trists per center . . . has diminished.

   The Community Mental Health Centers Act of 1963 funded a network
of mental health centers, and this gave way to a renewed belief in the
influence of environmental factors on mental health and therefore the
need for changing the environment. The CMHC program was implemented through many amendments and expansions:[34]

- Mental Retardation Facilities and Community Mental Health Centers (CMHC) Construction Act of 1963 (P.L.88–164)—states develop
  comprehensive mental health plans and list priorities, which led to
  the construction of CMHCs
- CMHC Construction Act Amendments of 1965 (P.L.89–105)—staffing under the 1963 act, deescalating over time
- 1967 P.L. 90–32—staffing and construction extended through FY
  1970
- Alcoholic and Narcotic Addict Rehabilitation Amendments of 1968
  (P.L.90–574)—construction, staffing, etc. relating to alcohol and nar-
  cotics addiction
- CMHC Amendments of 1970 (P.L.91–211)—increased federal funds
  for construction, staffing, administration, planning, child mental
  health, and consultation services, more for poverty areas, through
  June 1973
- P.L.91–513 CMHC Act amended—funding for drug abuse
- P.L.91–515 CMHC Act amended—staffing

- P.L. 91–616 CMHC Act amended—alcoholism prevention & treatment
- 1972 P.L. 92–255 CMHC Act amended—drug abuse funds
- 1973 P.L.93–405 CMHC construction and staffing through June 1974
- Health Revenue Sharing and Health Services Act of 1975 (P:L.94–63)—addresses organization, coordination, integration, response to the community, and quality and establishes a National Center for the Prevention and Control of Rape
- 1977 P.L.95–83 CMHC Act amendment—extended through September 1978
- 1978 P.L.95–622 CMHC Act amended—two-year extension, can carry over 5% of funds
- 1979 P.L.96–32 CMHC Act amendment—technical clarification
- 1980 P.L.96–398 Mental Health Systems Act—reauthorizes CMHC through FYs 81, 84
- 1981 P.L.97–35 Omnibus Budget Reconciliation Act—consolidates funding in block grant FYs 82–4; repeals CMHC Act and grants under Mental Health Systems Act

In Chapter 12, we will take note of P.L.97–35 of 1981 finally repealing the CMHC Act and grants, and changing from direct federal funding to CMHCs to block grants to states to assume responsibility for community mental health.

These implementation authorizations were accompanied by funding: Between 1955 and 1960, the NIH budget increased from $81 million to $400 million.[35] In 1948, when the NIMH was created, its budget was $4.3 million, in 1954 $18 million, in 1961 $100.9 million, in 1966 $300 million, and in 1977 $861 million[36]

Total expenditure[37]   1971 dollars

	Total expenditure[37]	1971 dollars
1971	294M	294M
1972	340M	329M
1973	469M	437M
1974	589M	502M
1975	776M	591M

1977 $237,846,000 appropriated[38]

Total federal expenditures under the CMHC Act as amended from 1965 to 1981 was $1,608,710,000.[39]

- Federal funding decreased from 37.5% to 29.1%.
- Direct services receipts increased from 22.5% to 32.3%.
- State, local, and other government funding remained fairly flat, from 35.8 to 34.3%.

Ideological support and resistance to a CMH approach to mental health and illness and societal implementation of these approaches through governmental action such as the CMHC program are succinctly described:[40]

> In that year [1960], the Democratic Party voted at its convention in favor of a plank in support of "greatly increased federal support for psychiatric research and training and community mental health programs to [help the hospitalized mentally ill live in communities]".
> President John F. Kennedy . . . appointment of a National Institute of Mental Health [NIMH] study group which recommended "comprehensive" CMHCs offering inpatient, outpatient, and rehabilitative services, as well as education and public information.

A coalition of mental health organizations supported a Kennedy proposal for CMHCs that would have provided funding for the construction of CMHCs and limited staffing grants:

> Congress approved the construction costs (Mental Retardation Facilities and Community Mental Health Centers Construction Act of 1964)[41] but not the staffing grants until President Lyndon B. Johnson requested them with . . . the Community Mental Health Centers Act Amendments, which passed in 1965.

Henry Foley, PhD, and Steven Sharfstein, MD, wrote in *Madness and Government* (APPI, 1983),

> In the beginning, then, CMHC services plus those of the state hospitals theoretically represented a balanced array, but the CMHC program alone did not. . . . The unanticipated consequence . . . was the failure of most CMHCs to develop even minimal rehabilitation and aftercare services for the mentally ill being discharged or diverted from state hospitals.

In 1972, President Richard M. Nixon argued that federal support for the CMHC program should be phased out and replaced by local support. Instead, in 1975 with new legislation, seven new services were added. The enactment of PL 94–63 in July 1975 over a presidential veto climaxed a seven-year struggle for program survival, which included appropriation battles and impoundment suits. By 1977 650 CMHCs had been funded, covering 43% of the population and serving 1.9 million people that year. The $1.5 billion federal investment generated another $2.5 billion in other sources of funds. "The bold new CMHC approach had little time and too meager resources to test its mettle before being overtaken by the urgent needs of patients with chronic mental illness. In 1977, President

Jimmy Carter established the President's Commission on Mental Health. After considerable debate within the administration, Carter submitted the Mental Health Systems Act to Congress in 1979. The Systems Act forcefully restated each of three missions without resolving priorities. The missions are adequate clinical care, particularly for those with serious mental illness; supportive services; and prevention.

President Ronald Reagan recommended that Congress cut the level of funding for the act by 25% and convert it into a block-grant program. In August 1981 he signed the Omnibus Budget Reconciliation Act, which "substantially repealed the Mental Health Services Act. . . . The federal government was entirely removed from the direction of the program and became a mere conduit of funds to the states".

The state mental hospitals constituted one of the constituencies most threatened by the CMHC program, fearing that they would be replaced. The Association of Medical Superintendents of State Hospitals fought the program. In fact, the Joint Commission had recommended that custodial institutions become therapeutic, and the APA urged that they expand into community work. Response varied from innovative outreach and community-based programs to old institutions retaining their old characters.

Note that federal Democratic administrations supported CMH programs and financing, while Republican administrations moved to limit their scope and funding. The decrease in mental health care resulting from the latter actions is described as an unintended consequence; it may be that it was an intended consequence of reducing government responsibility and financial expenditure while using the human costs to discredit the CMH approach.

The CMHC program took place in the context of US society's and its federal government's intensive exploration of the nature, needs, and consequences of CMH. The Mental Health Training Committee of the Policy and Planning Board of the NIMH met on October 2–3, 1964, for this purpose.[42] Most of the essential issues of the concepts of CMH, the changes that CMH brings, support of and resistance to these changes, and details of implementation were expounded and debated. Topics included the inclusion of biological factors in cause and treatment; the need for further research to justify approaches; individual and population perspectives and interventions; prevention, remediation, health promotion, and functional improvements; the involvement of nonmedical professionals and community members; specialization of training and separation of function and of location of clinical and CMH efforts; the appropriateness of the medical model and medical professionals to social problems and to leadership in CMH; the inclusion of political science, economics, and law in CMH; the place of private psychiatric practice, community centers, and state mental hospitals in comprehensive CMH; the effect of sociopolitical compromise on legislation, programming, and funding; the coordination of CMH with other large federal programs—Medicare, antipoverty, rehabilitation; what is desirable and what is feasible; broadening the range of people and roles (clinical and nonclinical) working for CMH; an expansion of training to include community issues perspectives and locations; the continuation of clinical psychotherapy training; CMH skills and education recognizing nonacademic sources and practitioners; new practitioner roles and team/program structure; CMH training for various health professions, including physicians and psychiatrists; the importance of training for interdisciplinary practice; and resistance to change even in the new CMH program. (More details of the report of committee deliberations can be found in the endnotes.[43])

The NIMH Training and Manpower Resources Branch's Study Section of the Subcommittee on Pilot and Special Projects and Public Health (on which Lindemann sat)[44] reviewed training grant applications from the Temple University Medical Center Department of Psychiatry (training of community paraprofessionals and professionals in mental health and community agencies), the University of Michigan School of Public Health Department of Health Development, and the New York University Medical Center (advanced study in legal aspects of psychiatry and psychiatric aspects of law). In its policy meeting, it addressed support for schools of public health regarding mental health education.[45] Its perspective is reflected in its preliminary report:[46]

> 10 years ago Robert Felix (then director of the NIMH) identified new areas of training for CMH "including action research, general knowledge of the social structure and social processes of the community, and new roles such as mental health consulting and program administration on local, regional or national levels". CMHCs are not much involved in measurement of mental health status and the contribution of non-clinical approaches to improved mental health. "If one views this new area with a greater emphasis on the community aspects of it, one can see the potentiality of instituting, and evaluating the effectiveness of, quite different approaches to community mental health from that represented in these existing and emerging agencies". It made recommendations regarding areas of training: evaluation components of CMH agencies, research components especially regarding social components and their impact on the community's mental health, flexibility in training programs and training for flexibility of staff in a new and changing field including training facilities in CMH programs, pilot and evaluation endeavors, exploration of new institutional functions, purpose, disciplinary roles, and broadening professional training (including community functions, CMH problems and problem individuals, preventive and corrective efforts, and the effectiveness of evaluation).

(pp. 1–3)

John Porterfield, the deputy surgeon general, cast these sentiments in public health terms:[47]

> Social work and public health share goals of epidemiology, preven-
> tion, and community planning: "The study of the epidemiology of
> mental illness within a community leads to a focus on such questions
> as what are mental illness and mental health, how do we measure
> them, what are the environmental conditions that maintain them,
> what are the agents that operate within a community of an individ-
> ual to endanger mental health, and how do we treat that individual
> or community? The concept of prevention leads to a focus on iden-
> tifying those many factors which may predispose a community or
> individual to mental illness and on evolving means of preventing the
> development of those conditions or strengthening resistance to them
> and hopefully therefore preventing the development of mental ill-
> ness. . . . From this perspective, it would seem that one could develop
> a comprehensive community mental health effort that was conceived
> in the public health-social work model. Agencies conceived accord-
> ingly would be comprehensive in that they were concerned with the
> epidemiology of mental illness, its prevention, and the mobilization
> of the citizenry in the service of mental health planning and the pre-
> vention of mental illness".

Sir Geoffrey Vickers (a member of The Special Committee on Social and Physical Environment Variables as Determinants of Mental Health—the Space Cadets—see more later on) saw the psychiatrist's role as not only extending to a community perspective but naturally encompassing ideol-ogy and policymaking:[48]

> And yet it [policymaking] is obviously important, not because we all
> suffer or benefit from the decisions of those who control our destinies
> but also because we all do it.
>
> (p. 465)

> Men, institutions, and societies learn what to want as well as how to
> get, what to be as well as what to do; and the two forms of adapta-
> tion are closely connected. Since our ideas of regulation were formed
> in relation to norms which are deemed to be given, they need to be
> reconsidered in relation to norms which change with the effort made
> to pursue them.
>
> (p. 467)

Norms are developed against which to measure and conform processes. Applying these norms regulates processes and also acts as precedents influencing norms in the future. People make experiences comprehensible and become ready to respond through experiencing them and developing schemata of meaning. Thus, the understanding of the world is artifactual. With sophistication, these schemata become more complex and comprehensive.

In applying norms to actions, we seek a *correct* answer by specified processes that can be proven. In developing norms, we seek a *good* answer by less-specifiable processes of judgment that can be approved by other judgments.

Changes in norms applied to practices challenge existing practices:

> It is no more pathological to fear a threat to one's appreciative system [system of understanding reality] than to fear bankruptcy or eviction. . . . Need we describe as pathological the reluctance to embark on massive reorganization of its appreciative system, or even its stark inability to admit the new until room could be found for it without disrupting the whole? . . . [This has] especial importance at a time when an appreciative system is unstable and under rapid change . . . most of all when many policymakers and others appear blissfully unaware that any appreciative system has an upper limit to its possible rate of change, which cannot be passed without disaster.
>
> (pp. 471–2)

> These new norms create or colour a great volume of policy in health, education and welfare, in housing and town planning and in much else besides; policy which should form a coherent whole, though the executive departments concerned are many. Its aim is to support the individual, internally and externally, and to reintegrate him into a physical and social environment more suited to his needs than that which we inherited or that which, impelled by the norms, we are busy making now. I believe that this development will be to our age what public health was a century ago, though in conception it is different and far more ambitious. For its aim is to humanize life or at least to combat the dehumanizing tendencies inherent in other aspects of our development; to provide what might be called a public humanizing service.
>
> (p. 475)

The humanizing services need a great variety of social workers. In politics and industry human relations develop their own professionals. Management consultants market new skills in organization. Planners, not least physical planners, make assumptions about the conditions best suited or least hostile to human life and sometimes ask social scientists to help in the task. Schools of social work, of business management, of public administration and of physical planning begin to root and grow in ever closer association with universities. New professions are emerging, based not on biological but on social sciences, on psychology, sociology, cultural anthropology and system theory applied to men and societies. I expect that some of them will soon equal medicine in their prestige and in their reliance on academic and professional training. When those days come, doctors, including psychiatrists, will no doubt be found working in interdisciplinary teams led by social scientists, no less than the reverse, the appropriate pattern being decided by the nature of the subject matter. Today such associations in either form are even more rare than they need be.

(pp. 475–6)

Where, in the course of these new humanizing policies, stands the profession of psychiatry? . . . . To humanize is a wider aspiration than to heal. . . . You may claim a special disability in dealing with normal men on the ground that you see so few of them. You may thus seek to barricade yourselves within the safe confines of a medical specialty.

May I suggest that you should not overcall this hand? You assure us, for example, that you aim to make mental hospitals into therapeutic—or at least non-pathogenic—communities; but those responsible for other organizations, industrial plants, schools, barracks are equally aware of some responsibility for the quality of the societies which they plan and administer. Is your experience irrelevant to these? Your success as therapists depends not only on hastening the recovery of your patients but on helping them, when well again, to re-establish themselves in the world from which they became displaced. Does not this require an understanding of the stresses of the world of the well? You must consider the effect of your patient's illness on his home and the strain which it, as well as he, can stand; and you will have to do still more, as domiciliary treatment increases. Does not this involve you in understanding the crises of the well? You sometimes advise parents who are not sick on the art of bringing up, and children who are not yet sick on the art of growing up. You are the best expert witnesses we have on criminal responsibility. You are potent influences in some juvenile courts. And what of your new responsibilities for and toward the psychopath? You teach those who are not psychiatrists what they need to know about mental illness and its pre-conditions. You are already educators, counsellors, planners and administrators in the field of preventive psychiatry, which is no frontier but a widening borderland. Moreover, you are today better qualified than others to do these things.

So I hope and expect that an increasing proportion of your (I hope) increasing numbers will be drawn into what I have called the public humanizing service. I hope so partly because your practical experience is necessarily so much wider than your professional claims. . . . The sanest like the maddest of us cling like spiders to a self-spun web, obscurely moored in vacancy and fiercely shaken by the winds of change. Yet this frail web . . . is the one enduring artifact, the one authentic signature of humankind, and its weaving is our prime responsibility. It is the realization of this which makes our age an age of ideology and one which, I think, will turn men's attention increasingly toward the first, the norm-setting half of the regulative cycle, to study its endemic appreciative process, of which one half-conscious instrument is policymaking and the total expression is social change.

(p. 476)

Among those dedicated to CMH, such as Leonard Duhl, these programs and resources bred enthusiasm, optimism, and hopes/expectations of great changes in psychiatry and society:[49]

[CMH Theory]

There is a new breed of psychiatrist today and there is a new style of social planning . . . Our professions themselves have been submitted to change. We have not so much defined our own work as we are having our work defined for us by the decade of social action in which we live . . . we have widened our view to encompass questions of social policy. In social planning, a new dimension has been added. The modern study of behavioral science, our knowledge of human behavior, is at last helping to shape our social endeavors. . . . The new breed of psychiatrist is one who is community-oriented. . . . Traditionally, those who are concerned with public health are occupied primarily not with the restoration of the sick, but with the prevention of sickness. Beyond the healing of illness, our sights are set on its cause and prevention. Furthermore, we seek not only the absence of disease, but the positive promotion of health, of physical and mental well-being.

In psychiatry we have been made more and more aware of the effect on the individual of the significant environment around him. Thus, the concerns of the psychiatrist have gone beyond the . . . treatment of the ill into the family, the community, the social structures surrounding.

We are increasingly aware of the deleterious effects of poverty, of crowding, of the need for each man to answer to the basic human inquiries such as, Who am I, and What shall I be? We have clocked dark evidence that the seeds of pathology lie in deprivation. We have clocked evidence that the nuclear family, shorn of extended support, must stand test again and again in its ability to manage life stress.

We are keenly aware, too, that the total structure of a community organization . . . may affect the normal development of young people and may play a role in the etiology and course of disease.

Many psychiatrists, therefore, have become involved in a variety of aspects of community psychiatry, working in ways unforeseen by our psychiatric pioneers, and participating in programs that are logical developments of our theory and practice.

Now we in mental health are engaged in developing a nationwide program of community-based mental health services. These services are designed to cope both with the problem of mental illness in our communities and with the protection of mental health. To this end, we are equipped with an abundance of psychiatric theories and psychiatric techniques. We possess a variety of sources for funding our mental health network. We seek to initiate these modern services and activities within a community atmosphere of acceptance and pliancy. This, of course, is essential if we would advance from old citadels of neglect.

Therefore, in preparing to institute our services, we find ourselves concerned with the formation of social policy, with the process of social change. They are as intimately related to mental health planning as are other plans on behalf of human need . . . my position as a psychiatrist in public health . . . is based upon a very broad view of mental health . . . expressed in the National Mental Health Act of 1946, which employs the phrase 'the mental health of the population of the United States.' Some of us have since interpreted this mandate as broadly as one might view the general welfare clause of the Constitution . . . to concern oneself with care, treatment, rehabilitation, and return to the community of the mentally ill person, one must be concerned with the total community, and with its competence. From a mental health view, the competent community contains within it not only mental health programs . . . but almost all of the programs that have any impact on the way people cope with problems which may lead to mental illness . . . we must arrive at some insight into the very nature of community functioning. . . . The scope of today's mental health policy has begun to transport some of us into the wide environment of the whole of the Nation, and at times into other parts of the world, in our desire to know firsthand the institutions which impinge upon human behavior.

(pp. 1–5)

Professionals may be hedgehogs (focus on 1 topic & avoid risk of looking into others—clinic, hospital, extension of services) or foxes ("He wanders widely, he circles the fields. Often he may not know precisely what he may catch . . . Eventually he reaches his quarry, even though he may not have been sure what the quarry might be when he started off").

(p. 5)

[CMH *Public Policy*]

Perhaps the widening world of mental health is a result of our greatly expanded budget . . . I think now, however . . . I believe it is the result of real changes and new realizations in our American society. The national interest in attacking mental illness has grown at a fantastic rate.

(pp. 6–7)

He enumerated mental health activities in the area of social policy: pre-school programs, mental retardation, VISTA [Volunteers in Service to America—a national service program designed to alleviate poverty], poverty programs, urban renewal, military industry conversion to community services (colleges, hospitals, planned cities), the Office of Economic Opportunity (OEO), the Job Corps, Youth Employment Centers. "The critical question is how to begin to understand in what manner all these systems affect the developing policy and programs, either directly or indirectly. If we as professionals would really like to make our contributions most telling, we shall have to discover ways of feeding into the system ideas and concepts which can shape policies as they are being evolved through the various channels".

(p. 12)

Another issue, and one which may cause deeper concern as new social programs emerge, is the need to establish ties between political functions and professional development, while keeping each quite separate.

On the neighborhood level, politics and professionalism frequently overlap. But moving up to the Federal establishment, it is extremely difficult for professionals to perform political functions. Yet bonds between the professional world and the political world must be strengthened, since each is involved in the formation of social policy.

In a sense, a new "politics" is already developing. In these times, everyone who is engaged in works of social consequence is actively participating in politics—which means in the governing of a community and dealing with its problems. Politics is a process of change, a process of beginning to allocate resources and energies toward achieving perhaps ever-more ambitious goals. But the professional must limit his concern with politics to those aspects which bear upon his professional activities, and leave to the politician—to traditional politics—functions which are outside the sphere of social service.

A new dynamic relationship is taking place between professionals who participate in political processes and the conventional partisan practitioners of politics. Professionals have begun to be subtlety aware of the complicated nature of the new politics, while many of the professional politicians are as yet unarmed with professional skills and knowledge that can be applied in social planning. However, many of our most effective politicians have proven to be highly apt students. [Vice President Hubert Humphrey, New York Senator Robert Kennedy regarding juvenile delinquency]. . . . this is an opportunity as well as challenge. It leads us to ask how can we as professionals bring our influence to bear more widely upon the political machinery on which many of our possibilities and our programs rest? Admittedly, the American social planner is presently engaged in what amounts to an open conspiracy. He is conspiring openly to press American society toward allocating its resources and funds for human services through a coordinated, integrated cooperative system.

A new discourse among professionals and politicians, as well as others involved in matters of social policy, has already begun to take place informally. . . . People in the political world, people in various government agencies, people in universities, people in cities, and people in business—all are concerned with the new social issues, and they have set up new vital communications.

(p. 17–19)

Robert Barra looked to a similar expansion of social welfare into the fields of social planning and structuring social institutions to prevent social problems, paralleling and extending Lindemann's ideas of changing social policy and institutions:[50]

Social welfare is thus at a crossroad in its evolution. Should it remain primarily service oriented, supplying protective and meliorative services to those unable to cope with the complexities of life, and offering the benefits of its experience and knowledge only when called upon by public or private policy makers and only in fields where it is unquestionably preeminent? Or, should social welfare seek a position of leadership to guide the formation of both public and private policy in all fields in order to prevent unfortunate social consequences?

The latter course would require major adjustments in the profession itself. This course would direct the attention of the social welfare profession toward the continuous study of the social order for the purposes of discovering, understanding, and correcting institutional inadequacies and cultural irrelevancies. Such study would also seek early recognition of emergent social problems in order to devise means for preventing them from coming into being, or for modifying them so as to minimize the social cost, or for assisting society to prepare for the problems before their impact . . . the need to correct the diverging trends of wealth production and distribution will involve some of [social welfare's] members in leadership roles.

(p. 13)

Then social welfare's role will be to premeditatedly invent and innovate the institutions and beliefs that will be required by society if it is to function successfully under the transformed basis of wealth distribution.

(p. 14)

He believed that society needs new approaches to adapt to new circumstances, as opposed to the perspectives from classical Rome, which looked back to simpler virtues that worked for exploration and conquest but were inadequate to social solidarity in the face of barbarians and ultimately failed.

Lindemann, too, was inspired by Kennedy's idealism:[51]

The efforts of psychiatrists and behavioral scientists until recently were concerned chiefly with evaluation and treatment of specified mental disease. They now include a much broader spectrum of concerns: with the maintenance of good mental health, with the recognition of hazards, and with the rehabilitation of the mentally impaired to their optimal level of functioning. This has led to the study of the patterns of adaptation to life crises and of the social stresses and adaptive challenges imposed by the ecological and human environment at various stages of the life cycle. The joint efforts between planners and decision makers for the development of cities and neighborhoods on the one hand and experts from the field of psychiatry and the social sciences on the other hand are beginning to produce new concepts and programs in which narrower concerns with health, education, and welfare as separate domains are integrated by a comprehensive approach.

(pp. 19–20)

We are reminded of Abraham Lincoln's second inaugural speech: "As the times are new so our thinking must be new, we must disenthrall ourselves and we will save our country". In the CMH era, this was opposed by conservative mental health professionals who recoiled from social responsibility to traditional medical secondary prevention.

Only later was Lindemann disappointed:

> For a while, when Kennedy was so successful in inspiring people
> and producing images of ideal types who would lead us to better
> things, I thought maybe there was an open pathway. I never thought
> that a person like that would probably be murdered, just as Socrates
> and Christ were killed, and as Faust says, "Die Wenigen, die Gefühl
> und Herz nicht warten, Dem Pöbel ihr Gefühl und Sehen offenbar-
> ten, Hat man von je gekruezigt und verbrannt".[52] ["The few who
> know something about it,/And foolishly do not guard their overflow-
> ing hearts,/But open their feelings, their responses to the mob,/Have
> always been crucified and burned".]

The CMHC program was one of a number of large-scale federal social
programs.[53] John McHale analyzed the politico-economic dynamics of
this major shift in values and policy—the details of the practical implementation of ideals discussed by Yarmolinsky earlier.[54] Historically, he
saw reciprocal invigoration between war and civilian industry:

> the growth of the defense establishment, the cutbacks, and the onset
> of the war on poverty. These must all be seen . . . as reflexive reac-
> tions rather than as parts of a considered and governable whole
> scheme. To state this is not to denigrate, for example, the worthwhile
> and often "visionary" efforts made at the executive level—such as
> the New Frontier, the Peace Corps, and the Great Society concepts.
> It is to recognize, rather, that the time available for political action is
> arbitrarily confined to the given terms of office. It is enormously dif-
> ficult to implement, within a four or even eight year period in office,
> a range of *ad hoc* solutions for conflict, overdue social changes, and
> economic dislocations, which may have been underway for anything
> from twenty-five years to a century. Politics has been called the art
> of the possible—but outside of the political sphere, our present time
> is characterized by the ease with which we have accomplished, and
> grown accustomed to achieving, the impossible.
>
> The most abrupt and fundamentally important of our recent
> achievements developed in physical science during the 19th century,
> when it began to probe into the subsensorial world of atomic and
> "radiation" phenomena. The competition for new raw materials
> and markets for growing industrial complexes, and the pressures of
> increased urban populations, detonated World War I. Its weaponry
> incorporated the new scientific discoveries and accelerated develop-
> ments in high strength alloys, energy conversion, air, surface and
> undersea transport, and radio communications. After World War
> I, the defense industry of the day "looked around in the domestic

market to find ways in which to exploit their super technical ability. The ex-government suppliers thus brought the dynamo, originally developed for the battleship, into the city to light man's streets, and the electric lights came thereafter to replace the candles in our domestic candelabra, but the candelabras were not changed".

(R.B. Fuller, *World Design Initiative*, 1964, pp. 6–7)

In his contemporary world, he saw a change in the national defense posture from massive confrontation to more local and flexible responses, resulting in an oversupply of strategic weapons, a decrease in federal defense spending, and consequently panic in industry and local government. The simultaneous growth of attention to social needs—civil rights, unemployment, pollution, delinquency, and urban dislocation—provided a rescue via defense industries contracting to support social programs.

The defense cutbacks in 1964 were accompanied by the official declaration of war on poverty—heralded by a series of bills. Chief among these was The Economic Opportunity Act of August 30, whose stated objective was "to mobilize local, state, and federal resources in a coordinated effort to assist the poor—especially children and youth—to achieve a better life". Its relatively miniscule budget has been given, and can bear, much criticism. . . . Nonetheless its influence and impact, even as a purely metaphorical declaration of war, is still reverberating. With its accompanying bills and budgetary provisions for increased expenditures for education, urban renewal and transportation, insurance and social welfare, and mental health, it represents an extraordinary legislative step towards comprehensive social policy and federal action in sectors that had been traditionally left to local initiative and "free enterprise". The state of California, one of the most heavily dependent on defense investment, "committed itself to putting aerospace engineers and scientists to work trying to solve earth-bound problems as successfully as they have coped with space" (*New York Times*, January 10, 1965). The areas in which it invited proposals were waste management, state information systems, crime and mental health, transportation systems.

(p. 5)

As just noted, these ideals and policies were followed by a great increase in federal funding inducements and guidelines (all unrealistically optimistic in historian David Musto's view).[55] The NIMH Study Section 1964–65 [Subcommittee on Pilot and Special Projects and Public Health, Training and Manpower Resources Branch] reported on the federal funding of programs and associated spending on people with mental illness:[56] Federal legislation in 1964–1965 included a CMHC construction program, grants in aid to states for comprehensive mental health planning, the Hospital Improvement Project Grants program, In-Service Training Grants Program for personnel in institutions for people with mental illness and people with intellectual disabilities, and intellectual disabilities legislation. "The extension of community mental health centers as the basic mental health facility may prove to be the most important development in the history of mental health in this decade." The report noted that the state hospital inpatient population had decreased since 1956 (since 1963, a 9.7% decrease, to 504,947), an increase in admissions since the 1940s (1963 = 285,439), an increase in releases since the mid 1940s (1963 = 247,423), staff increase (1955 = 146,392, 1963 = 194,516), reduction in patient-to-staff ratio (from 3.8 to 2.6), an increase in patient care cost (1955 = $3.06 to 1963 = $5.81 per patient per day), but an estimated cost per patient decrease due to a decrease in length of stay.

Much has been made of the availability of large funding as driving the social (including CMH) programs of this era and the subsequent simultaneous evaporation of both funds and programs. Slate acknowledged that "money motivates people to do what they wouldn't otherwise want to do".[57] However, he reminds us of other motivations that exert mutual influence with money:

> while money motivates people to expend energy it isn't the only thing that does so: people will work for friendship, for love, for the privilege of being part of a working group, for the enjoyment of service, for beliefs and convictions, or just to make their environment more attractive. . . . It isn't money that runs our economy but vanity. A corporation may justify its existence in terms of providing needed goods, but in fact only a small portion of its resources are devoted to this end.
>
> (pp. 170–1)

In 1960–1, early in the administration of President John Kennedy, the National Science Foundation had an increased interest in the behavioral sciences, and there was a desire in Congress to have foreign aid programs backed by behavioral science research.[58] This led to extensive maneuvering over the location of this field and control and use of the growing funds—the NIH Division of General Medical Sciences (a catchall for programs that did not fit in other institutes or crossed many, which focused on categorical programs training specific disciplines in non–mental health institutes such as heart and cancer) vs. the NIMH (championed by Assistant Surgeon General James A. Shannon). Leonard Duhl in the NIMH was concerned with the need to develop integrated conceptualization to meet the need for high-quality trained professionals. He saw the relation of mental health to developmental, environmental, and social institutions, not just illness prevention. Duhl remembers a major battle at the NIMH over the dispersion of mental health programming to all units

rather than confining it in a mental health empire.[59] An advisory committee of behavioral scientists appointed by Shannon to evaluate NIMH and
the Division of General Medical Sciences recommended a single program.
The directors of the NIMH (Stanley Yolles and Bertram Brown—the latter had been students of Lindemann's at the HSPH but did not implement
his belief in CMH) took the psychiatric empire route. In the end, the
NIMH was given responsibility for categorical mental health areas (e.g.,
disciplinary training) and for problem areas, systems, and general health.
Duhl saw this as resulting in CMHC continuing traditional clinical psychiatry practice in new packages; upon his retirement, Brown acknowledged that Duhl had been right. Duhl observed that Lindemann's CMH
ideas were implemented in tangential programs: Headstart, aging, the
early antipoverty programs, vocational rehabilitation, intellectual disability, civil rights, model cities, and community action programs.

There was increased lay interest in mental health as well as psychiatric interest in nonillness areas, leading to competition for mental health
resources and political power on federal, state, and private business levels.[60] There was change among psychiatrists from a hospital orientation
to that of the patient, environment, biopsychosocial issues, family, and
society. Psychiatrists were learning concepts of ecology, broader services,
and the social sciences. Within the Joint Commission on Mental Illness
and Health, there were battles over including only psychiatric organizations and finally including other professions and groups. It professed a
broad evaluation of psychiatric systems and community mental health
problems (NIMH's wish) but actually opted for a psychiatric report on
illness. The director purportedly represented the whole mental health
field (NIMH's wish) but actually represented psychiatry. Some of the staff
and outside forces pushed for a broader mental health and community
perspective, but the report focused on hospitals and improving state mental health systems, and they believed that prevention was impractical.
In contrast, NIMH innovators and researchers in intellectual disabilities
and psychopharmacology pushed for CMHCs, comprehensive services, a
public health approach, and hospitals as community mental health centers:[61] In 1963. . . a comprehensive community mental health program as
a *national public policy* had the support of the congress and the president of the United States . . . state officials were . . . generally supportive
and . . . thousands of citizens were ready to participate".

The 1963 Community Mental Health Centers Act was a compromise: it included non–mental illness services, but psychiatrists were to
be in charge. In the event, they varied from expanded hospitals and
clinics to the appreciation of and involvement in social issues and agencies. There was increasing overlap of professionals and organizations,
involvement in the political process, influence from public evaluation and
prioritizing resources, and broader databases and evaluation methods
influencing the assignment of roles. Vested interests—professional and

institutional—weighed in on more intense battles when authority passed from professionals to the public, Congress, federal executive departments, etc. The responses varied from defending parochial interests to alliances with other stakeholders for resources or selfless efforts for the greater good by seeing mental health problems broadly—including support of positive development, taking an ecological view of resources and stresses, and advocacy for programs covering all areas of need, including welfare, rehabilitation, poverty, and the work of the Department of Housing and Urban Development and the Model Cities Program. This could lead to the involvement of many institutions and professions and a change in the perspective and values of psychiatry.

Duhl and Leopold were disappointed that the NIMH did not take the step beyond the treatment of mental illness to dealing with social conditions—Greenblatt listed socioeconomic disadvantage, life styles, urbanization, the status of minorities and women, and population control.[62] The CMHCs were charged to integrate services and social institutions and to include a wide range of services: halfway houses, day treatment centers, cooperative apartments, home treatment programs, outpatient satellites, and aftercare facilities. It was envisioned that they would include paraprofessionals and address patient rights, standards for hospital care, and peer and government review of treatment. The idealists hoped to deal with social problems that precipitate casualties and respond to mental illness casualties but also mediate among institutions and community groups, with psychiatrists sharing authority. Too often, these differences led to bureaucratic battles.

Mental health professionals saw their role as manipulators of the environment and rode this spirit to national influence.[63] As one example, Steven Smith further traced the role of activists and political radicals (including psychologists):[64] He saw them view CMHCs as social change agents, resenting the conservative influence of psychiatry and medicine as a medicalization of social problems. Nonpsychiatric professionals and laypeople could seek to push aside psychiatrists in CMHCs, while nonpsychiatrists obtained not only staff but administrative and leadership positions.

As another example, Bernard Bandler, one of the implementers of a CMH approach through CMHCs, came from an interest in the epidemiology of mental health needs, the network of resources, and the coordination and maintenance of services.[65] He envisioned psychiatry practicing in the broad range that would include biology, intrapsychic dynamics, development, ecology, and organizational issues. That is, community psychiatry involves individual diagnosis and treatment skills too. He saw the CMHC embodying the widest range of services focusing on the mental health of a community. It would bring to bear a balance of primary, secondary, and tertiary prevention in regard to workforce, facilities, and goals. Multiple models would be applied with mutual understanding rather than conflict: medical/diagnostic, developmental, educational, organizational, and ecological. It would address all factors that affect mental health and well-being: general health, education, housing, employment, poverty, and urban and rural settings. The CMHC would be a consultant regarding planning and policy. The locus of activity would be mainly in the community and local facilities, including the influence of poverty on mental health. Special services would be located in the mental health center—such as individual and family therapy, training, and action research. In preparation for community mental health practice, he planned psychiatric residency training to include individual, family, and community dimensions as a complete foundation for future practice.

In Harry C. Solomon's 1957 presidential address to the APA, he stated that state mental hospitals were an anachronism.[66] In 1959, as commissioner of the Massachusetts DMH, his first report favored small local hospitals (he had grown up professionally at the Boston Psychopathic Hospital); and began establishing CMHCs in Lowell (named after him), Fall River, Boston (named in honor of Erich Lindemann) and helping to fund one affiliated with Boston University under the direction of Bernard Bandler. He associated CMHCs with expanded child guidance centers. He also tried to associate CMHCs with local hospitals, with the hospitals providing the land, local mental hygiene associations providing support administrative services and supplies, and the DMH funding staffing. In Ewalt's view, CMHCs varied, reflecting their own communities and institutions: some enlarged but kept their old characters, some became more multidisciplinary. Community involvement varied. Some focused only on social problems (and abandoned e.g. people with schizophrenia), while others treated only psychiatric problems (psychopathic hospitals with satellites—favored by Ewalt), and some did both. As president of the APA in 1964, Ewalt recommended that psychiatrists learn to deal with social problems (delinquency, poverty, etc.), because they had become defined as mental health problems. As commissioner of the DMH, he did not open a mental health clinic in a community until it was supported by the local medical society, bar association, school system, chamber of commerce, public health office, and labor unions, as demonstrated by their willingness to pay for housing and overhead expenses.

The implementation of CMHCs was complex. They were identified with the community mental health ideology, overlooking the heterogeneity of interpretations of CMH. Peter Whybrow saw the first CMHC law, PL 88–164 of 1963 as

> designed to change the focus of the public responsibility and to develop a bold new plan to care for the mentally ill. It was to change the locus of that care from the institution to community based centers and programs. . . . It was a radical and innovative move.[67]

Yet, as was predicted, the psychiatric profession had difficulty letting go of a focus on people with mental illness. A 1964 survey of CMHCs, thought to be representative of these institutions, found that most had the usual individual treatment services, with individual psychotherapy the back bone of the programs.[68] The range of clinical services was comprehensive. There was some consultation, but only about individual patients. Few provided mental health education programs, and there was limited research and evaluation.

Attitudes of psychiatric leaders varied. This was true even at the level of those charged with implementing CMH: Stanley Yolles, the director of the NIMH during the period of implementation of the CMHC program, had reservations: "many community psychiatrists believed that almost all mental patients could be treated in the community. This optimism was too euphoric . . . 15 percent . . . will require long-term residential care. A plan to meet this situation should have the highest priority".[69]

Jack Ewalt, who had been director of the Joint Commission on Mental Illness and Health, was at this time commissioner of the Massachusetts DMH. He was interested in HRS and in 1952 recruited Warren Vaughan, one of Lindemann's CMH colleagues, to develop mental health (not public health) facilities such as child guidance clinics, with clinicians adding community concerns to their treatment of mental illness. Ewalt recognized the accomplishments of the CMHC in decentralizing services, involving new people (laypeople, nonpsychiatric medical professionals), and improving knowledge on service needs. He had reservations about some social problem foci being too large for CMHCs to deal with.

Harry Solomon, another commissioner of DMH, acknowledged the battles involved in developing CMHCs—some won (such as convincing the federal government to allocate funds for them in Massachusetts, though the state had already appropriated some), some lost (land for a CMHC in the town of Quincy, Massachusetts, was denied because of community objections).[70] Solomon pursued the battles out of enjoying the challenges as much as out of championing CMH and was skeptical about prevention of mental illness. (Elizabeth Lindemann remembered him as self-important and controlling, including calling her on the carpet for developing a school consultation project with community agencies.)[71]

Gerald Klerman recalls that Elmer Gardner worked in the North Philadelphia Mental Health Consortium to develop good community clinic services but was caught in a political battle and "thrown out of town".[72] He then joined the administration of the federal drug and alcohol program and was again caught in political maneuvering and squeezed out of the agency. This led him to leave CMH entirely for a successful private psychiatric practice.

Paul Lemkau, a social psychiatrist, thought too little was known about social relations to demonstrate the practicality of prevention.

Gerald Caplan saw the causes of mental illness as both biological—genetics, congenital malformation, hazards of pregnancy, and medical errors—and social—cultural deprivation causing 70% of intellectual disabilities, family discord and disruption (e.g., early parental death causing a doubling of the children's risk of mental disease), parental mental illness, and school failures.[73] He saw institutional psychiatry (including the Joint Commission on Mental Illness and Health) fighting preventive mental health. He believed that he, Lindemann, and Robert Felix prevailed in including consultation and education programs in CMHCs. However, he thought they had utterly failed because consultants were untrained and were rejected or inactive. Educators and psychologists contributed more, and decreasing risk factors was more the field of politicians and primary caregivers than of mental health professionals. The proper preventive functions of mental health workers is consultation and education to caregivers, psychoeducational treatment in organized cognitive training programs, training parents in cognitive education skills, anticipatory guidance regarding life crises, preventive intervention in crises (with ego supplementation), convening supportive systems around people in need, and organizing mental help groups. Primary prevention should have been working with the highest-risk populations with the lowest competence and the fewest competence promotion resources.

The CMHC program is often identified with the ideas of Lindemann and other social and community psychiatry advocates, and its successes and failures are seen as reflecting on this ideology. This is a great misunderstanding of the ideologies and their values, goals, and sources of support. Years later, Lindemann presented in great detail his concept of community mental health as public health and preventive intervention, as differentiated from the community mental health centers as political and economic creations, and the ideological disparities between them. (See endnotes for the detailed exposition.[74]) In brief, he had focused on studies of transitions and crises and referred to the West End Study to demonstrate the relationship between change and casualties. He saw casualties (people with mental illness) as not just as examples of psychopathology but as the result of social role dysfunction and deviance. For instance, he was interested in alcoholism as a defense as well as psychopathology. He saw these social origins of mental illness as relevant to a consortium of community resources, including the state departments of public health, education, public welfare, and corrections, as well as the nongovernmental united community services as a source of coordination and funding. He was interested in experimenting with coordination and renewal among these agencies, as in his experience in Wellesley. Lindemann thought the clinicians who staffed the CMHCs had the wrong set of values for public health work and that child guidance clinics were inappropriate bases for community work: they were inefficient and had long waiting lists, and their long-term treatment reached few in the community

Erich Lindemann was always a professional and scientist. Therefore, he had reservations about unrealistic expectations, premature application, and overexpanding CMH, including in the CMHCs:

- "Sometimes I worry that public enthusiasm is doing harm to the slow building of sound foundations for a mental health program".[75]
- There has been a recent boom in the mental health movement . . . Mental health is the topic of the day. Legislatures . . . give increasing amounts of money. . . . Some of us feel that this may go too far too fast; that the public is being sold unsound merchandise; that we cannot keep the implied promises of happiness and success; that we have created a 'secular religion' which is supposed to supply the answers for . . . unanswerable questions, whereas for centuries philosophers and theologians have provided . . . various dogmas . . . the scientific method have become the source of prestige and validity . . . omnipotence and omniscience . . . tend to become attributed to the practitioner of scientific pursuits. . . . The very success of much . . . psychiatric research, and the public awareness that much may ultimately alter radically . . . dealing with mental illness . . . crime and with social dependence, leads to the stepped-up citizen demand for mental health services . . . premature application in the field of human engineering may lead to confusion and misunderstanding.[76]

Gerald Caplan seconded these concerns:[77]

An outstanding danger today is that community mental health will become a bandwagon, and that attractive slogans will impel us to undertake sweeping new programs which will be lavishly financed by federal and state funds because they are currently fashionable and politically expedient. . . . Preventive hopes of the . . . child guidance clinics turned out to be illusory, and so may those of the protagonists of the new community mental health centers. I do not agree with those who say that we should undertake no new program which is not based on scientifically validated research. In this field that would mean we should do nothing. Only by trying a new program can we find out if and how it works. On the other hand we must move with caution, lest we . . . provide disillusionment which will eventually leave us politically worse off . . . and lest we ill-advisedly stimulate a pendulum swing which may destroy the little we have already accomplished. We must build upon the best of what we have, and not destroy it merely to replace it by something new and fashionable. Unfortunately we can predict that the recent accelerating development of interest and support among the politicians and the public for comprehensive community programs to combat mental disorder, the excitement of new ideas . . . and the pressure of mounting public awareness of need in this field will . . . lead to the too hasty establishment of programs, staffed by workers untrained in the complexities of community practice, and deploying resources uncritically and overenthusiastically on the basis of untested ideas.

(p. 10–11)

Lindemann recognized the need for and complexities of community participation in community mental health.[78] He saw community participation as a vehicle for a public health approach to mental health: A February 1962 newspaper article reported on a meeting sponsored by the Dorchester (Massachusetts) Mental Health Association and the Dorchester United Neighborhood Association at the YMHA–Hecht House in Dorchester.[79] Lindemann spoke on his lecture "The Role of the Community Mental Health Center in the Prevention of Emotional Problems". Commenting on the state mental health clinic scheduled to open in the Robert White Health Center on Blue Hill Avenue that summer, he warned of long waiting lists. He called for a public health approach to mental illness akin to campaigns wiping out infectious diseases. He recommended sharing mental health information with community health workers, teachers, volunteers, and parents, believeing that some expertise was better than none. The Coconut Grove fire taught that emotional stress delays physical healing, that grief can be helped, and that nonphysicians see sorrow and can be taught to recognize and refer for treatment as well as other life crises (problems of adolescence, birth of a first child, etc.). Elizabeth Lindemann directed similar workshops in Dorchester community centers under the auspices of the State Division of Mental Hygiene.

In Lindemann's retrospect on community mental health and the community mental health center program, he commented on the practical problems with the massive federal/state program:[80]

[O]ne of the unfortunate aspects of it [the CMHC Program] was . . . a band wagon effect. All kinds of accretions came to this idea and all kinds of people climbed onto the band wagon. We never thought . . . that this would happen. We think it unfortunate that this should then be . . . a federal program providing for a large number of centers. Places . . . cannot be prepared in such a quick way. There is no solid base for knowledgeable operation. I have an awful fear that this thing will boomerang, that the hopes won't be fulfilled. I also am very sorry . . . that the federal money is channeled through the state authorities . . . there is no collateral channel to institutions.[81] . . . Though they may subscribe to the principle here, Massachusetts . . . really has the responsibility for its mentally sick people. . . . Harry Solomon might not like to see the transcript [of this interview], for as we social science workers know, when personal matters are involved, the studied professional attitude may change to something quite different. . . . Bob Hyde has been quite active in this before he went into the correctional side . . . A man. quite involved in the community side . . . whom I estimate very highly is [Belenden] Hutchinson [DMH Associate Commissioner and Director of the Division of Mental Hygiene] . . . had to believe, in the child guidance combine. . . . The South Shore guidance center is a shining example of what can be done. Arthur Hallock who went around with Warren Vaughan gathering citizens' groups alerted to . . . the mental health center. . . . [There are] very bitter feelings between the Mental Health Association and the state department division of mental hygiene because the division head organized citizens' groups . . . and had not always gone to the Mental Health Association . . . as an original citizens' organization.

John F. Kennedy's Mental Health and Intellectual Disability Message: Priming the Community Mental Health Centers Period

The process of federal support for healthcare continued to be tortured. During the Eisenhower presidency (1953–61), the Department of Health, Education, and Welfare sponsored the 1958 conference on problems of aging.[82] In 1960, the term "Medicare" was first used for a federal program of medical care for the aged; the proposal was rejected by the House of Representatives Committee on Ways and Means, though federal health appropriations had grown from $221 million to $840 million by that time. President John F. Kennedy (1961–3) proposed Medicare again and again, and it was rejected, though federal health appropriations had further grown from $1 billion to $1.6 billion by 1963, including a $6-million three-year program of research into the education of people with intellectual disabilities. There were complaints about the piecemeal and short-term character of this funding:[83]

Soon it became apparent that added manpower was the great need, and research fellowships and training programs were instituted. More adequate research facilities next appeared as the bottleneck, and the Congress passed legislation providing for the construction of medical research facilities. . . . Recently there has been increasing recognition in Washington of the integrated nature of educational institutions, and . . . long-term fellowship programs, and clinical center and general support grants have been made to support larger segments of the activities of the schools. . . . there has been essentially no change in the purely research focus of the National Institutes of Health. Research activities cannot exist in a vacuum. To flourish, a strong total academic environment is required. Support is needed for teachers and new teaching facilities, and for the general costs of our total programs. . . . Support is fragmented. Individual members of the faculty request funds for their particular interests. . . . Long-term planning is not easily possible in such a framework. . . . the duration of any particular grant is short. Long-term commitments cannot be based on mere assumptions of continuity.

An influential event in the area of mental health was President John F. Kennedy's "Message from the President of the United States Relative to Mental Illness and Mental Retardation" (referred to previously), elevating this area to the status of major societal issues.[84]

> But two health problems—because they are of such critical size and tragic impact, and because their susceptibility to public action is so much greater than the attention they have received—are deserving of a wholly new national approach and a separate message to the Congress. These twin problems are mental illness and mental retardation. From the earliest days of the Public Health Service. . . . the Federal Government has recognized its responsibilities to assist, stimulate, and channel public energies in attacking health problems. . . . But the public understanding, treatment, and prevention of mental disabilities have not made comparable progress. . . . Yet mental illness and mental retardation are among our most critical health problems (Quotes figures regarding patients, beds, and expenditures—perhaps from the report of the Joint Commission on Mental Illness and Health) This situation has been tolerated far too long. It has troubled our national conscience—but only as a problem unpleasant to mention, easy to postpone, and despairing of solution. The Federal government, despite the nationwide impact of the problem, has largely left the solutions up to the States. The States have depended on custodial hospitals and homes. Many such hospitals and homes have been shamefully understaffed, overcrowded, unpleasant institutions from which death too often provided the only firm hope of release. The time has come for a bold new approach. New medical, scientific, and social tools and insights are now available. A series of comprehensive studies initiated by the Congress, the executive branch, and interested private groups have been completed and all point in the same direction.

The address follows by giving first priority to prevention and dealing with community conditions, as favored by Lindemann, leaving the Joint Commission's emphasis on care of people with mental illness third, supporting Jack Ewalt's impression that the federal government's priorities differed from those of the Joint Commission:

> Our attack must be focused on three major objectives: First, we must seek out the causes of mental illness and of mental retardation

and eradicate them. . . . It is far more economical and it is far more likely to be successful. Prevention will require both selected specific programs directed especially at known causes, and the general strengthening of our fundamental community, social welfare, and educational programs which can do much to eliminate or correct the harsh environmental conditions which often are associated with mental retardation and mental illness. . . . Second, we must strengthen the underlying resources of knowledge and, above all, of skilled manpower. . . . We must also expand our research efforts if we are to learn more about how to prevent and treat the crippling or malfunctioning of the mind. Third, we must strengthen and improve the programs and facilities serving the mentally ill and the mentally retarded. The emphasis should be upon timely and intensive diagnosis, treatment, training, and rehabilitation. . . . Services . . . must be community based and provide a range of services to meet community needs. . . . I am proposing a new approach . . . designed, in large measure, to use Federal resources to stimulate State, local, and private action. . . . Emphasis on prevention, treatment, and rehabilitation. . . . In an effort to hold domestic expenditures down in a period of tax reduction, I have postponed new programs and reduced added expenditures. . . . But we cannot afford to postpone any longer a reversal in our approach to mental affliction. For too long the shabby treatment of the many millions in custodial institutions and many millions more now in communities . . . has been justified on grounds of inadequate funds, further studies and future promises. We can procrastinate no more. The national mental health program . . . warrants prompt congressional attention . . . a national mental health program . . . relies primarily upon the new knowledge and new drugs acquired and developed in recent years.

Prevention as well as treatment will be a major activity. Located in the patient's own environment and community, the [community mental health] center would make possible a better understanding of his needs. . . . Ideally, the center could be located at an appropriate community general hospital, many of which already have psychiatric units. In such instances, additional services and facilities could be added . . . to fill out the comprehensive program . . . an existing outpatient psychiatric clinic might form the nucleus . . . as affiliates of State mental hospitals, under State or local governments, or under voluntary nonprofit sponsorship.

The continued message's high expectations of success and low expectations of costs—doubtless designed to gain political support—set an unrealistic precedent that would lead to later disillusionment and justification of the counterrevolution against CMH and in favor of a return to biological psychiatry:

> [This approach will] make it possible for most of the mentally ill to be successfully and quickly treated in their own communities and returned to a useful place in society. . . . I am convinced that, if we apply our medical knowledge and social insight fully, all but a small portion of the mentally ill can eventually achieve a wholesome and constructive social adjustment. . . . If we launch a broad new mental health program now, it will be possible within a decade or two to reduce the number of patients now under custodial care by 50 percent or more. Many more mentally ill can be helped to remain in their own homes without hardship to themselves or their families. Those who are hospitalized can be helped to return to their own communities. All but a small proportion can be restored to useful life. We can spare them and their families much of the misery which mental illness now entails. We can save public funds and we can conserve or manpower resources. . . . The services provided by these centers should be financed in the same way as other medical and hospital costs. At one time, this was not feasible in the case of mental illness, where prognosis almost invariably called for long and often permanent courses of treatment. But tranquilizers and new therapeutic methods now permit mental illness to be treated successfully in a very high proportion of cases within relatively short periods of time—weeks or months, rather than years. . . . Long-range federal subsidies for operating costs are neither necessary nor desirable.

He then set the stage for implementing a CMH approach by drafting the CMHC program of building, staffing, and workforce development for mental health services, with a community perspective:

> Central to a new mental health program is comprehensive community care. Merely pouring Federal funds into a continuation of the outmoded type of institutional care which now prevails would make little difference. . . . I recommend, therefore, that the Congress (1) authorize grants to the States for the construction of comprehensive community mental health centers . . . with the Federal Government providing 45 to 75 percent of the project cost; (2) authorize short-term project grants for the initial staffing costs of comprehensive community mental health centers, with the Federal Government providing up to 75 percent of the cost in the early months, on a gradually declining basis, terminating such support . . . within slightly over 4 years; and (3) to facilitate the preparation of community plans for these new facilities as a necessary preliminary to any construction or staffing assistance, appropriate $4.2 million for planning grants . . .

the separate elements which would be combined. . . [services to include] diagnostic and evaluation services, emergency psychiatric units, outpatient services, inpatient services, day and night care, foster home care, rehabilitation, consultative services to other community agencies, and mental health information and education. These centers will focus community resources and provide better community facilities.

Plans for workforce development included an increase in the supply of psychiatrists, clinical psychologists, social workers, and nurses from 45,000 in 1960 to 85,000 in 1970. For this purpose, training funds would increase from $49 million to $65 million. Aid would also be provided to train more physicians and related health personnel.

Plans for financing were less detailed and more speculative—foreshadowing struggles that would limit the fulfillment of the dream: In the short term, declining federal funding should stimulate modest cost fee-for-service insurance, which the federal Department of Health, Education, and Welfare would encourage. Sources of funding might include third-party payments, voluntary and private contributions, state and local aid, mental health insurance, and redirecting state resources from custodial mental institutions to CMHCs, accessible to all.

The "storm decade", from Kennedy's assassination in 1963 to the resignation of President Richard Nixon in 1974, included the 1963 Kennedy civil rights bill that led to the 1964 Johnson Civil Rights Act. White contends that this legislation, intended to unify the country with civil rights for all was in fact the beginning of spawning fragmentated special interest/self-advocacy groups—black, gay, women, ethnic groups, students, etc.

With legislation driven by these social forces (including PL 88–164 1963, the CMHC Construction Act), community mental health activities grew rapidly and reached the proportions of a social movement in the 1960s,[85] sometimes referred to as the third psychiatric revolution (after moral treatment and psychoanalysis):[86] "To refer to community mental health as a 'social movement' signifies there was not only professional and scientific activity but that its ideas and goals had gained substantial support in public circles, particularly among governmental policymakers."[87] NIMH extramural research grant awards escalated:[88]

- 1948 = $3.3 million
- 1958 = $12.3 million
- 1968 = $66.9 million
- 1973 = $82.9 million.

In this era, government and industry turned to academia for information and guidance.[89] Grants, contracts, and consultantships turned professors' research and students' assignments and dissertations toward the grantors' interests: "the larger role played by the professor in guiding practical affairs has obviously benefitted society as well as himself".[90] Society was subsidizing professors' research on a vast and rising scale and seeking their advice:

> confronted with problems of enormous complexity and urgency— in business, in government, in international relations and economic planning and military technology—Americans have been turning for guidance to the scientists and scholars on university faculties. The universities themselves for the most part have been happy to give such guidance. (For one thing, it has enabled them to get badly needed financial support.) And in the process, the quality of academic life in America—and the whole shape of higher education— has been profoundly altered.[91]

Sponsored grants grew: in 1958 $60 million from foundations and corporations and $41 million from universities and in 1960 more than $500 million. The federal government was the largest source: in 1940 $15 million and in 1960 $460 million, of which $300 million went to universities.

Research areas and interpretations in educational institutions were shaped by academic traditions and control by more-senior and conservative faculty and administrators. The waxing and waning of CMHC policy also affected academic research, practice, and training. For example, one of the community-based programs supported by these funds was the James Jackson Putnam Children's Center.[92] This was the first therapeutic center treating children under five years of age by using a therapeutic nursery school. It was interested in the study of child development, including the child's ability to recognize its mother immediately after birth, multiproblem and poor families and their effect on child development, and the effect of physical conditions on children (flies, unrefrigerated food, etc.). It contacted families through public health and visiting nurses, and it collaborated with them and nursery schools and their teachers. When government funding for CMH progressively receded, community workers left for manual jobs, and the center closed.

Traditional psychiatric residency training programs did not train psychiatrists in comprehensive community-oriented mental health practice, as emphasized by CMH, including through the CMHC program.[93] Little of the training in community psychiatry involved medicine and social and behavioral science, which are needed by students, faculty, and practitioners. Local education programs varied:

> The western states are forced to be innovative by their need to make optimal use of their resources and to develop new ones. When

compared to those in areas richer in mental health resources, their activities illustrate a paradox: the inverse ratio between resources and innovation. Many of the major medical training centers are high on resources. The reader can draw his own conclusion as to their receptivity to innovation.[94]

Therefore, the NIMH supported university education centers' training programs that would integrate CMH into psychiatric residencies and augmented 20 post-residency programs specializing in CMH. In 1964, NIMH arranged four four-day regional institutes for chairpersons of departments of psychiatry and directors of psychiatric residency programs to encourage the inclusion of CMH in residency programs and then a series of two-week workshops for senior psychiatry faculty members. One of these was the visiting faculty seminars offered until 1967 by the Harvard Medical School Laboratory for Community Psychiatry. This expanded community psychiatry training was offered as a Harvard course and as continuing education for psychiatrists on leave from their jobs.[95] For example, Eliot G. Mishler, PhD, the program director for the Research Training Program in Social Psychiatry at the Massachusetts Mental Health Center (MMHC), reported to Lindemann that they had recruited a third trainee on an NIH grant and "thought you would like to know we were starting".[96] Columbia University has offered training in community psychiatry since 1956. By 1967, it also took place at other universities, including Baylor, Chicago, San Francisco, Duke, Pittsburgh, and Vermont. In 1966, the Southern Regional Education Board held a landmark conference on problems that medical schools have in planning CMH service as part of their education programs and on faculty acceptance of innovation without deterioration in communication and community, innovation vs. tradition, and concerns about professional identity (discussed in more detail later on).

There was criticism that NIMH general support for continuing education as needed for comprehensive professional education included little emphasis on CMH. There were many approaches to CMH education: continuing education, internship, joint university-community service agency appointments, etc. "Motivations of the training recipients frequently are suspect, and the long-term benefits certainly are".[97]

In terms of public health training in mental health, Viola Bernard noted that

Within the former area (i.e. the application of mental health concepts to public health activities), there has been considerable experience in teaching in various schools of public health. In the latter area (i.e. the training of mental health specialists), the experience is recent and limited; such special training has not yet been included in the educational programs of most of the schools of public health, and, in fact, is limited to just a fraction of them.[98]

The National Conference on Mental Health Teaching in Schools of Public Health saw the importance of the social sciences in education for and practice of public health mental health:[99]

> It is said that the problems which today confront sociologists, social workers and the like are problems of psychological maladjustment, and that these are symptomatic of a sick society. . . . Since World War II social science is involved in the study of child rearing, communication, perception, attitudes, group dynamics, and sociometry in shaping personality.
>
> (p. 16)

> The social sciences do not offer any panaceas for public health or mental health work. It is clear that they have made a contribution in calling attention to certain important areas which have a bearing on health and disease. The contribution comprises both knowledge and tools. Some remain to be explored in more precise fashion; some can be applied, but we still do not know all the ways in which application can be made. . . . Efforts are being made to develop interdisciplinary research under the auspices of such groups as the Institute of Human Relations at Yale, the Commission of Human Development at the University of Chicago and the Department of Social Relations at Harvard. Naturally, interdisciplinary research has its problems, but few of the problems that arise in collaboration between community health and the social sciences are unique to this specific area. They are generic to the larger area of teamwork, whether within as single field or between two or more fields, and differ only in terms of the degree or phrasing of collaboration.
>
> (p. 22)

Notes

1. Starr, Paul, *The Social Transformation of American Medicine* (New York: Basic Books, 1982). [also found in folder "History—Psychiatry, Medicine", David G. Satin files, Newton, MA]
2. "Special Message to the Congress on Mental Illness and Mental Retardation, February 5, 1963", *Public Papers of the President, John F. Kennedy, 1963*, pp. 126, 128.
3. Astrachan, Boris M., "Many Modest Goal: The Pragmatics of Health Delivery", *Connecticut Medicine 37*: 174–180 (1973).
4. Duhl, Leonard J., "History of Behavioral Sciences in the Federal Government", presentation at the Committee on Social and Physical Environment Variables as Determinants of Mental Health, 12th meeting, 10/27/65. [Erich Lindemann Collection, Center for the History of Medicine, Francis A. Countway Library of Medicine, Boston, MA]

5. Lindemann, Erich, letter to Zinberg, Norman, chairperson of the Massachusetts Associaton for Mental Health's Professional Advisory Committee, 9/20/1962. [folder "Mass. Association for Mental Health", Box IIIA 4 (I-Ma), Erich Lindemann Collection, Center for the History of Medicine, Francis A. Countway Library of Medicine, Boston, MA]

6. Thresher, Irene K., chairperson of the Action for Mental Health in Massachusetts Committee, letter to Lindemann, Erich, 5/11/1962. [folder "Mass. Association for Mental Health", Box IIIA 4 (I-Ma), Erich Lindemann Collection, Center for the History of Medicine, Francis A. Countway Library of Medicine, Boston, MA]

7. Action for Mental Health in Massachusetts, Minutes of Committee Meeting 4/24/62. [folder "Mass. Association for Mental Health", Box IIIA 4 (I-Ma), Erich Lindemann Collection, Center for the History of Medicine, Francis A. Countway Library of Medicine, Boston, MA]

8. Edwards, Carl, observations on social law and principles of responsibility in law and society. Informal discussion, Colloquium on the History of Psychiatry and Medicine, Harvard Medical School, Boston, MA, 10/21/2004.

9. Action for Mental Health in Massachusetts, Minutes of Committee Meeting 4/24/1962. [folder "Mass. Association for Mental Health", Box IIIA 4 (I-Ma), Erich Lindemann Collection, Center for the History of Medicine, Francis A. Countway Library of Medicine, Boston, MA]

10. Hallen, Philip, Director of the Maurice Falk Fund: Talk as part of the Wellesley Human Relations Service 30th Anniversary celebration, Wellesley, Massachusetts, 11/3/1978.

11. Correspondence between Lindemann and Charles I. Schottland, commissioner of the Social Security Administration, U.S. Department of Health, Education, and Welfare, 4/11–8/9/1956. [folder "Misc. Correspondence D, E,F 1956–57", Box IIIA 1–3, Lindemann Collection, Center for the History of Medicine, Francis A. Countway Library of Medicine, Boston, MA]

12. Klerman, Gerald L., "Better But Not Well: Social and Ethical Issues in the Deinstitutionalization of the Mentally Ill", *Schizophrenia Bulletin 3* no. 4: 617–631 (1977).

13. Goffman, Erving, *Asylums* (New York: Doubleday, 1961).

14. Jones, Maxwell. *The Therapeutic Community* (New York: Basic Books, Inc., 1953).

15. Feuerwerker, Elie, unpublished manuscript, fall 1985. [Erich Lindemann Collection, Center for the History of Medicine, Francis A. Countway Library of Medicine, Boston, MA]

16. Cited by Fein, Rashi, 1958, pp. 1, 135.

17. Joint Commission on Menta Illness and Health, *Action for Mental Health* 1961, pp. 2, 7–8.

18. Starr, Paul, 1982, pp. 3, 365.

19. Klerman, Gerald L., 1977, p. 622.

20. Klerman, Gerald L., 1977, pp. 2, 618.

21. Joint Commission on Mental Illness and Health, *Action for Mental Health* 1961.

22. Kennedy, John F., "Special Message to the Congress on Mental Illness and Mental Retardation", 2/5/63 p. 128.

23. Solomon, Harry C., 6/22/1978.

24. Gifford, Sanford; Lipsett, Don; Roazen, Paul; Apple, Roberta as part of Gifford, Sanford, "The James Jackson Putnam Children's Center 1943–1970s—Child Psychiatry and Social Change", Colloquium on the History of Psychiatry and Medicine, 12/16/2004.

25. Vaughan, Warren T., Jr., MD, "Local Mental Health Program Administration", Ch. 20 in Bellak, Leopold (ed.), *Handbook of Community*

Psychiatry and Community Mental Health (Grune & Stratton, 1964), pp. 388–408, 389.

26. Greenblatt, Milton, MD, "Profiles of Famous American Psychiatrists: Harry C. Solomon, M.D.", *Psychiatric Annals 10* no. 10: 71, 74–76 (10/1980).

27. Solomon, Harry C. letter to Hazard, Sprague W., 11/4/1960, p. 1. [folder "Child Psychiatry Unit", Box IIIA 4 (A-E), Erich Lindemann Collection, Center for the History of Medicine, Francis A. Countway Library of Medicine, Boston, MA]

28. Solomon, 11/4/1960, *ibid.* The committee included physicians Bernard Bandler, Walter Barton, Malcolm J. Farrell, Sprague W. Hazard, William F. McLaughlin, Charles G. Shedd, and Jackson M. Thomas as well as Rabbi Roland B. Gittelsohn, Mr. Wm A. Waldron, Mr. George A. Macomber, Mr. Gerald A. Ouelette, and D. Reginald Robinson, PhD.

29. Office of the Federal Register, National Archives and Records Administration, "Public Papers of the Presidents of the United States—John F. Kennedy" (1963). Also Kennedy, John F., message to Congress, 2/5/1963, "Community Mental Health Centers: The Federal Investment" (DHEW Publication No. (ADM) 78–677, 1978), p. iii. [folder "Federal U.S. Actions", David G. Satin files, Newton, MA]

30. Kelly, James G., The Ohio State University, "The Community Mental Health and the Study Of Social Change", in *Community Mental Health: Individual Adjustment or Social Planning; A Symposium, Ninth Interamerican Congress of Psychology, 1964* (Adelphi, MD: Mental Health Study Center, National Institute of Mental Health, 1965). [Also found in folder "CMH—Policy, Politics, Administration, Institutions", David G. Satin files, Newton, MA]

31. Smith, M. Brewster, University of California Berkeley, Hobbs, Nicholas, George Peabody College for Teachers, "The Community and the Community Mental Health Center", *American Psychologist* 449–509 (p. 499). [folder "SMITH + HOBBS—COMMUNITY+CMHC", IIIB3 d, Erich Lindemann Collection, Center for the History of Medicine, Francis A. Countway Library of Medicine, Boston, MA]

32. Sharfstein, Steven S., MD, "Will Community Mental Health Survive in the 1980s?", *American Journal of Psychiatry 135* no. 11: 1363–1364 (11/78) [found in folder "CMH—History", David G. Satin files, Newton, MA]; p. 1363.

33. Greenblatt, Milton, "To Complete the Revolution", *Psychiatric Annals 7* no. 10: 105–109 (p. 108) (October 1977). [also found in folder "CMH—Policy, Politics, Administration, Institutions", David G. Satin files, Newton, MA]

34. U.S. Department of Health, Education, and Welfare, Public Health Service, Alcohol, Drug Abuse, and Mental Health Administration, "Community Mental Health Centers: The Federal Investment" (DHEW Publication No. (ADM) 78–677, 1978).

Also Operations Liaison and Program Analysis Section, Community Mental Health Services Support Branch, Division of Mental Health Service Programs, National Institute of Mental Health, "The Community Mental Health Services Network: A Statistical Profile" (6/82). [folder "Federal U.S. Actions", David G. Satin files, Newton, MA]

35. Starr, Paul, *The Social Transformation of American Medicine* (New York: Basic Books, 1982), p. 347. [Also found in folder "History—Psychiatry, Medicine", David G. Satin files, Newton, MA]

36. "Introduction: Mental Health and Political Process", in Duhl, Leonard J. and Leopold, Robert L. (eds.), *Mental Health and Urban Social Policy* (San

Francisco: Jossey-Bass, 1968); Budget Office, NIMH, December 1976, in Lamb, Richard H. and Zusman, Jack, "Primary Prevention in Perspective", *American Journal of Psychiatry 136* no. 1: 12–17 (1/19/1979).

37. U.S. Department of Health, Education, and Welfare, Public Health Service, Alcohol, Drug Abuse, and Mental Health Administration, "Community Mental Health Centers: The Federal Investment" (DHEW Publication No. (ADM) 78–677, 1978); p. 56 CMHC funding sources 1971–5. [folder "Federal U.S. Actions", David G. Satin files, Newton, MA]

38. U.S. Department of Health, Education, and Welfare, Public Health Service, Alcohol, Drug Abuse, and Mental Health Administration, "Community Mental Health Centers: The Federal Investment" (DHEW Publication No. (ADM) 78–677, 1978); p. 51 federal investment in CMHCs. [folder "Federal U.S. Actions", David G. Satin files, Newton, MA]

39. Operations Liaison and Program Analysis Section, Community Mental Health Services Support Branch, Division of Mental Health Service Programs, National Institute of Mental Health, "The Community Mental Health Services Network: A Statistical Profile" (6/82). [folder "Federal U.S. Actions", David G. Satin files, Newton, MA]

40. Mulligan, Kate, *Psychiatric News* 2/6/2004, p. 7.

41. Newbrough, J.R., Mental Health Study Center, National Institute of Mental Health: "Community Mental Health: A Movement in Search of a Theory", in *Community Mental Health: Individual Adjustment or Social Planning; a Symposium, Ninth Interamerican Congress of Psychology, 1964* (Adelphi, MD: Mental Health Study Center, National Institute of Mental Health, 1965).

42. folder "NIMH", Box IIIA 4 (Mb-O), Erich Lindemann Collection, Center for the History of Medicine, Francis A. Countway Library of Medicine, Boston, MA. Committee members listed included: Erich Lindemann, David A. Hamburg, Reginald S. Lourie, Seymour B. Sarason. Staff included Dr. Eli A. Rubinstein (Chief), Dr. Raymond J. Balester (Asst Chief), Dr. Stephen Goldston, Dr. Harold Janney, Dr. Reginald S. Lourie, Miss Marie McNabola, Dr. Betty H. Pickett, Dr. Ralph Simon, Dr. Reber VanMatre; Community Mental Health Facilities Branch included Dr. Bertram S. Brown, Dr. Lucy Ozarin, Dr. Emory Ferebee.

43. Mental Health Training Committee, Policy and Planning Board, NIMH, Public Health Service, Health, Education, and Welfare Meeting, 10/2,3/1964. [folder "NIMH", Box IIIA 4 (Mb-O), Erich Lindemann Collection, Center for the History of Medicine, Francis A. Countway Library of Medicine, Boston, MA] The following were the essentials of the discussion:

[CMH theory]

[Dr. David A. Hamburg] viewed this movement as a point of view, the substance of which still needs to be filled in; in other words, that we are in a moment of social ferment, groping in essentially important and exciting directions, but that we lack highly developed conceptual schemes based on firm research evidence. While there are some areas in which large-scale and rapid applications of concepts can be justified, there are others where too little is known of the probable consequences to warrant the risk. . . . Dr. Hamburg discussed his analysis of the assumptions and stereotypes inherent in the concept of community mental health centers. Primary among these is the notion that professional services ought to be available more broadly, rather than restricted to the relatively well-to-do. Another implicit viewpoint is that mental health services will have to change in nature if they are to be actually provided to a larger segment of the population. Still another is that there must be a shift to more outpatient care. Although little is said regarding drugs in contrast to considerable discussion of large social units, group therapy, therapeutic environs, etc., in practice large-scale use of drugs has been and will be involved in treatment at centers. Another orientation is that toward early-case finding, perhaps explicitly linked to some type of preventive orientation. . . . Dr. Hamburg stated that there are a number of interesting and important questions . . . relevant to the value systems expressed in the actions of current community mental health practitioners (1) . . . there is some tendency to lose consideration of individuality and the variability among people and to have greater interest in human beings in the mass; . . . traditional patterns may have some merit in terms of focus on individual characteristics. He cited Dr. Lindemann's crisis approach as a very good example of an effort to retain focus on individuality while at the same time moving toward a broader availability of service. (2) What is to be the role of biological factors in these programs? Apart from the evidence derived from the use of drugs that points to the role of biological factors, consideration must also be given to genetics. . . . we are in the midst of an explosive advance in the biological sciences comparable to that of the physical sciences in the 1930s, and that a large-scale program which fails to take account of that situation is vulnerable. (3) How do we develop methods of preventive intervention with the social unit as the focus? This might have the greatest long-term preventive possibilities, and yet it is a very difficult area in which the mixing of personal values with professional judgement is very complex . . . urged against an attitude that 'we know pretty much all that is needed' and merely have to apply it quickly and on a large scale.

(pp. 19–21)

He emphasized the need for research in CMH, training in CMH research, research positions in CMHCs.

[Dr. Harold D. Chope] "Dr. Chope next called attention to the community mental health program that has developed in San Mateo County, California, over the past eight years, as being representative of some very crucial changes in philosophy and values in the field of mental health. In this program there has been a shift from the concepts of the Dorothea Dix philosophy of humane and kindly State care for the mentally ill and the traditional one-to-one therapeutic relationship, to a concern with the prevention and care of mental illness by better utilizing community and family resources along lines similar to those discussed earlier by Dr. Lindemann. In order to develop such community mental health services more is required than the one-to-one skills of the psychiatrist, the psychologist, the psychiatric social worker, and the psychiatric nurse. These professionals must learn to consider the community as their patient rather than the individual, just as the health officer of the last half century has had to learn to make a diagnosis of health needs of the community and design programs to combat community ill health, as contrasted with private physicians concerned with the individual patient".

(pp. 24–5)

Dr. Lindemann indicated that in public health programs, which are closely related to the rest of medicine, there are many sections of the community and many fringe operators (such as sanitary engineers) who are meaningfully related to public health programs, but are not themselves medical personnel. Public health and preventive medicine workers have to do exactly the same things which mental health specialists are doing; that is, become related to the total spectrum of disease over time and as it occurs in the community. One of the big problems of public health and preventive medicine is the integration of a concern with a population or community into the program of research and teaching. Another problem is that sections of the community not ordinarily defined as being of medical concern have to be invaded, sometimes against resistance, or have to be exploited for medical purposes. The same problem exists with respect to the community mental health centers.

A community mental health center wants to be a public health agency in the sense that it serves not individuals but populations, its rewards are the reduction of the incidence and prevalence of disease, strengthening healthy forms of living, and strengthening coping devices rather than removing only pathological devices.

In this role common purposes must be made with other sections of the community, such as the educator, the clergyman, the law enforcement agent, the social agent, and so on. We have to live with their particular investment and their special ways of remedial and preventative concerns which they don't call medical. Out of this reality grows the need for the community mental health agency to facilitate interaction and joint operations with other professional groups.

It is also necessary to be aware of the fact that a community has devised a variety of quasi-remedial procedures such as jails, schools, and so on, and that communities have an investment in these institutions. We cannot add any new procedures unless we have a conviction and are persuasive enough to see that our procedures add something to existing community-wide operations to cope with certain problems.

Furthermore, we are moving into areas of uncertainty. The diagnosis of a schizophrenic is something quite different from the diagnosis of an alcoholic, and certainly different from the diagnosis of a sexual deviant. If we include social deviancy and under-achieving as part of the mental health field, we get into an area where a social rather than a medical judgment determines the gravity of the situation. We find ourselves comparing different scales of measurement, and we have to learn to live with this.

Redlich, Leighton, Pasmanick seeking overview of community, social space, stratification disorders, define maladaptive responses and coping devices). . . . all this is a range of concern that is quite beyond the area of diagnosis and treatment but which now must be taken into account in a community mental health center.

Despite certain new and additional prescribed functions, Dr. Lindemann noted that the comprehensive community mental health center, while close to the community, is still a modified clinical operation. This poses the serious question of whether it is a good thing to have the same people who are the clinicians also the people who are concerned with the community issues mentioned above. These are not the same people nor is training the same for both types. These are two different regions of endeavor.

Dr. Lindemann indicated that some of the community mental health operations should not be in the community mental health center at all. They should be detailed operations being carried on in the several institutions within the community, but coordinated and controlled and researched in a particular center. If these things are kept in mind, one then might find it possible to collaborate with the community mental health centers which are not called by that label, but usually exist anyway. For instance it is quite impressive that the medical profession at large is taking up this point of view in the total health program and in the penetration of the community with respect to the general hospital. As a consequence, the metropolitan general hospital is changing its function.

Dr. Lindemann said that the social behavioral sciences do much better if they articulate with the whole spectrum of medicine rather than trying to be closer only to psychiatry. Medical casualties are just as serious and just as commonly casualties of the social process as are psychiatric casualties. He suggested closer contact with the evolution of preventive programs in medicine.

In subsequent discussion, the opinion was expressed that the extension of the medical model to a series of social problems at the community level poses a number of problems. First, that it requires a redefinition of social problems at the community level which will have disadvantages, inasmuch as problems such as underachievement, delinquency, etc. cannot best be understood by using any theories of behavior derived from the medical model. Second, it arouses spurious and inappropriate public understanding of these problems and of effective public alternatives to the resolution of these problems. Third, it may raise false hopes in the minds of the public because of the outstanding success that the medical model has achieved in areas where its competence is most appropriate.

It was stated that manpower shortages in the field are such that it cannot be expected that sufficient personnel can be mobilized in the next decade. If clinical expertise is to be given up in order to perform the new tasks required by the centers, it will have to be done at the expense of very important current responsibilities. Further, doubt was expressed that mental health knowledge is appropriate for the kinds of tasks that will have to be undertaken with regard to social community problems. Doubt was expressed that any of the mental health professions should be in charge of community programs.

Dr. Lindemann pointed out that the law establishing the centers dictates that those who wish to obtain this particular type of financial assistance must follow the dictates of this law; this does not dictate a pattern for all institutions and communities, which still have the freedom to develop along other lines if they do not wish to take advantage of this source of funds.

On the positive side of the issue, Dr. Lindemann added that the medical model can contribute to the field of social action in terms of a nonjudgmental approach, an approach which is scientific in the secular sense of basic process and procedure of evidence, and in the sense that it allows for case studies where all factors are evaluated and lead to a joint effort at determining decisions. The discussion closed with a reminder that three important basic services have been omitted from contributing, which are traditionally concerned with solution of social problems; namely, political science, economics, and the legal profession. However, it was pointed out that while these disciplines were not represented on the Policy and Planning Board, they are represented in the staff of the Community Mental Health Facilities Branch.

(pp. 27–31)

[CHM Public Policy and Administration]

It was pointed out that the funds appropriated would support the construction of about 75 [community mental health] centers, and that obviously there could be no expectation of doing away with everything now extant and translating all services into this new model.

(p. 23)

[Dr. Stewart T. Ginsberg] stated that in the discussion of comprehensive community mental health centers, the State mental hospital was sometimes overlooked as an integral part of a comprehensive community mental health program. He called attention to the fact that in the Inservice Training Program and the Hospital Improvement Program there is evidence that the State mental health hospital is playing an important role in over-all mental health programming and will continue to do so. In fact, in some instances it is possible that the State mental health hospital may be a core feature of comprehensive community mental health programming. . . . In fact, some important elements in a comprehensive mental health program probably could not exist without a State mental hospital being available. . . . For example, the clinic and community mental health center will need a State mental hospital for those patients beyond their treatment and care resources, e.g., for the aging mental patients in the community who need treatment and care for which there are no resources in the community, and for alcoholics and other chronic patients which, if they were not cared for in the mental hospital, would encumber community and university facilities with custodial problems. He urged that when thought is given to bold new approaches, the contributions State mental hospitals have been making for years to the community as well as their potential for making even greater contributions to community mental health services not be overlooked, but rather utilized appropriately as part of total community resources. Otherwise, a great deal of needed planning and programming for better services will suffer. . . . It was pointed out that private practice, community centers, and hospitals serve different groups of patients. The different socio—economic patient groups serviced in these different settings need further evaluation and study".

(pp. 25–6)

Dr. Bertram S. Brown, Chief, Community Mental Health Facilities Branch, pointed out that. . . . With the election of President Kennedy a new committee was appointed which had among its membership the Secretary of Health, Education, and Welfare, the Secretary of Labor, the Administrator of Veterans Affairs, an economist from the Council of Economic Advisors, and a representative of the Bureau of the Budget. The Committee drew on NIMH personnel for a great deal of background work. It arrived at a program to bring care back to the local community in a coordinated manner. Dr. Brown discussed the "socio-political" realities involved in the development of the plans, and pointed out that as is usually the case in American legislation, the law was a product of compromise among differing opinions. He also pointed out that the law is relatively unspecific as to a definition of a comprehensive community mental health center; that the regulations define 'comprehensive' in terms of ten services, and that regulations can be changed in three months. Dr. Brown pointed out that the list of services which defined 'comprehensive' is so broad that any desirable activity can be supported under its terms, which were designed to permit growth, modification, metamorphosis, and flexibility.

. . .

It was felt desirable also to include prevention as an essential; in anticipation of the need to define prevention, it was decided that in the present 'state of the art,' it is at least consultation and educational services to the community, and the principle of prevention is represented in the essential elements by those two services.

. . .

the myth constantly arises that there must be a single administration and a single physical facility for a program.

. . .

The failure of the staffing aspect of the legislation resulted in only "bricks and mortar" money, which leads to a distorted emphasis on a less needy aspect of the problem.

Dr. Brown pointed out that the requirements for the plans that the States must produce have had considerable impact and have already influenced the design of other programs, such as the drive on poverty, by virtue of the conceptual strength inherent in the types of coordination required within and between other plans, jurisdictions and activities.

. . .

if the Social Security and Medicare bill had passed, the Long amendment would have provided over $40 per day for the care of the mentally ill persons over 65 in State mental hospitals.

. . .

Dr. Brown expressed the opinion that ultimately this aspect of the legislation will become law and plans will have to be made to use it effectively. The large poverty and rehabilitation programs also present complex problems of coordination because of their overlapping boundaries . . . an objection was raised to the medical orientation of the entire conception of the centers as exemplified by the reiteration of the term 'care' of patients. The point was made that tying the centers to the medical profession constricts the potential development. . . . Dr. Brown pointed out that the reality of the situation is that the centers program represents social action stemming from trends of recent years and takes a form which is acceptable to the Congress. . . . Dr. [Eli A. Rubinstein, Chief, Training and Manpower Resources Branch, NIMH] remarked that the objection appeared to be an extreme one which did not take into account a variety of dramatic changes in the past few decades which had modified the 'traditional' patterns. He expressed the view that the concept of the centers has dramatic implications and offers a challenge and an opportunity for considerable constructive effort. The point was made that the discussion was centering about two attitudes, with one faction arguing in terms of doing what is desirable and the other in terms of doing the feasible. It was suggested that a sound approach would be to identify what is desirable and to relate this to what is feasible. . . . Dr. Rubinstein pointed to the importance for the Institute [NIMH] of the emphasis on the environment in this new program and the explicit recognition that the mentally ill exist in a community and that the solution to their problems must include more than merely the direct treatment of the individual. This emphasis brings the Institute into the field of urban health and gives it a broader mandate to concern itself with the play of forces in the community.

(pp. 31–5)

[CMH Education]

Training for comprehensive CMH work includes a broader scope, closer to the community roles of residents, increased integration among services, indirect services leading to extend mental health competence to nonclinical occupations and programs (p. 2). Work in and integration with community agencies. Dr. [Reginald S.] Lourie stated that the first big change in psychiatric training patterns would be a shift from intramural to extra-mural orientation . . . a shift in the balance of the training program to allow for much greater application of knowledge to the community. If the newer generation of psychiatrists is to accept professional responsibility for applying its basic information to larger groups and to the community, residents must be taken out of the intramural setting for at least part of their training.

(p. 6)

Dr. Seymour B. Sarason, psychologist, writes,

"An example of questions which were posed is the extent to which tradi-tional training in clinical fields is necessary at all . . . whether or not train-ing in any form of psychotherapy is necessary. . . . these issues have been prejudged, and the federal approach to community health implies that traditional training is needed. . . . This . . . merely unsupported convic-tion . . . a serious approach to prevention requires that all disciplines and fields involved must necessarily break to some extent with the traditional aspects of their fields or the consequences will be that these new programs will simply reflect more of what already exists.

(p. 16)

Dr. Donald R. Cressey, social science discussant, writes,

at present, there is a great need to operate flexibly in producing persons who can contribute to the mental health area; that it may be possible for instance, to work with people with bachelor's degrees so that they may contribute meaningfully to social science—mental health. He stated that in his experience, relatively untrained persons (e.g., the guard in a reform-atory, the aide in a psychiatric hospital, the bartender in a local commu-nity) can get close to the kinds of persons whom the mental health worker is trying to reach. Rather than retrain these persons so that they begin to conform to existing patterns of mental health work (with the danger that they lose whatever specific 'goodness' they have), Dr. Cressey suggested that it might be possible from study of these relatively untrained individu-als to evolve ways to become more effective in the various mental health programs. He stated that there is a very real danger in the tendency to reproduce existing patterns rather than absorbing new ways of effectively dealing with patients.

(p. 18)

There is a need for education for a new, flexible, broad approach to CMH practice:

Dr. [Erich] Lindemann stated that the anticipated tasks of the comprehen-sive community mental health center. . . . there is a concern for involving non-medical sections of the community in the mental health effort. This is done in variety of ways: training of non-medical personnel; adding a mental health component to an existing program of teaching; or sorting out from professional personnel a "new species" to work in the area of behavioral science of mental health.

(p. 27)

[Disciplines/CMH-Education]
On psychiatrist training, Dr. Reginald S. Lourie writes,

psychiatrists will have to be trained to work with many disciplines, and will also have to be trained to work on teams in which they are not the captains. The psychiatrist will need to know how to operate as a contributing member of the team where he is not the major focus nor providing the major component in the program. . . . it is necessary to think of new ways of working out broad team integration in training centers. Such modifications in practice would make new concepts of comprehensive community mental health tangibly available to the trainee. Trainees should be exposed to collaborative programs which are not compartmentalized by some of the artificial boundaries that arise from other needs.

(p. 7)

Comprehensive community mental health concepts should be introduced into medical schools at the undergraduate level. . . . Dr. Lourie wondered whether the Institute might not provide additional support on an incentive basis for medical schools that will develop these more comprehensive programs. He suggested that this might be considered instead of formula grants to undergraduate medical programs . . . some of the medical school deans . . . saw the introduction of such comprehensive concepts as useful for training deans. . . 'If we are not training our young people to fit into these new patterns that are emerging, I think we are short-changing them, because these will be the patterns in which they will have to function in the future.

(p. 8)

Dr. LeRoy W. Earley argues that CMH psychiatry training should occur both at undergraduate and at residency levels: "the best of these changes in training programs have come from the universities rather than from service units" (p. 8); "medical student training presents a special problem because of . . . the great time lag in introducing new knowledge into the medical school curriculum . . . it is difficult to obtain the curriculum time to present the concepts one would like to impart" (p. 9).

On nursing training, Mrs. Lorene Rowan Fischer writes,

problems of training for the future in the field of mental health . . . developing people who are flexible without being simply diffuse; delineation of the core of psychiatric nursing which must be retained; and selection of criteria to be used in training for extended and new service such as consultation, teaching and administration. . . . attention is being directed to new patterns of organizational structure and interprofessional orientation . . . as a special area of concern the preparation of nurses for leadership positions. . . . patterns and goals for community care need to be identified and tried to safeguard against superficial or patchwork approaches to planning for emotional and psychological support and for continuity of care.

(p. 9)

graduate [training] programs should . . . contain the theoretical concepts and experiences which will help nurses to accept strengths that exist within the family and the community, and to work within the framework of community care programs. . . . The organization of educational programs within universities and the interdisciplinary collaboration within agencies, particularly within the framework of teaching programs, are important factors in the development and facilitation of interdisciplinary collaboration. The collaborative development of content in the university should advance interdisciplinary kinds of training experiences. This . . . has implications for clarification of professional roles and responsibilities, and for effective professional interaction in terms of maximum treatment potential for all members of the team.

(p. 10)

Dr. Mary Kathryn Carl, nursing discussant, writes,

The interdisciplinary training aspect seems to be one key [to prep for work in CMHCs]. Interdisciplinary collaboration has become a part of therapeutic team activity, but it has not yet been extended to the training level. The psychiatric resident and graduate students in social work, psychiatric nursing, and clinical psychology are all learning in the same training center; therefore, collaborative experiences could be planned and implemented as part of the organized learning experience. Dr. Carl set a challenge for university training centers in which all mental health disciplines are represented to work out arrangements where learners in, at least, the four core disciplines can really participate in learning together with supervision, rather than having the collaborative experience as a graduation aftermath when each of the professionals is in the employment setting and this relationship has to be worked out.

(p. 12)

A new CMH subspecialty would include the incorporation of the behavioral sciences. On psychology training,—Dr. Seymour B. Sarason writes,

the danger of the new community mental health center programs reflecting nothing more than traditional styles of treatment in new settings. A principal part of this problem is the difficulty encountered when attempts are made to change the training methods of a profession, a field or an academic department, regardless of discipline. The established fields or disciplines all carry with them traditions which do not include the broad view of communities as presented by this newer theme. In many senses the staffs are victims of tradition and when faced with a need to change it is very likely that one will find resistance if not outright rejection. An even more critical problem will be a tendency to change the new into the old—to incorporate the new and make it into something familiar—since this would give the appearance of change when the status quo is actually being maintained. In the effort to institute the massive new programs in community mental health, one must start with the knowledge that this is an effort to graft something new and perhaps strange onto structures which are naturally resistant to the introduction of foreign elements. Therefore, . . . one must bring careful scrutiny to bear even in those areas where new programming seems to be taking hold. . . . In order to guard against the possibility that the mere appearance of change will suffice, these newer elements of programming should receive even more careful attention than older kinds. . . . In other words, a new housing does not necessarily incorporate a new idea.

(p. 15)

[Disciplines]

Dr. Brown indicated that . . . With respect to personnel, it is necessary to have a psychiatrist responsible for the clinical program and that the medical responsibility for patients be vested in a physician. This does not mean that the director or the leadership of a center has to be a psychiatrist or a physician, or that the coordinating agencies have to be centrally directed from the psychiatric component. There was some concern nonetheless that esixting [*sic*] state patterns will dominate the form of the center, which means that there will be less freedom for developing new models. Dr. Brown indicated that enlightened civic pressures can provide the necessary leverage to overcome this.

(p. 35)

[Civil Rights and Minorities]

There will be increased attention to certain problem populations and syndromes—a focus of effort to be directed toward school dropouts, culturally disadvantaged youths and the unemployed, among others.

(p. 3)

[CMH-Clinical]
Dr. Seymour B. Sarason, psychologist, writes,

A second problem is that those individuals seeking to promote the community mental health processes tend to approach the community with a missionary view. The difficulty is, according to Dr. Sarason, that there are no adequate definitions of community or of groupings, or population factors. The entire process of how one enters a community and the purposes for which entry is sought are critical questions. His suggestion is that thus far we have been naive and have not made a sufficient effort to obtain the services of social scientists such as anthropologists who are trained to understand these questions.

(p. 16)

Dr. Donald W. MacKinnon, psychology questioned the effectiveness of early intervention—predictions of future pathology are 70% wrong: those with early pathologies often become creative and mature through overcoming and controlling problems without treatment.

44. NIMH-Subcommittee on Pilot Spec. Proj. & Public Health—Training and Manpower Resources Branch. [folder "NIMH Study Section 1964–65", Box IIIA 4 (Mb-O), Erich Lindemann Collection, Center for the History of Medicine, Francis A. Countway Library of Medicine, Boston, MA]. Committee membership: as of 1/15/1963: Erich Lindemann, Dr. George W. Albee (Professor of Psychology, Western Reserve University), Dr. Roger W. Howell (Associate Professor of Mental Health, School of Public Health, University of Michigan), Mr. William J. McGlothlin (Vice President, University of Louisville), Dr. R. Nevitt Sanford (Director, Institute for the Study of Human Problems, Stanford University), Dr. Harvey L. Smithy (Professor of Sociology, University of North Carolina). Representatives from other subcommittees: Dr. C. Knight Aldrich (chairperson, Department of Psychiatry, University of Chicago), Dr. Bernard Bandler (chairperson of the Division of Psychiatry, Boston University), Dr. J. Mc Vicker Hunt (psychologist, University of Illinois), Dr. Elizabeth L. Kemble (nursing, University of North Carolina), Dr. Ronald Lipitt (social scientist, University of Michigan), Dr. Gardner C. Quarton (biological sciences, HMS/MGH), Dr. Lillian Ripple (social work, University of Chicago).

45. "NIMH Study Section 1964–65", Subcommittee on Pilot and Special Projects and Public Health, Training and Manpower Resources Branch. [folder "NIMH Study Section 1964–65", Box IIIA 4 (Mb-O), Erich Lindemann Collection, Center for the History of Medicine, Francis A. Countway Library of Medicine, Boston, MA]

46. Ad Hoc Committee of the NIMH Health Training and Manpower Resources Planning Board, preliminary report on Training for Comprehensive Community

Mental Health Efforts; 12/28/1964. [folder "NIMH Study Section 1964–65", Box IIIA 4 (Mb-O), Erich Lindemann Collection, Center for the History of Medicine, Francis A. Countway Library of Medicine, Boston, MA]

47. Porterfield, John, "Public Health Goals", in *Public Health Goals in Social Work Education* (New York: Council on Social Work Education, 1962); summarized in the Preliminary Report of the Ad Hoc Committee (NIMH Health Training and Manpower Resources Planning Board) on "Training for Comprehensive Community Mental Health Efforts", 12/28/1964, pp. 3–4. [folder "NIMH Study Section 1964–65", Box IIIA 4 (Mb-O), Erich Lindemann Collection, Center for the History of Medicine, Francis A. Countway Library of Medicine, Boston, MA]

48. Vicers, Sir Geoffrey, "The Psychology of Policy Making and Social Change", The Thirty-Eighth Maudsley Lecture, delivered before the Royal Medico-Psychological Association, 11/15/1963; *British Journal of Psychiatry 110*: 465–477 (1964).

49. Duhl, Leonard J., MD, Chief, Office of Planning, National Institute of Mental Health, NIH, Public Health Service, U.S. Department of HEW, "The Psychiatrist in Urban Social Planning", presented at Colloquium, Florence Heller Graduate School for Advanced Studies in Social Welfare, Brandeis University, 3/11/1965, pp. 17–19. [folder "NIMH", Box IIIA 4 (Mb-O), Erich Lindemann Collection, Center for the History of Medicine, Francis A. Countway Library of Medicine, Boston, MA]

50. Barra, Robert L., "Trends, Issues, and Social Policy: A discussion of economic and social trends and issues significant to the planning of social welfare policy in mid-century United States"; based on the introductory address before Trustees Seminar, Combined Jewish Philanthropies of Greater Boston and the Florence Heller Graduate School for Advanced Studies in Social Welfare, Brandeis University 10/23–25/1964; and keynote address before Annual New York State Welfare Conference, New York City, 11/17–19/1964. [folder "NIMH Study Section 1964–65", Box IIIA 4 (Mb-O), Erich Lindemann Collection, Center for the History of Medicine, Francis A. Countway Library of Medicine, Boston, MA]

51. Lindemann, Erich, "Human Ecology and Mental Health", part of Leonard J. Duhl's symposium "Environment of The City", 3/23/1962, pp. 19–20. [folder "Am. Orthopsychiatric Assn 1962, Duhl's "Environment of the City", Box IIIA6 2) A-M, Erich Lindemann Collection, Center for the History of Medicine, Francis A. Countway Library of Medicine, Boston, MA]

52. Lindemann, Erich, "Talk Given by Erich Lindemann to Staff of Student Health Department at Stanford, Nov. 12, 1971", p. 10; given in response to a request that he reconstruct some aspects of his own development as teacher and scientist. Quote from von Goethe, Johann Wolfgang "Faust, First Part of the Tragedy". [folder "Mental Health Services of MGH a setting for Community MH", Box VII 2, Erich Lindemann Collection, Center for the History of Medicine, Francis A. Countway Library of Medicine, Boston, MA]

53. Musto, David F., "The Community Mental Health Center Movement in Historical Perspective", in Barton, Walter E. and Sanborn, Charlotte J. (eds.), *An Assessment of the Community Mental Health Movement* (Lexington, MA: Lexington Books, 1977), pp. 1–11.

54. McHale, John, "Big Business Enlisted for the War on Poverty", *Trans-Action* 3–9 (5/6/1965). [folder "NIMH", Box IIIA 4 (Mb-O), Erich Lindemann Collection, Center for the History of Medicine, Francis A. Countway Library of Medicine, Boston, MA]

55. Musto, David F., 1975, *ibid.*

56. NIMH Study Section 1964–65" [Subcommittee on Pilot and Special Projects and Public Health, Training and Manpower Resources Branch], "Special Report: State Mental Health Programs", background material prepared for the Director of the NIMH to use in appropriation hearings regarding fiscal year 1965. [folder "NIMH Study Section 1964–65", Box IIIA 4 (Mb-O), Erich Lindemann Collection, Center for the History of Medicine, Francis A. Countway Library of Medicine, Boston, MA]
57. Slate, Philip, 1976, *ibid.*, p. 171.
58. Duhl, Leonard J. and Leopold, Robert L., 1968, *ibid.*
59. Duhl, Leonard, MD, Department of Public Health, University of California—San Francisco and Department of Psychiatry, University of California—Berkeley; interviewed by telephone at the University of California—Berkeley by David G. Satin, 4/2/1979, 8/16/2007. [Caddy 2, Box 4, X, Lindemann Collection, Center for the History of Medicine, Francis A. Countway Library of Medicine, Boston, MA]
60. Duhl, Leonard J. and Leopold, Robert L., 1968, *ibid.*
61. Yolles, Stanley F., MD [2nd Director of the NIMH 1964–6/2/1970". The Future of Community Psychiatry", Ch. 10 in Barton, Walter E. and Sanborn, Charlotte J. (eds.), *An Assessment of The Community Mental Health Movement* (Lexington, MA: Lexington Books, 1977), p. 169, based on Dartmouth Continuing Education Institute, Dept. of Psychiatry, Dartmouth Medical School, 1975. [folder "CMH—Theory", David G. Satin files]
62. Greenblatt, Milton, "The Revolution Defined: It is Sociopolitical", *Psychiatric Annals 7*: 24–29 (1977).
63. Musto, David F., 1977, *ibid.*
64. Smith, Steven, "Mental Health Policy and Community Mental Health" (interview by David G. Satin at the Countway Library of Medicine, Boston, MA, 10/23/1981). [Erich Lindemann Collection, David G. Satin files]
65. Bandler, Bernard, "Evolution of a Community Mental Health Center", in Bandler, Bernard (ed.), *Psychiatry in the General Hospital* (Boston, MA: Little Brown, 1966).
66. Solomon, Harry Caesar, 6/22/1978, *ibid.*
67. Whybrow, Peter C., "Forward", in Barton, Walter E. and Sanborn, Charlotte J. (eds.), *An Assessment of the Community Mental Health Movement* (Lexington, MA: Health, 1977), p. vii.
68. Glasscote, R.M.; Sanders, D.S.; Forstenzer, H.M.; Foley, A.R., *The Community Mental Health Center: An Analysis of Existing Models* (Washington, DC: The Joint Information Service [American Psychiatric Association-NAMH], 1964). [folder "NIMH Study Section 1964–65", Box IIIA 4 (Mb-O), Erich Lindemann Collection, Center for the History of Medicine, Francis A. Countway Library of Medicine, Boston, MA]
69. Yolles, Stanley F., MD, "The Future of Community Psychiatry", Ch. 10 in Barton, Walter E. and Sanborn, Charlotte J. (eds.), *An Assessment of The Community Mental Health Movement* (Lexington, MA: Lexington Books, 1977), p. 170, based on Dartmouth Continuing Education Institute, Dept. of Psychiatry, Dartmouth Medical School, 1975. [folder "CMH—Theory", David G. Satin files]
70. Solomon, Harry C., 6/22/1978.
71. Lindemann, Elizabeth B., interviews by David G. Satin in Wellesley and Boston, MA, 6/27/1978–8/1979. [Erich Lindemann Collection, David G. Satin, Newton, MA]
72. Klerman, Gerald, interview by David G. Satin, 8/17/1982. [Erich Lindemann Collection, David G. Satin files, Newton, MA]

73. Caplan, Gerald, "Preventive and Social Psychiatry", presented at Psychiatric Grand Rounds, Massachusetts General Hospital, 9/12/1978.
74. Lindemann, Erich, interview with two graduate students in sociology, 1965. [folder "Stanford—Misc.", box IV 3+4+5, Erich Lindemann Collection, Center for the History of Medicine, Francis A., Countway Library of Medicine, Boston, MA]

> When you say the name Lindemann, you think of one of the originators of the whole idea of the mental health center. What I really had in mind was an agency . . . now symbolized by the Wellesley Human Relations Service . . . that serves the community primarily in prevention and uses hospitals to refer casualties which can't be handled at the line where we are now functioning . . . would best be allied with public health's whole program and should not be singled out by the mental health program at all. When I developed this, I was a member of the Harvard [Univ.] Department of Social [p. 1] Relations and a member of the faculty of the Harvard School of Public Health. This agency, then, has four functions: 1. being available as a first-aid station for emotional disturbances. . . . 2. being a consultation resource for those emotional difficulties which are handled by the care-taking professions in the community 3. being able to help various civic and professional organizations and agencies . . . insofar as they might be . . . conducive to good or bad mental health . . . such as schools, the delinquency program, police, churches, etc. 4. to make joint investigative efforts with the community on such questions as . . . places in the community where high rates of emotional casualties emerge . . . disturbed kids often come from the fringe population. . . . newcomers in a community have . . . more trouble . . . society arrangements for. . . [people] protected . . . against the impact of stress situations . . . such as baptism, confirmation . . . marriage counseling, the "welcome wagon" . . . transitions in the community, as from family into school . . . a number of such places should evolve with very careful scientific supervision. A body of learning would then emerge on the social pathogenesis of emotional difficulties. . . . surely the mental casualties were sick in the narrow medical sense but that often they were unwanted people . . . cast out by the community, and . . . institutionalized. We became very much interested in . . . the tolerance of the community—the presence or absence . . . of deviant people. . . . the then-commissioner of mental health [Massachusetts], Jack Ewalt, became interested in Wellesley. He asked one of our charter members, Warren Vaughn, to become the fore-runner of Dr. Hutchinson [Deputy Commissioner and Director of the Division of Mental Hygiene providing community services]. They then evolved the notion that perhaps there ought to be other Wellesleys . . . not to be primarily public health oriented but . . . grafted onto existing child guidance organizations. . . . Within five years they developed 13 of these. At one of these, near Pittsfield they began to iron out the . . . problem of having clinicians add to their customary clinical operations some of . . . these community issues. . . . I didn't think clinicians were the ones to do this; you have to be dedicated to a different set of values. You mustn't get your reward from the gratitude of the patient but from the reduction in the rate of calamities. . . . child guidance clinics were getting into a . . . rut at the time. Long-term involvement with a small number of patients began not to pay off; the clinics all had long waiting-lists. Tacking on a certain amount of preventive work seemed a good idea. In this way developed programs that were forerunners of community mental health centers. . . .

But there was a strong segment of the psychiatry which had great doubts about this whole damn business. Dr. [Harry C.] Solomon [Massachusetts Commissioner of Mental Health] doubts this very much. . . . You might make people more comfortable but you won't prevent. And [Paul] Lemkau also felt that we still have to learn . . . a lot more . . . before we can demonstrate precisely what happens. And out of this developed on our side a . . . shift in focus to crises and examination of transition periods. The outcome . . . was putting a lot of money into the West End renewal program . . . the notion was . . . to show that some patterns of social change . . . are reliably related to casualties. Now out of this grew . . . that casualties . . . are not only the recognized forms of psychiatric disease, schizophrenia, depression, neurosis, and psychopathic disorders, but that there were . . . social patterns, namely . . . impairment of function, the defective breadwinner, the defective student, the underachiever . . . juvenile delinquency and rebellious behavior . . . alcohol as a defense against defective resources in meeting life crises. . . . The children of alcoholics. . . . That, however, related not to . . . mental health but to . . . public health. . . . we had gotten outside . . . the Mental Health Department, we spilled over into public health, and then . . . we found ourselves in . . . the Department of Education, the Department of Welfare, and the Department of Correction [sic]. . . . you need these departments lumped together . . . get them together with those people in the community, like the UCS [United Community Services] . . . concerned with financing and coordinating join [sic] efforts . . . established agencies . . . will be altered in their functioning . . . I was then a member of a committee . . . at the National Institute [of Mental Health—the Space Cadets] . . . to discuss the effects of human environment, social and physical, on emotional well-being. Out of this came . . . concern with transition points . . . in community life; with the relationship of planning to these transition points; with . . . marshaling knowledge appropriate for appropriate forecasting . . . in such a way that it isn't unwelcome to the powers in the community. We saw a five-circle pattern: the power structure of the community, the value structure of the community . . . the control of deviants . . . the education to make sure the kids will conform to these values . . . and . . . welfare and health collecting the casualties. With this . . . we have approached community mental health planning . . . keeping in mind that nothing will work unless the power figures are involved . . . this approach . . . was joined by quite a different stream . . . mental hospitals were craving greater proximity with the community . . . an after-care program . . . prepare the community for receiving their people back . . . educate the community to live with their casualties . . . have the community help them not to have to take so many casualties. . . . In addition . . . there was this need for a new role for the mental hospital. Then . . . the joint commission . . . a little underselling the trend for which I stand and putting a lot more emphasis on the survival of the mental hospital as the harbinger of all the good for sick people in a new form. Community mental health centers are . . . a political compromise of these issues, and they aggravate . . . grafting onto a clinical resource public health functions. . . . It has a refurbished mental hospital with a variety of new facilities for inpatients . . . and perhaps a vague notion about preventive services too [actually emphasis on severe, chronic mental illness]. . . . In the meantime, however, there was a totally different trend going on. I became professor here at the School of Public Health and was in charge of a General

Hospital [*sic*] psychiatric program, and I had to see that this psychiatric program embodied some of the values which we had tried to materialize in Wellesley and Public Health . . . we felt that . . . it could handle an inpatient capacity of 80. And . . . could be more effectively financed. we though we might . . . build something right next to the hospital as part of its campus. It turned out that . . . the [Roman Catholic] church owned a large part of the land . . . the entrepreneurs came in. . . . A building doing research at the molecular level was preferred to one working in the behavioral sciences. Personality study seemed damned fuzzy compared to studies . . . about cell protein formation. On the other hand, a new [general] director came to this hospital, John Knowles, and he . . . had to work out an issue between the McLean Hospital and our department . . . John Knowles and I became friends over this . . . and it looks now as though his future program is . . . emotional casualties . . . should take priority in the first contact in the hospital . . . so that we ought to have a vastly enlarged segment of the General Hospital . . . psycho-social predicament . . . would be considered entrance tickets to the General Hospital not just to [the] psychiatric service. . . . We would have a large psychiatric resource. . . . We have implanted the Wellesley system, namely, receiving casualties . . . being consultants during care by other doctors and nurses in terms of their own needs and the patient's needs, and . . . research and the administrative organization of the hospital. So . . . we have then become a part of the hospital administration. . . . my last year hear, I was the chairman of the central, general executive planning committee of the whole hospital. So psychiatry has lost some of its identity—it has become more of a kind of medical anthropology, as I like to call it [hearkening back to Lindemann's university studies]. . . . we thought maybe the state . . . could provide matching funds and then federal help so that we could have . . . a building. What is going up there . . . is a place for burnt children . . . developed by the Shriners [Shriners Burn Center] . . . where a new building <u>might</u> have been if . . . Dr. [Harry C. Solomon's [Massachusetts Commissioner of Mental Health] scheme of getting the Legislature to finance a mental health center in the government [center] complex hadn't developed. Dr. Solomon thought a building . . . by the hospital would be much more difficult because of the tremendous legal and cultural fear that the legislators have . . . that nothing should be done to help private enterprise, especially the church. . . . When I first talked with Dr. Solomon, Dean Clark [General Director of the MGH] was here. Then we established the principle that an enlarged psychiatric facility built and in some parts collaboratively financed as far as patient care goes between the state and Mass. General . . . later with John Knowles [General Director of the MGH] and with Dean [George Packer] Berry from the [Harvard] Medical School, saying . . . the senior posts . . . employment of the state would be joint appointments with the hospital . . . given appropriate faculty appointments by the Medical School. . . . this we don't want but this we have to accept. . . . Our wish is the pattern . . . with our alcoholism program . . . staffed by the MGH and the Medical School; we have our own budget and the [state] Department of Public Health, reimburses us . . . a contractual arrangement. . . . I believe the state should not be . . . running hospitals. They ought to be run by . . . people who know how to do it, and the state should . . . facilitate the . . . programs and not do it themselves. . . . I want to be an open hospital . . . patients are not . . . legally signed in . . . known on some roster as being peculiar in some illness which makes them second-rate citizens. This is against my feelings. . . . Harry Solomon . . . had this idea . . . to have the mental health center right in the center of governmental activities. It would always remind the people in the government of the reality of the mental health issue. . . . he has been running mental hospitals . . . for a long time . . . rather than . . . within the scheme of the general hospital . . . idea about the Blackstone School site [near and associated with the MGH]. . . . I'm not a terribly aggressive person myself so I didn't go fighting for this. . . . we would have run it as part of a general medicine program. . . . Our planning and efforts for the new center have lost a great deal of their enthusiasm . . . which we would have had for a place which we controlled. . . . an awfully lot more has gone into Dr. [Bernard] Bandler's [chairperson of the Division of Psychiatry at the Boston University School of Medicine and Superintendent of the Boston University Mental Health Center] proposed . . . center. . . . For quite a while it was taken for granted that Lindemann would take on this new hospital [as director][1] . . . and I provided the impetus. . . . We were allowed to modify it [plans for ELMHC] but we were not allowed a part in the developing of the pattern. . . . I would never have done it that way . . . the services which are . . . together in that building would have to be scattered throughout a community. . . . I would have said . . . build a number of different places . . . with different functions. . . . They were principal plans . . . for a hospital in general . . . a forty-bed model and a hundred-bed model. . . . Maybe Harry [Solomon, Massachusetts Commissioner of Mental Health] himself developed them. . . . he had . . . in mind the [Boston, MA] psychopathic hospital with some modification. . . . He was just convinced that the small mental hospital is the future of psychiatry and mental health rather than an aggregate of community agencies . . . which have as one of their specialized facilities a clinical resource where people can stay for a while . . . the mentally disturbed need a variety of environments . . . which cannot be had in a place where there are so many beds. . . . Our model . . . can be applied with settlement houses. Lincoln House, now torn down, was a wonderful example . . . where you have a variety of environmental supports for disadvantaged people of various kinds . . . in supportive experiences . . . occasionally they are so sick that they have to be kept in bed can be dealt with by . . . a hotel facility with the proper care. . . . That side ought to be underplayed. . . . There is a settlement house in Peabody where . . . that kind of remedial environment for underprivileged people . . . are just as much a target for psychiatric care as actually sick people. . . . I am now hoping to implement it [Lindemann's program/concept] in Palo Alto. You don't start with the hospital, and not with the commissioner. . . . Rather, you start with the people, as we did in Wellesley. You start a committee going such as the one of which I . . . being the chairman of—the Metropolitan Planning Committee . . . composed of a variety of people . . . concerned with various aspects of good emotional, mental functioning, including the paramedical and social. There are business people, union people, people from disadvantaged areas, people from churches, and some . . . dedicated citizens. . . . Mental health is appropriate and adaptable behavior and suitable experience, and it applies . . . to people . . . but also to organizations . . . the first thing for organizational mental health is better communication [re: the threat to mental hospitals]. . . . I would have the Mental Hospital man be an integral part of the plan in such a way that his position will have [a] more prestigious image than the declining prestige he has now . . . if some way could be found to extend their operations and to employ their under-used facilities . . . something that wouldn't just be treatment in the narrow, medical sense but rather . . . rehabilitation. . . . Mental hospitals do not provide treatment. . . . they provide a phase of later education, education we should have imparted to these poor people. long ago because they are terribly defective in social skills. In some form of adult education . . . provide them with the social skills . . . to met social crises. . . . [For example,] veterans' hospitals . . . have to have . . . a fresh, neutral field of thinking together. They can't do this thing in their own power hierarchy. . . [re: director of new CMHC]. . . . I thought I would be the one and I had to make a major decision whether to take on an administrative post or whether to return to a more scholarly kind of activity. Then I learned in Palo Alto that they wanted me there, so for the rest of my life . . . I had better do that. . . . [The CMHC director] should there be new organization: McLean and the Beth Israel [Hospitals] and then this hospital and the new Government Center. . . . we have agreed upon [with] Harry Solomon [Massachusetts Commissioner of Mental Health], that . . . we will not be three collaborating units, rather between the MGH and [Bowdoin] Square there will be one man in charge of outpatient services . . . a man for community interface operations . . . one man in charge of inpatient services and one in charge of the research laboratories. . . . It's a functional organization, not a spatial one. . . . ["And the man in what is your position now"] will be head of both. . . . This is final though I don't know if my successor will like it. He might throw this over. . . . ["What does it take to make this final?"] The nearest we could come . . . with Harry is our having discussions. . . . He never writes anything down so I have a notetaker to take minutes. . . . He has never written back. . . . We are up to the point now of the horizontal organization of the staff and a commitment expressed by the director here and by the dean . . . until we knew what our actual service area was going to be. . . . we could do only the most informal kind of contacting . . . experimental forms of state hospital voluntary collaboration with the Danvers State Hospital . . . as a blueprint for the Government Center. . . . we have informal and quite affectionate relationships with Raquel Cohen . . . in charge of the community mental health center in East Boston [North Suffolk Mental Health Association; later Superintendent of the ELMHC], which . . . emerged as [from] a child guidance preventive care program. . . . We have a similar relationship with some people in Salem. . . . I did not want it to get too mixed up with my name . . . on a community level it becomes personified in one person. . . [John C.] Nemiah [Acting Chief of Psychiatry after Lindemann] . . . will be considered as the man who will develop this relationship. . . . they will probably use the Wellesley pattern . . . get together a committee of the relevant people in professional agency life who . . . have something to do with mental health . . . get some ratios between actual services and needed services . . . greatly improved care of the acutely mentally ill . . . close to their home environment, and the interchange between hospital and home will be much better . . . a lot more community participation in the hospital program . . . excellent type of psychiatric therapy . . . a number of modified care programs such as the half-way houses . . . workshops and some infiltration of the labor situation . . . hopefully effective communication although none of that has happened so far . . . to reach disadvantaged people by educational methods, by the anti-poverty program . . . invasion of the facility by . . . the people heavily involved, the welfare people. . . . There will be a great deal of research going on . . . a breakthrough . . . on some forms of schizophrenia. . . . Whether they will become a pacemaker in the social system inquiry and the study of social casualties, that i don't know. a center like this is not exactly a catalyst for such processes because the image the people will hold is this: there is the hospital, the castle and there all is being done. My image is it's done right where you sit, in your own family, in your own factory, in your own school. . . . What arrive at the castle are the long neglected casualties . . . a set-up like Wellesley is probably more productive . . . a terribly important aspect . . . the image that a community has of . . . a hospital. . . . Will the community support the hospital or will there be an alienation effect or will the effect be that of surrender of responsibility? My central phrase . . . is responsible participation. If things are going on in the castle it means the professionals do it, if things are going on right under your nose then you . . . better pitch in and help . . . in the field of mental health. . . . there is a false conviction of competence which our colleagues in medicine often have and there is a justified conviction of competence because . . . in an experiential sense we all have learned a lot about our encounters with other people. This can be used . . . in terms of knowledge about the personalities involved and the social structure. We have tried as best we could [to improve the ELMHC interior structure]. I'm still smarting from a terrible defeat. We have done the best we could to fix our place to be . . . at least a living space. We hope to get the hospital to . . . give us one very large floor. . . [to be] a little community where people live together and share their daily experience . . . similar to community life . . . to demonstrate it to everybody. . . . To have them on beds is to put them on the experimental table. They are . . . there for the sake of the doctor. So we thought we could achieve that in connection with the rehabilitation service, which is re-education of people . . . a lot of the psychiatric disorders are also . . . having to learn a role in the proper way. . . . The head of rehabilitation was very excited about it and had very nice architectural plans for it. But then the trustees thought the hospital needs money, there are so many demands for beds . . . so now it becomes just a traditional set of rooms with beds . . . and T.V., underlining the passivity of the patients. . . . The trustees were terribly scared that organization for community, shared experience would do away with the anonymity of the wealthy patients . . . a curious aspect of privileged communication. . . . one of the important things . . . is to have . . . a mental health center include . . . a lot of people . . . involved in a community center, dealing with recreational, cultural and other aspects of the community. Unfortunately a mental hospital is not an attractive place for doing that. But a human relations service is a wonderful place to do it.

75. Lindemann letter to G. St. J. Perrott, chief of the Division of Public Health Methods in the U.S. Public Health Service, U.S. Department of Health, Education, and Welfare, 10/9/1956, in answer to his confirmation of Lindemann's introduction to the 10/29/1956 Josiah Macy Foundation conference at the Nassau Tavern, Princeton, New Jersey, 4/18/1956. [folder "Misc. Correspondence D, E,F 1956–57", Box IIIA 1–3, Lindemann Collection, Center for the History of Medicine, Francis A. Countway Library of Medicine, Boston, MA]
76. Lindemann, Erich, "The Nature of Community Mental Health Education", keynote address to be presented to the National Assembly on Mental Health

Education; Ithaca, New York; 09/11/1958, p. 3, 4. [file #56; "Lindemann—The Mental Health Educator + The Community 1958", Box XII #3, Lindemann Collection, Center for the History of Medicine, Francis A. Countway Library of Medicine, Harvard Medical School, Boston, MA]

77. Caplan, Gerald, MD, D.P.H., "Beyond the Child Guidance Clinic", in *Working Papers in Community Mental Health,* 2 no. 2 (Boston, MA: Laboratory of Community Psychiatry, Department of Psychiatry, Harvard Medical School, Summer 1964 (p. 11). [found also in folder "CMH—Policy, Politics, Administration, Institutions", David G. Satin files, Newton, MA]

78. Lindemann, Erich, and Spivak, McGrath, "Development of CMHCs (unpublished interview of Erich Lindemann by sociology students, 1965).

79. Dietz, Jean, "Attack on Mental Illness Urged by Dr. Lindemann", *The Boston Globe,* 2/1962. [folder "Correspondence 1962", Box IIIA 1–3, Lindemann Collection, Center for the History of Medicine, Francis A.Countway Library of Medicine, Boston, MA]

80. Lindemann, Erich, interview with two graduate students in sociology, 1965; p. 29. [folder "Stanford—Misc"., box IV 3+4+5, Erich Lindemann Collection, Center for the History of Medicine, Francis A., Countway Library of Medicine, Boston, MA]

81. Massachusetts, like other states, developed a community mental health center plan to qualify for federal funding for planning, building, and staffing. Those important in this aspect of state mental health were James Dykens, Robert Hyde (Department of Corrections), Belenden Hutchinson (expanded child guidance centers into community mental health centers), and Arthur Hallock (worked with Warren Vaughan to involve interested citizens groups). Lindemann, Erich, and Spivak, McGrath, 1965, *ibid.*

82. White, Theodore H., *In Search of History* (New York: Warner Books, 1978), pp. 501–502.

83. Meadow, Henry C., "The Federal Government and Harvard Medicine", *Harvard Alumni Bulletin:* 587 (5/5/1962). [folder "Meadow, Henry, Mr.; Harvard University—Accounting Dept.", Box IIIA 4 (Mb-O), Erich Lindemann Collection, Center for the History of Medicine, Francis A., Countway Library of Medicine, Boston, MA]

84. Kennedy, John F., "Special Message to the Congress on Mental Illness and Mental Retardation, February 5, 1963", *Public Papers of the President, John F. Kennedy,* 1963; Kennedy, John F., (88th Congress, 1st Session, House of Reps, Document No.58), 2/5/1963. [folder "K Miscellaneous", Box IIIA 4 (I-Ma), Lindemann Collection, Center for the History of Medicine, Francis A. Countway Library of Medicine, Boston, MA]

85. Barton, Walter E. and Sanborn, Charlotte J. (eds): *An Assessment of the Community Mental Health Movement* (Lexington, MA: Lexington Books, 1977).

86. Sabhin, Melvin, "Politics and the Stalled Revolution", *Psychiatric Annals* 7: 98–102 (1977).

87. Klerman, Gerald L., "Community Mental Health Developments in the U.S.A"., paper at William T. Grant Foundation workshop, New York City, 11/30–12/1/1984, p. 3; to be published in Rappaport, Robt N. (ed.), *Research and Action, A Collaborative Interactive Approach* (Cambridge, MA: Harvard University Press, 1985).

88. Frank, Robet G., Jr., Marshall, Louise H. and Magoun, H.W., "The Neurosciences", in Powers, John Z. and Purcell, Elizabeth F. (eds.), *Advances*

in *American Medicine: Essays at the Bicentennial*, vol. 2 (New York: Josiah Macy Jr. Foundation, 1976), pp. 552–613.

89. Klaw, Spencer, "The Affluent Professors", *The Reporter* 6/27/1960, pp. 16–25.
90. Klaw, Spencer, 1960, *ibid.*, p. 23.
91. Klaw, Spencer, 1960, *ibid.*, p. 1.
92. Pavenstedt, Eleanor (former MGH Chief of Child Psychiatry, Professor of Child Psychiatry at the Boston University School of Medicine), psychiatry conference, Cambridge Hospital, Cambridge, Massachusetts, 4/25/1983.
93. Foley, Archie R., "Prologue", in *Challenge to Community Psychiatry* (New York: Behavioral Publications, 1972), pp. 1–17.
94. Foley, Archie R., 1972, *ibid.*, p. 6.
95. Caplan, Gerald, MD, Laboratory of Community Psychiatry, Clinical Professor of Psychiatry, HMS, letter to Morrison, Miss Adele, The Grant Foundation, Inc., 5/11/1966:

> Proposed Program for Visiting Faculty Seminar in Community Psychiatry", Laboratory of Community Psychiatry, Department of Psychiatry, Harvard Medical School, [folder "G. Caplan/Visiting Faculty Seminar on Community Psychiatry", David G. Satin files, Newton, MA]:
>
> . . .
>
> The Laboratory of Community Psychiatry . . . has conducted 5 two-week sessions of the Visiting Faculty Seminar in Community Psychiatry since its inception in 1964. The Seminar is supported by a three year grant from The Grant Foundation. The topics of the Seminar have been:
>
> 1. <u>Meaning and Scope of Community Psychiatry</u> . . .
> 2. <u>Researches and Theories Which Form a Basis for Concepts and Methods of Community Psychiatry</u> . . .
> 3. <u>Studies Relating to Preventive Psychiatry</u> . . .
> 4. <u>Administration and Communication</u> . . .
> 5. <u>Consultation</u> . . .
>
> Three more sessions will be held in the coming fiscal year:
>
> 6. <u>Planning and Evaluation</u> . . .
> 7. <u>Community Organization</u> . . .
> 8. <u>Residency Training in Community Psychiatry</u> . . .
>
> the Visiting Faculty Professors. These 16 [minus Moody C. Bettis, MD, Baylor University Coll. of Med—deceased] are senior faculty persons . . . with responsibility for residency training in community psychiatry . . . plans are underway for this group . . . with the sponsorship of their departments of psychiatry, to offer, with us, an Inter-University Program for Faculty Education in Community Psychiatry to 60–70 senior psychiatrists throughout the country.
>
> (ltr p. 1)
>
> The purpose of this seminar is to provide senior faculty members of university departments of psychiatry with an opportunity to study the core content of community psychiatry over a three-year period in order to help them in organizing training in this subject for psychiatric residents . . . two-week visits to the Laboratory of Community Psychiatry . . . on eight occasions over a three-year period . . . three hours each morning in lectures and seminars . . . early afternoon visits of observation to a variety of community mental health and other community agencies in the health, mental health, welfare and education fields in the metropolitan Boston

area . . . to investigate the practical problems of implementing programs based upon the theoretical concepts (PROPOSED p. 1) . . . end of the day . . . group discussion . . . about their field observations . . . and the range of successful and unsuccessful ways . . . to deal with them . . . report on the residency training programs . . . establishing in his home university, and . . . theoretical and methodological problems.

(p. 2)

96. Mishler, Eliot L. memo to Lindemann 9/1/1965. [folder "Correspondence 1965", Box IIIA 1–3, Lindemann Collection, Center for the History of Medicine, Francis A. Countway Library of Medicine, Boston, MA]
97. Foley, Archie R., 1972, *ibid.*, p. 7.
98. Bernard, Viola W. (ed.), "The Training of Mental Health Specialists in School of Public Health", Ch. VI, *Mental Health Teaching in Schools of Public Health* (6 pre-conference committees & a national conference held at Arden House, NY 12/6–12/59, sponsored by Assn of Schls of Pub Hlth; Columbia Univ Schl of Pub Hlth & Admin Med.)
99. Committee I, "Historical Development of Mental Health Public Health": VI. Social Science and the Concepts of Mental Illness and Health [pp. 49–52], Report of the meeting of Committee I, "Historical Development of Mental Health Public Health", 4/23–4/59 at the Grosvenor Hotel, NYC, National Conference on Mental Health Teaching in Schools of Public Health, Columbia Univ. Chmn George Rosen, MD, PhD, Schl of PH & Admin.Med, Columbia U.; members James A. Crabtree, MD, GradSchlPH, UPittsburgh, Martha M. Eliot, MD, SchlPH, HU, Sol W. Ginsburg, MD, NYC, Benjamin Pasamanick, MD, CollMed, OhioStateU, Lindemann->Leona Baumgartner, MD, DeptHlth, NYC; see also final draft Ch. 1 "Public Health and Mental Health: Converging Trends and Emerging Issues", in Association of Schools of Public Health (eds.), *Mental Health Teaching in Schools of Public Health* (New York: Columbia University School of Public Health and Administrative Medicine, 10/1961).

3 Erich Lindemann's Projects

The Human Relations Service of Wellesley

The Wellesley Human Relations Service (HRS) predated the CMHC era, and during that era, it continued to be held up as an inspiration for CMH:

> Thirteen years ago Dr. Lindemann founded the first community mental health center in the United States, the Human Relations Service of Wellesley. A Massachusetts General Hospital spokesman said this center is a prototype for similar centers throughout the nation that President Kennedy requested in the Community Mental Health Act now before Congress.

In contrast, Clara Mayo (HRS staff member) believed that, for the most part, MGH saw the HRS as Lindemann's odd and irrelevant extraneous activity.[1]

After five years, the 1948 W.T. Grant Foundation grant ended. In anticipation of this, in October 1953, a charter of incorporation of the Human Relation Service of Wellesley was obtained, and on January 1955, the agency was admitted to the United Community Services of Metropolitan Boston (the agency coordinating regional community services funding) for funding.[2] By this time, the number of town residents who understood community mental health had grown from five to 50, but this cadre would have died out without a trace if the HRS had not continued.[3] They still fought for this perspective, which included the ideas of mental health consultation (especially in schools) and concern for early case finding and intervention (e.g., preschool screening) rather than treating illness:[4]

> the Administrative Director of the New England Medical Center and the Director of the Boston Home for Little Wanderers have joined the Board [of our Human Relations Service]. . . . We were also able to reassert our basic aim which is the development of the field of preventive psychiatry: we do not deal with sick persons individually but with networks of human relations, we are interested in the rate of

occurrence of emotional difficulties and are interested in community-wide planning for measures to decrease this rate. Rather than telling people how much we know we are asking for continued cooperation from all citizens in investigative work in this enormously complex field.

The tenth anniversary report of the HRS comprehensively described its range of goals and functions:[5]

> In 1953. . . a charter of incorporation from the Commonwealth of Massachusetts [stated goals]"To establish, maintain and operate an agency or agencies for the study and promotion of mental health . . . including without limitation, providing a consultation service to social agencies, physicians, ministers, teachers, and others whose work brings them in close association with people, and providing training for professional clinic personnel, engaging in research, participating in education in mental health through accepted community organization methods, and having as an important function participation with others in community service and planning for mental health". . . . Financial support was obtained from the United Fund of Greater Boston and from fees for services to institutions . . . individual clients also were charged fees on a sliding scale . . . for the second five years the Human Relations Service has functioned as a community agency with the major emphasis on giving service, it has carried on training and research functions as well. It is a field station for the Community Mental Health Training Program of the Massachusetts General Hospital . . . with funds [from] . . . the National Institute of Mental Health. . . . Small grants . . . have been available from time to time for research purposes, and further funds are actively being sought. [Collaboration] with the Harvard School of Public Health and the Harvard Medical School is insured by interlocking staff-faculty appointments.
>
> (pp. 3–4)

[theory and practice]

> the HRS approach to prevention . . . consists in trying to identify stressful situations and the factors which enable persons to master them successfully. . . . Doctors, nurses, clergy, teachers and other professional workers are at hand to reinforce families at each critical juncture. The responsibility for the prevention of emotional disorder falls heavily on members of these professions and on the arrangements which the community sets up for the provision of their services. . . . Consultation with Caretakers [mental health consultation function]. . . . An Experiment in Clinical Service [clinical

function].... the HRS clinic combines the function of a psychiatric first-aid station ... with that of a counseling center which specializes in situational analysis and offers a diagnostic service. ... Understanding the Community [CMH research function] ... study and evaluation which is basic to prevention. ... Good mental health involves the ability to respect oneself and view oneself realistically, to care deeply for others and to grow through meeting experience head-on, not evasively. It also involves making a constructive contribution to one's family, work group and community.

(pp. 7–19)

This kind of mental health is fostered, we think, in a community where children and adults alike have a sense of "belonging", where there is a clear consensus regarding acceptable and nonacceptable conduct so that standards are enforced in a predictable way, where social custom provides built-in supports for stresses in the life cycle, and where there are places to turn to in time of trouble. ... Looking at Transition [study of life crisis] ... learning how healthy people remain healthy even though they encounter the same stresses which cause others to succumb to mental illness ... study of other periods of change or transition ... the transition from home to kindergarten ... a study of nurses training ... when young people prepare themselves for a profession ... the experiences of newcomers to Wellesley ... Interpreting Mental Health to the Public [public relations] ... the Preschool Screening Program [planning help in coping with transition from home to school] ... more lasting immunity [to mental illness] ... any way of conferring it on children ... study a large number o children to see (1) what an emotionally healthy child would be like at each stage of his development; (2) whether he would stay healthy as he met the succession of stresses which all children must encounter; and (3) what ways he would have of mastering these stresses ... The "Export" of Mental Health.

(pp. 20–33)

The Wellesley community mental health program developed during a decade of rapidly increasing nationwide interest in the prevention of mental illness. ... Consequently, the Human Relations Service has found many ways to influence and assist those who are developing mental health services elsewhere. Through participation in workshops, conferences and training seminars in other communities and states, through meetings with visitors who come to Wellesley from many states and nations, and through special training opportunities for those wishing to specialize in community mental health, the HRS has been "exporting" its knowledge, methods and point of view regarding preventive psychiatry. . . . The Achievement of Collaboration [working relationship with the community] . . . [involves] four basic tasks which a community and a mental health agency must accomplish if they are to collaborate successfully: 1. Centrality . . . available to all groups . . . 2. Neutrality . . . to implement problem-solving. 3. Methods of communication . . . know enough about the operations of the agency to make intelligent use of it . . . confidentiality . . . must be preserved. 4. Boundaries . . . agreed on and . . . acceptable to staff, citizens and other agencies.

(pp. 36–44)

The basic CMH research focus aimed to answer the following questions:[6]

What is the actual and potential "case load of emotional disturbance" in the community? How could one recognize emotional disturbance early and see it in relation to the social arrangements in which people live? What would be an appropriate agency to help deal at an early stage with some of the identified neurotic and destructive patterns and deal alike with the creators and victims of these patterns?

(pp. 6–7)

This message was carried to many academic and professional audiences.[7] The range of projects documents this function:[8]

The clinical program, representing about 20% of staff time . . . follow-ups with former clients.

. . .

Consulting work and case finding—Wellesley Schools . . . Weston Schools, Clergy . . . Friendly Aid . . . Miscellaneous Consultation Screening—Hills and Falls Nursery School . . . Pre-School Checkup . . . Newton-Wellesley Hospital: Human relations seminars with all incoming student nurses . . . conferences with faculty groups

. . .

Community Planning—The Health Committee of the Wellesley Community Chest and Council . . . Interagency Committee of the HRS Board. . . Youth needs . . . Social Geography and Mental Health . . . After Care Program for returning mental hospital patients. . . Sex Ratio Research

. . .

Mental Health Education—Public Education . . . Professional Education:.seminars with pediatricians and physicians are indefinite. . . Fellowship Program.

Community mental health consultation, one of the cornerstones of CMH developed at HRS, reflected the philosophy of partnership with and strengthening the community:[9]

> OVERVIEW OF THEORY . . . public health philosophy and population centered orientation. . . "crises", early case finding, and epidemiology. The consultant adopts . . . an "ecological theory of emotional health" which assumes a dynamic equilibrium (homeostatic) between the consultee and his psychologically relevant environment . . . the focus of interaction shifts from individual diagnosis, sickness, and treatment, to appraisal of situations, health promotion and collaboration. The consultee, therefore, is not viewed as a client or patient but rather as a collaborator and co-professional. . . . the consultant seeks to assist the co-professional deal more effectively with that segment of the population which he serves by helping the consultee solve those problems in his work which have mental health implications. . . . the consultant also attempts to enhance the growth of the consultee so that his professional activities will become more attuned to the emotional needs of his clientele in the future. . . . The consultant . . . seeks to understand the setting within which the consultee functions and the relationships which he maintains within that setting. . . . three of the major components of the mental health consultant's "diagnostic theory" [are] (1) an ecological theory of emotional health or crisis theory; 2) health promotion; and (3) situational analysis.
>
> (pp. 2–4)

Upon his appointments at HMS and MGH on July 1, 1954, Lindemann relinquished administrative responsibility for HRS and assumed the office of medical director to focus on teaching and research. He left with a clear conception of CMH as HRS had pioneered and developed it and because he intended to duplicate it at the MGH:[10]

> Something has developed here since 1948. . . preventive psychiatry . . . a departure from the tradition of . . . look after sick individuals . . . for years to get them a little better . . . do for mental disease. . . [what was] done for typhoid fever and for small pox, to replace the presence of a lot of sick people . . . requiring a lot of doctors . . . illness would be anticipated and the right things . . . done to prevent it. Much of the work. . . [is] not be done by doctors. . . . it would have to be an enterprise of many people working together . . . all the "caretaking people", those responsible for the welfare and growth of people in a community. . . [p. 2]. . . . This would have to be a community enterprise rather than an enterprise of experts from Harvard who would come in and run something here. So we

have always had committees and citizens groups who were interested in . . . this enterprise, using us as resource people . . . to guarantee the standards . . . the Harvard School of Public Health, the [Harvard] Medical School, the [Harvard] Department of Social Relations, and the [Harvard] School of Education each. . . [sit] on a steering committee. . . [with] a group of citizens who would interpret us to Wellesley and who would also warn us of wrong steps. [It] became an executive committee . . . and had now . . . a board of directors. . . . One of our charter members, Dr. Warren Vaughn. . . [is] now the assistant commissioner of mental hygiene. . . [He] has now taken this pattern and. . . [to] transform child guidance clinics . . . into the pattern which we represent . . . not oriented to treat . . . severely sick people, these are referred to other psychiatric resources. . . . [It] is concerned with assessing troubled states . . . it tries to study crisis situations . . . distinguishing "well adaptive" from "maladaptive" responses. . . . Instead of seeing individual patients, we would see groups which were involved in a crisis situation. Furthermore we would be interested in analyzing the response to the crisis rather than think of a long term disease process which we were treating . . . Like the public health workers, we have also been interested in the carriers of emotional disturbance, just as there are carriers of typhoid fever . . . some people [have] ways with them which do not make them appear sick nor do people complain about them, but they have a lot of casualties arising around them. They are . . . disturbing individuals . . . we were also interested in . . . epidemiology . . . the distribution of mental illness . . . in what social circumstances and. . . [in terms of] human relations people are well adapted and . . . not well adapted. . . [We are concerned with] hazardous situations. . . [which] we can learn to identify. . . . The other big axis of concern was . . . determining the early signals of impending breakdown . . . the clergy group, the doctors group, and the social agencies . . . discuss with us problems which they handle themselves. . . [over the course of] mental health consultation. We do not see the people involved, but we talk about [them] . . . give directions and advice and ascertain the essential factors . . . what we call curriculum planning . . . what are the institutionalized factors which may be health making or sick-making. . . . The fourth item is the area of inquiry.

(pp. 1–7)

In 1958, Lindemann secured an NIMH grant for the training of psychologists in community mental health at the HRS.[11] Over the following years, he secured grants for the training of psychiatrists and social workers. Each grant had a project director: for psychology, originally Lindemann himself and later Donald Klein; for psychiatry, Helen Herzan; for social work, William Freeman; and Robert Bragg as coordinator.

These grants helped support a program generalized as a part of the entire Department of Psychiatry: "Training in Community Mental Health Theory and Practice for Psychiatrists, Psychologists, and Social Workers at the Massachusetts General Hospital and Affiliated Field Stations". Facilities involved included MGH, HRS, the Family Guidance Center (at Boston Department of Public Health's Whittier Street Health Center), and the Center for Community Studies (the West End Project). Stated areas of training were research, special clinical services and preventive, group, consultation, communication and public education, and community organization.[12] Seminars included Background in Public Health and Social Science, Approaches to Preventive Psychiatry, Applications of Crisis Theory in Mental Health Planning, Situational Appraisal and Preventive Intervention, Group Methods in Community Mental Health, Mental Health Consultation, Mental Health Education, The Epidemiology of Mental Health, The "Community" in Community Mental Health: What Is a Community?, Community Studies, and Role Development of the Mental Health Worker.

While this training program broadened the CMH program and funding at HRS and MGH and was the pride of the department, there were criticisms of its implementation. CMH trainees found that conferences were not productive and focused, field placements were not always receptive, physical and staff resources were overstretched, and project commitments were beyond the resources available and disappointing in achievement.[13]

The HRS staff drafted a proposal to the NIMH for training nonpsychiatrist physicians in the mental health opportunities in their work:[14]

> The Human Relations Service of Wellesley requests support for expansion of present training operations with non-psychiatric physicians and for the gradual evolution over a five year period of an integrated program of seminars and field experience in community mental health principles and practice for medical doctors. The purpose of the emerging program would be to enhance the physician's ability to perform his role as one of the "caretakers" of the community, to whom many people turn with their common life predicaments. To the program, therefore, would be brought personality insights afforded by psychiatry and the perspectives of group life and community afforded by social science and public health.

HRS recognized the need for improved communication with the town. The executive director and a social worker joined a public relations (later public liaison) committee consisting of community volunteers (many having served on the HRS Board of Directors) of increasingly diverse backgrounds. They arranged speakers, publications, gatherings, open houses, etc. It was also at the forefront of developing a new integration of professional mental health work into the community:[15]

> Another aspect of collaboration that had implications for the professional was the layman's multiplicity of roles in relations to the agency. It was a unique experience for the professional to encounter the same person as Board member, client, sponsor, or friend, within different social contexts. The layman's ability to perceive the mental health agency as one in which there were no clearcut demarcations between the kinds of people who became Board members and those who became clients made this fluidity in role relationship possible. Another feature contributing to ease in assuming different roles was the opportunity for the layman to share in a task-oriented situation with the professional. The attitude of the professional and the way he helped with the task often enabled the layman to make appropriate use of other mental health specialists for the resolution of personal concerns.

Derived from the collaborative experience was the notion that professional roles are more "blurred" in the mental health field than in traditional settings. In circulating widely among community people, the professional became aware of being "onstage" at all times, which necessitated a quick "shift in hats" appropriate to how he was being perceived. The varied contexts of interchange between professionals and laypeople fostered a feeling of mutual respect and friendship without impairing the dignity or objectivity of the expert. This required of the professional not only flexibility but also an inner assurance about the validity of maintaining proximity with community people.

From this experience, it became evident that emphasis on communication is essential in the preparation of specialists entering the mental health field. Although it is a complex and fluid field in which new insights are continually developing, basic to any effective enterprise in mental health is the professional's ability to establish meaningful patterns of communication not only within his own ranks but with citizens of the community as well.

This working group provided another articulation of the community mental health ideology:[16]

> Proximity and friendship were important factors in altering for layman and professional their perceptions of each other. As they explored together the verbal and non-verbal aspects of communication, they became aware of postures and attitudes that impaired effective interchange. Their continuous appraisal of <u>language</u> and <u>feelings</u> was essential to growth and change and enabled them to see

each other as human beings contributing in important but different ways to the mental health of community life.

John K. Brines, MD, the Wellesley pediatrician, an active HRS supporter and board member, continued to champion the social medicine approach. As symposium chairperson on the Committee on Mental Health of the Massachusetts chapter of the American Academy of Pediatrics, he asked Lindemann to attend the symposium, to strengthen the erratic fire kindled by his mentors, including Lindemann, Helen Herzan, and Donald Klein, for more effective communication and cooperation between physicians and others in the total life of child and parents.

HRS expanded its school consultation program to the Weston school system in Massachusetts, including assigning a psychiatric consultant (perhaps Richmond Holder or Peter Sifneos) in a project to sensitize elementary school teachers to observe and report on pupils in order to predict adolescent maladjustment.[17] In a letter to Lindemann from July 30, 1964, Charles K. Cummings, Jr., the guidance director of Weston High School, expressed warm appreciation for his help and insight and assurance that this spirit would continue. Several publications presented this approach to professional audiences.[18]

An important HRS project was preschool and school entering mental health screening, involving especially Elizabeth Lindemann, Kaspar Naegele, and Ann Ross.[19] Starting in 1950, it attempted to assess children's emotional readiness for kindergarten; prepare children, their parents, and school authorities for the transition of starting school; and identify children and families likely to have trouble with it and in need of monitoring and help.[20] Each year from April to June, free of charge, a one-hour evaluation of parents and children was followed by a half-hour report to parents. This developed into the observation of children during two hours of free doll play and one-hour parent interviews, followed by task-oriented play to predict school performance. In turn, from this developed a shorter screening test of child separation from mother and adaptation to new surroundings and activities. During 1953–1956, Klein and Ross evaluated parents' reactions to child school entry and documented stress for parents and children and shifts in family role and feelings. From 1958 to 1961, Ross and Lindemann's follow-up study of parents and teachers afterschool entry documented the ability of this screening to predict school adjustment. They found that mothers predicted adjustment problems of children that were not predicted by the screening procedure; this suggested either subtle cues sensed by mothers or self-fulfilling influences by the mothers. Other sub-studies focused on isolated vs. nonisolated children, friendship, and patterns of family relationships and roles. In 1962, Donald Klein organized at the American Orthopsychiatric Association meeting a gathering of nationwide preschool screening clinicians. This led to the conference *School Health* in the fall of 1964. Outcomes of these meetings were limited epidemiological research, case findings, child-rearing advice, and reassurance about normality. These HRS services and studies produced a number of publications and reports.[21]

In addition, HRS offered a nursery school mental health consultation program:[22] It offered understanding of the stresses on preschool children, especially stressed children; coping with problem children and parents; referrals for problems outside teachers' competences; and educational programs for parents.

Planned research projects included the following:[23]

1. A Study of Predicaments: The Prevalence of Mental Health Predicaments in Wellesley, Massachusetts, in March, 1959
2. Study of 3:1 Male:Female Prevalence of Mental Health Problems at HRS and US—epidemiological study
3. Neighborhoods and Their Patterns of Mental Health: A Study in Human Ecology (Wellesley)
4. A Comparative Study of Clinical Services at the H.R.S. and Psychiatric Treatment Centers
5. "The Prevention of Mental Illness", Human Relations Service of Wellesley, Inc.
6. Mental Health Aspects of Peer Relatedness in Pre-adolescence (Part of a longitudinal study of a school population).

Lindemann was more distanced from HRS by his responsibilities at MGH and on the national and international scenes, though he remained medical director. Bragg also found him more a thinker than the practical implementer that he would have expected and preferred.

Three of the principles of Lindemann's concept of CMH demonstrated at the HRS were community (as contrasted with professional) initiation, community implementation, and community direction. The practical management as well as review and reaffirmation of its philosophy took place at its board of directors, with community majority representation and leadership. Lindemann and the rest of the HRS staff were consultants, facilitators, and implementers of professional services. Thus, information about its direction comes from the board minutes, from its inception to this day, constituting a model of this form of CMH:[24]

> Major issues for HRS were the transition of leadership with Lindemann's shift to the MGH and HMS, and the agency's survival and character in the face of the massive CMHC character, controls, and resources.

At the board meeting on January 19, 1963, those present included Lindemann and John Wallace, Franklin Parker, and Howard Grimes (community residents). The important services of HRS were listed as school mental health, prekindergarten checkups, public liaison, consultation with Friendly Aid (town social service agency), and clinical services. In considering a successor to Lindemann as he shifted focus to the MGH,

> There was some question whether a psychiatrist could fill as easily such functions. There seemed to be considerable agreement that Wellesley does not want just a clinic but wants to continue the unique combination of community efforts and preventive psychiatry which have been developed over the last decade.
>
> (p. 1)

They considered race (Robert Bragg, MD—an African American psychiatrist), leadership capacity (William Freeman, HRS director of social work), and gender (Helen Herzan MD; Clara Mayo, PhD). Lindemann offered to administer HRS over the summer, with a senior team headed by Robert Bragg for daily services, draw up a list of candidates, and manage expected visits. A preliminary list of possible HRS directors included child psychiatrists—Leonard Weiner (Boston University and Boston City Hospital Child Guidance Clinic), Henry Work (head of Child Psychiatry at the University of California at Los Angeles), and David Reiser (James Jackson Putnam Children's Center); psychologists—William Ryan (Massachusetts Division of Mental Hygiene and Massachusetts Committee for Children and Youth), and Douglas Hooper (Tavistock Institute of Human Relations, London).

February 13, 1963, HRS Board Meeting: "after much discussion with Dr. Lindemann, the executive committee had decided to recommend that Dr. Bragg be appointed administrator and program director of HRS. . . . The Board voted unanimously to support these decisions" (p. 2).

The federal CMHC and other social programs brought with them not only massive funds but directions and limitations for their use, new institutions competitive with pre-existing ones (such as HRS), regulations, application and reporting requirements, and future changes difficult to predict, which made long-term planning uncertain to impossible. The citizen/professional collaboration at HRS struggled with this in the attempt to salvage HRS values and the program in the new politico-economic context. At the board meeting on February 12, 1964, Lindemann attempted to find a way:

> "How will the new Federal Bill on Mental Health [CMHC] affect the Wellesley Human Relations Service?"
>
> The pattern of prevention in mental health which HRS helped to initiate is now the accepted way of dealing with mental problems. It has become a part of mental health in the Commonwealth of Massachusetts.

Dr. Lindemann outlined what he saw as some of the accomplishments of HRS, from its inception to the present:

1. The original purpose of HRS still remains of helping to find out how mental health can be achieved. 2. HRS continues as an example of a good community clinic. 3. HRS is unusual in having achieved good cooperating participation by its citizens. 4. HRS can continue its leadership role in the state, but will now have many more partners. 5. Other clinics are using HRS ideas. In order to keep our position of leadership, it is more important than ever that HRS be efficient and creative.

Next, Dr. Lindemann outlined the factors to be considered in making decisions for the future of HRS:

2. The close supporting relationship between HRS, the Mass. General Hospital, and the Harvard School of Public Health may undergo changes. 3. Dr. Lindemann has to retire in 2 years as psychiatrist-in-chief at the Mass. General Hospital. No one can know now what the attitude of his successor towards community mental health will be. 4. The section of the Harvard School of Public Health under Dr. Gerald Caplan, with which HRS has had close ties, is about to be moved to the Harvard Medical School and is going to be known as the Laboratory for Community Psychiatry. Future relationship with HRS will have to be worked out. 5. The grant from the National Institute of Health to the Mass. Gen. Hospital which paid for the training program involving Fellows and staff at HRS also ends in 2 years. This might of course be renewed. 6. Dr. Lindemann's future plans are still uncertain. He is considering the direction of the new Bowdoin Square government center for mental health which is about to be built. This will be a unit for Community Psychiatry tied to the Mass. Gen. Hospital. He expressed some hope that he might be able to continue in some relationship to HRS.

(pp. 3–4)

POSSIBLE COURSES FOR HRS:

1. Remain as a community mental health clinic with federal support for physical facilities and money for research projects and community support for services provided to Wellesley. 2. Become a state clinic serving a larger community. . . . Dr. Lindemann . . . talked . . . to Dr. [Bellenden] Hutcheson, the present state director of State Clinics [Director, Division of Mental Hygiene, DMH]. . . . On April 1st he has to submit his budget for June 1965, so that HRS would have

to discuss this possibility . . . and make a decision if HRS is to be considered in this budget for 1965. Dr. Hutcheson told Dr. L. that HRS can become a state clinic and still retain independence in its activities. However, it would have to join with 2 other communities, possibly Weston and Wayland. . . . 3. Remain a community mental health center with a strong research component somewhat like the Judge Baker [guidance center]. This would require funds from a private source and these would have to be of considerable magnitude. Dr. Lindemann believes he could get a private grant to start a Research Center . . . attached to HRS. If the Wellesley Community agreed, this would be an addition to the established service-oriented part of HRS now operating. However, Dr. Alper expressed the fear that lack of an academic connection would be a serious drawback. Dr. Lindemann is still thinking of this plan as one possibility that would interest him after his retirement. 4. Become closer related to Newton-Wellesley Hospital and Medfield State Hospital. HRS would then be the community mental health center, Newton-Wellesley Hospital would be the general hospital and Medfield State the Mental Hospital.

(pp. 2–6)

At the board meeting on March 11, 1964, the option of becoming a state DMH clinic was considered:

There was a report on the staff meeting with Belenden Hutcheson, MD, Director of the DMH Division of Mental Hygiene: "He feels that HRS could be of great value in the state system in showing other clinics how to get community cooperation. He expressed considerable interest in providing all possible conditions that would enable HRS to consider becoming a state clinic. . . . The HRS pre-school program was especially interesting to Dr. Hutcheson. . . . Finally the following motion expressed by Dr. Wallace was passed: . . . Mr. Grimes, the president, would telephone to Dr. Hutcheson to indicate HRS interest in possibly becoming a state clinic. . . . It was to be understood that the Board did not wish at this time to commit itself".

(p. 2)

At the board meeting on June 10, 1964, it was noted that the board decided against becoming a state clinic. (This proved prescient in that state funding for staff salaries progressively waned and abruptly ended, leaving HRS scrambling for a viable identity and support.) "Mr. [Robin D.] Willits [HRS Treasurer] Report: Although the board has decided against becoming a state clinic, at least for the present, Mr. Willits said that the basic opportunity and need to evaluate the Agency's future still exists" (p. 2). The board saw the agency services they wanted to preserve as follows:[25]

"offer prompt psychiatric first aid in crisis situations, hazardous to the mental health of the affected individual"; assessment, short-term psychotherapy, and referral to 120 families per year. 2. Consultation Services—[Town of] Weston [Massachusetts]—consultation to school staff and parents, [Town of] Wellesley [Massachusetts]—emergency psychiatric consultation, in-service training, mental health consultation, administrative consultation, and curriculum planning. Family Counseling Service—Region West, Wellesley District—-psychiatric consultation. Nursery Schools—consultation to staff. 3. Newton-Wellesley Hospital Nurses' Groups—1952 the Director of the Newton-Wellesley Hospital School of Nursing arranged with HRS discussion groups with first year nursing students regarding class and ward experiences. Consequently the rate of dropping out of school decreased from 24 to six percent, there was better acceptance of patients and supervisors, and they identified areas of need for support. 4. Pre-School Check-Up Program—In 1950 worked with the first group of 50 mothers and children. 5. Research—staff members participated in research, attempting to develop methods of describing and analyzing the community. 6. Public Liaison Committee—community women speakers bureau led to neighborhood and organization coffee parties with HRS collaboration. 7. Other—participation with official committees, new organizations, expanding service organizations, speeches, and conferences with interested caregivers.

(pp. 3–4)

Lindemann's belief in and attachment to HRS—his offspring and realization of his ideals—was undiminished even amid these major shifts in interpretations of CMH and shaping of services by funding sources. He continued to speak to the agency about maintaining its place in mental health planning and chances/hopes regarding continued supports and relationships.[26] He started by placing HRS in the context of the historical development of CMH and the CMHC program:

Prior to the CMHC Act of 1963 he saw two trends in mental health center development: "1st Trend: many mentally sick are too far away from their community mental hospitals, that many state mental hospitals are too large in size and that hospitals must not limit themselves only to curing mentally ill but must think of prevention and early rehabilitation. Day Care Centers, Night Care Centers, Half Way Houses, etc. would be intermediate stations for patients between the hospital and the people of the community. . . . There would be closer relationship with families and friends. . . . There are many volunteer programs established. . . . <u>2nd Trend</u>: . . . recognition that there are casualties in communities which do not need hospitalization, including mental hospital care, emphasizes care of troubled people within the community itself. This involves welfare departments, family service agencies, jails, etc. and collaboration with the schools, police, ministers, etc. in the community. Mental health experts could be provided to help these people who deal with people and to draw agencies closer together in an effort to have coordinated activity in the care of those with emotional problems. H.R.S. pioneered with this trend".

The Mental Health Centers Act of 1963 tried to combine these two trends: to establish small mental hospital units with many waystations between people of the community and the mental hospital and to establish centers that emphasize some aspects of the HRS program. Through pressure of the American Medical Association, the workforce provisions of the Community Mental Health Centers Act of 1963 were eliminated, and at present, there are no funds for staff. Through this Act, funds are provided for the construction of buildings for mental health care (pp. 2–3). Massachusetts was planning on updating and reducing the size of mental hospitals before the CMHC Act and was planning CMHCs such as those at Bowdoin Square, Boston University, Tufts/New England Medical Center, and Boston State Hospital, including some features of the Massachusetts Mental Health Center. Different groups advocate focusing on state hospitals, general hospitals, and CMHCs, respectively. Belenden Hutcheson, MD, the director of the DMH Division of Mental Hygiene, fears his state mental health clinics will be satellites of state hospitals. The Massachusetts Medical Society's Mental Health Committee advocated for a mental health program like the TB [tuberculosis] program—wards in general hospitals and treated by family physicians. He then proceeded to assess HRS's place in this context:

it is not H.R.S.'s role to apply existing knowledge to a population. Rather, H.R.S. is a cooperative agency between citizens and professionals to increase existing knowledge—to devise new techniques, new methods. H.R.S. should remain a pilot organization for training manpower and developing methods for diagnosis, care and inquiry into various problems. Dr. Hutcheson is quite aware that the Board and Staff of H.R.S. are not too interested in being a State clinic. However, Dr. Hutcheson does feel that a center for research and training could be financed by his department.

(pp. 4–5)

In this case, there would be a proviso that H.R.S. would have to be different than what it is now. The emphasis would be on preventive mental health. Focus would be on such items as school entry. HRS could then have two major functions:

1. Function as a service organization to serve Wellesley uniquely and well.
2. Continue to be an academic institution adding to existing knowledge and training workforce in mental health.

<u>Relationship of HRS to other institutions</u>: H.R.S. could continue to be related to the Mass. General Hospital and Harvard University and there are no reasons why H.R.S. could not have relationships with other academic institutions. . . . Dr. Lindemann pointed out that M.G.H. has been a torch bearer for citizens supported programs and that the amount of work by many in developing the program at H.R.S. represents an investment that the Psychiatric Service at M.G.H. would not want to start over again. H.R.S. is a sort of child of M.G.H.'s.

(p. 7)

. . .

Dr. [John] Knowles, Director of the Mass. General Hospital . . . has stated that the modern metropolitan teaching hospital must alter its function—must do what H.R.S. did for the mental health field. The hospital must have anticipatory services, follow-up services and a network of ties with all kinds of agencies so that the medical care of the population may be more comprehensive. Mass. General might well develop this approach. (The Psychiatric Service at M.G.H. has served as a model for all the services of M.G.H. in involving family-social agencies, etc. in the prevention and rehabilitation treatment of patients.) Dr. Knowles will push the continuance of the relationship between M.G.H. and H.R.S. Dr. Robert Ebert, Chief of Medicine at M.G.H., is dedicated to this social approach to medicine. . . . Dr. Lindemann's successor will have an interest in H.R.S. . . . If this happens, H.R.S. could look to have academic support as in the past. . . . There has been a lull in research at H.R.S. because of limited staff time and financial support.

(pp. 4–5)

The Training Grants will come forth as in the past. M.G.H. would help direct applications for funds.

(pp. 5–6)

Mr. Willits [HRS Treasurer] then raised the question as to why does M.G.H. need H.R.S.? Dr. Lindemann sought hope for indirect support of social psychiatry on the basis of the interest of MGH and HMS in social medicine:[27]

Dr. Lindemann's Role: Dr. Lindemann stated that he has decided not to take the Superintendency of Bowdoin Square [CMHC]. He recalled a contact with Alan Gregg [Rockefeller Foundation] who stated there is a time to learn, to lead and to consult. Dr. Lindemann feels that it is now time for him to consult. He will continue his interest in H.R.S.

(p. 6)

The HRS Board gave further consideration to sources of support and remained ambivalent about joining the DMH vs. planning with Hutcheson for a protected/supported status.

The search for continuation of HRS's mission in the setting of weakening support and relationship with MGH (note John Knowles's uncertainty about them in the future and encouraging alternative supports), and HRS's reluctance to turn to DMH dominance was revealed in the board meeting of January 6, 1965:[28]

The Study Action Committee met 12/3/64 with Belenden Hutcheson, Director of the DMH Division of Mental Hygiene, and John Knowles, General Director of the MGH".Dr. Hutcheson stated that HRS could apply for State support: . . . 3) for the creation of a Primary Prevention Unit. Such a unit would be the first of its kind in the State of Massachusetts. . . . Dr. Hutcheson envisioned a 5 man team to carry out the work of the Primary Prevention Unit, requiring a budget of approximately $50,000. This 5 man team would have a director and staff approved by the State and by the HRS board. . . . Dr. Knowles expressed the opinion that. . . [t]he Chief of Psychiatry at Mass. General Hospital has tenure. This allows him some degree of freedom to do what he wants e.g. Dr. Lindemann's work with HRS. The prerogatives of tenure have to be protected. We want Dr. Lindemann's successor to be interested in HRS. However, he may not be. His tenure must allow him the prerogatives of choice. . . . Dr. Lindemann will retire by September 1965. We hope to have his successor come out here and take an interest in HRS or have someone as his delegate. . . . Dr. Lindemann raised the question of the relationship of a voluntary agency to that of a state agency. He pointed out that in the MGH Alcohol Program the state does not support a number of people . . . but rather contracts for services. He . . . would prefer this type of arrangement with the State. The HRS Board was exploring links, support from federal government, MGH, and Harvard University. Dr. Knowles spoke about the hospital and university's various interests, and that HRS should explore their interests in

HRS. "Dr. Knowles emphasized the fact that there is no substitute for a community supporting its own institutions". "Mr. [David] Parker [chairperson of the HRS Board's Study Action Committee] stated that the HRS Board prefers to not be involved with the State for this would mean a loss in some sovereignty. Dr. Knowles stated that Federal and State governments have always been in on mental health. This does provide an opportunity for HRS to shape policy . . . in a very positive fashion. Dr. Brines stated that it is important for HRS to make policy for if it is not done by HRS it will be done for us. . . . Mr. Grimes [Board President] remarked that this gives the Board good cause to continue with the Study Action Committee".

(pp. 1–5)

Dr. Knowles commented on the limitations of DMH affiliation:[29]

Dr. Knowles would like to have the Government Center Mental Health Unit operated by MGH on a contract basis because he feels this is best. However, this is not possible—at least, at present. . . . Dr. Knowles prefers [contractual] agreements with governmental agencies rather than placing services directly under them. He supported the concept of the role of voluntary health units.

An example of DMH relations with private entities was the consultation program of the Medfield State Hospital:[30]

Dr. Cummer stated that his interests in extra-mural activities and treatment involving individuals with emotional problems was greatly stimulated by Dr. Harry Solomon's inaugural speech at the American Psychiatric Association. At that time Dr. Solomon stated that the traditional state hospital, isolated and perched on a hill had to go. (The Medfield State Hospital was established some 80 years ago.) According to the newer concept, there would be smaller hospital units of some 50 beds with outpatient facilities and these would replace the state hospitals. . . . Medfield State Hospital planned and developed mental health training and service to local general hospitals (Framingham Union Hospital, Newton-Wellesley Hospital), clinics, guidance center, ministers, police chiefs, businessmen, expectant parents, and industrial physicians.

(pp. 1–2)

HRS continued to teeter between doubt and optimism about the future of its program. On February 12, 1965, Lindemann warned that

2. The close supporting relationship between HRS, the Mass. General Hospital, and the Harvard School of Public Health may undergo changes. 3. Dr. Lindemann has to retire in 2 years as

psychiatrist-in-chief at the Mass. General Hospital. No one can know now what the attitude of his successor towards community mental health will be.[31]

Yet he reported that there was no reason why NIMH funding cannot continue at least on the contemporary level of $40,013 for education in CMH ($21,445 for faculty, $18,568 for fellowships, and $24,038 for research and development in CMH.)[32]

The funding Grant Foundation was credited with HRS's influencing people and programs in the direction of CMH:

> the most significant contribution which the Grant Foundation made to the field of community mental health has been in enabling us to demonstrate the workings and the efficacy of a program so that it could be copied and further developed by workers who started with us. . . . Dr. Warren Vaughan through the Department of Mental Health of the Commonwealth of Massachusetts has by now developed seventeen agencies after the pattern of the Wellesley Project . . . and he is now working with Harvard Medical School, Boston University Medical School and Tufts Medical School to have mental health centers with similar research aims and similar practices. . . . Arnold Schwartz is now the person in charge of the mental health program in the State of California and Marie MacNabola. . . . the mental health social worker is now in . . . the central office of the Training Branch of the National Institute of Mental Health to encourage training programs similar to ours all over the country.[33]
>
> I was glad to hear Dr. Jack Ewalt [then commissioner of the Massachusetts] say the other day at a national committee meeting at the [National] Institute of Mental Health that his whole program of community mental health agencies in Massachusetts which now comprise twenty regional centers is based on the Wellesley experiment and is carried out in the light of our philosophy.[34]

Despite this glowing history, support for HRS shifted: Federal training and research grants phased down and out, the relationship to MGH became more tenuous and support waned, and HRS support shifted to local funding for its services. In the late 1960s, affiliation with the Massachusetts DMH with funding of staff positions brought an infusion of (temporarily) stable support.[35] This brought a shift in staff and the focus of responsibility toward clinical service. Donald Klein, its executive director, moved to Boston University as the director of its Human Relations Center.[36] He went on with work in community psychology, creative and nontraditional ideas about community relations and healthy communities, and consulting and teaching in these areas, including in the National Training Laboratory (NTL) Institute for Applied Behavioral Science at

Bethel, Maine. On June 8, 2007, he made some remarks at a community psychology conference in California, returned to his seat, and collapsed and later died.

Nevertheless, the HRS and its board of directors maintained their loyalty to primary prevention and preventive intervention in mental health:[37]

> The Human Relations Service of Wellesley, Inc. came into being in 1948 as an experiment in utilizing a public health preventive approach to mental health. Having demonstrated the practicality of this approach the experimental undertaking was closed-out and the organization was set up on a continuing basis with community support. However, three philosophical concepts or beliefs which underlay the original research endeavor continue to be fundamental to the goals and purposes of the Agency. The first concept is that mental health is amenable to a public health approach, i.e. that an individual's mental health is influenced by characteristics and activities of the community and can be fostered by joint action at the community level. The second concept is that mental health is amenable to a preventive approach, i.e. that individuals and society need not wait for illness to appear to take action but can act, before the fact, to prevent illness from occurring, both at the individual level and at the community level. Finally, the third concept is that life contains a range of "crises" which are potentially hazardous for even mature and stable individuals; crises which can "swamp" a basically healthy person, disrupt his effective functioning and generate a form of mental illness. . . . The basic goals of HRS are: 1. To improve the mental health of the Wellesley area. 2. To contribute to the body of professional knowledge in the mental health field. PROBLEM SOLVING . . . provide assistance to individuals and families in the resolution of emotional problems . . . directed towards providing assistance during crisis periods and with acute, "here and now" circumstances . . . but also entails preventing more serious illness. . . . It is our intention to provide <u>short term</u> professional assistance to "well" people as well as to "ill" people . . . it is <u>not</u> the policy of the Agency to provide service to those with a chronic emotional problem requiring long term treatment, but rather to refer such cases to other sources of assistance.
>
> (p. 11)

> . . .
>
> CONSULTATION . . . provide a consultation service to so-called "caretakers" and other organizations in the community . . . not only concerned with the resolution of specific individual problems but also with the increase of the caretakers' skills and knowledge. . . . RESEARCH . . . focus its research on the identification and understanding of <u>life crisis</u> situations, and to a lesser extent on "action"

research aimed at improving our diagnostic and clinical techniques. other aspects of community mental health, such as research aimed at identifying characteristics of the community, . . . can be undertaken with Board approval. . . . PLANNING . . . means the promotion of better mental health through reorganization of the community's resources. . . . Planning, as such, is not a sub-goal of the Agency.

(p. 2)

. . .

EDUCATION . . . is not a specific sub-goal of the Agency . . . Unless such activities are justified . . . for public relations, or are part of the established school consultation program . . . EVALUATION . . . on severe cases, referring them elsewhere for extended treatment . . . evaluation, per se, is not a specific sub-goal of the Agency.

(p. 3)

Bragg thought that HRS's long-term support and development allowed it to have a significant impact on how the school systems looked at students and the school environment. Charles Cummings, Jr., the director of Guidance in the Weston High School, expressed his appreciation of the HRS support of a study of pupil maladjustment:

your New Year's note moved me—to sadness in part, to pride in part, and to the reflection that it has been a real privilege to have been working with you over these years. . . . I do feel that the pride is justified, though, really, it seems to me that the steps we have taken toward building mental health are quite natural and sensible and that any one with sense would see how reasonable they were.[38]

Note that ultimately the counterrevolution in psychiatry was manifest in MGH's break with CMH and HRS (using Lindemann's analogy, MGH's stepchild rather than its child), the withering of HRS's research and training, and the shift of its focus to clinical service. DMH funding was rapidly withdrawn, leading to a break in that relationship in favor of self-support through independent contracts.

Explorations in Community Mental Health: "The Book"

Pulling together the experience and lessons of HRS was the vehicle for articulating a coherent picture of the public health, preventive interpretation of CMH. And it collided with a critical problem of Lindeman's.

Lindemann had an abiding and notorious difficulty in committing to print his broad perspectives and recommendations and their implementation in the HRS. He perceived the HRS enterprise as incomplete and ongoing, though he believed that he had done valid work and always referred to HRS.[39] He was wary of the finality of the written word and much preferred the creative interaction between a speaker and a live audience.[40] He acknowledged that "As you know, I find it very important to have a live audience as target for my presentations".[41] He also was uncomfortable about his ability to write in English.[42] At one point, he invoked his sensitivity to embarrassing the people whom he would be writing about and who had entrusted their ideas and feelings to him.[43] He also expected a hostile reaction.[44] Some suspected an abiding bitterness and sense of betrayal from his 1930s experience at the Iowa Psychopathic Hospital when he did prepare a book manuscript on psychopathology and believed that it was stolen in his absence by William Malamud. Elizabeth Lindemann noted the shifts in his concept of the book as his experiences with HRS changed: In 1953–1955, he was imbued with enthusiastic involvement in field work, and an outline shows the development of HRS and its various studies and interventions. In 1956, he retreated from a hostile field to an outline of theory and generalization.

Efforts at writing a book on community mental health and preventive intervention from the experiences at HRS continued spasmodically. Many people and organizations were eager to have it, and it was reported that Gerald Caplan and Elizabeth Lindemann resented Lindemann's taking so much time planning it without getting it done.[45] (Note that Caplan eventually wrote books on the topics.) Gerald Caplan included this project in his plans for the HSPH Division of Mental Health:

> Another plan which it is hoped will mature during the coming year is the publication by Drs. Lindemann and Caplan and their colleagues of a book, *Explorations in Community Mental Health*, which will describe the experiences in Wellesley and will document the current thinking and teaching of the Harvard School of Public Health Division of Mental Health in this field.[46]

This avoidance was demonstrated in his lack of positive response to many invitations: He received an invitation to write a book on suicide.[47] Elizabeth Lindemann referred to the book *Explorations in Preventive Psychiatry* to be published by Basic Books, New York.[48] Josenine Nelson, the director of public relations for the National Health Council, wrote to Lindemann: "Do you know when your book *Explorations In Preventive Psychiatry* will be available?"[49]

The W.T. Grant Foundation was interested in the book as a product of its support of HRS. It contributed funding for the project on the basis of Lindemann's reports of work on the project. Lindemann's responses to the foundation demonstrate his sensitivity to the many social and emotional effects of this action; his hesitation to present himself so irrevocably; and his avoidance:

- "This note is to inquire about the current status of the Foundation's appropriation of $7,500 to the Human Relations Service for publication of the book resulting from the Harvard-Wellesley project. . . . In your letter of May 10th last . . . you submitted an accounting of expenditures showing an unexpended balance of $476.70. . . . We should be interested to have news from you of the current status of the book."[50]

- "Please do bring me up-to-date on the famous (and invisible) book on the Wellesley project. Just where do we stand?"

- "You know I don't want to drive you to distraction and overwork but I would like to have some word of the present situation. I also hope that you can put a little optimism and even a tentative timetable into your reply".[51]

- "The book is coming along slowly but surely . . . it is our earnest expectation that we will have everything ready for the press sometime in June".[52]

- "Is here anything further to report on the publication of the book on the Wellesley experiment?"[53]

- "The work on our book has been proceeding with vigor. There have been several revisions of the organization and the material. Mr. Henry H. Balos, an experienced editorial writer, is helping us with the final version, and Dr. Gerald Caplan . . . is contributing considerably to the clear presentation of our concepts, methods and results. Mr. Rosenthal of Basic Books is working along with us. We hoped to have the material in the hands of the printers by the end of June but it seems now that we will have to work for two or three more months into the summer. . . . The subsistence sum which was generously given to us to aid in the publication of the book has been almost used up . . . Would you be willing to extend the final date for the use of this money to Sept. 1."[54]

- "Enclosed please find a check to cover your bill for . . . editorial consultation . . . concerning our book on the Wellesley Program. . . . We cannot hope at this time to finish the whole volume by the end of this academic year as we had hoped before. . . . Several members of our group will be very busy during the summer rewriting their sections of the work. . . . Mrs. Lindemann will contact you soon in connection with the revised out-line which we discussed."[55]

- "Thank you very much for your letters about our program and our book. . . . The slowness of the actual getting the work to the printer has something to do partly with my perfectionism and partly with the fact that I have been somewhat under the weather for several months and that my chest condition has gotten somewhat worse reducing my energy output. . . . However, I feel . . . a great urgency to get this important piece of work off my desk not only to fulfill my obligation but also to make a significant contribution to the development of our field of preventive psychiatry."[56]

- "I received your inquiry about the final report of the gift of $7,500. which was made to us for the publication of the book of our work in Wellesley. . . . I quite understand your concern about delay in having the manuscript of our book, 'Explorations in Preventive Psychiatry', in the hands of the printer by now. . . . Our original manuscript has had several revisions. A considerable difficulty was the sensitiveness of some citizens of Wellesley about anything published in book form rather than in scientific articles which would, like the book on 'Middletown' allow inferences about the aspects of community life which they consider as more or less private. A book like John Seeley's 'Crestwood Heights' would make many of the citizens quite uncomfortable and our first version was at least as revealing as Seeley's work. . . . We decided to rework the material in such a way that it included experiences in several communities . . . and disguising effectively the origin of a given description in Wellesley. . . . We expect to have all the significant material resulting from our Wellesley work . . . enriched by references to . . . Whittier Street Health Center in Boston and recently at the Massachusetts General Hospital. . . . We have kept in contact with Mr. Rosenthal of Basic Books about or progress and sincerely hope that the new version of the manuscript will be ready for publication before the first of April".[57]

There were many examples of Lindemann's delay and diversion: Henry Holt & Company urgently sought information on such a book and was referred to Donald Klein, the executive director of HRS;[58] Birton L. Beals inquired about publishing a book "on the burgeoning field of community mental health";[59] there was an expected chapter, "Preventative Intervention in Community Health", for Edwin Schneidman's multiauthored book on suicide, *Essays in Self-Destruction*;[60] finally, he delayed his article on grief for the *International Encyclopedia of the Social Sciences*.[61] To an invitation to write a book for interested laypeople, he replied that he was too busy and asked to be invited again later.[62] Later, he wrote that he had hopes that with his impending retirement he would have less administrative burden and be able to finally realize "a book about the basic issues and observations in the field of crises approaches in psychiatry and medicine".[63] A letter to Lindemann from Leonard Duhl (Professional Services Branch of NIMH and later chief of its Office of Planning) urged Lindemann to publish a small book of his papers on crisis theory, suggesting papers (starting with the Coconut Grove fire paper, then medical treatment, and finally the Hague paper), wanting to write the introduction, suggesting people to edit it, and noting that Basic Book publisher Arthur Rosenthal was enthusiastic.[64]

Lindemann felt responsible for a publication despite his reluctance to accomplish it:[65]

> I have felt from time to time a concern about an unfinished matter at home. Just before I left for India one of the associate directors of our Hospital, Mr. David Crockett, mentioned to me that one of the Trustees of the Grant Foundation at a luncheon had expressed to him his regret that I had failed to publish the book about the Wellesley program by this time. I was rather troubled by this and want to assure you, that of course I do feel as responsible as ever for the publication of the volume which pulls together at one place the many threads of the Mental Health Work started in Wellesley and continued there as well as at the School of Public Health and at the Mass. General Hospital. But I do want to do this publication when the time is just right so far as the content is concerned, and also as far as the reaction of our friends among the citizens of Wellesley is concerned. As you know there have been many discussions about techniques to assure the privacy of the families who have participated in the research; and combining work relating to families there with reporting work on other locations has seemed to be the safest course.—I do hope, however, that as planned earlier, the volume will be ready for the reader next October when we have our dedication of the new research laboratories in Psychiatry combined with a celebration reviewing the growth of Psychiatry and Mental Health Research at Harvard and at the M.G.H. since Stanley Cobb started the Unit in 1934.

There were "book meetings" that included potential contributors. The goals and audience for the book were discussed:[66]

> addressed to practitioners and investigators in . . . preventive psychiatry . . . psychiatrists, psychologists, and social workers and social scientists . . . Preventive psychiatry deals with the biological and sociological hazards to emotional and mental well being . . . conditions which produce illness . . . the kind and number of casualties. The psychiatric reaction types . . . as meaningful responses to the hazard or stress. Psychiatric symptoms . . . are not . . . result of breakdown of integration but . . . evidence of an adaptive process leading to reintegration or repair. The concern . . . is with the whole range of disorders including the behavior of visceral organs. From the . . . social sciences they may be considered . . . deviant behavior. Illness is . . . one class of attempt of solving a problem involving the relationship

of internal needs and environmental demands . . . a. From the point of view of the patient as proper balance of satisfaction and dissatisfaction. b. From the . . . social environment as equilibrium in rates of interaction of suitable types with suitable individuals in appropriate roles. [p. 1] c. From the demands made upon the patient a satisfactory level of achievement or production. Patterns of adjustment . . . become manifest at times of disturbance in equilibrium when readaptation to new distribution of interpersonal relationships is required. Patterns of adaptation . . . a. illness b. presence of a disturbing person in a neighborhood c. bereavement d. new arrivals e. problems of contingent social systems (job life to family adjustment) f. transition from one social system to the other (promotion, entering school) . . . study patterns of human relationships of relative suitability as contrasted with those . . . open to severe disturbances . . . the study of isolated individuals in contrast to individuals integrated with work groups or friendship systems. An appraisal of the supportive human environment . . . through formative years is a necessary next step. . . [to] the development or utilization of methods for the assessment of social relatedness at different age levels and . . . kinds of groups. It is the purpose of this book to describe . . . a special agency in which services were closely interwoven with research . . . provides access to populations for study . . . try modes of preventive intervention . . . involving families and small groups and . . . access to community institutions and professional groups for an appraisal of their functions in the community.

Some chapters were drafted, and the outline was repeatedly revised. Some participants became frustrated with blocks to progress.[67] Lindemann hoped

> my recent decision to start a new chapter in my life which is not one of large scale administration but a more scholarly form of assistance in which I hopefully make up for the low productivity in writing which has marred the recent years. I shall discontinue my administrative work . . . and will use the winter to bring to completion a book on mental health. . . . This can well be placed in the total perspective of the new convergence of social action in the service of welfare and education on the one hand and health services on the other hand.[68]

In parallel, John Baldwin, an exchange fellow in CMH at the MGH, proposed a monograph on CMH research based on HRS:[69]

> Introduction The place of research in community mental health ([James] Kelly, [Robert] Newbrough, [John A.] Baldwin, [Alvin] Simmons)

Chapter I The Human Relations Service of Wellesley: history of research and development of theory ([Donald C.] Klein)

Chapter II The evidently vulnerable population: a method of reporting mental health concerns (Kelly)

Chapter III Analysis of community: a social geographic method (Lewis)

Chapter IV Methods for the identification of potentially vulnerable groups (Baldwin)

Chapter V The caretaker in the community: a method of evaluating mental health agents (Newbrough)

Chapter VI Community research and community change: methods of translation of results of investigation and of maintenance of sanction with controlled effect on community (Simmons, The Massachusetts General Hospital [MGH])

This publication, too, was not realized.

Notes

1. Mayo, Clara, PhD, social psychologist, former member of the HRS staff and later member of the Section on Social Psychology at Boston University; interviews at Boston University 9/29/1978 and 12/15/1980.
2. Waring, Dorothy, "The Significance of Communication in a Community Mental Health Program", unpublished, 4/1963; 9/19/1964 HISTORY AND PRESENT PROGRAMS OF HRS, HRS Board Meeting minutes. [folder "Human Relations Service of Wellesley", Box IIIA 4 (F-H), Erich Lindemann Collection, Center for the History of Medicine, Francis A. Countway Library of Medicine, Boston, MA]
3. Parker, Franklin, member of the board of directors, Wellesley Human Relations Service, interviewd by David G. Satin in Boston, MA, 11/17/1978. [Erich Lindemann Collection, David G. Satin, Newton, MA]
4. Lindemann, Erich, letter to Galpin, Perrin C., Executive Director of the W.T. Grant Foundation, Inc., 4/25/1955, p. 1.
5. Bragg, Robert L., MD; Klein, Donald C., PhD; Lindemann, Elizabeth B., MS: "Tenth Anniversary Report of the Wellesley Human Relations Service, INC.; 1948–1958". [folder "Wellesley Human Relations Service of Wellelsely1961-2, 1964-5; DGS Fellowship", David G. Satin files, Newton, MA]

    The executive director, Donald Klein, reaffirmed this mission in the agency's practice:

    > Klein, Donald, memo to Lindemann, Erich, 3/10/1959, p 1. [folder "Lindemann-Caplan Application Material—[Site] Visit", p. 1 [IIIB2 c (box1 of 2), Erich Lindemann Collection, Center for the History of Medicine, Francis A. Countway Library of Medicine, Boston, MA]:
    > "The Human Relations Service of Wellesley, a project of the Harvard School of Public Health from 1948 to 1953 with financial support from the W.T. Grant Foundation . . . as a pilot project in preventive psychiatry, which seeks to apply epidemiological and other public health methods to the control of mental illness in a community.
    > Klein, Donald C., PhD, Executive Director of HRS: "HUMAN RELATIONS SERVICE OF WELLESLEY, INC. Calendar Year 1961; Copy of

Report submitted to the Research Division, U.C.S. [United Community Services]" (5/8/1962), p. 3. [folder "Wellesley Human Relations Service of Wellelsely1961–2, 1964–5; DGS Fellowship", David G. Satin files, Newton, MA]:

Function: The Human Relations Service of Wellesley is a preventively oriented mental health agency established for the study and promotion of mental health services. The agency offers clinical, consultative, group, educational, and research services. The services of the agency are divided into two broad areas: 1) direct services to individuals, families and groups, and 2) study and coordinated planning with groups, institutions, and agencies that would strengthen the mental health aspects of those programs. Individuals are encouraged to contact the agency on a preventive level. . . . Clinical assistance is offered on a short-term basis with follow-up contacts. Situations requiring possible long-term psychiatric or social service assistance are referred. In addition to established consultation programs with schools, hospitals, clergy, and family agency, consultation services are also offered to citizen groups regarding, for example, difficulties in handling neighborhood problems, establishing a discussion group for mothers, personnel programs in organizations and business, and community planning that may have mental implications (p. 1) . . . percents of professional time allocated . . . Clinical 27% . . . Consultation 30% . . . Screening 7% . . . Planning with community groups 30% . . . Education 3% . . . Administrative time of Dr. Lindemann and Dr. Klein 3%.

6. Naegele, Kaspar D., PhD; Department of Economics, Political Science and Sociology, Univ. British Columbia (former HRS staff member): "CASE STUDY: A Mental Health Project in a Boston Suburb", 1954.; Paul, Benjamin D. (ed.), *Health, Culture, & Community: Case Studies of Public Reactions to Health Programs* (New York: Russell Sage Foundation, 1955), p. 7. [folder "Wellesley Human Relations Service of Wellesley 1961–2, 1964–5; DGS Fellowship", David G. Satin files, Newton, MA]

7. Note summary of contributions to other agencies, meetings, training programs, and CMH planning efforts noted in Committee for the Tenth Anniversary Report (Robert L. Bragg, MD, Donald C. Klein, PhD, and Elizabeth B. Lindemann, MS), The "Export" of Mental Health in "Tenth Anniversary Report of the Wellesley Human Relations Service, Inc.: 1948–1958" (mimeographed), pp. 36–39.

Consultation and training:

Warren Vaughan, MD, became Director of the Massachusetts Division of Mental Hygiene, establishing child guidance clinics with preventive, consultation, and community liaison functions.

Consultation to Massachusetts towns, including Lincoln, Lexington, Concord, Belmont, Needham, Dover, Norwood, Brookline, and Natick.

Community mental health conferences with such programs as New York City, Nova Scotia, Toronto, St. Louis, and Prince George's County (Maryland).

Venderbilt University 1957 conference on interdepartmental training.

California Department of Mental Hygiene meeting of mental health professions on training for staffing community mental health programs. Requests for similar consultation from Kansas and South Dakota.

Over 200 visitors between 1954 and 1958. This included A[lexander] T[hompson] M[acbeth] Wilson, MD, chairperson of the Management Committee at The Tavistock Institute of Human Relations in London, interested in family and group studies and industrial management, who offered administrative consultation to Lindemann about establishing a social psychiatry department in a metropolitan hospital. [folder "Wilson, Dr. A.T.M"., IIIB1e 2), S-Z", Erich Lindemann Collection, Center for the History of Medicine, Francis A. Countway Library of Medicine, Boston, MA]

HRS staff have become director of the Massachusetts Department of Mental Hygiene (Warren T. Vaughan, MD), chief psychiatrist in the California Department of Public Health (Anold Schwartz, MD), and national consultant in social work training for the U.S. Public Health Service (Marie McNabola).

Publications:

Lindemann, Elizabeth B., "The Social Worker as a Mental Health Consultant", presented at the Massachusetts Conference of Social Work, 12/8/1955.

Lindemann, Elizabeth B., "Strengthening the Relation Between the School and the Community Treatment Facility" presented at the Fifth Institute on Preventive Psychiatry, University of Texas, 5/1965; published as Chapter V in American Psychiatric Association and the NIMH Joint Information Service, *The Community Mental Health Center: An Analysis of Existing Models* (Washington, DC: 1964).

[folder "Lindemann, Eliz. The Social worker as a mental health consultant—1955", file Human Relations Service via Elizabeth Lindemann, Erich Lindemann Collection, David G. Satin, Newton, MA]

Vallee, Natalie Kugris, Boston University candidate for EdD, "A Study of the Relationship of Physical Growth Patterns of Children and the Incidence of Maladjustive Behavior in a Period of 'Crisis'", 3/1955. Note consultants were Erich Lindemann and Nathan Talbot (MGH Acting Chief of the Children's Medical Service and HMS Associate Professor. [folder "Vallee, N.K"., Box IIIB1e 2), S-Z", Erich Lindemann Collection, Center for the History of Medicine, Francis A. Countway Library of Medicine, Boston, MA]

8. "Report of the Executive Director to the [HRS] Board of Directors 9–13–61". [folder "Wellesley Human Relations Service of Wellesley1961–2, 1964–5; DGS Fellowship", David G. Satin files, Newton, MA]

9. Simmons, Alvin J., PhD, Human Relations Service of Wellesley, Inc.: "Consultation Through a Community Mental Health Agency", p. 4. [folder "Wellesley Human Relations Service of Wellesley 1961–2, 1964–5; David G. Satin Fellowship", David G. Satin files, Newton, MA]

10. Lindemann, Erich, "Preventive Psychiatry", presented at a meeting of the HRS on 11/4/1954 from records by Paul Hare. [Box XII 2 folder "E.L. Preventive Psychiatry: HRS Meeting 11/4/54", Erich Lindemann Collection, Center for the History of Medicine, Francis A. Countway Library of Medicine, Boston, MA]

11. Bragg, Robert L., interview by David G. Satin at the Wellesley Human Relations Service, 7/13/1979. [Erich Lindemann Collection, David G. Satin, Newton, MA]

12. The following are some of the designated staff involved:

Research, Special Clinical Services and Preventive Intervention (staff: Erich Lindemann, etc.), Group Methods (staff: Pearl Rosenberg PhD, William Freeman, MSS, EdD, Laura Morris MSS, Donald Klein PhD), Consultation, Communication and Public Education, Administration (staff: Donald Klein, PhD, Laura Morris, MSS, Eleanor Clark, MSS), and Community Organization.

(staff: Laura Morris, MSS and Thomas Plaut MPH, PhD)

13. Mason, Helen; Messner, Edward, MD; Sarkela, Wiljo; Wheeler, Walker—
Fellows in Community Mental Health, Massachusetts General Hospital:
"An Analysis and Evaluation of a Training Program, 'Community Mental
Health Theory and Practice', with Recommendations", 7/25/1961. [folder
Community Mental Health Program 1961–63, Box IIIB3a-c, Erich Linde-
mann Collection, Center for the History of Medicine, Countway Library,
Boston, MA] [Messner became a vitriolic critic of EL]:

> I INTRODUCTION. . . . This paper is an attempt on the part of the
> four fellows in the Training Program in Community Mental Health at
> the Massachusetts General Hospital to evaluate the present training pro-
> gram and . . . ideas as to how such a program might be strengthened . . .
> because of some dissatisfaction with the formal seminar in Community
> Mental Health Theory and Practice. . . . II ANALYSIS OF EXPERI-
> ENCE . . . A. Problem of Multi-Disciplinary Approach Our experience
> would tend to negate one of the major aims of achieving a synthesis of
> knowledge and techniques from the fields of psychiatry, social science
> and public health. . . . There seemed to be a great deal of confusion as to
> what each discipline brought to the field and whether there is a generic
> base in the broad over-all Community Mental Health program for many
> disciplines. . . . B. Field Stations . . . the announcement exceeded the reali-
> ties of available opportunities. . . . two field stations which were listed
> were not available for trainee placement. . . . there was not a complete
> consideration of the fellows own wishes as to where they might fit in. . . .
> There was a deficiency of the coordination required to maximize the
> year's training potential . . . there were some excellent program[s] which
> provided a sound learning experience. . . . The school consultation pro-
> gram seemed to provide the most qualitatively as well as quantitatively,
> and met the standards as set forth in the training announcement. The
> clinical service at Human Relations Service fell short of expectations. . . .
> Conferences were productive. . . . other forms of more formal seminars
> and lectures, we had few. . . . C. Seminars, Lectures, Conferences. . . .
> the program did not measure up to its announced intentions. . . . the
> major seminar Community Mental Health Theory and Practice . . . was
> terminated by the faculty, and the fellows were given the option of car-
> rying on for themselves. . . . We did this and . . . our time spent together
> was productive and worthwhile. The seminar on 'Community Processes'
> which all social work fellows felt would be of inestimable value, was
> denied them. . . . It was felt by the faculty that it wasn't appropriate
> for social work fellows. The social work seminar was not a structured
> seminar setting . . . more like any informal 'bull session'. The seminar in
> 'Preventive Intervention' was goal directed. . . . Sometimes the group dis-
> cussion drifted toward a type of group supervision. The seminar in 'Crisis
> Consultation' was an excellent example of a superior effort. . . . Formal
> lectures were not included . . . could provide a much needed framework
> for orientation and understanding. . . . C. Supervision—Individual and
> Group. . . . its value varied. . . . III EVALUATION . . . A. Physical Plant
> and Staff Availability at the Human Relations Service, we felt that basic
> permanent staff was short . . . pressure on staff . . . frequently overex-
> tended their ability to function at the teaching level. . . . We feel strongly
> that staff time needs to be utilized in a different manner or additional staff
> hired to meet the demands of the training program. Physical space was a
> continuous problem. . . . B. Conceptual Understanding. . . . The year has

been a struggle in many respects, largely because of the difficulties of the trainee in not understanding the methods of the program, and also the staff not understanding the trainees.

(pp. 1–16)

Durant, Nancy, MD, "Impressions of the Fellowship in Community Mental Health", ?1958, pp. 1–3 [folder "Durant, Nancy, M.D." Box IIIB1 e2), A-E", Erich Lindemann Collection, Center for the History of Medicine, Francis A. Countway Library of Medicine, Boston, MA]:

It was my feeling in both Wellesley and the West End that the resources for secretarial help were quite inadequate and that this was detrimental to both the clinical and research activities.

Human Relations Service . . . I realize that this service is seriously understaffed but I also felt that it is very badly organized and apart from the clinical service, poorly run. . . . Though conferences may be considered imperative for trainees, I do not feel that excessive conferences should be fostered for staff . . . I also found that many of the conferences did not serve their announced purposes because gatherings of more than three people at the Human Relations Service seemed very prone to stray from the set aim off into vague generalizations, usually with the result that nothing was accomplished. . . . Dr. [Helen] Herzan . . . is to be commended for running the clinical service so well. It was my feeling that Dr. [Donald C.] Klein's administration of the agency was most inefficient and that he frequently committed the agency to programs of activity which it was ill-equipped to carry out with the result that the persons requesting the service are frequently disappointed. Two examples from 1957–58 are the parents groups in Weston and the present pre-school evaluation program.

(pp. 2–3)

14. Klein, Donald and Herzan, Helen, with cover letter by Lindemann, Erich, to Dr. Feldman, NIMH, 1/22/1959; p. 1. [folder "AMA Psychiatric Training Programs", Box IIIA6 2) A-M, Erich Lindemann Collection, Center for the History of Medicine, Francis A. Countway Library of Medicine, Boston, MA].

Proposed program staff were Director Erich Lindemann; Coordinator of Psychiatry Peter E. Sifneos, MD; Coordinator of Psychology John M. von Felsinger, PhD; Coordinator of Social Work William Freeman, MSS, EdD; Research Supervisor Marc Fried, PhD; etc.

15. Waring, Dorothy, "The Significance of Communication in a Community Mental Health Program", unpublished, 4/1963; pp. 20–21. [folder Waring, Peg—Communication in a Community M.H. Program, file Human Relations Service via Elizabeth B. Lindemann, Lindemann Collection, Center for the History of Medicine, Francis A. Countrway Library of Medicine, Boston, MA]

16. Waring, Dorothy, "The Significance of Communication in a Community Mental Health Program", unpublished, 4/1963; pp. 22. [folder Waring, Peg—Communication in a Community M.H. Program, file Human Relations Service via Elizabeth B. Lindemann, Lindemann Collection, Center for the History of Medicine, Francis A. Countrway Library of Medicine, Boston, MA]

17. Correspondence between Lindemann and Charles K. Cummings, Jr., guidance director of Weston High School, 6/29–10/5/1956. [folder "Misc. Correspondence C-1956–5", Box IIIA 1–3, Lindemann Collection, Center for

the History of Medicine, Francis A. Countway Library of Medicine, Boston, MA]

18. Evans, Robert L., EdD, Gochberg, Shayna, MSW, Kerzner, Arnold M., MD, Copel, Marcia, ACSW, "School Consultation: A System-Wide Approach", 55th Annual Meeting of the American Orthopsychiatric Association, New York City, 3/27–31/1978, *American Journal of Orthopsychiatry*.

19. Folder "Naegle—HRS", "Lindemann+Ross—Follow-Up Study of Predictive Test of Preschool Children from Caplan Book 52?" including, file Human Relations Service via Elizabeth B. Lindemann, Lindemann Collection, Center for the History of Medicine, Francis A. Countway Library of Medicine, Boston, MA.

20. 9/19/64 The Pre-School Check-Up Program. [folder "Human Relations Service of Wellesley", Box IIIA 4 (F-H), Erich Lindemann Collection, Center for the History of Medicine, Francis A. Countway Library of Medicine, Boston, MA]

21.

- Lindemann, Elizabeth B., MS, and Ross, Ann, MS, "A Follow-Up Study of a Predictive Test of Social Adaptation in Preschool Children", Ch. 4 in Caplan, Gerald (ed.), *Emotional Problems of Early Childhood* (New York: Basic Books, 1955), pp. 79–93.
- Lindemann, Elizabeth B., Rosenblith, Judy F., Allinsmith, Wesley, Budd, Linda M, and Shapiro, Sybil, "Predicting School Adjustment Before Entry", *Journal of School Psychology VII* no.1: 24–42 (Fall, 1967).
- Lindemann, Elizabeth B., Allinsmith, Wesley, Rosenblith, Judy F., Budd, Linda, and Shapiro, Sybil, "Evaluation of a Pre-School Screening Program", *American Orthopsychiatric Association*, 3/1963.
- Lindemann, E.B., "Summary of Experience with Pre-School Screening by Human Relations Service of Wellesley, Inc.", 7/1964.
- "Talk on Wellesley H.R.S. Pre-School Research at San Mateo County Mental Health Consultation Service", 05/17/1968.
- Wyatt, Gertrud L., PhD, Director, Psychological and Speech Therapy Services, Goodman, Richard H., Superintendent of Schools 1969–70, Chaffee, John B., Superintendent of Schools, 1968–69, Freeman, William J., Assistant Superintendent for Pupil Personnel Services, 1969–70, "Early Identification of Children with Potential Learning Disabilities: Final Report, Title VI Project, 1968–70" (consultants associated with H.R.S. included John K. Brines, Pediatrics, Dr. Helen M. Herzan, Psychiatry, Dr. William Freeman, Community Mental Health, Dr. Clara Mayo, Screening Techniques).
- Klein, Donald C., PhD, and Lindemann, Elizabeth, MSW, "Approaches to Pre-School Screening", *The Journal of School Health XXXIV* no.8: 365–373 (10/1964).
- "Human Relations Service Working Bibliography on Mental Health Consultation", September 1962.
- Mayo, Clara, PhD, research Social Psychologist Boston VA Hospital, "Selected Bibliography on Community Psychiatry", 1/1965.

    Mayo, Clara, PhD, "Bibliography on Community Psychiatry" [folder "Lindemann+Ross—Follow-Up Study of Predictive Test of Preschool Children from Caplan Book 52?", "EBL et al. Predicting School Adjustment Before Entry '67", "EBL et Al—Evaluation of a Pre-School Screening Program '63", "EBL—Experience with Pre-School Screening a HRS 64–68", "Wyatt—Pre-school 1975", "Klein + EBL Approaches to Pre-School Screening '64". [file Human Relations Service via Elizabeth B.

Lindemann, Lindemann Collection, Center for the History of Medicine, Francis A. Countway Library of Medicine, Boston, MA] [folder "Community Psychiatry—Lecture Bibliography", IIIB3 d, Erich Lindemann Collection, Center for the History of Medicine, Francis A. Countway Library of Medicine, Boston, MA]

22. 9/19/64 The HRS Nursery School Mental Health Consultation Program. [folder "Human Relations Service of Wellesley", Box IIIA 4 (F-H), Erich Lindemann Collection, Center for the History of Medicine, Francis A. Countway Library of Medicine, Boston, MA]

23. Folder "Lindemann-Caplan Application Material—Sight [*sic*] Visit", IIIB2 c (box1 of 2), Erich Lindemann Collection, Center for the History of Medicine, Francis A. Countway Library of Medicine, Boston, MA. Planned research projects included the following:

   1. A Study of Predicaments: The Prevalence of Mental Health Predicaments in Wellesley, Massachusetts in March, 1959
      (James G. Kelly, PhD, Research Fellow in CMH-coordinator; staff— Donald C. Klein PhD, HRS Executive Director; Alvin J. Simons, M.A., HRS Psychologist)
   2. Study of 3:1 Male:Female Prevalence of Mental Health Problems at HRS and U.S.—epidemiological study.
   3. Neighborhoods and Their Patterns of Mental Health: A Study in Human Ecology (Wellesley)
      Coordinator—Donald C. Klein, HRS Executive Director; Senior Reseach Psychologist—James G. Kelly, Research Fellow in CMH, Staff— Alan Eister, Professor of Sociology, Wellesley College; Alvin J. Simmons, HRS Psychologist; Lucy Thoma, MGH Anthropologist.
   4. A Comparative Study of Clinical Services at the H.R.S. and Psychiatric Treatment Centers
   5. The Prevention of Mental Illness", Human Relations Service of Wellesley, Inc. Klein, Donald C.
   6. Mental Health Aspects of Peer Relatedness in Pre-adolescence" (Part of a longitudinal study of a school population)
      Elizabeth B. Lindemann, MS, Mental Health Consultant, HRS of Wellesley, Inc.-Coordinator, Ann Ross, M.A.—Chief investigator

24. [folder "Human Relations Service of Wellesley", Box IIIA 4 (F-H), Erich Lindemann Collection, Center for the History of Medicine, Francis A. Countway Library of Medicine, Boston, MA]

25. 9/19/1964 History and Present Programs OF HRS (minutes of Board meeting). [folder "Human Relations Service of Wellesley", Box IIIA 4 (F-H), Erich Lindemann Collection, Center for the History of Medicine, Francis A. Countway Library of Medicine, Boston, MA]

26. Minutes of Board Meeting on November 18, 1964. [folder "Human Relations Service of Wellesley", Box IIIA 4 (F-H), Erich Lindemann Collection, Center for the History of Medicine, Francis A. Countway Library of Medicine, Boston, MA]

27. 11/18/64 Minutes of Board Meeting on November 18, 1964. [folder "Human Relations Service of Wellesley", Box IIIA 4 (F-H), Erich Lindemann Collection, Center for the History of Medicine, Francis A. Countway Library of Medicine, Boston, MA]

28. 1/6/65 Meeting of the Board of the Human Relations Service of Wellesley, Inc. [folder "Human Relations Service of Wellesley", Box IIIA 4 (F-H), Erich

Lindemann Collection, Center for the History of Medicine, Francis A. Countway Library of Medicine, Boston, MA]

29. 1/6/65 Meeting of the Board of the Human Relations Service of Wellesley, Inc., p. 4. [folder "Human Relations Service of Wellesley", Box IIIA 4 (F-H), Erich Lindemann Collection, Center for the History of Medicine, Francis A. Countway Library of Medicine, Boston, MA]

30. 12/17/64 HRS General Staff Conference: Summary of Dr. Fred Cummer's discussion of Some of His Activities. [folder "Human Relations Service of Wellesley", Box IIIA 4 (F-H), Erich Lindemann Collection, Center for the History of Medicine, Francis A. Countway Library of Medicine, Boston, MA]

31. 2/12/1964 Human Relations Service of Wellesley, Inc., Board Meeting: Dr. Lindemann's Report, p. 3. [folder "Human Relations Service of Wellesley", Box IIIA 4 (F-H), Erich Lindemann Collection, Center for the History of Medicine, Francis A. Countway Library of Medicine, Boston, MA]

32. Lindemann, Erich, letter to Howard Grimes, President of the HRS Board of Directors, 4/8/1964. [folder "Human Relations Service of Wellesley", Box IIIA 4 (F-H), Erich Lindemann Collection, Center for the History of Medicine, Francis A. Countway Library of Medicine, Boston, MA]

33. Lindemann, Erich, letter to Byler, John, Executive Director of The Grant Foundation, 3/5/1958, p. 1. [folder "Grant Foundation-1957–58", IIIB2 b (box2 of 3), Erich Lindemann Collection, Center for the History of Medicine, Francis A. Countway Library of Medicine, Boston, MA]

34. Lindemann, Erich, letter to Morrison, Miss A.W., The Grant Foundation, 5/4/1959, p. 1. [folder "Grant Foundation-1957–58", IIIB2 b (box2 of 3), Erich Lindemann Collection, Center for the History of Medicine, Francis A. Countway Library of Medicine, Boston, MA]

35. Human Relations Service, Inc., "HRS at Fifty" (10/15/1997) [folder "Wellesley Human Relations Service", David G. Satin files, Newton, MA]

36. [Folder "Klein, Donald Ph.D"., Box IIIB1e 2, and Klein, Donald C., PhD, "Consultation Processes as a Method for Improving Teaching" (undated). [folder "Klein—Consultation Processes as a Method for Improving Teaching", box Human Relations Service via Elizabeth Lindemann, Lindemann Collection, Francis A. Countway Library of Medicine, Boston, MA]

37. "A Statement of Policy by the Board of Directors of the Human Relations Service of Wellesley, Inc.", 2/13/1963. [folder "760–7554–5 Sapir Grant 9/1/62–8/31/63", IIIB2 b (box2 of 3), Erich Lindemann Collection, Center for the History of Medicine, Francis A. Countway Library of Medicine, Boston, MA]

A later restatement of these policies demonstrated the lasting inculcation of the CMH perspective independent of outside influences: Primary Prevention Unit, Human Relations Service of Wellesley, Inc., "Policy Statement", 3/31/1965. [folder "Hutchinson, B.R., MD, Director, Dept. of Mental Health Div. of Mental Hygiene, Com. of Mass."], [Box IIIA 4 (F-H), Lindemann Collection, Center for the History of Medicine, Francis A. Countway Library of Medicine, Boston, MA].

[B]ased upon a specific and professionally tested philosophy composed of three concepts: a) mental health can be promoted by a public health approach, i.e. an individual's mental health is influenced by characteristics and activities of the community and can be fostered by action at the community level; b) mental illness can be prevented, i.e. individuals and society need not wait for illness to appear to take action but can act, before the fact, to prevent illness from occurring at the individual level and through community action; c) life contains a range of situations which are potentially hazardous for even mature and stable individuals; events can overwhelm even a basically healthy person and disrupt his effective functioning.

(p. 1)

GENERAL PURPOSE The general purpose of the Human Relations Service of Wellesley, Inc. (Primary Preventive Unit) is primary prevention of emotional disorders. Its mission is to undertake programs, with a primary preventive orientation, designed to reduce the incidence of mental and emotional disturbances among the members of the community, through helping to prepare individuals for anticipated life hazard events. It also maintains an ongoing effort to measure and analyze the effectiveness of its programs, including evaluation of method, further exploration of the nature of life hazard events and the determination of causes and effects, for the benefit of all other mental health programs now in existence or to be established, especially in Massachusetts".

(pp. 1–2)

Primary prevention means reduce the incidence of illness by working with potential victims and factors which cause illness; not "working with individuals who have already become victims of illness", or work with caretakers. Life hazardous events include "childbirth, entrance into kindergarten, high school or college; marriage and divorce; retirement; death; surgical operations and relocations to another community".

(p. 2)

The members of the board of directors are predominantly residents of Wellesley.

38. Cummings, Charles K., Jr., letter to Lindemann, 1/24/1965. [folder "Correspondence 1965", Box IIIA 1–3, Lindemann Collection, Center for the History of Medicine, Francis A. Countway Library of Medicine, Boston, MA]

39. Lindemann, Elizabeth Brainerd, interviews by and letters to David G. Satin in various settings, 8/14/1999–8/22/2006. [David G. Satin files, Lindemann Collections, Newton, MA]

40. Lindemann, Elizabeth, remarks at the HRS 30th anniversary luncheon, 11/4/13, p. 4. [folder "EBL-HRS Anniversary Reports 1978–1988–1998 (+1991)", box Human Relations Service via Elizabeth, Lindemann Collection, Center for the History of Medicine, Francis A. Countway Library of Medicine, Boston, MA]

41. Lindemann, Erich, letter to Duhl, Leonard J., 6/8/1964. This remark related to a draft of a chapter on HRS that he had coauthored with Robert Bragg, and he (vainly) offered "hope to send you a revision of this draft".

42. Lindemann, Elizabeth Brainerd, 8/14/1999–8/22/2006, *ibid.*

43. Haylett, Clarice, Division of Mental Health, San Mateo County Health Department: interview by David G. Satin at her home in Palo Alto, CA. [Erich Lindemann Collection, Center for the History of Medicine, Francis A. Countway Library of Medicine, Boston, MA]

44. Lindemann, Erich, Duhl, Leonard and Seeley, John, interviews of Erich Lindemann 6/15,22/1974 (caddy 4, tape 3A, 4B,7, Erich Lindemann Collection, Rare Books Department, Francis A. Countway Library of Medicine, Boston).

45. Lindemann, Elizabeth Brainerd, 8/14/1999–8/22/2006, *ibid.*

46. Division of Mental Health, Department of Public Health Practice, HSPH, "Annual Report, 1954", *ibid.*, p. 6.

47. Crossman, John S., the editor in chief of the Health Education Department of the Blakiston Division of the McGraw-Hill Book Company, to Lindemann, 9/20/1955 asking his interest. Lindemann had been recommended by Paul V. Lamkau, who thought that this would be outstanding.

48. Lindemann, Elizabeth B. and Ross, Ann, "A Follow-up Study of a Predictive Test of Social Adaptation in Preschool Children", Ch. 4 in Caplan, Gerald (ed.), *Emotional Problems of Early Childhood* (New York: Basic Books, 1955), pp. 79–93.

49. Nelson, Josenine, letter to Lindemann, 6/1/1956. Lindemann's reply does not address the issue. [folder "Misc. Correspondence M-N 1956-7", Box IIIA 1–3, Erich Lindemann Collection, Center for the History of Medicine, Francis A. Countway Library of Medicine, Boston, MA]

50. Morrison, A.W., Associate Director and Secretary, The Grant Foundation, Inc., letter to Lindemann, Erich, 1/14/1956. [envelope "Grant Foundation 1955–56", IIIB2 b (box2 of 3), Erich Lindemann Collection, Center for the History of Medicine, Francis A. Countway Library of Medicine, Boston, MA]

51. Galpin, Perrin, C., president of the Belgian American Educational Foundation, Inc., former executive director of the Grant Foundation, Inc, to Lindemann, Erich, 1/26/1956. [envelope "Grant Foundation 1955–56", IIIB2 b (box2 of 3), Erich Lindemann Collection, Center for the History of Medicine, Francis A. Countway Library of Medicine, Boston, MA]

52. Lindemann, Erich, letter to Galpin, Mr. Perrin C., Belgian American Educational Foundation, Inc., former Executive Director of the Grant Foundation, Inc., 2/1/1956. [envelope "Grant Foundation 1955–56", IIIB2 b (box 2 of 3), Erich Lindemann Collection, Center for the History of Medicine, Francis A. Countway Library of Medicine, Boston, MA]

53. Byler, John G., Executive Director of The Grant Foundation, Inc., letter to Lindemann, Erich, 5/9/1956. [envelope "Grant Foundation 1955–56", IIIB2 b (box2 of 3), Erich Lindemann Collection, Center for the History of Medicine, Francis A. Countway Library of Medicine, Boston, MA]

54. Lindemann, Erich, letter to Byler, Mr. John G., Executive Directof of the Grant Foundation, Inc., 5/10/1956. [envelope "Grant Foundation 1955–56", IIIB2 b (box2 of 3), Erich Lindemann Collection, Center for the History of Medicine, Francis A. Countway Library of Medicine, Boston, MA]

55. Lindemann, Erich, letter to Balos, Mr. Henry B., Newton, MA, 5/10/1956. [envelope "Grant Foundation 1955–56", IIIB2 b (box2 of 3), Erich Lindemann Collection, Center for the History of Medicine, Francis A. Countway Library of Medicine, Boston, MA]

56. Lindemann, Erich, letter to Galpin, Mr. Perrin C., Belgian American Educational Foundation, Inc., 11/15/1956. [folder "Grant Foundation-1957-58", IIIB2 b (box2 of 3), Erich Lindemann Collection, Center for the History of Medicine, Francis A. Countway Library of Medicine, Boston, MA]

57. Lindemann, Erich, letter to Morrison, Miss A.W., The Grant Foundation, pp. 1–2. [folder "Grant Foundation-1957-58", IIIB2 b (box2 of 3), Erich Lindemann Collection, Center for the History of Medicine, Francis A. Countway Library of Medicine, Boston, MA]

58. Robinson, Henry Wallace, Executive Editor of Henry Hold & Company to Lindemann, 9/13–10/11/1959. [folder "Misc. Correspondence H,I,J 1956-57", Box IIIA 1–3, Lindemann Collection, Center for the History of Medicine, Francis A. Countway Library of Medicine, Boston, MA]

59. Birton L. Beals, an editor at W.W. Norton & Company, publishers, to Lindemann, 1/27/1964. [folder "B Miscellaneous 2 of 2 file folders", Box IIIA 4 (A-E), Lindemann Collection, Center for the History of Medicine, Francis A. Countway Library of Medicine, Boston, MA]

60. Schneidman, Edwin G., PhD, the president of the Suicide Prevention Foundation, Inc., letter to Lindemann, 5/26/1965. [folder "Correspondence 1965", Box IIIA 1–3, Lindemann Collection, Center for the History of Medicine, Francis A. Countway Library of Medicine, Boston, MA]

61. Gochman, David S., the staff editor for psychology for the International Encyclopedia of the Social Sciences, letter to Lindemann, 7/27/1965; and from David L. Sills, editor, to Lindemann on 12/7/1965. [folder "Correspondence 1965", Box IIIA 1–3, Lindemann Collection, Center for the History of Medicine, Francis A. Countway Library of Medicine, Boston, MA]

62. Jarrett, William, an associate editor at Little, Brown and Company, pubiishers, correspondence with Lindemann, Erich, 4/29–7/8/1964. [folder "L Miscellaneous", Box IIIA 4 (I-Ma), Erich Lindemann Collection, Center for the History of Medicine, Francis A. Countway Library of Medicine, Boston, MA]

63. Lindemann, Erich, letter to Jarrett, William, Editorial Department, Little, Brown and Company, publishers in Boston, 3/30/1965. [folder "J Miscellaneous", Box IIIA 4 (I-Ma), Lindemann Collection, Center for the History of Medicine, Francis A. Countway Library of Medicine, Boston, MA]

64. Duhl, Leonard J. letter to Lindemann, 12/3/1965. [folder "Correspondence 1962", Box IIIA 1–3, Lindemann Collection, Center for the History of Medicine, Francis A. Countway Library of Medicine, Boston, MA]

65. Lindemann, Erich, letter to Morrison, Miss Adele, secretary and treasurer of the W.T. Grant Foundation, New York City, 2/18/1960; pp. 2–4. [folder "E.L. Notes on India Trip", Box IIIA5 2), Erich Lindemann Collection, Center for the History of Medicine, Francis A. Countway Library of Medicine, Boston, MA]

66. "Comments on Book on Preventive Psychiatry for Staff Discussion on June 4th, 6/4/?19 55". [folder "Lindemann: Comments on Book on Preventive Psychiatry June 1955?", box V 4–8, Erich Lindemann Collection, Center for the History of Medicine, Francis A. Countway Library of Medicine, Boston, MA]

67. Naegle, Kaspar and Lindemann, Erich, correspondence11/30/54–7/4/55 regarding his contribution to the "Wellesley book", and Naegle's skepticism about its planning and organization.

68. Lindemann, Erich, letter to Duhl, Leonard J., 11/7/1964, p. 1. [folder "Leonard Duhl—NIMH Corr"., Box IIIA 4 (A-E), Lindemann Collection, Center for the History of Medicine, Francis A. Countway Library of Medicine, Boston, MA]

69. PROPOSED MONOGRAPH SUGESTED GENERAL OUTLINE, 3/30/1961. [folder "BALDWIN, JOHN A., M.D.", Box IIIB1 e 2), A-E", Erich Lindemann Collection, Center for the History of Medicine, Francis A. Countway Library of Medicine, Boston, MA]

4   Societal Influences and Efforts

The Civil Rights Movement

The CMH movement and consumer activism of the 1950s to 1970s flowered in the context of the anger and anguish of civil rights, minority rights, and racial tensions; the drug scene; the anti-Vietnam war activism; the expressed contempt for the establishment, for professionalism, and for merit based on knowledge of substance; and rebellion against traditional authority.[1] Psychoanalysts also interested in social psychiatry recognized this.[2] White described the factors driving the Civil Rights Movement:

> Consider that year [1954] as the opening of an era: the next twenty years of American history were to fall clearly away from . . . the two most spectacular peaks thrust up within seven weeks of each other in spring of 1954. On May 7. . . in Vietnam, the elite strike force of French general Christian de Castries, surrounded at Dienbienphu . . . was forced to surrender by the Vietminh. On June 29. . . the French gave up, dumping the protection of a "South Vietnam" on a willing John Foster Dulles. . . . [This] would, even twenty years later, be causing the deaths of young Americans. But within that same month, on June 17, the Supreme Court of the United States outlawed segregation by race in all American public schools . . . in Brown versus the Board of Education of Topeka, it set a domestic revolution under way. . . [which would] change the color and character of American cities, alter the nature of American society, free millions of black people, but hammer into categories other millions of Americans previously unaware of their differences. Youngsters . . . in the summer of 1954. . . would grow up to fight, to riot, to march, some to protest, some to die because of these two watershed spring events. . . . Furthermore, the push for changes in mental health service delivery, itself a sociopolitical issue, occurred in the dynamic context of social ferment with which it became inevitably enmeshed: the civil rights movement, the "war on poverty", the black protest movement, student unrest, and Vietnam with all its psychosocial repercussions.[3]

Abrams wrote that[4]

> What had been a profound impatience with a political system that
> refused honestly to confront racial injustices, poverty and prob-
> lems of personal dignity having to do with mass living, working
> and educational conditions has . . . turned into angry desperation.
> The mounting violence we are experiencing expresses that despera-
> tion . . . the [Vietnam] war must bear primary responsibility for the
> changed mood. . . . [It] has presented . . . young men with the awe-
> some choice. . . . Many of the "tough" among them have "got going"
> with civil disruption. . . . What has happened at Columbia [Univer-
> sity] . . . the faculty's discontent with their role in the governance of
> the University . . . the estrangement of the faculty and students from
> the administration . . . remains the one outstanding explanation of
> the disaster that has struck.
>
> (pp. 13–15)

These issues were international, as in China's communist revolution:[5]

> Phrases like "rebellion against authority", "revolution in educa-
> tion", "destroying an old world so a new one could be born", and
> "creating new man"—all of which attracted many in the west in the
> 1960s—were interpreted as calls for violent action.

The Civil Rights movement overlapped the CMH movement, and they
intersected in several ways: They both drew from the well of the search
for recognition, valuation, and care for previously neglected populations.
Through this association, each drew from the other validation and support. And through this association, enemies of each included the other in
their attacks.

Prompted by the black and poor rights movement, Robert Felix and
Stanley Yolles, directors of the NIMH, insisted that "powerless" community populations be represented on the CMHCs' area boards (community
involvement structures).[6] Community influence—and, in some views,
dominance—persisted in various styles for some time. Antiprofessional
stances occurred, and some argued that they were justified. Jack Newfield
extolled young radicals and groups (the Student Nonviolent Coordinating Committee, Students for a Democratic Society, the Northern Student Movement—NSM) that took direct action on current social ills, as
distinct from older radical groups (the Communist Party, the Trotskyite
group, socialist parties, the National Association for the Advancement
of Colored People [NAACP], and the United Auto Workers Union).[7] He
valued their attacks against the war in Vietnam, segregation, the death
penalty, authority, and capitalism. They espoused humanist-anarchist
principles, community organizing, and empowering the poor: "insurgent

forces disrupting society" (p. 6), including (NSM) "attacks on middle-class control of the war on poverty" (p. 4). He also noted the extremist left fringe, including the Peking splinter group and Progressive Labor Movement.

Whereas Leonard Duhl sought alliance in the effort toward betterment and mental health,[8]

> we could not anticipate the appearance of a cult of the indigenous population who now tend to under-rate vital professional skills. The turn-about seems to be that any indigenous person, by some indigenous magic, is better for the program than any professional could be. I believe that both the professional and the local helper can together translate services into real help.
>
> (p. 17)

Thomas Gladwyn of the NIMH saw the connection between (community) mental health programs and one of the civil rights projects, COFO (Council of Federated Organizations), as a coincidence:[9]

> the goals of this intervention, indeed the goals of much of the entire civil rights movement, fall in the same psychological domains as do the goals of mental health programs. These include changes in attitude, in self-expectation and self-perception, in access to opportunity, and in stereotyping and prejudice. In striving toward these goals, people experience self-doubt, fears and anxieties both rational and irrational, and a host of other "symptoms" which mental health programs regularly try to relieve. In other words, both the civil rights movement and its agents are at least in the same league with, if not actually part of, mental health programming as it has developed in the mid-1960s. As we look at the failures and frustrations of COFO we must simultaneously inquire into the degree of success <u>we</u> have had in dealing with the problems of minorities through our mental health strategies. As we look at the dilemmas of the COFO workers, we must be equally realistic regarding the psychological hazards besetting the "mental health worker", the "urban agents" and other indigenous volunteer workers.
>
> (p. 7)

He gives more details of the project goals, participants, supporters, and results for community and individuals.[10]

Anticipating future cases of political cooption, Lindemann believed that architects of mental health programs should promote responsible participation by community residents and separate those with a false conviction of competence from those with justified experiential competence in regard to personality and social structure. The CMHC program attracted a variety of groups. It was not ready to be a large federal program. Many places were unprepared, there was no solid knowledge base for operation, and there was the danger that hopes would be disappointed, leading to negative reaction:

> Not all of us are happy about this rapid rise of interest and hope [in CMH], knowing only too well how enthusiastic excessive expectations which lead inevitably to disappointment may be followed by an aversion and renewed neglect of the whole field. It is, therefore, both appropriate and timely for us to consider with each other soberly the basic ingredients of mental health which can be defined and approached in a systematic manner, trying to separate sound principles from vague hopes which are being pursued with almost religious fervour and prayerful assurance of fulfillment.[11]

The CMH and civil rights movements shared some of the same motivations: disadvantaged and neglected populations' needs, injustices, rights, and desire for participation in control. They both encompassed a broad range of manifestations. And they could overlap in identifying with one another. Thus, they could share support and opposition, their distinctions could become blurred, and their fates could be shared. In judging and acting on them, it is important to understand them as intertwined and not identical and to pursue their futures as they deserve.

The Joint Commission on Mental Illness and Health

The Joint Commission on Mental Illness and Health was a landmark effort to develop a comprehensive long-term plan for US mental health policy. It was developed at a time of struggle for change in the care of psychiatric illness and patients.

In the late 1950s, previous attempts at reform of the treatment of mental illness had been brief and impermanent.[12] Both society and the professions did not face the requirements for overcoming mental illness, including the need for cooperation among disciplines and social classes. More recently, the federal government had assumed more leadership and responsibility, especially by establishing the National Institute of Mental Health (NIMH) and expanding the resources and purview of the Veterans' Administration (VA), followed by the states taking increased responsibility. However, only 20% of the 277 state mental hospitals had adopted an updated treatment approach, with more than half of psychiatric patients in custodial care; 80% of them were in state hospitals, amounting to 540,000 patients at any time and about a million in any year. When mental illness was designated as the nation's most important health problem, its funding from the National Institutes of Health (NIH) increased from being the fourth largest in 1950 to the second largest in

1960, and funding from voluntary sources advanced from the eighth to the seventh largest category. The states responded by decreasing their funding in favor of federal sources: spending on psychiatric patients averaged \$4.44 per patient per day, as compared with \$31.16 for general hospital patients and more than \$12 in VA and tuberculosis hospitals. Staff-to-patient ratios were 0.32 in state mental hospitals compared with 2.1 in general hospitals. Interest in and optimism about mental illness increased, with more interest in information, volunteer work, humane and noninpatient treatment and shorter hospital stays, and progressive decreases in mental hospital populations even before the advent of antipsychotic medications, though those with chronic major mental illness were still rejected. More people were applying for mental health treatment: 10% of treatment requests were for mental health problems and 1% for severe mental health problems; it was estimated that 25% of these problems would have benefited from treatment. Of those with mental health problems, 14% sought help, especially with marital, adjustment, and children's problems; 42% were referred from clergy, 29% from physicians, 18% from psychiatrists or psychologists, and 10% from social and marital agencies. More than half presented with (in decreasing order of frequency) physical and external problems, psychological and internal problems, personal adjustment problems, and marital problems. The lack of workforce reflected a lack of training programs and societal disrespect for mental health issues.

Jack Ewalt traces the origins of the Joint Commission to the 1950s, when William Menninger, as director of the NIMH, increased budgets and fellowships, and Kenneth Appel, the president of the APA, addressed the Council of State Governments about the need for a "Flexner Report" to evaluate mental health service needs over the next ten years.[13] A governor's conference was concerned about the size of budgets for mental health services—their largest item. In 1946, Senator J. Lister Hill and Senator Harold Burton's legislation provided federal subsidies to improve small hospitals. Senator Hill and Representative John E. Fogarty, interested in the results of a study of service needs, increased funding for the NIH. Questions arose about the direction that mental health should be taking, and there was interest in developing a ten-year plan for it. A group assembled to plan for a study of and the direction for the future of mental health services: Appel (president of the APA), Daniel Blaine (medical director of the APA), Leo Bartemeier (chairperson of the American Medical Association's Council on Mental Health), and Robert Felix (director of the NIMH). With funds from the Mary Lasker Foundation, pharmaceutical companies, and the Federal National Mental Health Study Act of 1955,[14] the APA and AMA created the Joint Commission on Mental Illness and Health.

Jack Ewalt was important in the history of CMH. His original interests were in research in pharmacology and surgery and in the care of patients.[15] He became a Commonwealth Fund Fellow under Franklin Ebaugh. Ewalt was interested in traveling to psychiatric clinics at the Colorado Psychopathic Hospital but preferred the study of neurosyphilis. He became advisor to the Texas director of state health services and then joined the Hogg Foundation for Mental Health, with an interest in training teachers in mental illness prevention. He developed the University of Texas School of Medicine's postgraduate school seminars in small towns. He was then called to Massachusetts, jointly funded by the Massachusetts DMH and Harvard University as director of the Massachusetts Mental Health Center and commissioner of the DMH, where he developed a network of psychiatric services. In seeking a director of the Joint Commission study, Alan Gregg of the Rockefeller Foundation refused and Gunnar Myrdal was considered. Ewalt, a member of the Joint Commission planning committee, was appointed chairperson.

While others contributed ideas (including the First Hoover Commission, whose recommendations were not implemented), Ewalt was empowered to plan and carry out the project. A broad range of stakeholders was involved, including nurses, social workers, psychologists, the American Hospital Association, and the Catholic Hospital Association. To improve the chances for implementation, consumer organizations were represented, such as organized labor, the American Legion, and the United Auto Workers Union (see endnotes for a fuller list)[16]—all represented by good mental health professionals,[17] indicating the broad reach of mental health issues. Representatives for people with intellectual disabilities opted for a separate research study. As evidence of serious interest, funding also came from a broad range of government, philanthropic, professional, and business sources.[18] The AFL-CIO voted against the commission. Erich Lindemann served on one study section but preferred to work on his own, though he was thanked for contributions to some of the working groups and was included in a gathering at HMS of heads of psychiatry departments to consider the Joint Commission's new ideas about patient care and psychiatry.[19] He did not have a large formal constituency and so was not nominated to represent a large body. However, his ideas had spread and were represented on the project.

Some topics were scheduled for separate study with private funding: intellectual disabilities, child psychiatry (not funded but still pursued by a separate joint commission with federal funding), geriatrics (not addressed at the time), delinquency (intended as part of the child psychiatry project), and drug and alcohol abuse (done later).

The Commission took note of this heterogeneity of stakeholders:[20]

> [W]e are obliged to remain in full view of certain intervening observations that provide little cause for hope except as we can dispose of them. We must note, for instance, the curious blindness of the

public as a whole and of psychiatry itself to what in reality would be required to fulfill the well publicized demand that millions of mentally ill shall have sufficient help in overcoming the disturbances that destroy their self-respect and social usefulness. Further, we must rise above our self-preservative functions as members of different professions, social classes, and economic philosophies and illuminate the means of working together out of mutual respect for our fellow man.

The Joint Commission saw its mandate as follows:[21]

The Mental Health Study Act of 1955 directed the Joint Commission on Mental Illness and Health, under grants administered by the National Institute of Mental Health, to analyze and evaluate the needs and resources of the mentally ill people of America and make recommendations for the national mental health program.

Studies were made of mental health needs, reactions to experiences with mental health care, available resources, and obstacles to their use. There were considerations of the mental health functions of schools, self-help groups, churches, hospitals, clinics, etc.[22] Populations were studied to discover what factors had desirable or undesirable effects, where people sought help, the economic impact of mental illness, etc. The results of these studies were published in a series of monographs in addition to the summary report *Action for Mental Health*.[23] They were edited by a science writer on the commission staff, published within 90 days by Arthur Rosenthal at Basic Books in New York, and sent free to members of Congress and federal and state officials for maximum impact. (The exception was Schwartz *et al*.) The following is a comprehensive list of these monographs:

- Jahoda, Marie *Current Concepts of Positive Mental Health*, 1958
- Fein, Rashi: *Economics of Mental Illness*, 1958
- Albee, George W.: *Mental Health Manpower Trends*, 1959
- Gurin, Gerald; Veroff, Joseph; Feld, Sheila: *Americans View Their Mental Health: A Nationwide Interview Survey* (New York: Basic Books, 1960)
- Robinson, Reginald; DeMarche, David F.; Wagle Mildred K.: *Community Resources in Mental Health*, 1960
- Plunkett, Richard J.; Gordon, John E.: *Epidemiology and Mental Illness*, 1960
- Soskin, William S.: "Research Resources in Mental Health", appendix to *Action for Mental Health*, 1961
- Allinsmith, Wesley; Goethals, George W.: *The Role of Schools in Mental Health*, 1962
- McCann, Richard V.: *The Churches and Mental Health*, 1962

- Schwartz, Morris S.; Schwartz, Charlotte Green; Field, Mark G.; Mishler, Eliot G.; Olshansky, S.; Pitts, Jesse R.; Rapoport, Rhona; Vaughan, Warren T., Jr.: *Social Approaches to Mental Patient Care* (New York: Columbia University Press, 1964)

The next steps would be to mobilize public and Congressional opinion and assemble a Committee of Consultants to develop standards and requirements for federal implementation. The Joint Commission made several proposals for a future mental health system for the country:

- Improve current psychiatric facilities' community services, associate services with general hospitals for hospital treatment, rehabilitation for chronic patients, hospitals smaller and nearer home, preventive education, increased use of semi-professionals and nonprofessional workers.
- Efficient treatment including prevention should especially focus on schizophrenia and arteriosclerotic organic brain syndrome—which represented the majority of hospital patients.
- Preventive services are not recommended: The Commission was sympathetic to this ideal, but there were no good studies supporting this approach.
- Mental health programs should not be involved in socioeconomic or racial change. Though these factors can contribute to psychiatric illness, this is not the province of psychiatry, and society will not empower psychiatry for these purposes. Psychiatry may interpret the pathological reactions to pathological environments. (It was noted that the Joint Commission on the Mental Health of Children made sweeping recommendations on environmental change, which were ignored.)
- Expand required basic and long-term research communication between researchers and practitioners.
- Flexible and experimental research must involve a larger number of centers (not just a few major universities and their medical centers). Funding should be long term, to stimulate fundamental studies, rather than short term, and individual researchers should focus on specific topics, which favors applied research.
- Funding of the commission was 57% federal and 20% state, 17% pharmaceutical corporations, and 6% private and other. Expand funding, especially federal. Federal funding sets the trend and should be expanded and longer term, for stable programming.
- Support science and education.
- Increase funding for basic research and less for applied research.
- Increase the number of venturesome people and ideas, with the NIMH developing and holding young scientists with ten-year and lifetime support.

- Increase support for the establishment of scientific and educational institutes.
- Capital investment should establish research centers, both independent and associated with educational institutions, in underdeveloped regions.
- Diversify areas receiving support.

It found that the majority of state mental hospitals were custodial and punitive. There was a need to do the following:

- eliminate political patronage
- integrate hospitals into their communities
- provide staff with good pay, training, and the opportunity for good jobs
- extend care into the community
- broaden the concept of treatment
- individualize patient care
- make hospitals open, providing a social treatment milieu
- provide aftercare
- provide treatment relationships via supervised laypeople and mental health professionals.

Policy recommendations:

- incorporate a broad philosophy regarding personnel and practices, since there was no definitive knowledge of mental illness etiology
- medical and psychiatric-neurological procedures should be under appropriate physician supervision
- depth psychotherapy should be practiced only by adequately trained professionals
- nonmedical mental health workers should practice short-term superficial psychotherapy under the supervision of recognized mental health agencies.

Recruitment and training recommendations:

- expand all categories
- include professional training, short courses, and on-the-job training
- upgrade partly trained workers.

Services to people with mental illness:

- community counseling by mental health professionals or those with mental health training and orientation
- expert consultation as needed
- secondary prevention.

Immediate care of acute mental health patients:

- community-based immediate/emergency care by professionals.

Intensive treatment for the acutely ill:

- first priority to those with major mental illness who constitute the core problem
- community mental health clinics, preventive hospitalization
- require a clinic for each 50,000 population group.

A summary statement included the following:

> A national mental health program should recognize that major mental illness is the core problem and unfinished business of the mental health movement, and that among those with severe mental illness the intensive treatment of those with critical and prolonged breakdowns should have first call on fully trained members of the mental health professions. . . . The objective of modern treatment of persons with major mental illness is to enable the patient to maintain himself in the community in a normal manner.[24]

Means should be found to include private practice psychiatrists. General hospitals of 100 or more beds should include psychiatry wards to provide as much psychiatric treatment as possible, with mental hospitals reserved for more-intensive treatment. Existing state mental hospitals should be reorganized and all new state mental hospitals should be established as intensive treatment centers for patients with acute mental illness and a good prognosis. No new state mental hospitals should be built for 1000 patients or more, and existing ones should not be enlarged. All existing large state mental hospitals should be converted to the rehabilitation and resocialization of patients with chronic mental and physical illnesses and the aged. Services for after care (care after hospitalization), intermediate care, rehabilitation, day and night hospitalization, public health nursing, foster families, nursing homes, vocational services, and groups for former patients should avoid or minimize hospitalization and maintain patients in the community as long as possible, with funding of demonstration projects to this end.

The commission advocated increasing public funding for these services: "we can see only one matter that takes priority over all others in the program we propose and that is to obtain vastly increased sums of money for its support".[25] Funding should double in five years, triple in ten years. The federal portion of this funding via Congress and the NIMH should support treatment, in addition to research and training. State laws should be changed to require treatment of people with mental illness, and county and municipal contributions should be encouraged.

Under its encouragement of public information about the nature of mental illness, the rejection of people with mental illness and optimism about treatment, the commission in many places warned against excessive expectations and suggested skepticism about primary prevention and a community locus for mental health programs:[26]

- "A national mental health program should avoid the risk of false promises in "public education for better mental health" and focus on the more modest goal of disseminating such information about mental illness as the public needs and wants in order to recognize psychological forms of sickness and to arrive at an informed opinion in its responsibility toward the mentally ill" (p. 13).
- "The extension of these new services is not always carefully planned. . . . At times, there seems to be a desire to create new services out of the wish to do something, and perhaps the belief that the creation of a mental health clinic, or a counseling and guidance service, will automatically care for the social ills and unhappiness of a community. In some instances, there is a trend toward substituting a mental health service for intelligent leadership and planning" (p. 5).
- "There is much talk extolling the virtues of small hospitals without too much thought or attention being given to problems in staffing. To date, the construction of small hospitals occurs only in the psychiatric units in the community general hospitals. . . . The enthusiasm for building small-unit state hospitals has been principally at the verbal level, however, and those buildings actually under construction . . . are for the most part continuations of the large, multi-bed, multi-purposed buildings, most of them beautifully designed, at least according to modern architectural views". (p. 17).
- "Our surveys . . . disclose that this [community resources substituting for professional services] is a fantasy and not a fact. The plain answer is that without proper resources for handling problems, they are neglected. Informed community people may be concerned but blocked by lack of personnel. Family physicians, clergyman, and welfare workers are most involved but uneducated, unmotivated, overworked, and need training. A Federal education bill should stimulate undergraduate and graduate schools to meet mental health professional shortages" (p. 18).
- "Creating unsatisfied demands can only result in a generation of quackery with a yet-to-be-determined effect on the mental health of the nation" (p. 21).

Ewalt, the Joint Commission's director, claimed that it modeled its recommendations for CMHCs on the Massachusetts Mental Health Center, the Judge Baker Guidance Center, and the Massachusetts General Hospital's Psychiatry Service. He had invited Lindemann to give information to its subcommittee on mental health education, though Lindemann begged off and recommended Peter Sifneos of the MGH and Donald Klein of the HRS as contributors.[27] Psychopathic hospitals did not include community involvement, though the Colorado Psychopathic Hospital under Franklin Ebaugh incorporated child guidance clinics and traveling clinics. Ewalt believed that the Joint Commission recommendations moved the mental health system into the community, made it more flexible, and provided more appropriate services. It recommended community involvement and training of paraprofessionals.

Warren Vaughan, formerly with the HSPH and directing the Massachusetts DMH's Division of Mental Hygiene to develop CMHCs, became a research psychiatrist for the Joint Commission. He felt strongly about and (presumably) worked toward primary prevention: "Many of the Wellesley ideas, especially that of early intervention, were built into the Joint Commission recommendations. Linkage between helping agencies and growth-promoting agencies were especially stressed".[28] However, his outline of the commission's report indicates an emphasis on treatment of the severely mentally ill, with social and preventive services included, if at all, peripherally and by implication:[29]

> the Joint Commission on Mental Illness and Health . . . formed a task force on new perspectives of mental patient care. . . . the general recommendations [sought] . . . the reorganization, reconceptualization, and further development of psychiatric care.
>
> (p. 237)

A. Outpatient themes of concern:

1. providing immediate help for the emotionally disturbed
2. extending the outpatient system in the community
3. broadening the conception of help.

B. Inpatient themes of concern:

1. individualizing care and treatment
2. breaking down the barriers between the hospital and community
3. developing a therapeutic milieu.

C. Expatient themes of concern:

1. tailoring care to expatient's needs
2. grading stress
3. providing continuity of care.

Joint Commission monograph "Social Perspectives of Mental Patient Care" discusses each of these themes. . . . Extending the outpatient care in the community means . . . the development of mental health consultation services to the many community agencies . . . to develop . . . the helping role of nonmedical "caretakers" who work with individuals and families in community settings, such as schools, public health and social agencies, industry, and others. preservice and continuing education in mental health. . . . Broadening the conception of help means . . . awareness of the complex biological, sociological, cultural, and psychological factors that underlie most psychiatric problems . . . a fuller utilization of nonmedical practitioners.

Ewalt believed that NIMH priorities differed from those of the commission and, without discussion with senior members of the commission, "took the play away from them". The commission saw CMHCs as clinics from general hospital departments of psychiatry with nonprofessionals on their boards and staffs, as was done in San Mateo County, California, and in CMH clinics in Massachusetts, Florida, and North Carolina. The NIMH made the programs more comprehensive. President Kennedy put implementation into the hands of his cabinet, resulting in the Community Mental Health Act of 1963. Ewalt observed that the CMH programs that succeeded concentrated on casualties; those that failed were involved in broader social issues of racism, poverty, and education. He thought that it takes time for community boards to learn to function effectively. There is a need to integrate mental health into federal comprehensive health planning.

Clearly, the Joint Commission's perspective and conclusions represent a different school of thought and group of stakeholders than did the one Lindemann represented, as Gerald Caplan recognized:[30]

Their [politically dominant psychiatric professional groups committed to an individual patient ideology] attitudes and influence were expressed in the report of the Joint Commission on Mental Illness and Mental Health in 1961 that recommended increasing governmental support for existing psychiatric institutions and programs without significant changes in patterns of service delivery [toward a population perspective].

The title of the commission, "Mental Illness and Health", signifies its higher priority for the treatment of mental illness: "secondary or tertiary prevention" in public health terms. It recommends control of the mental health system by a central, federal body and professionals.[31] Top priority is given to severe and chronic mental illness rather than to nonsick people and populations at risk of mental illness. It looks to mental health professionals and the tools of what is sometimes termed "medical psychology" to lead, provide primary expertise, and supervise care. The community aspect of this mental health policy consists of adding group and environmental modes of treatment, making psychiatric institutions more active and effective in treating mental illness, and making the treatment of mental illness available in a larger array of settings, including outside psychiatric institutions. More money, personnel, training, and dispersion of resources are recommended for the treatment of people with mental illness. The term "prevention" is used in the sense of secondary prevention (prevention of chronic disease) and tertiary prevention (the rehabilitation of people with mental illness). Addressing mental health is considered a false promise. The social approach to mental health and illness and the perspective of the social sciences are treated warily as unproven:

> The behavioral sciences on the other hand express considerable dissatisfaction with the focus on "sick behavior", and argue for a new and broader perspective of interest in mental health as a positive force. . . . Some social scientists even questioned the value of the concept of mental illness.
>
> (p. 7)

> Since there is substantial evidence to indicate that mental illness and anxiety are communicable, or transmissible, from one person to another, however, [there is] little or no effort to study the effect on the family, or the community, of having ill persons of this type cared for at home and in the community, rather than isolating them in a hospital. We do not yet know whether mental illness of the acute, aggressive sort is communicable like tuberculosis or malaria, or whether, like vitamin deficiency and malnutrition, illness in one member of a group may or may not be reflected in the other members, depending on the social circumstances. There can be no doubt that this is a high priority area for research. . . . We cannot be other than optimistic concerning the future of our knowledge of how to treat the ill and perhaps even prevent the development of illness. . . . We may hope that further research will develop more precise knowledge of the effect of drugs on the mental processes, more detailed knowledge of the psychologic mechanisms involved in getting sick and recovering, and more complete understanding of the social setting necessary for recovery.
>
> (pp. 14–17)

Lindemann's comrades in CMH, Leonard Duhl and John Seeley, credited themselves and Nicholas Hobbes with preparing a design for the Joint Commission based on Lindemann's ideas of the lifeline, life crises and tasks, supportive resources, and workforce and training, which was accepted by the NIMH grantee organizations but largely ignored by Ewalt.[32] Lindemann made many references to conflict with Ewalt and saw him as competitive and devious rather than cooperative.[33] Lindemann's reaction to the commission report was that the stimulus to a policy study was the wish of mental hospitals to have the community participate in preventing hospital admissions, receiving discharged patients, and supporting community-based aftercare.[34] The pressure for community-based mental health service threatened the continued existence of a large mental hospital industry involving large budgets and a large group of employees—it had become one of the largest items in state economies. He saw the Joint Commission underselling a public health approach and emphasizing the importance of mental hospitals. Lindemann himself thought that, for a group of psychiatrists, the Joint Commission accomplished more than expected in terms of closing psychiatric hospitals. He was critical of the failure of the second half of the process: throwing patients out into the community without follow-up crisis intervention. Through the report of an interview with him by Warren Vaughan, acting as a researcher for the commission, Lindemann took the opportunity to comprehensively lay out his perspective on mental health and illness and its diametrical contrast with the commission's approach (see the following sample; the balance of exposition in endnotes). Perhaps this accounted for his election not to participate:[35]

> He mentioned as reality "social forces, the idea that people are victims of forces over which they have no control" which include economic forces, socio-cultural forces. He decried what he spoke of as "shallow optimism" on the part of some mental health workers that manipulation of human relations in some simple fashion can control the destructive forces in society and human nature . . . formulations . . . of Utopian societies . . . were perhaps necessary for the mental health movement and the morale of the mental health workers, but perhaps had within them some denial of the realities of social forces and human nature".
>
> (p. 1)

> The New England Protestant ethical Puritan tradition led to individualism as compared with San Francisco where it was easier to initiate new programs, so that mental health programs were tailored to the backgrounds of various regions. Is this discussion "dealing only with remedial resources or were we dealing broadly with mental health, that is with hospitals and clinics being only one part of the total issue as it would be viewed by public health–oriented people".
>
> (p. 1)

Caplan thought that the Joint Commission's recommendations were set aside by President Kennedy in his 1963 message to Congress and in the community mental health center legislative acts.[36] The CMHC program was a political compromise, grafting public health functions on a clinical resource (an approach doomed to failure), while improving clinical services and planning.

Rashi Fein, who collected and analyzed data on the economics of mental health and illness, clearly identified the social values and social policy basis of mental health policy and programming:

> which can we best afford, cost in human misery caused by mental illness, or the cost in dollars to provide the best care we know how to give? Could greatly increased expenditures be justified from an economic and humanitarian point of view? . . . All that is necessary to spend more on one thing is to spend less on something else. What will be spent depends on the tax rate and the value system we embrace.
>
> (pp. 23–5)

Adam Yarmolinsky, assistant secretary of defense, remarked on the importance of political implementation in forwarding a set of values:[37]

> the significant fact . . . about some of the criticisms of contemporary institutions and policies . . . is not that they rest on moral judgments, but that the moral judgments are consciously offered as a substitute for political judgments . . . a particularly violent critic of our policy . . . was proud to base his arguments on emotion; mind you, not that he held his view with strong emotion, but that his arguments themselves were based on emotion. . . . But in any case, hearts are not relevant to the issue; neither racial affinities nor racial hostilities are rooted there. It is institutions—social, political, and economic institutions—which are the ultimate molders of collective sentiments. Let these institutions be reconstructed today, and let the ineluctable gradualism of history govern the formation of a new psychology.
>
> (pp. 1–3)

My quarrel with the "no-win" tendency in the civil rights movement (and the reason I have so designated it) parallels my quarrel with the moderates outside the movement. As the latter lack the vision or will for fundamental change, the former lack the realistic strategy for achieving it. For such a strategy they substitute militancy. But militancy is a matter of posture and volume and not of effect. Bayard Rustin was quoted on p. 3: "I suggest that the new moralists are perhaps concentrating on a critical examination of the morality of our politics without sufficient attention to the politics of their own morality. A movement that focuses on moral goals, no matter how noble, without addressing itself to the institutional means to achieve those goals, reflects neither a meaningful commitment to morality nor a practical hope of improving the human condition".

(p. 5)

Note that Yarmolinsky does not recognize that the same values are the basis of the social, political, and economic institutions as they are of the programs and policies whose implementation is determent by them. See McHale, later on, for a delineation of the politico-economic implementation of CMH and other contemporary social programs.

A similar reaction in Massachusetts was the Action for Mental Health in Massachusetts Committee.[38] It met on January 10, 1962, to express concern about the risk of false promises about the benefits of education about mental health; oversimplification, including the analogy with physical health (though this makes mental health more acceptable); doubts about the appropriateness of general hospitals as the location for mental health units; psychiatrists' disagreement with the Joint Commission report; the inability to meet community needs with limited resources; and the need to emphasize education and the encouragement of addressing mental health in the education system.

> The fact is that the Joint Commission Report is primarily a report to Congress requesting Federal funds for state hospitals. There seemed to be agreement that resources of the Federal Government were needed in mental health. . . . All agreed that the problem of mental health and mental illness was one for years of study. . . . If State funds cannot be obtained for training mental health professionals and the ancillary personnel, like the school teacher and clergy who have such a profound effect on the lives of children and families, federal funds should be sought.
>
> (p. 3)

It was noted that in Massachusetts some important legislative action has been achieved quietly without much citizen support. . . . The best way is the middle ground, i.e. for a group that is well informed and reasonable to inform their legislators of health needs. For example, at the national level, parent groups achieved the passage of the National Mental Health Act, and its implementation has been taken over by professional "mental healthers" with not a parent represented on the policy-making bodies of the Institutes of Health. Recommended for Massachusetts: An Advisory Committee on Mental Health on the state level. . . . Members should represent a good cross section of the community close to the grass roots . . . consideration of councils or advisory committees to represent government, voluntary service agencies and the public.

(p. 4)

Voluntary Community Mental Health Planning: The Mental Health Planning Committee of Metropolitan Boston and the Boston Mental Health Survey

The contrast between community mental health via understanding and collaboration among community resources vs. imposition of mental health planning and services by professions and institutions is illustrated by the history of the Mental Health Planning Committee of Metropolitan Boston. In contrast to the Joint Commission's national plan for expanded mental health treatment services for individuals and the CMHC Program's massive funding of professional and institutional resources, there was interest in a collaboration of local agencies and government for preventive services for communities.

In metropolitan Boston, the question arose in many minds as to why mental health services were disjointed. It began with the United Community Services of Boston (UCS)—the centralized charity distributor—appointing a committee (with Gerald Caplan as chairperson) to review the agency's function.[39] This committee recommended the establishment of a UCS section on mental health. It undertook a survey (with William Ryan as director) of mental health resources in the area, the characteristics of patients, and possible gaps in or duplication of services during the period 1960–2.[40] In conjunction with the Survey, Lindemann and Dr. Belenden Hutcheson, the director of the Division of Mental Hygiene, convened a Mental Health Urban Renewal Luncheon Group on April 24, 1962, "in order to discuss the problems of mental health involved in the on-going and future programs for urban renewal in this area".[41]

The survey found a lack of planning and coordination.

> There was agreement that the Boston Mental Health Survey Summary was a credit to Dr. Ryan. His summary evidences a broadly inclusive approach which not only relates to the professional, but the "lay" people and the community agency viewpoint as well.[42]

As a result, the committee recommended a broadly representative regional planning agency to redress the maldistribution of mental health services. Lindemann was helpful in setting direction and dealing with resistance (including from traditional psychiatry) and was courageous in supporting Ryan and the survey report, including against Eveoleen Rexford, a psychiatrist member of the committee who wrote to dissent.

Energized by the findings of the survey, in 1960 the UCS, the Massachusetts Association for Mental Health (the successor to the Massachusetts Committee for Mental Hygiene) and the DMH Division of Mental Hygiene (addressing outpatient services) were dissatisfied with the disjointed and inadequate state of mental health services and therefore formed the Mental Health Planning Committee of Metropolitan Boston and invited Lindemann to join its advisory committee.[43] The ideology behind the committee and its view of its history is articulated by its leaders:[44] They read a long- and short-term historical shift in the delivery of human services: private to public, voluntary to legislated, reparative and remedial to preventive and promotive, serving special groups to serving larger groups and the community, narrow and exclusive (professional) participation in decision-making to a broader and inclusive direction, and a local base to a national base.

> These trends are certainly not accidental or random. They reflect what might be termed an historical and sociological "pull". In all industrialized and economically advanced nations, particularly those with strong democratic and egalitarian principles and traditions, the needs of citizens have resulted in a variety of governmental actions to insure some minimum provision of services in a standardized, orderly manner.
>
> Its Statement of Purposes and Functions aimed to "promote sound comprehensive mental health planning . . . an effective, responsible, and viable citizens' planning body which will promote active collaboration among voluntary agencies and citizens . . . development of comprehensive networks of mental health services . . . to all segments of the population".[45] Though not providing these services directly. It was composed of 50 distinguished professional and lay members, part-time staff, and offices, with *ad hoc* financial support from the sponsoring agencies. There was much optimism and commitment, as from Edward Kovar, Director of the Health Division of United Community Services of Metropolitan Boston, appreciating Lindemann's concept of CMH via the collaboration and education of voluntary/private groups, and participation in establishing and chairing the Committee:[46] "In view of my own personal investment (as well as that of UCS) in the concept of voluntary citizen effort as a vital part of the planning process in the field of mental health service, I feel particularly grateful to you for the contribution you have made to the successful launching of this new regional planning venture".
>
> (pp. 13–14)

The committee and its work were recognized in the popular press as working for comprehensive mental health regional planning via a broadly representative, effective, viable citizens planning body:[47]

> A volunteer group of citizens headed by Dr. Erich Lindemann . . . has been charged with responsibility for planning a more rational pattern of mental health services for Greater Boston. . . . Formation of the committee was announced jointly by Robert H. Gardiner, president of United Community Services of Metropolitan Boston; Pliny Jewell Jr., president of the Massachusetts Assn. for Mental Health, and Dr. Harry C. Solomon, state commissioner of mental health . . . formed in response to findings of the recent Boston Mental Health Survey which called for creation of a regional planning mechanism here in the mental health field.

While cooperation among participants, agencies, and the public improved, the committee did not develop the intended plan. A principle reason was that it was overtaken by the federally funded CMHC Program: in 1965, the federally mandated State Mental Health Planning Project recommended regional mental health planning and oversight boards, and in 1966, state legislation funded mental health regional directors to implement comprehensive mental health services. These regional mental health agencies were official and public and had budgets and directors, as compared with the committee's tripartite, private–public sponsorship with neither a regular budget nor permanent, full-time staff. The committee was unable to engage in active planning, uncertain regarding its raison d'être, duplicated the planning function aspect of the Community Mental Health Center Act, lacked agreement among the sponsoring agencies as to their responsibilities (and one felt threatened by competition), and failed to procure basic funding and to recruit full-time professional staff. In 1968, the committee disbanded, having inadequate resources, sanction, and authority to compete with the massive government program: community-based efforts were overwhelmed by institutional might. In March 1968, its chairperson wrote,[48]

> I must advise you of my decision to resign as chairman of the Mental Health Planning Committee of Metropolitan Boston. . . . the capacity to create change by the present structure of the Mental Health Planning Committee is meager, indeed. . . . In my opinion the vast array of forces, some of which are quite formidable, to be encountered are more than a part-time voluntary effort can materially influence.
>
> A number of efforts . . . to obtain significant funds in order to mount a continuing program of negotiation and conversation. . . [was] to no avail. Endorsement of the importance of continuing mental health planning . . . was never very convincing. . . . There was verbal assent

that "it was a good idea" but convincing investment of energy and recognized skills and reputation from individuals within the sponsoring organizations have not been impressive. . . . it is my opinion that the structure, the Mental Health Planning Committee of Metropolitan Boston, should be disbanded.

A similar approach of voluntary collaboration among community agencies was the 1962 work with the Boston Social Service Exchange, Inc., which liaised among community social service agencies.[49] Lindemann approached this body about cooperating in a project to use "human ecology" data for broad mental health purposes. As an example, he reported that[50]

> at MGH the hospital's whole <u>concept of responsibility is changing</u>, to cover not only its immediate patients but also the surrounding community, not only medical illness but also emotional, not only treatment but also prevention. [An example was John Baldwin's work compiling CMH agencies, research, and data for epidemiological and preventive work.[51]] No one agency, however, can properly define its own responsibility without also taking into account the function and resources of the other agencies in the community. To provide a truly effective network of services the agencies must coordinate their planning. And for sound planning, they must have research data available, and on an on-going basis.

The Boston Social Service Exchange had long and full data on human needs that was accepted by the community. Lindemann incorporated this resource into broader data:

> his current thinking is the outcome of three prior projects: the de Koos study (following the Coconut Grove Fire); the outgrowth of the Wellesley Human Relations Center study; and the outgrowth of THAT, the West End research project conducted by the Center for Community Studies. In each case the <u>basic question</u> has been: given a crisis situation, a "predicament", what are the factors that tax an individual beyond his adaptive powers, what prompts him to turn to an agency for help, what resources does he use, what help does he get, and what are his unmet needs?
>
> (p. 2)

In response, the Boston Social Service Exchange created a subcommittee on long-range development, including "social ecology" studies.[52]

Yet another voluntary effort among community agencies involved the Dorchester Mental Health Center Association and its effort to develop the Dorchester Neighborhood Center Project. It also involved Boston

University, the Settlement [House] Council, and the Division of Mental Hygiene of the Massachusetts DMH (represented by Elizabeth B. Lindemann as mental health consultant).[53] It addressed multiple agency, population, and social issues, such as racial conflict and prejudice. It provided staff training in mental health skills; developed activity programs; and enhanced the recognition of settlement, neighborhood, and community houses involvement in mental health issues.

Another project was a multisession mental health workshop to sharpen the awareness of settlement and community center executives of their agencies' roles in dealing with the mental health needs of their communities.[54] Its purposes were to make group work effective, pursue case finding, support professional mental health intervention, and stimulate and educate the community about mental health.

A sociological analysis of ideological perspectives on human services was developed by Willensky and Lebeaux. It conceptualizes the disparate approaches of the Joint Commission, the Mental Health Planning Committee, the CMHC program, and likeminded community efforts:[55]

> developments in the delivery of human services will disclose . . . historical trends . . . from private to public arrangements; . . . from voluntary to legislated; . . . from the reparative or the remedial to the preventive or promotive; . . . from programs directed to specially defined groups to . . . much larger groups or even for the community at large; . . . from a narrow, exclusive base of . . . decision-making to a broader, more inclusive base; and . . . from locally based to nationally based arrangements.
>
> (pp. 57–8)

> Two conceptions of social welfare seem to be dominant in the United States today: the <u>residual</u> and the <u>institutional</u>. The first holds that social welfare institutions should come into play only when the normal structures of supply, the family and the market, break down. The second, in contrast, sees the welfare services as normal, "first line" functions of modern industrial society. . . . The residual formulation is based on the premise that there are two "natural" channels through which an individual's needs are properly met: the family and the market economy. These are the preferred structures of supply. However, sometimes the institutions do not function adequately: family life is disrupted, depressions occur. Or sometimes the individual cannot make use of the normal channels because of old age or illness. In such cases, according to this idea, a third mechanism of need fulfillment is brought into play—the social welfare structure. This is conceived as a residual agency, attending primarily to emergency functions, and is expected to withdraw when the regular social structure—the family and the economic system—is again

working properly. . . . the "institutional" view implies no stigma, no emergency, no "abnormalcy". Social welfare becomes accepted as a proper, legitimate function of modern industrial society in helping individuals achieve self-fulfillment. The complexity of modern life is recognized. The inability of the individual to provide fully for himself, or to meet all his needs in family and work settings, is considered a "normal" condition: and the helping agencies achieve "regular" institutional status.

[We can construct a] hypothetical single dimension . . . the Exceptional-Universal (E-U) dimension. The Exceptionalist position . . . perceives social problems and needs for human services as exceptions to the general run of affairs, as accidental, unpredictable, arising from special, individual circumstances . . . arrangements for service . . . are unusual and temporary, and . . . voluntary [and] depend on continuously renewed consensus . . . a Universalist outlook . . . sees social problems as rooted in societal and structural contradictions, as general, regular and expected. . . . [It will] approach the problems with systematic arrangements that are . . . ordered, . . . with a goal of systematic and structural change that can be institutionalized. [The] framework is . . . the collective, the group, the social system. . . . the Exceptionalist wants to change attitudes, the Universalist acts to change laws.

(pp. 61–4)

These public and private approaches to mental health clearly are ambivalent—nay conflicted—about, or perhaps have not even recognized, this duality in social policy.

The Local Arena: The Massachusetts Mental Health Planning Project

The CMHC program mandated planning groups in the individual states to implement the CMHC Act. The Massachusetts Mental Health Planning Project (MMHPP) was funded for two years to implement the CMHC Act by developing a comprehensive analysis of mental health services and assisting the state DMH in developing a long-range program. It reflects in the state arena attitudes toward and the tension between concepts of CMH. Its task forces were 1. Adult Crime and Juvenile Delinquency, 2. Adult Mentally Ill, 3. Alcoholism, 4. Communication and Health Education, 5. Drug Addiction, 6. Emotionally Disturbed Children, 7. Epilepsy, 8. Occupational Mental Health, 9. Research, 10. Aging.[56] A Task Force on Community Mental Health also submitted a report.[57]

Lindemann accepted the invitation to join the Advisory Council[58] and became a member of its Task Force on Adult Mentally Ill.[59] On this task force, he encountered members representing adult and long-term treatment programs in favor of a CMH perspective to mental health services as well as presumably those with a treatment-oriented perspective. He suggested expanding the focus from major mental problems, psychosis, and alcoholism to include all those emotionally disturbed and provide both intramural treatment and extramural treatment, without separating hospital and community in a continuity of treatment. He proposed a study of conditions and interventions that would prevent hospitalization, including abolishing the concept of mental health and sickness in favor of identifying needs in a social psychology perspective. He advocated pushing rehabilitation further and establishing a variety of centers to deal with relationships other than illness, shorten hospital stays, and prevent readmissions. He drew attention to aftercare clinics, Alcoholics Anonymous and Al Anon, referring physicians, psychiatrists making home visits, community agencies collaborating with hospitals, and physical and mental health services to the elderly.[60]

This state-level task force duplicated the national level in the persistence of conflicting factions with opposing definitions of mental health and the goals and priorities for a mental health program, despite the charge to revamp it in accordance with the president's special message and the evolving CMHC program. The report of the subcommittees and the task force reflected this ambivalence:

> Most consumer interest in mental health is in primary preventive activities and in individual treatment for less serious conditions. For these reasons, members of the Task Force . . . agreed nearly unanimously that in planning services for the mental health needs of Massachusetts citizens, the bulk of effort should be aimed at the acutely disturbed and chronically ill.
>
> (p. 2)

The various subcommittees reported the following:

- Statistics—Need objective evidence of effectiveness of treatment approaches. Age 15–34 (the baby boom) is the fastest growing subpopulation and traditionally contributes to chronic mental hospital patient population.
- Public Mental Hospitals—The state will continue to need the state hospital to attend to the care of chronically ill and to aftercare. It called for improved support of mental hospitals from the community and community agencies. The expected increase in the volume of admissions calls for the development of emergency treatment and diversion services.
- Outpatient Clinics—There is need for increased consultation activities and emergency and early treatment services.

- Community Care—Recommendations were for treatment within the community. It encouraged recognition of help for people with mental illness by other helping professionals and nonprofessionals, community agencies, welfare departments, family service agencies, mental health services in other agencies, rehabilitation agencies, aftercare services, and mental health clinics. Public education is important. There is need to address treatment patterns in the community and the effect of mental illness on the family and community. Important also are mental health research, coordination among services, and the allocation of psychiatric services. In terms of resources, there was concern for an increase in social work treatment of low-status diagnoses, a review of independent practice by nonmedical professionals, and the training of mental health personnel. It recommended local mental health commissions plan and coordinate services and local comprehensive CMHCs and support all mental health services. Finally, it took note of the study of sound family life and the evaluation of treatment methods.

- This task force concluded that we cannot prevent mental illness and should aim for early recognition, effective treatment, and minimizing disability in incurable disabilities: 5%–10% of new admissions and a future total of 600, as compared with the present total of 2000.

Lindemann was a member of the Task Force's Sub Committee on Community Services,[61] also referred to as the Task Force on Community Mental Health Programs, which first met on October 2, 1964.[62] It was more hospitable toward a CMH perspective. It produced a report thoughtfully outlining CMH responsibilities of a state mental health program. Its first report addressed the origins and focus of contemporary CMH efforts:[63]

> Twentieth century America has witnessed the emergence of a new social need, psychological security, and, in response to this need, a new social movement, the mental health movement. In what appears to be an inverse relationship, as Americans more and more are spared the burden of basic economic survival, they can, and do, concern themselves with emotional survival. Increasingly, there is being expressed a widely felt need for psychic well-being and personal security, revealed most recently as a demand for organized mental health services. The achievement of positive mental health, it can be said, has become a social goal and cultural value. As the country's current concern with poverty suggests, the passage of social legislation over the past 30 years has not eliminated the problems of economic security. Security in 1964 has come to mean something more than what it meant in 1930. The real test of the future may not be whether we

can provide for those who do not have enough, but whether we can make life tolerable for those who do.

(p. 2)

The task force put this perspective in the form of four historical stages in the care of people with mental illness in the US:

1. superstition and fear leading to segregation and abuse
2. moral treatment by a small group of reformers focusing on social attitudes rather than space, which eventually was extinguished
3. the deterioration of care, with prevention and early diagnosis almost outlawed, and the growth of large, custodial institutions and isolation
4. the current era of early diagnosis and treatment; integrated drug, social, and psychological treatment in the community rather than in isolation; and voluntary hospital admissions.

The second draft of the report expanded on the contemporary CMH perspective:[64]

> In spite of the widespread support which is now being evinced for community mental health programs, it is important to remember that this concept still represents many different things to different people. To some, the essence of a community mental health service is its physical location in the very midst of a population center, thus bringing regular psychiatric services closer to its patients and permitting the utilization of such facilities as the general hospital. To others, the distinguishing feature of the community mental health service . . . lies in its philosophy that provision of comprehensive mental health services (direct and indirect) requires the cooperation and participation of all segments of the community's power structure and caregiving system. Consequently, the skills of more than the traditional psychiatric team are utilized. . . . To still others, the essential quality of a community mental health program is not rooted primarily in the character of he services which it provides but more importantly in the fact that a local citizen group assumes responsibility for program planning and development.
>
> (pp. 3–4)

In fact, it has been theoretically conjectured that primary prevention potentially stems most from the areas of economics and politics, and is mainly outside the social, health, and welfare systems entirely. On the other hand, most social-welfare agencies are more than glad to turn over responsibility for an actively psychotic individual to the mental health center. The broad middle area of joint concern may be a source of much friction in the years to come.

(p. 22)

Because of the diversity in background and theoretical predilection brought to bear by the Task Force members, unanimous agreement could not be reached in regard to all of the detailed issues considered by the group. However, consensus could be achieved as to the major elements of community mental health program development. . . . The concept of community mental health has not yet completed its theoretical gestation but the Task Force agrees that in its final form, such elements certainly will be highlighted: The patient must always remain the central focus of a comprehensive program which is designed to meet his, and not the institution's needs; continuity of care must be provided by institutions in the same way that private practitioners have always done; and active cooperation must be engendered between the mental health center and other community health and welfare agencies if a comprehensive variety of services is to be provided the citizens. With the expanded range of programs available to the community, increased emphasis will be placed upon programs of primary and secondary prevention. Mental health professionals will be expected to be proficient not only in the provision of direct clinical services but also in such indirect functions as community consultation, education, and interagency planning. If the truly ambitious scope of a community mental health program is to be achieved, the use of complementary resources will be imperative since no single agency can diagnose and treat adequately each member of the community who is mentally disturbed.

(pp. 41–2)

The Task Force cannot express too strongly its affirmation of the principle of citizen participation in the development and operation of community mental health centers. . . . The Task Force recommends that every mental health center have formally affiliated with it a Community Advisory Council whose composition and functions are such as to reflect the true needs and desires of the citizens residing in the region. The membership of the Council should include all significant community forces but the Task Force thinks that professionals should not compose more than 1/4 of the total Council's membership. The Task Force recommends a variety of functions to be assigned the Council, including those of establishing policy and program priorities, and responsibility for long-term planning.

(p. 45)

The subcommittee produced some operational specifics to implement this ideology.[65]

There was a contrast between the CMH approach of the subcommittee on CMH Programs and that of the mental illness treatment approach of the committee as a whole:

- In the final report of the Task Force on Adult Mentally ill, the community subcommittee recommended treatment within the community. It encouraged recognition of help for people with mental illness by other helping professionals and nonprofessionals, community agencies, welfare departments, family service agencies, mental health services in other agencies, rehabilitation agencies, aftercare services, and mental health clinics. It stated that public education is important. There is need to address treatment patterns in the community and the effect of mental illness on the family and community. Important also are mental health research, coordination of services, and allocation of psychiatric services. In terms of resources, an increase in social work treatment of low-status diagnoses, a review of independent practice by nonmedical professionals, and the training of mental health personnel are of concern. It recommended local mental health commissions to plan and coordinate services; local, comprehensive CMHCs; and coordination among and support for all mental health services. Finally, it took note of the study of sound family life and the evaluation of treatment methods.
- In contrast, the Task Force as a whole concluded that we cannot prevent mental illness and should aim for early recognition, effective treatment, and minimizing disability in incurable disabilities—5%–10% of new admissions and a future total of 600, as compared with the present total of 2000.

Psychopolitics

Politics is the process through which social institutions—including mental health—are created, implemented, and adapted to changes in social ethos. Thus, it is appropriate to contemplate the experience of politics in regard to mental health goals, practices, and programs.

Milton Greenblatt, variously professor of psychiatry at Harvard and Tufts Universities and the University of California at Los Angeles Medical Schools, superintendent of the Boston State and Boston Psychopathic Hospitals and various Veterans Administration medical centers, and Massachusetts commissioner of the DMH, had much opportunity to observe the politics of the choice and implementation of mental health care.[66] He provides information, insight, and thoughtful responses.

Greenblatt saw changes in expectations of rehabilitation causing changed views of the mental hospital and new ideas about facilities and systems. The custodial-authoritarian model existed before 1930. It was followed, from the 1930s to the 1950s, by the therapeutic-egalitarian model, with institutions more open to outside contributions toward effective biological, milieu, and activity therapies. The mental health center model, from the 1950s to the 1960s, involved the community and community professionals in the treatment system, more treatment taking place in the community, and more interaction between hospitals and community. He believed that the comprehensive community mental health center model, stimulated by the Joint Commission report in 1961 was backed by national policy and funding, had a more public health perspective, gave community forces more voice in the mental health system, and addressed social causes of mental illness and social action to rectify them. Beyond these, he posited a total healthcare model, comprehensively addressing mental health, physical health, education, and welfare and requiring the political and administrative integration of these programs, public and private sectors, and professional resources. He saw the process of the conversion of state hospitals, psychopathic hospitals, mental health and guidance clinics, general hospital psychiatric units, and university psychiatry services to community mental health centers stalled when federal focus and funding turned to welfare, crime, and urban problems; and lack of financial resources when state mental hospitals were not phased out as quickly as expected resulted in inadequate local funding, in turn resulting in inadequate community services for discharged patients.

"In the long run a mental health system can move only as far as the legislature will let it, and, in turn, the legislature will usually move only as far as the citizens will approve".[67] The administrator is subject to influence by patients, families, staff, legislators, and citizen groups. There is an inherent contradiction between benevolent goals for human good on the one hand and on the other hand political tactics involving an adversarial relationship to other powers and competitors and political actors serving constituents vs. serving themselves. The culture of government bureaucracy imposes on the mental health system mistrust, the assumption of wrongdoing, self-serving materialism, rivalry, formal and authoritarian communication and relationships, large structures and distant relationships, exploitation, delays, stifling of creativity, political interference with professional and scientific practice, and public disillusionment. Politicians can be expected to be more blunt, self-aggrandizing, emotional, and used to trading favors; on the other hand, mental health professionals are likely to be more subtle, client oriented, and interested in honors. To be politically successful, professionals must avoid the taint of politics while being close enough to it to be effective. Politicians deal with mental health as a political issue demanding resources or a vehicle to political prominence whether by supporting its success or attacking its wrongdoing. When conditions are ripe, mental patients in public facilities may attract attention regarding inadequate funding, poor living conditions, and other failures, making the mental health system vulnerable to attack. The increase of citizen involvement through governance, review, or volunteer participation positions them to be critical of conditions and the mental health professions, leading to legislative investigation. In an election year, this increases, and the speaker of the House of Representatives and president of the Senate may join mental health foes on investigating committees that, added to system maintenance burdens, overload the mental health system. The press is powerful and sometimes negativistic. The mental health system can deal with it by being open, honest, impartial, and patient and by seeking the support of friends.

The legislature is crucial for funding and is subject to many pressures. It may plan with the governor rather than with the commissioner of mental health, want pet projects, appoint people to the DMH for purposes of control or patronage, and seek to discredit the governor through the way it deals with the DMH.

Greenblatt's experience of the interplay of mental health and politics sensitized him to the issue of psychopolitics in "Psychopolitics and the Search for Power". He found Machiavellian traits with politicians: affectless, value-free, manipulating people and resources, and disliking structure and goals. Alternative value systems were authoritarianism (strong superego and weak ego, hostile, and unproductive) vs. democratic (spontaneous, non-authoritarian, group spirit, warm, productive) vs. laissez-faire (poor productivity). A custodial mental health approach is judgmental, pessimistic, and authoritarian, whereas a humanistic approach is optimistic and treatment oriented. Power is needed to forward programs: this may come from statutory delegation, expertise, or an effective administrative team. It requires coordinated support from committed constituencies. Power, an important basic motivation, shifted in location and usage during the 1950s to the 1970s period of decline in authority; the breakup of social institutions; the alienation of youth; and the radicalization of minorities, women, the poor, and liberals. All these affected the source of support and the direction of mental health programs.

"[P]rivate motives displaced onto public objects and rationalized as in the public interest equals political man".[68] Power corrupts: the holder of power may feel superior, distant, exempt from common morality, protected from reality, and deprived of loving relationships. However, it is possible for power to be used compassionately and jointly. Is it possible and appropriate for psychiatry to evaluate and advise political leaders toward insights into their motivations and the benevolent use of power? Lindemann embraced the CMH political goal of influencing policy and ecology while avoiding partisanship and the loss of a collaborative acceptance:[69]

Some of my colleagues believe that people who are interested in the socio-psychological component of illness ought to be chaplains or school teachers, and not doctors. There is a widespread feeling that the boundary between health concerns and those of the other legitimate care-taking operations in the <u>community</u> has become a bit fuzzy, and should be made tighter. My point of view has been the opposite. However, it requires skill, and the maintenance of a friendly give-and-take, to have open access to the areas of the well person—to get past the gate-keepers of the schools, churches, welfare agencies and police. . . . Our objectives are political: we are fighting for making <u>concern for people</u> a first priority of social planning. . . . The punitive, repressive approach . . . which is usually handled by the people in power as their method of keeping others in line, has shown itself wanting . . . so here is also a feeling that the health and medical experts might be allowed in, because . . . scientific competence makes it legitimate to present to the decision-makers the alternate outcomes of different procedures. . . . The important thing to remember is, <u>we must not take over</u>. We must only tell the power people the consequences, and let them consider where they will lead them. If we step beyond this line, we will be out in no time. . . . There is a subtle balance between forces in the community making for the status quo and those wishing to introduce new patterns of dealing with problems.

Citizen groups, of which Greenblatt identified 200 at the time, provide volunteer services, support mental health programs, attack those who block their special interests, and were growing more powerful.

The administrator's job was more and more often that of mediator between various citizen partisan groups, between citizens and professionals, and between citizen groups and the political sector—rather than promulgator of a master plan for which he was the accepted leader with a natural assumptions of citizen support.[70]

The tradition had been for universities and professionals to fill the post of commissioner of mental health with joint appointments at the Harvard Medical School and the state Boston Psychopathic Hospital, addressing treatment, training, and research. After World War II, the great influx of federal funds was designated for these purposes to specific projects that bypassed the state legislature. The legislature was suspicious that the universities were using staff time and research funds for university purposes. And there was also some competition between universities and local communities for these resources, though overall, he found good collaboration. Organized labor, too, could test and challenge the mental health administration and compete for control, though they were helpful when they were consulted and understood the program. Patience and persistence were required to earn the respect, understanding, and cooperation of entrenched individuals and interests.

Consumers can participate in the scientific evaluation of community needs while avoiding the administration of services or battling for control. To avoid battles for control, train administrators and define authority clearly. Otherwise, citizens have superior weapons in a battle: They appeal to and pressure government, demonstrate, boycott and riot, appear more unselfish, and are uninhibited by accusations and distortions. Families and communities are more able and willing to care for people with mental illness than they are credited for. The resistance of mental health professionals and institutions to community-based treatment includes personal bias; resistance to change; lack of understanding of and preparation for community services; fear of giving up hard-won treatment techniques; fear of losing professional dignity and identity; concern over blurring of role boundaries; loss of institutional structure, protection, and empire; and the burden of population-wide responsibility.

Notes

1. Yolles, Stanley F., M.D, second director of the NIMH 1964–6/2/1970, "The Future of Community Psychiatry", Ch. 10 in Barton, Walter E. and Sanborn, Charlotte J. (eds.), *An Assessment of The Community Mental Health Movement* (Lexington, MA: Lexington Books, 1977), pp. 21–34, based on the Dartmouth Continuing Education Institute, Department of Psychiatry, Dartmouth Medical School, 1975. [folder "CMH—Theory", David G. Satin files, Newton, MA]
2. Committee on Community Psychiatry, American Psychoanalytic Association, Wadeson, Ralph W. Jr., MD, ""Psychoanalysis in Community Psychiatry: Reflections on Some Theoretical Implications", *Journal of the American Psychoanalytic Society* 23: 177–189 (1975) report of Panel (Viola Bernard, Chmn) at Annual Meeting of the American Psychoanalytic Association 5/1974, Denver, CO; p. 177. [Research Papers, Lindemann Collection, Center for the History of Medicine, Countway Library of Medicine, Boston, MA]
3. White, Theodore H., *In Search of History: A Personal Adventure* (New York: Warner Books, 1978), p. 373.
4. Abrams, Richard M., Assoc. Professor of History, University of California-Berkeley, "When the Tough Get Going", *Psychiatry & Social Science Review* 2 no. 7: 13–15 (7/1968)—volume on student political activity at Columbia University. [folder "Civil Rights/Minorities", David G. Satin files, Newton, MA]
5. Chang, Jung, *Wild Swans: Three Daughters of China* (New York: Anchor Books/Doubleday, 1952), p. 283.
6. Ewalt, Jack, Supt., Mass. Mental Health Ctr, Commissioner of Mental Health, MA, interview by David G. Satin, at the U.S. Veterans Administration, Washington, DC, 1/26/79
7. Newfield, Jack, "Revolt Without Dogma—The Student Left", *The Nation* 5/10/1965. [folder "NIMH Study Section 1964–65", Box IIIA 4 (Mb-O), Erich Lindemann Collection, Center for the History of Medicine, Francis A. Countway Library of Medicine, Boston, MA]
8. Duhl, Leonard J., MD, chief, Office of Planning, National Institute of Mental Health, NIH, Public Health Service, U.S. Department of HEW, "The

Psychiatrist in Urban Social Planning", p. 17. Presented at the Colloquium, Florence Heller Graduate School for Advanced Studies in Social Welfare, Brandeis University, 3/11/1965. [folder "NIMH", Box IIIA 4 (Mb-O), Erich Lindemann Collection, Center for the History of Medicine, Francis A. Countway Library of Medicine, Boston, MA]

9. Gladwin, Thomas, Dr., Consultant in the Social Science and Community Research and Services Branch "A Visit to COFO [Council of Federated Organizations]", 5/1965. [folder "NIMH", Box IIIA 4 (Mb-O), Erich Lindemann Collection, Center for the History of Medicine, Francis A. Countway Library of Medicine, Boston, MA]

10. Gladwin, Thomas, 5/1965, *ibid.*

> Council of Federated Organizations (COFO) 1964 summer project to develop cultural and educational resources in Mississippi Negro communities, voter registration drives, independent Freedom Democratic Party with mock elections, local leadership and activism. Organized by the highly activist Student Non-Violent Coordinating Committee (SNCC), and only slightly more conservative Congregation of Racial Equality (CORE), and other civil rights organizations. Energized by the murder of three workers (importantly two were white). "Undoubtedly many of those who joined this crusade did so in an attempt to resolve their own uncertainties regarding race relations or to fulfill some need within their own maturing selves. Nevertheless, whatever their reasons they served effectively". In the fall most dispersed back to their own lives, few kept the offices open. Mostly from SNCC. Small weekly expenses, automobiles. They have been harassed. The staffs came to know the communities and are accepted and trusted. "They represent, therefore, agents of change of a sort we in mental health and other 'helping' programs hope to see in many kinds of settings in ever increasing numbers in the United States. Psychologically they have been domestic counterparts of the Peace Corps Volunteers—although Peace Corps Volunteers found far less difficulty in explaining to their friends and families why they were volunteering".
>
> (pp. 1–2)

> Gladwin reported on a 24 hour observation of a local project in a small Mississippi town. "Without any question the Project has brought something valuable and valid to its community. This is evident in the fact that, although the Project has produced no material gains and has led to turmoil, trouble, and even bloodshed, the staff are accepted with complete trust and affection. . . . Yet what that something might be is not at all clear. Virtually none of the overt goals of the Project have been met in any substantial degree. Voter registration has been a failure. No facilities except a few lunch counters which were not integrated before have been integrated during the past months. The Freedom School has been abandoned. Although individuals can express themselves and think through issues more clearly. . . . the evening meeting . . . was a disaster in community organization. . . . It must therefore be concluded that what has been added by the Project is completely intangible. The people have given their trust and affection in return only for a measure of hope and perhaps a little more faith in the future. What will grow from this in the months and years to come only the future can tell. Much depends upon the opportunities which are brought to bear by outside forces, many of which were, of course, themselves mobilized largely on the basis of the dramatic confrontations created by COFO and similar activities. These

include a variety of Federal programs, most notably the voting rights bill. . . . It seems unlikely that the poverty program will reach many Mississippi Negroes in the immediate future. The outside forces also include the organizations sponsoring COFO. At present this is almost entirely SNCC. . . . As the Civil Rights Movement has become more successful all of its organizations have moved, or been forced, into more activist strategies. SNCC has always seen itself as the most radical among these organizations. So, in order to show that they still qualify as way-out types many Snickers have felt they had to assume more and more radical postures. Increasingly, this more extreme element seems to be against the Federal Government, biting the hand that others believe is feeding the Movement. The resulting contrast between responsibility and radicalism, between compassion and hate, charged the air even within the tiny confines of the Project office. . . . [The Project] staff . . . shares the parochialism and myopia of crusaders everywhere. They have not time nor bent for extensive reading or the broad sampling of evidence and points of view which are necessary to an informed and balanced opinion. As a result the project staff have accepted this almost nihilist interpretation and are disillusioned with their own Government and incredibly ignorant of the processes by which their Nation is in fact ruled. . . . I find quite incomprehensible the purpose which anyone who supposedly is working for civil rights might have in subjecting these young people to such destructive and disheartening propaganda".(pp. 3–4) His conclusion was that COFO was ineffectual, obstructing more effective sophisticated pressure on unyielding whites. Professionals have not addressed civil rights of Mississippi Negroes; naive volunteers were available and inspire the community. Without success hope fades; the COFO project must withdraw but not seem a failure. "The prospect of withdrawal raises another kind of dilemma, a personal one. . . . Work in the Movement for all of these young people has been a climactic experience, the first and greatest climax of their adult lives, and in fact perhaps the experience which made them adults. . . . they have found themselves through their experience. . . . But it rests upon an individual way of life which pulses too strongly to be a good model for campus or on the job. In other words, the COFO experience has had a meaning so powerful that it has become for each his whole self and being. A transition to anything else is hard to imagine and will be hard to bear". For undereducated Negroes return to work or school is hard, their radical past is a burden. White radicals, previously rejected, found meaning and acceptance, and will return to rejection. "Having in the past groped in vain to find a meaningful role for themselves in the world these people are now faced with losing again the precious identity so recently found. While their uneducated Negro colleagues will return to a status of nonperson, these white young people will return to a status of unwanted persons. . . . Their situation is one in which their reasons for staying with and maintaining the Project, however well these may be rationalized, are in fact increasingly personal and serving their own needs, and decreasingly useful to the community. . . . Perhaps this is a special case of the old saying that revolutions always in the end devour their own".

(pp. 6–7)

11. Lindemann, Erich, "Fundamentals of Community Mental Health: A. Contributions of the Psychiatrist", p. 1, presented as part of a symposium at

the American Orthopsychiatric Association meeting, 3/15/56. [Erich Linde-mann Collection, Center for the History of Medicine, Francis A. Countway Library of Medicine, Boston, MA]

12. "Action for Mental Health: Digest of the Final Report of the Joint Commission on Mental Illness and Health", *The Modern Hospital* 3/1961.
13. Ewalt, Jack, "The Birth of the Community Mental Health Movement", Ch. 2 in Barton, Walter E. and Sanborn, Charlotte J. (eds.), *An Assessment of the Community Mental Health Movement* (Lexington, MA: Lexington Books, 1977).
14. Newbrough, J.R.[obert], Mental Health Study Center, National Institute of Mental Health: ""Community Mental Health: A Movement in Search of a Theory", in *Community Mental Health: Individual Adjustment or Social Planning; a Symposium, Ninth Interamerican Congress of Psychology, 1964* (Adelphi, MD: Mental Health Study Center, National Institute of Mental Health, 1965). [also found in folder "CMH—Policy, Politics, Administration, Institutions", David G. Satin files, Newton, MA]
15. Ewalt, Jack, 1/26/1979, *ibid.*
16. *Action for Mental Health: Digest of the Final Report*, 1961, *ibid*.: Organizations participating in the Joint Commission: American Academy of Neurology, American Academy of Pediatrics, American Association for the Advancement of Science, American Association on Mental Deficiency, American Association of Psychiatric Clinics for Children, American College of Chest Physicians, American Hospital Association, American Legion, American Medical Association, the Coordinating Council of the American Nurses Association and the National League for Nursing, American Occupational Therapy Association, American Orthopsychiatric Association, American Personnel and Guidance Association, American Psychiatric Association, American Psychoanalytic Association, American Psychological Association, American Public Health Association, American Public Welfare Association, Association for Physical and Mental Rehabilitation, Association of American Medical Colleges, Association of State and Territorial Health Officers, Catholic Hospital Association, Central Inspection Board of the American Psychiatric Association, Children's Bureau of the U.S. Department of Health, Education, and Welfare, Council of State Governments, U.S. Department of Defense, National Association for Mental Health, National Association of Social Workers, National Committee Against Mental Illness, National Education Association, National Institute of Mental Health, National Medical Association, National Rehabilitation Association, Office of Vocational Rehabilitation of the U.S. Department of Health, Education, and Welfare, U.S. Department of Justice, U.S. Veterans Administration, United Auto Workers.
17. Third Annual Report of the Joint Commission on Mental Illness and Health, 1958. [folder "Jt Comm. on Mental Illness & Health (Ewalt)", Box IIIA 4 (I-Ma), Lindemann Collection, Center for the History of Medicine, Francis A. Countway Library of Medicine, Boston, MA]

Members of the Joint Commission were listed as: Appel, Kenneth E., MD (Philadelphia), Baer, Walter H., MD (Peoria), Bartemeier, Leo H., MD (Baltimore), Barton, Walter E., MD (Boston), Bettag, Otto L MD (Springfield, Illinois), Bingaman, George (Purcell, OK), Black, Kathleen RN (New York City), Blain, Daniel, MD (DC), Braceland, Francis J., MD (Hartford)., Carmichael, Hugh T., MD (Chicago), Casey, J. Frank, MD (DC), Cunningham, Jas M., MD (Dayton), Davis, John E ScD (Rehoboth

Beach, DE), Dayton, Neil A., MD (Mansfield Depot, CT), Dunn, Loula (Chicago), Fabing, Howard D., MD (Cincinnati), Frawley, Patrick J., Rev, PhD (New York City), Gorman Mike (DC), Hewitt, Robt T., MD (Bethesda), Hilleboe, Herman E., MD (Albany), Hobbs, Nicohlas, PhD (Nashville), Hogan, Bartholomew W., Rear Adm, USN (DC), Jacobs, Louis, MD (DC), Kaufman, M. Ralph, MD (NYC), Langford, Wm S., MD (New York City), Lay, Madeleine (New York City), Masur, Jack, MD (Bethesda), Mattison, Berwyn F., MD (New York City), Mayr, Ernst, PhD (Cambridge MA), Morse, Robt T., MD (DC), Ojemann, Ralph H., PhD (Iowa City), Overholser, Winfred, MD (DC), Potter, Howard W MC (New York City), Schlaifer, Chas (New York City), Smith, Lauren H., MD (Phila), Smith, M. Brewster, PhD (New York City), Spector, Sidney (Chicago), Tarumianz, Mesrop A., MD (Farnhurst, DE), Tiedman, David W EdD (Cambridge), Tompkins, Harvey J., MD (New York City), Wade, Beatrice D. OTR (Chicago), Whitten, E.B. (Washington, DC), Witmer, Helen, PhD (Washington, DC), Woodward, Luther E., PhD.

(New York City)

Officers of the Joint Commission were listed as follows: President—Appel, Kenneth E., MD; chairperson of the Board of Tustees—Bartemeier, Leo H., MD; Vice-President—Smith, M. Berwster, PhD, Secretary-Treasurer—Schlaifer, Charles; Vice-chairperson of the Board of Trustees—Hobbs, Nicholas, PhD

Staff of the Joint Commission were listed as: Director—Ewalt, Jack R., MD (Boston); Consultant for Scientific Studies—Sanford, Fillmore H., PhD (Austin); Consultant in Social Science—iBlackwell, Gordon W., PhD (Chapel Hill); Consultant in Epidemiol—Gordon, John E. (Boston); Associate Director for Administration—Plunkett, Richard J., MD (Boston), Director of Information—Williams, Greer (Boston); Associate Director and Consultant on Law—Brewton, Charles S. LLB (Boston); Librarian—Strovink, Mary R. (Boston)

18. NIMH $1,250,000 authorized by Congress, American Legion $10,000, American Occupational Therapy Association $100, American Psychiatric Association $500, Benjamin Rosenthal Foundation $10,000, Carter Products Company $5000, Catholic Hospital Association $500, Field Foundation $10,000, National Association for Mental Health $5000, National Committee Against Mental Illness $5,000, National League for Nursing $300, National Rehabilitation Association $500, Rockefeller Brothers Fund $60,000, Smith, Klein and French Foundation $30,000. "Action for Mental Health: Digest of the Final Report", 1961, *ibid.*

19. Soskin, William F., Task Force on Research, Mishler, Elliot G., Research Associate on the Task Force on Patterns of Patient Care, 2/21/1958, Ewalt, Jack R. 4/4/1960 letters and memos to Lindemann, Erich; HMS Dean memo to all psychiatry department heads re meeting with Warren Vaughan, Jr. and Dr. Mark G. Field, research Associate in the Joint Commission, 1/13/1958. [folder "Jt Comm. on Mental Illness & Health (Ewalt)", Box IIIA 4 (I-Ma), Lindemann Collection, Center for the History of Medicine, Francis A. Countway Library of Medicine, Boston, MA]

20. Joint Commission (1956–1961) (on Mental Health & Illness): *Action for Mental Health* (Basic Books) digest reprinted from *The Modern Hospital*, 4/1961, p. 1. [folder "Joint Commission (1956–1961) (on Mental Health & Illness)", Box IIIA 4 (I-Ma), Lindemann Collection, Center for the History of Medicine, Francis A. Countway Library of Medicine, Boston, MA]

21. Action for Mental Health, Digest: Digest, 3/1961, *ibid.*, p. 1.

22. See, for instance, the form letter from Warren T. Vaughan, Jr., MD, representing the Task Force on Patterns of Patient Care, to Lindemann asking for

his critique of the Joint Commission's questionnaire. Appended was a hand-written note wanting to discuss the "state-MGH situation", with a diagram of the MGH Psychiatry Service, its relationship to outside agencies, and its projects. 7/19/1957. [folder "Misc. Correspondence T-Z—1956-7", Box IIIA 1–3, Lindemann Collection, Center for the History of Medicine, Francis A. Countway Library of Medicine, Boston, MA]

23. Joint Commission on Mental Illness and Health, *Action for Mental Health: Final Report of the of the Joint Commission on Mental Illness and Health 1961* (New York: Basic Books, 1961).

24. Joint Commission on Mental Illness and Health, 1961, *ibid.*

25. Action for Mental Health, Digest: Digest, 3/1961, *ibid.*, p. 16.

26. Action for Mental Health, Digest: Digest, 3/1961, *ibid.*, p. 13.

27. Correspondence between Lindemann and Jack R. Ewalt, MD, Director of the Joint Commission, 2/13,21/1956. [folder "Misc. Correspondence D, E,F 1956–57", Box IIIA 1–3, Lindemann Collection, Center for the History of Medicine, Francis A. Countway Library of Medicine, Boston, MA]

28. Vaughan, Warren T., Jr., Burlingame, CA, "In Honor of Erich Lindemann", *American Journal of Community Psychology* 12 no. 5: 531–532 (1984). [found also in folder" Kelly, James G.", David G. Satin files, Newton, MA]

29. Vaughan, Warren T., Jr. MD, FAPHA, and Field, Mark G., PhD, "New Perspectives of Mental Patient Care", *American Journal of Public Health* 53 no. 2: 237–242 (pp. 237–240) (2/1963).

30. Caplan, Gerald, MD [professor of child psychiatry and chairperson, Department of Child Psychiatry, Hadassah University Hospital, Ein Karem, Jerusalem], Epilogue: "Personal Reflections by Gerald Caplan", in Schulberg, Herbert C. and Killilea, Marie (eds.), *The Modern Practice of Community Mental Health: A Volume in Honor of Gerald Caplan* (San Francisco: Jossey Bass, 1982), pp. 540–564.

31. Musto, David F., "Whatever Happened to Community Mental Health?", *The Public Interest* no. 39: 53–77 (Spring 1975).

32. Lindemann, Erich, with Duhl, Leonard, Lindemann, Elizabeth, and Seeley, John, interview at Lindemann's home in Palo Alto, CA by Leonard Duhl, 7/15/74. [caddy 4, tape 8A, 9B;7, Erich Lindemann Collection, Center for the History of Medicine, Francis A. Countway Library of Medicine, Boston, MA]

33. [folder "Dean George Packer Berry", Box IIIA 4 (A-E), Lindemann Collection, Center for the History of Medicine, Francis A. Countway Library of Medicine, Boston, MA]

34. Lindemann, Erich, and Spivak, McGrath, "Development of CMHCs (unpublished interview of Erich Lindemann by sociology students, 1965).

35. Vaughan, Warren T., "Conference with Dr. Erich Lindemann, Saturday, July 27, 1957". [folder "Joint Commission (1956–1961) (on Mental Health & Illness)", Box IIIA 4 (I-Ma), Erich Lindemann Collection, Center for the History of Medicine, Francis A. Countway Library of Medicine, Boston, MA]

Balance of Lindemann's exposition:

There are problems of personnel shortage and the type of personnel and training needed: "He said that the trend was toward more intensive training and expensive training for fewer and fewer highly trained specialists who would then be working with fewer and fewer patients. . . . the parallel was in the medical field where specialism with more gadgets has developed to such an extent that hospitals are pricing themselves out of business; it is happening that smaller and smaller segments of privileged people are eligible or able to afford hospitalization. . . . He sees the future psychiatrist as a policy determiner and supervisor, with non-medical people in the role of the 'doers'. . . . He uses an analogy here comparing this field to the field of nursing, where the R.N.s are becoming the managers and administrators in nursing, where bedside care for patients is in the hands of practical nurses, nurse's aides, and volunteers etc.".

(p. 2)

The patient role is of low social status and stigmatization. "He further spoke of the hospital, general hospital, as an aristocratic institution looking for a 'rare' profitable disease, that psychiatric illness fell into neither of these categories. It's impossible to sell the psychiatric patient on either of these bases, then the psychiatric patient is one of a number of people who are taken care of by the state through social action and social medical planning . . . a public role of psychiatric institutions, which in many senses involves the assigned task of segregating and excluding people from society. . . . private money is very hard to come by for mental health, mentioning that recently some 3–6000 [*sic*] large industrial corporations were canvassed with respect to supporting mental health activities; almost none were interested".

(p. 3)

[He noted] a dilemma, namely that of interfering with individual freedom (patient's or people in general) for the sake of a program, that professionals may not always see what will happen when they start a program; they may fail to appreciate the social forces to the point of denial of their presence.

(p. 4)

The greatest contributions to the solution of mental health problems: a contribution of Freud's namely, there is a continuity between "everyday troubles" and segregatable troubles among people. . . . [There is a] filtering . . . of this type of thinking into all levels of functioning in communities and in the public concern . . . A second great contribution is the idea that the patient can be a responsible co-planner in his care and programming. Here Dr. Lindemann mentioned Maxwell Jones, the Northfield experiment, milieu therapy and what he refers to generally as the "war experience". A third contribution . . . is the fusion at the theoretical and practical levels of psychology and bio-physiology . . . assumed under the term "psychosomatic" and Dr. Lindemann refers to the work of Stanley Cobb among others . . . especially important for the development of mental health research work in the future. A fourth great contribution has been the utilization of social science and community methods in health programming in the community mental health and psychiatric field. He obviously feels that this is the contribution that lies for the most part in the future.

(pp. 4–5)

Dr. Lindemann hopes that someday it will be possible to view all categories of behavior that are now lumped under terms like "crazy", "criminal", "sick", and "neurotically impaired" as "troubled or disturbed people in need of help" (medically) . . . some psychosocial planning group, perhaps mental health maintenance group—mental health center, would "watch all of these four groups of individuals in the community, ready to pour resources in to help these people at critical points". We need to define what we mean by emotionally disturbed. There are people with symptoms which are "normal expressions of adaptation to pathological situations, and on the other hand, there are people who have pathological situations within themselves".

(p. 5)

Difficulties that stand in the way of achieving [this approach] "(1) the structure of society, (2) traditional practices, (3) class differences with different values and prejudices built in". Plan of attack: "communities need broad mental health programming, that the clinic-structured outfits of a traditional sort are not the answer, that psychotherapy is not the answer, that we need thorough community analyses and epidemiologic orientation and concern; we need situational analyses and we need the development and utilization of preventive resources".(p. 5) What stands in the way of this?: "he stressed psychiatric training, suggesting that (1) we do not have trained people for this community approach; (2) that the choice of personality types among people going into psychiatry is not that which you would ordinarily think of as working in a community situation, but the personality type for the one-to-one clinical situation, and that (3) professional values are such that this community approach does not have much value attached to it by psychiatrists and the profession. In his present training program, Dr. Lindemann is exposing third and fourth year psychiatric trainees to this approach. During the second year, he says, this approach is too threatening to most psychiatric trainees, because they are not secure in their work with and understanding of the individual patient. After this has been achieved, their work in the community context becomes of real value of them".

(pp. 5–6)

Treatment goals: "the basic definition of the patient being disturbed or having a 'predicament' must be carefully made, because treatment means dealing with the predicament and solving the predicament by (1) changing the predicament situation itself or (2) changing the patient himself in some way to be able to deal with the life situation which has become a predicament. This involves . . . the educative process or re-education. It may also involve a process of strengthening bodily resources. Drug therapy would certainly come under this latter category. Drug intervention for large categories of people may prove to be more desirable than psychotherapy, which is based on personal relationship with the therapist and is, accordingly, very expensive. Dr. Lindemann is also interested in who the non-professional 'informal people' are who give emotional support in the community. Who are they; how can we strengthen them further?".

(p. 6)

Present treatment facilities: "Dr. Lindemann . . . referred as important developments to the open hospital and the general hospital wards, where the treatment is short-term, highly technical with many gadgets, in contrast to psychotherapy which takes more time and depends on the development of human relationships".

He wondered whether a lot of treatment could be de-centralized with treatment including not only the psychiatric contact with the patient but also work in a mental health consultation framework, pastoral care, welfare work, etc. He was sure that there was such a thing, especially in mental hospitals today, which would be seen as "negative treatment", highly damaging. . . . a lot that goes on in our mental hospitals is not "treatment" but detention, with the hospital serving the role of an inexpensive hotel or boarding home. . . . For instance, there are undoubtedly many old people who don't belong in mental hospitals but if there was planning for them or management of them, they would be in some other life situation . . . psychiatric out-patient services with the idea of psychiatrists participating in treatment planning with other medical men, playing a consultant role. . . . Dr. Lindemann stresses the importance that the role for semi-professional people be stimulated by and under the supervision of psychiatric personnel of great skill and experience.

(pp. 6–7)

We need development of roles and ideas of competence in mental health. "There are many practices that go on side by side with each other representing diametrically opposite philosophies. For instance, the roster of speakers at the forthcoming Mental Health Institute of the American Psychiatric Association does not impress Dr. Lindemann as representing the best standards in the field".

(p. 8)

Psychoanalysis offers benefits vs. is an expensive luxury for a few; private psychiatric hospitals are good for demonstration but expensive and available only for a few. Government mental hospitals are too big; size should be limited e.g. to the size of a general hospital (about 800 beds)—this would "'bring people closer together, be closer to the community, which would have an open door policy. . . [have] many activities of interest to the healthy segment of the population", leading to a transformation of mental hospitals' appearance, and have an effect on patients, and function as community institutions.

(p. 8)

Administration: Psychiatrists are leaders but not good administrators. Policy could be made by committee with psychiatric leadership. Administrators could be lay people (e.g., psychologists) who lay out programs and implement policy. Social scientists could be active agents—study or provide services in the community ("sociatrics"); "Expertness and understanding in dealing with community dynamics is just as important as understanding and dealing with individual dynamics."

(p. 9)

Programming: "With respect to dividing responsibility, Dr. Lindemann says that in his view de-centralization, individual, locally initiated programs with voluntary agencies serve traditionally to play the role of pathfinding with the state taking on the solid and proven parts of the new programming. This is the traditional pattern in New England, certainly. He said, however, in mental health work it seemed that the government was getting involved in more than simply developing programming, but was also playing a role as a motivator, an initiator, a developer of pilot projects. This seems almost like a change in the role and function of government, to be not only a law-making and enforcing agent for the people, but to get into the whole field of planning and promoting for the people".

(p. 9)

The origin of treatment facilities: Seek small community treatment units; state hospitals disappear. Need for state department of mental health to pool and compare experiments in CMH and psychiatric services. "He says that these community treatment centers and community treatment programs should not be discriminating or mixing up categories using such concepts as mental illness, criminality etc. but that implicit is the idea that communities would essentially develop an 'accepting attitude toward deviant behavior'". Tap & pull together community interest groups. Involve family, friends, and volunteers. Need more emphasis on rehabilitation, job placement, occupational therapy, and handicapped facilities.

(p. 10)

Lindemann wondered about this approach to mental health programming: "Is this medicine or religion or crusading or social work or economics etc.?"

(p. 9)

36. Caplan, Gerald, MD [professor of child psychiatry and chairperson, Department of Child Psychiatry, Hadassah University Hospital, Ein Karem, Jerusalem], Epilogue, "Personal Reflections by Gerald Caplan", in Schulberg, Herbert C. and Killilea, Marie (eds.), *The Modern Practice of Community Mental Health: A Volume in Honor of Gerald Caplan* (San Francisco: Jossey Bass, 1982), pp. 540–564.
37. Yarmolinsky, Adam, "The Politics of Morals", address to the Ethical Culture Society of Long Island, Garden City, Long Island, New York, 5/9/1965. [folder "NIMH", Box IIIA 4 (Mb-O), Erich Lindemann Collection, Center for the History of Medicine, Francis A. Countway Library of Medicine, Boston, MA]
38. Minutes 1/10/1962. [folder "Boston Mental Health Survey", Box IIIA 4 (A-E), Lindemann Collection, Center for the History of Medicine, Francis A. Countway Library of Medicine, Boston, MA]
39. Ryan, William, interview by David G. Satin in Ryan's office at Boston College, Boston, MA. [Erich Lindemann Collection, David G. Satin, Newton, MA]
40. Bigelow, Edward L., President of United Community Services of Boston, letter to Lindemann 12/30/1960. Lindeman letter to William Ryan accepting this invitation, 1/23/1961. [folder "Boston Mental Health Survey", Box IIIA 4 (A-E), Lindemann Collection, Center for the History of Medicine, Francis A. Countway Library of Medicine, Boston, MA]
41. Lindemann letters to invitees, 4/18/1962. [folder "Boston Mental Health Survey", Box IIIA 4 (A-E), Lindemann Collection, Center for the History of Medicine, Francis A. Countway Library of Medicine, Boston, MA] Among the invitees were Mr. Walter Ehlers (UCS), Mr. Edward V. Kovar (Health Division of UCS and Survey staff member), Mrs. Laura Morris (MGH Mental Health Unit), Mrs. Erich Lindemann (HRS), Dr. Marc Fried (Center for Community Studies/West End Project), Dr. Edward Ryan, Dr. William Ryan (Director of the Survey), Dr. Gerald Caplan (Division of Mental Health, HSPH), Dr. Thomas Plaut (Massachusetts Commissioner of Alcoholism), Ted O'Donnell, and Dr. Beals.
42. Advisory Committee meeing minutes, 5/27/1964, p. 2. [folder "Boston Mental Health Survey", Box IIIA 4 (A-E), Lindemann Collection, Center for the History of Medicine, Francis A. Countway Library of Medicine, Boston, MA]
43. Bigelow, Edward L., 12/30/1960, *ibid.*
44. Ryan, William, PhD and Banuazizi, Ali, PhD, "Mental Health Planning in Metropolitan Areas", *Community Psychology Monograph Series No. 1* (Boston, MA: Boston College, 1971).

45. Ryan, William, PhD and Banuazizi, Ali, PhD, "Mental Health Planning in Metropolitan Areas", *Community Psychology Monograph Series No. 1* (Boston, MA: Boston College, 1971), p. 14.
46. Kovar, Edward B. letter to Lindemann, 10/8/1965. [folder "Correspondence 1965", Box IIIA 1–3, Lindemann Collection, Center for the History of Medicine, Francis A. Countway Library of Medicine, Boston, MA]
47. Dietz, Jean, "Citizen Group to Plan Mental Health Changes", *Boston Globe*, 3/14/1965. [folder "Mental Health Planning Committee of Greater Boston", Box IV 1 + 2, Erich Lindemann Collection, Center for the History of Medicine, Francis A. Countway Library of Medicine, Boston, MA]
48. Hazard, Sprague W., MD, letter to Rhome, Mr. John O., President, United Community Services, Boston, 3/11/1968, p. 1. [folder "Correspondence 1968", Box IV 1 + 2, Erich Lindemann Collection, Center for the History of Medicine, Countway Library of Medicine, Boston, MA]
49. [folder "Boston Social Service Exchange Inc.", Box IIIA 4 (A-E), Lindemann Collection, Center for the History of Medicine, Francis A. Countway Library of Medicine, Boston, MA]
50. Minutes of the Joint Conference to Explore Data Collection for Research and Administrative Planning, First Meeting, 6/11/62, pp. 1–2. Present were (from MGH) Lindemann, John Baldwin, Fred Dewell [Duhl], Mark [Marc] Fried, Mrs. Laura Morris; Eleanor Clark unableto attend; from the Boston Social Service Exchange) Mr. C. Eliot Sands—president, Ruth Darr, Edward Landry, Dr. Katherine Spencer, Katharine Toll; Ruth Butler and Elizabeth Rice unable to attend. See also Toll, Katharine, executive director of the Boston Social Service Exchange to Lindemann, 10/19/1962. [folder "Boston Social Service Exchange Inc.", Box IIIA 4 (A-E), Lindemann Collection, Center for the History of Medicine, Francis A. Countway Library of Medicine, Boston, MA]
51. Annual Report Hall Mercer Hospital 1960–1961, 4/5/61:

> Investigative Work in the Stanley Cobb Laboratories for Psychiatric Research Involving the Staff Members of the Hall Mercer Hospital [p. 12]. . . . Dr. [John] Baldwin . . . 1. Research and work of compiling a book, Community Mental Health and Social Psychiatry: A Reference Guide. . . 2. An attempt to integrate some aspects of previous research work in the area of epidemiology of mental illness at the Human Relations Service at Wellesley. The objective is primarily the development of methods of estimating the distribution of mental health problems in a community and include: methods of identification and reporting of known mental health concerns, methods of evaluating mental health agents and other caretakers as percipients of mental health problems, and a method for spatio-temporal analysis of community populations which it is hoped might facilitate the identification of groups believed to be particularly vulnerable to mental ill health; 3. A design for a pilot study on prevalence of psychiatric and social problems in an Emergency Ward caseload . . . attempt to estimate the proportion of patients who come to the Emergency Ward for what is in effect a psychiatric or social problem and is designed to test the suggestion that very many more do so than in readily apparent from their initial complaint.
>
> (p. 13C)

[folder "Hall-Mercer Hospital Report 1948? + 1960–61", Box IIIB1b box 1 of 2, Erich Lindemann Collection, Center for the History of Medicine, Francis A. Countway Library of Medicine, Boston, MA]

52. Toll, Katharine, letters to Lindemann, 10/19 and 12/13/1962. [folder "Boston Social Service Exchange Inc.", box Human Relations Service, Elizabeth B. Lindemann, Lindemann Collection, Center for the History of Medicine, Francis A. Countway Library of Medicine, Boston, MA]

53. [folder "DMH—Blume Res—Project 1959–60"., box Human Relations Service, Elizabeth B. Lindemann, Lindemann Collection, Center for the History of Medicine, Francis A. Countway Library of Medicine, Boston, MA]

54. Dorchester Mental Health Center "Report to the Project Advisory Committee", 5/25/1961. [folder DMH—Blume Res—Project 1959–60, Lindemann Collection, Center for the History of Medicine, Francis A. Countway Library of Medicine, Boston, MA]

55. Wilensky, Harold L. and Lebeaux, Charles N., *Industrial Society and Social Welfare* (New York: Free Press, 1965), pp. 138–140, excerpted from Ryan, William, PhD, and Banuazizi, Ali, PhD, "Mental Health Planning in Metropolitan Areas", *Community Psychology Monograph Series No. 1* (Boston, MA: Boston College, 1971).

56. [folder "Mass. Mental Health Planning Project(2)", Box IIIA 4 (I-Ma), Erich Lindemann Collection, Center for the History of Medicine, Francis A. Countway Library of Medicine, Boston, MA]

57. "Massachusetts Mental Health Planning Project: Report of the Task Force on Community Mental Health Programs to the Advisory Council of the Massachusetts Mental Health Planning Project", 2/1965. [folder "S Miscellaneous", Box IIIA 4 (P-S), Erich Lindemann Collection, Center for the History of Medicine, Francis A. Countway Library of Medicine, Boston, MA]

58. Peabody, Endicott, Governor of Massachusetts, letter to Lindemann, Erich, 3/5/1964; and Lindemann, Erich, letter to Harold Demone, Director of the MMHP and Massachusetts Governor Endicott Peabody, 3/13/1964. [folder "Mass. Mental Health Planning Project(2)", Box IIIA 4 (I-Ma), Erich Lindemann Collection, Center for the History of Medicine, Francis A. Countway Library of Medicine, Boston, MA]

59. Solompn Harry C., chairperson of the Advisory Council and Massachusetts commissioner of mental health, letter to Lindemann, Erich, 12/6/1963, and Lindemann, Erich, letter to Demone, Harold, director of the MMHPP, 12/18/1963. The membership of this task force was listed as follows:

Alice Dempsey (Visiting Nurses Association, Boston)
Charles J. Littlefield (director, Public Assistance, Cambridge)
David Kantor, PhD (MMHPP)
Donald Moreland (Family Service Association of Greater Boston)
Elvin Semrad, MD (MMHC)
Erich Lindemann (MGH)
Francis DeMarneffe, MD (McLean Hospital)
Irving Fishman (state representative-Newton)
jack Consnsein (Mental Health Association of The North Shore, Inc.)
John J. Toomey (state rep).
Leston Havens MD (MMHC)
Lilly Siskind (Lawrence Guidance Center, Inc.)
Louisa Howe, PhD (HSPH)
Morris Schwartz, PhD (Brandeis University)
Murray Cohen, PhD (Boston University)
Philip Solomon, MD (HMS, Boston City Hospital; co-chairperson)
Samuel Tarnower, MD (psychiatrist, Pittsfield)
Theodore Lindberg, MD (Medfield State Hospital, chairperson)
Thomas Pugh, MD (DMH; chairperson)
William Malamud, MD (Boston University School of Medicine)

Sub Committee on Statistics:

Thomas Pugh, MD (DMH; chairperson)
Robert Hyde, MD (DMH)

Sub Committee on Public Mental Hospitals:

David W. Moriarty, MD (Worcester State Hospital; chairperson)
Dorothy Mathews (Boston State Hospital)
John Arsenian, PhD (Boston State Hospital)
Kathleen Coutou (Worcester State Hospital)
Lewis J. Sherman, PhD (Brockton Veterans Administration Hospital)
Paul Foran (Worcester State Hospital)
Fr. Wm. P. Sullivan (Metropolitan State Hospital)

Sub Committee on Private Mental Hospitals:

Francis deMarneffe, MD (McLean Hospital, chairperson)
George Macomber (Cambridge Trust Company)
Libbie Bower, PhD (Massachusetts Association for Mental Health)
Martha Brunner-Orne, MD (New England Hospital)
William. Malamud, MD (Boston University School of Medicine, University
    Hospital)
Most Rev. Thomas J. Riley (Auxiliary Bishop of Boston).

Sub Committee on Private Practice:

Jack Mendelsohn, D.D. (Arlington Street Church)
John A. Larson, MD (psychiatrist, Springfield)
Leon N. Shapiro, MD (Tufts-New England Medical Center; chairperson)
Philip Quinn, MD (St. Elizabeth's Hospital)

Sub Committee on Outpatient Services:

Elvin Semrad, MD (MMHC)
Irving Fishman (state representative—Newton)
John A. Armstrong (state representative—Plymouth)
Leston Havens, MD (MMHC; chairperson)
Louisa Howe, PhD (HSPH)
Reuben Margolin, PhD (Northeastern University)

"Report of the Task Force on Adult Mentally Ill to the Advisory Council, Massachusetts Mental Health Planning Project", 9/1964". [folder "Mass. Mental Health Planning Project(2)", Box IIIA 4 (I-Ma), Erich Lindemann Collection, Center for the History of Medicine, Francis A. Countway Library of Medicine, Boston, MA]

60. Lindemann, Erich, notes to Lindberg, Theodore, F., MD, chairperson of the Task Force on the Adult Mentally Ill, MMHPP, 1964. [folder "Mass. Mental Health Planning Project(2)", Box IIIA 4 (I-Ma), Erich Lindemann Collection, Center for the History of Medicine, Francis A. Countway Library of Medicine, Boston, MA]

61. "Report of the Task Force on Adult Mentally Ill to the Advisory Council, Massachusetts Mental Health Planning Project", 9/1964. [folder "Mass. Mental Health Planning Project(1)", Box IIIA 4 (I-Ma), Erich Lindemann Collection, Center for the History of Medicine, Francis A. Countway Library of Medicine, Boston, MA]

62. Schulberg, Herbert C. PhD, staff liaison between the MMHPP and the Task Force on Community Mental Health Programs, memo 9/18/1964. In the 1/27/1965

reports of the Task Force the following were listed as members: chairperson Jack Ewalt MD (Massachusetts Mental Health Center), Rev. Joseph Alves, PhD (Catholic Family Counseling, Inc.), Robert Arnot, M.D (Association of General Hospital Psychiatrists), Libbie Bower, PhD (MAMH), Gerald Caplan, MD (Harvard Medical School), Saul Cooper (South Shore Mental Health Center), Bardwell Flower, MD (Worcester State Hospital), Bellenden R. Hutcheson, MD (Massachusetts DMH), Erich Lindemann, MD (MGH), Howard Parad MSW (Smith College School of Social Work), John L. Quigley (Massachusetts Hospital Association), Wiliam Ryan, PhD (Massachusetts Committee on Children and Youth), Philip Solomon, MD (HMS and Boston City Hospital), Norman Zinberg, MD (Beth Israel Hospital, Boston); staff liaison Herbert C. Schulberg, PhD (MMHPP). [folder "Mass. Mental Health Planning Project(2)", Box IIIA 4 (I-Ma), Erich Lindemann Collection, Center for the History of Medicine, Francis A. Countway Library of Medicine, Boston, MA]

63. Report of the Task Force on Adult Mentally Ill to Advisory Council, Massachusetts Mental Health Planning Project, 9/1964. [folder "Mass. Mental Health Planning Project(2)", Box IIIA 4 (I-Ma), Erich Lindemann Collection, Center for the History of Medicine, Francis A. Countway Library of Medicine, Boston, MA]

64. Report of the Task Force on Community Mental Health Programs to the Advisory Council of the Massachusetts Mental Health Planning Project, Second Draft, 1/27/1965. [folder "Mass. Mental Health Planning Project(2)", Box IIIA 4 (I-Ma), Erich Lindemann Collection, Center for the History of Medicine, Francis A. Countway Library of Medicine, Boston, MA]

65. Massachusetts Mental Health Planning Project: Report of the Task Force on Community Mental Health Programs to the Advisory Council of the Massachusetts Mental Health Planning Project, Second Draft, 2/1965.

"The major goal assigned the Mental Health Planning Project in July 1963 was the development of a comprehensive plan through which the Commonwealth's mental health services could assume a community orientation". The task force met weekly 10/64–2/65 and included representatives from the cities of Pittsfield, Lowell, and Quincy. It developed concepts of CMH, their implications for the provision of services, and the relationship between mental health programs and local communities. "With the passage of Public Law 88–164 in October 1963, the new age of community mental health was officially ushered onto the scene. Regulations pertinent to the Community Mental Health Centers Act were published by the U.S. Public Health Service on May 6, 1964. . . although the concept of community mental health is not an entirely new one. . . . widespread acceptance and implementation of this concept is expected to produce radical changes in the national picture during the coming decades. . . . The concept of community mental health may truly be said to have undergone much of its theoretical gestation and experimental development in this state. However, . . . a significant gap still remains between what is now available and what is actually necessary".

(pp. 1–2)

Basic rationale: 1. Patient needs is the focus, 2. Programs should be comprehensive (case finding, screening, investigation, diagnosis, treatment, rehabilitation, and consultation), 3. The goal is to return the patients to their ordinary life situations (not remake them), 4. Minimize intervention to maximize patient and environment strengths. 5. Move patients through systems as quickly as possible to avoid regression. 6. Maintain continuity of treatment relationships. 7. Establish communication and participation (among psychiatric units, medical resources, community agencies, and institutions). Differences in philosophy should not prevent primary and secondary prevention, coordination with other resources, staff allocation to indirect services (to spread limited resources), recognize the capabilities of others (e.g., at South Shore Mental Health Center 45% of staff time is spent in consultation and education work; at Northland MHC (Minnesota) 47% is so spent), Mental health professionals have varied roles. There is a need for preplanning by CMHC director with the community, and stability of unique personnel. There is a need for readjustment of practices and organization; DMH needs to reorient the use of mental health resources to CMH, including state hospitals, child guidance clinics, teaching hospitals and medical schools, and general hospitals.

(pp. 12–13, 17)

C. Citizen Participation in Programs . . . the need to have the community mental health center obtain true citizen participation in its efforts via some type of formal administrative structure". . . . "the Task force recommends the establishment of a <u>formal</u> Community Governing Board . . . it is recognized that the Governor may well be unwilling to forsake his power of making political appointments. . . . it is suggested, therefore, that the Governor retain this prerogative but that the new Governing Board be augmented through the selection of at least a majority of its members by other sources, e.g. the Commissioner of Mental Health, selectmen and community council, etc. to insure representation for such community interests as local government, community welfare councils, mental health associations, medical and other professional societies, clergy, schools, business, labor, etc. Such diverse interests are influential in the community's general decision-making process and their involvement will become increasingly meaningful and valuable as the mental health program becomes an integral force for serving the community's needs. The Task Force recommends that the Board's total membership be composed of a ratio of one professional to three non-professionals so that technical information will be available while also insuring that the broad interests of the community are represented. . . . The Task Force recommends that the Board . . . be delegated these types of authority: 1. Establishing policy and program priorities for the services offered by the community mental health center. (. . . The manner of actually providing clinical services is a professional decision and should remain within the clinician's scope of responsibility.) 2. Bearing responsibility for approving the center's annual budget request to the Department of Mental Health. 3. Bearing responsibility for providing long-term planning and continual surveillance of the changing needs of the community so that service programs may be modified as indicated. 4. Approving the Department of Mental Health's nomination for the Center's Director and Associate Director. 5. Serving as a primary liaison between the local community and its mental health center. 6. Serving as primary liaison between the local mental health center and the Department of Mental Health and the Legislature. . . . It is the Task Force's understanding that a major facet of the Planning Project's current activity is directed toward clarification of . . . how to promote citizen participation in mental health programs . . . and reaffirms its fullest support for this truly basic principle in the concept of community mental health.

(pp. 20–3)

U.S. Department of Health, Education and Welfare Regulations: Community Mental Health Centers Act 1963, Federal Register, 5/6/64: The state plan

> shall provide for adequate community mental health facilities for the provision of programs of comprehensive mental health services to all persons residing in the state and for furnishing such services to persons unable to pay therefore.
>
> (pp. 7–8)

For CMHC to serve a population of 75,000–200,000, it requires at least five essential elements: inpatient, outpatient, partial hospitalization, emergency, consultation, and education. For "adequate" services, include also diagnosis, rehabilitation (including vocational and educational), community precare and aftercare, training, and research and evaluation. Services may be given by a combination of agencies with formal agreements.
  CMH-Theo

B. Principles of Community Mental Health

In spite of the widespread support which is now being evinced for community mental health programs, it is important to remember that this concept still represents many different things to different people. To some [traditionalists], the essence . . . is its physical location in the very midst of a population center, thus bringing regular psychiatric services closer to its patients and permitting the utilization of such facilities as the general hospital. To others [Lindemann,] . . . the essence of the program lies in its philosophy that provision of comprehensive mental health services . . . requires the cooperation and participation of all segments of the community's power structure and caregiving system. Consequently, the skills of more than the traditional psychiatric team are utilized . . . increased involvement of the community's lay and professional network. . . . To still others [social radicals], the essential quality of a community mental health program is not rooted primarily in the character of the services which it provides but more importantly in the fact that a local citizen group assumes responsibility for program planning and development.

(p. 2)

Some traditional mental health professionals restrict their practices to patient groups of interest to them; CMH professionals accept responsibility for all in the community, who are defined as having psychiatric disorders; are diagnosed as being physically ill; or are socially, educationally, occupationally, or religiously disordered. The CMH professional function is fundamentally different—it deals in large populations, indirect services, and prevention and considers a total population.

> the Task Force. . . [had] differing viewpoints, which . . . can be described as representing the medical and social system models. The medical model was characterized as having a structural arrangement in which the mental health center, under medical leadership, assumes responsibility and supervision for all of the community's mental health services. The resources of other agencies are clearly seen as being of value but as functioning in a basically supporting role. The other model posed was the social system one, whose structural arrangement and network of liaisons are such as to designate the mental health center as just one of a variety of relevant community resources. All participate in cooperative ways to serve the mental health needs of the citizens. . . . This problem will become even

more widespread as mental health programs develop interest in the area of primary prevention and begin to engage in activities which traditionally have been within the domain of social and welfare agencies. When attacking the disturbances produced by such problems as economic deprivation the classical medical model is clearly not applicable since the initiative and active participation of social-welfare agencies is necessary for therapeutic success. In fact, it has been theoretically conjectured that primary prevention potentially stems most from the areas of economics and politics, and is mainly outside the social, health, and welfare systems entirely.

(p. 13)

III Summary

The patient (not institution) is the central focus of the program, there is continuity of care, there is cooperation between the CMHC and community health and welfare agencies, there is increased emphasis on primary and secondary prevention (consultation, education, and interagency planning) and less on direct services, complementary resources are used (including evaluating the potential constructiveness of others), local programs are tailored by community consensus including early in the process of hiring the director and then prepping the community for the program, involving and coordinating existing resources, integrating government and general hospitals and private practitioners, in the DMH expanding state hospitals and mental hygiene clinics to participate in CMH, and citizen participation via Community Governing Boards (no more than one quarter traditional professionals) to do long-term planning and policy and program priorities.

(pp. 25–6)
[folder "S Miscellaneous", Box IIIA 4 (P-S), Erich Lindemann Collection, Center for the History of Medicine, Francis A. Countway Library of Medicine, Boston, MA]

66. Greenblatt, Milton, *Psychopolitics* (New York: Grune & Stratton, 1978).
67. Greenblatt, Milton, 1978, *ibid.*, p. 6.
68. Laswell, Harold D., *Psychopathology and Politics* (New York: Viking Press, 1960), pp. 74–77.
69. Lindemann, Erich: "Relationships with Decision-Makers; from 'Preventive Intervention as an Instrument in Community Psychiatry", talk at dedication of the Suicide Prevention Center, Los Angeles, CA., 4/7/1963, pp. 1–2. [Box XII 2 folder "Lindemann—Relationships with Decision-Makers-4-7-63", Erich Lindemann Collection, Center for the History of Medicine, Francis A. Countway Library of Medicine, Boston, MA]
70. Greenblatt, Milton, 1978, *ibid.*, p. 43.

5 Academic and Professional Involvement

The Medical School and the Community Mental Health Center: The Southern Regional Education Board Meeting, December 13–15, 1966

Because of the special status of and the influence on society and CMH of the professions of psychiatry and medicine, and of academia and academic institutions, they merit specific exploration.

Psychiatry had been considered the dominant discipline in mental health, including in CMH.[1] This was ensconced in legislation, including the administration of mental hospitals. As CMH practice grew, psychiatry faced overt and covert challenges from other disciplines considering themselves more appropriate or supplemental to psychiatry, leading to tension and turmoil, jurisdictional battles, and/or adjustments among collaborators in this quickly growing field. While psychiatry staked out fields of practice and status, social work, psychology, and psychiatric nursing grew through theoretical justification, skills, training, hiring, and an expansion of functions. It became clear that roles and jurisdictions had to be negotiated in each institution; professional theory and law could not settle these relationships.

Financial support for behavioral science teaching in medical schools came mainly—90%–95%—from the NIMH and NIH, with the Department of Defense making large contributions and the National Science Foundation much less.[2] Most was focused on psychiatry and mental health. There was much resistance to expanding psychiatry beyond mental illness, such as to human development and the behavioral sciences more generally. Only two medical schools had independent behavioral science programs, including the Department of Behavioral Science at the University of Kentucky under Robert Strauss.

A greatly illuminating view of the relationship of medical education to CMH came out of the conference held in Atlanta, Georgia, December 13–15, 1966, sponsored by the Southern Regional Education Board and the National Institute of Mental Health (contract no. PH-43-67-43). It clearly shows the apprehensions and conflicts within psychiatry and academia in regard to social psychiatry and CMH on the eve of massive efforts in this direction, and it merits a detailed review here.[3]

I Introduction

In 1965–6, almost all departments of psychiatry in the US South paid attention to community psychiatry, though varying from a cursory exposure of residents "with a feeling that community psychiatry was perhaps only a passing fad"[4] to the development of divisions of community psychiatry with post-residency training programs. However, almost all shared the idea that residents should be prepared for CMHC work in the future. Some medical schools were constructing CMHCs or affiliating with them for teaching purposes. All shared the same problems. The NIMH enthusiastically supported a conference of regional medical centers and states, including 25 medical school departments of psychiatry; schools and departments of nursing, social work, vocational counseling, and psychology; departments of public health and mental health; and community agencies. Dr. Leigh Roberts defined "community psychiatry" as "a subspecialty of psychiatry, focusing on the prevention, diagnosis, treatment and rehabilitation of emotional illness and its sequella in a given population".[5] In community psychiatry, individuals and the CMHC are responsible for clinical service to individuals with a population/catchment area focus, "and the center is responsible for the development of generally good mental health in that population".[6] Medical schools and departments of psychiatry were used to placing service secondary to teaching and research and not having total service responsibility, including community planning and action. In contrast, these community and social responsibilities were familiar to agricultural college extension programs and in the community extension arms of academic programs in business, welfare, engineering, industrial relations, urban planning, public health, etc. Clark Kerr, president of the University of California listed in his key book *The Uses of the University* as a major use of the university "involvement in the life of society", especially public service. Since disciplines other than psychiatry work in the CMHC, multidisciplinary practice is a characteristic of CMH. Questions arise about the CMHC having the function of teaching training, how to include research and the roles of social scientists, how to organize mental health services, sources of funding (including for teaching), the administrative organization, staff scopes of service and appointments, and relations with the university, community service agencies, and government entities.

II Is Community Psychiatry a Medical School Obligation?

Reference is made to Israel Zwerling and Milton Rosenbaum of the Albert Einstein College of Medicine, who saw community psychiatry as new in terms of including the social sciences and scientists; diagnostic formulations, including social reactions in addition to intrapsychic conflicts; etiology, including social systems; treatment, including intervention in social and environmental structures; and the locus of practice in community sites. Community psychiatry receives much attention because of the increasingly inadequate supply of psychiatrists and the increasing demand for mental health services due to third-party financing, welfare programs, and the civil rights movement. Psychiatry must meet CMH needs; otherwise, other disciplines will take leadership. Psychiatry has traditionally focused on research, teaching, and the private practice of individual therapy. Will it take up a community focus including non-medical factors? General psychiatric training can include community psychiatry or separately recruit community psychiatry trainees. Training in treatment of individuals can be scheduled before or after community psychiatry. Medical students can be taught community psychiatry via medical sociology courses. Service obligations can be of various sizes. Increased federal funding for community psychiatry vies with the dedication of the department chairperson and senior faculty to individual therapy. While community psychiatry is taught as a subspecialty in departments of psychiatry,[7] "We believe that in time we will witness the emergency of social and community psychiatry as a related but separate discipline from psychiatry", focusing on mental illness as an interpersonal and social process.

Several problems arise in establishing community psychiatry in academic departments traditionally oriented to individual biological and psychological medicine practice: difficulty in defining goals and means, doctor–patient vs. ecological focus, and blurring of disciplinary roles without guides (such as the question of medical leadership). CMH is needed, and medical schools and universities need to be informed and play their roles with CMHCs as training and practice sites. Difficulties arise regarding the relationship of the medical school and the CMHC:

> Some of us see service and education as not only compatible, but also mutually beneficial. Some of us, however, are fearful that too heavy a commitment to community service by a medical school may be detrimental to its primary educational function. . . . Many persons conceived of community psychiatry as dealing with a few selected community agencies; almost none conceived of it as assuming responsibility for the comprehensive mental health of the entire population.[8]

III Planning the CMHC—Problems the Medical School Encounters

The medical school administration and the department of psychiatry faculty need a clear idea of what a CMHC is. They can then continue traditional organization and practice or change and innovate. At the Southern Regional Education Board conference there was consensus that teaching centers should use CMHCs as teaching sites but wariness about overloading trainees with service responsibilities. Types of involvements was reported: CMHCs only as clinical teaching sites and medical schools in charge of training and community and government bodies in control of services and funding or the CMHC as one elective site with affiliated faculty supervising at the CMHCs. It suggested that it would be a problem for senior medical students and psychiatric residents to have non-medical professionals (nurses, social workers, etc.) take on independent clinical responsibility, leading to administrative responsibility. Should psychiatrists direct the CMHCs or only the clinical services? Would this decision influence medical centers regarding delegating administration to nonphysicians? Team treatment and supervision would decrease the responsibility of individual physicians. This situation would offer the opportunity for the department of psychiatry to lead the medical school toward community relations and treatment innovation:

> Those departments that feel psychiatry has a major contribution to make in resolving social crises facing us today will find the comprehensive community health center an excellent vehicle for channeling these efforts. Those who do not, will find it a disturbing interruption in "business as usual".[9]

Thus, there was clear disagreement between those who favored the university taking responsibility for the total CMHC, including cost and service, and those favoring using part of the CMHC and leaving the community responsible for cost and service.

IV *Programming the Services*

Adult and child services must be changed, not just expanded. This involves working with social milieu factors and agencies, population responsibilities, and community sites. Nonclinical services are important and federally mandated, including mental health education, promotion, prevention, consultation, and social action. CMHC services should not take funds only for clinical service; like medicine, it is responsible for prevention. The programs must be worthy of community support and be a part of the community. Discussion focused on nonclinical services to be offered mostly by nonpsychiatrists and consultation mostly to clinical service agencies. There was no discussion of education and prevention.

V *Training of All Kinds of Workforce in Teaching CMHCs*

Practice should develop toward comprehensive healthcare, including social factors and function, not just the model of medical diagnosis and treatment. Contact between psychiatric and other medical specialties should be increased, and the training of nonmedical professions and pre-professionals should be considered.

VI *Financing and Administration*

Finances: In fiscal year 1966, the NIMH funded 126 CMHCs, 15 of which were sponsored by or affiliated with medical teaching centers: 70% of teaching center–affiliated CMHCs were in metropolitan areas. The average staffing grant for new services in these teaching CMHCs ($300,000) approximated that for nonteaching CMHCs ($280,000), but the initial total costs were higher ($1,260,000 vs. $780,000) and they had higher state support promised for the future (40% vs. 22%), lower local funding (1% vs. 9%). Of these CMHC programs, 86% were focused programs within older organizations (e.g., departments of psychiatry) that continued broader programs; all had more comprehensive programs; and 84% started all services immediately. They had more staff for the centers (most not grant funded), had more psychiatrists (average of six new and more not grant funded vs. average of 3.4), and had limited community liaison: one planned by the community and two by local board sanction and one active and one planned community advisory board. Trainees needed training for a nonacademic setting.

Administration: There was need for experience in public administration and financing and for careful planning and staging:

> Those who represent the leadership of your department will have the responsibility of cushioning the reverberations set off within a university department of psychiatry with the introduction of a major community-oriented service, teaching, and research program. The new enterprise may be seen as the intrusion of a foreign body into a well-functioning system or the painful but natural growth of a dynamic department. . . . Another factor that will surely strike at some stage of developing of such an enterprise is the total unpreparedness many of you have had for the tasks facing you. . . . The university must decide what business it is in. If learning is its mission, each department must decide learning for what, and for whom. Each of you must also come to understand the particular place your medical school plays in your community.[10]

VII *CMHC Relations*

To the university:[11] Social psychiatry is the application of social science to psychiatric problems. Community psychiatry and CMH apply social psychiatry to treatment and research but are not tied to application. It must stick to research, training, and the university; otherwise, it will fail as the mental hygiene movement did: "lost momentum because it was not sufficiently university connected".[12] The CMHC is a laboratory for natural research and training. The university recruits its staff, helps the state plan for CMH, and addresses community health and social factors in medical schools. Universities and psychiatrists should avoid self-aggrandizement and exceeding legitimate expertise.

In the discussion, it was suggested that community psychiatry can be taught without a CMHC affiliation, "but it was emphasized that teaching is usually effective only where teachers do what they teach".[13] There was ambivalence about catchment area responsibility, with the suggestion that local authorities have responsibility for the CMHC and the state for psychiatric service and that the medical school should not extend too far into service responsibility. The state department of mental health would take prime responsibility for the CMHC and include universities in funding-expanded facilities and in planning. Universities should take advantage of this opportunity.

To community agencies: Opt for limited relationships for fear of overwhelming service demands.

To the state: Patient care is a state responsibility, 75%–90% of patients are transferred to CMHCs with state support. Changed and expanded professional roles lead to creative developments but role confusion.

After experience in academia, CMHCs, and administration, Miles Shore observed that although academic medical centers resisted CMH, they were influenced by it: They developed community approaches to medicine, such as community health centers.[14]

Viola W. Bernard

Viola Bernard was a psychoanalyst who expanded this foundation to a dedication to and activity in social and community psychiatry in New York as Lindemann had in Boston. Her dedicated and broad efforts to install social psychiatry and CMH in academia and in the community strikingly parallel Lindemann's and show the multiple foci of such CMH development. It is an example of academic insularity that these two pioneers knew little of one another and worked independently.[15]

Bernard came from a liberal, public-spirited family of multiple outstanding talents:[16] Her father owned the United Cigar Company and cofounded the Federated Jewish Philanthropies. Her brother, Maurice Wertheim, briefly owned the journal *The Nation*. Her daughter was the social historian Barbara Tuchman.

In 1936, Bernard was one of the few female graduates of the Cornell Medical College and completed psychoanalytic training at the New York Psychoanalytic Institute. Before World War II, she worked for refugees: from 1939 to 1945, she opened her family home in Nyack, New York, as a hostel for war refugees, and she sponsored many immigrants who were fleeing the Nazis. In 1942, she was a cofounder of the Columbia

University Center for Psychoanalytic Training and Research, and in 1946, she was a cofounder of the Group for the Advancement of Psychiatry (GAP)—the liberal counterbalance to the American Psychiatric Association. Kelly, her colleague and biographer, characterized her as devoted to the poor and disadvantaged, an activist for social justice and world peace, and an opponent of bigotry in social and professional settings— e.g., in the 1950s and 1960s, she worked to open psychiatric and psychoanalytic training to black physicians. From 1963, she was active in the Pugwash Conferences on Science and World Affairs, involving behavioral scientists in scientific efforts to reduce the risk of nuclear war. And she participated in the 1960 Mediterranean Congress of Culture—a forum to promote world peace; a publication in 1970 addressed psychological aspects of chemical and biological weapons.

"Dr. Bernard was committed to the fundamental principles of psychoanalysis, but remained open to new concepts and techniques that met the realities of a changing world".[17] She was inspired by Marion Kenworthy, one of the first psychiatrists to bring psychodynamic psychiatry into the teaching of casework in schools of social work. As a first-year psychiatric resident at Cornell University, she found the training dull until she met the dynamic Kenworthy and audited her courses. Bernard was concerned about the inequity and injustice of the financial obstacles that limited access to psychiatric help. Her political and sociological interests in interracial, interprofessional, and nonpsychiatric settings led her into community psychiatry and community mental health. She applied psychoanalytic and public health (prevention as well as treatment) approaches to social problems, including war (conventional and nuclear), urban unrest, poverty, and racism:[18]

> contributions from psychiatry and psychoanalysis to the understanding of social issues can and should be made, insofar as those issues bear on mental health and illness. Furthermore, it is my conviction that we carry a responsibility to seek the effective use of our understanding, through professionally appropriate measures.

She addressed the objections to professional involvement in social issues, namely that psychiatrists would lose objectivity and exceed their competence and mission: "such social problems do have relevance for mental health and illness, and that we would be failing in our proper professional responsibilities if we didn't address ourselves to them".

Bernard convinced the New York Psychoanalytic Institute board of directors to allow third-year training credit for two half-years of work in the Harlem Unit of the New York City Board of Education's Child Guidance Clinic. Thereafter, she became a psychiatric consultant to adoption and other social agencies, the Bank Street College of Education, guidance programs in the Ethical Culture Society schools, and (through a close family relation with a judge) the Domestic Relations Court.

Experience with social work brought to the fore the multiplier effect of a consultation approach as compared with the limited efficiency of treatment of individual patients by psychoanalysts or psychotherapists. Recognizing the interaction rather than mutual exclusion of the social and inner world led to conviction in favor of the collaborative, biopsychosocial approach.[19] This led to her editing a book on the reciprocity between psychoanalysis and social psychiatry and writing the article "Some Applications of Psychiatry and Psychoanalysis to Social Problems".[20] After chairing the Commission on Children and Adolescents, she brought the issue of social psychiatry to the American Psychiatric Association's Ninth Council on Children, Adolescents, and Their Families. She maintained her identity as a physician, child psychiatrist, and psychoanalyst, though she believed that she was always drawn to stepchildren, whether they be individuals, minority populations, or unconventional professions (such as psychiatry) and professional interests (such as child and social psychiatry).

In the 1940s, Bernard helped establish the Columbia Psychoanalytic Institute, one of the first university-based analytic institutes, for analysts who broke away from the New York Psychoanalytic Institute, eliciting mixed reactions. She was also the first administrator of a low-fee clinic, later emulated by other psychoanalytic institutes.

At Columbia University, Bernard developed the Division of Community Psychiatry, a collaboration between the College of Physicians and Surgeons (the medical school) and the School of Public Health and Administrative Medicine. It developed many programs in child psychiatry, administration, etc. and sought to convince the National Board of Psychiatry and Neurology (which credentials psychiatrists) to include in its examination the test of knowledge of community mental health. In the 1960s, when the NIMH funded four regional programs for leaders in university psychiatry programs, Bernard was on the planning committee and directed the New York conference. She was involved in the Citizens Committee for Children, composed of volunteer professionals and sophisticated citizens and functioning as a watchdog over government services for children in New York City. This and other evaluation and advisory projects encouraged child mental health services to become more comprehensive and to incorporate community services. The division also developed within the Columbia Psychiatry Institute a community service program for local residents, through which all psychiatry residents rotated for training.

The Special Committee on Social and Physical Environment Variables as Determinants of Mental Health

The Special Committee on Social and Physical Environment Variables as Determinants of Mental Health (in the period of enthusiasm for space exploration fondly referred to by its members as the Space Cadets) is an interesting example of an influential voluntary interest group demonstrating CMH's stimulation of creative thinking in experts from a wide range of disciplines and nations. It began with Leonard Duhl, psychiatrist, psychoanalyst, and public health officer, who had a career in the US Public Health Service (USPHS) under the Kennedy administration and then continued a public health, social psychiatry career in academia and national and international organizations. He made use of his position as psychiatrist in the Professional Services Branch of NIMH and later as chief of the NIMH Office of Planning to convene a discussion and mutual consultation group,[21] meeting twice a year, including people from the fields of animal behavior, architecture, astronomy, biology, community development, environmental protection, futurists, international relations, international studies, landscape architecture, law, mathematics, medicine, military quartermaster office, opinion surveying, pediatrics, planning, political science, politics, psychology, psychiatry, public health, public policy, publishing, sociology, urban studies, and zoology.[22] He saw it as a forum for incubating ideas on social psychiatry from many disciplinary sources.[23] John Seeley saw it as a group offering support for many nonconformists who overlapped traditional fields, such as biological mathematics (Nicholas Rashevsky), astronomical mathematics (John Q. Stewart), animal ethology (John Calhoun), sociology (Herbert Gans), psychoanalysis and community psychiatry (Erich Lindemann), and philosophy (Center for the Study and Democratic Institutions).[24] Seeley saw his role as interpreting and clarifying the commonalities among the contributions.

The first meeting took place on May 28, 1956, in which its members learned to communicate and agreed that the physical environment modifies behavior.[25] It recognized that practical planners wanted a formula for this effect, but scientists had not yet developed a theory or formulated the concept for its practical use. At the second meeting, on October 11–12, 1956, the goal was to formulate a definition of this effect and make it practically available. Lindemann chaired one of the sessions on communities facing imminent drastic change in the physical environment (an interest no doubt stimulated by his experience with the urban development of the West End of Boston and the West End Study). This committee's focus was on transition points in community life, forecasting them and planning interventions that would be acceptable to community powers. It explored patterns in community power structure, community values and preservation, the education of children in these values, controlling deviance, and how welfare and health resources deal with casualties. Lindemann gave papers on his consultation in India[26] and the South Pacific Commission regarding urbanization.[27] The committee contributed to the publication *The Urban Condition*[28] and studies of those who served in the Peace Corps.

Duhl thought this environment contributed to Lindemann's appreciation of the social dimension of CMH.[29]

Lindemann benefited most from the sharing of substance and attitude.[30] He believed that he developed few close relationships—Duhl, journalist Robert Gough, and (sharing some interests with) psychiatrist Louis Jolyon ("Jolly") West (though he remembers West going through a year of crisis and choosing opportunities for power rather than wisdom). However, in some ways, he maintained a network of relationships with the group.

Meetings were devoted to clarifying concepts and sharing research projects, including some of the seminal issues and projects of the time. (Topics and presenters are listed in the endnotes.)[31] The Space Cadets met again in March 1966. At that time, Leonard Duhl changed his position from NIMH to the office of the undersecretary of Housing and Urban Development, and there was concern that this project of his would end.[32] The Space Cadets are credited with supporting funding of three major CMH research studies: Herbert Gans's *The Urban Villagers* (1982), Eliot Liebow's *Tally's Corner* (1967), and Lee Rainwater's *Behind Ghetto Walls* (1973).[33]

The US federal government struggled with these social and intellectual currents in deciding on the government's role in healthcare. Duhl reported to the committee on the NIMH's broader program in the behavioral sciences. He was involved in planning for large research grants, though the decision was made to develop this area (except for projects with mental health relevance) through the NIH Division of General Medical Sciences, excluding Duhl from official involvement in program development.[34]

Among those who participated in the Space Cadets, Robert Felix (founder and first director of the NIMH) also looked to a broad concept of mental health and the federal government's role in it:[35]

> Any attempt toward solution which rests on one-shot schemes and neglects the application and integration of our total human resources and knowledge, is doomed to fail. Our considerations cannot and must not rest solely on a treatment basis—on therapies to the exclusion of prevention, on repair to the neglect of positive mental health. Important and pressing as treatment requirements are, the total effort must be built upon the sum of all of the talents and facilities which every community can muster. Fundamental to strategic planning is the recognition of individual community needs and responsibilities. . . . Too frequently they [mental health services] have arisen as creations of expediency and in response to special group pressures. Fragmented services and special autonomous operations that serve only a segment of the total community needs have added to the confusion and uncertainty that beset the public mind and have complicated and interfered with the professional and organized

approaches. . . . not infrequently there later appears a tendency to resist the development of community-wide, well-integrated programs because of fear of loss of prestige, prerogatives or independence on the part of the established agencies. This . . . has resulted in reliance on improvisations rather than soundly conceived service

. . .

A second and overlapping [with professional mental health workers] group of people whose activities must be integrated are those who have been called the community's opinion leaders and caretakers. . . . Ultimately we might expect the efforts of the key persons to be a major force in creating a therapeutic environment in which a contagion of health might exist. Such an environment would tend to reduce the incidence of mental illness and permit the management and treatment of the less seriously ill in the community.

John Knowles quoted several authors in seeing a public health and moral obligation here:[36]

- "The high esteem of psychology and science in the American culture both emphasizes and expresses this sense of dependency in the search for good health. . . . In relative terms, the individual may come to feel more dependent on psychotherapy, on medical science, on the doctors; less on his own inner resources". (Titmuss, R.M., "Essays on the Welfare State" [New Haven: Yale University Press, 1959] pp. 133, 134)
- "[H]ealth has become a basic human birthright in America and like other birthrights, it is being identified by increasing numbers as a function of government". A healthy citizenry is not only a nation's most important "natural resource" but also a prime aspiration of any government whose effectiveness is defined in terms of its ability to serve the best interests of all the individuals who make up the society. (National Advisory Committee to the Surgeon General, "Medical Care in the United States", U.S. Dept. of Health, Education and Welfare, U.S. Public Health Service, 3/61; [pp. 1, 2])

He was apprehensive about the biological ideology that was later incorporated: "I cannot believe that this is all good, what with such problems as . . . excessive emphasis on biological research".

This brief report of the Space Cadets adds another bit of color to the tapestry of efforts—pro and con—in the CMH movement.

Psychoanalysis

As discussed previously, psychoanalysis was conflicted over social and community psychiatry. The American Psychoanalytic Association's Committee on Social Issues was founded in 1962 at the time of the

Berlin airlift[37],[38] feeling that "analysts, by virtue of their theory of human motivation and their experience with patients, might make meaningful contributions to the understanding of national and international social problem". On the other hand, Shore skeptically wondered whether psychoanalysis contributed to CMH indirectly via motivating those rejected for analytic training to fight back by attacking it in the name of CMH.[39] Early committee members "showed great initiative in tackling a wide range of issues. They were more active, while we today are more reactive"—regarding threats to personal liberty, privacy and professional confidentiality, and the Department of Health and Human Services rule requiring gynecologists to notify parents of minors seeking contraception or abortion. The committee studied social issues, including homosexuality, abortion, racism, and child abuse. The committee, study groups, and workshops developed an instrument to describe the development, course, and problems of CMH programs.[40] It was tried out on presentations about the Cincinnati and Pittsburgh programs, was found to need concrete examples, and was too sensitive to exploding events, and so it was not used. An early interdisciplinary group studied the psychological development of international political leaders through their biographies. Analysts worked with police departments on the selection of recruits and coping with the stresses and anxiety of their job. Robert Dorn at the UCLA Medical School studied children at high risk for social trauma. Viola Bernard initiated a 25-year-long vulnerable child seminar, and Stanley Cath initiated a paternity seminar.

The Boston Psychoanalytic Society and Institute maintained the identity of psychoanalysis separate from CMH:[41]

> we in Boston believe that psychoanalysis is a science in its own right, separate and distinct from other disciplines. . . . The American Psychoanalytic Association was alerted to the dangers in permitting the confusion and diffusion of psychiatry, psychotherapy and psychoanalysis to take place.

If we as a local group can constantly remind our parent organization that it must stand firm, take a position for psychoanalysis, and that it is strong within, then there is nothing to fear from without—be it the American Psychiatric Association or the Academy of Psychoanalysis.

It resisted the incursion of other therapies:[42] "Dr. [John M.] Murray felt that the economic and social pressures of our changing times would create a new situation in terms of available therapy and a lowering of standards; that we should take whatever steps were necessary to retain priority and our standards". There was some suggestion of more openness in the 1960 Code of Professional Ethics (revised):[43]

> 2. The Analyst in Relation to the Institute . . . 3) Every instructor should be free to present the concepts of psychoanalysis according to

his convictions and understanding. Differences of opinion should be expressed openly in a scientific manner by the objective presentation of pros and cons of the differences for further discussion.

In 1961, Roy Grinker invited Lindemann to become a fellow of The Academy of Psychoanalysis.[44] This group promoted communication among analysis and other science and humanities, was interested in inquiry into individual motivation and social behavior, encouraged psychoanalytic research, and fostered the acceptance of analysis and its integration into university study.

In the mid 1960s, the Boston Psychoanalytic Society and Institute initiated some exploration into social psychiatry and CMH:[45]

- On December 11, 1963, Frances Bonner was elected a member of the APA's Committee on Social Problems.
- On May 2, 1963, Joseph Michaels proposed that this committee initiate its first project on the prevention of mental disease on the basis of psychoanalytic knowledge.
- On May 2, 1963, the Committee on Public Information (Dr. Burness E. Moore, chairperson) proposed a study of psychoanalytic knowledge applicable to the prevention of mental disease, a questionnaire to APA members about their interests and activities in this area, and the formulation and communication of psychoanalytic knowledge. It planned a conference about such projects that was attended by analysts representing institutes. It considered a classification of problems:

  a) group psychological processes including the influence of leadership which would have bearing on international tensions, etc.; b) the effect on individuals of modern culture including the changing family structure, urbanization, etc. . . . d) socio-clinical areas including alcoholism, delinquency, drug addiction, etc.[46]

- There was discussion of a position statement by the APA, *Action for Mental Health*, presented by Burness Moore.[47] It addressed comprehensive care, focusing on the mentally healthy as well as the ill and emphasizing prevention.
- On January 8, 1964, a report of recent library acquisitions included Leonard Duhl's *The Urban Condition*.

After Lindemann's painful experiences with the Boston Psychoanalytic Society and Institute in the 1950s, he was discouraged about organized psychoanalysis. He worked outside organized psychoanalysis and as much with the social sciences as with medicine. He was spread so thin with his many interests and responsibilities that he had only a peripheral involvement with the American Psychoanalytic Society, unlike Viola

Bernard, who worked to bring social psychiatry into organized psychoanalysis. He did continue some involvement in the Boston group through 1955, serving as training analyst for Benjamin D. Paul, PhD (a "C" candidate in the Institute),[48] and accepted an invitation to serve as one of two discussants of Alfred Stanton's presentation of ideas on his program for McLean Hospital: "Psychoanalysis and Psychiatry: Considerations Regarding a Psychiatric Hospital Program" on February 29, 1956.[49] Also, in 1957, Lindemann was invited to write one of a continuing series of articles on psychoanalysis in response to articles by D. Fedotov, the director of the Institute of Psychiatry in the USSR Ministry of Health. Despite its claimed respect for scientists in all fields and nationalities, it labeled psychoanalysis and Freud as antiscientific and retrogressive in thinking in science in comparison with Pavlov's materialist concept of the higher nervous system and science.[50] However, Lindemann was not listed as an officer, committee member, or in attendance at the society in 1957–1958.

Despite the ambivalence and sometimes hostility toward CMH of organized psychoanalysis, his personal experience of its criticism, and his disappointment at the inhumanity of some of its internal relationships, Lindemann never wavered in seeing psychoanalysis as the basis of CMH. He adhered to the psychoanalytic approach as basic to human understanding.[51]

Group for the Advancement of Psychiatry

In 1946, Viola Bernard joined William Menninger and colleagues from the U.S. Army Medical Corps in forming the Group for the Advancement of Psychiatry (GAP),

> appalled by the weakness of the American Psychiatric Association and its inability to assume professional leadership. They hoped "to galvanize the American Psychiatric Association (APA) for promoting better mental health hospitals and the grave inadequacies in community mental health facilities".[52]

They fielded an unprecedented opposition slate of officers for the APA; elected Menninger, Appel, and Thomas Rennie; and established the Committee on Social Issues.[53] In 1970, the APA polled its members regarding the APA's taking a position on the Vietnam War; the APA trustees refused to release the results, GAP fielded an opposition slate of officers, Bernard was elected vice president, and, in 1971, a new APA board of trustees issued a resolution of concern over the effect of the Vietnam War on the morale of and destructive effects on the American people. The GAP continued to confront the APA and psychiatry with study group reports, papers, and conferences with social implications:

- "The Social Responsibility of Psychiatry: A Statement of Orientation"
- on September 21, 1956, circular letter #265[54] and on July 26, 1957,[55] circular letter #271 "Psychiatric Aspects of School Desegregation"
- on September 1, 1957, Leighton, Alexander H. "Explorations in Social Psychiatry"[56] regarding collaboration between psychiatry and the social sciences (see content in endnotes)
- on October 22, 1957, circular letter No. 272 regarding the epidemiology of psychopathology and social environment[57]
- during October 31–November 3, 1963, GAP meeting on Community Psychiatry in relation to psychiatry, social sciences, and politics (more content in notes)[58]
- in 1964, "Psychiatric Aspects of the Prevention of Nuclear War".

GAP found that a majority of its committees dealt with community psychiatry and opted to bring together this interest as part of its Committee on Preventive Psychiatry.[59]

At this time, the equivalent of community mental health was developing in other countries too. In the UK in the 1950s and 1960s, there was an interest in mental health reform in the form of a transition from institutional to community care with an integration of medical, social, and psychiatric services.[60] After several successful experiments, interest in mental health reform decreased, and patients were discharged from institution to inadequate community care. Maxwell Jones concluded that professional specialization and unification of services is needed for effective mental health care in all settings, rather than the diffusion of skills and goals advocated in the US.

Notes

1. Strauss, Anselm, Schatzman, Leonard, Bucher, Rue, Ehrlich, Danuta, and Sabshin, Melvin, 1964, *ibid.*
2. Duhl, Leonard F., 10/27/1965, *ibid.*
3. Southern Regional Education Board, *The Medical School and the Community Mental Health Center* (Washington, DC: Superintendent of Documents, U.S. Government Printing Office, Public Health Service Publication No.1858, 1968).
4. Southern Regional Education Board, 1968, *ibid.*, p. 1.
5. Southern Regional Education Board, 1968, *ibid.*, p. 1.
6. Southern Regional Education Board, 1968, *ibid.*, pp. 1–2.
7. Southern Regional Education Board, 1968, *ibid.*, quoting Israel Zwerling, p. 7.
8. Southern Regional Education Board, 1968, *ibid.*, p. 8.
9. Robert H. Barnes, Professor and chairperson, Department of Psychiatry, University of Missouri, Southern Regional Education Board, 1968, *ibid.*, p. 11.

10. John F. O'Connor, Administrator, Connecticut Mental Health Center, in Southern Regional Education Board, 1968, *ibid.,* p. 30.
11. Melvin Sabshin, chairperson, Department of Psychiatry, University of Illinois College of Medicine, in Southern Regional Education Board, 1968, *ibid.*
12. Melvin Sabshin, in Southern Regional Education Board, 1968, *ibid.,* p. 31.
13. Southern Regional Education Board, 1968, *ibid.,* p. 32.
14. Shore, Miles F., 1/28 and 4/24/1981.
15. Bernard, Viola W., Chief of the Division of Community Mental Health, College of Physicians and Surgeons, Columbia University, interviewed at her home by David G. Satin, 4/26/1979 [caddy 1, Box 4, X, Erich Lindemann Collection, Center for the History of Medicine, Francis A. Countway Library of Medicine, Harvard Medical Area, Boston, MA] Lindemann reported: "Unfortunately, I have no personal acquaintance with Viola Bernard beyond the type of contact which is developed through occasional encounters at meetings". Lindemann, Erich, letter to A.T.M. Wilson, Tavistock Publications, Ltd, 8/26/1957. [folder "Wilson, Dr. A.T.M.", IIIB1e 2), S-Z", Erich Lindemann Collection, Center for the History of Medicine, Francis A. Countway Library of Medicine, Boston, MA]
16. Kelly, Kathleen, "Viola W. Bernard, MD, 1907–1998: Pioneer in Social Psychiatry", press release 3/25/1998. [folder "Bernard, Viola W.", research papers, Erich Lindemann Collection, Center for the History of Medicine, Francis A Countway Library, Boston, MA]
17. Kelly, Kathleen L., 3/25/1998, *ibid.,* p. 2.
18. Bernard, Viola, "Some Applications of Psychiatry and Psychoanalysis to Social Issues", *Psychoanalytic Review* 85 no. 1: 139–170 (p. 142) (2/1998).
19. Engles, George L., "The Need for a New Medical Model: A Challenge for Biomedicine" *Science* 196: 129–136 (4/8/1977).
20. Bernard, Viola W., 2/1998, *ibid.*
21. Duhl, Leonard J., memo:

> Seven years ago, under the sponsorship of the National Institute of Mental Health, a committee on the Social and Physical Environment Variables as Determinants of Mental Health was organized. This group made up of approximately 30 persons has met twice a year since that time. The participants included psychiatrists, psychologists, sociologists, planners, economists, newspaper men, political scientists, biologists, philosophers, and others. We have recently produced, under my editorship, a book entitled <u>The Urban Condition</u>.
>
> > [folder "4/25-27/63 SPACE CADETS, NIMH Bethesda, MD", Box IIIA6 Da GAP, Erich Lindemann Collection, Center for the History of Medicine, Francis A. Countway Library of Medicine, Boston, MA]

22. Committee on Social and Physical Environment Variables as Determinants of Mental Health. [Box III A6, Erich Lindemann Collection, Center for the History of Medicine, Francis A. Countway Library of Medicine, Harvard Medical Center, Boston, MA] Participants in the various meetings included the following:

> Bazelon Judge David L.—U.S. Court of Appeals, DC;
> Bell, Wendell—professor of sociology and anthropology, University of California
> Birch, Herbert—Department of Pediatrics, Albert Einstein College of Medicine, New York

Blum Dr. Henrick—public health officer, Contra Costa County Health Department, CA

Buchanan, Dr. Scott—philosopher and educator, Santa Barbara, CA

Calhoun Dr. John B.—Laboratory of Psychology, NIMH; Animal Zoology Center for Advanced Study in the Behavioral Science, Stanford University, CA

Caspari, Ernest W.—Biological Laboratories, University of Rochester, Rochester, New York

Chayes, Toni—former president, Commission on the Status of Women

Cohen, Henry—Office of the Mayor, City of New York

Coke Dr. James G.—Kent College, OH

Connery, Robert H.—Department of Political Science, Duke University, Durham, North Carolina

Cook Dr. Donald A.—Technical Planning and Evaluation, Xerox Corp, NYC; Basic Systems, Inc., NYC

Cook, Daniel

Deevey, Edward S., Jr.—Osborn Zoological Laboratory, Department of Biology, Yale University, New Haven, CT

Dennis, Larry

Duhl, Leonard J.—psychiatrist, Professional Services Branch, NIMH

Ehrenkrantz Ezra—president, Building Systems Development Inc, San Francisco, CA

Elkes, Dr. Joel, St. Eliz Hsp., DC

Fried, Marc—social psychologist, Director, Center for Community Studies, MGH, Boston, MA

Galamison, Milton

Gans, Herbert—Center for Urban Education, NYC; Institute for Urban Studies, University of Pennsylvania, State College, Pennsylvania

Gladwin, Thomas—Community Research and Services Branch, NIMH

Goe, Robert—executive assistant to the mayor, Los Angeles, California

Goffman, Irving—Laboratory of Psychology, NIMH

Grennan Miss Jean—president, Webster College, St. Louis, MO

Guilliam, R.B.

Hayes, Fred—Urban Renewal Administration

Hayes, Ray H.

Heimann John G., vice president, E.M. Warburg and Co., Inc., New York City

Henschal, Austin—environmental protection research director, Natick Quartermaster Research and Development Center, Natick, Massachusetts

Hollingshead, August B.—chairperson, Department of Sociology, Yale University, New Haven, CT

Holmberg, Allen

Iatrides, Demetri—Athens Technical Institute, Greece; Boston College, Boston, MA

Isaacs, Harold R.—research associate, Center for International Studies, Massachusetts Institute of Technology, Cambridge, Massachusetts; Center for Cultural and Technological Interchange Between East and West, University of HI

Jackson Lady Barbara Ward—c/o Barclays Bank, London

Jackson Mr. John B.—editor, "Landscape", Santa Fe, NM

Jahoda, Marie—Department of Psychology, New York University, New York, NY

Kennedy, Robert Woods—architect, Cambridge, MA

Knowles, John H.—general director, MGH, Boston, MA
Larrabee Mr. Eric—associate editor, "*Harper's Magazine*", NYC
Leopold Dr. Robert—Philadelphia, PA
Lewis Dr Hylan—Howard University
Lindemann, Erich—chief, Department of Psychiatry, MGH, Boston, MA;
    Department of Psychiatry, Stanford University, Palo Alto, CA
Lohman, Joseph—dean, School of Criminology, University of California
Meier, Richard L.—Mental Health Research Institute, University of Michigan,
    MI; Assistant Professor of Planning, University of Chicago, Chicago, IL
McHarg, Ian L.—chairperson, Department of Landscape Architecture, Uni-
    versity of Pennsylvania, State College, Pennsylvania
Meier Dr. Richard—Chem and Social Planning, Athens Technol. Institute,
    Athens, Greece; Mental Health Research Institute, University of Michigan
Meikeljohn Dr. Alexander—Educator, Philosopher, Berkeley, CA
Michael Dr. Donald—Institute for Policy Studies, DC; director of research,
    The Peace Research Institute; Ctr for Res on the Utilization of Scientific
    Knowledge, University of Michigan;
Miller, James—Director, Mental Health Research Institute, University of
    Michigan
Miniclier, Louis—Office of Technical Cooperation and Research, Agency for
    International Development, Department of State, DC; Chief, Community
    Development Division, International Cooperation Administration
Morris, Laura—Department of Psychiatry, MGH, Boston, MA
Moynihan, Daniel—US assistant secretary of labor
Nemerovski, Mr. Howard—Howard, Prim, Smith, Rice, and Downs, San
    Francisco, CA;
Perloff, Dr. Harvey—economic planner, Resources for the Future, DC
Poston, Richard W.—director, Department of Community Development,
    Community Organizer, Cooperative Community Resources, Southern
    Illinois University, IL
Rashevsky, Nicholas—chairperson, Committee on Mathematical Biology,
    University of Chicago, Chicago, IL
Richmond, Julius—director, Peace Corps
Rustow, Eugene—dean, School of Law, Yale University, New Haven, CT
Saqalyn Mr. Arnold—chief, Law Enforcement, Treasury Department, DC;
Schneirla, T.C.—Department of Animal Behavior, American Museum of
    Natural History, New York, NY
Schon Dr. Donald—Office of Science and Technology Innovation, Cam-
    bridge, MA
Seeley, John R.—Center for the Study of Democratic Institutions, Santa Bar-
    bara, CA; York University, Toronto, Canada; Community Surveys, Inc.,
    Indianapolis, IN
Smit Mr. Hank—Xerox Corporation, NYC
Snyder, Benson—psychiatrist, Homberg Memorial Infirmary, Medical
    Department, Massachusetts Institute of Technology, Cambridge, MA
Stewart Dr. John Q.—astro-physics and social physics, Princeton University
    Observatory
Sutton Mr. Frank—Behavioral Science Division, Ford Found, NYC
Vickers, Geoffrey—lawyer, Goring-on-Thames, UK
Warburg E.M.—Warburg and Company, Inc., NYC
Webber, Melvin M.—city planner, Resources for the Future, DC; Department
    of City and Regional Planning, University of California, Berkeley, CA
Whyte, William—editor, *Fortune Magazine*

Wilner, Daniel M.—School of Public Health, University of California, Los Angeles, CA; School of Public Health, Johns Hopkins University, Baltimore, MD

Wofford Mr. Harris L.—president, State University of New York, Albany, NY

Wurster, Catherine Bauer—Department of City and Regional Planning, University of California, Berkeley, CA

Young Dr. Michael—Institute of Community Studies, London.

23. Lindemann, Erich, and Spivak, McGrath, "Development of CMHCs (unpublished interview of Erich Lindemann by sociology students, 1965).

24. Seeley, John, interview by David G. Satin by phone, 4/12/1979. [caddy 5, Erich Lindemann Collection, David G. Satin, Newton, MA]

25. Duhl, Leonard J. letter, 9/7/1956, and "Summary of Conference in Washington October 11–12, 1956 on "The Physical and Social Environment Related to Mental Health" held by Professional Services and Research Section, N.I.M.H".—possibly written by Laura Morris. [folder "Columbia-Washington Heights Community Mental Health Project", Box IIIA6 Da GAP, Erich Lindemann Collection, Center for the History of Medicine, Francis A. Countway Library of Medicine, Boston, MA]

26. Meeting #9 at the NIMH, Bethesda, MD, 5/19–21/1960. [various boxes and folders, Erich Lindemann Collection, Center for the History of Medicine, Francis A. Countway Library of Medicine, Boston, MA]

27. Meeting #12 Department of Health, Education, and Welfare Public Health Service, National Institutes of Health; Twelfth Meeting of the Committee on Social and Physical Environment Variables as Determinants of Mental Health; Conference Room "A", Stone House, National Institutes of Health, Bethesda, Maryland, 10/26–28/1961. [various boxes and folders, Erich Lindemann Collection, Center for the History of Medicine, Francis A. Countway Library of Medicine, Boston, MA]

28. Duhl, Leonard J. and Powell, John, *The Urban Condition: People and Policy in the Metropolis* (New York: Basic Books, 1963; Clarion/Simon & Schuster, 1969).

29. Duhl, Leonard, Department of Public Health, University of California—San Francisco; interview by telephone at the University of California—Berkeley, CA by David G. Satin, 4/2/1979, 8/16/2007. [caddy 2, Box 4, X, Lindemann Collection, Center for the History of Medicine, Francis A. Countway Library of Medicine, Boston, MA]

30. Lindemann, Erich, with Duhl, Leonard, and Seeley, John, interviewed at his home in Palo Alto, CA by Duhl, 6/15,22, 1974. [caddy 4, tape 3A, 4B;7, Erich Lindemann Collection, Center for the History of Medicine, Francis A. Countway Library of Medicine, Boston, MA]

31. Agendas found in various boxes and folders, Erich Lindemann Collection, Center for the History of Medicine, Francis A. Countway Library of Medicine, Boston, MA.

5/28–29/1956 first meeting: Achieving mutual understanding and agreement that the physical environment modifies behavior but lacking understanding of how. Decision makers need a rationale for their decisions, but scientists have not formulated or communicated this rationale.

10/11–12/1956 in Washington, DC: Discussion of definitions of mental health; the influence of aspirations, support, and participation in community decisions; and research issues and technical services needs and policies. The Committee and Duhl provided consultation and helped arrange grant support for Lindemann's study, "Relocation and Mental Health—Adaptation

Under Stress" ("The West End Study"), and Lindemann reported on its progress. Richard Poston discussed the project in Cairo, Illinois.

10/23–4/1958 in the American Psychological Association building in Washington, DC: Agenda included Robert Goe's study of the effect on society of crime, including organized crime's investment; Lindemann's update on the West End Project; Henrik Blum's report on the West Coast group; Daniel Wilner's material; and background reading on the importance of the individual and the characteristics of the politician.

5/19–21/1960 in Stone House of the NIMH in Washington, DC: Agenda included Hollingshead's discussion of the epidemiology of schizophrenia; Taylor's discussion of social dynamics in a college dormitory; and John Stewart's presentation of energy physics as a model for the social sciences.

10/20–21/1960 at the Brookings Institution, Washington, DC: Agenda included preliminary articles about the planning of the new Brazilian capital of Brasilia; Finchenden Manor and psycho-education; use of airplanes in sociological research; criticism of modern Freudianism; criticism of redevelopment from the points of view of architecture and historical heritage; planning in Puerto Rico; predictive theory; conservation and planning movements; the mental health effects of change in home; and social science and the law.

4/27–29/1961 11th meeting at the Brookings Institution, Washington, DC: John Seeley discussed the environment and mental health; Connery explored how NIMH and other federal mental health monies got to Philadelphia, New Orleans, and the Piedmont crescent in North Carolina, and what it was used for; Calhoun discussed "Are There Inherent Limits on the Adaptive Capacity of Social Systems?"; Hollingshead presented "Planning for a Study of Mental Health in Puerto Rico"; and Miller presented general systems theory.

10/26–28/1961 12th meeting at Stone House, NIMH: Frederick Duhl was to discuss the Development of the Behavioral Sciences in the Federal Government; Miniclier on ICA and AID.

10/11–12/1962 13th meeting at Stone House, NIMH: Wendell Bell—social policy and social change in the Caribbean; Richard W. Poston—studies of Colombia, the Peace Corps and community development; Leonard Duhl—Development of the Youth Volunteer Corps in the US; and John H. Knowles—Changing a Traditional Hospital into a Community Hospital.

4/25–27/1963 at the Park Plaza Hotel, Washington, DC: hosted by Basic Books, Inc. to honor authors they had published.

Melvin M. Webber—resources for the future; Richard Maier—researches in Athens; John Stewart—background materials on black–white relations, urban redevelopment, planning and social responsibility; Melvin Webber—services to youth with special needs; Leonard Duhl—issues in long-range planning and the development of new programs (the Peace Corps, a domestic peace corps, CMH); Leonard Duhl—the federal role in justice-involved youth and education; Ray Hayes, MD—rural CMH programs; Hebert Gans—study of mass media; Fred Hayes—the Urban Renewal Administration; Allen Holmberg—Peru; Marc Fried—the West End Study; Larry Dennis—education for a changing world.

11/7–9/1963 in Washington, DC: John Calhoun—African ecology; Donald Michael—planning for a new town; Henry Cohen—urban youth programs; Milton Galamison—black people in urban New York City; Harvey Peloff—behavior and the social sciences in international consultation; Daniel P. Moynihan—problems of youth employment and Herbert Gans's ideas;

also supporting documents: Calhoun—social change research in East Africa; Galamison—Bedford-Stuyvesant conditions; and Gans—government policy regarding the changing economy and employment.

3/26–28/1964 at the American Psychiatric Association, Washington, DC: Harold Isaacs—adolescence worldwide; Harlan Lewis—black child-rearing in Washington; R.B. Guilliam—Canadian manpower training; and Daniel P. Moynihan and Marc Fried—the West End Study.

3/8/1965 in Bethesda, MD: Meeting with Peace Corps staff and some returned volunteers in the Conference on Returned Peace Corps Volunteers regarding their role in the US, and lessons in sound mental health planning.

32. Webber, Melvin M., Cashier, College of Environmental Design, Department of City and Regional Planning, University of California, Berkeley, to Lindemann, Erich, 3/30/1966. [folder "General Correspondence T-Z 1966", Box IV 1 + 2, Erich Lindemann Collection, Center for the History of Medicine, Countway Library of Medicine, Boston, MA]

33. Kelly, James G., "The National Institute of Mental Health and The Founding of the Field of Community Psychology", in Pickren, W.E. and Schneider, S.F. (eds.), *Psychology and the National Institute of Mental Health* (Washington, DC: American Psychological Association, 2002). [copy in file "Kelly—NIMH + Founding of Community Psychology", Box XII #3, Lindemann Collection, Center for the History of Medicine, Francis A. Countway Library of Medicine, Harvard Medical School, Boston, MA]

34. Duhl, Leonard, chief of the Office of Planning, NIMH, to the Committee on Social and Physical Environment Variables as Determinants of Mental Health, 1/8/1962. [folder "Leonard Duhl—NIMH Corr"., Box IIIA 4 (A-E), Lindemann Collection, Center for the History of Medicine, Francis A. Countway Library of Medicine, Boston, MA]

35. Felix, Robert H., "The Dynamics of Community Mental Health", Contrib. to Panel Discuss. on "Creating a Community Climate Conducive to Mental Health", National Health Forum, Cincinnati, OH, 3/21/1957. [folder "NIMH-Misc. Material 1956–1958", Box IIIA6 Da GAP, Erich Lindemann Collection, Center for the History of Medicine, Francis A. Countway Library of Medicine, Boston, MA]

36. Knowles, John H., "Medical School, Teaching Hospital and Social Responsibility: Medicine's Clarion Call", delivered at the Second Institute on Medical Center Problems, Association of American Medical Colleges, Miami, Florida, 12/91964 and Panel Meeting, Task Force on Economic Growth and Opportunity, U.S. Chamber of Commerce, Washington, DC, 12/10/1964). [folder "Dr. John Knowles, Medical Director—MGH", Box IIIA 4 (I-Ma), Erich Lindemann Collection, Center for the History of Medicine, Francis A. Countway Library of Medicine, Boston, MA]

37. Committee on Social Issues, "American Psychoanalytic Association", *The American Psychoanalyst* 25 no. 4: 17–18 (1991). [folder "Psychoanalysis", Research Papers, Lindemann Collection, Center for the History of Medicine, Francis A. Countway Library of Medicine, Boston, MA]

Early members included Raymond Raskin (chairperson), Frances Bonner, Robert Dorn, Edward Joseph, Robert Ivory, Seymour Lustman, Joseph Michaels, Bernice Moore, Bernard Pacella, Calvin Settlage, and Alberta Szalita.

38. Cath, Stanley, telehone interview by David G. Satin, 3/12/1998. [Erich Lindemann Collection, Center for the History of Medicine, Francis A Countway Library, Boston, MA]

39. Shore, Miles F., interview by David G. Satin at the Massachusetts Mental Health Center, 1/28 and 4/24/1981. [Lindemann Collection, David G. Satin, Newton, MA]

40. Bernard, Viola W. MD—chief, Div. of CMH, College of Physicians & Surgeons, Columbia University, CMHCs and studies by the Standing Committee on Community Psychiatry and Psychoanalysis, American Psychoanalytic Association Study Group. Interviewed by David G. Satin at Bernard's home, 4/26/79. The Group collected many tape recordings and drafts but had not edited them for a report. [caddy 1, Box 4, X, Lindemann Collection, Center for the History of Medicine, Francis A. Countway Library of Medicine, Boston, MA]

41. Michaels, Joseph J., Annual Reports A. p. 2, Annual Meeting of the Boston Psychoanalytic Society and institute, Inc., First Session: II, 4/1/1959. [folder "The Boston Psychoanalytic Society and Institute, Inc. 1959–60", Box IIIA6 2) A-M, Erich Collection, Center for the History of Medicine, Francis A. Countway Library of Medicine, Boston, MA]

42. Annual Meeting of the Boston Psychoanalytic Society and institute, Inc., Second Session, 4/8/1959. [folder "The Boston Psychoanalytic Society and Institute, Inc. 1959–60", Box IIIA6 2) A-M, Erich Collection, Center for the History of Medicine, Francis A. Countway Library of Medicine, Boston, MA]

43. Code of Professional Ethics, The Boston Psychoanalytic Society and Institute, Inc. (revised), 7/1/1960, p. 2. [folder "The Boston Psychoanalytic Society and Institute, Inc. 1959–60", Box IIIA6 2) A-M, Erich Collection, Center for the History of Medicine, Francis A. Countway Library of Medicine, Boston, MA]

44. Grinker, Roy (president) correspondence with Lindemann, 7/18,27/1961. [folder "Misc G", Box IIIA 1–3, Lindemann Collection, Center for the History of Medicine, Francis A. Books Department, Countway Library of Medicine, Boston, MA]

45. [folder "Boston Psychoanalytic Soc. & Inst"., Box IIIA 4 (A-E), Lindemann Collection, Center for the History of Medicine, Francis A. Countway Library of Medicine, Boston, MA]

46. Ad Hoc Committee on Social Problems APA, Appendix B, 5/2/1962, p. 2. [folder "Boston Psychoanalytic Soc. & Inst"., Box IIIA 4 (A-E), Lindemann Collection, Center for the History of Medicine, Francis A. Countway Library of Medicine, Boston, MA]

47. *Journal of the American Psychoanalytic Association II*: 436–438 (1963):

> The Association applauded the new comprehensive, multidisciplinary evaluation of needs and resources for mental disease. "The Report of the Joint Commission is concerned primarily with the large central core of the mentally ill, the psychotic patients who may or do require hospitalization". . . . It indicates a large-scale expansion of resources. "An important, but as yet unwritten chapter on the prevention of mental illness will have to be added in the future.
>
> (p. 436)

> "The emphasis given in the Report to treatment which is centered in the community deserves special commendation. Early, intensive treatment in mental health clinics and general hospital psychiatric units would do much to eliminate the need for hospitalization in State Hospitals. . . . The patient should be less isolated from his community, and the resources of the community less isolated from responsibility for the continuing care

of the patient. . . . Psychoanalysis, as part of the complex of organized medicine, and psychoanalysts as individuals, will give vigorous support to the implementation of these phases of the mental health program". . . . 1. The psychotic, neurotic, and well should not be separated; "conflicts and mental mechanisms contributing to the defensive and adaptive need of the human organism at all levels of mental health" should be studied.

(pp. 436–7)

2. Research should focus on areas where there is already important constitutional, developmental, and motivational knowledge. 3. Include applied research as well as basic. 4. A "therapeutic attitude" (kindness, care) is good for all people, and especially psychiatric patients, but restorative therapy must not be ignored. . . . The promotion of ancillary care to the status of therapy by nonpsychiatric personnel, whose training at best is likely to be inadequate, is a solution of dubious value, subjecting patients to dangers as well as possible benefits".

(p. 438)

Hope for the future . . . is not based so much on the extension of therapeutic efforts, however desirable and indicated that may be, as on the prevention of mental illness. . . . Preventive measures include not only education but also therapy at appropriate and critical times. Thus, the dissemination of information regarding normal growth and developmental patterns and the significance of family and cultural interactions will have to be combined with psychological counseling during periods of environmental and intra-personal stress. . . . Psychoanalytical research suggests that the principles on which prevention may be based will be derived primarily from the study of childhood experiences and the investigation of child-rearing practices, and the effective prevention of mental illness will be implemented largely through measures that aim at the attenuation of unavoidable traumata of childhood and at the improvement of the emotional atmosphere in which children grow up.

(p. 438)

48. Lindemann, Erich, correspondence with Eleanor Pavenstedt, MD, Secretary of the Students Committee, Boston Psychoanalytic Society and Institute, 2/17, 3/15/1954. [folder "Boston Psychoanalytic Soc. & Insti. 1954–58", Box IIIA6 2) A-M, Erich Lindemann Collection, Center for the History of Medicine, Francis A. Countway Library of Medicine, Boston, MA]
49. Lindemann, Erich, correspondence with Helen H. Tartakoff, MD, chairperson of the Program Committee, Boston Psychoanalytic Society and Institute, 12/16/1955, 1/6/1956. [folder "Boston Psychoanalytic Soc. & Insti. 1954–58", Box IIIA6 2) A-M, Erich Lindemann Collection, Center for the History of Medicine, Francis A. Countway Library of Medicine, Boston, MA]
50. Huberman, Leo of the *Monthly Review* to Lindemann, 11/22/1957. A reply was written by Norman Reider, the chief of psychiatry at Mt. Zion Hospital in San Francisco, and former president and then director of education at the San Francisco Psychoanalytic Society. [folder "Misc. Correspondence H,I,J 1956–57", Box IIIA 1–3, Lindemann Collection, Center for the History of Medicine, Francis A. Countway Library of Medicine, Boston, MA]
51. Lindemann, Elizabeth B., Interviews by David G. Satin including 8/23/1998, 11/29/1998. [David G. Satin files, Newton, MA]
52. Bernard, Viola W., 2/1998, *ibid.*, pp. 148–149.
53. Members included Sol Ginsburg (chairperson), Helen McLean, Nathan Ackerman, Charlotte Babcock, Bernard, and others.

54. 9/21/56 "Some Psychodynamic Aspects of School Desegregation, Report of the GAP Committee on Social Issues" (draft circulated to GAP members under cover of Circular Letter No. 265): Table of contents: I. INTRODUCTION; II. PSYCHODYNAMICS OF RESPONSES TO DESEGREGATION, A. Functions of Racial Myths and Prejudices, B. Psychodynamics of Changing Attitudes, 1. Some Aspects of Attitude Change, 2. Effect of Group Processes on Attitudes, 3. Role of Authority, C. Responses of Various Groups to Desegregation, 1. The Children, 2. The Educators, 3. The Parents, D. Reactions to Anticipated and Actual Desegregation; III. CONCLUDING STATEMENT; ANNOTATED BIBLIOGRAPHY. Committee on Social Issues: Chair Viola W. Bernard-New York, Nathan W. Ackerman-NY, Charlotte Babcock-Pittsburgh, Mabel B. Cohen—Chevy Chase MD, Donald L. Gerard-NY, Joel S. Handler-Chicago, Harold Lief-New Orleans, Joseph J. Michaels-Belmont, MA, Arthur A. Miller-Chicago, Angel N. Miranda-NY, Edward Stainbrook-Syracuse, Ruthreford B. Stevens-NY, Ian Stevenson-New Orleans) [folder "Group for the Advancement of Psychiatry (GAP) 1956–57", Box IIIA6 Da GAP, Erich Lindemann Collection, Center for the History of Medicine, Francis A. Countway Library of Medicine, Boston, MA]

55. 7/26/57 Circular Letter No. 271:

> The report by the Committee on Social Issues on "Psychiatric Aspects of School Desegregation" has been well received in most quarters. At the time of its publication a press conference was held in Chicago, which was attended by about 25 representatives of newspapers and news services. . . . A copy of the report was sent in June to each member of the Congress and the Supreme Court. A great many courteous replies have been received, some of them commenting favorably on the contents of the report. No critical replies have as yet been received.
>
> (p. 1)

[folder "Group for the Advancement of Psychiatry (GAP) 1956–57", Box IIIA6 Da GAP, Erich Lindemann Collection, Center for the History of Medicine, Francis A. Countway Library of Medicine, Boston, MA]

56. 9/57 Leighton, Alexander H., "Explorations in Social Psychiatry", *Social Science Research Council Items XI* no. 3: 26–29:

> In the years following World War II there came into existence a number of community-oriented research projects concerned with the relationship of the socio-cultural environment to mental health and mental illness. The Wellesley Study, work at New Haven, Syracuse, Phoenix, and the Stirling County Study may be cited as examples. Those of us engaged in these researches became aware shortly of a strong need for sharing the problems of theory and method, and this was made possible in a series of meetings sponsored by the Milbank Memorial Fund. Such meetings, together with the progress of the work, increased our desire for some kind of broad, yet integrative, study. . . . Early in 1950 the Social Science Research Council . . . brought together two conferences of social scientists and psychiatrists to consider the common ground in their fields of interest. Those attending these meetings were: Nathan W. Ackerman, Henry W. Brosin, Donald T. Campbell, John A. Clausen, Robert A. Cohen, Kingsley Davis, John Dollard, Joseph W. Eaton, Clements C. Fry, Herbert Goldhamer, Ernest M. Gruenberg, Allan R. Holmberg, Marie Jahoda, Alexander H. Leighton, Erich Lindemann, Quinn McNemar, A. R. Mangus, Ørnulv Ødegaard, Thomas A. C. Rennie, John Romano, Leo W. Simmons, Raymond Sletto, and M. Brewster Smith . . . From these

two conferences and a panel discussion held at the spring meeting of the Council the same year, there was formulated a proposal for a committee on research in psychiatry and the social sciences. The basis for this proposal was as follows: . . . 2. *Need for a concept of mental health.* . . . 3. *Relation of mental illness to social pathology.* . . . 4. *Sociocultural change.* . . . The desired committee on research in psychiatry and the social sciences was appointed by the Council in the spring of 1950. The original members, together with some later additions, include: Henry W. Brosin, John A. Clausen, Joseph W. Eaton, Herbert Goldhamer, Ernest M. Gruenberg, Clyde Kluckhohn, Erich Lindemann, F.C. Redlich, the late Thomas A.C. Rennie, James S. Tyhurst, Edmund H. Volkart, and myself as chairperson. The committee has directed its attention to the following matters: (1) a comparative and analytic review of concepts and methods relevant to understanding the nature of mental health and disease (2) the definition of significant problem areas that invite research attention. . . . The resultant manuscript bears the title *Explorations in Social Psychiatry* and is to be published by Basic Books, Inc. in December 1957.

(pp. 26–7)

[folder "Group for the Advancement of Psychiatry (GAP) 1956–57", Box IIIA6 Da GAP, Erich Lindemann Collection, Center for the History of Medicine, Francis A. Countway Library of Medicine, Boston, MA]

57. 10/22/57 Circular Letter No. 272:

Committee on Preventive Psychiatry . . . The Committee is at present engaged in a review of changes in rates of occurrence of different psychiatric illnesses over the last two decades in order to derive information which may be of value in deciding which psychiatric illnesses can be influenced by changes in social and cultural conditions.

(p. 4)

[folder "Group for the Advancement of Psychiatry (GAP) 1956–57", Box IIIA6 Da GAP, Erich Lindemann Collection, Center for the History of Medicine, Francis A. Countway Library of Medicine, Boston, MA]

58. 6/12/63 Circular Letter No. 325:

Community Psychiatry: An ad hoc committee was appointed, consisting of Dr. Modlin, chairperson, Dr. Bernard, Dr. Coleman and Dr. Caplan, to explore the possibilities of GAP activity in the field of Community Psychiatry, which has recently received considerable impetus on the national scene.

(p. 5)

10/11/63 Circular Letter No. 326:

SUNDAY MORNING SYMPOSIUM: We are indebted to Dr. Leonard J. Duhl, chairperson of the Committee on Preventive Psychiatry, for his preparation of the Sunday Morning Symposium to be held November 3rd, on URBAN AMERICA AND THE PLANNING OF MENTAL HEALTH SERVICES. Dr. Duhl writes that 'during the past few years and especially in the last few months there has been a tremendous pressure to increase the availability of mental health services in the United States. . . . One of the criteria for the plans is the integration of planning in mental health services with other related programs. For example, health, welfare, housing, alcoholism, mental retardation, the law, etc. The problems of urbanization are such that each issue, whether it be mental health or delinquency or hospital planning, becomes an infinitely complex one, tied in with many relevant problems of politics, economics, law, etc. . . . In many of our major metropolitan areas comprehensive programs for physical and social planning are under way. There will be a need therefore for a careful consideration of how mental health planning is related and should be integrated with these other activities.

(p. 4)

Speakers: Leonard Cottrell (sociologist at Russell Sage Found., former member National Advisory Mental Health Council, member President's Committee on Juvenile Delinquency) "Social Planning, the Competent Community and Mental Health"; Harry Bredemeier (Rutgers University Urban Study Center) "Strategic Points of Intervention: A Theory", Daniel P. Moynihan (assistant secretary of labor) "Manpower, Employment and Minority Groups in the Urban Environment", Marc Fried (psychologist, director at the Center for Community Studies) "Social Change, Social Programs and Psychopathology"; Stanley Yolles (deputy director at NIMH) relate papers to current mental health developments in the US.

11/3/63 Revision of Dr. Lindemann's "Discussion" remarks at the GAP Meeting, November 1963 (discussant of GAP symposium "Urban America and the Planning of Mental Health Services"):

The gentlemen from the other professions have presented before us a panorama of activities and possibilities which are challenging and promising but also frightening. How do we react to this challenge? . . . It seems that the range of activities which are new and untried before us [psychiatrists] today are immense. The question of our competence as psychiatrists, as leaders and participants is much a matter of debate. . . . Being accustomed to a central and pivotal role on the psychiatric team we are asked here to consider patterns of participant roles with fuzzy definition as to leadership and division of labor. We would like to search for certain well defined operations which psychiatrists are competent now to accomplish or for which they can be properly prepared. As psychiatrists, we prefer a gradual evolution of functions to sudden changes and to abrupt reorganization. . . . we have not turned away from the solid base of patient-centered work and many of us might feel that it would be presumptuous to do so. Should we really go beyond this and begin to manipulate social institutions on the basis of psychodynamic insight? Should we advise the city planner where to turn next? Should we tell the school superintendent how to fix his school curriculum in terms of mental health requirements? Should we, indeed, deal directly with politicians and try to win political support in a game of conflicting interests? For some of us this may be an appealing challenge, for others it will be difficult and objectionable. They would be reluctant to do this type of work themselves and would not even wish other psychiatrists to engage in it. . . . Scientific advance is proceeding with an accelerating pace in the laboratories of the behavioral scientist . . . molecular biology . . . advances in the social sciences but we learn today about aspects of social structure and social processes which is becoming an area of special study for some psychiatrists. . . . In any case, we will be closer to community life than ever before. . . . we will be a bit more aware of the influence of politicians and other power persons in the community in shaping our professional lives.

(pp. 1–2)

Original draft: "I sort of feel like the Sorcerer's Apprentice today. We have pulled out the stopper somewhere and don't know where this is going to go" (p. 1).

[folder "10/31–11/3/63- G.A.P. Meeting", Box IIIA6 Da GAP, Erich Lindemann Collection, Center for the History of Medicine, Francis A. Countway Library of Medicine, Boston, MA]

59. 12/26/63 Group for the Advancement of Psychiatry Circular Letter No. 329: "1. to What Extent are Gap Committees involved in aspects of community psychiatry at present?" (p. 5). The committee chairman circularized an inquiry: 21 responded—eight were current projects centrally related to community psychiatry, five were peripherally related, and eight were not related. Ad Hoc Committee on Community Psychiatry recommended that no new Community Psychiatry Committee be formed; that the definition of community psychiatry, social psychiatry, etc. be addressed as an introduction to the upcoming report by the Committee on Preventive Psychiatry; and that the Ad Hoc Committee on Community Psychiatry be discontinued. [folder "4/16/64–6/19/64-G.A.P. Mtg. Phila, PA", Box IIIA6 Da GAP, Erich Lindemann Collection, Center for the History of Medicine, Francis A. Countway Library of Medicine, Boston, MA]

60. Jones, Kathleen (Department of Social Administration and Social Work, University of York, York, England), "Mental Health Administration: Reflections From the British Experience", *Administration in Mental Health 14* no. 2: 3–10 (1977). [folder "Group for the Advancement of Psychiatry (GAP) 1956–57", Box IIIA6 Da GAP, Erich Lindemann Collection, Center for the History of Medicine, Francis A. Countway Library of Medicine, Boston, MA]

6 Introducing Community Mental Health at Harvard University

The Harvard School of Public Health

When Lindemann shifted his appointment and attention from the HSPH to the MGH and HMS on July 1, 1954, Gerald Caplan replaced him as associate professor of mental health in the Division of Mental Health of the HSPH Department of Public Health Practice.[1] Caplan was seen as having an abrasive personality, resenting authority, and not relating well with the HSPH director of the Department of Mental Health Practice.

Lindemann continued his HSPH affiliation as advisor and consulting psychiatrist. In those capacities, he continued to participate in mental health training as part of the training of all public health students; developed workshops for practitioners and teachers of mental health; gave papers and seminars around the United States, other countries, and the Tavistock Clinic in London; consulted for the Peace Corps under Joseph English, Leonard Duhl, and Robert Leopold; and participated in visits from eminent workers in social and community psychiatry.[2] On July 1, 1954, a new public health field station was opened at the Whittier Street Health Center of the Boston Health Department, funded by a Commonwealth Fund grant.

Caplan's first annual report for 1954 reviewed the activities of the Division of Mental Health (more details of content and participants are presented in the endnotes):[3]

Teaching:

A. participation in introductory course for all students in biological and social ecology
B. Specialized courses

   Public Health Practice 3B—Psychosocial Problems
   Course 14c,d—Problems in Mental Health:.[4]
   Public Health Practice 40c,d—Group Dynamics:

C. Special training of Mental Hygiene Concentration
D. Special research seminars

   Review of Division projects, selected seminars in HDSR and HGSE.

E. Plans for next year

> Dr. Lindemann, advisor and consulting psychiatrist, medical director of HRS, with Gerald Caplan to guide division policy.

MGH:

> "an attempt will be made to integrate the teaching program in the Harvard School of Public Health with that which is being developed at the Mass. General Hospital. The collaboration of the two units will further be aided by the active participation of Dr. Caplan in the Policy Committee of the Department of Psychiatry at the Mass. General Hospital. It is envisaged that such a pooling of resources will provide a whole gamut of therapeutic and preventive services". MGH and other sites will provide for teaching of public health students and postgraduate training for CMH specialists.

The new Whittier Street Family Guidance Center complements the HRS. There will be a study of the collaboration of mental health and public health workers concerning family adaptive and maladaptation reactions to premature or congenitally deformed babies or the diagnosis and hospitalization for tuberculosis, to help and test the mental health of family members.

Course case material will come from the two field stations and the MGH. Lindemann will "give a number of the systematic lectures". Field station staff will teach. It is expected that there will be progress toward field training in the State Division of Mental Hygiene with the support of its director, Dr. Warren Vaughan.

W.T. Grant Foundation funding of HRS and the partial salary of the secretary of the HSPH Division of Mental Health ended on June 30, 1954. HRS "incorporated as a local community supported agency. Its close professional association with the Harvard School of Public Health continues as before".

From May 18 to May 20, 1955, Caplan chaired the Community Mental Health Organization Conference.[5] Erich Lindemann was the vice-chair, and Leonard Duhl of NIMH and Arthur Halleck of the DMH participated. There were discussions of the definitions of mental health, mental health promotion, sources of mental illness, and ways of researching mental health and illness in the community. Emphasis was on poor and disorganized communities. Examples of health promotion projects were reviewed: Richard W. Poston's efforts to decrease the prejudice about mental health issues in southern Illinois towns; the Tavistock Clinic in London, which offered clinical evaluations of communities and worked through resistance to this approach; and the DMH had ten projects in which the state and community collaborated in developing mental health clinics into CMHCs, including projects to serve the entire cities of Brockton and Worcester; the HRS; and projects in Israel.

Caplan proposed a CMH research program and structure that mirrored those at the MGH, articulating the ideals and hopes of CMH centers that faced the political and economic difficulties of implementation:[6]

> Introduction and Overview . . . the Harvard School of Public Health and the cooperating unit at the Massachusetts General Hospital. . . [occupy a] national and international leadership role in the field of community mental health . . . increasing demands are therefore being made upon these units . . . for aid and direction in research, in training, and in consultation. . . . This necessitates an expansion and development of the mental health facilities in the two institutions. . . . The plan calls for the creation of seven new senior staff positions—four at the Harvard School of Public Health and three at the Massachusetts General Hospital . . . a cadre of leaders who will be given long-term appointments and will not be budgetarily dependent upon any circumscribed research or training project. They will thus be free to plan and supervise an orderly development of the community mental health field . . . each of these specialists will conduct reconnaissance and pilot studies within the areas of his interests . . . develop plans for special projects which will be separately funded and staffed. . . . he will withdraw from major administrative responsibility for its operations, but will maintain technical supervision . . . so that he may devote his energies to initiating and developing other projects. . . . In addition, . . . these workers will exercise a leadership role in the development of the specialist training programs. . . . They will also be available as consultants both for research projects in these and other Harvard units as well as . . . in other parts of the country. . . . It is hoped that it will also bring them into closer articulation with allied endeavors in the fields of social science and psychiatric research and training at Harvard University—in the School of Public Health, in the Medical School, in the School of Education, and also in the Department of Social Relations. . . . The program proposed for Harvard School of Public Health will create four new staff positions: (a) Psychiatric Director- Dr. Gerald Caplan, MD (b) Sociologist with Clinical Training . . . Dr. Louisa Howe, PhD (c) Psychoanalyst with Social Science Training . . . Dr. Rhona Rapoport [PhD] (d) Specialist in Community Organization and Administration . . . If suitable long-term salaried positions were to be made available together with appropriate working conditions, it is felt that a group of leaders would be attracted by the existing possibilities of making a signal and timely contribution to this field, and this group would ensure the development of present facilities to act as a vanguard of community mental health in this country and abroad. . . . We are suggesting, therefore, the provision of three new positions in each of the cooperating units to be financed by the N.I.M.H. as a ten-year

program. In addition, it is suggested that Dr. Caplan be transferred
to this program. . . . An informal liaison group has recently been
established, consisting of Drs. [Erich] Lindemann [MGH], [Gerald]
Caplan [HSPH], [Benjamin] Paul [HSPH], [John] Spiegel [Harvard
Department of Social Relations], Wilson, and [Daniel] Levinson
[Massachusetts Mental Health Center] . . . Advisory Committee of
the Harvard School of Public Health Family Guidance Center at
Whittier Street . . . Dean George Berry, Harvard Medical School, Dr.
Jack Ewalt, Massachusetts Mental Health Center; Professor Talcott
Parsons and Dr. Robert White, Harvard Department of Social Rela-
tions; Dr. George Gardner, [chief of psychiatry] Children's Medical
Center; Dr. John Whiting, Harvard School of Education; Dr. Harry
Solomon, director [actually commissioner], Dept. of Mental Health
of the Commonwealth of Massachusetts.

In 1959, Caplan and his colleagues initiated a research project to test
the effects of mental health consultation on public health nurses in Boston, which was expanded with the commissioner of public health to all
public health nurses and was funded by the NIMH.[7] After the study,
the HSPH community mental health program continued its consultation
with the public health nurses and was invited to work also with the Boston Visiting Nurse Association. These service programs also provided
placements for the education of NIMH students as part of a highly developed theory and curriculum for teaching public health mental health.

From 1954 to 1971, John Crayton Snyder, head of the HSPH Department of Microbiology, succeeded to the deanship of the school, disappointing Leavell's candidacy and redirecting the school's emphasis from
social to biological healthcare. In light of this change in institutional
support, Caplan moved to the Harvard Medical School to carry on the
public health mental health approach at the Laboratory for Community
Psychiatry:[8]

our Community Mental Health Program will transfer from Harvard
School of Public Health to Harvard Medical School on July 1st, 1964.
A new unit will be established under my direction in the Department
of Psychiatry of Harvard Medical School. It will be called the Laboratory of Community Psychiatry and will be devoted to professional
education and the development and evaluation of new methods in
community mental health and to research on problems of preventive
psychiatry.

This was recognized by the HMS:[9]

Gerald Caplan and his group transferred from the School of Public Health to the Medical School last year in order to move into a

sympathetic environment where the intellectual climate would be consonant with their aims and activities. His programs have flourished enormously since this move was made.

Lindemann was also acutely aware of the changing fate of his CMH place in the HSPH. He thought of Caplan as

> my spiritual son . . . came up in the fourth year of the Wellesley operation, and he became my successor at the [Harvard] School of Public Health. We evolved the notion of crisis theory and mental health consultation together . . . it turned out that [due to] the ever increasing orientation of that school [HSPH] (as of the [Harvard] medical school) towards micro-biological inquiries,[10] that his operations were not given as much support as he would have wished, so he . . . switch[ed] to the Medical School. I went to the dean and strongly supported that. Then because of my impending departure, he wasn't sure how much support he would get here at the hospital [MGH] and so he went to Jack Ewalt [Massachusetts Mental Health Center superintendent] and has there a Laboratory of Community Psychiatry which carries on our ideas beautifully.[11]

Lindemann believed that he shared much of CMH with Caplan, wanted him to succeed at his post and perhaps become a Harvard professor of community psychiatry, and felt bad for the obstacles that Caplan encountered.[12]

Leavell recognized this loss of HSPH support for public health mental health:[13]

> I learned some time ago about Gerald Caplan's new arrangement, and suppose from his standpoint that it is a very good thing. Of course, I am sorry to have the School of Public Health losing out after the very fine start that you gave. No doubt, losing a battle does not mean losing the war.

He left HSPH for the Ford Foundation and planned some years of consultation in New Delhi, India.[14]

Still frustrated with the lessened support for a social psychiatry ideology, Caplan believed that CMH's time had passed except in rural and other resource-poor settings. In 1977, he took early retirement from HMS and returned to Jerusalem, where he organized child psychiatry programs and wanted to "extend the boundaries of the crisis model to the support systems model and of the method of consultation to the methods of collaboration".[15] Niels Poerksen wrote that at the Hadassah Medical Center Department of Child Psychiatry, he abandoned CMH and primary prevention in a population-based practice and returned to secondary and tertiary prevention.[16]

Massachusetts General Hospital: Community Mental Health in the Cauldron of Academia

It was in this context that on July 1, 1954, a 54-year-old Erich Lindemann assumed the positions of chief of the psychiatry service at the MGH and professor of psychiatry at the HMS.[17] (His wife, Elizabeth Lindemann, believed it was an injustice to him that Stanley Cobb's joint appointment in psychiatry and neuropathology was split into the psychiatry professorship for Lindemann and the neuropathology professorship for Raymond Adams, the chief of the MGH Neurology Service.)[18] Lindemann had achieved the long-sought position of respect and influence from which he expected to change medicine to humane caring and social concern through his advocacy for CMH. He clearly remembered a lesson from his youth: "At this time I acquired a new view of knowledge, namely, knowledge is a weapon, and you find ammunition, so to say, to fight battles with each other, and to defend what has become very valuable to you".[19] The MGH is a good example of the strong conflict that social and community psychiatry met in the professional and academic arena.

Years before Francis Weld Peabody, professor of medicine and director of clinics and laboratories at the Harvard Medical School, pointed out the influence of the chief of a medical department:[20]

> Thus, the administration of the department of medicine, with its large teaching and clinical staff, its responsibility for the welfare of a considerable number of patients, its interrelations with the hospital administration and its sub-departments (social service, dietetics, physical therapy) is a very different thing from the administration of a department of physiology or biologic chemistry . . . If the chief has any conviction as to the relation of doctors to their patients, to scientific research, or to any other aspect of his profession, this is his opportunity to bring it out, and in so doing he will determine the character of the clinic. . . . Provided the chief has anything in himself to offer, here is his chance to turn out every year a group of selected men who shall represent his ideas and his clinic all over the country, and it is to be hoped that they will gradually affect the type of medicine in many remote communities.

Even before Erich Lindemann's appointment as chief of the Psychiatric Service, the MGH was encouraged to commit itself to community service:[21]

> V The Committee listened with interest and approval to Dr. [p. 1] [Dean A.] Clark's [MGH general director] presentation of opportunities for the Hospital to experiment with the extension of its community services. The Committee believes that the Hospital has

a unique opportunity and obligation to move in this direction and recommends that aggressive steps be taken to develop specific plans.

A biography of Lindemann, published upon his appointment, clearly stated his goals for the department:[22]

> On July 1, 1954, Dr. Lindemann became Professor of Psychiatry at the Harvard Medical School and is undertaking now to develop a mental health service at the Massachusetts General Hospital and to develop a teaching program for medical students and the resident staff with special emphasis on preventive psychiatry.

From the beginning, this put him in a contentious relationship with his setting: He and his predecessor, Stanley Cobb, had their differences that made collaboration difficult. As Lindemann became more emphatic in his commitment to CMH and social psychiatry, Cobb became more disenchanted with him, concerned that Lindemann had abandoned solid drug and psychosomatic research, though he admired his initiative and ability to obtain funding.[23]

Upon Lindemann's appointment, the MGH, like the search committee that had recommended him, officially welcomed his eclectic interests, especially in social psychiatry:[24]

> On July first Dr. Erich Lindemann takes over the Psychiatry Service of the Massachusetts General Hospital, as Chief of Service, and becomes Professor of Psychiatry at the Harvard Medical School. By training he is both a psychologist and psychiatrist. . . . In recent years he has held important teaching positions in the Department of Social Relations at Harvard University and in the Harvard School of Public Health. His varied activities in psychiatry attest to the breadth of his interests and his versatility. . . . he was actively engaged in the diagnosis and management of psychotic patients. . . . he discovered the effect of sodium amytal on the mental functions of the depressed and schizophrenic patient. . . . he carried on several studies of the psychological effects of other pharmacological agents. . . . [He] was in charge of the Psychiatric Out-Patient Department and also supervised the consultation services. His pioneering studies of patients with ulcerative colitis and his observations on the somatic effects of grief. . . . He also published papers on the emotional reactions following hysterectomy and on hysteria and other neuroses. In recent years Dr. Lindemann has turned his attention to the sociological aspects of psychiatry. The Human Relations Service of Wellesley, Incorporated . . . is now well known as a highly original approach to the understanding of mental disease in an American community.

Dr. Lindemann comes to us at a time when psychology, sociology, and medicine are beginning to cooperate in important investigations. The well substantiated sciences in the Medical School will continue to be basic, but the behavioral sciences are bringing new techniques to the physician. It can hardly be doubted that in the next decades these will improve not only the treatment of the individual patient, but the relation of the general hospital to the community in which it functions. We welcome Dr. Lindemann with enthusiasm. . . . Our Psychiatry Service was one of the first psychiatry units in a general hospital. The idea was initiated by Dr. [C. Howard] Means [MGH Department of Medicine] and supported by the Rockefeller Foundation as a demonstration. . . . Thus we have aided in an important trend in modern psychiatry—to get it out of the isolated special hospital and integrate it with general medicine.

The task was to bring psychiatry to a great general hospital and make the physicians and surgeons of the staff realize that psychiatric problems occur in almost all patients with chronic, and many with acute, illness. Psychiatry is not confined to crazy people; far from it; we now regularly get consultations and patients to treat from every service in the Hospital. A great many of the staff members in departments other than psychiatry are truly interested in our work and cooperate to a most gratifying degree. They realize that much of psychiatry is the understanding of human motivation, and that such knowledge is of benefit to practically all people who suffer illness. . . . Another aspect of our work has been more controversial. We have tried to make psychiatry dynamic in every way: (1) By supporting and teaching a psychology of personality. . . . Many of the postulates upon which such a psychology is based originated with Freud, but others came from Meyer, Thorndike, Pavlov, and many contemporary psychiatrists. This point of view is eclectic, and is criticized both by the orthodox Freudian and by the anti-Freudian. Nevertheless, we have pursued it with some measure of equanimity and therapeutic success. (2) By developing and teaching a theory of mind. This holds that mind is a function of the living brain. . . . This point of view has brought us into close and fruitful collaboration with the neurosurgeons and neurologists. (3) By supporting the thesis that all function is organic. . . . Having rid ourselves of the anachronistic dichotomy, "either functional or organic", we can see that not only do lesions produce symptoms . . . but prolonged dysfunction produces lesions. . . . This is the basis of "psychosomatic medicine". (4) By studying lesions of the brain and their effect on personality.

Ellsworth Neumann, then Associate Director of the MGH, thought Lindemann was appointed chairperson of psychiatry because he was by far the most internationally known of the MGH psychiatrists and would take the hospital in the direction in which it wanted to go.[25] He saw one-third of the hospital elite (staff and administration) seeing community medicine as extremely necessary, while two-thirds wanted to stay within the hospital walls, though he saw the hospital moving increasing toward community medicine. He thought there was within the MGH— including its general directors Dean Clark and John Knowles—a general interest in community medicine. He acknowledged that there also was a strong bias toward the physical side of medicine. The hospital's direction was a matter of the number of chiefs of services with strong personalities. He was confident that with administration support, a strong enough community medicine leader could succeed and had succeeded where this was tried and that the trend would continue with good community people interested in more than one-to-one therapeutic relationships.

In seeking support for his ideas of institutional change, Lindemann and the Psychiatry Service developed a working relationship with the MGH administration. The two General Directors of the MGH during Lindemann's tenure both had sympathy for a public health perspective, reflecting the agenda of the hospital and medical school powers at that time. Clark had been a public health professional who developed groundbreaking public health programs, including the Health Insurance Program (HIP) of New York City, a pioneer in prepaid health insurance programs. Support came also from associate directors such as Ellsworth Neumann and Henry Murphy and, of course, John Knowles. Together, they were concerned about hospital personnel and administration in terms of social organization, process, and motivation. They addressed the hospital's Emergency Ward Program, developing a rehabilitation service, a nursing administration, and personnel policies.[26] The hospital administration responded to this social setting perspective. Its general executive committee (GEC) recognized that "Once considered as a place for the cure of the ill in the narrower sense, it is becoming more and more a health center including prevention of illness and rehabilitation of the chronically sick in its scope".[27] This view of mental health consultation, crisis intervention, and mental health consultation was echoed in almost one-third of the GEC report. The administrators' response for Lindemann's perspective and efforts was supportive, but at the MGH service, chiefs and professors determined hospital values and programs.

John H. Knowles's impending appointment as general director of the MGH gave Lindemann the opportunity to outline to this man with a public health background his efforts and experience in introducing a social approach to the MGH.[28] Knowles was a clinician who understood that the hospital and academia had a professional and moral responsibility to meet the needs of the community:[29]

> health has become a basic human birthright in America and like other birthrights, it is being identified by increasing numbers as a function of government

(p. 1)

Only recently have some of our medical school research plans included studies of the patient care and community service functions. This type of "applied" research has a better chance of giving something to the community which will improve the organization and distribution of health services. . . [a component of] the proper balance of university and hospital function. I do believe that the attitude of the hospital must be geared to its primary function of caring for the sick . . . I cannot agree with the statement made repeatedly today by medical faculty that "A university hospital should offer long-term patient care to the extent needed for optimum teaching and research which should be its major goals". [Letter to the Editor from Dr. Robert Williams. *New England Journal of Medicine* 271 1121 (1964)]. . . . There is one crucial area here I believe both teaching hospital and medical school have failed, and this is the area of planning for the health needs of communities. . . . Demographers, economists, city planners and architects, public health disciplines, sociologists and so on are readily available and invaluable to such planning [note the participants in the Space Cadets]. . . . the medical curriculum has not kept pace with the presently emerging, major issues of medical care.

(pp. 17–18)

It is important to know Lindemann's perspective and goals in order to understand his programs and advocacy at the MGH and the reputation and responses they engendered from the MGH social system. Lindemann's wife and colleague in community mental health thought that he was interested not in history but in the present and future.[30] For instance, he gave no evidence of knowing about the Emmanuel or psychopathic hospital movements, which were forerunners of many of his ideas and efforts and had much to teach about reactions to and results from them.

Lindemann consistently emphasized the psychoanalytic basis for his professional approach. He always reaffirmed his identity as a psychoanalyst and psychoanalytic psychiatry as the main therapeutic contribution in clinical psychiatry and psychosomatic medicine:

we believe that the psychoanalytic formulation of concepts concerning personality functioning are still the most useful theoretical forms in which to make inquiries, supplemented by learning theory and systems theory.[31]

He presented to a group of pediatricians this perspective on psychiatry:[32]

professional identity in psychiatry is changing. . . . I would think of myself as a mental health worker . . . who applied psychoanalytic theory and some psychoanalytic routines to the understanding and modification of societal processes, which may be influencing the well being of individuals.

(p. 1)

I believe that a great strength in the psycho analytic approach is it is closer to ideology than to a set of theories . . . psychoanalysis is embedded in the culture. . . . The culture is moving on in certain quite specific directions. . . . people no longer handle problems by punitive approaches, reward-punishment constellations, or reconditioning, but by understanding the people involved and understanding the problems they are meeting . . . in terms of their patterns of mastery and . . . to add to their efforts of mastery, knowing . . . anxieties and what unconscious or conscious obstacles might interfere.

(p. 2)

While he affirmed the importance of brain function in comprehensive psychiatry, he relegated biological therapeutics to a secondary role and was uncomfortable with electro-convulsive therapy as something imposed on and not in collaboration with patients. He also saw psychoanalysis as the basis of his social psychiatry, as in his talk at the Boston Psychoanalytic Institute: "The Use of Psychoanalytic Constructs in Preventive Psychiatry". MGH staff and medicine in general had mixed feelings about psychoanalysis, with pockets of disdain and rejection. Avery Weisman at the MGH wrote an exploration of the place of psychoanalysis in psychiatry and the MGH.[33] This hostility was sensed as a constituent of the hostile petition circulated in regard to the choice of Lindemann's successor (see later on). Thus, this was another component that Lindemann had to deal with in promoting his program.

Lindemann stated succinctly the evolution of the theoretical basis of the social psychiatry perspective of his program: "We might hopefully say that by expanding our orbit of concern from individual disease to crisis behavior and then to problems of human ecology, we may lay the groundwork of community-wide innovations of care and prevention".[34] He expanded on this in a discussion with one of his likeminded supporters at MGH, General Director John Knowles:[35]

A useful notion in such preventive intervention has been the concept of "crisis" in an emotional or social context in contrast to the concept of "disease". We considered medical patients on the medical and surgical wards, as well as those appearing in the Emergency Ward, as proper candidates for psychiatric appraisal and intervention even if they do not have established mental disease in the form of psychoses or psychoneuroses. Many of these persons are deeply troubled about overwhelming adjustment problems and many of the members of their families are endangered in terms of their emotional adjustment even though they are not sick in the narrower sense of the word. Our impetus to this type of crisis-intervention came from studies of bereaved states and grief reactions since the Coconut Grove fire in which we learned to diagnose and to prognosticate the severity of reactions at the time of a severe loss in the network of human relationships. From these studies it became apparent that the context of the roles played by the patient vis-a-vis other individuals, one of whom died or was removed, had to be changed into a new role profile and that this role transition constitutes a crisis attended by severe emotional reactions: a temporary disintegration of psychological and some aspects of physiological functioning. We were able to extend the study to other patterns of role transitions related to the work life and to the typical crises in life which are constituted by adolescence, marriage, childbearing, and bereavement. A series of studies on the medical and surgical wards was interested in the crisis reactions related to surgery and to anticipated death. The Human Relations Service in Wellesley was created to study in detail the reactions to role transitions engendered by school entrance and shift from elementary to high school and by entering job training after school. The information obtained in this context then was used for the problems encountered in the Emergency Ward. With this new orientation to crises and emotional adaptation relating to changes in the social context, rather than to established disease, there has been a very considerable extension of the range of psychiatric problems.

Lindemann further elaborated on the mental health perspective that he encouraged—social context as primary, from which followed professional responsibility for improving the community context through mental health consultation—and transferring this perspective from the Wellesley community to the MGH community:[36]

> Modern psychiatry means effective intervention in clusters of human beings concerned with the predicament which often is signaled by the disturbed state of one person who comes with an entrance ticket. . . . If you take social context seriously and are really willing to abide by your convictions that each patient arriving in your orbit of power is only a fragment of a disordered social system then your relationship to the participant in this social system is very much enhanced. You will become concerned with the family. . . . you will become concerned with the power structure to which the patient belongs, to those people who control his life. You will become concerned with [the] institutional organization [in] which he is embedded. You will become concerned with city planning, the housing which he has, the prospects for advancement in his life situation, and so on, and, you will not only look

common cause in the face and say—isn't it too bad—there you are. But you will decide to work out those psychological, sociological issues in the community which you can use as admonition vis-a-vis the power structure decision-makers in the community to tell them perhaps your next decision might be of such order that there will not be so many casualties, of a psychiatric kind anyway. And it will be at that point where our intervention of psychological disorders by social means comes about. This is a young field, a field very much attacked by others, a field considered by many as strange and paramedical for medical sciences, but a field which has tremendous enthusiasm in some other places.

(pp. 7–11)

Caplan saw this as introducing a population/community approach, adapted from HRS:[37]

> Erich Lindemann, when he moved from the Harvard School of Public Health to the Harvard Medical School in 1954, promoted a population orientation in the Department of Psychiatry at Massachusetts General Hospital. There he pioneered the modification of the concepts and skills that he had developed in his community program at the Wellesley Human Relations Service for use inside the hospital. He tried to deal not only with the community of patients but with the community of the hospital staff and the intrahospital social system, as he had become accustomed to do in dealing with the social systems of community agencies and with the field of social forces in the town of Wellesley.

In his new position, Lindemann carried over both the public health perspective and his relationship with the HSPH: he maintained an appointment at HSPH, and Gerald Caplan, who assumed Lindemann's former position at HSPH, was appointed to MGH.[38] Lindemann made it clear that he envisioned introducing CMH in many spheres:[39] mental health as part of public health education, a CMH approach to the MGH hospital community as well as its surrounding neighborhoods, a redirection of hospital services to a social medicine approach, and CMH services and research to influence community agencies and city planning. He saw the roots of this in the HRS, the West End Study, and the Mental Health Service in the MGH Psychiatry Service.

In practical implementation, Lindemann sought to have prevention and rehabilitation principles guide the MGH Psychiatry Service:[40]

> In general we are approaching a program of which intensive psychotherapy and systematic steps for the care of psychoneurotic patients is still the focus, but which is expanding its horizon to include

systematic consideration of rehabilitation and preventive psychiatry as part of an overall health program.[41]

He reported the following:

- adding psychiatry consultants to the MGH Family Health Program and Medical Social Service rounds
- addressing the problem of long, dependent hospital ward stays—Lindemann's public health and John Nemiah's (psychiatry senior staff member) rehabilitation background combined to develop a program of improvement in social skills and dealing with human relations and of developing an occupational therapy program
- accepting patients as "boarders" on the psychiatry ward to study and care for "casualties" of medical treatment (ACTH, cortisone, psychosomatic illness)
- supporting Nemiah's studies of back pain from surgery and work injury developing into a rehabilitation program on the Psychiatry Service in conjunction with the MGH and Bay State Medical Rehabilitation Clinic; they were aware that patients with activity defenses become passive in treatment, leading to chronic disability, and such patients were to be treated with psychotherapy and prevention of disability
- psychiatric consultation with the MGH Orthopedic Department and the Peabody Home for Crippled Children.

He envisioned research programs in the following:

- language style (by Maria Lorenz)
- the neurophysiology of language (Stanley Cobb)
- psychosomatics and personality structure in different disorders (Nemiah and Frances J. Bonner)
- social determinants of asthma, rheumatoid arthritis, and other psychosomatic disorders (child psychiatry group)
- reactions to severe stress such as surgery in children and burns (Robert Long, Oliver Cope—MGH Surgical Service)
- suicide in critical situations (Peter Sifneos)
- experimental psychological-behavioral effects of sedatives and intoxicants (John von Felsinger, Henry S. Beecher—chief of the MGH Anesthesia Service)
- motivation, cognition, and planned social behavior of people with neurosis in task groups (George A. Talland—new from the HDSR).

Lindeman was indefatigable in teaching the social and public health ideology, advocating for its adoption, and proposing structures and programs that would embody it, though many achieved little or limited implementation. An early outline of the prospective implementation of these principles in a reconstructed psychiatry department appeared in the department's annual report:[42]

> Additions to the department included George Saslow (professor of psychiatry, George Washington University, St. Louis) to develop the Out-Patient Department, and Alfred Stanton to increase staff integration between MGH and McLean Hospital. "<u>The Mental Health Service</u> The third important development during this year was the inauguration of the 'Mental Health Service' of the Department of Psychiatry. This group of workers representing not only psychiatry but also experts in social science, community organization and child development is concerned with the protection of mental health and the prevention of mental disease. This group is working closely with the Family Health Service under the direction of Dr. [David] Rutstein [chairperson, HMS Department of Preventive Medicine] to contribute to the diagnosis of disturbed family situations and to render assistance to the members of the families who are endangered in their emotional adjustment. The Mental Health Service is concerned with the emotional problems of the population in the area surrounding the hospital. Many families in the West End will be moved from their present location and a new housing development is expected to bring into the neighborhood of the hospital families from a different level of society. The Mental Health Service serves as a consultation resource to social agencies and professional groups in the neighborhood in such crises. <u>A Behavioral Science Laboratory</u> Widening the horizon of psychiatric activities in this manner has necessitated the development of a strong and active program in basic behavioral science. Within the last year we have added four psychologists well trained in clinical and experimental methods; one expert in child development; one worker in community organization and an outstanding sociologist to our group. Their influence has been marked both in greater precision of diagnosis and prognosis, and in developing our research program".
>
> (p. 2)

Liaison Work with Medical Services—with Walter Bauer, MD (chief of MGH Medical Service), a senior fellow on each ward, joint fourth year HMS teaching with Bauer re emotional and social factors in medical illness, and an effort to care for psychiatric problems without transferring patients to psychiatry ward. Joint work with MGH Rehabilitation and Orthopedic services, and Peabody Home for Crippled Children regarding emotional needs.

<u>Training Program</u> . . . We carried a large part of the psychiatry teaching for first-year and second-year medical students. . . . To the

training of residents and fellows in psychiatry and to that of social workers, now has been added a training program in clinical psychology. The USPHS [United States Public Health Service] has made a considerable grant to us to further this kind of training with particular emphasis on the preparation of future workers in community mental health. This program is being developed in close cooperation with Dr. Gerald Caplan of the Division of Mental Health of the Harvard School of Public Health and with Dr. Donald Klein of the Wellesley Human Relations Service. Both agencies provide field training opportunities in community aspects of mental health of a type which is not yet available through our own mental health service.

Research . . . We are beginning the precise study of the social behavior of patients in small groups.

(pp. 5–6)

Lindemann saw a trend toward shorter stays for acute psychiatric illness, aftercare, and preventive intervention in the general hospital looked to the McLean Hospital to care for and rehabilitate chronic conditions.

In another effort to support this public health/CMH effort, Lindemann submitted a proposal for the Cooperative Program of the Department of Psychiatry of the Massachusetts General Hospital and of the Harvard School of Public Health:[43]

a ten-year program of research and development in community mental health . . . assemble a core group of high level research workers . . . long-term appointments and adequate technical assistance . . . a series of studies in the theory and practice of community mental health and preventive psychiatry . . . development of the specialist training programs in the two units . . . consultants both for research projects in these and other Harvard Units as well as for pioneer community mental health programs in other parts of the country.

Lindemann suggested several other administrative approaches to the major restructuring and redirection, broadening the department in perspective, space, and integration with other services—proposed and advocated before MGH governing bodies:

We propose the establishment of a new organization to be called the M.G.H. Institute of Mental Health. This shall be located on the grounds of and closely associated with the services of the Massachusetts General Hospital, and shall incorporate the Psychiatric Department of the hospital as well as the Community Mental Health Services. It shall also be a teaching unit of the Harvard Medical School. . . . It is proposed that the ward and the ambulatory services occupy one floor of the Baker Memorial [Building] and the contiguous floor of the Pathology Building . . . Baker 10 and Baker roof, and floors 10, 11, and 12 of the Pathology Building.[44]

. . .

The change from the designation Pathology Building to the broader title of Medical Science Building is correct when it is considered that in addition to Pathology the building will house what might be called an Institute of Neurology and Psychiatry. . . . it establishes a link between the Hospital and the great scientific resources of Harvard University and Massachusetts Institute of Technology. . . . psychiatry has found joint interest with the behavioral sciences.[45]

. . .

The new chapter in developing of psychiatry in this hospital which started with Dr. Lindemann's arrival can perhaps best be described as the systematic application of concepts and methods of behavioral and social science to clinical problems.

There seems to be an urgent need to get away from the diffuseness of impressions gained from the verbal productions of patients and to arrive at a more objective, quantifiable description of individual and social behavior:

Social scientists in the field of experimental psychology, social psychology, sociology, and anthropology have made considerable strides in the last decade in developing such methods. . . . Dr. George Saslow and Dr. Joseph Matarazzo are using the interaction chronograph. . . . The so-called process of interaction analysis which was developed by Robert Bales holds promise.[46]

[The department] Shows modest increase in in- and out-patients and child psychiatry patients. . . . We would like to continue a 17 bed medical psychiatric service and we would like to develop a 15 bed service for psychoses and a 15 bed neuroses rehabilitation center.

Laboratory Division

1. a section for experimental psychology
2. a social interaction study unit
3. a bio-chemistry section
4. a psychodynamics study section
5. a mental health section:

    a.   for demographic and community studies
    b.   for systematic observation of children's groups

6. a unit for behavioral science in pediatrics.[47]

Your application for a Health Research Facilities Grant . . . Grant request: $106,625 Title of Project: Psychiatric Floor, Warren Medical Sciences Building Principal Investigator: Erich Lindemann, M.D.[48]

(Note that plans included an office for Dr. John Seeley—a likeminded sociologist.)[49]

And reports of the activities of the MGH Psychiatry Service show a persistent, recurrent integration in the structure of the department of the social origins of mental health, social crises in the origins of mental disability, and social reconstruction in achieving mental rehabilitation.[50] The earlier years of Lindemann's tenure indicate efforts to expand psychiatry into other aspects of medicine and to collaborate with them in the care of patients and preparation of trainees. One example of the interests of the department is the list of journals to which it subscribed:[51]

JOURNALS IN THE SUPPLY CLOSET & JOURNALS WHICH MAY BE FOUND IN THE SUPPLY CLOSET: [scattered issues or brief sequences] American Anthropologist, Am. J. Medicine, Am. J. of Orthopsychiatry, Am J. of Psychiatry, Am. J. of Psychology, Am. J. of Public Health, Am. J. of Sociology, Am Psychologist, Am Sociological Review, Archives of Neurology and Psychiatry, British J. of Psychology, Bulletin of the Menninger Clinic, Group Psychotherapy, Human Organization, Human Relations, International J. of Psychoanalysis, J. of Abnormal and Social Psychology, J of the American Medical Association, J. of the American Psychoanalytic Association, J of Clinical and Experimental Psychopathology, J. of Experimental Analysis of Behavior, J. of Experimental Psychology, J. of the Hillside Hospital, J of Medical Education, J. of Mental Science, J. of Nervous an Mental Diseases, J of Neurochemistry, J. of Neurophysiology, J. of Personality, J. of Social Issues, Neurology, New England J. of Medicine, Psychoanalytical Quarterly, Psychological Abstracts, Psychological Bulletin, Psychological Review, Psychosomatic Medicine, Sociological Abstracts, Sociometry, Transactions of the New York Academy of Sciences.

Lindemann's hopes for a robust CMH research program were reflected in his outline of an array of research projects in the department exploring aspects of social psychiatry (see endnotes for specifics).[52]

G. Ronald Hargreaves, with whom Lindemann shared warm mutual appreciation, had moved from the World Health Organization (WHO) to become the Nuffield professor of psychiatry at the University of Leeds (United Kingdom). In an undated letter, Lindemann wrote,

I am trying at present to transform the Psychiatric Service here at Harvard and at the Mass. General into a Mental Health Service which extends all the function of a good mental health agency into the various departments and layers of the hospital and its surrounding community. Perhaps it will help a little to make the hospital a better servant to the community.[53]

This was reflected in the development of a psychiatric consultation service embedded in the other services in the hospital:[54]

> The [medical] consultation service . . . is an important new development in our relationship to the total [MGH] hospital program. On the basis of last year's experience we have been asked to arrange for a psychiatric resource to each medical ward.
>
> 1. The consultant will be available during one morning a week for either participation in medical social service rounds or participation in another weekly rounds.
> 2. The liaison work with the Medical Department also includes active participation in the care of ambulatory patients in the Medical Out-Patient Department. . . . This program will include participation in the training of a medical assistant resident. . . . The program also will involve an active teaching participation in the training of 3rd year medical students. . . . It further includes psychiatric participation in the development of the family health service under Dr. [Joseph H.] Stokes [III—MGH chief of family and preventive medicine] and Dr. [David] Rutstein [chairperson, HMS Department of Preventive Medicine]. [There were multiple joint projects with the MGH Medical Service, whose chief, Walter Bauer, was sympathetic to psychiatry and contextual medicine.[55]]
> 3. The further development of our program may be described as a joint medical-psychiatric service involving the joint planning of medical care of patients with chronic medical disease. Some of these patients may be treated on the medical wards either by a medical student with psychiatric supervision or by a medical resident with psychiatric consultation or a psychiatrist may undertake the psychotherapeutic work with . . . close articulation with the medical regime which remains the responsibility of the medical resident.
> 4. Close scrutiny of the problems which arise in such joint programs of medical care especially with respect to nursing care, social work and occupational therapy.

Some patients may be located on Ward B-7 [open psychiatry ward] in a special research section devoted to this purpose. The care of these patients would be handled jointly by overlapping medical and psychiatric administration. Here we may have the opportunity to [p. 1] work out the respective roles of the medical and psychiatric personnel and the best living arrangements and arrangements for human relations . . . to facilitate total medical care. The work of this Service will reach into the Out-Patient follow-up and also be concerned with the care of the patients' families and with the development of a health maintenance program for these families. This development will be carried forth by a planning group consisting of Drs. [Walter] Bauer [MGH Chief of the Medical Service] . . . [Erich] Lindemann [MGH chief of the Psychiatry Service] and [Carl] Binger [MGH director of psychiatry Medical Consultation Service] with the necessary specialist advice". [John Knowles—later MGH general director—and Lindemann supported the involvement of a medical resident September 1955–August 1956.]

Lindemann's efforts to implement CMH goals early in his tenure encompassed training as well.[56] Note that the department's program sought to incorporate social psychiatry and social medicine programs into departments and schools located around Harvard University.

at the Division of Mental Health at the Harvard School of Public Health . . . it appeared that a training program to prepare future mental health workers has to start much earlier in their career than the time at which they would reach the School of Public Health. This concern was one of the reasons which motivated Dr. Lindemann to accept the Professorship at the Harvard Medical School with the opportunity of developing a program of service, training, and research at the Massachusetts General Hospital . . . to provide preparation in the field of preventive psychiatry for workers in the various contributing professions, starting with psychiatrists, and later expanding to psychologists, social scientists and social workers. the Massachusetts General Hospital . . . now deals with psychosomatic and psychoneurotic problems primarily but is expected to expand in the near future to take care of severe behavior disorders also. This facility is closely linked with the work at the McLean Hospital. . . . On the one hand, and with the field training unit in the Whittier Street Health Center and the Wellesley Human Relations Service on the other hand. . . . It is this continuum from Health to illness, called by John Gordon [HSPH epidemiologist] "the biological gradient of disease", which provides the basis for the development of preventive programs. The concern with hazardous social situations which become critical and traumatic for predisposed people and the study of possibly pathogenic individuals ("carriers of mental disease") is an important facet of this program. As a first step we plan to develop a three-year program for psychiatrists, aimed systematically at preventive psychiatry. Such a program would provide its trainees with a solid basis in clinical and dynamic psychiatry and with a conceptual frame of reference developed in modern social psychiatry and would teach them the skills for becoming established in the field of "preventive intervention" and mental health consultation. At the end of this training such trainees should be ideally suited to direct and develop mental health agencies in various communities. . . . Facilities . . . A Family Service Program has been started here under the leadership of Dr. David Rutstein, Professor of Preventive Medicine [HMS], which will provide an opportunity for an integrated preventive psychiatry program. . . . Staff: At the M.G.H. . . . The psychiatrists who will supervise this program directly are: Lincoln D. Clark . . . Peter Sifneos. . . Whittier Street [Boston community health center] Dr. Gerald Caplan. . . McLean Hospital . . . Wellesley [HRS]. . . . Donald C. Klein. . . Department of Social Relations [Harvard] including such well known men as Tacoltt Parsons, Clyde K.M. Kluckhohn, Charles F. Mosteller, Henry A. Murray, Robert W. White.

(pp. 1–8)

Simultaneously, there was a sustained project to integrate training institutions and ideologies, seeking to interrelate all HMS psychiatry training programs in a graduate school of psychiatry.[57] Lindemann hosted these meetings, which would develop another avenue by which to introduce social psychiatry in all HMS-affiliated psychiatry departments: MGH; Beth Israel, Peter Bent Brigham, McLean, and Boston City Hospitals and the Massachusetts Mental Health Center (MMHC).

Lindemann pursued CMH training for psychiatric residents by embedding it in psychiatric residency training and in the culture of the MGH:[58]

Training Program for Psychiatrists in Community Mental Health $73,666 7/1/58–6/30/59–4th yr of 5 yr prog. (funding to expand Dept to 3 yr MGH+McLean psychiatric residency) . . . 7. Describe the training program.

We believe that we have been much more successful this year in communicating to the total staff the validity of our program within the hospital as exemplified by ward-wide consultation on the medical and related services by explicit concern with the rehabilitation of medical and orthopedic patients who cannot be cured and by ecological surveys of the patient population in the medical clinic and in the Emergency Ward. The staff has also been stimulated to become interested in the social system aspects of the administrative arrangements in the different segments of the hospital in the relationship of administrators, clinicians, nurses and maintenance personnel and in the use of mental health consultation methods . . . as distinct from the traditional patient-centered consultation of the past.

These efforts of our training faculty in community mental health go far beyond the influence on the specific trainees of our program . . . a series of seminars covering . . . psychiatric ecology, community mental health practice, preventive intervention and mental health consultation to which is added . . . group dynamics. . . . The more important experience of the trainees is the joint participation with the other professions in organized mental health programs in our three field stations . . . the West End Neighborhood Program, the Whittier Street Study of Families in Crises and the Community-Wide Program of the Service in Wellesley. [The course lectures are listed in the endnotes.[59]]

. . .

During the last year . . . we have gradually created a "felt need" in the hospital community and are being asked more and more in consultation concerning questions not related to individual patients but to administrative problems and to the organization of the social system within the hospital community. . . . With a more confident faculty and with a more accepting atmosphere in the hospital as a whole, the students will have heightened opportunities for enthusiastic participation. . . . A crucial development of the next year. . . [is] the reorganization and enrichment of our basic program in training psychiatrists in such a manner that the mental health orientation becomes an integral part of clinical instruction, diagnosis and therapeutic planning. . . . When Dr. Lindemann took over the Service and Dr. Stanton became the chief of the McLean Hospital. . . . there was the opportunity for the development of a basic program . . . with special focus on social psychiatry and the social sciences while at the same time providing solid ground work in the biological approaches. with the expectation that many students in this program will choose to do advanced work in community mental health, social psychiatry, dynamic psychiatry or in one of the physiological approaches to behavioral disturbances. . . . we would like support for an integrated program in basic psychiatry leading to a program in community mental health and also offering opportunities for advanced work in other specialties.

Information Concerning the Massachusetts General Hospital Psychiatric Training Program: Fourth and Fifth Years. . . . There are five major areas:

1. Advanced Psychotherapy . . .
2. Community and Preventive Psychiatry . . .
3. Research . . .
4. Teaching . . .
5. Administrative Psychiatry.

(pp. 6–10)

Lindemann also envisioned subspecialty training in CMH, as in correspondence with Dr. Robert H. Jones, coordinator of the MGH Rehabilitation Service.[60]

These principles were also reflected in the psychiatric residency training program:[61]

> Psychiatric Residency Programs Massachusetts General Hospital . . .
> III FACILITIES A. The General Hospital Division . . . 6. The Mental
> Health Unit provides training for advanced fellows in the techniques
> of community and preventive psychiatry. The unit is closely associ-
> ated with the Harvard School of Public Health, the Wellesley Human
> Relations Service, the Whittier Street Clinic, and the Department of
> Social Relations of Harvard University.
>
> (p. 3)

> Fourth and Fifth Years . . . 2) Community and Preventive Psychiatry.
> Opportunity is provided here for advanced training in the techniques
> and methods of community and preventive psychiatry through the
> training program of the Mental Health Unit. Requests for further
> information about this program should be directed to: Dr. Erich
> Lindemann Chief of Service Psychiatric Department Massachusetts
> General Hospital
>
> (p. 9)

Simultaneous with these efforts to expand the span of mental health and incorporate psychiatry into other medical specialties and into the social sciences, there was advocacy for a public health role for the general hospital. There were MGH and HMS forays into family health, social medicine, and preventive medicine that Lindemann supported and with which he collaborated. None of these endured.

Operationally, Lindemann wanted to increase the number of psychiatric beds to 80,[62] improve financing, and add HRS values.[63] On one occasion, he recalled that "There was the wish to have at the M.G.H. a 40-bed unit where long-term psychiatric care could be given—e.g., for ulcerative colitis",[64] which was rejected by MGH, whether as part of the chronic competition among the services for resources, depreciation of psychiatry and/or Lindemann, or its being financially unsupportable.

An incubator of ideas and planning for the MGH Psychiatry Service was a regular meeting between the MGH Mental Health Service, the HSPH Division of Mental Health and other interested divisions, and other public health mental health organizations, including the Whittier Street Family Guidance Center (a field training unit of the HSPH), HRS, the Greater Boston Council for Youth, the Harvard Medical School, the DMH, the City of Boston Health Department, the HDSR, and visitors from the US and other countries.[65] On July 22, 1954, it discussed the Family Guidance Center, established in July 1954 with a grant from the Commonwealth Fund to develop a mental health unit as an integral part of a public health center that would demonstrate the practice of public health mental health. Research projects as a part of the professional activities of public health workers included family adaptation to stresses such as the premature birth of a child, birth of twins, birth of children with congenital defects, Rh negative pregnancies, and family members admitted to and discharged from the hospital for tuberculosis. It also wanted to study the interaction of mental health and public health workers, among mental health workers, and between government public health mental health workers and associated mental health workers in the community.[66] There was discussion of the study tools, related dynamics, case referral, instant availability, inclusion in planning, full information sharing, etc. HMS Dean George Packer Berry was greatly interested in the project. Lindemann related it to the experience in HRS and "spoke of the possibility of seeing in the reorganization of the Psychiatric Department of Massachusetts General Hospital an application of some of the things discussed at the Family Guidance Center".[67]

On October 21, 1954, there were presentations by Lindemann on the foundational theory and its implementation in the HRS; by Donald Klein on various projects at the HRS; by Clara Mayo on the HRS program of preventive intervention in a nursing school; and about several CMH-related research projects.[68] The agenda for the meeting on November 18, 1954, focused on Lindemann's projected program for the MGH Department of Psychiatry, especially its CMH aspects.

On May 19–20, 1955, the Community Mental Health Organization Conference was held.[69] There were presentations on the implementation of CMH and its consequences, which presaged important issues in the CMH movement:

- Dr. Lindemann restated three levels of inquiry: "1.) verification of a social science theory; 2.) initiation of actions which are presumed useful; and 3.) using the community as an object of observation which one does not yet know how to describe fully. He thought that the third choice offered the most possibilities and that one could watch the community in crisis, rationalizing the purpose as being to help such a community, but mostly to observe with this community what actually occurs" (p. 1).

- "Mr. [Arthur] Hallock [DMH Division of Mental Hygiene] spoke of work toward a partnership between the areas being organized under the CMHCs Act and the Massachusetts Department of Mental Health, and that there were now ten such arranged. The mental health program includes, besides therapy, consultation and education as well. . . . The Commonwealth is now proposing that two field trial projects be set up in Brockton and Worcester with the aim of service to the community as a whole, using some of the CMH techniques, and then determining what community changes can take place. He was asking quite directly for support and ideas from this conference" (p. 1).

- "Dr. [Leonard] Duhl stressed the danger that the large amount of money available is forcing the establishment of programs. He felt that this would backfire, because such programs would not fulfill all needs promised and that it would be better to have an overall plan toward which to work slowly and solidly to the same end" (p. 4).

At these joint meetings in 1954, Gerald Caplan presented A Proposal for a Community Mental Health Center (nine years before the Community Mental Health Centers Act).[70] It envisioned the need for preventive mental health work. This was seen as the responsibility of a community psychiatry clinic:

> This responsibility is very often unwelcome. . . . the clinician feels that his participation in preventive work is a diversion from his main concerns. There are few clinicians who believe that preventive work is as important, interesting, or rewarding as treatment and diagnosis. This situation is a serious handicap to the development of good preventive programs. . . . if preventive work is to be done effectively at the present time, it must be made the responsibility of a separate agency whose primary function is prevention. Our proposal is for the creation of a Mental Health Center that will have the responsibility for developing a complete and integrated program of prevention in the community. Such a program should provide for: 1) a continuing research program aimed at developing a basic theoretical guide for activities: 2) continuing experimentation with a wide variety of new activities and evaluations of their utility: 3) a serious attempt to develop sources of personnel and adequate training facilities.
>
> (p. 1)

I Research: (a) epidemiology (community conditions, illness prevalence and incidence, health, influence on health & illness); (b) analysis of health and illness (apply research); (c) cultural analysis (describe groups, effect on health, illness, and service utilization); (d) evaluation (program evaluation)

II Activities: Planning committee of "leading workers in the Boston area". Experience of HRS, Harvard Field Training Unit at the Whittier Street Health Center. Community participation (e.g., Roxbury interested citizens, agencies, Unit Council, settlement houses, churches, nursery schools, housing projects, well-baby clinics). (a) Community education (psychiatry concepts to community, focus on key people/professionals—teachers, physicians, clergy, settlement house workers, public health nurses). (b) Community planning (social institutions for good mental health—e.g., cooperation between social groups, nursery schools, recreational facilities; possible work in large, inter-racial public housing projects). (c) Counseling (focus on successful management of specific situations—not basic character change; mothers at nursery schools and well-baby clinics, people in distress, bad risk case finding of those at great psychiatric risk). (d) Consultations to key community workers and social agencies about psychiatric problems (similar to HRS—meetings with groups). (e) Group work (many groups, orientations, purposes; mothers about child care, psychotherapy, community action, health education, etc.).

III Personnel and Training: Model for other CMHCs. Traditions/ contributions from psychiatrist (leadership), social worker (psychiatric, group, community planning), public health nurse, clinical psychologist (especially skilled bridging psychiatry and social science); social psychology, sociology, social anthropology (especially research). Train HSPH Division of Mental Health students, other key centers of academic and professional training.

Relate to existing community psychiatry services: Fill gaps and enhance services and act as a channel and framework for their preventive work. Liaison group.

Implement Planning committee of prominent professional workers in the Boston areas in early spring [?1954] develop the philosophy and implement the plan. An advisory committee of community professionals (e.g., clergy, settlement house workers, physicians, community leaders). Locate in Roxbury [a Boston neighborhood known for a large minority population]. Citizens group (Roxbury residents) organize and carry out the activities of the center; they are included in planning and activity, feel ownership of the program.

Location: Housed in Whittier Street Health Center in Roxbury [a field site of the HSPH Division of Mental Health]. Administrative control by the Field Training Unit of the HSPH. This is near HSPH, HMS, Boston public health clinics, in a racially neutral population. Maintain a relationship with the Boston Health Department (encourage its interest in mental health). Near two large housing projects.

Budget: Team of one each psychologist, psychiatric social worker, psychiatric public health nurse, health educator, social scientist (social psychologist vs. social anthropologist); ½ time clinical psychologist. Staff from the HDSR and HSPH. A psychiatrist as advisor and providing a consultation service.

Perhaps because it was attributed to Gerald Caplan, it seemed to rely heavily on mental health professionals and Harvard-affiliated institutions, and not on Lindemann's HRS approach of growing out of and with the community.[71]

The Psychiatry Service saw rehabilitation as close to its mental health and preventive goals. It took an interest in the hospital's Rehabilitation Service as well as the rehabilitative and habilitative functions, with a holistic, social perspective:[72]

> The Psychiatric Department in consultation with this Service made use of its resources of psychologists and social scientists in systematic observation of the activities of both the patients and the personnel to track down these difficulties which stood in the way of the most effective division of labor and distribution of roles within the Unit helping to better motivation of the patients and relieving anxiety on the part of the nurses and administrators.
>
> . . .
>
> Much consideration is being given to the rehabilitation of the chronically ill by strengthening the social services and extending psychiatric and social diagnosis to all patients who may have difficulties integrating in home and in community. With respect to the large patient population of the Medical Clinics, there are beginnings of systematically investigating the ethnic and cultural aspects of the excessive dependency on physician and clinic which is a common problem in medical care of these individuals. Much thought is being given in the Pediatric Department to the personality development and motivation of children who have to live and grow in family and neighborhood with diabetes, obesity or deforming illness. Finally, there appears on the part of industrial concerns a growing readiness to seek the help of the hospital [for accident victims] . . . and of those among their staff whose state of health and effectiveness is impaired by the emotional consequences of crisis situations.
>
> (p. 3)

> The Family Health Service, a joint enterprise of the Department of Medicine, Department of Pediatrics, Department of Preventive Medicine, and Department of Psychiatry, extends services to families in the neighborhood of the hospital, thus teaching medical students the orientation to family groups and environmental factors which the hospital now shares with the general practitioner. At the same time supported by a grant from the United States Public Health Service, the Mental Health Service of the Psychiatry Department is working with social agencies and with the relocation authorities of the West End in assisting families in their adaptation to the enforced change of their homes. Through these services new insight is gained about family life in a slum area as it contributes to ill health and emotional instability.
>
> (p. 4)

The perspective of rehabilitation as re-education rather than dependent care was clearly articulated by Lindemann at the GEC: Patients were seen as students and physical therapists as teachers rather than as having a patient–therapist relationship; weekly discussion sessions integrated the roles of caretakers; and the spouse was seen as consultant to the community setting.[73]

This adaptive and learning approach to mental illness fit well with Lindemann's social psychiatry, and he followed it in many settings at MGH. He developed a special understanding with John H. Knowles, the general director of the MGH (1962–72) with a social responsibility view of the general hospital. He met Knowles over planning for the future of the McLean Hospital.[74] They addressed financial problems, ideas of administration, and treatment planning privileges for the staff and town physicians. Lindemann supported the ideas of Alfred Stanton (McLean psychiatrist-in-chief) that mental illness is an effort at adaptation; the need to evaluate personality and life adjustment to correct the illness by working with patients' adaptive resources via psychotherapy and education; that medications and electro-convulsive therapy (ECT) were only auxiliary; and that improvement is faster with vigorous treatment and return to family and community rather than the disease concept of neurological and brain disorder and custodial care. Stanton's treatment philosophy reflected this set of priorities (see the endnotes for more).[75]

The dedication of the McLean Hospital Rehabilitation Center in 1963 (Lindemann was toastmaster) was an occasion for several authorities to speak on behalf of social medicine and psychiatry.[76] George Packer Berry, HMS dean, supported plans to bring the hospital into the community:[77]

> to use Doctor de Marneffe's [director, McLean Hospital] apt phrase—the distinguished staff will seek "to bring the hospital closer to patients living in the community, and the community closer to patients living in the hospital". This far-ranging objective, which Dr. John Knowles, has effectively articulated for the Massachusetts General Hospital also, holds great significance for progress in the mental health field, a field long frustrated by its isolation.
>
> (p. 1)

Dana Farnsworth concurred:[78]

> Physicians, both psychiatrists and others, may <u>learn</u> about the late effects of long-continued emotional stress. They <u>digest</u> and <u>organize</u> this information and <u>pass it on</u> to all members of the auxiliary mental health professions and to the non-professional attendants. They <u>teach</u> patients and their relatives.

He saw students in a broad range of disciplines learning about society while working with patients and about prognosis. This had been true in government and private hospitals. It required the development of community care, such as halfway houses, daycare, and family participation. He saw American society tending toward desegregation of people with mental illness, just as the general hospital changed toward shorter patient stays, community and home care, rehabilitation, re-education, and convalescence for the chronically ill:[79]

> The general hospital originally conceived as a curative resource care for medical and surgical care of established disease is forced to accept new responsibilities relating to total health care mainly in rehabilitation of those with chronic sickness and in preventive measures in the anticipation of future illness, particularly health education. It also is confronted with vast economical changes demanding service to specified, defined populations such as occurring in industry, insured segments of the population and in specified communities outside the center of the metropolitan district.
>
> (p. 1)

He supported the division of psychiatric care between the MGH for acute care and McLean Hospital for chronic illness and rehabilitation.

The issue of turning medicine toward social medicine was taken up in detail in the Space Cadets. John Knowles, Lindemann's likeminded general director at the MGH, shared the view of the general hospital and the MGH as a resource for community health, including mental health in 1962.[80] It reflects Erich Lindemann's perspective:

> *MGH needs direction, integration, and autonomy. Knowles' plan was to establish social science in medicine: "So we are either going to try to do it through the [Harvard] Medical School or establish sociologists, demographers, ecologists, and so on within the framework of the [MGH] administration . . . because the administration is the only neutral observer in the hospital".*[81] *. . . Hospital function increasingly deals with social, economic, and political change. Doctors can be inept in non-pathological situations: isolated, intimidated, and blocked communication with nurses and the nursing services. The hospital plans a series of lectures to the staff about social, economic, and political changes bearing on medicine to help prepare the hospital for change. It plans to find out about community needs and expectations, and has asked for help in this endeavor from Dean Schottland of Brandeis University, the HSPH, and the HMS Department of Preventive Medicine. It wants to expand ambulatory services to Logan International Airport; shift from a traditional acute, curative institution to preventive, public health, and chronic care*

functions; and add staff people with traditional training but interest in this perspective.

The MGH needs to concentrate education on vocation and technology, rather than science and intellect or the traditions and customs of medicine. Modern medicine is focusing on technology and specialization. It is losing the time, understanding, and interpersonal relationship that patients need. Patients are sophisticated in technology from the mass media, and demand it. Doctors lose charisma, authority, and understanding of patients' backgrounds. Dealing with community and CMH is an open-ended commitment. Lindemann is doing it, but most of the MGH doesn't know what he is doing.

Responses from committee members include Leonard Duhl seeing implications for a new definition of medicine and doctors. Lindemann saw a new definition of help-seeking, which challenges the compartmentalization of the medical profession. Marc Fried saw the doctor's status unchanged, but the role of doctor and hospital changed, requiring a redistribution engendering conflicts with vested interests. Benson Snyder saw the doctor caring more about technology and less about participation and knowledge. Lindemann objected to the separation of technology from social and community focus, since patients expect the latter and are disappointed when they don't get it from doctors. He thought that this area can now be studied systematically. Knowles asked why not include social science in the intellectual development of doctors? Lindemann observed that when doctors confront social issues they panic, feeling overwhelmed, discouraged, and guilty, thus leading them to avoid this perspective. He suggested introducing it only when control over social processes can be demonstrated. Harold Isaacs thought that charisma was being passed from doctor to psychiatrist and social scientist; however, they are not that effective, and are not desirable as social manipulators. Joseph Lohman thought that doctors look at medical and social issues in mechanistic terms of causes and solutions. Duhl was concerned that there was no place to train psychiatrists to be social manipulators.

Discussants argued against impulsively embracing a comprehensive health service plan to avoid the control of medicine by a central hierarchy. They saw the need to recognize that change (social, political, and technological) is constant, gradually becomes incorporated in the social/political process, and affects the practice of medicine as well as other institutions. The sociologist John Seeley saw medicine defined as physicians curing diseases (including personality) and solving all problems, without considering values in medicine, setting goals, and weighing the authority to do so.

Knowles reaffirmed that the MGH staff was oriented to acute, curative medicine and not interested in social and preventive medicine except for Lindemann and the Department of Psychiatry. He

was optimistic about and proud of the medical staff and their intel-
lects, but recognized that staff members are now uneducated about
social issues and change, and thus resistant, and therefore should
not be allowed the traditional control of the hospital. He argued
that the hospital administrator must and can educate and then lead
the medical staff to a social responsibility, and should do this inde-
pendent of national medical organizations (such as the AMA and
American Association of Medical Colleges) and the medical school.
He was interested in defining community and community functions,
and including patients, doctors, health agencies, and services. Public
health and preventive medicine cannot deal with specific cases in hos-
pitals, and so are not eager to collaborate. Community patients want
big hospital technology. No longer are there great clinicians with
bedside clinical research; all are technology-oriented. MGH should
try to involve itself in all of the community with health services (such
as the Logan International Airport clinic), rotate house staff through
them for three months a year, develop a prepaid group medical prac-
tice near the hospital ambulatory services, and attempt to integrate
specialties. However, he saw the community so poorly organized that
they do not communicate their needs (a conception soon to be chal-
lenged by the civil rights and community control movement).

From his position as General Director of the MGH Knowles
continued to note and take the university and medical school to
task for continued failure in their social and community service
responsibilities:[82]

The medical school has always occupied a unique and sometimes
difficult position amongst the graduate schools of the University.
Other faculty members have looked upon medicine as a more vocational pursuit than their own scholarly interests. . . . Finally the
medical school has been concerned with the development and maintenance of a very expensive social service instrument—the teaching
hospital. This has been an uncomfortable relationship and a trying
responsibility, and no other department of the university has a similar obligation.

(p. 14–15)

There is one crucial area where I believe both teaching hospital and
medical school have failed and this is the area of planning for the
health needs of communities. The greatest blame falls on the medical
school for it could have assumed the role of coordinating agent and
provided for rational health planning on a university basis, drawing
on its tremendous intellectual wealth for help. Demographers, economists, city planners and architects, public health disciplines, sociologists and so on are readily available and invaluable to such planning.
Certainly with the median number of affiliations for medical schools

lying between 5 and 7 hospitals, some interest could have been demonstrated by now in assessing the medical wants and needs of communities and in bringing about regional planning for health facilities. Instead University regional planning has concerned itself only with the needs for "teaching material" admittedly enlightened but also short-term, self-interest.

(p. 18)

However, Knowles drew a distinction between hospitals and universities in this regard:[83]

There is considerable question in my mind as to whether any university should own and operate a hospital. I do not . . . think they are in the position to resolve effectively certain crucial conflicts of interest involving University function versus community service. Involve themselves with the social issues, yes, but do not subject the budget of the rest of the university to the possible losses of a teaching hospital, nor the hospital's necessary funds for community service to the needs of the Biochemistry or the Fine Arts Department.

Lindemann, too, saw general hospitals increasingly as facilities for the care of acute mental illness, community aftercare, and community preventive intervention, thus decreasing mental hospital referrals. He advocated for the "crisis" concept of emotional adaptation to change in a social context, rather than seeing mental health problems as established diseases. A model was grief, comprising the loss of a meaningful person, causing role transitions, which may lead to illness and surgery. Parallels were the HRS study of transitions in education, the Emergency Ward, and medical and surgical patients facing adjustment problems that affect families.

He saw an enhanced role for general hospital psychiatry in bringing mental health services closer to communities and early therapeutic intervention to prevent chronic illness. He saw it developing in the directions of home care, rehabilitation, and convalescence:[84]

the general hospital is now and will be more specialized for acute, short term care while the McLean Hospital might well develop more and more effective resources for the care and rehabilitation of chronic conditions. . . . the [Massachusetts] General Hospital is assuming a larger and larger share of the care of the acute phase of psychiatric disorders, many of whom can be returned to their families. . . . With the provision of resources for after care in the community, many persons previously in need of mental hospital care can now be looked after by the general hospital. it means larger facilities in the general hospitals for mental patients, and an extension of the program of the hospital into the community for after care and for preventive intervention to <u>forestall</u> the more serious conditions. . . . From this discussion it appeared that it might well be possible to look forward to a program of strengthened services jointly executed by McLean and the Massachusetts General [Hospital] both at the private and public levels which would alleviate the financial problems and make a significant contribution to the revolution of patterns of psychiatric care in this country.

. . .

Dr. Lindemann believes there is a remarkable opportunity in the next five or ten years in the future planning of this Hospital as regards McLean and the Department of Psychiatry to develop an outstanding Institute of General Hospital Psychiatry.[85]

In an experiment encompassing both short-term resources and long-term resources for the comprehensive mental health care of the community, Lindemann developed a working relationship with a local state mental hospital. He reached out to the Danvers State Hospital in Massachusetts to help it move from custodial to community care.[86] He sought an affiliation to share training and staff appointments. He discussed with its superintendent, Peter B. Hagopian, a joint residency training program[87] and Hagopian's appointment as clinical director and chief psychiatrist in order to maintain the hospital's residency certification. With Dr. Elizabeth Crossfield, the clinical director of Danvers and Charles L. Clay, MD, the assistant director of the MGH, he arranged that MGH psychiatric residents would work at the state hospital

[a]s part of our contribution to the psychiatric care of the people of the Commonwealth and in order to strengthen the opportunities for our residents to see certain clinical psychiatric conditions. . . . In order to increase our liaison with Danvers State Hospital and to add to the clinical experience of our residents.[88]

In 1964, Lindemann won approval from the American Board of Psychiatry and Neurology for the development of psychiatric residency training involving Danvers.[89],[90] He expected that within two and a half years, MGH would staff and direct a state mental health center, leading to an increase in resident staff and a training program including residents rotating through Danvers. To bring Danvers into the training orbit earlier, Hagopian and Crossfield were given MGH appointments; several senior MGH staff members had half-time appointments to Danvers to teach residents and medical students there; and residents were assigned to Danvers as an alternative to McLean Hospital for their second-year training.

Many people who later distinguished themselves in the fields of psychiatry, psychoanalysis, psychology, and public policy applied to the MGH Psychiatry Service for training and staff appointments, whether or not they ultimately jointed the service:[91]

Berman, Leo (developed technique of mental health consultation with teachers)

Blane, Howard, PhD (psychologist, research in alcoholism)

Dibner, Andrew (psychologist, philanthropist)

Geiger, H. Jack (community medicine, Tufts Medical School; founding member of Physicians for Human Rights, Physicians for Social Responsibility)

Katchadourian, Herant (faculty member at Stanford Medical Center Department of Psychiatry)

Lifton, Robert J. (psychiatrist researching cultural influences on personality and psychopathology)

Mandell, Arnold Joseph (psychoanalyst)

Mudd, Merle William (later executive director of The Medical Foundation, Boston)

Reimer, Delilah (rehabilitation psychiatrist)

Vaillant, George Eman (psychiatrist studying the life course of personality and mental health)

Wynne, Lyman (psychiatrist teacher, organizational member)

Zwerling, Israel (CMH psychiatrist, director of the Division of Social and Community Psychiatry at the Albert Einstein School of Medicine at Yeshiva University in New York and director of the New York Bronx Psychiatric Center).

Lindemann was eager to attract to the department social psychiatry professionals of stature. Lindemann corresponded with Dr. Christopher Heinicke (during his temporary stay at The Hampstead Child-Therapy Course in London) and invited him to join MGH's efforts in preventive psychiatry:[92]

The Department of Pediatrics and the Department of Psychiatry are jointly interested in developing a program of studies in behavioral science relating to sickness and health at different stages of physical and emotional development. . . . The program is part of our overall efforts of bringing a preventive point of view and a health orientation into a large metropolitan teaching hospital. . . . I left the School of Public Health to become the Professor of Psychiatry at the Harvard Medical School and hope very much to make useful what we learned in Wellesley and the insights which we gained from contacts with such groups as yours at the Palfrey House. The development of a laboratory of behavioral science to the study of sickness and health in children is one significant step in this direction.

He welcomed the inquiry of Marvin K. Opler (formerly at the HDSR) about a new placement where social and preventive psychiatry was active or planned.[93] He explored appointing Harris Peck (director of several community mental health programs) to head the MGH CMH program, integrating child psychiatry with pediatrics and community psychiatry.[94] He noted that "Maxwell Jones [noted British social psychiatrist] now at Stanford, temporarily based at Chico Village Rehabilitation Center for psychopaths, is coming here for two weeks in May. May conceivably be interested in running McLean".[95] He invited Erik Erikson (then in the HDSR) to sample the department's activities, especially presentations by the Research Unit on Human Development.[96]

An interesting episode involved Timothy Leary, a brilliant young psychologist who was a lecturer in clinical psychology in the Center for Personality Studies of the HDSR.[97] Leary was attracted by Lindemann's social psychiatry perspective: "I believe that you are one of the important leaders in a groundswell of realistic and humanistic psychology that is just coming into its own".[98] "As you know I am very dissatisfied with the current theories of clinical training for psychologists. In particular I'm concerned with the pseudo-objectivity, the secrecy, the depersonalization, the tendency to ignore the realities of the human situation in favor of abstractions".[99]

Lindemann was enthusiastic about Leary's interest in social influences on personality and a more humane approach to psychology.[100] They made plans for Leary to have a position at MGH:[101]

> Leary's interested in working half time at MGH starting July 1st combining community activities with psychopharmacology. . . . T.L. and Dr. [John] Hill [recommended by Leary] will give staff meeting here on November 21st. E.L. to see David [McClelland, chairperson of the Harvard Department of Psychology] next week discussing overall program and successor for clinical psychology and in Wellesley.

McClelland was receptive to Leary's spending half time at MGH taking a leadership role in developing predoctoral and postdoctoral psychology training programs in personality and interpersonal psychology, as well as community activities regarding psychopharmacology.[102] Elizabeth Lindemann remembers Leary as being odd and impolite, and she and Lindemann discussing something developmentally wrong with him. In the end, Leary's views on the therapeutic use of psychedelic drugs and the academic and legal problems that they caused prevented the implementation of these tentative plans.

Lindemann was also selective about whom to involve in the MGH Psychiatry Department. John A. Abbott, MD, retired from the MGH electroencephalography laboratory and on several occasions proposed his involvement with MGH psychiatry; Lindemann was evasive.[103] Raymond D. Adams, the MGH chief of neurological medicine, asked Lindemann to contribute a chapter on social science approaches to medical problems as part of his textbook of medicine; Lindeman was resistant and referred Adams to Gardner Quarton, who was the acting chief of psychiatry while Lindemann was a visiting professor at Stanford Medical Center.[104]

Many visitors came through the MGH Psychiatry Service and the HRS, drawn by the community mental health ideas and experiments that were rare or unique at that time. Many went on to develop careers in this field:

> Donald C. Klein, as a newly minted psychologist, was recruited by Lindemann to administer the HRS. He later joined the social psychology department at Boston College, and then social psychology training programs nationally.

James Kelly's father died when he was in college, and in 1957, he came to Boston with a new doctorate in psychology, a family, and unfocused career goals.[105] He was touched that Lindemann took a personal interest and helped guide him to a career in social, organizational, and community psychology. He spent a year as a postdoctoral research fellow in community mental health at the MGH and HRS, and his interest in this perspective led him to a degree program at HSPH with Gerald Caplan in 1958–60.[106] Thereafter, he became an active figure in developing community psychology as a subspecialty recognized at universities and professional organizations.

Lindemann continued to search entrance points and structures to combine, expand, and solidify the CMH component of the MGH Psychiatry Service. In 1964, he wrote to Gerald Caplan:[107]

> An administrative rearrangement of our [MGH Psychiatry Service] program which under the heading of Division of Community Services combines a crisis information center and a very active acute service in the Emergency Ward with our crisis approach to alcoholism as a community problem and the Wellesley Human Relations Service as a suburban multi-purpose facility ought to help to lend more solid structure to our program . . . in an article which John Knowles [MGH general director] contributed to a symposium on mental health in the Atlantic Monthly in which he commits himself to the future of this hospital as a health center devoting a considerable portion of its resources to crisis intervention and community work. Since, as of today, I have become the chairperson of the central

General Executive Committee of the hospital, I may have an opportunity in some measure to contribute to this development.

The logistics and politics of the transformation that Lindemann envisioned were complex, involving the MGH and the DMH:[108]

> Dr. Lindemann mentioned that the [Massachusetts] commissioner of Mental Health, Dr. Harry Solomon, had invited the [MGH] Psychiatric Service to develop; and staff a psychiatric mental health unit to be located in the new government center near Bowdoin Square. The Psychiatric Group has been reluctant to accept a program so far distant from the hospital but has been keenly interested in the development of a psychiatric service within the confines of the hospital or adjacent to it which would reflect the new responsibilities of the general hospital for the medical care of mental disorders and disturbed behavior. A number of attempts which have been made such as the securing of a floor in the Warren Building have not succeeded so far. However, efforts continue for support and the necessary space in the hospital.
>
> (p. 3)

MGH never accepted such an expansion of mental health responsibilities and dedication of resources to it.

Introduction of the Social Sciences Into Medicine at the Massachusetts General Hospital

One of Lindemann's major campaigns was to integrate the social sciences and social scientists into the MGH and medicine more broadly through the development of social psychiatry and CMH. He learned from, was validated by, and continually tried to incorporate into the MGH Talcott Parsons, a sociologist and chairperson of the HDCR. Parsons had been influenced by psychoanalysis and had a major interest in the sociology of medicine, which Lindemann adapted. Parson set forth the concept of psychological medicine as dealing with patients more broadly, as well as learning from and collaboration with the social sciences. (See endnotes for his presentation of this view of modern medicine.[109])

Lindemann struggled to introduce social science concepts, have them accepted among applied social scientists (perhaps including physicians), and make this a respected perspective.[110] His recruitment, support, and administrative arrangements for Alfred Stanton was a part of this campaign. Stanton's biography indicated that[111]

> he was much influenced by [Harry Stack] Sullivan's ideas [social psychiatry] and by his contact with David Rioch and Frieda

Fromm-Reichmann [psychoanalysts]. He developed a strong interest in the potential of social science to provide a better understanding of psychopathological processes. He developed a collaborative
effort with the sociologist Morris Schwartz, resulting in a series of
quite new and provocative observations concerning the sociological
and psychological events on the disturbed ward [of the mental hospi-
tal]. . . . Dr. Stanton's move to the Veteran's Administration Hospital
in Framingham [Massachusetts] from Chestnut Lodge [a psychiatric
hospital in Maryland] was a logical next step in his interest in the
group structure as related to the processes of psychiatric disorder . . .
with Talcott Parsons and to a lesser extent with Grete Bibring [psy-
chiatrist-in-chief, Beth Israel Hospital, Boston], he was a central person in organizing and carrying on for about six years a small group
of psychiatrists and social scientists who met regularly. . . . It was
at this time that Dr. Lindemann, who had become profoundly interested in the systematic study of social processes in the community in
relation to personality and emotional well-being, became attracted
to Dr. Stanton's work and persuaded him to move to Harvard and to
take over the leadership of the McLean Hospital. He now began to
take part in the reorganization of the program at McLean and the
[Massachusetts] General Hospital in a new direction, emphasizing
intensive psychotherapy, the focus of clinical efforts and social psychiatry as the research focus.

Clearly, Stanton was appointed because of his background and promise in bringing social science and social psychiatry to the HMS-MGH-
McLean collaboration:[112]

he is a person whose interests and aims in developing McLean would
foster the intimately related activities and institutional integration
with the [Harvard] Medical School and M.G.H. . . . [He] is one of
the few psychiatrists who have become thoroughly acquainted with
the concepts and methods of social science. He is especially qualified, therefore, to contribute effectively in a co-operative program
of investigations with the Department of Social Relations at Harvard. His studies . . . have laid the groundwork for the development
of a new field of knowledge concerned with the precise relationship
between variations in social structure and individual behavior. . . .
it could be expected that the McLean Hospital would become an
important center for the advancement of knowledge of the relation
between social science and the etiology and treatment of mental illness . . . an exceptional opportunity for the development of social
psychiatry exists at the McLean.
      [signed] Raymond D. Adams, MD [MGH chief of neurology],
Walter Bauer, MD [MGH chief of medicine], Dean A. Clark, MD

[MGH general director], Ralph Lowell [MGH trustee], Henry A. Murray, MD [chief of the Harvard University Psychology Clinic and member of the HDSR], Talcott Parsons, PhD [Harvard professor of sociology and chairperson of the HDSR], George Thorn, MD [Harvard professor of medicine and Peter Bent Brigham Hospital chief of medicine], and Allan M. Butler, MD [MGH chief of children's medicine and committee chairperson]

Years later, this choice of social psychiatry leadership at the McLean Hospital was reconfirmed:[113]

Stemming primarily from the vision of Erich Lindemann, a major effort was undertaken in 1954–1955 to develop the scientific as well as the clinical psychiatric program to include what was now easily recognized as a remarkably powerful clinical tool—systematic psychotherapy, informed by psychoanalytic insight and theory. . . . Lindemann, noting these developments, foresaw that the next period would include a rapid development of the practice of social psychiatry—in the community, in schools, in psychiatric and perhaps in general hospitals, in group and family therapy—and that its practical application would greatly outrun the understanding of its methods and action. . . . in this setting, the clinical program at McLean was placed in the hands of a psychiatrist whose research had been in the field of social psychiatry.

Stanton suggested plans for the reorganization of the McLean Hospital's program—embodying a small group and social perspective for the institution:[114]

Dr. Stanton suggested three basic areas of inquiry . . . also attempting to gain a new kind of "objectivity" which would transcend the limits of the culture and class orientation of these workers. . . . The second was the problem of communication from one profession to the other. . . . The third was dealing with the proper articulation of studies concerning intrapsychic processes leading to predictions concerning future behavior. . . . He proposes to ask for a senior social scientist such as [John] Seeley who would be available also to the Massachusetts General Hospital for consultation in social science and would be especially interested in statistics. . . . The proposal from the Massachusetts General Hospital will at this time . . . concentrate on a program to investigate the interpersonal aspects of the personality organization of persons with neuroses. This requires. . . [a] group of workers closely allied with Fried Bales [social psychologist HDSR] and using a laboratory set-up to study examples of social behavior. 1. The development of a center for more long range study of social behavior by assigning meaningful roles in a cooperative household to various individuals with psychoneurotic difficulties.

Stanton's efforts were published in collaboration with sociologist Morris Schwartz in an essentially sociological treatise, *The Mental Hospital*, on the social dynamics of mental hospitals.[115]

In another example of Lindemann's efforts toward social science and psychiatry projects, Benjamin Paul, anthropologist, presented A Proposed a Program for The Cross-Cultural Study of Mental Illness.[116] This was to be a seven-year interfaculty (interdisciplinary) research program in cross-cultural and cross-community aspects of mental illness. It would involve field studies in foreign and domestic communities. The staff would be interdisciplinary but mainly psychiatrically oriented anthropologists, including Clyde Kluckhohn, Cora DuBois, John Whiting, Benjamin Paul, David Schneider, and William Caudill—many of whom had formal training in psychoanalysis. There would be people from the departments of anthropology, HSDR, HGSE, and HSPH. There would also be sociologically oriented psychiatrists, including George Gardner, Erich Lindemann, Gerald Caplan, and Alfred Stanton.

Yet another expression of the increased involvement of social science in psychiatry was the Seminar on Social and Cultural Aspects of Psychiatry in 1957, involving many close to Lindemann.[117] It was arranged by Carl Binger, MD, an education consultant to the sponsoring Psychiatric Training Faculty of Massachusetts, Inc., a collaboration of psychiatric training programs in the Boston area. Presentations included Clyde Kluckhohn's "The Meaning of 'Cultural' and its Significance for Psychiatry"; Frederick Redlich's "The Significance of Social Class for Psychiatric Theory and Treatment"; Talcott Parsons's "The Role of the Psychiatrist in American Society"; Oscar Handlin's "The Immigrant: His Effect Upon American Attitudes"; Gordon W. Allport: "Prejudice"; John H. Finley's "Psychological Themes in Greek Tragedy"; Paul J. Tillich's "Christian Concepts of Guilt and Sin"; Perry G.E. Miller's "Social Themes in American Literature"; Eric A. Havelock's "The Beginnings of Scientific Anthropology among the Greeks"; Herbert H. Marcuse's "Psychology and The Science of Politics"; and Harry A. Wolfson's "Spinoza".

Lindemann was disappointed that Talcott Parsons did not want the HDSR to join in applied social science but rather wanted to make his department a great academic think tank. Later Elvin Semrad, a senior psychiatrist and psychoanalyst at the Massachusetts Mental Health Center and HMS, traced the chronology of several HMS committees and study groups addressing the inclusion of social scientists in HMS faculty appointments, promotions, and department structure:[118] There were negotiations with the HDSR, HGSE, and Harvard Divinity School. Lindemann was involved in an April 1957 Interfaculty Committee, which also included George Gardner (psychiatry), Henry Meadow (HMS associate dean), and George Stofford (chairperson pro tem). A June 1957 committee reviewed social science faculty appointments in the Department of Psychiatry (Lindemann as chairperson with George Gardner, Henry Meadow, and Elvin Semrad). In April 1958, an HMS committee included Lindemann and George Thorn regarding psychiatry at HMS; it recommended setting up a professorship at the HMS central campus to develop the basic science of psychiatry, including that section of the biological sciences involved in mental health; developing a section of social science in mental health; developing a section of pedagogy and research; and cooperating with teaching units in the Harvard orbit. Names were proposed for the unit: the Department of Social Science in Medical Behavior, the Department of Psychobiology, etc. In June 1958, Lindemann proposed a social science laboratory for multidisciplinary work on the relative contributions from various sources to problems of sickness and health. On January 8, 1963, Lindemann introduced the problems of the social and psychological sciences in health and planned a meeting on February 12, 1963.

There were problems in incorporating social science and social scientists within the MGH Psychiatry Service too. Irving Zola, a young sociologist working on the medical consequences of the West End relocation (and later a distinguished medical sociologist), critically described his experiences:[119]

> The Problems . . . the authority structure of the institution . . . the lines of authority were blurred. Clearance at the top did not necessarily mean cooperation at the lower levels. Because of the admixture of many staff . . . the chief of service occasionally appeared as a general without an army . . . the clinics were more likely to be managed by the head nurses or in some cases the chief clerk. . . . It was necessary to "sell" the research (as well as the integrity of the investigator). . . . this did . . . mean a considerable lag between the completion of the design and data collection. . . . the initial suspicion a researcher encounters . . . it . . . becomes necessary to assuage this anxiety. . . . The most difficult problem . . . was . . . no real academic or institutional standing for the social scientist. Appointment . . . carried no real status or meaning, no voice in Departmental or Medical School policy even where it impinges on the social sciences. . . . there was no consistent opportunity for teaching . . . being supported on "soft funds", as most social scientists in this institution are, hardly gives one a sense of financial security.
>
> Finally, there is the matter of recognition. Whether this is indicative of the regard for social science in this institution or of me . . . I continually felt my work was more appreciated, influential, etc., outside my home base. My gauge in this regard, is the number of requests for information or speaking engagements . . . my greatest

problem. . . . I became more and more isolated from my discipline and its practitioners. If people like myself are a bridge between social science and medicine and if they are supposed to infuse the insights from their own discipline into the medical field and vice-versa, then they have to have their feet in both fields. . . . There was little communication with those who were straight and simple social scientists. . . . I am skeptical of two trends in the organization of social science, a) for hospitals to have their own social scientists or units of social scientists with only nominal academic affiliation, b) for these units or individuals to be incorporated into existing departments or units such as Administration. Either of these solutions leads to both an isolation from his "parent" discipline and an emphasis on "operations" research (i.e. tendencies toward focusing on applied problems). . . . Two possibilities suggest themselves. One is the founding of a relatively independent unit or department, with formal teaching responsibilities, with the possibility of doing both basic as well as applied research, with some solid base of financial support, with some official ties with a Medical School and a voice in . . . general planning. In the instance, where social scientists work only on a project-by-project basis . . . explore the possibilities of joint appointments, not just in the Medical School which . . . is in a real sense without substance, but with departments of their own discipline at local universities . . . encouraged to make use of this departmental affiliation and perhaps even . . . some teaching responsibility. . . . some mechanism of integrating the various social scientists within the institution . . . give the individual . . . a place where he can read, write and think. Some funds . . . for . . . typing, travel and . . . the purchase of relevant documents.

(pp. 4–7)

An alternative perspective on this situation is the recognition by Frank Ervin, an MGH biological psychiatry researcher, of lacks and encouragement of growth in a comprehensive psychiatry that encompasses biological and social factors and incorporates the social sciences:[120]

It is necessary . . . that the clinical program within the hospital have active and reciprocal links with McLean [Hospital], the new Bowdoin Square Hospital [later the Erich Lindemann Mental Health Center], local guidance centers, etc. Pediatric psychiatry is not well integrated with the general pediatric medical-surgical program nor with the special needs in preventive intervention in children with prolonged, crippling, or especially traumatic disorders. . . . the consultation service needs to be expanded with more active involvement in other medical services. . . . We should turn out graduates who are equipped to become leaders in community, academic, and research medicine and initiate the future developments in psychiatry. We are not doing so at present. . . . Practical community experience with courts, with social agencies, with public health agencies, and in case sharing with other physicians is also limited. . . . Even less attention has been paid to the importance of environmental influences not uniquely individual, i.e. cultural patterns, social crises, group identity, etc., in determining behavior. It is in this area that Dr. [Erich] Lindemann has been an important pioneer. While these are many facets to social psychiatry, in pragmatic application to the hospital, it would seem to be increasingly possible to predict aspects of an individual's behavior from information about his cultural, social, and economic background, independent of his unique intra-personal development. Extensions of our knowledge in this area and its application to prevention of behavioral disorder or its rapid control by appropriate social intervention, is most important if we are to deal meaningfully with the problems reflected in mental health statistics. . . . Research in psychiatry then must concern itself with at least three areas". Analysis of clinical syndromes via computer, biological research, and social research. "Third, building on Dr. Lindemann's start, we must both increase our understanding of social psychiatric issues in our hospital population and the community from which it comes. This development calls for close collaboration with the program started by Dr. [Victor] Sidel [MGH epidemiology] and careful delineation of the areas of appropriate concern for the two groups and their proper interface. In addition, it requires a senior staff member of superior competence as a social scientist . . . At present there are so few psychiatrists trained in any of the biological or social sciences that it is difficult to recruit competent staff members. This means that we must have a training program which leads young psychiatrists to seek further basic science training and return to work, as has happened in medicine and surgery. In addition, we must for some time find Ph.D. scientists with appropriate skills and interests to collaborate in our investigations and teaching. Adequate academic and hospital appointments for such senior scientists remain a barrier to development in this young field. This problem . . . must be resolved for further progress to take place . . . social and biological sciences in the past decade, however, have indicated routes to a systematic understanding of human behavior and the MGH should be in the forefront of this exciting period described in different context as a "race between the success of the behavioral sciences and nuclear physics".

(pp. 1–7)

The struggle in the MGH over incorporating social science in medicine took place not only on the clinical service and training levels but also on the level of the hospital administration. Lindemann introduced to MGH

Scientific Advisory Committee this change in the direction of the Psychiatry Service:

> The new chapter in developing of psychiatry in this hospital which started with Dr. Lindemann's arrival can perhaps best be described as the systematic application of concepts and methods of behavioral and social science to clinical problems.[121] Some Questions Concerning the Future Development of Research in Psychiatry at the Massachusetts General Hospital: 1. Are we right in thinking of psychiatric research in its broader meaning as including behavioral and social science and as being concerned with a total mental health program. 2. Is it proper to have a behavioral science laboratory considered as part of the Psychiatric Department. 3. Is the emphasis on the study of motivational factors and social organization as related to health and illness justified in comparison with the great importance of progress in the study of somatic structure and biochemical and biophysical processes. 4. Should behavioral scientists be represented on basic science planning committees.

Even seven years later, Lindemann continued his campaign to encourage the committee to accept the social science perspective on health and illness and to incorporate it into the hospital's mission:[122]

> The agenda for today was to help me clarify and obtain some sort of consensus among ourselves on what we consider the nature of behavioral science research and the future of behavioral science research at this hospital. . . . on Monday noon possibly at subsequent meetings also will be Ray[mond] Adams [MGH Chief of Neurology], Henry Beecher [Chief of Anesthesia], William Sweet [Chief of Neurosurgery] and myself are supposed to elaborate on our ideal plan for behavioral science for the hospital. . . . The consensus of Oliver Cope [MGH surgery, MGH Research Committee] and John [Knowles, MGH general director] says that behavioral science should be the next push of the hospital in whatever form it will take . . . just a few minutes ago. . . [we] hear John Knowles make a great plea for the use of social science for the scientific description and formulation of the actual social process within the hospital. He knows about our work in the community and he seems to actually know almost nothing about how the hospital actually functions. . . . It was explicit that the administration had a very great stake in this sort of work, [suggesting] one central department in the hospital. . . . So I encourage the thought that social science might be related directly to the whole spectrum of hospital activities and necessarily being [incorporated] by psychiatry. . . . In this area it is an important scientific hitch because rather than being primarily able to use the experimental

design familiar to biologists which they would like to extend to everywhere. . . . we are including in this, what I believe, certain aspects of procedures and types of verification and arriving at consensus which are useful in the historical sciences in contrast to the experimental, natural sciences. They take evidence from the past, put it together, and interpret a probably previous state of affairs.

The Scientific Advisory Committee recommended against the establishment of research centers (such as social science), supporting instead the existing various clinical disciplinary services and their chiefs.[123]

Still a year later, the issue of more attention to the social aspects of disease was raised in the committee and (cautiously) supported:[124]

A respected senior member of the staff of the Massachusetts General Hospital presented to the Committee a concern lest the hospital was being insufficiently attentive to sociological and psychological problems related to health and disease. He pointed out that the factors in these general areas lay back of many of the cases appearing in the accident room. For example, at Massachusetts General Hospital the emergency room sees more than two suicide attempts a day, on the average. A viewpoint expressed was that a gulf exists between a continent of solid knowledge based on health and disease and an island of interpersonal, sociological and psychological problems underlying disease processes and the welfare of the people. The viewpoint held that there might be an insufficient number of bridges crossing this gulf. The questions were raised: Should the Massachusetts General Hospital establish a strengthened series of bridges extending into the behavioral and sociological sciences? Should the hospital embark on an extensive research program directed toward solving sociological and psychological problems related to health and disease?

The Committee was pleased to see the attention of influential staff members directed toward these problems. . . [and] noted the overwhelming medical importance of the reactions of persons to their social environment. The Committee was of the view that a cautious search for sound opportunities to expand into the areas outlined might be worthwhile. . . . As in any field of science, problems must be taken on and solved a little bit at a time.

The Committee was pleased to recall that the Massachusetts General Hospital has a long and distinguished tradition for emphasizing the importance of environmental and sociological factors on health. . . . This splendid tradition at the Massachusetts General Hospital will undoubtedly continue to maintain its healthy balance and will not be obscured by exclusive emphasis on the hard sciences.

And a year after that, it was raised again under the agenda item "Some Social Approaches to the Problem of Health and Disease by Erich Lindemann, MD, and Colleagues".[125] There followed an exchange of criticism of social medicine research, a defense of it, and reassurances of continued interest on the part of the MGH:[126]

3/19/1964 letter from Bennett, H. Stanley, MD, chairperson, Scientific Advisory Committee [MGH] to Gray, Francis C., chairperson, Board of Trustees, MGH:[127]

report and recommendations of that Committee, formulated during its recent meeting at the hospital on January 3 and 4, 1964. . . . As in previous years, samples of research work from various disciplines represented in the hospital were presented to the Committee. Some of the studies were of high quality and of great relevance. . . . Especially noteworthy were a series of reports dealing with the molecular mechanisms underlying the restructuring of connective tissue and the specificity of biosynthesis of cell surface antigens. . . . The Committee, however, was less enthusiastic over some of the presentations dealing with sociological aspects of illness. Last year, in recognizing the need for valid new knowledge in this area, the Committee emphasized the caution, astuteness, and superb quality of scientists which are necessary if research in these complex domains is to be fruitful. The Committee was unconvinced that these criteria have been sufficiently met in attempting the studies in question. . . . methodologies brought to bear on the problems seemed to be feeble and the conclusions attempted were not novel. . . . [A] profound understanding of complex social systems is unlikely to emerge from simple correlative studies invoking very few variables.

7/9/1964 letter from Lindemann, Erich to Lawrence, John E., chairperson, Board of Trustees, MGH:

I am profoundly concerned about the unfavorable impression which the members of the Committee gained from the report about some of the presentations dealing with the sociological aspects of illness. To my deep regret a severe pneumonitis prevented me from making my own contribution that day. This would have set a frame of reference for the other more focused papers and would have given us an opportunity to interpret individual findings in terms of larger concepts and goals.

It would be most regrettable if the result would be a reduction of interest in the application of the social sciences to medical problems. We have made only a quite modest beginning in an extraordinarily difficult field of inquiry and we need all the courage we can muster to forge ahead to more respectable attainments.

I sincerely hope there will be an opportunity to belatedly correct at least in some measure this unfortunate situation.

7/21/1964 letter from Lawrence, John E. to Lindemann, Erich:

I . . . would like to assure you that there is no reason whatsoever for concern on your part. I do understand the unfortunate combination of circumstances that resulted in a misunderstanding on the part of the Committee of what has actually been taking place in this field, and you may rest assured that there is no reduction in interest on our part in the application of the social sciences to medical problems.

While the MGH wrestled with incorporating the social sciences, the HMS recognized their increasing involvement in health and medicine and explored the establishment of relevant administrative structures and policies:

IV. Dr. Lindemann presented the problem of the behavioral sciences and personnel therefrom working in medical settings . . . providing, or at least insuring, their progress on the academic ladder. The relative merits or demerits of such a department existing as an entity was discussed quite thoroughly . . . in the vein that setting up a separate department at this time was premature and that we needed to observe more thoroughly the development of these people and their work in the Department of Psychiatry, especially in relation to their contribution to the overall problem of health and mental health.[128]

. . .

III. Dr. Lindemann introduced for discussion the problem of the social and psychological sciences in the health area. . . . He knew of the Department of Social Relations' interest in this development and their concern with the growing numbers of Social Relations people working in the health areas and the problems . . . in terms of appointment. . . [and] academic progression of these workers. . . . It involves in the neighborhood of seventy-five people . . . invite [Dr. McClelland] to our next meeting . . . invite Doctors Newman, Gerald Caplan [HSPH], Dana Farnsworth [Harvard University] and [Talcott] Parsons [HDSR].[129]

. . .

Dr. Lindemann surveyed the past and recent plans for the representation of the social sciences and clinical psychology in the medical area. Dean [of HMS George Packer] Berry reviewed briefly the medical school's plans for implementation of such a program when approximately 5 million dollars can be raised. He expressed the belief it would take approximately 2 million dollars to give proper staffing for such a unit to start as a separate operation. The problem

of creating a separate department of behavioral sciences, social relations or psychology in the quadrangle as opposed to the departments
in the college and university in Cambridge was discussed. Using the
analogy of biochemistry, it was the general consensus that the medical school and school of public health's needs were sufficiently large
to require setting up a second department. . . . This could not be
accomplished until funds are available to give the people status in
the university.[130]

The evidence suggests MGH's hesitant acceptance of the social aspects
of health and perhaps the contributions of the social sciences but also its
redoubtable resistance to accepting social science and scientists into full
membership in medical society.

The Massachusetts General Hospital Mental Health Service

While Lindemann intended to redirect the MGH Psychiatry Service, the
MGH as a whole, and influence medicine at large in the direction of
CMH, he sought to establish a core specialized CMH unit within the
Psychiatry Service—the Mental Health Service (MHS).

In a manifesto written around 1956, he described the departmental
social psychiatry ideology that he intended to create as a model:[131]

"The major objective underlying this program I would prefer to
express as a question . . . although I am more than a little optimistic
about the answer: *Can health considerations be added to the medical
objectives of the hospital in such a way that the medical staff member
will view himself as a health officer?*" Psychiatrist consultants will
introduce concern with the relationship of patients to the ward population, and thus "the mental health representative hopes to interest
the staff in the emotional well-being of the total patient population
of the medical or surgical ward, including those who are allegedly
mentally healthy". For instance, on the orthopedic ward screen for
patients needing activity to maintain their mental health before they
become casualties from immobilization. Study ward hazards and
supports. "Ward curricula, while in harmony with medical considerations, often rest largely on staff as vs. patient needs; they may
sometimes in actuality conflict with the latter's emotional requirements. A basic principle of this work emphasizes that a given state
of affairs is almost always maintained by a set of forces, which must
be understood and altered before constructive and lasting changes
can be effected. Consequently, our consultants have been broadening
their focus to include a concern for the mental health of the staff as
well as the patients". The mental health officers recognize the staff

and institution's defensive patterns of interprofessional relations and isolation from/control of patient emotions. They can help confront and alter these to benefit patients and prevent staff casualties, and thus maintain and enhance staff emotional wellbeing.

(pp. 3–5)

On the rehabilitation ward, strains among staff lead to worsening of patients (see Stanton and Schwartz, *The Mental Hospital*). The chief of these services, the staff, and the program director are interested in a mental health team (psychiatrist, social worker, and social anthropologist) to review with staff the flow of social events; deal with stresses; consider staff roles, status, and ward systems; and thus develop new professional self-perceptions.

The Mental Health Service will review the flow of psychological casualties and apply field epidemiological techniques to reduce pathological reactions. For instance, the Massachusetts Eye and Ear Infirmary changed from applying bilateral to unilateral eye patches: "a great many staff operations for coping with physical conditions may carry with them features hazardous for mental health. It is possible to identify such hazards on a population-wide basis and to try to achieve policy alterations consistent with medical prudence" (p. 9).

"The hospital itself is embedded in a larger community, represented, on the one hand, by those patients relating to the caretaking institution on an outpatient basis and, on the other hand, by the population and events within the residential area contiguous to the hospital. The Mental Health Service has been concerning itself with both these groups". The chief of the medical service allowed exploration of the patient population flow, discovering that the staff inadvertently contributed to a dependent patient population, and then attempting to stop impeding referral to more suitable help.

The West End Project gives access to the population around the hospital. This allows training for social and medical scientists—the Mental Health Service and the HDSR, staff, and fellows—to confront and learn about issues of medical practice as well as social and cultural issues. This raises research questions of adaptation to stress for the Center for Community Studies in the MGH Department of Psychiatry.

As the pattern of the Mental Health Service unfolds, its multifaceted nature becomes apparent. It continues to offer direct help with psychiatrically disturbed patients as before. It moves out increasingly into the flow of life in the hospital, relating as it can to significant segments of this community. Yet it recognizes that as part of the community itself, it is often perceived as having vested interests of its own, including values, that may clash with those [of] others, and strivings for satisfactions and rewards, which do not always exist in abundance for all those who seek them. Therefore, it moves toward the development of independent and autonomous activities, which may represent a secure base of operations from which workers can go forth with some security in their efforts to work cooperatively with others. Most important, it finds stimulation and security in the development of a coherent frame of reference whereby: (1) the hospital moves into focus as a community with its several segments, a hierarchy of dominant values, typical reactions to major stresses, and favored modes of work; (2) staff groups move into focus as caretakers whose methods of handling medical concerns and intra-staff relations affect groups of patients; and (3) the patient group moves into focus as a component of the community composed of sub-groupings according to a. socio-economic characteristics, b. the specific nature of the medical problem and its consequent emotional hazards and c. personality predispositions, which render some individuals and not others rather more vulnerable to special sets of circumstances encountered in the course of their treatment.

(pp. 11–12)

There were expressions of interest from the MGH as an institution in the preventive, holistic, and collaborative approach, which Lindemann encouraged when he was chairperson of its General Executive Committee.[132]

The administrative plan was to develop the MHS for clinical service and preventive psychiatry,[133] to introduce CMH in the hospital. This would be more complex and less preplanned than was the HRS. It would include a service team for diagnosis and preventive intervention; an interdisciplinary investigative team looking into the origins of social maladjustment and reactions to emotional crises; and a study of the mental health needs of the surrounding community. In the first year of his tenure, Lindemann included the following in the description of the department's training program:[134]

A mental health service is being established in the Clinic, which will be concerned with services and research in preventive psychiatry. A team of psychiatrists, psychologists, social workers, and social scientists will be organized for diagnosis and preventive intervention in crises which are known to produce stress. An investigative team will be concerned with the origins of social maladjustment and with the spectrum of reactions to emotional stress.

Lindemann described its inception as a "proposed integrated program of service and research in the field of community mental health":[135]

> INTRODUCTION The staff of the Mental Health Service of Massachusetts General Hospital has been engaged in laying foundations for an integrated program of service and research in the field of community mental health. The approach and the activities to be described represent the planning and work that have been carried on during the past year. In designing the program, it has been the aim of the staff to implement the general approach of Dr. Erich Lindemann. This approach is to be characterized, in part, by emphasis upon:
>
> (a) the practice of preventive psychiatry (early case finding, promoting wholesome living conditions, etc.)
> (b) the application of public health concepts to the study and psychopathology (epidemiology, etc.)
> (c) the integration of information and methods derived from social science with the principles and skills of the clinician
> (d) the study of human behavior under conditions of crisis (the conception of crises as special opportunities for reaching people, and for effecting psychotherapeutic changes that may result in lasting improvement; crisis, as an opportunity to study effective "coping" behavior)
> (e) the importance of research as an integral aspect of the program
> (f) the active participation of residents and organizations within the community in developing, and in carrying out the program.
>
> (p. 1)

The Mental Health Service of Massachusetts General Hospital was established in the fall of 1955. It is composed of a small core staff, and a larger advisory committee. The core staff consists of a psychiatrist, a social worker, a child psychologist, and a teacher. The larger committee includes other members of the Department of Psychiatry of Massachusetts General Hospital, and of the Department of Mental Health of the Commonwealth of Massachusetts.

(p. 2)

The minimum core staff for the MHS was (at the time) executive coordinator 1/2 time Dr. Peter Sifneos,[136] Staff Psychiatrist 1/2 time, Social Case Worker full time, Social Worker in Community Organization Mrs. L.[aura] Morris, M.A., Research Fellow in psychology an Demography 1/2 time Elizabeth Gellert, EdD; Research Assistant full time, secretary full time; Part time consultants: Sociologist Paul Hare Ph.D., Clinical Psychologist Michael von Felsinger Ph.D.,

Fellows in training in CMH 2 psychiatrists, 2 postdoctoral psychologists, 1 social worker.

He drafted an organizational chart for the MHS, with a budget of $50,000:[137]

Projected Administrative Chart for Community Mental Health Unit
in Psychiatry Department (M.G.H.):
Chief of Psychiatry—Dr. Erich Lindemann
Community Mental Health Coordinator (psychiatrist half-time)

Research Coordinator	Asst CMH Coordinator	Dir. CMH Prog
(full-time, psychol or sociol)	(CO s.w. full-time)	(CMH Coord->separate)
Sociologist		MH Consultant in Psychiatry
Psychologist (part time)		MH Consultant in Psychology
		(part time)
Research Graduate Assistants ½ time:		(Mental Health Trainees 1/2 time):
1 psychiatrist		1 psychiatrist
2 psychologists		2 psychologists
1 social worker		1 social worker
1 secretary		1 secretary—part-time

1. It might be most desirable to see any mental health project or mental health research integrated into the above structure whether it operates in the outside or hospital communities.
2. An over-all advisory committee might be considered.

FUNCTIONS OF COMMUNITY MENTAL HEALTH UNIT IN PSYCHIATRY DEPARTMENT (M.G.H.)
Research Program (to develop in this trend)

1. Priority on projects related to Urban
2. Linked with community program
3. Other projects when staff and time available

1. Individual Consultation to agencies and Redevelopment Institutions
2. Group Consultation to Agencies and Institutions
3. Inter-Agency Consultation Group

From the beginning of Lindemann's tenure, he described the institution of this service as a departure from Stanley Cobb's approach:[138]

This has been a year of transition from the active and vigorous leadership of Dr. Stanley Cobb to the guidance of Dr. Erich Lindemann. . . . Our program will be enriched by the addition of a Mental Health Service, being primarily services and research in Preventive Psychiatry. Generous support for this work has been provided by the Grant Foundation. This project involves the development of a service team for diagnosis and, if necessary, preventive intervention, plus an investigative team concerned with the origins of social maladjustment and with the spectrum of reactions to emotional crises. This team will include psychiatrists, psychologists, social workers and social scientists.

(p. 1–2)

An important aim of this program will be the study of the Mental Health needs of the neighborhood surrounding the hospital. Dr. Morris Chafetz is already working closely with Dr. Stokes of the Family Service Program to develop the design for psychiatric participation in this important program.

The MHS was approved by the MGH Trustees in May 1955[139] and established in the fall of that year by a planning committee, including Lindemann as chairperson; MGH adult and child psychiatry, psychology, and psychiatric social work; the DMH, represented by Warren Vaughan, MD, director of its Division of Mental Hygiene; the HSPH, represented by Gerald Caplan, MD, director of the Division of Mental Health; and the HRS, represented by its executive director, Donald Klein.[140]

It was intended to follow Lindemann's approach:[141]

- preventive psychiatry—early case finding, promotion of wholesome living, etc.
- public health concepts—epidemiology
- integration of the social sciences with clinical skills
- the study of human behavior in crisis—increased opportunity to reach people, effect changes, and study coping behavior
- research
- the participation of community residents and organizations in program development and implementation

Consideration was given to filling the core staff of psychiatrists, social workers, child psychologists, and teachers as well as social psychologists, anthropologists, sociologists, epidemiologists, and public health administrators. (See endnotes regarding people involved.)[142] An Advisory Committee would include representatives of the MGH Department of Psychiatry and the DMH.

John Spiegel, MD, was a social psychiatrist whom Lindemann often included in the list of resources at Harvard University. He was a lecturer in the HDSR, and in January 1957, Lindemann spearheaded an effort to gain him an appointment as an associate clinical professor of psychiatry at HMS, Boston Children's Hospital, and the Department of Social Relations. He wrote about bridging psychoanalysis and the social sciences such as sociology, psychology, and anthropology (this happened nine years after the Lindemann and Dawes confrontation with the Boston Psychoanalytic Society and Institute on this topic).[143]

John Seeley was a significant figure in Lindemann's constellation of CMH comrades. He was a sociologist committed to the ideals and spirit of social psychiatry more than the practicalities of their acceptance and implementation. Lindemann included him in the Space Cadets, various conferences, and especially as a spiritual confidant—including during Lindemann's deathbed interviews with Leonard Duhl. He was notably mentioned by Lindemann in his retirement banquet speech. Seeley was effusive in his idolization of Lindemann and defense of him in contrast to "lesser" lights such as Gerald Caplan. Lindemann floated various plans to bring Seeley to the MGH to augment a growing cadre in CMH:[144]

the application for support by the National Institute of Mental Health of our program in community mental health has been approved. I am therefore now in a position to repeat on a more solid basis the expression of our desire to have you with us here at Harvard as a senior member of our group. . . . I am inviting you to consider joining us. . . . We would picture you as the senior social scientist at the Massachusetts General Hospital. You would be free of administrative duties, and we would hope that a variety of workers in the field of social science and in other departments of the hospital would avail themselves of your advice in connection with social science implications of medical care and clinical research.

So far as the academic post at Harvard is concerned, I infer from our discussions . . . that perhaps you would feel most satisfied to be appointed not at the Medical School or in the School of Public Health, but become associate professor of Urban Research in the new Center for Urban Studies of Harvard and Massachusetts Institute of Technology. I had an opportunity to discuss these matters in detail with Professor [Martin] Meyerson [Harvard-MIT Center for Urban Studies]. He would undertake to initiate the faculty procedures. . . . We also discussed . . . the problem of lifelong tenure for this position. . . . The National Institute of Mental Health has guaranteed $15,000 a year and secretarial assistance for five years. . . . We would . . . do everything to make this particular post a tenure post in the narrower sense before the five-year period is over. . . . you would have the assurance that I will be here for another seven years before retirement, that Martin Meyerson is a young man, and that the hospital is working hard to develop a system by which senior scientists have guaranteed tenure posts. . . . This new program of the hospital . . . reflects efforts to become a university type of organization, like the Rockefeller Institute. . . . Your very presence [at the Center for Urban Studies] would be a significant gain for our mutual interests. . . . You . . . would symbolize the growing relationship between our work in the health area and the program of the Center for Urban Studies. . . . I am writing mainly to see whether you are still interested, and . . . how we could arrive together at a satisfactory set of arrangements. . . . I could come to Toronto, or you might want to pay us another visit here.

(pp. 2–3)

Seeley opted out of these plans for closer collaboration and found himself in a series of limited-time consulting and planning positions in the United States and his native Canada.[145] There were suggestions of Seeley's neurotic problems in these ambivalent relationships and plans.

The author's experience in entering the MGH CMH program may serve as an example of the rise and fall of recruitment to this specialty.[146] His undergraduate major was sociology, and in medical school, he was drawn to psychiatry and preventive medicine. He spent time in the public health mental health program of the HSPH in the Boston Public Health Department's Whittier Street Clinic, as well as volunteering with Joseph Matarazzo's Interaction Chronograph research on documenting human interaction. Gardner Quarton (MGH Psychiatry Service) found him committed to social psychiatry, and Lindemann gave him high priority for the MGH CMH fellowship program. However, Merton Kahne, MD, the director of residency education at McLean Hospital, was concerned that his gifts in psychiatry might be derailed by social psychiatry:

There is one problem which I think needs careful guidance; that has to do with his substantial interest in social psychiatry. It is entirely possible for an individual of his caliber to catapult himself into this field without adequately preparing himself in individual psychology and in the problems of clinical medicine. It would be unfortunate if his considerable gifts in social psychiatry were developed without taking adequate precaution to see to it that he knows the other areas reasonably well.[147]

Nevertheless, the author was appointed to an NIMH CMH fellowship at MGH and HRS, implemented a CMH consultation approach during his mandatory military service, and was invited by Lindemann to return to the MGH as a CMH fellow and then a junior staff member to work part time at HRS, part time in epidemiologic studies at the MGH and settlement houses, with participation in planning for the developing CMHC. He was appointed to an exchange fellowship at the University of Aberdeen, Scotland, to bring psychodynamic psychiatry there and learn mental health epidemiology with John Baldwin, a former CMH fellow at the MGH. As Lindemann was preparing for his retirement, there were suggestions that the author should study at the Harvard Department of Social Relations with John Spiegel and the HSPH with Lenin Baler, as well as analysis of the medical and mental health components of the West End Study. The author repeatedly stated, "My intention is to continue in a career in community mental health and the ecology of human behavior and social organization. I plan to spend full time in research and teaching in academic medicine".[148] The implementation of these various plans would be left in the hands of John Nemiah, the acting chief of psychiatry at the MGH, and Robert Bragg, the director of the CMH program and HRS. As noted, after Lindemann's departure, the MGH Psychiatry Service quickly phased out CMH and social psychiatry, and HRS gradually lost MGH support and involvement. The author completed the second year of CMH fellowship and then migrated to the Boston University Division of Psychiatry that was vigorously applying CMH under Bernard Bandler. When John Nemiah was passed over as the chief of the MGH Psychiatry Service, he transferred to the chairpersonship of the Psychiatry Department at the Beth Israel Hospital, accompanied by other senior MGH psychiatry staff members Peter Sifneos and Fred Frankel as well as other staff members. When the author later spoke with Nemiah about a position in the Beth Israel Hospital psychiatry department, he was firmly rejected as having a psychiatric perspective inappropriate to that department and being associated with antipsychiatric community mental health practices. And after a few years of bravely representing HRS and community psychiatry, Robert Bragg returned to his roots in Florida academia.

In the first year of Lindemann's tenure, the MHS was described as an exemplar of applying CMH to a broad range of care and collaboration activities both in the MGH and in the surrounding community:[149]

> This service is concerned with the development of a program in preventive psychiatry inside and outside the hospital . . . supported this year by a generous grant from the Grant Foundation. . . . The intra-hospital functions of the M.H.S. are under the leadership of Prof. George Saslow who joined the Service on July 1st. Our preventive work focuses less on sick individuals but [rather] on the "hazardous situations" of which they are victims. We are particularly interested in other apparently healthy individuals in the social orbit of a given patient who were exposed to the same or similar hazardous situations. This has led to a gradual reorganization of the consultation service which was operating along traditional lines in this hospital.
>
> We have begun to concentrate our efforts on the "Family Service Program" of the hospital where whole families are being followed . . . and where the health hazard to each member of the family is being determined. On the . . . wards of the hospital . . . we are gradually winning access to the whole patient population for behavior assessment and social appraisal. This is being done instead of waiting for referrals. . . . Consultation work concerning persons with emotional difficulties is being applied according to the principles of "mental

health consultation" with due respect for the emotional problems of the physicians and nurses involved in the care-taking process, as well as for the social structure of the ward. This intensified participation of mental health workers in the care-taking program of the hospital community has been much facilitated by the whole-hearted support of Dr. Walter Bauer, chief of medicine [diagnosed as manic-depressive and interested in mental health] and Dr. Allan Butler, chief of pediatrics. We also have made some headway with the Orthopedic Service. Progress will be slower in the Neurological Service. A particular opportunity for our mental health service occurred with the influx this fall of 140 acutely ill patients with poliomyelitis, about 40 of whom were in respirators for a number of weeks. The reactions of the patients themselves to the impairment of their motor systems, the reactions of their families and neighborhoods, the processes of group formation among relatives and the changes in their attitudes and participation in the care-taking program—all these were an object of study by our group interested in preventive psychiatry. It was possible then to be of assistance to the internists and nurses at times of faltering morale and to help them master the challenge which turned out to be a considerable organizational and emotional crisis for the whole hospital. . . . These opportunities for teaching and demonstration have markedly increased the interest on the part of the overall psychiatric staff and of the Fellows in training . . . with respect to preventive programs and community mental health work.

Outside the hospital much attention has been given to a major crisis in adaptation threatening the population in the neighborhood of the hospital. This community is threatened by the demolition of a large segment of the houses. . . . Our mental health service has been active in interesting the hospital administration and the steering committee of the staff in a program of studies to define the relationship of the hospital to the surrounding community using the staff of the mental health service as resource people concerning problems of social organization and health planning for the out-going and incoming populations.

Efforts to make contact with key persons in the community, organization of committees to anticipate the disturbances and to document the occurrence of emotional casualties as a consequence of this crisis have . . . stimulated interest in community mental health work.

Further MHS collaborative projects included the following:[150]

The Mental Health Service, which serves the population of the West End, has gradually defined its role as a family counseling center and as a center for psychiatric consultation with the social agencies in the area. We have met regularly with the heads of the welfare agencies in the neighborhood and have assisted them in planning for a number of families which have difficulty in adapting to the anticipated redevelopment program in the West End. Being family centered, the Mental Health Service has an important relationship to the Family Health Service in the Medical Department, and to the Child Psychiatry program. . . . Dr. Sifneos and Mrs. Laura Morris, a community organization specialist, have charge of this Service. The Department has continued to give advanced training to psychologists who are preparing for a career in community mental health. Five advanced Fellows are having such training during this year under Dr. John M. von Felsinger.

The Mental Health Service also has developed a liaison with the Department of Pediatrics. A program of activities and teaching for the children who are patients on this Service to counteract the hazard of being in the hospital separated from their families and undergoing considerable stress has been designed by Dr. Beth Gellert who came to us from the Laboratory of Child Development at Harvard. Systematic observations are made on groups of children in a nursery school type of setting and these observations are used for teaching student nurses, occupational therapy students and student dietitians. . . . With our growing orientation to families and to community neighborhoods, the demands on the Social Service Department are steadily rising. Our experienced social workers are developing new methods of liaison with neighborhood resources and are doing an excellent job in training young social workers in the integration of hospital and clinical services with community needs. . . . The Mental Health Service is continuing its program of studies of the adaptation of families who are involved in the West End redevelopment program. We are interested in the distribution of mental illness in the West End population at successive stages of its relocation. . . . In addition to consultations within the hospital the Child Psychiatry Unit [Gaston E. Blom, MD chief] has been asked for consultation by a number of agencies outside the hospital, to mention a few: West End Guidance Center of the Commonwealth of Massachusetts, Dept. of Mental Health; Associated Day Care Service of the United Community Services; and Consultation with 92 social agencies in Massachusetts and New Hampshire.

(pp. 3–7)

Lindemann's persistent search for financial support for the MHS provided opportunities for elaboration on its actual and potential scope and structure. Applications to the W.T. Grant Foundation, Inc., a sympathetic source of support from the early days of Lindemann's CMH work at HRS, illustrates the varied and evolving MHS plans and support (see endnotes for details).[151]

Lindemann proposed for support both the theoretical issues he would like to pursue[152] and the building of a comprehensive mental health system to implement them:[153]

> for the remainder of my active career in mental health work I hope to bring to fruition the natural growth of our Department in three important directions.
>
> The first . . . is the development of adequate facilities for the short term care in a general hospital of patients at times of major emotional crises. The facilities within the hospital . . . will be properly matched with agencies in the community concerned with the anticipatory and preventive phases of community work . . . and with the re-integration of people who have succumbed to stress with mental or emotional breakdown. . . . The second goal is a natural outgrowth. . . . [As] in Wellesley . . . systematic investigations in various phases of human development related to predictable crises . . . are absolutely necessary if we ever hope to have a solid basis for programs of community action. . . . [Create] at the Massachusetts General Hospital a Center for Studies in Human Development. . . [for] studies on groups of normal children with studies on sick children. . . . Search for the types of human environment which are facilitating emotional growth in contrast with those that impeded emotional growth. . . . the third target. . . [is] comparative studies of different social settings and practices in child care as they relate to patterns of personality development, create special kinds of strength and also special kinds of liabilities . . . as he will meet the challenges for his adaptation in his particular culture. My recent visit to India has convinced me. . . [of] most promising opportunities for comparative studies . . . a cooperative program with an Indian university for joint investigations.
>
> The McLean Hospital serves private patients with mental disease. . . . The general hospital service provides for the care of the emotional complications of physical disease and for the acute emotional disorders. . . . Both units have solid facilities for neurobiological research. However, much significant growth is envisaged in the area of the <u>application of the social sciences to the study of behavior</u> and in the speedy <u>utilization of new knowledge to the actual care of the sick</u>. The leaders of both units also have a keen sense of responsibility for the detection of early signs of threatening future emotional disorders and for <u>preventive programs</u> which reach into the family, neighborhood and community institutions to safeguard the population by suitable methods of preventive intervention.
>
> At this juncture a bold new program in preventive psychiatry is envisaged which would involve operations in both units. It would organize preventive services to the families of patients and to others in the community who would be encouraged to take advantage of preventive

counsel. The families and relatives of the mentally sick as well as of general hospital patients would constitute a very large medium for health education which is used but little at present. Previous work supported by the Grant Foundation in Wellesley, a middle class suburb, and in the Boston West End, a low income population . . . have provided insights and skills on how to reach the families and to motivate them to cooperate in a preventive program. A small beginning has also been made in dealing with the families of patients seeking help in the emergency ward and in the medical and surgical services. It is apparent now that a new organization combining services and research . . . would [bode] . . . well to bring forth a significant advance in our understanding and anticipatory control of the interpersonal pathological causes of disease whether physical, emotional or psychological.

Components of the Program:

A. A laboratory of behavioral science at the McLean Hospital devoted to the intensive study of interpersonal relationships among patients and their families and the community.
B. A center at the Massachusetts General Hospital devoted explicitly to preventive psychiatry. . .

  1. Studies of clinical populations as they appear in the Emergency Ward, Out-Patient Services, In-Patient Services, and Social Agencies . . . composition, community background and typical predicaments leading to seeking help at the hospital
  2. Intensive studies of critical phases of human development. . .
  3. The application of the approaches developed in these studies to cross-cultural comparisons . . . about the differential effects of various patterns of child rearing and family structure . . . to provide health services which take due cognizance of the cultural forces which may block or facilitate the acceptance of a healthier way of life. . . . We have learned that a five year period is not sufficient for top level staff. However, a period of eight to ten years may be expected to be acceptable (pp. 2–3).

The Grant Foundation contributed significant and crucial funding.[154] Its interest and support highlight many of the MGH Psychiatry Services programs. In the effort to shift the psychiatric approach in the MGH,[155]

We, also, have been fortunate to secure further support for the work of Dr. [Eliza]Beth Gellert concerning the emotional needs and the activities of sick children on our Pediatrics Service. . . . The work which Dr. [George] Saslow together with Dr. [Joseph] Matarazzo began in the Medical Clinic under the name Comprehensive Medicine is being continued by Dr. Gerald Davidson and Dr. [Michael] von Felsinger. . . [who] renamed this program "Studies in Medical Care". It is aimed at understanding and helping sick people as persons and social human beings in contrast to the treatment of disease from the purely organic point of view. It is also concerned with the families of the patients and with the neighborhoods from which they come . . . the considerable number . . . suffer from . . . chronic alcoholism and have become one focus of attention both with respect to study and to improved care of these families. The Commonwealth of Massachusetts has developed a special agency to facilitate this program. . . [including] an Alcoholism Clinic . . . psychiatric consultations concerning in-patients on medical and surgical cases. . . . Rather than restricting the inquiry to the condition of the patient alone, inquiries are made concerning the organization of medical care on the particular services and . . . the frequency with which a given type of problem occurs. . . . We are also. . . [planning to] survey from the psychological and social points of view. . . [of] all the patients who are entering certain services . . . so that . . . the whole care-taking process can be planned in the light of a given patient's make up, his motivation and the life in the community to which he will have to return. . . . plans are being made for their rehabilitation to the best possible level of function in in their particular life situation.

All this has led to very vigorous participation of the mental health staff with the staff of other services. The Psychiatric Service rather than being a specialty service in the narrow sense is becoming . . . a mental health agency which assists both the staff and the patients in the solution of crises and in organizational planning. . . . Part of this program is being absorbed by the hospital and supported by general funds. The specific research enterprises . . . may well be supported . . . by the Commonwealth Fund. . . . May I take this opportunity to express . . . the profound appreciation . . . for having made possible the development of our mental health program which was a natural further development and application of the principles developed with your support on the Wellesley project.

(pp. 1–3)

The MHS also had work and teaching ties to a wide range of programs around Harvard University:[156] the Division of Mental Health at the Harvard School of Public Health, the HDSR, the Harvard-MIT Joint Center for Urban Studies, the Harvard Center for Studies on Personality, and the Laboratory for Human Development. Education programs included the following:[157]

- Community Mental Health Program Child Psychiatry 1957–8 (diagnosis, limited psychotherapy, mental health consultation in the West End, Boston, Massachusetts)

- Community Mental Health Program for Psychiatrists 1962–3
- Community Mental Health Program for Psychologists 1962–3
- Community Mental Health Seminars—1959–62 MGH
- Community Mental Health Survey 1963 HSPH
- Community Processes Workshop 1961 MGH
- Future West End-Beacon Hill; Dr. Dean A. Clark and Laura Morris
- Seminar on Cultural Aspects of Psychodynamics (Spiegel, Caudill, Lifton)—1958–62 MGH[158]
- Community Mental Health Seminars—1956–7 MGH-HRS
- Psychiatric Training in Community Mental Health
- Seminar on Community Processes 1964—Dr. [Frederick] Duhl
- Seminar—Preventive Intervention 1961
- Seminar: Issues in Community Mental Health. Dr. Lindemann, 1962[159]
- Visiting Faculty Seminar 1965 (Gerald Caplan) includes Levinson, Daniel J. PhD "Program on Careers in Mental Health" (NIH, July 1, 1965–June 30, 1966); Caplan, Gerald MD "Training in Community Processes" (NIH, September 1, 1964–June 30, 1965).

Lindemann determined the following CMH training needs of psychiatry trainees:[160]

1. They need to learn how to work with a lot of other people on the team in a different way.
2. They need to learn how to "deal with" people in agencies and groups in the larger community.
3. They need to learn how to be concerned with hazardous situations and the components of hazardous conditions and know what is nonpsychiatric material and what psychiatry can contribute to this material.
4. They need to follow populations (rather than an individual), people's value orientations, the social systems in which they are involved, and what can be done about some of the problems coming out of all of this.
5. They need to learn the epidemiological approach to the study of mental illness.
6. They need to change the basic attitude of therapeutic concern for individuals to that of populations.

(p. 2)

The HMS Department of Psychiatry, through the Massachusetts Mental Health Center, announced the Research Training Program in Social Psychiatry:[161] "An interdisciplinary postdoctoral program for social scientists and psychiatrists offering specialized advanced training in the application to mental health problems of the systematic concepts and methods of the social sciences". Several HMS-affiliated social psychiatry units participated:

- Laboratory in Social Psychiatry; Director: Elliot G. Mishler, PhD
- Laboratory of Community Psychiatry; Director: Gerald Caplan, MD
- Laboratory in Social Behavior and Autonomic Physiology; Director: David Shapiro, PhD
- Community Mental Health Training Program; Directors: Robert L. Bragg, MD; William J. Freeman, M.S.W., EdD; Robert C Misch, PhD
- Department of Behavioral Sciences, Harvard School of Public Health; Director: Alexander H. Leighton, MD.

Psychosocial research proposals and projects included the following:[162]

- Frankel, Freddy H., MD "Mental Health Telephone Information Center" (NIH submitted January 18, 1965; rejected)
- Koumans, Alfred J.R., MD "Community Extensions of the Acute Psychiatric Service" (The Medical Foundation, submitted April 21, 1965; rejected)
- Rutherford, Robert F. (director, Simmons College School of Social Work) and Lindemann, Erich, MD (chief of psychiatry, MGH) "A Survey Course for Advanced Practicing Social Workers in Community Mental Health, Theory and Practice" (Charles H. Hood Foundation, application April 21, 1959)

In the interests of providing mental health consultation with community agencies, a pilot joint consultation seminar was developed with the Boston Department of Public Welfare workers, social workers, and supervisors addressing an assessment of community mental health hazards and a consultation with staff about mental health dynamics. The seminar was evaluated in terms of its process and use with other agencies. It was planned that when the MHS staff increased, so would its services: the mental health consultation with the settlement house, boys club, Boston Departments of Health and Public Welfare, churches, and civic organizations that had no mental health staff of their own and turned to the MHS for this expertise. The MHS would develop techniques for dealing with hardcore mental health problem families, including an "anchor agency" for local service, and would clarify which subpopulations were appropriate for family agencies or for mental health services. From the HRS experience of mental health consultation with the Wellesley public schools, Lindemann also explored mental health research and early case finding with the Boston Public School Department.[163] He communicated with Joseph Lee, a member of the Boston School Committee (related to HMS-affiliated James Jackson Putnam in neurology, Mollie Putnam in child psychiatry, and Tracy Putnam in neurosurgery); Dr. Frederick Gillis, superintendent of schools; and Dr. Martin Spellman, director of school hygiene.

Another early MHS project implementing Lindemann's plan to convert the MGH Psychiatry Service to a CMH approach to mental health services was a program of collaboration with the Public Welfare Department of the City of Boston:[164]

> After a series of discussions at Mental Health staff meetings (at M.G.H.) regarding the advisability of organizing a group consultation project with the City's Public Welfare Department, it was agreed that L.[aura] Morris should proceed along this course. Our early discussions included some of the following notions: In light of the experiences at the Wellesley Human Relations Service in consultation with school teachers and at the Family Guidance Center in consultation with public health nurses, it seemed desirable that this part of the core staff in Mental Health activities begin consultations with another type of professional "caretaker", namely the welfare worker in a public agency. In conjunction, also, with some thinking that mental health workers should apply their resources and skills to those spots where greater numbers of people might be influenced or helped, it seemed logical to look to the Public Welfare Department. It was another source which not only reached masses of people, but, also, whose staff of workers, mostly untrained in the field of human behavior could benefit from such consultative work. It was our further understanding that within the structure of the Public Welfare Agency, both locally and nationally, major efforts were being initiated to strengthen the skills of their workers and to raise standards of services, beyond financial assistance, to the clientele, particularly in the Aid to Dependent Children and Disability Assistance categories. For this reason we felt there might be an atmosphere congenial towards us for the project. We also felt strongly that field workers could give direct and vivid impressions of the people and their problems in the neighborhoods in which we might well work at a later date. It was agreed, therefore, in staff meeting that a two-way process would be involved. Approval for carrying out the project was given by E.L. [Erich Lindemann] and P.S. [Peter Sifneos] and it was presented briefly to the Mental Health Planning Committee. [There follows a description of the process of planning, negotiation, identifying, and recruiting key supporters.]
> (p. 1)

We get a hint at Lindemann's doubts as well as confidence in his plans to make over the MGH Psychiatry Service, MGH, and medicine: Perrin C.

Galpin, the executive director of The Grant Foundation, Inc., encouraged him:

> May I make one suggestion, and that is when you dictate your presentation of this new proposal which we discussed yesterday [Program of Service and Research in Preventive Psychiatry to be carried out by the Mental Health Service, at MGH], you do it in what you once referred to as "one of my more optimistic moments".[165]

Lindemann wanted the MGH to formally endorse the MHS. The MGH Executive Committee discussed the MGH developing as a community hospital, including collaboration with the physicians in the West End of Boston, where the hospital was situated. Lindemann, the MGH general director Dean Clark, and one of the orthopedists recommended that a subcommittee be appointed to study an extension of this role. Clark, with a professional history of social medicine, was sympathetic to a mental health consultation approach and sat on the West End Planning Board and Neighborhood Council. The DMH said it looked to the MGH to lead in exploring the need for the MHS in this community. It pressed the MGH to commit itself to provide service not only to the West End but also to the North End, Charlestown, and East Boston. Arthur Hallock, staff member of the Division of Mental Hygiene, tried to direct this program but refused to share with the MGH control over the state staffing blocks. The city of Boston Department of Public Health was interested in developing a mental health service and in-service training in mental health consultation (along the lines of Gerald Caplan's approach). The Boston Redevelopment Authority was interested in and cooperated with MGH psychiatry's study and service to the 2600 residents who remained in the West End during the relocation process. Belenden Hutchinson, director of the state Division of Mental Hygiene, proposed a collaboration with the MGH Department of Psychiatry to train homemakers for preventive intervention in family crises and assign them to Multi-Service Centers in the Boston communities of Charlestown Roxbury and the South End.[166] Lindemann tried to embed a social approach in medicine in the MGH:[167]

> I believe that we are now at the point where the study of social, economic, and group dynamic issues, which until recently was fostered by the Department of Psychiatry, becomes so much a concern of the overall hospital program that a social science center related to the office of the General Director of the hospital would seem a logical and promising next step.
>
> I am counting on much help from you [John Knowles, MGH general director] in the efforts of the Committee on the Development of

Behavioral Sciences at the Massachusetts General Hospital which is to report to the Committee on Research in the not too distant future.

(p. 2)

In reaction to all these opportunities for collaboration, the MGH staff tended to want to operate autonomously, in contrast to the characteristics of CMH, and its Advisory Committee was vague in terms of function and investment. Lindemann felt called upon to appeal to the MGH Scientific Advisory Committee:

> I am profoundly concerned about the unfavorable impression which the members of the Committee gained from the report about some of the presentations dealing with the sociological aspects of illness. . . . It would be most regrettable if the result would be a reduction of interest in the application of the social sciences to medical problems.[168]

Robert S. Shaw, MD, of the MGH spent three months at McLean Hospital and reported the following: "My observation and experience amply reinforce your concept of social psychiatry—which I found to be not very popular at McLean".[169]

The staff members and trainees associated with the MHS and its branches created a number of publications that enriched community mental health.[170]

Notes

1. Caplan-Moskovich, Ruth, "Gerald Caplan: The Man and His Work", Ch. 1 in Schulberg, Herbert C. and Killilea, Marie (eds.), *The Modern Practice of Community Mental Health: A Volume in Honor of Gerald Caplan* (San Francisco: Jossey Bass, 1982), pp. 1–39.
2. Lindemann, Erich, correspondence with Caplan, Gerald regarding visits by Alexander Leighton, Nicholas Greydburg, Jane Murphy, and representatives of Cornell University. Also correspondence with Lenin A. Baler regarding a luncheon at MGH with Alexander Mitscherlich of the University of Heidelberg, Germany, and Erik Erikson. [folder "HSPH", Box IIIA 4 (F-H), Erich Lindemann Collection, Center for the History of Medicine, Francis A. Countway Library of Medicine, Boston, MA]
3. Division of Mental Health, Department of Public Health Practice, HSPH, "Annual Report, 1954". [folder "HSPH Courses + Seminars 1950s; 1954 Annual Report of Div. Ment. Hlth (HSPH)", Box IIA&B, Lindemann Collection, Center for the History of Medicine, Francis A. Countway Library of Medicine, Boston, MA] Curriculum:

Teaching:
A. Participation in introductory course for all students in biological and social ecology—lectures, seminars, and case studies. Participation in general and specialist courses in the Departments of Public Health Practice, Maternal and Child Health, Epidemiology, and Industrial Hygiene. Sensitize all students to the mental health implications of their activities.[1]

Public Health 1a—Ecology: Biological and Social: Topics and faculty: Whittlesey (regional geography), Benjamin Paul (culture, communication), Robert Reed (demography, community), Taylor (population dynamics), Chernin (animal populations), Jean Mayer (nutrition), Levine (public opinion), Stuart (human maturation), John Spiegel (family), Miller (authority), and Ozzie G. Simmons (social class)

B. Specialized courses:

Public Health Practice 3B—Psychosocial Problems (2nd half of 1st semester): Sources of psychosocial disturbance, public health implications of etiology and behaviors; including shared, biological, early physical and emotional trauma, physiological and pharmacological relationships, interpersonal and intrapsychic processes (especially life crisis and support), community control of these factors.

Course 14c,d—Problems in Mental Health: Mental Health programs, history of psychiatric disorders (MGH cases), function of the mental health team (psychiatrist, clinical psychologist, psychiatric social worker, social scientist), group dynamics and community attitudes and practices, existing mental health programs.[1]

Public Health Practice 40c,d—Group Dynamics: (new) Pearl Rosenberg, Health Education Unit, Department of Public Health Practice. Students from mental health and other departments. Group process, cohesion, productivity, leadership, structure, and communication.

C. Special training of Mental Hygiene Concentration:

Supervised field work in Division Field Station at the Wellesley HRS. Also include students from the Harvard Department of Social Relations [HDSR], Harvard Graduate School of Education [HGSE], HMS psychiatry. Past year concentration on mental health consultation—Wellesley school system, Caplan weekly seminar. Action research projects at HRS—NIMH trainee Dr. Natalie Valee and Dr. George Talland (HDSR psychologist) preschool screening. Dr. Paul Hare (on an NIMH research fellowship) preschool screening and school children leadership. Dr. Peter Sifneos (MGH psychiatrist) USPHS prevention techniques regarding family crisis pathogens. Dr. Trawich Stubbs work toward doctorate in public health under Dr. Lindemann—group techniques to sensitize teachers to mental health implications.

D. Special research seminars:

Review of Division projects, selected seminars in HDSR and HGSE.

4. Course 14D "Mental Health Problems", Division of Mental Health, Department of Public Health Practice, HSPH 1954. [folder "HSPH Courses + Seminars 1950s; 1954 Annual Report of Div. Ment. Hlth (HSPH)", Box IIA&B, Lindemann Collection, Center for the History of Medicine, Francis A. Countway Library of Medicine, Boston, MA] Course topics and faculty:

Ecology—Dr. Frederick Richardson; Discussant—Dr. Hans Helweg-Larson
Culture—Dr. Beatrice Whiting; discussion of cultures and psychiatry—Miss Mary Kozeff
Group Membership—Dr. Hubert Coffey; discussion of minorities and prejudice—Dr. Holland Carter
Group Leadership—Dr. Hubert Coffey; discussion of transitioning community leadrship—Miss Ruth Huenemann and Miss Catherine Leamy
Childhood and school—Dr. Warren Vaughan; discussion of marriage—Miss Katherine Fitzgerald and Miss Asenath Cooke

The mental health industry—Dr. Frederick Richardson; disussion of the public health nurse—Mrs. Veronica Marks, Miss Madeline Phaneuf

DMH Program—Dr. Peter B. Hagaopian; discussion of alcoholism—Miss Dorothy Woodcock, Miss Doris Boulware

Volunteering and the Massachusetts Association for Mental Health—Mrs. Irene Malamud, Mrs. Dorothy Parker; discussion of child guidance clinics

5. "Community Mental Health Organization Conference" [Box II B1, Erich Lindemann Collection, Center for the History of Medicine, Francis A. Countway Library of Medicine, Harvard Medical Area, Boston, MA]

6. Caplan, Gerald, proposal to Lindemann, Erich, "Research and Development in Community Mental Health", undated (possibly 1958). [envelope "From Dr. [Gerald] Caplan, Research in Community Mental Health; [to] Dr. Erich Lindemann, Department of Psychiatry, Massachusetts General Hospital", IIIB2 a+b (box1 of 3), Erich Lindemann Collection, Center for the History of Medicine, Francis A. Countway Library of Medicine, Boston, MA]

7. Caplan, Gerald, MD, D.P.M., "Problems of Training in Mental Health Consultation", lecture delivered at the Institute on Residency Training in Community Psychiatry, University of Texas, Dallas, Texas, 11/7/1963. [folder "Caplan—Problems of Training in M. H. Consultation, box Human Relations Service via Elizabeth Lindemann, Erich Lindemann Collection, Francis A. Countway Library of Medicine, Boston, MA]

8. Announcement by Gerald Caplan, p. 1. [folder "Caplan, G. papers", Box IIIB1 e 2), A-E, Erich Lindemann Collection, Center for the History of Medicine, Francis A. Countway Library of Medicine, Boston, MA]

9. Berry, George Packer, HMS Dean, letter to Quigg Newton, president of The Commonwealth Fund, 12/21/64, p. 2. [folder "Dean George Packer Berry", Box IIIA 4 (A-E), Lindemann Collection, Center for the History of Medicine, Francis A. Countway Library of Medicine, Boston, MA]

10. HSPH choice of new dean passed over Hugh Leavell (social medicine) and chose John C. Snyder, working with infectious diseases, professor of population and public health, as part of HSPH shift from social to biological medicine:

> "had dignity and certain stern countenance." Alexander Leighton, brought to the School by Snyder to head up a newly created behavioral sciences department in the 1960s . . . careful and conservative (p. 83) . . . in 1946, Snyder was appointed to head the [HSPH] School's new Department of Public Health Bacteriology (p. 85) . . . Snyder was named dean in October 1954, a few months after the sudden death of Dean James Stevens Simmons . . . when American faith in health and medical science—and science more generally—was sky-high. The country was euphoric about . . . the Salk polio vaccine . . . Professor Thomas Weller's shared Nobel Prize for research that made the vaccine possible. . . . controlling and preventing infectious disease still remained the pivotal mission of much of public health . . . Snyder also established the Center for the Prevention of Infectious Diseases near the end of his deanship, in 1970. But Snyder was not afraid to break new intellectual ground. In 1962, he created the Department of Behavioral Sciences. . . . That same year he founded the Department of Demography and Human Ecology . . . and a year later, the university-wide Center for Population Studies.
>
> (p. 86–7)

"1922–1971 Harvard School of Public Health: Evolution of a Global Leader", *Harvard Public Health Review, 75th Anniversary Issue vol.1* (Boston, MA: Office of Development and Alumni Relations, Harvard

School of Public Health, 1997); "John Crayton Snyder Dean 1954–1971", pp. 82–88. [folder "Harvard School of Public Health", David G. Satin files]
    While dedicated to biological public health, he is credited with "modernizing and expanding the scope of HSPH, Snyder founded the Department of Behavioral Sciences, now known as the Department of Health and Social Behavior, and the Center for Population Studies".
    "John C. Snyder, class of 1935", *Harvard Medical Alumni Bulletin*, Autumn, 2002; p. 60. [folder "Harvard School of Public Health", David G. Satin files]

11. Lindemann, Erich, interview with two graduate students in sociology, 1965, p. 26. [folder "Stanford—Misc.", box IV 3 + 4 + 5, Erich Lindemann Collection, Center for the History of Medicine, Francis A., Countway Library of Medicine, Boston, MA]
12. Lindemann, Erich, with Duhl, Leonard, and Seeley, John, interview at Lindemann's home in Palo Alto, CA, by Leonard Duhl, 6/15,22/1974. [caddy 4, tape ee3A, 4B;7, Erich Lindemann Collection, Center for the History of Medicine, Francis A. Countway Library of Medicine, Boston, MA]
13. Leavell, Hugh R., letter to Lindemann, Erich, 1/2/1965. [folder "Correspondence re India 1964–65", Box IIIA5 1), Erich Lindemann Collection, Center for the History of Medicine, Francis A. Countway Library of Medicine, Boston, MA]
14. Leavell, Hugh R., letter to Farrell, Jean, administrative assistant to Lindemann, 8/11/1963. [folder "L Miscellaneous", Box IIIA 4 (I-Ma), Erich Lindemann Collection, Center for the History of Medicine, Francis A. Countway Library of Medicine, Boston, MA]
15. Caplan-Mosovich, Ruth, 1982, *ibid.,* p. 37.
16. Poerksen, Niels, CMH psychiatrist at the University of Heidelberg, interview by David G. Satin in Wellesley, Massachusetts, 9/9/1978. [caddy ?, Box 4, X, Lindemann Collection, Center for the History of Medicine, Francis A. Countway Library of Medicine, Boston, MA]
17. Lindemann, Elizabeth file #105 Press Notices; also folder "Erich Lindemann—Biographies", Box IV 1 + 2, Lindemann Collection, Center for the History of Medicine., Countway Library of Medicine, Boston, MA. "Erich Lindemann, Professor of Psychiatry. *(Consent given by the Board of Overseers, June 17, 1954.)*". *Harvard University Gazette XLIX* no. 39 (7/17/54), p. 295. [folder "Lindemann—Personal Documents", David G. Satin files, Newton, MA]
18. Lindemann, Elizabeth B., interviews by David G. Satin at Wellesley and Boston, MA, 6/27/1978–8/1979. [Erich Lindemann Collection, David G. Satin, Newton, MA]

> "Scientists in the News. . . Eric [*sic*] **Lindemann**, associate professor of psychiatry, has been appointed professor of psychiatry in the medical school and psychiatrist-in-chief at Massachusetts General Hospital; and **Raymond DeLacy Adams**, associate clinical professor of neurology has been named Bullard professor of neuropathology in the medical school and continues as chief of the Neurological Service of the Massachusetts General Hospital. The appointments create a new professorship in psychiatry in the Faculty of Medicine and fill two posts vacated by **Stanley Cobb**, who has retired as Bullard professor of neuropathology and as chief of the Psychiatry Service at the Massachusetts General Hospital" *Science 120*: 126.

(1954)

19. Lindemann, Erich, "Talk Given by Erich Lindemann to Staff of Student Health Department at Stanford, Nov. 12.1971" (in response to a request that he reconstruct some aspects of his own development as teacher and scientist). [folder "Mental Health Services of MGH a setting for Community MH", Box VII 2, Lindemann Collection, Rare Books Department, Countway Library of Medicine, Boston, MA]

20. Peabody, Francis W., "The Soul of the Clinic", *Journal of the American Medical Association 90* no. 45: 1193–1197 (pp. 193–194) (4/14/1928).

21. Recommendations of the Scientific Advisory Committee Massachusetts General Hospital, 12/2,3/1949, p. 4. [folder "Brazier, M.A.B"., Box IIIB1 e 2), A-E", Erich Lindemann Collection, Center for the History of Medicine, Francis A. Countway Library of Medicine, Boston, MA]

22. 10/1954. [folder "Dr. Erich Lindemann—Personal Misc. Material (old", Box IIIB1e 2), F-Ma", Erich Lindemann Collection, Center for the History of Medicine, Francis A. Countway Library of Medicine, Boston, MA.]

23. Lindemann, Elizabeth B., phone communication 7/30/2002. [folder "Dr. Erich Lindemann—Personal Misc. Material (old", Box IIIB1e 2), F-Ma", Erich Lindemann Collection, Center for the History of Medicine, Francis A. Countway Library of Medicine, Boston, MA]

24. "Stanley Cobb, MD, Retiring Chief of Psychiatry Service", "Psychiatry Service", *M.G.H. The News* no. 136 (7 and 8/1954); 6/54 *Harvard Medical Alumni Bulletin* 6/1954. [folder "Cobb, Stanley", Box IIIB1a box 2 of 2, Erich Lindemann Collection, Center for the History of Medicine, Francis A. Countway Library of Medicine, Boston, MA]

25. Neumann, Ellsworth, MGH Associate Director. Interviewed by David G. Satin at the Rockefeller Foundation, New York City, 4/27/1979. [caddy 5, Box 5, X, Lindemann Collection, Center for the History of Medicine, Francis A. Countway Library of Medicine, Boston, MA]

26. Lindemann, Erich: memo to John H. Knowles, 9/29/1961.

27. "Annual Report of the General Executive Committee 1957 (final)" (p. 1). [folder "G.E.C.—Annual Report from all MGH Depts. 1957", Box IIIB1b box 1 of 2, Erich Lindemann Collection, Center for the History of Medicine, Francis A. Countway Library of Medicine, Boston, MA]

28. Lindemann, Erich, memo to Knowles, John H., 10/6/1961. [folder "Dr. Knowles, John 1961", Box IIIA 4 (I-Ma), Lindemann Collection, Center for the History of Medicine, Francis A., Countway Library of Medicine, Boston, MA]

29. Knowles, John H., "Medical School, Teaching Hospital and Social Responsibility", Second Institute on Medical Center Problems, Association of American Medical Colleges, Miami, FL 12/9/1964, p. 17–18; also Panel Meeting, Task Force on Economic Growth and Opportunity, U.S. Chamber of Commerce, Washington, DC, 12/10/1964.

30. Lindemann, Elizabeth B., interviewed by David G. Satin including 8/23 and 11/29/1998. [David G. Satin files, Newton, MA]

31. Lindemann, Erich. [Box XII 2 folder "Incomplete or Unidentified", Erich Lindemann Collection, Center for the History of Medicine, Francis A. Countway Library of Medicine, Boston, MA]

32. Lindemann, Erich, "Talk to Pediatricians '56?". [Box XII 2 folder "Lindemann—Talk to Pediatricians' 56?", Erich Lindemann Collection, Center for the History of Medicine, Francis A. Countway Library of Medicine, Boston, MA]

33. Wisman, Avery quoted in Eisenberg, Leon, "Psychiatry After Lindemann: 'A View from the Bridge'", Ch. 18 in "Psychiatry Service", in Castleman,

Benjamin, Crockett, David C. and Sutton, S.B. (eds.), *The Massachusetts General Hospital 1955–1980* (Boston, MA: Little Brown, 1983), pp. 168–175:

> For many years MGH was known as 'anti-analytic', meaning that psychoanalytic concepts or even psychoanalysts were said to be scoffed at here and regarded as a contaminating influence. . . . When it came time to appoint a new chairman, both to replace Cobb and Lindemann, the Search Committee explicitly said that it wanted to get away from someone who was "heavily psychoanalytic" and turn MGH psychiatry back to medicine, where it belonged. [MGH biol tradit, psychiat not perm rooted by Cobb—MGH wanted to put it in its subordinate place] Thus, two views prevailed: the notion that MGH opposed psychoanalysis and the belief that MGH psychiatry was "too analytic". I can attest that neither accusation was ever correct. . . . In the early years after Hitler came to power, psychoanalysts who had been among Freud's followers became refugees. Many landed in East Coast cities. . . . But it was through the help of Stanley Cobb that several outstanding psychoanalysts were able to settle in Boston. . . . He invited a few to participate in the department's teaching program. . . . Shortly after World War II, however, the link with psychoanalysis became stronger with the popularity of analytic training among psychiatric residents. . . . I must emphasize that in those days there was no other opportunity for post-graduate training than in psychoanalysis. . . . Although the medical community may feel that psychoanalysis can be rooted out of departments of psychiatry, we must recall that long before the influx of refugees psychoanalysis had imprinted itself throughout the artistic and literary world. Consequently, it is part of our common culture and cannot be denied. . . . psychoanalysis has disappointed our naive, early expectations, but . . . it is no longer a question of being analytic or not, but rather how well one learns the importance of psychotherapy.
>
> But I cannot explain the antagonism expressed for psychoanalysis by medical colleagues who are otherwise fair and objective. Why the establishment feels threatened by the mild, inconspicuous efforts of some staff members with analytic training is a mystery. . . . Cobb, Eisenberg, and Hackett, along with John Nemiah, encouraged residents to get training in anything that might broaden their psychiatric weaponry and perspective".
>
> (p. 183)

34. Lindemann, Erich, "The Dynamics of Bereavement, presented at the Annual Meeting of the American Orthopsychiatric Association, New York City, 3/24/1961, p. 9. [Box XII 2 folder "Lindemann—The Dynamics of Bereavement March 1961", Erich Lindemann Collection, Center for the History of Medicine, Francis A. Countway Library of Medicine, Boston, MA]

35. "Summary of the Discussion between Dr. John Knowles and Dr. Erich Lindemann on September 29, 1961", p. 2. [folder "GEC Report by Dr. Lindemann for Dept. of Psychiatry—Dec. 6, 1961", Box IIIB1b box 1 of 2, Erich Lindemann Collection, Center for the History of Medicine, Francis A. Countway Library of Medicine, Boston, MA]

36. Lindemann, Erich, "The Role of Psychiatry at the M.G.H"., 7/1/1965, pp. 7, 10–11. [folder "The Role of Psychiatry at the M.G.H. July 1, 1965", IIIB3 a-c, Erich Lindemann Collection, Center for the History of Medicine, Countway Library of Medicine, Boston, MA]

37. Caplan, Gerald, MD, Professor of Child Psychiatry and chairperson, Department of Child Psychiatry, Hadassah University Hospital, Ein Karem, Jerusalem, Epilogue, "Personal Reflections by Gerald Caplan", in Schulberg,

Herbert C. and Killilea, Marie (eds.), *The Modern Practice of Community Mental Health: A Volume in Honor of Gerald Caplan* (San Francisco: Jossey Bass, 1982), p. 660.

38. Lindemann, Erich, "The Mental Health Service of the Massachusetts General Hospital: A Setting for Community Mental Health Training" (given at a conference, possibly in 1956) and included in edited form in Lindemann, Erich and Lindemann, Elizabeth (eds.), *Beyond Grief: Studies in Crisis Intervention* (New York: Jason Aronson, 1979), Ch. 9 "Community Mental Health Training at the Massachusetts General Hospital", pp. 155–166.

39. Lindemann, Erich, "Outline of Introductory Comments Concerning the Community Mental Health Program at the Massachusetts General Hospital". [folder "Lindemann-Caplan Application Material—Sight [*sic*] Visit", IIIB2 c (box1 of 2), Erich Lindemann Collection, Center for the History of Medicine, Francis A. Countway Library of Medicine, Boston, MA]

The cooperative program in Community Mental Health of the Harvard School of Public Health and the Massachusetts General Hospital. . . . the division of mental health at the Harvard School of Public Health had developed a program of teaching for students in public health. . . . This type of program had been discussed . . . at an NIMH sponsored conference in 1950. . . of advanced training for future specialists in . . . Community Mental Health . . . need of bringing to younger psychiatrists, psychologists, social workers, and . . . care-taking professions in their formative years . . . information about . . . preventive work in the area of mental health . . . discussed . . . at a conference called by the NIMH in the spring of 1954. . . the MGH service which already had established a Mental Health Unit, and started a program to bring to psychiatrists . . . psychologists . . . and to social workers . . . a program of studies in Community Mental Health which might stimulate some . . . to make this new field the focus of their professional careers, but particularly to help . . . to include a mental health orientation in their program of professional activities . . . the Mental Health Service of the hospital, which was created by the trustees to develop preventive measures in the field of mental illness and health, both inside the hospital and in the community areas adjacent to it, undertook a teaching program . . . Such a program would also serve to weld together a multidisciplinary faculty from the three psychiatric professions, and permit infiltration [sic—need for deviousness recognized] of the other faculties of the hospital with a mental health orientation which would become part of the system of medical care in a large metropolitan hospital . . . it appeared imperative to have an ongoing research and field work on mental health problems . . . We also needed a theoretical frame of reference . . . which differed from the traditional nosological categories. We found this frame in the crisis theory and studied . . . the spectrum of mal-adaptive and well-adaptive responses to life situations demanding new solutions. . . . The practical application . . . in crisis situations inside the hospital as well as . . . the non-medical care-taking professions in the community at different class levels also seemed desirable . . . clarification of community organization issues and group processes involved in health education, particularly the relation of city planning to possible mental health factors . . . for inquiry and for teaching.

The program is based on the small existing service staff at the Massachusetts General Hospital and on the Human Relations Service at Wellesley . . . further enriched by the West End Relocation Study Project. A faculty . . . a didactic program and a syllabus . . . field station experiences in the areas of preventive intervention, mental health consultation, community organization and research . . . program would be tremendously strengthened if we could assemble a group . . . in certain branches of the social sciences . . . give guidance and consultation to the . . . research program and the training courses . . . continue their own work . . . contributing to and stimulating . . . by developing their own research . . . facilitate and enrich the exchange with other departments of the university . . . lend stature to our Community Mental Health Program as a source for consultation for other developing programs throughout this country.

(pp. 1–4)
[folder "LINDEMANN-CAPLAN APPLICATION
MATERIAL—SIITE VISIT", IIIB2 c (box1 of 2),
Erich Lindemann Collection, Center for the History
of Medicine, Francis A. Countway Library of
Medicine, Boston, MA]

40. Psychiatry Service, "Massachusetts General Hospital", Annual Report—1951, *ibid.*

41. Psychiatry Service, "Massachusetts General Hospital", 1951, *ibid.,* Psychiatry Service 1954–5, p. 5.

42. "Annual Report for the Department of Psychiatry for the Year 1955 Statistical Summary from October 1, 1954–September 30, 1955". [folder "Annual Reports from Staff Members 1955", Box IIIB1b box 1 of 2, Erich Lindemann Collection, Center for the History of Medicine, Francis A. Countway Library of Medicine, Boston, MA]

43. A Program of Research and Development in Community Mental Health. [folder "Lindemann-Caplan Application Material—Site Visit", IIIB2 c (box1 of 2), Erich Lindemann Collection, Center for the History of Medicine, Francis A. Countway Library of Medicine, Boston, MA]

44. "The Massachusetts General Hospital Institute of Mental Health (penciled: "New Unit", 7/19/1955. [folder "The New Unit—M.G.H. Warren Building", IIIB2 c (box1 of 2), Erich Lindemann Collection, Center for the History of Medicine, Francis A. Countway Library of Medicine, Boston, MA]

45. Bauer, Walter, Chief of the Medical Services, and Churchill, Edward D., Chief of the Surgical Services, to Gray, Mr. Francis C., chairperson, Board of Trustees, Massachusetts General Hospital, 12/1/1955. [folder "The New Unit—M.G.H. Warren Building", IIIB2 c (box1 of 2), Erich Lindemann Collection, Center for the History of Medicine, Francis A. Countway Library of Medicine, Boston, MA]

46. "Outline "Considerations About a New Psychiatric Unit at the Mass. General Hospital, presented by Dr. Lindemann to the Scientific Advisory Committee". [folder "The New Unit—M.G.H. Warren Building", IIIB2 c (box1 of 2), Erich Lindemann Collection, Center for the History of Medicine, Francis A. Countway Library of Medicine, Boston, MA]

47. "Psychiatric Service of the Massachusetts General Hospital", (undated). [folder "The New Unit—M.G.H. Warren Building", IIIB2 c (box1 of 2), Erich Lindemann Collection, Center for the History of Medicine, Francis A. Countway Library of Medicine, Boston, MA]

48. Schmehl, Francis L., chief of Health Research Facilities Branch, Division of Research Grants, Department of Health, Education, and Welfare, U.S. Public Health Service, letter, 10/24/1956. [folder "The New Unit—M.G.H. Warren Building", IIIB2 c (box1 of 2), Erich Lindemann Collection, Center for the History of Medicine, Francis A. Countway Library of Medicine, Boston, MA]

49. New Plan in Warrent Bldg: PLAN A and Plan C, (undated). [folder "The New Unit—M.G.H. Warren Building", IIIB2 c (box1 of 2), Erich Lindemann Collection, Center for the History of Medicine, Francis A. Countway Library of Medicine, Boston, MA]
50. Knowles, John H., letter to MGH physicians, 1/26/1962, p. 1. [folder "MGH GRAND ROUNDS", IIIB3 d, Erich Lindemann Collection, Center for the History of Medicine, Francis A. Countway Library of Medicine, Boston, MA]

> Have one wing of the Baker Memorial for 9–10 beds for people under continuous supervision. The rest of the floor to be a regular Baker floor, which might attract patients with psychiatric difficulties. The new building will be called Neuropsychiatric, for Neurology, Pathology, and Psychiatry. This will have recreational facilities for the Baker patients. For the psychoneurotic patients, we will have a dormitory where patients will do the housekeeping, and will have cooperative living. These patients will come to offices for interviews. B7 [psychiatry ward] will be for Medicine and Psychiatry. Dr. [Walter] Bauer [Chief of Medicine] thought we might have another medical house officer there. This will be for psychosomatic patients. The first year it will be run by Psychiatry.
>
> [folder "Staff Conference Schedule 1957–58 Dept. of Psychiatry—1959–60", Box IIIB1a box 1 of 2, Erich Lindemann Collection, Center for the History of Medicine, Francis A. Countway Library of Medicine, Boston, MA]
>
> December, 1959 MASSACHUSETTS GENERAL HOSPITAL PSYCHIATRIC SERVICE [schedule of meetings/rounds including] Tuesdays, 2:00–4:00 Seminar: Cultural Aspects of Psychodynamics. Dr. Wm. Caudill and Dr. John Spiegel. . . . Dec. 1—Individual formulation of the Italian-American case materials. Dr. Spiegel Dec. 8 —Presentation of the Italian-American case materials. Dr. Spiegel Dec. 15 -Wednesdays, 2:30–4:00 Community Mental Health Seminar. . . . Dec. 2—Discussion. Dr. Wilson Dec. 9—Community Organization and Process. Laura Morris, MSW., and Lester Huston, MSW. Dec. 16—Discussion. Mrs. Morris and Mr. Huston 3:30–5:00 Seminar on the Etiology and Community Mental Health Aspects of Alcoholism. . . . Thursdays, . . . 9:00–10:00 West End Staff Meetings. . . . Dec. 3 —Ethnic Cultures in West End. I. Edward Ryan Dec. 17—Student Mental Health Study. Charles Bidwell, PhD Mondays, Wellesley Human Relations Service Staff conference.
>
> > [folder "Some Recent Developments in the Activities of the psychiatric service 1964 (MGH)", Box IIIB1a box 1 of 2, Erich Lindemann Collection, Center for the History of Medicine, Francis A. Countway Library of Medicine, Boston, MA]

> Some Recent Developments in the Activities of the Psychiatric Service E. Lindemann, MD November, 1964:
>
> Dr. [Stanley] Cobb began his administration of the [MGH Psychiatric] Service with an emphasis on neurophysiology, to which he gradually added a program of psychological and personality studies including psychoanalytic considerations. He was also interested in the early efforts at introducing social science into the study of clinical problems. At his retirement, Dr. Adams was made Bullard Professor of Neuropathology. . . . Dr. Lindemann, as new Professor of Psychiatry at the Massachusetts General

Hospital developed a fourfold approach to problems of integration. Our studies have to do with: first, the integrative functions of the central nervous system; second, the integration of personality function; third, the integration of individuals into social systems; and fourth, the developmental aspects of integration at various stages of the life cycle of individuals and of communities. As was natural with Dr. Lindemann's selection as Chief of Service, major emphasis has been placed on the development of the field of personality studies and of social psychiatry. This emphasis has led to considerations of human ecology: of the habitat from which a person comes to the hospital and to which he returns. It has been concerned with hazards to the emotional health of close relatives of the patients and with possible preventive measure as part of an overall health program rather than a program which is restricted to remedial efforts with established disease. The expansion of activities has been particularly marked in the area of <u>basic research</u> which is carried on both in the Stanley Cobb Laboratories and in the social psychiatry units in Wellesley and in the West End of Boston. The integration of psychiatric services into the general hospital in this transition from a "[psychoneuroses] unit" to a 'mental disease unit' has been difficult and has not been completely successful up to now. There are complaints about us at times, and there are swings of opinion, changing from excessive admiration and expectations to discarding our services altogether.

(pp. 1–2)

. . .

The development of a separate psychiatric section for the special care of patients with emotional difficulties appears desirable to many staff members. We are now experimenting with the provision of certain forms of physical treatment, such as shock therapy, to the depressed patients in the private section of the hospital. Points of real advance are in the Emergency Ward [greatly increased population seen, especially people with alcoholism], in the community services, in the development of a substantial research program on the integration of behavior, and in our liaison with the suitable parent departments at Harvard University.

(pp. 16–17)
[folder "Ward Plans", Box IIIB1a box 1 of 2, Erich
Lindemann Collection, Center for the History of
Medicine, Francis A. Countway Library of
Medicine, Boston, MA]

51. [folder "Miscellaneous Journals Catalog & File directions", Box IIIB1a box 2 of 2, Erich Lindemann Collection, Center for the History of Medicine, Francis A. Countway Library of Medicine, Boston, MA]
52. "Massachusetts General Hospital—Unit of Psychiatry in Harvard Medical School", pp. 1–6. [folder "RESEARCH—1955", IIIB2 a+b (box1 of 3), Erich Lindemann Collection, Center for the History of Medicine, Francis A. Countway Library of Medicine, Boston, MA]. Specific research areas included the following:

This [MGH Psychiatry] unit is in the process of re-organization aimed at providing facilities for access to the total biological gradient of mental health and disease. . . . it is being related on the one hand to a private mental hospital with an orientation to social psychiatry (McLean) where severe illness and fatal outcomes are studied and on the other side to organizations providing access to normal populations such as: the "West End Guidance Center" in the City Health Department; the Human Relations Service in Wellesley giving access to a normal school population; and to a rehabilitation center for victims of accidents and physical illness developed by the Massachusetts General Hospital. There is also a strong tie to the activities of the Division of Mental Health of the School of Public Health at the Whittier Street Family Guidance Center. The individuals concerned with the development of the behavioral science aspects of the mental health work . . . form a planning group for the total research program. While they agree that the social science approach to mental health provides an essential next step they do not lose sight of the great importance of simultaneous developments in bio-chemistry and neuropathology to provide a better understanding of host factors in behavior disorders. . . . It is therefore an essential part of the program to provide the neurological department with behavioral scientists especially interested in the details of cognitive processes and with the organization of action as it is related to the structure and function of the central nervous system.

However, the central enterprise of the Department would be an investigation of the relationships of interpersonal processes to personality structure and functioning. Dr. [Alfred] Stanton will have the opportunity at the McLean Hospital to investigate in detail those aspects of the caretaking environment of mental patients in a hospital setting. . . . Dr. Lindemann will have the opportunity at the Massachusetts General Hospital through the development of a new unit . . . to start a program for the study of the behavior in small groups of patients whose personality structure and psychopathology has been ascertained by psychoanalytically-oriented studies. . . . The progress which Dr. [R. Fried] Bales [Harvard Social Relations Department] is making in clarification of dynamics of behavior in small groups would be immediately useful. . . . To these . . . would be related a study of children in nursery school groups as envisaged as part of the program of the new Mental Health Service of the Massachusetts General Hospital utilizing the insights . . . from the Laboratory of Human Development under Dr. Whiting and from the Human Relations Service of Wellesley. The program further envisages making use of the facility for the study of social behavior provided by a special unit for the rehabilitation of patients suffering from psychoneurosis. Instead of having such patients treated in the conventional setting of a psychiatric ward they will be living together in a unit in which meaningful social roles are assigned . . . in joint housekeeping as well as in a variety of job and recreational pursuits. . . . A useful focus for this program appears to be a study of the changes in personality functioning and in social behavior which are necessitated by various types of role transition such as bereavement, disabling accidents, including unsuccessful suicide, leaving home for school and changes in occupational role. All of these require re-organization of role behavior and may be followed by well-adaptive and mal-adaptive responses both personality-wise and within the primary social group. Earlier studies of bereavement and of behavior in social crises indicate that individuals are particularly open to inquiry at such periods and that even minor efforts at intervention may be effective in determining the course of such responses. . . . This program is aimed at basic investigations concerning personality functioning and social integration. . . . we would select those individuals who offer opportunities for study with respect to our

particular problem and would actively search . . . inviting for a period of
stay not only "patients" whose role is well defined but also individuals
not belonging to the sick category such as recently bereaved people and
other persons facing a major role transition. This would . . . include a
good many key persons in the human environment of individuals being
studied. . . . There is . . . another program. . . [that] deals with the kind
of joint personality functioning which is seen between certain specific
individuals of a patient's primary group. The co-ordination of the role
behavior of two individuals seems to be so close and in a special way so
instrumental for each partner . . . that separation leaves on both sides a
truncated personality which cannot be related to other persons because
the requirements for role behavior are excessively stringent. A number of
patients with psychosomatic disorders . . . are related . . . in this manner
but the partners do not appear as sick. A detailed study of such "pathogenic individuals" has been started. . . . our present focus on interpersonal behavior and what is often called "social psychiatry" . . . serves
only to re-emphasize the importance of studies on somatic processes
which are correlated with, impaired by or occasionally even facilitated
by the type of social and personality events which we are studying. . . .
These studies will require joint work with the Department of Internal
Medicine and with the Department of Neurology involving not only the
re-organization of certain caretaking facilities on the medical and psychiatric services but also close contact . . . with the behavioral scientist who
is primarily concerned with the behavioral manifestations of variations
of the functioning of the central nervous system.

(p. 1–6)

53. [folder "Misc H", Box IIIA 1–3, Lindemann Collection, Center for the History of Medicine, Francis. A. Countway Library of Medicine, Boston, MA]
54. (Carbon copy of typed manuscript.) [folder "MEDICAL SERVICE 1956–
57", Box IIIB1a box 1 of 2, Erich Lindemann Collection, Center for the History of Medicine, Francis A. Countway Library of Medicine, Boston, MA]
55. "Annual Report Hall Mercer Hospital Massachusetts General Hospital Division 1955–1956", pp. 1, 2. [folder "Hall-Mercer 1955", Box IIIB1b box 1 of
2, Erich Lindemann Collection, Center for the History of Medicine, Francis
A. Countway Library of Medicine, Boston, MA]

[The Mental Health Service/Hall Mercer Hospital] staff is working closely
with the Family Service under the direction of Dr. [David] Rutstein [chair-
person, HMS Department of Preventive Medicine] to contribute to the
diagnosis of disturbed family situations and to render assistance to the
members of the families who are endangered in their emotional adjustment. . . . we have made considerable effort to increase our usefulness to
patient and physicians in other wards and in other clinics . . . a program
of close cooperation with Dr. [Walter] Bauer [MGH Chief of Med] and
the Medical Service . . . training program of the fourth year [HMS] medical students in a joint exercise [EL] with Dr. Walter Bauer where problems
raised by the students dealing with emotional and social factors in medical illness have been discussed.

56. National Institutes of Health Application for Training Grant, 12/10/1957.
"Training Program in Preventive Psychiatry at the Massachusetts General
Hospital", NIMH grant proposal 2169-M, 1955–6 2M-6198 760 7540–5.
Details of training grant application:

12/11/54 Department of Health, Education, and Welfare, Public Health Service, National Institutes of Health: Application for Training Grant Under National Mental Health Act:

Period July 1, 1955 TO June 30, 1956... Amount Requested... $24,093... 5. Estimate of future support to be requested . . . First Additional year $27,693. Second additional year $30,693. Third additional year $30,693 Fourth Additional year $30,693.

(pp. 1–4)

12/13/54 Grant Application Cover Sheet (MGH letterhead):

Training Program in Preventive Psychiatry at the Massachusetts General Hospital . . . Granting Agency: U.S. Public Health—Mental Hygiene . . . Principal Investigator: Erich Lindemann, M.D. Support requested for 5 year(s) . . . Active Date July 1, 1955 Expiration June 30, 1961. . . Total $24,093.

(p. 1)

[envelope "USPHS Training in Preventive Psychiatry 1955–6 2M-6198 760 7540–5", IIIB2 b (box2 of 3), Erich Lindemann Collection, Center for the History of Medicine, Francis A. Countway Library of Medicine, Boston, MA]

57. [folder "MINUTES ** AD HOC SUBCOMMITTEE ON GRAD PSYCH. TEACHING", Box IIIC1 c, Erich Lindemann Collection, Center for the History of Medicine, Francis A. Countway Library of Medicine, Boston, MA]

"4/19/57 Minutes of 1st Meeting of Committee on the Organization of a Graduate School of Psychiatry" (pp. 1–2):

held in Dr. Erich Lindemann's office . . . Members present: Dr. Erich Lindemann, chairman, Drs. [Beth Israel Hospital—Thomas] Dwyer, [Peter Bent Brigham Hospital—Sanford] Gifford, [McLean Hospital—Merton] Kahne, [MGH—John] Nemiah, [MMHC—Elvin] Semrad, and [Boston City Hosp.—Donald] Wexler . . . Dr. Lindemann outlined a possible organization for a graduate school in psychiatry which would utilize the facilities and teaching personnel of the now discrete psychiatric teaching units at the Harvard Medical School. The purpose . . . would be to promote the training of psychiatric residents along academic lines, and to encourage them to participate in ongoing research projects. It would provide more elementary courses in general and dynamic psychiatry . . . more advanced seminars in specialized topics. As examples of comparable programs . . . the Harvard School of Public Health and the Department of Social Relations at Harvard University. . . . By pooling the resources . . . it would . . . eliminate the gaps in interest and ability . . . provide for cross-fertilization among the various members and their interests . . . give residents a wider body of teachers . . . strengthen psychiatry in the medical school as a whole . . . have direct effect upon under-graduate psychiatric teaching. . . . there was considerable enthusiasm for the idea. . . . matters discussed. . . [the] relationship of such a faculty to the Massachusetts Training Faculty, the Boston Psychoanalytic Institute, and other departments in the behavioral sciences in the University.

"5/3/57 MINIUES OF 2ND MEETING OF COMMITTEE ON THE ORGANIZATION OF A GRADUATE SCHOOL OF PSYCHIATRY" (p. 1):

held in Dr. Erich Lindemann's office at the Massachusetts General Hospital . . . Members present: Dr. Erich Lindemann, chairman, Drs. Dwyer, Gifford, Kahne, Nemiah, Semrad and Wexler . . . Dr. Lindemann cited a an example that a seminar in preventive psychiatry could include the approach used at the Beth Israel Hospital of searching for indications of early emotional disturbance in medical and surgical patients . . . and the orientation at the Massachusetts General toward searching out hazardous situations in the community at large.

"7/15/57 MINUTES OF 5TH MEETING" (pp. 1, 3):

[Held at Lindemann's office, MGH] . . . Members present: Dr. Erich Lindemann, chairman, Drs. Dwyer, Gifford, Kahne, Marcotty, Nemiah, and Semrad. Present by invitation, Dr. George Gardner, Chief of Psychiatry, Judge Baker Clinic. . . . Dr. Lindemann . . . asked Dr. Gardner two specific questions: 1) How should one schedule a central course of didactic lectures so as not to conflict with the individual units involved and at the same time to act as a rallying point for these varying units? 2) How could one best build a federation of the various units into an active and vigorous graduate school of psychiatry? . . . It was generally felt that . . . a course of didactic exercises should be organized to be ready by July of 1958.

(p. 1–3)

"4/7/61 Minutes of the Planning Committee of the Department of Psychiatry, Harvard Medical School":

To: Dr. Grete Bibring [BIH], Dr. Jack Ewalt [MMHC], Dr. Henry Fox [PBBH], Dr. George Gardner [Judge Baker Clinic], Dr. Erich Lindemann, Dr. Elvin Semrad [MMHC], Dr. Philip Solomon [BCH], Dr. Alfred Stanton [McLean Hospital]. . . . The committee meeting was held by telephone.

58. [folder "USPHS Preventive Psychiatry Training Grant 1958–59 2M-6198-C3", IIIB2 c (box1 of 2), Erich Lindemann Collection, Center for the History of Medicine, Francis A. Countway Library of Medicine, Boston, MA]
59. [folder "USPHS Preventive Psychiatry Training Grant 1958–59 2M-6198-C3", IIIB2 c (box1 of 2), Erich Lindemann Collection, Center for the History of Medicine, Francis A. Countway Library of Medicine, Boston, MA] Courses proposed:

- The Meaning of Culture and its Significance for Psychiatry. by Clyde Kluckhohn, PhD [Anthropol., H.U.]
- The Significance of Social Class for Psychiatric Theory and Treatment. by Frederick Redlich, MD [soc psychiat rsrchr, Columbia U.]
- The Role of the Psychiatrist in American Society by Talcott Parsons, PhD [chairperson, Harvard Department of Social Relations]
- The Immigrant: His Effect Upon American Attitudes by Oscar Handlin, PhD [historian, H.U.]
- Prejudice by Gordon W. Allport, PhD [psychol, H.U.]
- Psychological Themes in Greek Tragedy by John H. Finley, PhD
- Christian Concepts of Guilt and Sin by Paul J. Tillich, D.D. [theologian, Princeton U.]
- Social Themes in American Literature by Perry G.E. Miller, PhD
- The Beginnings of Scientific Anthropology among the Greeks by Eric A. Havelock, PhD

- Psychology and the Science of Politics by Herbert H. Marcuse, PhD [polit. sci, H.U.]
- Spinoza by Harry A. Wolfson, PhD

60. 7/8, 12/21/1960. [folder "Dr. Robert Jones Rehabilitation", Box IIIB1a box 2 of 2, Erich Lindemann Collection, Center for the History of Medicine, Francis A. Countway Library of Medicine, Boston, MA]

61. Application for Approval of Residencies and Fellowships in Psychiatry, American Medical Association Council on Medical Education and Hospitals, 7/15/1958. [folder "American Medical Association Inspection 1958", Box IIIB1a box 2 of 2, Erich Lindemann Collection, Center for the History of Medicine, Francis A. Countway Library of Medicine, Boston, MA]

62. Sifneos, Peter E., memorandum to Lindemann, Erich, 5/20/1960. Space for psychiatry was requested in the new Clinics Builidng being constructed: "(1) The Mental Health Service a. The Adult Psychiatric Clinic proper . . . b. The Child Psychiatry unit . . . c. The Community Mental Health unit with 3–4 offices and a receiving room. (2) The Social Service section (3) Rehabilitation Center a. Alcoholism Clinic . . . b. Day Care unit". [folder "MGH—New Clinics Bldg", Box IIIA 4 (Mb-O), Erich Lindemann Collection, Center for the History of Medicine, Francis A. Countway Library of Medicine, Boston, MA]

63. Lindemann, Erich, and Spivak, McGrath, 1965, *ibid*.

64. "Notes on Erich Lindemann's Talk at Lindemann Mental Health Center, April 13, 1971", p. 1. [Box XII 2 folder "Discussion with Colleagues re Lindemann Mental Health Center April 13, 1971", Erich Lindemann Collection, Center for the History of Medicine, Francis A. Countway Library of Medicine, Boston, MA]

65. Box II A&B, folder "Joint Meetings HSPH Commun. Health Projects 1954 [and 1955]", Center for the History of Medicine, Francis A. Countway Library of Medicine, Boston. Those present included Dean Berry of Harvard Medical School; Dr. Robert Reed and Miss Lena DiCicco of the Field Training Unit Staff; David Austin, Director of the local delinquency program of Greater Boston Council for Youth; Ed Wellan, social anthropologist from the Department of Nutrition, Harvard School of Public Health; Dr. [Thos] Pugh of the Department of Epidemiology, Harvard School of Public Health and the Department of Mental Health of the Commonwealth of Massachusetts. Other guests included Dr. Esther Lucille Brown of the Russell Sage Foundation; Dr. Ed. Abramowitz, Chief Psychologist, Wisconsin Department of Mental Health; Miss Vuorikosky, mental health nurse from Finland, Dr. Donaghue, psychiatric fellow at Massachusetts General Hospital, Dr. Hugh R. Leavell, Professor of Public Health Practice, HSPH; Mr. Arthur Hallock, Supervisor in Education, DMH; Dr. Andrew H. Henry, HDSR s, Dr. Mildred Creak, Head of Psychiatric Department, Great Ormond St. Hospital for Children, London; Dr. G.D. Fraser Steele, Lecturer in Psychiatry, University of Dundee, Scotland. Other visitors included Bengt Berggren, Professor of psychiatry in Sweden: "It was such a long time ago, September [*sic*] 1963. . . my stay in Boston because of Erichs [*sic*] generosity turned out to become a most important ingredients [*sic*] in my professional life. Indirectly also very important for great changes in the Swedish Mental Health system, upon which I have had some influence. . . . I wanted to follow up the Wellesley-project [*sic*], which I visited in 1963, thanks to Erich, of course". [Berggren, Bengt, letter to Lindemann, Elizabeth, 1/1/1996]

66. "Joint Meetings HSPH Commun. Health Projects 1954 [and 1955]", *ibid*. Family Guidance Center staff involved included Dr. Edw Mason

(psychiatrist), Miss Mary Foster (mental health nurse consultant), Mr. Howard Parad (social worker), Mrs. Barbara Ayres (social scientist), and Dr. Harold Stalvey (psychiatrist).

67. "Joint Meetings HSPH Commun. Health Projects 1954 [and 1955]", *ibid.*, p. 9.

68. "Joint Meetings HSPH Commun. Health Projects 1954 [and 1955]", *ibid.*, pp. 1–3, etc.

Lindemann on the theory behind and its operationalization in the HRS:

From his [EL] experience with bereavement reactions and from other clinician's observations, it became clear that social events, such as bereavement, may be followed by serious emotional disease. This observation was followed by an interest in intervening in such social events so as to reduce the number and severity of emotional casualties resulting from them, in contrast to remedial work which focusses on suffering individuals. It was clear that a knowledge of social events was not the province of the clinically oriented professions and so assistance was requested from Harvard School of Public Health and the Social Relations [Department] at Harvard University. As these groups from divergent backgrounds worked together, it became clear that many of their notions regarding each other's areas of knowledge and skill were quite unrealistic. Much of the past five years' experience has been essentially a shared learning marked by heightened ability to communicate and make use of one another's frames of reference. In the beginning the attempt was primarily to develop an organization permitting access to people with methods of work and patterns of investigation not yet fixed. The group did not at that time try to define mental health but rather assumed only that there were a great number of people who were complaining in the areas of behavioral or emotional disturbances. The objective was to be on the lookout for such people and the human environments in which they were operating. . . . Fortunately the project had the counsel of a Steering Committee of which Dr. Leavell was chairman. . . . In the first place, problems arose within the staff group, reflecting status questions, varying orientations, problems of wishing to be heard by the other group more than the other group would agree to, etc. In the second place, there was the problem of integration with the community, seeking ways to help the community accept an organization not basically oriented towards remedy. A guiding principle was the execution of activities as enterprises of citizens' groups, rather than of the agency itself. There were several citizens' committees for which staff members were appointed as resource people. These citizens' groups themselves accepted responsibility for the campaign to establish the Service in the community. No doubt community acceptance was more readily forthcoming because Wellesley is not representative of communities at large but is composed of many upper-middle class citizens interested in intellectual pursuits and seeking intellectual solutions of their emotional problems.

The organization which has evolved includes a certain pattern of functions which can be enumerated: First, remedial work with individual and family problems carried out on a relatively small scale—work which is now called preventive intervention. Second, work with various key individuals and professional groups who are in the community life recognized as caretakers of other people. Third, the development of mental health consultation which has gradually become a rather complicated set of operations carried on with the area of work which might be roughly described as mental health education.

. . .
these activities have been accepted by the community as its own concern. Thus, for the past year the agency has operated under the aegis of the community, with a caseload of families, a program of education and a mental health consultation program—all backed by continuing research interests and activities.

(pp. 1, 2)

Donald Klein on the operations of the HRS:

After the initial grant funding, in 1953 HRS was incorporated and became a member of the United Community Services of Greater Boston. The community wondered if increased emphasis on clinical service would satisfy the agency's res aims or whether it would close. Care was taken in making stable staff task assignments and transitions to new staff. Mental health consultation was provided to schools in the towns of Wellesley and Weston, and to clergy, family case workers, nurses, and physicians with the "objectives of clarifying with these professional groups the emotional needs of the people with whom they work and of supporting them in their efforts to meet these needs most constructively within the scope of their individual profession".

(p. 3)

Clara Mayo described the mental health seminar for student nurses and reviews with the nursing faculty regarding students' adjustment to nursing training. In the first six months of the program, student dropout from the training program decreased from 24% to 6%.

Research projects included correlates of suicide and psychosis. In 1951, Warren Vaughan (formerly on the staff of the HRS and then director of the Division of Mental Hygiene of the Massachusetts Department of Mental Health), Seymour Halleck of the DMH, and Jack Ewalt (commissioner of mental health) made a survey of the distribution of psychiatric facilities, published as Vaughan, Warren T., Conwell, Margaret Devitt, and Kaplan, Bert, "Survey of Community Psychiatric Resources in Massachusetts", 1952. There was interest in solidifying the relationship between the DMH and the HSPH and in the formation of a council of state agencies involved in CMH. Research addressed the family's reaction to emotionally charged events and crises and in meeting discipline problems. Research on the father's occupational role resulted in the publication Aberle, David F. and Naegle, Kaspar D., "Middle Class Fathers' Occupational Role and Attitudes Toward Children", *American Journal of Orthopsychiatry XXII* no. 2 (4/1952). There was study of social interrelatedness and intrapsychic features as antecedents of disturbed behavior. Research on school entry of children and their families included the social relatedness of children entering school (Ann Ross) and the patterns of social adjustment and leadership behavior of children in play groups (Paul Hare).

69. Box II A&B, folder Joint Meetings HSPH Commun. Health Projects 1954, Center for the History of Medicine, Francis A. Countway Library of Medicine, Boston. In attendance were Dr. Hugh R. Leavell [HSPH], Dr. Stanley Cath, Dr. Paul Hare, Dr. Robert B. Reed, Miss Beryl J. Roberts, Miss Lena DiCicco, Dr. Richard W. Poston, Mr. Arthur C.K. Hallock (DMH), Dr. Leonard J. Duhl (NIMH), Dr. Erwin Linn, Dr. Erich Lindemann, Dr. John M. von Felsinger, Mrs. Elizabeth Lindemann, Dr. Pearl P. Rosenberg, Mrs. Barbara C. Ayres, Miss Mary L. Foster, Dr. Edward A. Mason, Dr. Harold D. Stalvey, Mr. David M. Austin and Mr. Walter Miller.

70. Caplan, Gerald, folder "Joint Meetings HSPH Commun. Health Projects 1954", Box II A&B, Erich Lindemann Collection, Center for the History of Medicine, Francis A. Countway Library of Medicine, Boston.

71. "A Proposal for a Community Mental Health Center, *ibid*. Those involved included Drs. Dooley, Ipsen, [Gerald] K[C]aplan, Leavell, [Erich] Lindemann, [Benjamin] Paul [lecturer in social anthropology, HSPH], Pugh, Reed, Schmidt, Stuart, Miss. [Elizabeth P.] Rice [social worker, assistant professor, Department of Maternal and Child Health, HSPH], Miss [Beryl J.] Roberts [assistant professor of health education, HSPH], Miss Trulson, and Miss [Margaret L.] Varley [assistant professor of public health nursing, HSPH].

72. "Annual Report of the General Executive Committee 1957 (final)" (pp. 3–4). [folder "G.E.C.—Annual Report from all MGH Dept.s 1957", Box IIIB1b box 1 of 2, Erich Lindemann Collection, Center for the History of Medicine, Francis A. Countway Library of Medicine, Boston, MA]

73. [folder "GEC Report by Dr. Lindemann for Dept. of Psychiatry—December 6, 1961", Box IIIB1b box 1 of 2, Erich Lindemann Collection, Center for the History of Medicine, Francis A. Countway Library of Medicine, Boston, MA]

74. Lindemann, Erich, and Spivak, McGrath, 1965, *ibid*.

75.

> Good psychiatry means a thorough investigation of a patient's personality and his life adjustment, followed by psychotherapy and educative measures to help him master his problems more effectively. Medication and, under special circumstance, shock therapy can be considered only as auxiliary measures in such a program. Mental abnormalities are understood as adaptive devices which are open to correction in terms of a person's adaptive resources. This approach is quite different from the approach using the disease concept as exemplified by neurological brain disease. . . . The development of the Social Relations Department and its Psychology Division at Harvard have separated from the Psychology Department qua experimental psychology on much the same grounds and in the same manner in which we have somewhat of a distance between Neurology and Psychiatry at the MGH. It may require a considerable advance in existing theory and in our body of knowledge before a common ground can be found for all workers in the field of human behavior.
>
> (pp. 1–3)

76. "McLean Rehabilitation Center to be Dedicated", *The Massachusetts General Hospital News* 10/1963. [folder "Correspondence 1963", Box IIIA 1–3, Lindemann Collection, Center for the History of Medicine, Francis A. Countway Library of Medicine, Boston, MA]

77. Berry, George Packer, "The McLean Hospital Rehabilitation Center", remarks by George Packer Berry, Dean of the Faculty of Medicine, Harvard University, at Dedication Banquet. [folder "McLean Hospital", Box IIIA 4 (Mb-O), Erich Lindemann Collection, Center for the History of Medicine, Francis A. Countway Library of Medicine, Boston, MA]

78. Farnsworth, Dana L., Director of the Harvard University Health Services and Henry K. Oliver Professor of Hygiene, at the dedication of the McLean Hospital Rehabilitation Center, 10/18/1963. [folder "McLean Hospital", Box IIIA 4 (Mb-O), Erich Lindemann Collection, Center for the History of Medicine, Francis A. Countway Library of Medicine, Boston, MA]

79. Lindemann, Erich, memo to Claude E. Welch, MD [MGH Surgical Service], comments for the report of the committee regarding the future of MGH activities at the McLean Hospital, 3/7/1962. [folder "McLean Hospital",

Box IIIA 4 (Mb-O), Erich Lindemann Collection, Center for the History of Medicine, Francis A. Countway Library of Medicine, Boston, MA]

80. Knowles, John H., Thirteenth Meeting of The Special Committee on Social and Physical Environment Variables as Determinants of Mental Health, National Institutes of Health, Public Health Service, Department of Health, Education, and Welfare, Bethesda, Maryland 10/12/1962, stenographic transcription, pp. 49–153. [Erich Lindemann Collection, Center for the History of Medicine, Francis A. Countway Library of Medicine, Boston, MA]

81. Knowles, John H., 1962, *ibid.*, pp. 76–77.

82. Knowles, John H., "Medical School, Teaching Hospital and Social Responsibility: Medicine's Clarion Call", p. 15, delivered at the Second Institute on Medical Center Problems, Association of American Medical Colleges, Miami, Florida 12/9/1964 and Panel Meeting, Task Force on Economic Growth and Opportunity, U.S. Chamber of Commerce, Washington, DC 12/10/1964. [folder "Dr. John Knowles, Medical Director—MGH", Box IIIA 4 (I-Ma), Erich Lindemann Collection, Center for the History of Medicine, Francis A. Countway Library of Medicine, Boston, MA]

83. Knowles, John H., "Medical School, Teaching Hospital and Social Responsibility: Medicine's Clarion Call", p. 15, delivered at the Second Institute on Medical Center Problems, Association of American Medical Colleges, Miami, Florida 12/9/1964 and Panel Meeting, Task Force on Economic Growth and Opportunity, U.S. Chamber of Commerce, Washington, DC 12/10/1964. [folder "Dr. John Knowles, Medical Director—MGH", Box IIIA 4 (I-Ma), Erich Lindemann Collection, Center for the History of Medicine, Francis A. Countway Library of Medicine, Boston, MA]

84. "Summary of the Discussion between Dr. John Knowles and Dr. Erich Lindemann on September 29, 1961", p. 2. [folder "GEC Report by Dr. Lindemann for Dept. of Psychiatry—Dec. 6, 1961", Box IIIB1b box 1 of 2, Erich Lindemann Collection, Center for the History of Medicine, Francis A. Countway Library of Medicine, Boston, MA]

85. "A Meeting of the General Executive Committee was held in the Trustees' Room, White Building, at 8:30 a.m. on Wednesday, December 6, 1961", p. 4. [folder "GEC Report by Dr. Lindemann for Dept. of Psychiatry—Dec. 6, 1961", Box IIIB1b box 1 of 2, Erich Lindemann Collection, Center for the History of Medicine, Francis A. Countway Library of Medicine, Boston, MA]

86. Correspondence between Lindemann and Hagopian, 2/4–4/11/1957. [folder "Misc. Correspondence H,I,J 1956–57", Box IIIA 1–3, Lindemann Collection, Center for the History of Medicine, Francis A. Countway Library of Medicine, Boston, MA]

87. Lindemann correspondence with Peter B. Hagopian, MD, Superintendent of Davners State Hospital, 1/19/1959–8/1/1961 re MGH psychiatry staff teach and MGH residents cover weekends. [folder "Misc H", Box IIIA 1–3, Lindemann Collection, Center for the History of Medicine, Francis. A. Countway Library of Medicine, Boston, MA]

88. Letters from Lindemann to Dr. Elizabeth Crosfield and Dr. Charles L. Clay, 8/25,9/15,1961. [folder "Misc D", Box IIIA 1–3, Lindemann Collection, Center for the History of Medicine, Francis A. Countway Library of Medicine, Boston, MA]

89. Lindemann letter to David A. Boyd, Executive Secretary-Treasurer of the American Board of Psychiatry and Neurology with this proposal, 2/5/1964; and Boyd letter to Lindemann with approval, 2/11/1964. [folder "Amer. Bd. of Psychiatry & Neurology", Box IIIA 4 (A-E), Lindemann Collection, Center for the History of Medicine, Francis A. Countway Library of Medicine, Boston, MA]

90. Lindemann, Erich, letter to Hagopian, Peter B., 3/24/1965: "This letter is written to affirm the cooperative psychiatric training program between Danvers State Hospital and the Psychiatric Service of the Massachusetts General Hospital". Letters from Lindemann to Hagopian and the American Medical Association's Medical and Hospital Training Program supporting the Danvers State Hospital's application for an accredited residency training program; Peter Sifneos and John Nemiah negotiated this program for the MGH. [folder "Danvers State Hosp. Psych Res. Tr. Program", Box IIIA 4 (A-E), Lindemann Collection, Center for the History of Medicine, Francis A. Countway Library of Medicine, Boston, MA]

91. [folder "Old Applications, Box IIIB1 e 1), Box 1, 2", Erich Lindemann Collection, Center for the History of Medicine, Francis A. Countway Library of Medicine, Boston, MA]

92. Lindemann, Erich, letter to Heinicke, Christopher, 3/29/1957. [folder "Misc H", Box IIIA 1–3, Lindemann Collection, Center for the History of Medicine, Francis. A. Countway Library of Medicine, Boston, MA]

93. Opler, Marvin K. (Social Psychiatry group, Department of Psychiatry, Cornell University Medical College and the New York Hospital) letters to Lindemann, 6/1,4/1957. Lindemann replied that he was delighted and was eager to meet and wished to attract men of Opler's scope. [folder "Misc. Correspondence O,P,R—1956–7", Box IIIA 1–3, Lindemann Collection, Center for the History of Medicine, Francis A. Countway Library of Medicine, Boston, MA]

94. Lindemann correspondence with Leo M. Davidoff, chairperson of the Department of Neurological Surgery at Albert Einstein College of Medicine, 2/28/1961. [folder "Misc D", Box IIIA 1–3, Lindemann Collection, Center for the History of Medicine, Francis A. Countway Library of Medicine, Boston, MA]

95. Minutes of a meeting with Jack Ewalt, MD, 3/31/1960. [folder "Misc E", Box IIIA 1–3, Lindemann Collection, Center for the History of Medicine, Francis A. Countway Library of Medicine, Boston, MA]

96. Lindemann letter to Erik Erikson, 9/18/1961. [folder "Misc E", Box IIIA 1–3, Lindemann Collection, Center for the History of Medicine, Francis A. Countway Library of Medicine, Boston, MA]

97. Leary, Timothy correspondence with Lindemann 4/21/1960–10/23/1961. [folder "Misc L", Box IIIA 1–3, Lindemann Collection, Center for the History of Medicine, Francis A. Countway Library of Medicine, Boston, MA]

98. Leary letter to Lindemann, 5/30,1960. [folder "Misc L", Box IIIA 1–3, Lindemann Collection, Center for the History of Medicine, Francis A. Countway Library of Medicine, Boston, MA]

99. Leary letter to Lindemann, 7/30/1960. [folder "Misc L", Box IIIA 1–3, Lindemann Collection, Center for the History of Medicine, Francis A. Countway Library of Medicine, Boston, MA]

100. Lindemann, Elizabeth—telephone interview by David G. Satin, 7/1/1999. [folder "Misc L", Box IIIA 1–3, Lindemann Collection, Center for the History of Medicine, Francis A. Countway Library of Medicine, Boston, MA]

101. "Luncheon Meeting with T.[imothy] Leary, 10–23–61". [folder "Psychiatry Service—Misc. + Budgets", Box IIIB1c box 2 of 2, Erich Lindemann Collection, Center for the History of Medicine, Francis A. Countway Library of Medicine, Boston, MA]

102. Lindemann letter to Leary, 7/21/1960, and from Leary to Lindemann, 10/23/1961. [folder "Misc L", Box IIIA 1–3, Lindemann Collection, Center for the History of Medicine, Francis A. Countway Library of Medicine,

Boston, MA] Also letter from Lindemann, Erich, to Wittkwoer, Dr. E.D., Alan Memorial Institute, McGill University, 2/23/1961: "Drs. David McClelland and Timothy Leary are cooperating with us in the Advanced Predoctoral Training Program for psychologists who are interested in the community aspects of clinical work". [folder "Wilttkower, Sylvia D. Ph.D"., IIIB1e 2), S-Z", Erich Lindemann Collection, Center for the History of Medicine, Francis A. Countway Library of Medicine, Boston, MA]

103. Abbott, John A. correspondence with Lindemann, 1/41962–7/27/1964. [folder "A Miscellaneous", Box IIIA 4 (_A-E), Lindemann Collection, Center for the History of Medicine, Francis A., Countway Library of Medicine, Boston, MA]

104. Lindemann letter to Raymond D. Adams, 3/14/1063. [folder "A Miscellaneous", Box IIIA 4 (A-E), Lindemann Collection, Center for the History of Medicine, Francis A., Countway Library of Medicine, Boston, MA]

105. Kelly, James, interview by David G. Satin at the Francis A. Countway Library of Medicine, Boston, MA, 4/29/1983. [Erich Lindemann Collection, David G. Satin, Newton, MA]

106. Kelly, James G., "Gerald Caplan's Paradigm: Bridging Psychotherapy and Public Health Practice", presented in the symposium "Gerald Caplan's contributions to American Psychology: Views from the Discipline" at the 98th annual meeting of the American Psychological Association, Boston, MA, 8/13/1990.

107. Lindemann, Erich, letter to Caplan, Gerald, 7/1/1964, pp. 1–2. [folder "Caplan, G. papers", Box IIIB1 e 2), A-E", Erich Lindemann Collection, Center for the History of Medicine, Francis A. Countway Library of Medicine, Boston, MA]

108. "Summary of the Discussion between Dr. John Knowles and Dr. Erich Lindemann on September 29, 1961", p. 3. [folder "GEC Report by Dr. Lindemann for Dept. of Psychiatry—December 6, 1961", Box IIIB1b box 1 of 2, Erich Lindemann Collection, Center for the History of Medicine, Francis A. Countway Library of Medicine, Boston, MA]

109. Parsons, Talcott: "Some Trends of Change in American Society: Their Bearing on Medical Education", 54th Annual Congress on Medical Education and Licensure, Palmer House, Chicago, IL, 2/9/1958. Excerpt:

> The Significance of Health and Illness in American Society . . . values of active achievement in instrumental contexts. . . . Health is vital because the capacity . . . to achieve is ultimately the most crucial social resource. Illness is . . . a disturbance of this capacity to perform in socially valued tasks and roles . . . capacity to achieve . . . comes to flower . . . in the individual's capacity, at the level of personality, to live with and to utilize complex systems of symbols, and to conduct highly sophisticated transactions with other persons in human relations . . . which makes understandable the rapidly increasing importance in our own time attributed to problems of "mental" as distinguished from "somatic" health. many phenomena of disturbance of behavioral capacities at the higher levels of social participation. . . [are] brought within the health-illness complex which previously were thought of as simple "misconduct". The field of phenomena defined as illness has been steadily broadening and . . . more highly differentiated. . . [and] the prominence of the mental health problem and . . . it becomes a basis of organizing medical thinking which is not oriented simply to organ-systems.
>
> (pp. 2–3)

Some Aspects of the Scientific Background of Medicine. . . . A second development in science . . . is the emergence within about the last forty years, in their relevance to medicine, of the so-called "behavioral sciences", notably psychology (including psychoanalysis), sociology and anthropology. . . . they are destined to take their place . . . in their ultimate contribution to our understanding of ourselves and of the world we live in, and . . . providing the knowledge . . . to control events in the interest of human values and goals.

(pp. 4–5)

. . .

A Few Implications for Medical Education . . . both the relative importance of mental illness in the whole field, and the scientific knowledge necessary for its competent handling are destined to grow very greatly in the coming half century . . . to be competent to handle mental cases the physician must . . . have more clinical experience with them, but learn much more psychology, sociology, etc. train the future "psychological physician" in general medicine in much more general terms. . . . The differentiation between psychological and somatic medicine must reach much farther back than now. And "psychological medicine" must become . . . one of the two great primary branches of the profession. . . . This high responsibility must increasingly. . . [be] discharged in a setting where the patient leads a more complex life and is harder to "get at" as a total person. . . . the profession itself must learn to cooperate with many different lay agencies, starting with the sciences which are not as such primarily medical . . . physicians must be trained for it . . . medicine will have a brilliant future . . . in a combination of agencies which will ensure a future level of health on all fronts which would have been beyond the most optimistic dreams.

(pp. 14–17)

110. Lindemnn, Erich with Duhl, Leonard and Seeley, John, interviewed at Lindemann's home in Palo Alto, CA by Leonard Duhl, 6/15,22/1974. [caddy 4, tape 3A, 4B;7, Erich Lindemann Collection, Center for the History of Medicine, Francis A. Countway Library of Medicine, Boston, MA]
111. Professional Biography, Alfred H. Stanton, MD, Associate Professor of Psychiatry, Harvard Medical School, Psychiatrist-in-Chief, McLean Hospital (undated), pp. 1–3. [folder "Stanton, Dr. Alfred", Box IIIB1e 2), S-Z", Erich Lindemann Collection, Center for the History of Medicine, Francis A. Countway Library of Medicine, Boston, MA]
112. "Recommendation for appointment of Dr. Alfred H. Stanton; Report of the ad hoc Committee appointed to represent the joint interests of the Faculty of Medicine, the McLean Hospital and the Massachusetts General Hospital in seeking a Psychiatrist-in-Chief for the McLean Hospital", 1/12/1955. [folder "Dr. Stanton", IIIB2 a+b (box1 of 3), Erich Lindemann Collection, Center for the History of Medicine, Francis A. Countway Library of Medicine, Boston, MA]
113. "Appendix B a Program for Mclean Hospital—The Psychiatric Research Program". [folder M.G.H. General Executive Committee 1965, Erich Lindemann Collection, Center for the History of Medicine, Francis A. Countway Library of Medicine, Boston, MA]
114. Review of Discussion with Dr. Alfred Stanton, 6/15/1955, pp. 1–2. [folder "Stanton, Dr. Alfred", Box IIIB1e 2), S-Z", Erich Lindemann Collection, Center for the History of Medicine, Francis A. Countway Library of Medicine, Boston, MA]

115. New York: Basic Books, 1954.
116. Paul, Benjamin, associate professor of social anthropology at HSPH. folder "Seminar—Health + illness in Cross-cultural Perspective HSPH 1952", Box II A&B, *ibid.*
117. [folder "Teaching—Misc."., Box IIA&B, Lindemann Collection, Center for the History of Medicine, Francis A. Countway Library of Medicine, Boston, MA]
118. Semrad, Elvin memo to Lindemann, Erich, "Social and Psychological Sciences in the Health Area", 2/8/1963. [folder "Dr. Elvin Semrad", Box IIIA 4 (P-S), Erich Lindemann Collection, Center for the History of Medicine, Francis A. Countway Library of Medicine, Boston, MA]
119. Zola, Irving Kenneth, PhD, assistant sociologist, Department of Psychiatry, Massachusetts General Hospital. "Final Report of the Work of: Irving Kenneth Zola, PhD, Assistant Sociologist, Department of Psychiatry, Massachusetts General Hospital". [folder "Further Development + Res. in Community Mental Health—Sapir Report 1966", IIIB2 a+b (box1 of 3), Erich Lindemann Collection, Center for the History of Medicine, Francis A. Countway Library of Medicine, Boston, MA]
120. Ervin, Frank, MD, "Considerations for Further Development of MGH Psychiatry Department", 1965. [folder "Hall-Mercer Res. Symposium—1965", IIIB2 a+b (box1 of 3), Erich Lindemann Collection, Center for the History of Medicine, Francis A. Countway Library of Medicine, Boston, MA]
121. "Considerations about a New Psychiatric Unit at the Mass. General Hospital Presented by Dr. Lindemann to the Scientific Advisory Committee", 12/16/1955, p. 1. [folder "MGH Scientific Advisory Committee 1955–61", Box IIIB1d, Erich Lindemann Collection, Center for the History of Medicine, Francis A. Countway Library of Medicine, Boston, MA]
122. "1/3/62 Meeting with Dr. Stanton, Dr. Quarton, etc. (Preparation for Scientific Advisory Comm Mtg.)", pp. 1–3. [folder "MGH Scientific Advisory Committee—MGH 1962–65", Box IIIB1d, Erich Lindemann Collection, Center for the History of Medicine, Francis A. Countway Library of Medicine, Boston, MA]
123. Agenda Massachusetts General Hospital Scientific Advisory Committee Meeting January 5 and 6, 1962, p. 7:

> Institutional Research Grants . . . Organization of Staff: The second administrative question related to the possible disrupting effect of large categorical research 'centers' upon the departmental organization of the hospital staff. Despite the realization that the continued growth of research centers, which must inevitably cross departmental lines, will undoubtedly compound the future administrative problems of the various chiefs of services, it was agreed by all that the basic departmental structure of the staff must be preserved. Were it eventually to be replaced by a center-oriented organization, the quality of clinical teaching as well as patient care would inevitably deteriorate.
> [folder "MGH Scientific Advisory Committee— MGH 1962–65", Box IIIB1d, Erich Lindemann Collection, Center for the History of Medicine, Francis A. Countway Library of Medicine, Boston, MA]

124. "Report of the Scientific Advisory Committee of the Massachusetts General Hospital January 4 and 5, 1963", pp. 4–5. [folder "MGH Scientific Advisory Committee—MGH 1962–65", Box IIIB1d, Erich Lindemann Collection, Center for the History of Medicine, Francis A. Countway Library of Medicine, Boston, MA]

125. "Agenda Massachusetts General Hospital Scientific Advisory Committee Meeting January 3 and 4, 1964", p. 3. [folder "MGH Scientific Advisory Committee—MGH 1962–65", Box IIIB1d, Erich Lindemann Collection, Center for the History of Medicine, Francis A. Countway Library of Medicine, Boston, MA]

126. [folder "MGH Scientific Advisory Committee—MGH 1962–65", Box IIIB1d, Erich Lindemann Collection, Center for the History of Medicine, Francis A. Countway Library of Medicine, Boston, MA]

127. pp. 1–2.

128. "12/14/1961 Harvard Medical School Planning Committee of the Department of Psychiatry (Ad hoc)". [folder "Ad hoc Subcommittee on Graduate Education in Psychiatry/Subcommittee on Psychiatry Education of Dept. of Psychiatry HMS—Meeting on September 30, 1958 P.M"., Box IIIC1 c, Erich Lindemann Collection, Center for the History of Medicine, Francis A. Countway Library of Medicine, Boston, MA]

129. 1/8/63 Harvard Medical School Planning Committee of the Department of Psychiatry (AD HOC). [folder "(Ad hoc) Planning Committee of Dept of Psychiatry—HMS 1963–65", IIIC1 c, Erich Lindemann Collection, Center for the History of Medicine, Francis A. Countway Library of Medicine, Boston, MA]

130. 2/12/63 Planning Committee Meeting—Department of Psychiatry Harvard Club Feb. 12, 1963 7:00 p.m. [folder "(Ad hoc) Planning Committee of Dept of Psychiatry—HMS 1963–65", IIIC1 c, Erich Lindemann Collection, Center for the History of Medicine, Francis A. Countway Library of Medicine, Boston, MA]

131. Lindemann, Erich: "The Mental Health Service of the Massachusetts General Hospital: A Setting for Community Mental Health Training" (unpublished) [folder "Mental Health Services of MGH a setting for Community MH", Box VII 2, Lindemann Collection, Center for the History of Medicine, Francis A. Countway Library of Medicine, Boston, MA]; edited in Lindemann, Erich, and Lindemann, Elizabeth, 1979, *ibid.*, pp. 155–166.

132. "General Executive Committee Annual Report for 1964 Final Draft" [folder "GEC Annual Report 1964", Box IIIB1b box 1 of 2, Erich Lindemann Collection, Center for the History of Medicine, Francis A. Countway Library of Medicine, Boston, MA]:

> The need to apply preventive considerations to many conditions now reaching the hospital led to the development of a new program in the Department of Medicine under the leadership of Dr. Victor Sidel. He will undertake studies of the composition of the patient population, its ethnic and cultural background as well as the various phases of the patient's career as he moves through the hospital to recovery or aftercare.
>
> (p. 3)
>
> Subcommittee to study teaching on private patients including "new experimental units specially designed for collaborative teaching and care by different services. . . . The collaborative methods required in order to integrate the several specialties demanded much attention from the [Gen'l Exec] Committee. . . . Greater integration of the staff of the several services in the Clinics both for the teaching of medical students and house officers must be achieved and articulation between the clinical services and other care-taking agencies in the community has to be developed. [from John Stoeckle, chief of medical clinic] . . . Another field requiring interdisciplinary cooperation involving Orthopedic, Medical.,

Neurological and Psychiatric services is that of rehabilitation. . . . There was also discussion of possible expansion of the 'educative phase' of medical care of those handicapped by the sequelae of accident or chronic disease on the grounds of the McLean Hospital where the rehabilitation and re-education of emotionally disturbed persons has reached a high level of effectiveness. . . . The Emergency Ward is increasingly oriented toward prevention through concern with hazardous situations and precipitants of sickness. . . . The role of the social worker in helping patients and their families deal with the stress of hospitalization has attained special importance".

(pp. 4–5)

133. Psychiatry Service, Massachusetts General Hospital: "Annual Report—1951". [IIIB1b box 1, Erich Lindemann Collection, Center for the History of Medicine, Francis A. Countway Library of Medicine, Boston, MA]

134. "Description of Teaching Activities of the Psychiatric Service during 1954", p. 1; also "Training for Residents and Fellows Psychiatry, Massachusetts General Hospital, 6/13/1955". [folder "AMA Questionnaire 1955,56,57,58", Box IIIB1a box 2 of 2, Erich Lindemann Collection, Center for the History of Medicine, Francis A. Countway Library of Medicine, Boston, MA]

135. "Proposed Plans for an Integrated Program of Service and Research in the Field of Community Mental Health 4/56 Submitted by the staff of the Mental Health Service Massachusetts General Hospital". [folder "Columbia-Washington Heights Community Mental Health Project", Box IIIA6 Da GAP, Erich Lindemann Collection, Center for the History of Medicine, Francis A. Countway Library of Medicine, Boston, MA]

136. Lindemann included Sifneos in his CMH plans, including warding him an NIMH fellowship in CMH at the HRS. However, Sifenos was not committed to CMH and did not continue this work, focusing his interests instead on "short-term anxiety-provoking psychotherapy" and teaching this, including via videotape. Harvard Medical School Public Affairs public_affairs@hms.harvard.edu: "Flag at half-staff notice, Thu, 8 Jan 2009 11:12:44–0500".

137. "Projected Administrative Chart for Community Mental Health Unit in Psychiatry Department (M.G.H.)", undated. [folder "RESEARCH—1955", IIIB2 a+b (box1 of 3), Erich Lindemann Collection, Center for the History of Medicine, Francis A. Countway Library of Medicine, Boston, MA]

138. "6/3/55 Psychiatry Service 1954–5", Annual Report—1954, 6/3/1955, p. 10. [folder "Annual Report—1954", Box IIIB1b box 1 of 2, Erich Lindemann Collection, Center for the History of Medicine, Francis A. Countway Library of Medicine, Boston, MA]

139. "12/12/55 Application for Training Grant under National Mental Health Act". [folder "MGH Budget Preps 1964–65", Box IIIB1c box 2 of 2, Erich Lindemann Collection, Center for the History of Medicine, Francis A. Countway Library of Medicine, Boston, MA]

140. Morris, Laura B., "Mental Health Service—Massachusetts General Hospital", Minutes of the Mental Health Service 1955–7. [File 1 drawer 1, Erich Lindemann Collection, Center for the History of Medicine, Francis A. Countway Library of Medicine, Harvard Medical Area, Boston, MA]

141. Staff of the Mental Health Service, Massachusetts General Hospital, 4/1956: "Proposed Plans for an Integrated Program of Service and Research in the

Field of Community Mental Health". [Box III A6 folder "Duhl Caplan", Erich Lindemann Collection, Center for the History of Medicine, Francis A. Countway Library of Medicine, Harvard Medical Area, Boston, MA

142. Vaughan, Warren T., Jr., Burlingame, CA, "In Honor of Erich Lindemann", *American Journal of Community Psychology 12* no. 5: 531–532 (p. 531) (1984). [folder "Kelly, James G"., David G. Satin files, Newton, MA] The following were some of the staff involved:

> Important among these was Laura Morris, a community organization social worker who was a knowledgeable advisor and facilitator for Lindemann. He encouraged Peter Sifneos, a young staff psychiatrist, to commit himself to CMH; he worked for a time at HRS, and was then designated as the Director of the Mental Health Service. Lindemann also brought in social scientists: Donald C. Klein, PhD and Mark A. Fried, Associate Psychologists; and A. Paul Hare, PhD, Associate Sociologist (and Harvard University Assistant Professor of Sociology), Ray H. Elling and Louisa P. Howe, Assistant Sociologists, and James G. Kelly, research Fellow in Psychology. Eventually other CMH professionals had Psychiatry Service appointments: Gerald Caplan, MD; Assistant Psychiatrist Helen M. Herzan MD; Assistant in Psychiatry Jason A. Aronson, MD, Robert L. Bragg, MD, and Robert J. Lifton, MD; Psychologist John M. von Felsinger, PhD; Associate Psychologist Clara Weiss May, PhD; and Assistant Sociologist Irving K. Zola, PhD John Baldwin, an exchange fellow from the University of Aberdeen, Scotland, brought an interest in the epidemiology of mental health and illness, and in CMH research. Lindemann tried to incorporate some of his valued associates, who were not funded and/or opted not to transfer to this endeavor: John Seeley (sociology), Hendrick Blum (public health), and John Stoeckle (medicine).

"Annual Report Hall-Mercer Hospital 1959–1960". [folder "Hall-Mercer Hospital Annual Report 1959", Box IIIB1b box 1 of 2, Erich Lindemann Collection, Center for the History of Medicine, Francis A. Countway Library of Medicine, Boston, MA]

"Minutes of the Annual Meeting of the Directors of the Hall-Mercer Hospital May 26, 1956". [folder "Hall-Mercer 1955", Box IIIB1b box 1 of 2, Erich Lindemann Collection, Center for the History of Medicine, Francis A. Countway Library of Medicine, Boston, MA], "Annual Report Hall Mercer Hospital, Boston 1958". [folder "Hall-Mercer Annual Report 1958", Box IIIB1b box 1 of 2, Erich Lindemann Collection, Center for the History of Medicine, Francis A. Countway Library of Medicine, Boston, MA]

"Annual Report Hall Mercer Hospital Massachusetts General Hospital Division 1961–1962". [folder "Hall-Mercer Hospital Annual Report 1961–62", Box IIIB1b box 2 of 2, Erich Lindemann Collection, Center for the History of Medicine, Francis A. Countway Library of Medicine, Boston, MA]

"Annual Report Hall-Mercer Hospital Massachusetts General Hospital Division 1963". [folder "Hall-Mercer Hospital Report 1963", Box IIIB1b box 2 of 2, Erich Lindemann Collection, Center for the History of Medicine, Francis A. Countway Library of Medicine, Boston, MA]

[folder "Baldwin, John A. M.D.", Box IIIB1 e 2), A-E", Erich Lindemann Collection, Center for the History of Medicine, Francis A. Countway Library of Medicine, Boston, MA] Baldwin earned Oxford University degrees in Liberal Arts and Social Work (B.A. with honours), then University of Aberdeen MB, ChB with honours. "My chief interests, however, centre on what is perhaps best called social psychiatry, by which I mean the study of psychiatric aspects of social or cultural and family problems and the epidemiology of psychiatric disorder, from both clinical and research points of view". (Baldwin, John A. letter to Lindemann, Erich, 8/22/1958) He obtained training in social psychiatry, including his one year at the MGH and HMS.

He was involved in several research projects, including developing a psychiatric case register and the application of the sociological concept of deviance to psychiatric phenomena.

Lindemann, Erich: "Further Development and Research in Community Mental Health". [box XII 2 folder "Grant Application to NIMH 1956", Erich Lindemann Collection, Center for the History of Medicine, Francis A. Countway Library of Medicine, Boston, MA]

143. Spiegel, John P., "Applications of Psychoanalysis in Sociology", in Masserman, Jules H. (ed.), *Science and Psychoanalysis IV* (Grune & Stratton, Inc., New York, 1960), pp. 39–48.

144. Lindemann, Erich, letter to Seeley, John, 8/4/1959, p. 1–3. [folder "Dr. John R. Seeley", Box IIIB1e 2), S-Z", Erich Lindemann Collection, Center for the History of Medicine, Francis A. Countway Library of Medicine, Boston, MA]

145. [folder "Dr. John R. Seeley", Box IIIB1e 2), S-Z", Erich Lindemann Collection, Center for the History of Medicine, Francis A. Countway Library of Medicine, Boston, MA]

146. [folder "Satin, David, M.D.", Box IIIB1e 2), S-Z", Erich Lindemann Collection, Center for the History of Medicine, Francis A. Countway Library of Medicine, Boston, MA]

147. Kahne, Merton J., MD, letter to Nemiah, John, director of MGH Psychiatric Residency Training, 12/13/1960. [folder "Satin, David, M.D.", Box IIIB1e 2), S-Z", Erich Lindemann Collection, Center for the History of Medicine, Francis A. Countway Library of Medicine, Boston, MA]

148. Satin, David G., "Autobiography". [folder "Satin, David, M.D.", Box IIIB1e 2), S-Z", Erich Lindemann Collection, Center for the History of Medicine, Francis A. Countway Library of Medicine, Boston, MA]

149. "12/12/55 Application for Training Grant Under National Mental Health Act". [folder "MGH Budget Preps 1964–65", Box IIIB1c box 2 of 2, Erich Lindemann Collection, Center for the History of Medicine, Francis A. Countway Library of Medicine, Boston, MA]

150. Annual Report Hall-Mercer Hospital Massachusetts General Hospital Division 1955–1956: Essentially the same as ANNUAL REPORT FOR THE DEPARTMENT OF PSYCHIATARY FOR THE YEAR 1955 Statistical Summary from October 1, 1954–September 30, 1955, 5/19/1956; see also 1/22/57 report from John M. von Felsinger [chief psychologist, Psychiatry Service, MGH] "Annual Report of the Psychology Unit of the Psychiatry Department 1956", Annual Report Psychiatric Service Massachusetts General Hospital 1959: "Introduction, Annual Report Psychiatric Service Massachusetts General Hospital 1959, (undated) News—M.G.H., 5/55 Needs for the Development of the Research Program in Psychiatry at the Massachusetts General Hospital. [folder "Annual Report—Psychiatric Service, MGH '55-'56 and 1959", Box IIIB1b box 1 of 2, Erich Lindemann Collection, Center for the History of Medicine, Francis A. Countway Library of Medicine, Boston, MA]

151. Grant applications to the W.T. Grant Foundation for plans and activities of
the MGH MHS:

Title of Project: Program of Service and Research in Preventive Psychiatry to be carried out by the Mental Health Service; II. Granting Agency: Grant Foundation; III. Principal Investigator: Erich Lindemann, M.D.; c. Active Date July 1, 1955 Expiration June 30, 1956 D. Budget: Salaries $66,900, total $92,398 (revised 5/19/55):

I. <u>Field of Operations</u> It is planned to develop at the Massachusetts General Hospital in Boston a mental health service based on the knowledge and skills developed in the Wellesley Human Relations Service. Its purpose will be to make available to the Hospital community and to the surrounding neighborhoods of the North and West End the services in "preventive intervention" and mental health consultation which have been evolved so far and to create an opportunity for further investigative work in this area with the hope of accumulating further basic knowledge concerning the manner in which the human environment of a person influences his good or bad adjustment and his emotional well being. . . . we would hope that the methods of medical care in the hospital would include more and more concerns about the mental health not only of the patients but of their families and relatives and an increasing concern for the hospital clinics with the population in the surrounding neighborhoods. A very special added opportunity for service and investigation is expected to arise . . . when part of the West End area will become the place for a large housing development at which time our agency might render substantial help . . . with the planning for the mental health of the future residents while . . . view the effect . . . of this considerable degree of social change. . . . 3 <u>Plan of Development</u> The pattern of operations as developed in Wellesley, namely the combination of a service team for the purpose of diagnosis and care with an investigative team concerned with the problems of social maladjustment and with the various reactions to social crises has proved to be an auspicious type of organization and we would plan to have the service team of psychiatrists, psychologists and social workers available for preventive intervention and counseling while our social scientists would provide the skills necessary for penetrating this particular community with its schools, professions and agencies and would help us design the research on the groups in the population which have become accessible to our work. The first year will perhaps be used in exploring the mental health needs both of the hospital community and the neighborhoods and in involving an organization similar to the committee structure used in Wellesley for the purpose of activating our services. The second and third years would see the beginning of accumulation of new information and of comparative studies between the populations of our new neighborhoods and the data assembled previously. By the end of the third year the agency and its investigative program ought to be well under way. We ought to then have a thorough knowledge of the neighborhood as it is then existing and would then be ready for the social changes related to the development of the housing program. . . . The third year should see the agency as a fully developed program both in service and research established as a training center in close cooperation with the Wellesley agency [HRS] and the Division of Mental Health at the [Harvard] School of Public Health. . . . We would by that time be known for our training and have established contact with other groups which work in the field. Much exchange would take place between our group and the Tavistock Clinic in London [social psychiatry]. The third period of three years would be . . . consolidating our gains. We then would be ready for developing textbooks in this field and would have established a profession of mental health workers who are respected by the community as persons with special skills and special insights. . . . 6. What Outcomes Will Lead to We hope that our group can contribute to the establishment of a new field of science, namely the field of mental health and preventive psychiatry. 7. Cooperation Between Groups All the contacts made by the Wellesley Human Relations Service remain open to us as before. Dr. [Hugh] Leavell [chairperson Department of Public Health Practice] of the [Harvard] School of Public Health as well as Dr. [Walter] Bauer [HMS Professor of Medicine and MGH Chief of Medicine] of the [Harvard] Medical School and Dr. [Samuel] Stauffer, [Harvard Professor of Sociology] of the Department of Social Relations [Harvard] and Dean [Francis] Keppel of the [Harvard Graduate] School of Education remain much interested in this new development. We also have won the interest and support of the Dean of the [Harvard] Medical School, Dr. George P.[acker] Berry, and the [General] Director of the Massachusetts General Hospital, Dr. Dean A. Clark. . . . 8. Organization The work will be initiated by the Massachusetts General Hospital which will be responsible for the administration of the service. . . . It is expected to begin July 1, 1955. The operation will be directed by Dr. [Erich] Lindemann with the help of Dr. George Saslow and with the advice of a committee consisting of Dr. Ellsworth T. Neumann, Associate Director of the Massachusetts General Hospital; Dr. Thomas Pugh, Epidemiologist to the [DMH] Commonwealth of Massachusetts; Dr. Gerald Caplan, Director of the Division of Mental Health, Harvard School of Public Health; Dr. John Whiting, Professor of Anthropology, Harvard University, [Graduate] School of Education; Dr. Joseph Stokes, Executive Head of the Family Health Service of the Massachusetts General Hospital; Dr. Warren T. Vaughan, Director of the Mental Hygiene Division of the [DMH] Commonwealth of Massachusetts, and finally Dr. Nathan Talbot, Associate Professor of Pediatrics, Harvard Medical School [and MGH Chief of Children's Medical Service].

(pp. 1–7)

Dr. Lindemann and the committee will consult with experts such as Professor John Gordon [HSPH] in epidemiology; Professor Franz Goldmann in problems of medical care; Professor Talcott Parsons for problems involving social science. . . . We believe that a sum of approximately $75,000 per year would be a sound financial basis for our program.

(p. 8)

. . .

4/29/55 Budget Administration Erich Lindemann, M.D. Richmond Holder, MD [child psychiatrist] . . . Service Program Lincoln Clark, MD [Adult Psychiatrist . . . Morris Chafetz, MD [Adult psychiatrist] . . . John Lamont, MD [Child Psychiatrist] . . . Lydia Dawes, MD [Child Psychiatrist], Doris Gilbert, Ph.D., Psychologist . . . Irene Prentice, Social Worker. . . Research Program George Saslow, M.D. Joseph Matarazzo, Ph.D. . . ., psychologist. Lois Paul, M.A., anthropologist . . . Ann Ross, M.A., sociologist . . . Wyman Richardson, Ph.D., statistics . . . TOTAL $79,831 (p. 10).

We do have now a Mental Health Service at the Massachusetts General Hospital which functions as part of the overall hospital program. Dr. [George] Saslow is our key worker with the Family Health Service of the hospital for the neighborhood surrounding the hospital. Dr. Peter Sifneos is working on the Community Program. Dean Clark, the [General] Director of the hospital, has become the chairperson of a committee from the various hospital services and will review the relationship of this large hospital to the population in the surrounding neighborhood. Our Mental Health Service serves as a research program supplying information about the social structure of the neighborhood and about the prospective developments. . . . The second major interest . . . is the prediction of future mental and emotional disturbance from behavior at earlier age levels. . . . We are developing an investigative team. . . . Several groups of nursery school children . . . will serve as an opportunity for the detailed analysis of the development of patterns of human relations. . . . Thirdly, the Mental Health Service is operating as a group which becomes active at the time of catastrophic events. The influx into the hospital last summer of 140 acute cases of poliomyelitis, 40 of which became respirator cases of more than two months duration presented a remarkable challenge just as the Coconut Grove Fire did years ago to study the reactions of the patients, their families, the various professions in their care and the neighborhoods of these families.

(pp. 1–2)

Administration: Erich Lindemann, MD, . . . Peter Sifneos, MD Service Program: Gardner Quarton, MD, Morris Chafetz, MD, . . . John Nemiah, MD, Ingrid Sondergaard, MD, . . . Thomas Plaut, PhD Laura Morris, M.A. Mary McCarthy, secretary . . . Research Program: George Saslow, M.D. Joseph Matarazzo, PhD Elizabeth Gellert, PhD Ann Ross, M.A. Paul Hare, PhD, Sociologist . . . William Fitzgerald, PhD Jaclin Lindau, M.E. Elizabeth Klingensmith, secretary.

I am at this time submitting to you a second report on our activities in the Mental Health Service at the Massachusetts General Hospital. . . . Our overall goal remains that of the evolution of an effective program of preventive psychiatry and of mental health activities based on a large general hospital. . . . Fortunately, this way of thinking has met with an auspicious attitude on the part of the hospital administration especially Dr. Dean Clark [General Director] and with the Chiefs of the various services particularly Dr. Walter Bauer [Chief of Medicine] who was . . . a member of the Steering Committee of the Wellesley Human Relations Service. . . . 1. A program of comprehensive medicine. Dr. George Saslow. . . . Dr. Joseph D. Matarazzo. . . . Dr. Morris Chafetz . . . have developed in the General Medical Out-Patient Service a Mental Health Center . . . concerned with the psychological and emotional problems of all the patients and their families who come to the clinic . . . an effort is made to appraise the overall adjustment load. . . . and to learn . . . about the manner in which they master the crisis involved in the illness and other life problems. . . . his team had a fine opportunity to develop their procedures at the time of the polio epidemic which hit Boston in August, 1955. . . . Dr. Saslow has also been active in working with the staff of the Family Service. . . . 2. another segment . . . has been naturally concerned with the mental health of children . . . who enter the hospital for the care of physical illness and have to be separated from their parents . . . give mental health consultation . . . to a group of normal children, the children of staff members and nurses, in a day care program which the hospital maintains . . . while the children are in the hospital is a fine opportunity for assisting the overall development and adjustment and to assist the parents in their efforts to understand the children and to help them to grow into mentally healthy individuals. . . . 3. the most important focus . . . is the gradual penetration of the neighborhood around the hospital . . . learning something about the mental health of the population. predominantly a low income area. . . . Present Organization of the Mental Health Service: a. Advisory Committee Dr. Dean Clark, [General] Director, Mass. General Hospital, Dr. Warren Vaughan Commissioner of Mental Hygiene, Comm. of Mass. Mr. Arthur Halleck, Director of Community Organization, State Dept. of Mental Health. Dr. John Whiting, Professor of Child Development, Harvard Graduate School of Education. Dr. Gerald Caplan, Assoc. Professor of Mental Health Harvard School of Public Health Dr. Hugh Leavell, Professor of PHP [Public Health Practice], HSPH. Dr. Walter Bauer, Chief of the Medical Service, MGH. b. Staff Members: Dr. Erich Lindemann. . . . Intramural Mental Health Services: Comprehensive Medicine Dr. George Saslow Dr. Joseph Matarazzo. . . . Dr. Morris Chafetz . . . Mr. William Fitzgerald, psychologist . . . Secretary 2. Studies on Child Development: Dr. Elizabeth Gellert, child development specialist Miss Ann Ross, M.A., educational psychologist. Miss Jaclin Lindau, nursery school teacher Dr. John Lamont, child psychiatrist. Community Studies and Services: Dr. Peter Sifneos, Community Psychiatrist, Dr. Paul Hare, Sociologist,.Mrs. Laura Morris, Community Organization Specialist . . . Mr. Thomas Plaut, psychologist . . . Dr. Ingrid Sondergaard, psychiatrist training in comm. mental health. . . . Plans for the Future: . . . our new enterprise in which the mental health principles and procedures worked out in Wellesley were carried into a large teaching hospital and its surroundings. . . . We do expect that part of our research activities . . . will be financed from Washington. Our training program also will be financed by the USPHS [United States Public Health Service]. There remains, however, the main core of mental health services to individuals and families. . . [and] our investigative program in child development. . . . We therefore would appreciate support from the Grant Foundation for two more years. . . . We confidently expect that after that time the work of our Service can be carried on the basis of community support.

(pp. 1–7)

PROPOSED PLANS FOR AN INTEGRATED PROGRAM OF SERVICE AND RESEARCH IN THE FIELD OF COMMUNITY MENTAL HEALTH Submitted by the staff of the Mental Health Service Massachusetts General Hospital:

INTRODUCTION . . . it has been the aim of the staff to implement the general approach of Dr. Erich Lindemann . . . characterized, in part, by emphasis upon:

(a) The practice of preventive psychiatry; (Early case finding; promoting wholesome living conditions, etc.).
(b) The application of public health concepts to the study and psychopathology; (epidemiology, etc.).
(c) The integration of information and methods derived from social science with the principles and skills of the clinician.

(d) The study of human behavior under conditions of crisis; (the conception of crises as special opportunities for reaching people, and for effecting psychotherapeutic changes that may result in lasting improvement; crisis as an opportunity to study effective "coping" behavior).

(e) The importance of research as an integral aspect of the program.

(f) The active participation of residents and organizations within the community in developing, and in carrying out the program. The Mental Health Service of Massachusetts General Hospital was established in the fall of 1955. It is composed of a small core staff, and a larger advisory committee. The core staff consists of a psychiatrist, a social worker, a child psychologist, and a teacher. The larger committee includes other members of the Department of Psychiatry of Massachusetts General Hospital, and of the Department of Mental Health of the Commonwealth of Massachusetts. THE AREA TO BE SERVED It is planned to concentrate work in the West End, an area surrounding the Massachusetts General Hospital.

(1) Massachusetts General Hospital is moving toward offering increased services in many aspects of medicine to members of the immediate community. . .

(2) . . . a large portion of the present West End population faces evacuation . . . this upheaval will disturb the equilibrium of many residents. For some . . . may result in increased needs for psychiatric help. They also offer an opportunity for studying individuals under conditions of heightened stress (crisis).

(3) The West End (and some adjacent neighborhoods) has the highest rate of juvenile delinquency in the city. It is an area characterized by poverty, social instability, by chronically dependent "multiproblem" inhabitants, and by concomitant earmarks of decline. . . . Present Activities of Mental Health Project. . . . it is not desirable to impose a program of service on a community without first becoming intimately acquainted with the nature and needs of the community. Furthermore, . . . the introduction of a new Community Mental Health Program must be carried out in close articulation with services and organizations that are already in operation in the area. . . . the social worker on the staff has been engaged in an exploratory survey of health, welfare, and religious organizations serving the West End area.

. . .

1) To gain an understanding of the major social and emotional problems. . .

2) To find out what kind of professional services . . . the agencies are in need of.

3) To assess the major gaps in the services offered. . .

4) to learn what the effect of Urban Redevelopment Planning will be upon individual agencies. . .

5) To become aware of the ideas and the level of thinking of social workers. . .

6) to "open the door" for developing constructive relationships with established organizations and resource persons. . . (2) The Joint Consultation Seminar of the Mental Health Staff With Boston Department of Public Welfare Workers. . . . The participants . . . are some 16 public welfare field workers, two head social workers, the district supervisor and the Department's In-Service training supervisor, the present core staff of the Massachusetts General Hospital Mental Health Service, and guest "specialists" the stated purpose of the seminar:

1) To assess . . . the existing hazards to the mental health of the community.
2) To offer . . . professional insights and understanding of the dynamics of behavior, as well as of social and educational problems
. . .

It is planned to evaluate . . . a) group process and techniques b) information gained and c) attitudes expressed . . . and evidence of changes in attitudes. Future plans—MH consultation to community agencies, consultation and demonstration programs re dealing c "hard core" cases, multi-problem families. Research Plans and Interests . . . A. The Assessment of the Emotional Health of Residents of the Area, as Reflected in their Responses to the Crisis of Relocation . . . a research project, combining clinical and sociological approaches, in studying the impact of a crisis . . . upon a community . . . B. The Evaluation of Group Consultation as a Technique for the practice of Preventive Psychiatry . . . C. A Clinical Analysis of "Deserted" Families, and of Men Who Have "Deserted" Their Families. . . . D. A "Matched" Comparison of Multi-Problem Families, with "Normal" Families Living in the Same Area. . . . It is hoped that such a study may contribute to a deeper understanding of the causes of delinquency. . . . Minimum Core Staff for the Mental Health Service Executive Coordinator of Services and Research (half-time). . . . Dr. Peter Sifneos. . . Staff Psychiatrist (half-time) . . . Social Case Worker (full-time) . . . Social Worker in Community Organization, Mrs. L.[aura] Morris, M.A. Research Fellow in Psychology and Demography (half-time) Elizabeth Gellert, Ed.D. Part-time Consultants: Sociologist, Paul Hare, PhD, Clinical Psychologist, Michael von Felsinger, PhD.

Fellows-in-training in Community Mental Health: (part-time)
2 Psychiatrists
2 Postdoctoral Fellows in Psychology
1 Social Worker
Estimated Budget, July 1956–July 1957 . . . Total $41,000.00

. . .

the grant made available for the Mental Health Service of the Hospital. . . . The Family Health Service Program in which Drs. Saslow and Matarazzo are participating. include now more than 200 families in the immediate neighborhood of the hospital. We have further infiltrated the West End community, have had regular mental health consultation sessions with the welfare departments and with the personnel of the Peabody House, a neighborhood house. . . . Dr. Gellert's so-called Activities Program on the Pediatrics Service has by now become well established. . . . The keen interest which the Division of Community Services at the National Institute of Mental Health has developed in our program. . . . we are expecting to have support for our research program . . . from the United States Public Health Service. The service operations . . . are expected to be continued with the help of the Department of Mental Hygiene of the Commonwealth of Massachusetts. It is natural that Dr. Warren Vaughan who is a charter member of the Wellesley group and who is now Director of the Commonwealth of Massachusetts Mental Hygiene Program would wish to support this mental health agency.

(pp. 1–2)[1]

152. Lindemann, Erich, letter to Morrison, Miss Adele, The Grant Foundation, Inc., 7/25/1960. [envelope "Grant Foundation", IIIB2 b (box2 of 3), Erich Lindemann Collection, Center for the History of Medicine, Francis A. Countway Library of Medicine, Boston, MA]

153. "Memorandum in Connection with Discussion at the Office of the Grant Foundation of the Program in Psychiatry of the Massachusetts General Hospital", 9/20/1960. [envelope "Grant Foundation", IIIB2 b (box2 of 3), Erich Lindemann Collection, Center for the History of Medicine, Francis A. Countway Library of Medicine, Boston, MA]

154. "a sum not to exceed $75,000 was appropriated for the development of a 'Program of Service and Research in Preventive Psychiatry to be Carried Out by the Mental Health Service of the Massachusetts General Hospital' under your direction". Galpin, Perrin C., executive director, The Grant Foundation, Inc., letter to Lindemann, Erich, 5/19/1955.

> we are enclosing [a] check of The Grant Foundation in the amount of $37,500. . . . This represents the second and final payment on account of the sum of $75,000 of the appropriation by the trustees for the development of a "Program of Service and Research in preventive Psychiatry to be Carried Out by the Mental Health Service of the Massachusetts General Hospital" under Dr. Lindemann's direction. Upon termination of the project on or before June 30, 1956.
>
> > Byler, John G., Executive Director and Treasurer,
> > The Grant Foundation (Incorporated), letter to
> > Weld, Mr. George S., Assistant Treasurer
> > The Massachusetts General Hospital, 1/12/1956

> let me thank you for the . . . conversation which you had with me a few days ago. I am . . . happy . . . that you and the trustees will continue to be interested in seeing us further through the initial period of our new work at the Massachusetts General Hospital, and that you will consider helping us on a smaller scale for one or two years. . . . I was also very happy . . . that the Foundation may be willing to provide an adequate stipend for one or two somewhat senior psychiatrists or psychologists who want to spend a year with us and then apply our techniques and our findings in their own area.
>
> > Lindemann, Erich, letter to Byler, Mr. John G.
> > Executive Director The Grant Foundation, Inc., 2/29/1956

> I have received your letter recommending that we consider a stipend for Dr. Robert J. Lifton to enable him to participate in your program during the next year. We are sorry to inform you that lack of funds will prevent us from making such a grant.
>
> In connection with the appeal for the Mental Health Service of the hospital, we are setting aside in our estimates from uncommitted funds $42,720 to cover the appeal for the general budget for one year. . . . we feel we should restrict further support to one year only with the expectation that additional outside support will be forthcoming.
>
> As for Dr. Gellert's research proposal in child development. . . . we would not wish to initiate support . . . due to the same lack of funds.
>
> > Byler, John G., Executive Director The Grant Foundation,
> > Inc., letter to Lindemann, Erich, 6/5/1956

> I was thoroughly delighted to receive . . . the announcement that the Grant Foundation is setting aside $42,720 to cover our general budget. . . . We had become rather concerned about the possible need of terminating our activities.

Lindemann, Erich, letter to Byler, John G., Executive Director of The Grant Foundation, 6/7/1956[envelope "Grant Foundation 1955–56", IIIB2 b (box2 of 3), Erich Lindemann Collection, Center for the History of Medicine, Francis A. Countway Library of Medicine, Boston, MA]

155. Lindemann, Erich, letter to Byler, Mr. John, Executive Director of The Grant Foundation, 1/14/1958. [folder "Grant Foundation-1957–58", IIIB2 b (box2 of 3), Erich Lindemann Collection, Center for the History of Medicine, Francis A. Countway Library of Medicine, Boston, MA]

156. "Developments in the Activities of the Psychiatric Service Dr. Lindemann's Report to General Executive Committee, December 7, 1961", p. 13. [folder "Comments GEC Dec.1961", Box IIIB1b box 1 of 2, Erich Lindemann Collection, Center for the History of Medicine, Francis A. Countway Library of Medicine, Boston, MA]

157. Psychosocial Teaching, IIIB3 a-c, Erich Lindemann Collection, Center for the History of Medicine, Francis A. Countway Library of Medicine, Boston, MA.

158. Taught by Caudill, William; Lifton, Robert; Spiegel, John; then Spiegel, John, MD; Kluckhohn, Florence, PhD; and Vogel, Ezra, PhD:

> This seminar will attempt to explore the effects of culture upon various aspects of psychodynamics, emphasizing the interplay between specific environmental influences and individual personality traits. . . . The seminar will work towards developing an approach to the study of individual behavior which includes a systematic appraisal of cultural influences.

> [folder "Course: Cultural Aspects of Psychodynamics. Caudill, Lifton & Spiegel. '58", Box IIIC2 a+b, Erich Lindemann Collection, Center for the History of Medicine, Francis A. Countway Library of Medicine, Boston, MA]

159. Baler, Lenin, Professor of Public Health Practice, Harvard School of Public Health: notes on lecture "New Directions in Community Mental Health", CMH Course, MGH 2/16/1965, p. 1. [folder "Community Mental Health Course, MGH 1961–62, 1964–5", David G. Satin files, Newton, MA]:

> Many current mental health practices labeled "community mental health" are really only slight modifications + expansions of clinical practice
> what is really needed is adoption of traditional public health procedures. . .
> mental health planning haphazard + opportunistic
> often on basis of advantage to mental health professional + his goals.
> Appropriate public health approaches:
> accept responsibility for mental health of definite, circumscribed total community. . .
> study + know community
> incidence + risk of mental illness
> carriers + high risk to mental health areas
> efficient deployment of personnel and facilities
> mental health professionals not in total charge
> true equal cooperation with other professionals
> comprehensive services—direct treatment . . . priority is socially deprived patients indirect treatment prevention—priority service (at least 75% of staff time)
> probably largely through social + economic improvement
> Program evaluation + research
> public support depends on this in the long run.

160. Summary of Meeting with Faculty Connected with the Training Program in Community Mental Health" (Mass. Gen'l Hsp., 7/12/56. [folder

"Community Mental Health Training Faculty Meeting July 1956", IIIB3 a-c, Erich Lindemann Collection, Center for the History of Medicine, Francis A. Countway Library of Medicine, Boston, MA] Faculty included Lindemann, Erich; Sifneos, Peter; McNabola, Marie; vonFelsinger, Michael; Klein, Donald; Perry, Sylvia; Gellert, Beth; Morris, Laura.

161. [folder "MGH-Community Mental Health Fellowships", IIIB3 a-c, Erich Lindemann Collection, Center for the History of Medicine, Francis A. Countway Library of Medicine, Boston, MA]

162. Research projects and applications, IIIB2 c (box2 of 2), Erich Lindemann Collection, Center for the History of Medicine, Francis A. Countway Library of Medicine, Boston, MA.

163. Lindemann correspondence with Joseph Lee, 10/13/1960–2/9/1961. [folder "Misc L", Box IIIA 1–3, Lindemann Collection, Center for the History of Medicine, Francis A. Countway Library of Medicine, Boston, MA]

164. "The Development, Content and Evaluation of the Group Project (Mental Health) with the public welfare department city of Boston, Spring 1956" [note: typographical errors corrected]. [folder "Columbia-Washington Heights Community Mental Health Project", Box IIIA6 Da GAP, Erich Lindemann Collection, Center for the History of Medicine, Francis A. Countway Library of Medicine, Boston, MA]

165. Galpin, Perrin C., letter to Lindemann, Erich, 3/4/1955. [envelope "Grant Foundation 1955–56", IIIB2 b (box2 of 3), Erich Lindemann Collection, Center for the History of Medicine, Francis A. Countway Library of Medicine, Boston, MA]

166. 3/6/1964 letter from Elizabeth Lindemann, Head Psychiatric Social Worker at the HRS, to Lindemann. [folder "Correspondence 1964", Box IIIA 1–3, Lindemann Collection, Center for the History of Medicine, Francis A. Countway Library of Medicine, Boston, MA]

167. Lindemann, Erich, letter to Knowles, John H., 7/30/1962, (p. 2). [folder "Dr. John Knowles, Medical Director—MGH", Box IIIA 4 (I-Ma), Erich Lindemann Collection, Center for the History of Medicine, Francis A. Countway Library of Medicine, Boston, MA]

168. Letter from Lindemann to John E. Lawrence of the MGH Scientific Advisory Committee dated 7/9/1964. [folder "Correspondence 1964", Box IIIA 1–3, Lindemann Collection, Center for the History of Medicine, Francis A. Countway Library of Medicine, Boston, MA]

169. 9/9/1964 letter to Lindemann. [folder "Correspondence 1964", Box IIIA 1–3, Lindemann Collection, Center for the History of Medicine, Francis A. Countway Library of Medicine, Boston, MA]

170. Gelfand, Sidney B. and Kelly, James G.[ordon] (Dept. of Psychiatry, Harvard Medical School), "The Psychologist in Community Mental Health: Scientist and Professional"

Gelfand, Sidney and Kelly, James G.[ordon], "Community Mental Health a Selected List of References" (1959).

Kelly, James G.[ordon] and Newbrough, J.R.[obert], "Community Mental Health Research: Some Dimensions and Policies"; prepared for symposium Community Mental Health Research; Facts from Fancies, 69th Annual American Psychological Association Convention, NYC, 8/31/61.

[folder "Kelly, James", Box IIIB1e 2), F-Ma", Erich Lindemann Collection, Center for the History of Medicine, Francis A. Countway Library of Medicine, Boston, MA]

[folder "Materials for—Sight [*sic*] Visit on Lindemann-Caplan Application", IIIB2 c (box1 of 2), Erich Lindemann Collection, Center for the History of Medicine, Francis A. Countway Library of Medicine, Boston, MA]

1. Weisman, Avery D. and Hackett, Thomas P., "Psychosis After Eye Surgery: Establishment of a Specific Doctor-Patient Relation in the Prevention and Treatment of 'Black-Patch Delirium'", *New England Journal of Medicine 258*: 1284–1289 (1958)
2. von Felsinger, John M. and Klein, Donald C., "The Training of Psychologists for the Mental Health Field" (submitted for publication—*The American Psychologist*)
3. Bibliography of Human Relations Service of Wellesley, Inc.—First Draft (mimeographed)
4. Sifneos, Peter E., MD, "Preventive Psychiatric Work with Mothers", *Mental Hygiene 43*: 230–236 (4/1959)
5. Kaplan, Bert (University of Kansas), Reed, Robert B. (Harvard University), Richardson, Wyman (University of North Carolina), "A Comparison of the Incidence of Hospitalized and Non-Hospitalized Cases of Psychosis in Two Communities", *American Sociological Review 21*: 474–479 (8/1956)
6. Lindemann, Erich, "The Nature of Mental Health Work as a Professional Pursuit", *Psychology and Mental Health*, Appendix A, 136–145 (1957)
7. Gordon, John E., MD, O'Rourke, Edward, MD, Richardson, F.L.W., Jr., PhD, and Lindemann, Erich, MD (Department of Epidemiology and Division of Mental Health, Department of Public Health Practice, HSPH), "Preventive Medicine and Epidemiology: The Biological and Social Sciences in an Epidemiology of Mental Disorders", extracted from *American Journal of Medical Sciences 223*: 316–343 (3/1952)
8. (undated, no authors) Research and Development in Community Mental Health
9. Lindemann, Erich, MD, Further Development and Research in Community Mental Health

7 Practicing Community Mental Health at Harvard

Resistance to Community Mental Health

Benjamin White had remarked that the MGH was conservative, competitive, adherent to Yankee social structure, and dedicated to "hard science" medicine.[1] Stanley Cobb had the "Proper Bostonian" social roots and history of hard science work to effectively defend the "soft science" represented in the new field of psychiatry. Though Lindemann was appreciated for his past psychopharmacological research, he did not have the social credentials to win acceptance of his attempts to introduce social psychiatry. His plans encountered resistance from a number of quarters: HMS and MGH put a higher priority on molecular research than on the behavioral sciences. The hospital also was intolerant of the psychiatric concept of personality development and functional adaptation; some rejected any conceptualization other than biological disease. At the MGH, the psychiatry clinical service orientation and structure differed from those of public health, and it objected to a change in focus from treating people with mental illness to working with a nonpatient population. HMS objected to a change in the service name from psychiatry to mental health and to surrendering a secure professional and academic retreat to a federation of academics with community professionals and agencies. It insisted that psychiatry was an all-inclusive, respected discipline and objected because "mental health" sounded amateurish. The West End Study of the need to take into account the mental health consequences of public policy (see more later) conflicted with Boston urban renewal plans that sought increased tax revenues from displacing a working-class population with upscale housing that would attract wealthier citizens and tax revenues, and the Roman Catholic Church owned much of the property in the West End (the neighborhood encompassing the MGH) and imposed strictures on its use.

Community mental health is defined in different ways by different schools of thought that represent different stakeholders. Clearly, Lindemann represented the school that defined community mental health as dealing with the social and interpersonal conditions that were seen as major determinants of mental health and illness and the basis of "primary prevention" in public health terms. This school was informed by and collaborated with public health and the social sciences. It saw the role of mental health professionals as discovering these conditions and their methods of effect and as intervening to change these conditions to enhance mental health and prevent mental illness. It was prepared to work through community residents, leaders, agencies, and institutions and to influence social and political policies and practices.

Lindemann experienced resistance when he presented his projected program to the MGH.[2] There was conflict with the public health viewpoint of a wide preventive frame of reference with behavioral disorders as casualties to be found amid the population, where the hospital and psychiatry play a limited remedial function. It was difficult to establish a unit (the MHS) for the studying and teaching of mental health as based on the concept of a biological gradient of disease and behavior disorder on a continuum from health to sick and on the psychosomatic concept of the whole person and focusing on the hospital's neighborhood citizens rather than statewide hospitalized patients. HMS dean George Packer Berry looked at the integration of the MGH and McLean Hospital for the convenience of caretaking personnel and not in accordance with the comprehensive needs of the community population.

This social psychiatry ideology brought Lindemann into conflict with some aspect of biological treatments. Reportedly, he was especially uncomfortable with electro-convulsive treatment (ECT), which seemed to be the use of force rather than enabling patients—perhaps reminiscent of his maternal grandmother's treatment in the authoritarian mental hospital. "Medication and, under special circumstances, shock therapy can be considered only as auxiliary measures in such a program" addressing personality and life adjustment treated with psychotherapy and education to master problems more effectively.[3] He was subject to some pressure to sanction such treatments[4] and established an ECT service, directed by Gerald Caplan (who had been trained in this biological treatment modality in the United Kingdom), which treated private patients in the MGH private pavilion—the Phillips House.[5] While psychiatry cooperated well with neurosurgery—such as in the care of intractable pain—neurology rejected social and psychological approaches in the same way that the experimental Psychology Department differed from HDSR.

This approach represented a significant change in ideology and professional identity. Many MGH physicians thought the West End Project wild and strange and did not fit the traditional model of research and clinical service. Lindemann's teaching of situational context, loss, prevention, and grief exceeded narrow constructs and was disdained and resisted by many staff members. He was a major source of new ideas in the MGH: he was a nonconformist, not confined to ideological orthodoxy and introduced continually widening thought and action. George

Packer Berry, the HMS dean, noted the glacial progress of the movement of the social sciences into medicine[6] and hoped it would progress:[7]

> Perhaps you will agree that some of these problems are not as horrendous as they seem to be . . . the next steps whereby social and behavioral scientists can achieve in the realm of Harvard Medicine not only a more effective but a happier and more satisfying modus vivendi.

Berry appreciated Herbert Gans's publication, *The Urban Villagers*, as part of the West End Study: "Of course I do not need to tell you how grateful I am for the privilege of working with you during the last decade and more, coming to know you well, and benefitting from your wisdom and friendship".

Lindemann aggressively sought to influence the MGH in many ways, serving people differently than did the tertiary care that had been the tradition. He wanted CMH training for psychiatrists, psychologists, and social workers to provide innovative and available psychiatric clinical services for the people living in the West End section of Boston surrounding the MGH.[8] He used ideas from HSPH: analyze hazardous environmental situations and behavioral responses to them, and institute short-term help to return people to functional equilibrium. Previously there had been no short-term treatment, and the psychiatry senior staff members in charge of clinical services had difficulty with changes in their orientation.

Lindemann had to consider the timing and pace of the introduction of his ideas.[9] Later in his career, Lindemann tried to help a young disciple struggle with the resistance to change:[10]

> One forgets sometimes how fundamentally the values of Community Psychiatry have changed *vis a vis* the traditional psychiatric position, and how difficult the transition is, and above all, how slowly one must go forward in order not to be brought to a halt by the inevitable [resistance to change].

Gerald Caplan thought that Lindemann's 1964 election to the chairpersonship of the MGH GEC would help gain support for his approach:[11] "I am sure this will provide you with an important opportunity to make an even greater mark on the hospital community". He emphasized the importance of the MGH mental health program and Lindemann as a senior consultant in its collaboration with the HSPH.

Another support came when, in 1962, John H. Knowles became general director of the MGH. He had a public health background and sought to inject this social responsibility value into the MGH:

> Striving for the proper balance [of hospital activities—teaching/research vs. community service] we recognize the necessity for

nurturing academic excellence and, at the same time, the necessity for maintaining a strong social conscience and a direct relationship to the community in terms of service.[12]

He could speak forcefully about the medical center and medicine's opportunity—nay, responsibility—for the health and prevention of illness in the community.[13] He developed a relationship with Lindemann and psychiatry that could at times lend Lindemann authority. Caplan noted Knowles's article emphasizing the contributions of the Wellesley Project. While it was difficult to change this tradition at the MGH, outreach services and community health centers gradually developed, though not attributed to Lindemann.

Lindemann was given pause in his efforts by recognizing the dissonance between traditional hospital structure and tradition on one hand and his mental health concept of social adaptation as opposed to disease on the other:[14]

Whether or not the location of a mental health agency in a general hospital is the most auspicious location is at the moment very doubtful. Its concern and operations are so different from the traditional operations and culture patterns of a psychiatric department that interpersonal crises and emotional tension as well as some role confusion among the members of the department can hardly be avoided, at least we have found this difficulty. Furthermore, the inclination of health workers to penetrate the whole population of a given community, in this case the hospital, can easily lead to resistance and misinterpretation in the competitive striving of the various departments. Perhaps the location of the health agency elsewhere in the community but cooperating with the hospital may be a better pattern of organization.

The later resurgence of resistance at the MGH validated his doubts.

Relationships With Other MGH Services

Lindemann was active in developing the Psychiatry Service also through increased communication between psychiatry, medicine, and surgery, including through the appointment of psychiatrists who also had credentials in other medical fields, such as Gerald Davidson, who was an internist, and Benjamin Gill, who was a gastroenterologist.[15] Psychiatrists began to be part of the medical team, participated in patient rounds, discussed all patients rather than only those referred for psychiatric consultation, and addressed the ward population as a whole—thus following the HRS mental health consultation model according to which the identified person offered access to understanding the consultee and their organization.

Receptivity to and the success of these efforts varied widely among the MGH specialty services and were influenced by both theoretical and personality factors.

Lindemann and Walter E. Bauer (MGH chief of medicine) corresponded about the state's offer of new facilities in general hospital psychiatry to facilitate active collaboration between medicine, psychiatry, and the social sciences, including fostering cross-service teaching (MGH Psychiatry's Jerome Weinberger met with junior medical staff) and the study of the treatment of medical patients.[16] In retrospect, Bragg believed that Lindemann was not as successful in this as he wanted to be.

While the chief of the MGH Neurology Service, Raymond Adams, appointed at the same time as Lindemann, had sat on the committee that recommended Lindemann's appointment, he and some in his department were resistant to the Psychiatry Service's approach. Lindemann's efforts to involve neurology in collaborations were largely frustrated. He saw this as a reflection of the nationwide incompatibility between neurologists and personality/adaptive (psychodynamic) psychiatry:[17]

> The Neurological Service [MGH] has shown itself particularly intolerant of this form of psychiatric approach. . . . [For instance] Mandel Cohen . . . carries on psychiatric practice and psychiatric teaching of a nature which appears completely out-moded and inappropriate to many well-trained psychiatrists. . . . [The Psychiatric Service] has not found a completely satisfactory mode of cooperating so far as the psychoneuroses and personality disorders are concerned. . . . The development of [the] Social Relations Department and its Psychology Division at Harvard have separated from the Psychology Department qua experimental psychology on much the same grounds and in the same manner in which we have somewhat of a distance between Neurology and Psychiatry at the MGH.[18]
>
> Dr. Lindemann is concerned that. . . . Dr. Adams does not see eye to eye regarding the type of psychiatry to be developed and therefore is reluctant to grant him any funds [from the Joseph P. Kennedy, Jr. Laboratories for Research on Mental Retardation]. He is laboring under the misconception that Dr. Lindemann only plans a study in psychoanalysis, which I find from Dr. Lindemann is far from true. . . . Drs. Sweet and Mark [MGH Neurosurgery Service] who have equal interests in this space feel that: 1) Difficulties with [the] Neurological Service have been increasing steadily to the extent of constituting a major problem.

Mandel Cohen is an exemplar of the differences in conceptualization and acceptance of psychiatry at the MGH. His professional biography includes training, appointments, and membership in professional societies in both psychiatry and neurology.[19] He stood out in the cadre of biological psychiatry that was loudly hostile to Lindemann's Psychiatry Service and was vigorously rejected by Lindemann. Some psychoanalysts rationalized his failings as the product of an unresolved transference in his incomplete analysis by Hanns Sachs, an Austrian psychoanalyst known for these problems. Negotiations over his place on the MGH staff were reported by Raymond Adams, the chief of neurology:

> After much discussion with Drs. Lindemann [MGH chief of psychiatry], Bauer [MGH chief of medicine] and [Edward F.] Bland [MGH Chief of the Cardiac Unit] concerning the status of Dr. Mandel Cohen in the Massachusetts General Hospital, it has finally been recommended that he be given an appointment in the Neurology Service. In view of his rather senior status and very creditable accomplishments in the field of clinical investigation, I believe this appointment should be that of associate neurologist. . . . We shall recommend that he be made a clinical associate in neurology at Harvard Medical School though we should at least consider the possibility of an appointment in the Department of Preventive Medicine. . . . it is understood that he will devote himself mainly to clinical investigation of disorders of the nervous system and that he will not function as a psychiatrist. Whenever psychiatric problems arise on the Neurology Service or in the other wards of the hospital, we shall call the psychiatric resident and senior staff. This is necessary in order to maintain the closest possible cooperation between the Psychiatry and Neurology Services. Any estrangement of this Service through criticism of the members thereof would, I feel, be detrimental to the best interests of the hospital. Dr. Cohen and I both appreciate the delicacy of these relationships.[20]
>
> . . .
>
> I talked to Mandel Cohen regarding an appointment in our department + he accepted it on the terms stated in the accompanying letter to Dean Clark. I hope this will prove to be the best arrangement for everyone concerned.[21]

There were shared interests and better cooperation in research with the Neurosurgery Service.

The relationship with the MGH Children's Medical Service (pediatrics) was strained. Its chief during Lindemann's early tenure was Alan Butler, who recognized that mental health issues were prominent in pediatric practice:[22]

> Demands requiring hospitalization . . . were but a small per cent of the total demands [for pediatric care]. . . . practicing pediatricians stated that from 50% to 85% of their practices concerned anticipatory psychological or emotional health care. During the early years

most of this . . . concerned with the behavior and problems of parent rather than infants. . . . A pediatrician . . . stated that 65% of his consultations concerned primary psychological or emotional disturbances.

However, he was reported to be "violently" opposed to psychoanalysis as well as cool to psychiatry as a whole.[23] The Psychiatry Service report noted that

It appears that with the change in pediatric orientation in the recent past there has come a somewhat altered emphasis in the demand for child psychiatrists in the joint care of pediatric patients. . . . and the best distribution of roles in diagnostic and therapeutic procedures has not always been easy to find.[24]

Gaston Blum, former chief of the Child Psychiatry Unit, described his experience:[25]

some of my opinions and impressions concerning the difficulties between Child Psychiatry and pediatrics at the Massachusetts General Hospital. . . . The basic problem was the attitude of Dr. [Alan] Butler himself which was never a scientifically critical attitude, but always a highly emotional diatribe. This gave support to negative attitudes of other senior staff. Dr. [Nathan] Talbot [successor as MGH chief of Children's Medicine Service] himself also shared Dr. Butler's point of view. . . . In this kind of situation I do not see how one could be very successful in the teaching and training of pediatric residents. What was done was undermined both directly and indirectly. Dr. [Philip] Dodge [MGH pediatric neurologist] also got involved in this.

There was frequent difficulty with pediatrics in carrying out our research and obstructing collaborative treatment of children. . . . one frequently felt . . . criticism and lack of respect by many hospital personnel. . . . These people (Butler, Talbot, Dodge) could not accept and understand the psychological approach to emotional problems. When staff people had interest in the psychological aspects of pediatrics, they were open to criticism. . . . In spite of these difficulties, there are a number of pediatricians at the Massachusetts General Hospital who have varying degrees of interest and acceptance of psychiatry.

Butler concurred:[26]

2. While the contributions of the General Surgical, Neuro-surgical, Neurological. Orthopedic, Dermatology, Ophthalmology, Oto-laryngology, Medical and Physical Therapy services to our pediatric

education and patient care and, I trust, the contributions of the Children's Medical Service to these services are gratifying, the complementary relationship between the Child Psychiatry Unit and the Children's Medical Service is not so gratifying. As the personal relations are good, this seems to result from: one, the hesitancy or scepticism of pediatricians to accept the emphasis and validity given certain hypotheses and theories used by the Child Psychiatrists in explaining the etiology of behavioral, psychological or emotional disturbances and in treatment; and, two, a feeling on the part of the Psychiatrists that the pediatricians are unreceptive to current psychiatric teaching. However, while this is not satisfactory, it should under the circumstances of conflicting opinions derived from differing points of view and associations with children be more constructive than an uncritical avoidance of resolution of differing opinions.

There was a hope (in the end vain) for research collaboration among MGH units in this area

to provide for a combined unit to study Emotional and Central Nervous System disorders. The combined unit would consist of child psychiatry, child neurology, child neurosurgery, and pediatrics; each group would be independent, but all would have adjacent office space and would work collaboratively.[27]

James C. White, the chief of the MGH Neurosurgical Service, reported on the NIH grant application for this, though he identified it as "a laboratory for pediatric neurology".[28] Butler concurred in hopes for this collaboration:

the excellent collaboration between the neurologists, neurosurgeons, psychologists, psychiatrists and pediatricians of the hospital there is the opportunity of developing an outstanding unit for the collaborative study of diseases of the central nervous system in children. Plans have been drawn and staff designated for such a unit . . . to contribute to the knowledge of the etiology, pathological physiology and therapy of this important and too little understood and unsatisfactorily treated category of diseases of childhood.[29]

He did not mention psychiatry's contribution to The Children's Recreation Service, though psychiatry claimed the project was initiated by a child psychiatrist.

Butler's successor, Nathan Talbot, was much interested in mental health but had his own ideas about it and wanted to develop care within his own department. For instance, on December 1, 1955, he submitted a grant application to the Behavioral Science Program of the Ford Foundation to support a pediatric mental health unit at MGH to study the divergent ways that children and parents manage social and medical problems of illness (motivation influencing coping vs. feeling helped is useless) leading to interventions to improve adaptation. This he based on Lindemann's studies of grief and the Coconut Grove fire, and he suggested Lindemann's collaboration. He spoke about "psychologic malnutrition" and behavior problems in adolescents and the role of the pediatrician in dealing with them.[30] Lindemann reached out to him in a letter:[31] "I enjoyed very much reading your report. . . . It is exciting and promising. . . . I hope we have at least a chance to talk". There is no record of a response.

Moral and Religious Contributions to Lindemann's Perspective and Goals

To more fully understand Lindemann's professional theory and practice, it is important to be aware of the moral principles that help guide and energize them. While he was not attached to organized religion, spiritual and moral values were strong influences.

Ernst Raeker, Lindemann's maternal grandfather and mentor, had a formative influence on his perspective and career: he taught and demonstrated a commitment to social justice, morality, and the importance of human and family lives. Later in his life, Lindemann recalled his grandfather's expectation that he would enter the ministry.[32] This moral strain echoes throughout his education and professional life, inclining him to a "guru" rather than power role.[33] And it channeled his professional interests toward the social and caring application of psychiatry and psychoanalysis. It was later remarked that in his advocacy of social and community psychiatry, he had a long career as an evangelist.[34] He was drawn to philosophy, religion, and humanistic psychology in his university education. In his psychiatric work, he felt bonds with clergymen and religious institutions as sources of psychological expression and support. He thought about the relationship of religion and science in dealing the mental health issues:[35]

> The Mental Health Movement is . . . one manifestation of the . . . secularization and the professionalization in contemporary society. . . . beliefs and practices can be based on tradition, values and goals, as in religious groupings, [p. 1] or they can be based on scientific evidence. Religion prescribes that it is good to help your neighbor. . . [including in regard to] complications of his mental health. . . . we here are an example of a characteristic tendency toward professionalization . . . will it profit us, or the receiver? We do not want to be missionaries or do-gooders. We want to be agents of progress towards a better society . . . lay people want to participate as citizens . . . and

want to leave to the government . . . only those arrangements which can be enforced on the basis of general acceptance.

At the MGH, he took a great interest in the chaplains and the pastoral counseling program. Upon Lindemann's retirement, Rev. Allan W. Reed, MGH Protestant chaplain and supervisor of clinical pastoral education, expressed his debt to Lindemann:[36]

> No mystery about it: I have found your work with grief and bereavement to be the single most helpful insight to come to me from the behavioral sciences . . . this also has been most helpful to me in my dealing with my own maturation and losses. I shall continue to call the attention of my students and fellow clergy to your work, but even more important, to your evident respect for your fellows, and the effect that respect has had on the Department of Psychiatry here at M.G.H.

On November 5, 1956, Lindemann led a seminar titled "Care of the Dying and Bereaved" at the Fifth Annual Workshop on Pastoral Care at the Boston University School of Theology.[37] His long-term assistant and admirer Ina Greer, then working in the Protestant Episcopal Diocese of Massachusetts, corresponded with him about joining regular meetings of a discussion group of psychiatrists and theologians.[38] Topics included the nature of humankind. In 1957, he gave a talk at the Mid Winter Ministers' Institute at Exeter, MA.[39] In 1961, he talked with students of the Crane Theology School of Tufts University about the role of the minister in the situation of death.[40]

Lindemann was a member of the advisory committee of an NIMH-funded project of the Harvard Divinity School (HDS) (Dean Douglas Horton as chairperson and Hans Hofmann—a theologian with a background in psychotherapy—as secretary) to develop an understanding of the mental health function of community clergy—very much in line with his work at HRS:[41]

> Project: Pilot and Evaluation Project designed to develop and make available a curriculum for the training of theological students in the laws of mental health and psychiatric procedure.
> The Need. With the great advance in the therapy of people with mental illness during the last two generations, the psychiatrist has become an indispensable man in the community. The day has now come, however, when the psychiatrist needs the help of other leaders, such as the minister of the local church, both to disseminate information concerning mental health and to aid in guiding the unwell to those who can cure them. The minister is, in fact, a key figure in the

public health scene because he works with a cooperating group, a congregation, through which he has access to a relatively large sector of the community and in which he has a social instrument, if wisely used, of no little therapeutic power. The minister can be of little use in ameliorating mental ills, however, if he does not know the rudiments of psychiatric principles and methods and is not able to work with the local psychiatrist in a relationship of mutual understanding and respect.

A supervisory committee included Lindeman, Dana A. Farnsworth, MD (director of the Harvard University Health Services), Prof. Paul J. Tillich (theologian), Dr. Cora A. DuBois (cultural anthropologist), Rev. Samuel H. Miller, D.D. (chairperson of the HDS Department of Pastoral Theology) ex officio, Prof. Robert Bonthius (psychologist at Wooster College), and clinical psychologists, a behavioral scientist, an expert in education methods, a community leader, and a member of the clergy with training in psychology. Additional consultants were sought from the National Academy of Religion and Mental Health; Rev. George A. Buttrick, D.D. (HDS Department of Homiletics); and Gordon W. Allport, PhD (Harvard Department of Psychology). Simultaneous studies took place at Yeshiva University and Loyola University with the aims of investigating mental health issues in Protestant ministry, designing curriculum, training seminary teachers, and preparing texts.

The project began in July 1957. It produced several publications:

- Tillich, Paul, Niebuhr, Reinhold, Miller, Samuel, Appel, Kenneth, *et al, Making the Ministry Relevant* (New York: Scribner, 1960), addressing the role of the minister
- Hofmann, Hans (ed.), Tillich, Paul, Parsons, Talcott, McClelland, David, Kuether, Frederick, Douglas, William, Booth, Gotthard, Leslie, Robert, Dittes, James, Westberg, Granger, Loomis, Earl, Hoffmann, Hans, *The Ministry and Mental Health* (Hew York: Association Press, 1960), addressing theological education vs. pastoral function
- Stern, Paul (New York: van Nostrand, 1961), addressing psychology for theology students
- *Religion and Mental Health* (New York: Harper, 1961), a collection of annotated cases with a bibliography
- *The Christ Symbol* (1961), addressing a phenomenological study of Christian faith as regards human development.

Hofmann sat in on MGH staff seminars and audited medical sessions. Lindemann was looked to for seminars and courses in psychopathology psychotherapy and existential psychotherapy and for contributing an article for the symposium Making the Ministry Relevant.[42] Relevant to criticisms of Lindemann's organization and dependability, throughout the correspondence, three were repeated references to Lindemann's influenza, upsurges of his chronic chest affliction, illnesses, and an absence in Europe as reasons for his delays and nonattendance. Note that there were also criticisms of Hofmann's administrative inefficiency and grandiosity.[43]

The final report of the project stated the following:[44]

> <u>THE MINISTRY AND MENTAL HEALTH</u> This is the final report of the Harvard University Project on Religion and Mental Health to the National Institute of Mental Health on Grant No. 2M-6406. In 1956 Harvard University was invited to set up a pilot study at its Divinity School, a pilot study in which several departments of the University would cooperate in designing and testing various ways in which Protestant theological education could be implemented with appropriate consideration of communal mental health problems. The goal of this Project has been to complement existing efforts in this area by offering textbook material and suggestions about curriculum which would help other theological schools either to initiate or broaden their instruction in the relationship between religion and mental health.

Then–HDS Dean Samuel H. Miller wrote to Donald Klein at HRS that the end of government funding left them in financial embarrassment; although they were uncertain about being able to continue, they would like to try to keep collaborative channels open.[45]

Lindemann's consultation with India enriched these values in him through the Hindu focus on morality and communal life. He noted the Indian (Hindu) belief in past and future lives and focus on inner moral status in order to achieve better future lives. Therefore, health practices were developed to conform to these moral laws with the guru (wise teacher) as arbiter, teacher, and problem solver. They resist critical views and assertive behavior as morally disrespectful and destructive. Instead, they try to discover emotional conflict as the basis of disability and seek moral guidance and correction from a guru. They reject the dyadic, warm, uncovering treatment method. Thus, there are two distinct approaches to emotional issues: values and traditions dictate behavior and feeling, and technology is used to enable specific results. From his background in community mental health, Lindemann recommended the development of the guru role as therapeutic in collaboration with the physician. The gurus preserve and collaborate with traditional values, with the Western consultant available, but the Indians make responsible choices. In his report, he reveals the moral, humanistic basis of his ideology and life.

He regretted the spiritual poverty of Western life but also the lack of response to human need in Indian life:[46]

> I find our life what I call a rat race very often, not a commendable life. A large percent is spent in a spiritually highly unproductive kind of existence in the competitive life. There are a few moments which are dedicated to another aspect of existence with perhaps, some moments of ecstasy or religious preoccupation or artistic preoccupation or fusion with another human being. They are hellishly rare in our culture. The Indians have much more, but they are buying it at the price of something I couldn't stand. I couldn't stand seeing all those sick people and dying people and nobody caring. A man begs on the street and is practically ready to die from starvation or thirst and there is a cow who gets the water, not the man. I couldn't stand that. My level of values is different.

George Saslow

George Saslow was involved in a tumultuous and painful episode in MGH social psychiatry, which Lindemann thought almost blew the department apart.[47] This was a significant event in the history of CMH at MGH. It also demonstrated Lindemann's impulsive optimism about relationships in CMH as well as his capacity for a firm defense of his program and himself.

Saslow got some of his training at HMS and the MGH,[48] and Lindemann remembers a warm relationship and shared interests.[49] In 1943, Saslow was appointed as a professor of psychiatry at Washington University. Lindemann met him at professional conferences and, as he often did, felt an affinity of interests that made him look forward to comradeship in CMH work. He saw Saslow as an excellent organizer and teacher, and the families were friends.[50] Saslow returned the enthusiasm and warmth:[51]

> We are both better at communication by face-to-face interaction than by other methods. . . . I am not at all ambivalent about willingness to share the rest of my life with you in the enterprise you have undertaken. As I realized how different a situation I would find in Boston from what has developed here, and how disturbed and disappointed an atmosphere my leaving will apparently create, I had a good deal to work through. But I have now done that, and am settled about my willingness to move to Boston.
>
> Saslow also explored promising relationships at HMS, such as with David Rutstein, chairperson of the Department of Preventive Medicine, who responded "It was great fun to have the opportunity to discuss joint problems with you. . . . I hope . . . that plans will

work out so that we may be able to do cooperative research. . . . With kindest personal regards".[52]

Over Stanley Cobb's objections, Lindemann invited Saslow to come from St. Louis to join the MGH Psychiatry Service on July 1, 1955, as a senior member—with the intention of developing a comprehensive social medicine program in the MGH Medical Clinic and to measure human interaction.[53] Saslow drafted extensive plans for changing residency training in medicine and psychiatry and the medical student curriculum, as well as outpatient and inpatient treatment.[54] He sought general agreement from Dean A. Clark (MGH general director), George Packer Berry (HMS dean), Walter Bauer (chief of the MGH Medical Service), and Lindemann—the MGH and HMS enthusiasm for comprehensive medicine is what he had found lacking at George Washington University. He also laid out his expectations for appointments and support. He wrote again seeking specific confirmation of receptivity to his plans:[55] "I need to learn what implicit moves must be made, by you or them [Berry, Clark, Bauer], so that I can regard myself as moving into a situation in which at least certain basic elements have been stated clearly and agreed upon". He also urged hiring a psychologist and internist with whom he worked.

Lindemann negotiated support for Saslow's academic appointment and logistical support:[56]

> As suggested, I communicated with Drs. [Harry C.] Solomon [Director of the Boston Psychopathic Hospital and senior HMS psychiatrist], [Raymond D.] Adams [Chief of the MGH Neurology Service], and [Derek] Denny-Brown [Chief of Neurology at the Boston City Hospital] concerning the appointment of Dr. Saslow as Clinical Professor . . . All three men expressed their agreement with the plan.

Saslow, Lindemann, and Clark corresponded about arrangements for transfer from Washington University to MGH/HMS, including research space, office location, positions for Joseph Matarazzo and George Murphy (fellow in internal medicine and psychosomatic medicine), salary, pension, etc. However, Lindemann avoided commitments about the changes in training and clinical service in favor of future negotiations with the existing academic system and culture:[57]

> Thank you for your note of Saturday. . . . It seems to me that the details of the arrangement, so far as shifting the curriculum in the Medical School goes will have to be left to joint planning after you are here. The [HMS] Dean could hardly commit himself at the present time to the details of a program which will have to be integrated bit by bit with the traditional teaching here. You would not wish in

any case to superimpose a ready-made program upon an organization which works in terms of its own social forces and which you would have to come to know pretty well first. . . . So far as finances go . . . we will have to find in our budget the resources for your salary. I am reasonably sure that another $3,000 can come from the Rutstein Family Service project. . . . To count on an additional sum, as a "buffer sum" beyond $15,000 would be risky. I would certainly find it hard to justify this with the budget committee. Perhaps the fact that the Department also provides you with an office and secretarial help, will do instead. So far as moving expenses go, Dean Clark expressed reasonable confidence that the [MGH] General Executive Committee would approve of a contribution towards that expense. So far as space in the Hospital goes. . . . So far as personal assistants go.

This vagueness set the stage for the future disappointments, conflicts, and failures in this project and relationship. However, Saslow committed himself to this move:[58]

On Friday, May 6, I submitted my resignation formally, to take effect on June 30. . . . I then sent a letter of acceptance to Dean Clark with regard to the appointment at the Hospital, and one to the secretary of the Harvard Corporation with regard to the appointment in the university. . . . I shall try to get to Boston as close to July 1 as we can manage.

Saslow brought with him psychologist colleagues Joseph D. and Ruth Matarazzo.[59] Lindemann supported Saslow's research proposals before the MGH Executive Committee of the Committee on Research.[60] Joseph Matarazzo was active in proposing projects involving psychologists: psychology and psychologist teaching of MGH psychiatry residents[61] and enhancing the teaching of behavioral sciences as part of medical education (one of Lindemann's goals).

Saslow expected to train new generations of physicians in a social science outlook and had many expectations and requests for salary and rank for himself and his colleagues, changes in HMS curriculum, research space, etc. He expected to be the effective (administrative and educational) head of the department, while Lindemann focused on CMH research at the HRS (Lindemann later wondered whether that might have been a good arrangement[62]). Lindemann was disturbed by Saslow's focusing on conditioning and unconditioning and also by bringing the psychologist Joseph Matarazzo, who was intolerant of psychoanalysis and making the department edgy, and his association with a well-known developmental psychologist in the department, who began to sabotage by organizing a psychology group that sought to create a developmental psychology committee.[63]

The conflict grew (see correspondence involving Lindemann, Saslow, Dean Clark, and Berry).[64] Saslow believed that he could have made community mental health successful at MGH if he were in charge. In 1956, Lindemann objected to Saslow's isolating his unit rather than integrating it into the department as a whole, his failure to attend executive meetings, his expecting to be appointed as associate director of the department, and his moves toward control of his work independent of Lindemann and the department. An alternative view of the relationship by Avery Weisman, a member of the psychiatry staff who was critical of his chief, saw Saslow as

> an outstanding, enthusiastic, assertive, knowledgeable man, who had strong opinions which he did not bother to temper. . . . [He] found that Lindemann encouraged him to make decisions and then would fail to support him on grounds that he was usurping authority.[65]

Lindemann directed Saslow to head a comprehensive medicine program and the alcoholism clinic, continue his research, and teach the second-year medical student course in psychiatry. Saslow resented what he saw as a repudiation of their original agreement, including his expectation that he would be Lindemann's deputy; share in general departmental planning, decisions, and relationships with other groups; and direct ambulatory and consultation psychiatry.[66] They disagreed over salary, use of research salaries, and salary supplements. Lindemann reported that Saslow did not fulfill his clinical responsibilities. In turn, Saslow thought CMH would not go anywhere and complained to the HMS dean. Harry Solomon, senior member of the Harvard Medical School psychiatry program, saw Saslow as trying to organize a group to remove Lindemann and felt forced to take action to resolve this: He told Saslow that Lindemann had precedence due to Lindemann's tenure and that Saslow would have to leave, though he allowed him to complete his three-year contract.[67]

In 1956, Lindemann noted that the relationship was hopeless, began restricting the functions of Saslow's psychologist colleagues and his funding, did not renew Saslow's appointment, and advised Saslow to prepare another placement for himself.[68] In March 1957, Saslow resigned, effective June 30, 1957.[69] He became a professor and chairperson of psychiatry at the Oregon Health and Science University School of Medicine, where he served for a long time and with distinction.[70] Joseph and Ruth Matarazzo joined Saslow in resigning from MGH and assuming positions at Oregon.[71]

Massachusetts General Hospital Community Mental Health Center/Erich Lindemann Mental Health Center

Lindemann had long-standing shared interests with the DMH's Division of Mental Hygiene. Warren Vaughan had learned CMH in the HSPH and

MGH and was recruited as the associate commissioner of mental health, heading the division to start the development of CMHCs growing from the state child guidance centers. In 1957, Lindemann met with him to explore planning:[72]

> The State Department of Mental Hygiene is interested in contracting with the three medical schools—for each school to have a so-called mental health center which would be financed and staffed by the Commonwealth but completely independent to follow its own focus of interest. They would not be bound to a specific region [changed later] but rather would determine a special focus of concern. In this manner Boston University—Eleanor Pavenstedt, who was approached via Dr. [William] Malamud, is now instrumental in organizing a program of service to the DCG [state Division of Child Guidance] children . . . Similar plans are made with Dr. Tiza at Tufts Medical School. Dr. Vaughan would prefer that the development of a mental health center would take place at the MGH and that Dr. Blom [chief of the child psychiatry unit] in consultation with Dr. Lindemann would develop the program and be the director of the mental health agency. The Commonwealth would provide a salary in the neighborhood of $12,000. . . . Dr. Lindemann agreed to talk with Dr. Blom about this proposition and also to talk to [HMS] Dean Berry about the matter. . . . <u>Very tentative budget</u>: Psychiatrist 12,000. Psychologist 8,000. Co-ordinator 6,000. Social Worker 4,000. Secretary 2,500.

There were suggestions for encompassing the MGH, McLean Hospital, and the planned CMHC,[73] all under the MGH chief of psychiatry. Each would chair an advisory committee on the collaboration; each would be involved in training, teaching, and clinical service; and all three directors would sit on a central administrative committee chaired by the MGH chief of psychiatry.

An early CMHC initiative in collaboration with community agencies is illustrated in the minutes of the Dorchester Mental Health Association's first annual meeting:

> the Dorchester Mental Health Project . . . was initiated in September 1959 with weekly seminars in which the Executive Directors of the settlement houses and community agencies in Dorchester participated under the leadership of Mrs. Eric Lindeman, Mental Health Consultant of the Wellesley Human Relations Service. The purpose of these seminars has been to explore and strengthen the mental health role of these facilities in an urban area which is undergoing change; and to arrive at a common understanding of mental health needs in this area. Participating in this Project are . . . William Ryan,

PhD, Research Director of the Crisis Treatment Project at the South Shore Guidance Center.

(p. 5)

The MGH Psychiatry Service applied for state funding to expand the contacts and collaboration that it had already established with community agencies:[74]

In view of the interest the State Department of Mental Health has in seeing [explorations] made into the communities of East Boston, North End, West End and Charlestown program [eventually the Erich Lindemann Mental Health Center (ELMHC) catchment area] for purposes of developing a mental health, we should like to indicate our contact with those health and welfare agencies to date which serve and influence the population of those neighborhoods: 1. Department of Public Welfare, Boston, East Boston District 2. Family Society of Greater Boston, Somerset office 3. International Institute 4. Department of Public Health, Boston, Central office Bureau of Nursing 5. Boston Juvenile Court, Probation Dept. 6. Mass. Dept. of Public Welfare, Division of Child Guardianship, Greater Boston District 7. Children's Aid Association of Boston, Neighborhood Group Dept. 8. Visiting Nurses' Association 9. United Community Services of Greater Boston, Divisions on Health, and Services to Families and Children 10. Mass. Council of Churches, Research Division 11. Associated Day Care Centers 12. West End Child Guidance Clinic 13. Catholic Charitable Bureau, Family Division 14. Mass. Society for Prevention of Cruelty to Children 15. Mental Health Association of Massachusetts 16. Big Brothers' Association 17. Mass. Eye and Ear Hospital, Social Service 18. Mass. General Hospital, Psychiatric Out-Patient and Alcoholic Clinics and Child Psychiatry

. . .

the 6 series [of] meetings held this spring with the East Boston District office of the Department of Public Welfare. . . . One staff member (L. Morris) is now a full member of two community groups: The West End Neighborhood Council.

Correspondence documented DMH payments to MGH, including for staff:[75] Harold Wolman psychiatrist, Eleanor Clark social worker, Laura Morris social worker, Donald Weston Ph.D. psychologist, Miss Ferguson followed by Patricia McSheffrey stenographer.

In line with our interest to expand both group and individual consultation to the professional personnel . . . and to eventually provide direct client service, we request an addition in staff to be financed via the State Dept. of Mental Health for one full time psychiatrist and two full-time psychiatric caseworkers.

(pp. 1–2)

Vaughan's successor, Belenden Hutchinson, continued this collaboration with much correspondence between them regarding mental health planning for Boston. In 1959, a study, "Delineating the Role of the Settlement or Neighborhood House in Developing a Community Mental Health Program in a Metropolitan Area", was proposed with Donald Klein funded to contribute.[76] President John Kennedy's "Message from the President of the United States Relative to Mental Illness and Mental Retardation" specifically mentioned "Ideally, the center could be located at an appropriate community general hospital, many of which already have psychiatric units. In such instances, additional services and facilities could be added . . . to fill out the comprehensive program".[77] In 1961, Lindemann proposed state staff positions to plan an emergency ward information center and mobile task force to go to community disasters, family crises, and individual breakdowns based on DMH Commissioner Solomon's encouragement of general hospitals to share in state mental health services.[78] There was progressive planning specifically for a CMHC:[79]

> The establishment of a new state center, to be located in a concentrated area in Boston, has been proposed by Foster Furcolo, Governor. . . . This would include a Mental Health Center for the Department of Mental Health, a Reception and Classification Center for the Department of Corrections, a State Laboratories Building, and (by 1965) a second state office facility to house the Health, Welfare, Education and Rehabilitation agencies of the state government. This proposal has the support of Harry C. Solomon, MD, Commissioner, Massachusetts Department of Mental Health. . . . Dr. Solomon cited the inadequacy of the present facilities for the care and treatment of the mentally ill. . . . He indicated the great need for the prevention of hospitalization, when possible, through outpatient clinic and day hospital facilities which such a project would make available. The provision of a small number of beds, in addition, for intensive treatment would help patients to remain as near as possible to their homes and communities. Dr. Solomon estimated that the average stay of patients in this in-patient facility would be no more than 45 days, and that from 75–90% of the acutely ill would be returned to their homes. The establishment of a Reception and Classification Center of the Massachusetts Department of Correction (with 50 beds for psychiatric cases) adjacent to the mental health facilities would ease staffing and budget problems through an arrangement between the two state Departments by which the Department of Mental Health would furnish treatment, and the Department of Correction security aids. This centralization of activities, said Dr. Solomon, would mean "a concentration of a large number of professional individuals, consisting of psychiatrists, psychologists, social workers, correctional,

probation and parole authorities who would work as a team in evolving improvements of the varying aspects of social welfare".

There were innumerable legal, policy, and stakeholder issues. David C. Crockett, the MGH associate director, described exploring with Dr. Frechette (State Department of Public Health) the location of an MHC: on the MGH 12th floor or in part of the urban development adjacent to the MGH research building. In 1961, Lindemann voiced one scenario:[80]

> Dr. Lindemann spoke of plans for <u>future development</u> and of money which has been granted by the State Legislature as part of a plan for erection of a Mental Health Center and Hospital under the direction of MGH Psychiatry to be located in the proximity of Scollay Square [s short distance from MGH]. The Psychiatric Department is trying to acquire property nearer the Hospital, such as the West End House. The development of community psychiatry is part of the State Department's plans as well as those of the Hospital. Dr. Lindemann hoped that some statement might be forthcoming from the Hospital Trustees in which they would support the importance of such a unit being close to the Hospital. . . . the program concerning psychoneuroses and psychosomatic disorders would remain at the Massachusetts General Hospital.

Harry C. Solomon (DMH commissioner) was determined to situate it within the Government Center complex of state health, welfare, and state office buildings (where it ultimately stands).[81] He suggested that if there were need to return to the state legislature for additional funds, the siting issued might be reopened. Later, Dr. Solomon was reported willing to negotiate with the MGH to build the MHC on hospital grounds.[82] While MGH was a pioneer in collaboration between the DMH and a private agency, the state at that time could not reimburse private agencies for services or supply DMH staff. However, it could locate a state clinic at a private agency if the agency's policies met the state's standards.[83]

> The following plan is outlined as an endeavor to do the following: a. Show how the Department of Mental Health, the Division of Mental Hygiene can work collaboratively with a general hospital. b. Provide a facility needed by the general hospital. c. Attract young child psychiatrist directors into the Division of Mental Hygiene's psychiatric clinics by providing for their professional stimulation through the activities that might be provided by a general hospital.
>
> (p. 1)

The Mystic Valley Clinic and the Boston City Hospital child psychiatry clinic were offered as prototypes.

A meeting with Dr. Solomon on January 18, 1963, addressed a number of practical issues concerning the new institution:[84] There was general agreement that overhead and salaries would be funded by the Commonwealth, except some medical staff might be funded jointly with the MGH and HMS. The superintendent would select personnel; if the superintendent has appointments at HMS, then HMS and MGH will help choose them. Staff will have close relations and joint appointment with MGH and HMS. The MGH Psychiatry Service would be an important participant in decisions on staff and policies. The impression was that Dr. Solomon was eager to have MGH psychiatry involved in planning and operating the center. A memo from John H. Knowles (MGH general director) to Lindemann and Nemiah stated that Dr. James Curren (Massachusetts Medical Society)

> is looking into the feasibility of the present plans for a Government Mental Health Center. He called me to ask if I would write a letter stating it would be best and desirable to have the Massachusetts Mental Health Unit immediately across the street from us.

Dr. Knowles was willing—this was the original preference.

In preparation for this meeting with Harry Solomon, a manuscript was prepared:

> A Cooperative Program of the Massachusetts General Hospital, the Commonwealth of Massachusetts, and Harvard Medical School for the Development of a Community Mental Health Center to be Located at Bowdoin Square. Suggested Titles: Massachusetts Institute of Preventive Psychiatry or Massachusetts Center for Community Psychiatry.
>
> (p.1)

It would be an extension of MGH psychiatric care to acute psychoses and behavioral disintegrations. If this were not feasible in the MGH and adjacent locations, it would be directed to the Bowdoin Square center. The center would provide comprehensive evaluation as well as follow-up care, information and education, consultation with social agencies, daycare, halfway hospital care, and participation by government and community agencies in the development of a model program. Multiple planning meetings were contemplated to include Lindemann and discussions with [HMS] Dean Berry. A core planning and implementation group and advisory committee were recommended to include relevant government, academic, and community agency representatives.[85] The Advisory Committee would develop the program, an epidemiological appraisal of the service population, and an appraisal of community resources and develop an information center, recruit staff, and develop a building program. Federal funds via DMH would be sought for planning, the core executive group, and travel and per diem payment for the Advisory Group. There was developed a "Proposal for the Expansion of Psychiatric Facilities at the Massachusetts General Hospital":

> I. Aims and Purposes ... 1. To create a Community Psychiatric Center for this area of the city of Boston, with special emphasis on prevention and crisis intervention. 2. To increase patient care facilities to enable us to diagnose and treat a greater number of emotionally sick people in in-patient, out-patient and day-care settings. 3. To increase our opportunities for research and for the teaching and training of students at an undergraduate, graduate and post-graduate level.
>
> (p. 1)

> it is imperative that the present quality and unique characteristics or our department be preserved. We must remain an integral part of the functioning of the entire hospital, and must not become a large psychiatric institution only loosely connected with the other facilities.
>
> (p .1)

An intimate teaching atmosphere would be maintained. A 20-bed patient ward would be located at the MGH for patients with neurotic, psychosomatic, and behavioral disorder problems. There would be a new 80-bed unit predominantly for patients with psychoses. Also, there would be a new, 15-bed unit for children. Fifteen psychiatric residents per year (a total of 45 at any given time) would be trained in clinical practice, including consultation, neurology, child psychiatry, community psychiatry, and research.

The Massachusetts Medical Society passed a resolution "that the Massachusetts Medical Society enter into negotiation with the Department of Mental Health with the view to making possible joint control of a mental health center" (p. 12), with debate about delaying state action pending the society's preparation of a report by its Committee on Mental Health.[86] However, the executive director of the Massachusetts Hospital Association reported that the Massachusetts Medical Society's committee preferred DMH financial assistance to general hospitals for the care of psychiatric patients over establishing state units near general hospitals.[87]

A later meeting in 1964 with the commissioner of mental health developed more-specific plans for MGH's involvement in the planned mental health center, including CMH projects at the MGH, and designated Lindemann in charge:[88]

> The following are the main points which ... were discussed during the conference on Monday, June 8th in Dr. Solomon's office. Future plans for cooperative efforts ... between the Department of Mental

Health and the Massachusetts General Hospital ... 1. ... construction of the Government Center mental health unit ... begin in August and the building ... about two years. 2. Once the corner stone is laid in the early fall ... assign to Dr. Lindemann the task of preparing the staff and the details of the collaboration between the Department of Mental Health and the Massachusetts General Hospital and the Harvard Medical School. ... In each of the major units of the Psychiatric Department of the Massachusetts General Hospital ... a senior person. .. [will] develop that section of the program in the Government Center ... Acute Services and the Emergency Ward ... Psychiatric Clinic, Psychiatric Ward Services, liaison services with other medical specialties ... community services ... research laboratories. ... Key staff members of the new unit must be eligible for and ordinarily will hold staff appointments at both the Massachusetts General Hospital and the Government Center unit. ... appointments at Harvard Medical School will correspond to the contributions ... to the academic teaching and research program of the new Center. 3. Dr. Lindemann and Dr. Solomon then will prepare a budget for the year beginning July 1965. ... a small group of key persons ... develop the organization of services, and plans for the internal structure ... relationships to the communities to be served and ... to other agencies ... plans for a preliminary budget to finance the first year of actual operations ... beginning ... summer of 1966. Dr. Solomon anticipates considerable autonomy of the new unit ... expects the financial support to be at a similar level as that now available to the Massachusetts Mental Health Center. 4. .. work out collaborative efforts ... a joint residency program between the Massachusetts General Hospital Department of Psychiatry and the Danvers State Hospital ... organization of an Information Center to be called the Mental Health Information Center or the Crisis Information Center of the Massachusetts General Hospital ... provide on a twenty-four hour basis first aid information and advice ... a unit of the community services of the Psychiatric Service of the Massachusetts General Hospital and located in the Emergency Ward.

(pp. 1–2)

Despite the general identification of the community mental health movement with the community mental health centers program, Lindemann did not want a CMHC affiliated with the MGH.[89] He pressed for strengthening the MGH Psychiatry Service, including increasing its inpatient beds from 20 to 60 to handle an increase in acute and preventive intervention services:[90]

Such a facility within the general hospital would be vastly preferable to the extension of the program of the Psychiatric Service of the Massachusetts General Hospital into a state operated psychiatric institution which might be built in the immediate vicinity of the hospital, but more likely is going to be constructed as part of the Government Center.

(p. 1)

He saw it as forced by politics, the state legislature, the state DMH commissioner, architectural plans, and city of Boston plans: "we never wanted the center—it has caused us a great deal of frustration. . . . it was forced on us . . . by political realities, by a number of architectural plans, city plans . . . the work of the legislature and the commissioner [of DMH], and the blocks [obstacles—possibly referring to the interests of the Roman Catholic Church] in the way in the area around the hospital [MGH]" (p. 1).[91]

In contrast with a mental hospital, he wanted a public health facility not specifically limited to mental health, an idea that he had developed when he worked at the HSPH and HDSR and implemented in the HRS. He was interested in a preventive function with 24-hour first aid for emotional disturbance and in people with mental illness being referred to mental hospitals. It would offer case consultation with community professionals dealing with people with emotional problems, program consultation with community organizations that affect mental health, research jointly with the community about high-risk populations and life stresses, and preventive methods. He believed that there was need for more such facilities to develop knowledge, such as the desegregation of schools (a contentious issue at the time), provoking interest in community outcasts and tolerance for deviance.

Lindemann's preference for the future of CMH was supplanted by what he rejected when the CMHC program came to dominate public mental health planning and funding. He had to become involved with State Commissioner of Mental Health Harry C. Solomon, MGH General Director Dean Clark and his successor General Director John Knowles, and HMS Dean George Packer Berry in planning a state-funded mental health program affiliated with the MGH and located adjacent to it and with joint CMHC and MGH appointments for the staff. Lindemann wrote,

there is now pending a new mental health center which will be under the direction of our staff. The center is to be built and financed by the state and used for teaching and research by us. It will be finished some time in 1966 and approximately one year before that we will begin to assemble the staff for the program.[92]

The negotiations were tortuous: The state legislature was resistant to funding a private enterprise, and the Roman Catholic Church had other plans for its West End real estate. The MGH was reluctant to take on large clinical responsibilities and a second site separate from the hospital. Efforts to develop an enlarged psychiatric service in or near the MGH were stymied by space and financing.

When a state CMHC near the MGH was decided upon Lindemann accommodated to planning the MGH's involvement. He tried to envision his CMH approaches in this setting:[93]

> John Nemiah who is in charge of our residency training program and will be a key person in the new Commonwealth Center for Community Psychiatry which is expected to start operations about two years from now in the new government center buildings in Boston adjacent to the Massachusetts General Hospital. . . . You will be interested that we are planning to make the new Center for Community Psychiatry a model for a program of services, training and research in all phases of community mental health, serving a defined population in the metropolitan area.

In a memo from Lindemann to Solomon, he outlined steps in developing this affiliation:[94] He expected the CMHC construction during 1964–1966.

> 2. Once the corner stone is laid in the early fall, it will be possible to assign to Dr. Lindemann the task of preparing the staff and the details of the collaboration between the Department of Mental Health, the Massachusetts General Hospital and the Harvard Medical School.
>
> (p. 1)

In a letter to HMS Dean George Packer Berry, he outlined his recommendations (or hopes) for this element of CMH even after his retirement:[95]

> long range plans . . . for the development of psychiatry beyond my tenure. . . . The first . . . a community mental health unit in the Government Center at Bowdoin Square . . . plan that our Department at the Massachusetts General Hospital become [involved] intimately and for research in addition to . . . the further development of social psychiatry. . . . Dr. Solomon suggests that since the opening of this center almost coincides with the end of my tenure that I should become the Superintendent of the Mental Health Unit. . . . [Have] John Nemiah move with me. . . [to] coordinate the residency training program there as he does now at the Massachusetts General Hospital. . . [to develop] into one integrated training center. . . . [He will receive a] promotion appropriate to the extension of his responsibilities.
>
> (p. 1)

The second concern is the future relationship of the Massachusetts General Hospital program proper to this new center. . . . [It will] considerably strengthen . . . psychosomatic medicine and . . . acute care for mental illness arising in a medical context . . . developing a new unit . . . at the MGH, probably the twelfth floor of the Warren Building and Baker Memorial combined, adding 30–40 beds . . . new federal funds available for community psychiatry programs . . . match with . . . private sources. . . . [This is] a necessary balance to the large increase in the public sector . . . by the Bowdoin Square Unit.

(pp. 1–2)

the new professor might take over the directorship of . . . both facilities with an associate at Bowdoin Square . . . psychiatric, psychological, and basic science research . . . primarily appointed . . . to the Massachusetts General Hospital unit . . . auxiliary professions, nurses, social workers, aides, and maintenance personnel, would operate under . . . the Commonwealth.

(p. 2)

Another urgent concern . . . is the . . . solid strength of the community psychiatry and child psychiatry programs. . . [which I] hope to see survive . . . beyond my tenure. The problem is . . . energetic and imaginative leadership. . . . A crisis at the School of Public Health might make it possible . . . to attract Gerald Caplan to move to our Department in the Medical School. Since the departure of Dr. [Hugh] Leavell. . . . Gerald's departure would be a great loss for Boston".

(p. 2)

He expected senior staff members in MGH Psychiatry units to develop parallel units in the CMHC and, if possible, staff these new units with those familiar with the MGH. Ordinarily, they would hold joint appointments at the CMHC and MGH; HMS appointments would be arranged as appropriate. He looked forward to he and Dr. Solomon preparing the July 1965 fiscal year budget for a small group to plan the CMHC organization and structure, relationships to communities and other agencies, and a preliminary budget for the 1966 inaugural year. Solomon anticipated considerable autonomy in the development of financial support, similar to the Massachusetts Mental Health Center. They would begin the collaboration between the DMH and MGH, including initiating a psychiatric residency training program shared by the MGH and Danvers State Hospital. He also suggested organizing a mental health information center or crisis information center at MGH, available 24 hours a day, offering first aid information for psychological and emotional predicaments and operating in collaboration with the poison information center and other agencies. "It will be a unit of the community services of the Psychiatric Service of the Massachusetts General Hospital and located in the Emergency Ward orbit" (p. 2). DMH would fund, for example, the afterhours service. In subsequent letters, they explored an MGH-Bridgewater State Hospital Dangerous Sex Offenders unit. Solomon was eager for this academic involvement, Lindemann was reluctant about the intrusion of law-medicine interests from Boston University and on the part of Jack Ewalt, and MGH was resistant to an appointment for the Dangerous Sex Offender Director Harry Kozol.[96]

The multiple nominations, suggestions, and assumptions that Lindemann would return from academic administration to CMH research and demonstration as superintendent of the CMHC were put to rest by Lindemann in consultation with HMS Dean Berry on the grounds that Lindemann's successor as chief of the MGH Psychiatry Service should decide on its involvement in the CMHC.[97] As an alternative, Lindemann requested and Berry and MGH General Director John Knowles appointed an ad hoc committee, chaired by Robert Ebert (new professor and chief of the MGH Medical Service and future HMS dean), to explore the future of the MGH Psychiatry Service relationship to the CMHC:

> This committee can now consider the overall plans for Harvard and Massachusetts General Hospital psychiatry and the proper place of the new center in this program. It seems to me absolutely essential that the closest form of integration of the activities at the two centers in service as well as in teaching and research will be guaranteed. . . . If it should turn out in the end that all those concerned including my successor consider it essential that I contribute further to the development of this program I will, of course, give this very serious consideration, but I think it only proper for me to make alternate plans.
>
> (p. 1)

This was a part of Lindemann's difficult struggle to relinquish his campaign to bring the MGH, psychiatry, and medicine into a social perspective and professional identity. Further letters and meeting minutes document meetings to explore philosophies, personnel, and institutional relationships between MGH and the CMHC.[98]

A good deal of publicity and associated activities grew up, some idealizing the mental health center and its support by the MGH and HMS:

- A state mental health center, operated in cooperation with Massachusetts General Hospital and Harvard Medical School, will be established in the Government Center. . . . Its functions will be patterned on a center pioneered in Wellesley 14 years ago by the hospital.[99]
- Massachusetts General Hospital, which already has moved outside its doors twice to help meet the mental health needs of entire

communities—the West End and the town of Wellesley—is hoping to move out a third time, to serve a large area of Boston. Dr. Erich Lindemann . . . revealed . . . in the sixth Lowell Lecture, the hospital, Harvard Medical School and the state Department of Mental Health are discussing ways the resources of the hospital can be tied in to the new mental health center to be built as part of the government center. Some criticism already has been leveled against the new mental health center . . . because it appeared to be isolated from a general hospital, contrary to recent trends. Under . . . proposals . . . being worked on among the state, M.G.H. and Harvard Medical School this would not be so. The new unit would be very close to the hospital and utilization of its resources would be easy geographically. . . . Dr. Lindemann's lecture stressed that the hospital has a great responsibility for meeting the health needs of the community, and this means mental health and prevention of illness as well as curative functions. . . . Working with the two groups [West End, Wellesley], MGH psychiatrists have found that a hospital as a whole can do a great deal toward keeping people out of hospital beds through total programs for health maintenance. "What is at stake here", he said, "is the transformation of the hospital into a resource for maintenance of community health. The enormous load of demand for beds, more beds than for all other diseases together, has forced us to seek better understanding of the community conditions conducive to mental breakdown. . . . This concerns populations and communities rather than dealing with individuals. We may have to influence population-wide attitudes and prejudices to win proper consideration for preventive measures. We must develop a total program for health maintenance".[100]

In this atmosphere, the Lowell Institute's regular series of lectures on public affairs was devoted to the topic "The Hospital's Responsibility to the Community" and was given in the Mosely Rotunda at the MGH.[101] The topics and speakers were listed as follows:

- 2/6/1963 Knowles, John H. (General Director of the MGH): The Social Conscience and the Primary Function of the Hospital Viewed in Historical Perspective
- 2/13/1963 Reader, George G.: The Contribution of the Behavioural Sciences to Medicine: Some Studies in the Evaluation of Hospital Function
- 2/20/1963 McKeown, Thomas: An Examination of the Traditional Concept of Medical Care
- 2/21/1963 McKeown, Thomas: Changes in Medical Education Appropriate to an Enlarged Concept of Medical Care

- 2/27/1963 Cherkasky, Martin: The Hospital as a Social Instrument—Recent Experiences at the Montefiore
- 3/6/1963 Lindemann, Erich: The Health Needs of Communities
- 3/13/1963 McKittrick, Leland S.: Privileges and Responsibilities of the Physician in the Hospital
- 3/20/1963 Nelson, Russell A.: The Hospital in the Continuing Education of the Doctor
- 3/27/1963 Churchill, Edward D. (chief of surgery, MGH): Pre- and Post-Doctoral Medical Education in the Hospital
- 4/3/1963 Peterson, Osler L.: Research in Medical Care
- 4/10/1963 Masur, Jack: The Relationship of Government to Hospitals
- 4/17/1963 Somers, Herman M.: Health Insurance: Programs, Pressures and Problems
- 4/18/1963 Somers, Herman M.: (Continuation of the same topic)
- 4/24/1963 Schotland, Charles I.: The Past, Present and Future of the American Social Security System—Its Implications for Health and Medical Care Programs
- 5/1/1963 Trussell, Ray E. (Columbia University School of Public Health and Administration): The Problems of Maintaining Quality in Hospitals
- 5/8/1963 Pollack, Jerome: The Voice of the Consumer: Cost, Quality and Organization of Medical Services
- 5/15/1963 Rutstein, David D. (chairperson, HMS Department of Social Medicine): At the Turn of the Next Century

Lindemann expressed his interest in the CMHC, still hoping that it would be within the MGH as part of the Department of Psychiatry:[102]

> Let me tell you again today how much I am interested in the development of a mental health center adjacent to the Massachusetts General Hospital. I do believe that the Trustees of the hospital can be persuaded to make available space adjacent to the hospital for such a program once we can present them with a fairly concrete image of our joint plans. I am still somewhat uncertain as to the legal patterns of such cooperative ventures and would be grateful for a few minutes of your time in the near future so that I know better what steps to take next.

However, a letter from Solomon to Lindemann on March 20, 1962, reported on a pleasant meeting with Mr. David C. Crockett (MGH associate director for resources and development) and John Nemiah (representing the Department of Psychiatry):[103]

> Mr. Crockett indicated that the Hospital could afford no money for land that it would have to buy. I explained to him that this would

simply stop anything because I thought there was no likelihood of my being able to get a sum of money sufficient for this job.

He suggested that Crockett and the trustees explore this issue with the (state legislature's) Committee on Ways and Means. HMS Dean Berry noted evolving plans:[104] There were new plans for a building much nearer to MGH—80 inpatient beds plus 20 daycare places and a child psychiatry unit

> to be used as a teaching and research facility by the Psychiatric Service of the Massachusetts General Hospital and staffed jointly by the hospital, the Commonwealth, and Harvard University. . . . [with evolution toward] more usefulness for an expanded mental hospital program under Lindemann's guidance in the center of town. This would be in some way a balance to McLean Hospital, which serves only well-to-do persons. He suggested that after Dr. Ewalt's return from Geneva, we arrange for a meeting with Dr. Knowles, Dr. Ewalt, and Dr. Solomon, to get a definite understanding before Dr. Solomon's retirement.

Lindemann refused to make a state-licensed hospital part of the MGH Psychiatry Service, because he feared that involuntary commitment would stigmatize the department's programs. Solomon planned independently, believing in the small psychopathic hospital model based on his experience with the state Boston State and Boston Psychopathic Hospitals: He rejected a contractual relationship with the MGH in favor of direct state employment of staff. He decided to locate a mental hospital separate from the MGH in the newly built Government Center (within sight of the state house) in order to bring mental health issues to the attention of other state agencies. Under these conditions, MGH became less enthusiastic and more distant, falling back on the previous practice of joint academic and state appointments for physicians and administrators but not for nurses and social workers (who were subject to different standards). Recognizing these complexities, Lindemann wrote (swallowing his disappointment with much diplomacy) that[105]

> One of the most important challenges to my successor will be the new government mental health center. We have collaborated in the architectural design and believe it will be a superb facility for psychiatric research and training. John Nemiah, Morris Chafetz and Jack Mendelson [MGH psychiatry staff members] are working closely with Dr. Solomon and myself in preparing the details of the organization. I do believe that my successor will wish to consider the whole complex network of collaborative efforts existing at the Massachusetts General Hospital, at the McLean [Hospital] and at the Government

Center facilities and we all hope that a decision can soon be made about the leadership as it involves the new program. This development in psychiatry is particularly important because it constitutes a new venture in coordination of psychiatric work in a general hospital with the Commonwealth of Massachusetts.

(pp. 1–2)

All this betokens the tortuousness of the MGH's participation in the development of CMHCs during Lindemann's tenure.[106] The psychiatry czars in the Boston arena included Lindemann, Bernard Bandler (later superintendent of a Boston University mental health center), Harry Solomon (commissioner of mental health with ideas of hospital complexes), Jack Ewalt (at Harvard Medical School and the Boston Psychopathic Hospital, which was later renamed the Massachusetts Mental Health Center), Tufts Medical School, and Boston State Hospital (a stepchild in the process). Laura Morris observed that the DMH staff was "playing political games" and there was a move to lock the Lindemann/MGH group out of the planning of the building and the mental health catchment areas and regions. Lindemann expressed a rare emotional outburst and phoned the DMH to intervene. He and Solomon came to an agreement about the division of turf in partnerships between teaching hospitals and the DMH in the development of CMH programs. Fred Frankel represented Lindemann in these efforts. Negotiations involved HMS, MGH, and DMH. For instance, in seeking research staff, Peter Dews of HMS and Gardner Quarton and Lindemann of the MGH corresponded with David A. Drachman at the National Institutes of Health:[107]"a new psychiatric unit to be directed by our Department and located in the new governmental buildings . . . at the edge of the development area on Bowdoin Square" (Lindemann, December 3, 1962):

the state of Massachusetts plans to build a new hospital in the Bowdoin Square region which would be administered and staffed by the Massachusetts General Hospital. The goal is to develop a center for the care and treatment of mental disorders with primary concern for the interrelations between hospital and community. This new venture will give us an opportunity to expand our staff, and we shall require individuals with a variety of special interests. As director of research in the department, I am interested in adding individuals who have research potentials.

(Quarton)

Lindemann's long-term administrative assistant, Jean Farrell, continued her dedication to his efforts and his deserved rewards by leading an indefatigable mission to name the CMHC for him.[108] Their petition to the state senate read as follows:[109]

[The mental health center is to be named] in honor of Dr. Erich Lindemann, pioneer in the development of community mental health concepts and founder of the first community mental health center in this country, The Human Relations Service of Wellesley. Dr. Lindemann established a firm foundation in the community mental health field, setting up training programs for psychiatrists, psychologists and social workers. He carried out several research projects dealing with problems of community mental health including the study of the effects of forced relocation on the former residents of the West End of Boston which study today is most helpful to the federal government in coping with the emotional stress involved in such relocation processes. Dr. Lindemann formulated the initial plan for the Government Center Mental Health Center and has great hope that it will serve a truly important role in maintaining good mental health for the citizens of Massachusetts. The commissioner of mental health shall cause a suitable tablet bearing said designation and commemorating his pioneer efforts in community mental health be erected within the said building and he shall also cause suitable lettering to be placed upon the outside of said building bearing said designation.

The dedication of the Erich Lindemann Mental Health Center (ELMHC) amply expressed the ambivalence of this building and its role between the CMH/social psychiatry concept of enhancing the community's mental health and the psychopathological tradition of professional treatment of people with mental illness on a larger, community-wide scale. Gerald Klerman, the first superintendent of the ELMHC and Harbor Area Mental Health director, came from the mixed experience of having been a psychoanalyst and the superintendent of the socially active Connecticut Mental Health Center and since then reforming himself to be a biological psychiatrist conforming to institutional roles and norms.[110] He saw that the goal of the reorganization of the state mental health services under the federal CMHC act

was to provide an effective local mechanism whereby mental health services, training and research would be brought closer to the residents of the local communities. Moreover, Area Boards were created to provide a mechanism for direct community participation in the planning and delivery of services.

(p. 1)

The CMHC

> will be the location of inpatient services, special outpatient services, research and administration. We see our responsibility as providing a comprehensive network of mental health and intellectual disabilities services for the citizens in the Harbor Area. . . . Our overall goal is to develop a network of dispersed and decentralized services to meet the needs of this diverse group of communities.
>
> (p. 2)

To begin, there would be 110 staff members at the CMHC or 150 staff if community facility staff are included: 12 psychiatrists, nine psychologists, 12 social workers, 24 nurses, 27 mental health workers (a goal was to employ 31 unemployed or economically disadvantaged community residents so that they could contribute their knowledge as well as the ELMHC contributing to the reversal of unemployment). It was estimated that ultimately there would be 400–500 staff members.

> I . . . hope that this monumental building will serve as a home base, backing up a dispersed network of community mental health services. This would fulfill the dream of Dr. Lindemann who first put forth some of the basic concepts of social psychiatry and community mental health three decades ago.
>
> (p. 3)

Dr. Lindemann characteristically tried to empathize with the situation that he faced and see potentials for more constructive adaptation. His associations and reactions included the following:[111]

> a ceremony of transition . . . baptism . . . acceptance into the kinship group. . . . <u>namegiving</u> . . . powerful processes, intercessionary. . . . Immediately the joy of the honour is blended with a sense of having to give something. . . . Can this be in a service? . . . Integration of biologic into psychologic as addressed by Cobb . . . Allen Gregg . . . priests—government . . . remember Harry Solomon then the. . . [MGH] internal—[Francis O.] Schmitt [MGH trustee] . . . Worcester. . . . Danvers (internal planning) and finally an architectural structure to enfold a social structure . . . my pleasure in being at the meetings—the contrasts, the complexity . . . the flexibility. . . . All this is also an aspect of the social network, Inside: the many branches . . . Outside—Administration, Professionalism, Community. . . . Those who receive services want to know . . . want to share responsibility . . . want to give in a small measure. . . . John Knowles is a pioneer in community medicine. . . . Another Allen Gregg who 50 years ago founded [psychiatric services in general hospitals]. . . .

And now I extend my best wishes to Dr. Klerman and indeed to the whole magnificent group of . . . the Medical School and the Hospital and will be watching eagerly how it all goes!

This mixed result of the mixed interests of the CMH movement, MGH, HMS, state and federal governments, the local Roman Catholic Church, the mental health area community, and Lindemann and his colleagues was nevertheless marked by a triumphant reception.[112] It included an introduction by Joseph V. DeLena, EdD, president of the Harbor Area Board; an invocation by the Reverend Elfrid T. Bouvier, SJ, past president of the Harbor Area Board; the foregoing welcome by Gerald L. Klerman, MD, superintendent of the ELMHC; greetings of the Commonwealth of Massachusetts by governor Francis W. Sargent; recognition of the Massachusetts General Court (the state legislature) by the Hon. Mario Umana, senate majority leader; the speech "Mental Health in the 70s" by Milton Greenblatt, MD, commissioner of the DMH; a presentation of the plaque by Dr. Milton Greenblatt and its acceptance by Robert H. Ebert, MD, dean of the HMS, Leon Eisenberg, MD, chief of the MGH Psychiatry Service, and John H. Knowles, MD, MGH general director; a response by Erich Lindemann, MD, professor of psychiatry, emeritus, HMS; and the speech "Community Mental Health: A Center of Focus" by Bertram S. Brown, MD, director of the NIMH. A reception and tour of the building followed. The plaque installed on the building reads as follows:[113]

THE ERICH LINDEMANN MENTAL HEALTH CENTER; This building is dedicated to Erich Lindemann, MD, PhD, a pioneer in the development of community mental health concepts. Dr. Lindemann founded in 1948 the first community mental health center in this country and was one of the first to help develop techniques for community consultation and crisis intervention. An important part of his work was done in the West End of Boston.

Reactions to this dedication reflect the mixture of the gratification of this recognition and its contrast with reminiscences of Lindemann's community-based concept of CMH:

GERALD KLERMAN:[114] "So many have commented on your so naturally warm and personally effective manner. . . . We . . . firmly pledge a continuous effort to provide a totally functional community mental health service always in appreciation of the time and effort put forth by the brilliant and devoted men as yourself. It is an honor and privilege to be directing the Erich Lindemann Mental Health Center. I thank you".

ALEXANDER LEIGHTON, MD, HEAD OF THE HSPH DEPARTMENT OF BEHAVIORAL SCIENCES:[115] He regretted that it was not possible to get to the dedication but sent his congratulations and strong sense of fitness of the occasion: "You help us re-dedicate ourselves".

MARION NILES, WELLESLEY RESIDENT, A KEY SUPPORTER OF THE DEVELOP-MENT AND MAINTENANCE OF THE HRS:[116] "As I read the fact sheet, I felt that the building would be a center for carrying out those pro-grams in which you have been a pioneer always emphasizing the close touching with people and community—not as I think you feared might be just a building for offices and committees—far removed from community concepts. Those first days with H.R.S. under your leadership are some of the most cherished reminiscences of my life and I love to think I defied Bill Rice in wanting to waylay you on your way to catch the boat back to Portsmouth from Star Island. It was the beginning of a friendship in which Betty has joined".

PEG WARING, HRS STAFF MEMBER:[117] "I recall a conversation with Erich a long time ago in which he ruefully commented that he had failed to fulfill his grandfather's expectation that he would enter the minis-try. . . . I impetuously remarked that Erich had had a long career as an evangelist".

HUGH R. LEAVELL:[118] "You have done so much for the entire field of men-tal health in Massachusetts, that a finite memorial is in order. Even more significant in my opinion, are the many memorials written in the lives and the careers of your students and your associates. I am glad to be among those who have been stimulated and encouraged by the association with you. Your inspiration and patience have been very important to me, and I am eternally grateful for them".

ERICH LINDEMANN:[119] "It gives me great satisfaction that the development of the new building and the community program it will facilitate is part of the broader enterprise in social and community medicine which is being fostered by the Medical School".

The result for MGH was a mental hospital, ironically later named after Erich Lindemann.

Mental Health Center had responsibility for clinical services to defined areas, but Lindemann would have preferred decentralized services, including supportive day programs (as in the former West End's Lincoln House settlement house) and a hotel for inpatient care. The MGH direc-tor of social work, Eleanor Clark, held negotiations for social work staff-ing, which eventually broke down.

"Relocation and Mental Health—Adaptation Under Stress" (The West End Study)

A major focus of MHS work would be the West End (WE), the neighbor-hood of Boston around the MGH. The hospital seemed to be moving toward providing service to this local community for which it was the major medical resource. In addition, the Boston Redevelopment Authority was preparing to remove these 2500 families, lower-class and lower-middle-class Italian, Jewish, Slavic, and other immigrants and residuals of past immigrant waves. This population presented a high level of need and research opportunities, with high rates of justice-involved youth, poverty and welfare use, people with several problems, and social instability. Lindemann described this project as an outgrowth of the family and community mental health work at the HRS:[120]

> As we reach the end of the pilot period in our program in mental health [HRS] which the Grant Foundation so generously supported we are looking forward to a five-year support of our efforts by the Professional Services Branch of the National Institute of Mental Health. In the form of a community laboratory of the Department of Psychiatry of Harvard and the Massachusetts General Hospital the focus of our effort . . . will remain the careful study of the adaptation of families of the West End of Boston who will be relocated in other areas of Boston . . . to make room for a redevelopment program with the hope that our studies will provide significant material for future planning of redevelopment projects in various cities.

In fact, he saw the West Project as expanding CMH from influencing community life to influence national policy:[121]

> we have received word . . . that a substantial grant was given to us for a period of five years to continue the work concerning mental health problems in the neighborhood of the Massachusetts General Hospital. . . . Perhaps we will have an opportunity to make a modest contribution to the future of city planning in relocation areas.

Before launching new programs, MHS-affiliated social workers surveyed the area to learn about the community and coordinate work with community agencies. Between 1955 and 1958, a planning group got support from the director of the DMH Division of Mental Hygiene (Arthur C. K. Hallock), the MGH general director (Dean Clark), the director of the Boston Redevelopment Authority (Kane Simonian), and some members of the MGH GEC (including the chief of orthopedics) in regard to consultation with West End agencies and a survey of its residents. It started to develop a mental health program for the West End, which extended to the neighborhoods of Charlestown, East Boston, and the North End.[122] The MHS proposed a nursery school/program of children's activities at the MGH and a research program in social behavior in early childhood. They were interested in learning about community problems, the needs of community agencies and the effect redevelopment would have on them, and attitudes toward mental health programs and in developing cooperation with community agencies regarding mental health issues. In the process of this work, a rich collection of formal and informal studies and proposals was generated.[123]

The study was presented as an example of the MHS's introduction of CMH-integrated service and research:[124]

> The focus was on the WE: MGH was moving toward more services to this community. Planning for the evacuation of this population constituted a major crisis with the consequent need for mental health help and the opportunity for study of this phenomenon. The West End and vicinity exhibited the highest rate of juvenile delinquency in the city. "It is an area characterized by poverty, social instability, by chronically dependent 'multiproblem' inhabitants, and by concomitant earmarks of decline". [Note that this characterization contrasts with later concepts of the West End as a vital and healthy society.] Activities of the Mental Health Project: The Area Survey of health, welfare, and religious organizations serving the WE. The Joint Consultation Seminar of the Mental Health Staff With Boston Department of Public Welfare Workers—the Department of Public Welfare provided insights into hazards to the mental health of the community, and MGH provides increased knowledge and skills; five sessions; evaluation of process and outcome would lead to planning further work with the Department of Public Welfare and other agencies. Plans for Expansion of the Program: Depends on grown in staff. Consultation to other WE agencies. Demonstration projects with "anchor agencies" to experiment with reaching hard core, multi-problem families. Research and demonstration projects regarding identified cases likely to be helped. Research Plans and Interests: Assess the emotional health of residents resulting from the relocation crisis. Evaluate group consultation as a technique in preventive psychiatry. Clinical analysis of deserted families and the men who have deserted families. Comparison of multi-problem vs. normal families.

The West End Study was looked to for further expansion of these ideas, their use as a vehicle for the further introduction of social psychiatry into the MGH, and collecting hard data validating them. The study proposal was presaged in a funding application that may have been submitted to the W.T. Grant Foundation, Inc., which had contributed to CMH in the HRS and the MHS:[125]

> The primary object of this investigation is to clarify the personal and communal significance and consequences of a special stress: the geographical relocation of the residents of a Boston slum area. Our aim is to study the expectations and the actual changes which come about and to [relate] the differences in attitude and adaptive behavior to

personal, social, and cultural variables. . . . [It] provides a unique opportunity for studying: (a) the expectations, problems, and consequences of a change in geographical and social space; and (b) the meaning and significance, positive and negative, of many aspects of the physical and social environment of a slum. We plan, therefore, to study the interrelationship between psychological, social, and cultural factors which serve as stabilizing or disruptive factors in a slum community, and the satisfaction and dissatisfactions they promote, and the range of adaptations to a new physical and social environment which are possible to the former inhabitants of a slum . . . a number of . . . questions and hypotheses have already emerged. 1. . . variations in reaction to leaving the slum environment . . . the desire to leave the slum and ability to take such actions as opposed to a determination not to leave (a) For some people, the positive values of the slum location lie in the freedom to maintain a life style which . . . is deviant from non-slum, American norms . . . demographic variables (e.g., ethnic background) and psychological characteristics (e.g., regressive defenses) . . . may correlate with these values (b) . . . one of the most critical features of the slum for many people . . . is the extended family interaction. Leaving the slum . . . appears to signify a major loss of stability . . . We wish to know whether the primary significance of such extended kinship units lies in the affectional ties, in its structured stability, or in its adaptive significance (requiring character adaptations to a group which are incompatible with the middle class "isolation" and independence . . . we would like to know the range of . . . adaptations . . . once relocation takes place. (c) . . . We should like . . . to know some of the correlates of . . . a pseudo-family relationship to care-taking agencies: Cultural, social, and psychological (d) . . . for some of the population, the press to move out of the slum may appear as an opportunity to create a new and more desirable way of life. . . . [They] differ in many respects from those who can see only the disadvantages of moving . . . differences in social characteristics and in psychological characteristics . . . the difference in adaptation . . . to the new environment of those who had some positive expectations as compared with those who expected only the worst. . . . 2. An essential feature of the study . . . is a social psychiatric investigation of a slum community. Our knowledge of lower socioeconomic class communities, from either a social or psychological point of view, is very meager . . . for control purposes we have . . . data, and facilities for obtaining further comparative data, from middle class communities in Wellesley; or we may consider studying a non-slum working class group (a) . . . we would like to study . . . the patterns of social attitudes and values in this lower socio-economic group . . . we wish to inquire into the ways in which those . . . attitude and value formation, personal dispositions and social experience, are incorporated into the attitudinal framework and value orientation (b) . . . a number of survey studies have suggested an inverse relationship between social class and incidence of psychiatric disturbance . . . we hope both to evaluate this hypothesis and to study . . . the sociocultural variables . . . and the psychological variables . . . involved. . . . [We look forward to] the establishment of criteria of mental health and illness one can meaningfully apply to this slum population. . . . C. Significance of this research . . . 1. Adaptation under the special stress of relocation. . . . The practical importance of such knowledge . . . will allow us, in future programs, to modify relocation plans . . . 2. An understanding of the psychosocial problems of a slum . . . this is an essential prerequisite for evaluating problems of mental health and for preventive public health planning which takes full account of the needs and wishes of people in the slum . . . 3. Mental health problems in a slum community. . . . The study should contribute markedly to our present understanding . . . of the nature and correlates of psychiatric disturbance . . . it also will allow us to expand our knowledge of the relations between mental illness and environment; and to develop an ecological model. . . . 4. Training in mental health research . . . an opportunity for teaching research methods in Mental Health to clinically trained personnel. It should also provide a wider background in community mental health for social workers, psychologists, psychiatrists, and graduate students. . . . 5. Community laboratory . . . a division of the Department of Psychiatry of Harvard Medical School and the Massachusetts General Hospital, would be dedicated to the multi-disciplinary investigation of community life . . . already available in middle class community (Wellesley, Massachusetts). We would hope to expand into other areas for comparative studies and to make data and facilities available to other interested research groups.

(pp. 1–8)

An advisory group to the study was assembled to include both those who could contribute a wide range of expertise and those who could be educated in CMH to become its supporters:[126]

George P. Berry, MD, [dean] Harvard Medical School; Dr. Leonard Duhl, Professional Services Branch, National Institute of Mental Health; Dr. Alex Inkeles, professor of sociology, H.U.; Mr. Robert W. Kennedy, 8A Eliot St, Cambridge, MA; Professor Martin Meyerson, Center for Urban Studies, H.U.; Dr. Ben Paul [anthropologist], HSPH; Dr. Robert Rapaport, McLean Hospital; Dr. Robert Reed, HSPH; Dr. John Seeley, director of research, Alcoholism Research Foundation, Toronto, Canada; Dr. Joseph Stokes, III, [director] Family Health Service, MGH; Dr. John Whiting, Department of Social

Relations, Harvard University; Dr. Dean A. Clark, [general director] MGH; Dr. John Stoeckle [director, Medical Outpatient Department, MGH]; Dr. Herbert Gans, Institute for Urban Studies, Philadelphia, PA; Dr. Lawrence Frank; Dr. Riesman, Dr. Erich Lindemann, Dr. Gerald Caplan, Dr. Marc Fried, Dr. Peter E. Sifneos, Mr. Lawrence Frank, Belmont.

Early in the project, a planning group gave careful thought to the effect that this study might have on those with political, economic, and ideological stakes in the West End renewal:[127]

> Extension of planning for the WE project included Gerald Caplan, Leonard Duhl, and Laura Morris. This included "c) Since more urban redevelopment projects are anticipated throughout urban centers, it was felt that a 'look-at' some of the problems involved for the people and the neighborhood via this change could be useful material to put in the hands of officials and communities elsewhere who would attempt similar projects". [This foreshadows later claims of having changed urban development policies.] "It was further felt that the project might benefit by an independence from the M.G.H. setting. This was particularly brought out in view of the fact that M.G.H. upholds the present urban redevelopment plans and might well view our activity at some point as 'stirring up trouble' and could attempt presumably to sabotage. It was recognized that there are techniques which must be employed to keep several power forces from misunderstanding the project. It was suggested that the objective for the project was to report and observe what was happening, that the project would not be involved in the politics or policies around the present project in the West End. There was recognition of the fact that this latter point would be difficult to maintain and to interpret".

Despite the demurs, the study of the mental health significance of urban renewal and forced population relocation carried CMH further into social policy and political decision-making:[128]

> When we started out in the West End we thought about . . . crisis behavior in a predicament affecting a population . . . in terms of health and disease, of well being and possible disintegration . . . but much more important seems a new orientation which breaks down the boundary between health and welfare agencies and includes the component of human development over time as affected by the circumstances of a historical situation. It is perhaps not surprising, therefore, that the life style, the cognitive orientation and the central adaptive problems of a working class population had to be considered in detail in order to form a basis for inference about agency use

and agency function not only in the medical field but also in that of welfare and education.

There has emerged in our minds the necessity for fostering and training professional persons dedicated to social action and to the scientific basis of social action, utilizing the resources not only of the health sciences but also those inquiries which deal unabashedly with issues of the "good life", satisfaction and achievement, of poverty and access to community resources, and of class and ethnic conflict.

I believe we have learned to see community problems in a new way and are asking questions in a way which might make us more useful to city planners, to welfare agencies and to political decision makers. This new venture of inquiry is about community-wide well being or failure at times of crisis and transition.

We are deeply grateful to you for your eager participation in our thinking and to the Professional Services Branch for the generous support it has given us.

The West End Study exemplified the community mental health approach. Lindemann referred to it and the emotional reaction of families forced to find new homes because of slum clearance, families displaced by the West End housing project.[129] The West End Study embodied an important step in the expansion of Lindemann's concept of the centrality of psychosocial crisis to life stress and coping, from the individual and family to society at large. He had always theorized that the loss and repair of key social relationships applied not only to individual grief but to populations as a whole, and he suggested the appropriateness of preventive intervention on a social policy level.

The predecessor of the West End Study was initially the attempt to have the MGH duplicate with its West End setting HRS's involvement in the fabric and health of its host community. It deepened into the effect on the community of rumors of urban renewal of its homeland. The opportunity to test this enlargement of the purview of CMH to the effects of public policy came when Boston mayor John F. Collins (a champion of renovating cities), through the Boston Redevelopment Authority, decided on an urban redevelopment policy of clearing a working-class population from a financially underperforming and potentially profitable city property to make way for land use profitable to private housing developers and the city's tax income. This affected an area of 47.9 acres, encompassing 3075 families—2122 eligible for public housing.[130] The project would cost $13 million and took place from June 1956 to April 1962. Private housing developers lobbied for this as a profit windfall. Local institutions saw opportunities to advance their interests—for example, the Massachusetts General Hospital to acquire land for expansion, and the Roman Catholic Church to make use of dormant land holdings. The first- and second-generation immigrant working-class population had little political influence on these decisions. There were loud protests from social advocacy groups and local political representatives—Massachusetts State Representatives Christopher Ianella and Charles Caprano, State Senator Mario Umana, and Boston School Committee chairperson Joseph Lee—aimed at the Urban Redevelopment Section of the Boston Housing Authority, which was sensitive to charges of being unfeeling. There were efforts to redirect policy, legal challenges, and public protests. They ultimately failed in the face of determined political and economic interests.

Lindemann saw the West End renewal as an inevitable human-caused disaster for the population affected and a bad form of urban renewal.[131] He looked out the windows of the MGH psychiatry unit at the wrecking balls demolishing rows of tenement houses and, with tears in his eyes, murmured, "They don't know what they are doing!" (to this human community). He saw the destruction of the web of social relations of an entire community that did not figure into public policy decisions and decided that documenting a study of it would be a natural experiment with his strategy of influencing public policy through teaching rather than political action.

Leonard Duhl, who shared Lindemann's social sympathies and CMH perspective, had been appointed to the Professional Services Branch of the NIMH. He was interested in mental and general hospitals as foci of community development and in city planning.[132] He collaborated with Lindemann in developing the West End NIMH research grant to address the impact of and level of coping with the stress of forced urban relocation and the crisis of urban renewal generally. The Space Cadets, which looked upon the physical environment from this social perspective, understood this project and helped modify the application and secure the grant to study this phenomenon in order to document crisis theory on a community-wide basis and to translate these findings into public policy as mental health preventive intervention for the larger society. Duhl remembers involving Herbert Gans,[133] Marc Fried, and others, some of whom also joined the Space Cadets. Lindemann met with Dean Clark, then general director of the MGH, and Martin Meyerson, a noted urban planner and, at the time, director of the Harvard Joint Center for Urban Studies, to look into health problems brought on by new real estate development in the MGH neighborhood as a vehicle for studying urban planning in this area.[134] Funding for the project officially began on December 1, 1957.[135]

Lindemann corresponded with Kane Simonian, the director of urban redevelopment in the Boston Housing Authority, asking for a meeting with the MGH MHS headed by Peter Sifneos and including Laura Morris.[136] He suggested they make themselves useful to the relocation authority and the families to be relocated by bringing their understanding of family problems in moving, why people are attached to a substandard neighborhood, and how to plan for them. William B. Spofford, Jr., the supervisory chaplain at MGH, invited Laura Morris to talk to a student chaplain group about the West End Project. He also appreciated the Psychiatry Service staff, including Clemens Benda, John Nemiah, and clinical psychologists, as well as Peter Sifneos' contributions to a couple of his students consulting in the outpatient department.[137]

There was wide interest in this study, both as social science research and in terms of political policy. Ray Elling saw it as a major step in the development of medical sociology and wrote a critique of his mixed experience with it:[138]

> [This promoted] the opening up of the field [medical sociology], especially in various medical- or health-related settings (as opposed to departments of sociology). Also, the Yale program had begun to receive recognition. . . . August Hollingshead, whose groundbreaking work on social class and mental illness had already become recognized, was a key sponsor in opening up opportunities. The most promising position seemed to be in the Harvard University Department of Psychiatry at the Massachusetts General Hospital with Professor Erich Lindemann and his many colleagues in social psychiatry. . . . Lindemann was a very engaging and impressive person. When he interviewed me . . . in the spring of 1957, he penetrated easily . . . my major intellectual and perhaps emotional and family concerns. . . . I should have been much more concerned with the specifics of the position and related research. At first the return [from a study trip to Germany] was exciting. . . . Erich Lindemann suggested at an early point that I talk with Dr. John Stoeckle, head of the Medical Outpatient Department at the Massachusetts General Hospital. . . [which] turned into an exciting exchange which we repeated often during the year. His interest in medical linguistics . . . and my concern with conceptions and expressions of self seemed to form a natural match. We discussed events which precipitated persons from the West End or elsewhere coming to the clinic, also the training of medical and nursing personnel and division of labor in caring for "nonorganic" problems. . . . Some of his later work with Irving Zola reflects in part a systematic pursuit of the themes. . . . The weekly staff meetings of the study center were very exciting a first. All kinds of visiting firemen dropped by and tidbits of information from the West End were spun up into more or less appropriate-seeming connections with one grand theory or another. Leonard Duhl, Gerald Caplan, Benjamin Paul, and Eliot Mischler were among the more frequent visitors. . . . the director [Marc Fried—social psychologist] . . . was much taken by [Talcott] Parsons' grand theorizing . . . when this colleague confided to me . . . that his real ambition was to develop a theory which would integrate Freud, Durkheim, and Weber, I became uneasy.

Real disillusionment set in when I realized that there was no systematic "before" measure of the West End population's orientations and behavior to compare with their adaptive patterns wherever they located. Among other things, the theorizing and talk had kept the first-wave interviewing from entering the field on time. . . . with the surplus of exciting talk, opportunities for recouping on remaining segments of the sample while they were still in the West End were being lost by a not very rigorous or energetic approach to the scheduling of interviews. . . . When I looked through the interview schedule . . . self-conceptions and the full range of social participation were key spheres either missing or much underdeveloped . . . in terms of significant losses.

After making my concerns known and finding some defensiveness . . . I decided to follow [Herbert] Gans's [sociologist in the West End Project] rather independent course . . . for a study of . . . first- and second-generation Italian males in the West End of Boston . . . my first sharp encounter with disciplinary jealousies and conceptions. Had the director . . . been an NORC-trained sociologist, I believe I would not have resisted or encountered the resistance I did . . . considering the brief tenures of Gans and myself, as well as a Michigan-trained sociologist who followed me . . . support for my ideas and concerns came from medically oriented and medically trained colleagues with a direct interest or experience in social aspects of medicine who did not have or exercise hierarchical relations with me. There were basic disagreements and difficulties with the project director which involved authority and jealousy over autonomy of decision making.

Note that Elling found that "Lindemann was very supportive and did not act in a directive hierarchical manner, even though he had overall authority".

(pp. 62–7)

In the political area, Howard W. Hallman, who was about to take charge of the New Haven (Connecticut) urban renewal for Middle Ground (aiming at neighborhood improvement rather than clearance) wanted to learn about the West End Study's findings about the effects of relocation on people; Lindemann referred him to Marc Fried for research findings.[139] With Gerald Caplan's introduction, Lindemann corresponded with Kalman J. Mann, MD, medical director of the Hadassah Medical Organization in Jerusalem, Israel, who had experience in providing comprehensive medical and recreational care for new immigrants.[140] Lindemann wrote,

We are in the process of studying the reaction of a population in the neighborhood of the hospital to forced relocation to other parts of metropolitan Boston and we are now turning to preparations for a program of medical care for a new population which will be located in the rebuilt area. Our interest is centered on mental health issues. Your experience in Israel may be very helpful to us in clarifying our ideas.[141]

G. Ronald Hargreaves, the Nuffield professor of psychiatry at the University of Leeds (Great Britain) was warmly appreciative of visits by social workers, psychologists, a senior registrar (resident), and Hargreaves to the West End Study, HRS, MGH, and McLean Hospital.[142] Lindemann's careful scientific and professional approach to CMH is illustrated by his insistence on waiting for solid data before taking social action: William B. Collins, reporter for the *Cincinnati Enquirer*, saw the parallel of the West End Study with the Cincinnati plan to relocate 10,000 African American families from its own West End slum as part of a massive urban redevelopment project. There was concern about the social but not emotional effects, and he wondered whether the West End Study could contribute to the newspaper's story—the paper had a standing interest in community matters. Lindemann refused because the West End Study was not far enough advanced to provide valid experience.[143]

The Center for Community Studies and Social Science Research Laboratory

The Center for Community Studies was the closest that Lindemann got to establishing a social science unit for basic research and informed mental health practice—something he proposed many times. The Center was established to house the West End project. Lindemann was the grant's principle investigator, and he appointed Marc Fried, a young social psychologist, as research director.[144] Community organization, social and clinical psychology, sociology, and anthropology research projects were undertaken. The project carefully avoided judgment about urban relocation but sought to advise other relocation programs based on the West End experience. Efforts we made to study the adaptation of the population as well as mental and physical health casualties and basic cultural and community structure.[145] They worked with community "service-oriented" caretakers. The project operated independently of the MGH because that institution favored redevelopment and might see the study as troublesome and creating problems. However, the MGH MHS work with the West End continued simultaneously.

In the early period of the West End Study, when it was located at the MGH, Lindemann's ideas were always discussed, for instance with Herbert Gans, the compatible sociologist on the project. Though he wrote in the language of sociology, Gans included these ideas in his participant-observer studies of the character of working-class life and its reaction to relocation.[146] When the project moved to another location with researchers who had not worked with him, Lindemann became an occasional and irrelevant visitor whose clinical and epidemiological thrust was discarded in favor of social structure and dynamics.

An abiding conflict developed between Lindemann and Fried over the direction of the project:[147] Lindemann, a mental health clinician, looked forward to case studies of the clinical effects of disruption of the social environment on mental health, the power and influence of poor and middle-class cultures, and "responsible participation" in informing and influencing the power structure (an echo of his outspoken gymnasium professor). Fried, a social psychologist, saw an opportunity to study the social structure, with mental illness as only one of its many products. Lindemann was surprised and disappointed at the statistics[148] but, being modest, nonhurtful, and reluctant to force obedience on others, refused a direct clash. Perhaps his preoccupation with MGH administration and his approaching retirement also lessened his influence. He let Fried take his own direction as he had when he left the HSPH education program to Gerald Caplan.[149] He felt left out but was proud of the project, satisfied that he had put his stamp on it, and he distanced himself from the study without giving it his clear blessing. Fried resented this lack of blessing and participation, and the researchers developed their own contacts with the funding source and their sense of autonomy. He saw Lindemann as an innovator in psychiatry who showed the importance of the social network, meaningful relationships, their relationship to psychopathology, and thus implications for real prevention of mental illness. He shared ideas openly with Gerald Caplan. Fried thought that these were not new ideas in the social sciences, in which Lindemann was not sophisticated, and that CMH did not take up this important redirection. He saw Lindemann as too preoccupied with the reactions that others might have to his activities and preoccupied with his MGH responsibilities. Because of this feeling of a lack of appreciation and support, Fried maintained an abiding hatred of Lindemann.

Lindemann's clinical concern reared its head in the social science research findings: To the social science researchers, grief was only incidentally included as a possible response to relocation, and it came as a surprise that it was a major issue. It was not a surprise to the clinicians: Laura Morris and Peter Sifneos consulted with welfare, nursery school, church, settlement house, and gang workers who saw behavioral evidence of grief: Gang members hanging around turf that had been cleared of buildings, two old sisters refusing to move, and aberrant behavior in medical settings were all linked to loss of community and place. And in the Space Cadets, there had been exploration of the meaning and use of space—ethologists' ideas of claiming territory. The West End Project observed people having problems leaving their space when they had never crossed the community's major boundary streets and were unused to detached houses. Lindemann was receptive to adding this new idea to the research plan.

The MGH MHP's work with the West End community predated and then fed into the West End Study.[150] Lindemann understood the significance of the relationship of institutions and the MGH to the community and hired Laura Morris in 1955–1956 to deal with this relationship, act as liaison with the West End Community, and do preliminary planning before the formal research project. She respected community feelings and later helped develop a home care program. She was appointed associate director of the MGH Social Work Training Program and an MGH staff member. Since she was paid from the Child Psychiatry Unit before training grants and West End Study grants were available, social workers resented her.

Morris found Lindemann committed to learning about people and applying resources to strengthening their function. She thought inner-city people, street behavior, and settlement houses were new to him, though his wife, a social worker, worked in settlement houses, including in the West End. His mental health consultation with a young settlement house group worker made her more effective than hospital treatment by social workers and psychiatrists, as his consultation with gang workers helped them be available to upset children. These were Lindemann's concepts of community mental health.

Morris and Sifneos had lunch with the director of the Boston Redevelopment Authority to discuss the problems of the dislocated population. The mental health professionals learned about the bureaucracy from an old politician, and the director was fascinated that MGH doctors were interested. The program met with gang workers, public welfare staff, nursery school staff, etc. about their observations, before the research project; developed links with them; and continued mental health consultation with these groups. There was a complex and delicate relationship among the urban renewal forces, which wanted the land for economic purposes; the MGH, which wanted land for expansion; the MGH Department of Psychiatry, which had contradictory reactions to this process; and Lindemann; who wanted research to be supportive of mental health and not detrimental to the community. In the community, there were strong feelings against the MGH, which had not served the community but would be staying in their homeland. "Left-wing" politicians identified Lindemann with MGH's self-interests, which led to a negative incident involving Lindemann. Morris was put in the uncomfortable position of explaining that Lindemann and the Psychiatry Department's interests were different from those of the MGH, including making it possible to address the sources of this hostility. She contacted key West End people who facilitated Lindemann's talks in the community, which changed his image to one of a friend. In another instance, Frieda Rogalsky, a worker in the Peabody House settlement house, knew John Knowles,

MGH general director, and how to break through the system so that hospital rules changed and its Emergency Ward was made accessible to the community.

As mentioned earlier, one of Lindemann's first projects in developing social and community psychiatry in the department was the following:

> A Behavioral Science Laboratory: Widening the horizon of psychiatric activities in this manner has necessitated the development of a strong and active program in basic behavioral science. Within the last year we have added four psychologists well trained in clinical and experimental methods; one expert in child development; one worker in community organization and an outstanding sociologist to our group. Their influence has been marked both in greater precision of diagnosis and prognosis, and in developing our research program.[151]
>
> (p. 2)

As part of the plan to further develop social psychiatry as a major unit in the MGH Psychiatry Department, Marc Fried and Judith Rosenblith proposed a Psychosocial Research Laboratory. Its goals were to provide leadership in social science investigation, participation in planning psychosocially related research, and coordination among MGH social scientists.[152]

> Proposals Concerning a Psychosocial Research Laboratory: most of the problems of personnel, space, financing, and relations with clinical services and facilities are quite similar for both the biological and the social psychiatric units. Yet, the Psychiatric Laboratories have been able to deal with these issues systematically as a unit, composed of several senior staff members working together in a single laboratory. . . . The isolated nature of these [social science] investigations appears to contribute to the fact that social psychiatric thinking occupies a relatively peripheral position in relation to departmental activity as a whole in spite of the large scale of social psychiatric and social science commitments. In view of your own work in these areas, the importance of these considerations in your own thinking, and the great expansion of social science and social psychiatric investigation in other institutions, the possibility for more basic integration and coordination would seem to warrant our attention. . . . The different research units which have a social science orientation should be integrated into a single unit, a psychosocial research laboratory. Minimally this should include the current Center for Community Studies and the Center for Studies in Human Development . . . among these current units which might bear different types of relationship to a central psychosocial research laboratory. . . . The Emergency Ward Study (Duhl), the Alcoholism Research (Chafetz-Blane),

social science research at Wellesley [HRS] ([Ozzie] Simmons), and the work of individuals such as John Hill and Ralph Switzgabel. . . . The administrative model might well follow the same lines as that of the Stanley Cobb Psychiatric Laboratories. One might envision a set of relatively independent research units headed by their respective professional chiefs and coordinated through an overall director. . . . A more consistent affiliation with other social science research activities and social psychiatric investigations in our local, geographic area appears desirable. One possible means of achieving this might be the establishment of an advisory board composed of senior social scientists working in the Boston area. . . . Relatively long-term support should be considered for at least several senior investigators . . . spell out some of the common issues concerning community studies, studies in human development, and other related issues . . . a broad program of research for community studies or child development studies or both. . . . It would be ideal to have a full-scale laboratory with both office and research space in addition to adjunct facilities, e.g. computer equipment, etc. Short of this. . . [a] common conference room, common location of office space, and common basic technical facilities. . . . A Psychosocial Research Laboratory should develop meaningful ties and programs related to (a) the Stanley Cobb Psychiatric Laboratories, (b) the clinical psychiatric services, (c) other hospital facilities and units.

(pp. 1–4)

There were explorations of leadership and a location for the center.[153] A Research Center for Studies in Human Development was designated with Judy F. Rosenblith, PhD, as coordinator. She wrote to Lindemann about the need to add research staff to achieve a viable mass of workers. The arrival of Jerome Kagan at the HDSR gave hope for increased interaction with that body. Rosenblith and Marc Fried recommended the development of a behavioral research center,[154] which presaged the Center for Community Studies, directed by Fried, and mainly occupied with the study of the social and mental health dynamics of a working-class community and the mental health effects of forced urban relocation (the West End Study). In 1964, the annual HMS Department of Psychiatry research conference was devoted to social science in psychiatry, including the function of psychiatric facilities in the community, and the registration of psychiatric predicaments and conditions in a general medical population.[155] However, in that year, funding for the continuation of the human development failed, and the uncooperative bent of the MGH Children's Medical Service interfered with collaborating with Jerome Kagan of the Harvard Psychology Department.[156]

Fried saw MGH as aloof and showing only a passing, superficial interest in the project. Presentations, new insights (e.g., in this culture, dependency was adaptive and not pathological), and papers drew no response. When Herbert Gans, a sociologist who had trained under David Riesman and was recommended to the project by Leonard Duhl, became too identified with and an activist for the population, Lindemann charged Fried with controlling him.

The reports and publications from the resultant research project The Mental Health Effects of Forced Urban Relocation would contribute to a major change in the incorporation of psychosocial and cultural needs and crises in the making of public policy.[157] Fried noted its influence:[158]

> Many of our experiences of participation involve exploring the possibilities of stimulating or encouraging effective planning and action programs on the basis of our findings, an objective strongly supported by the Special Grants Review Committee in the past. The very earliest results of our work, even the existence of such a study, stimulated concern among housing, renewal, and planning circles about exclusive attention to the physical objectives of slum clearance and redevelopment. At a very early date, before many findings were available, reports from the Housing and Home Finance Agency and the Urban Renewal Administration singled our study out for the implications our work carried for future policy decisions. In general, we have found that the willingness to consider our findings rests largely on the conception of planning and to some extent, its political purpose.

In a memo dated September 10, 1962, from Leonard J. Duhl, MD, a psychiatrist in the Professional Services Branch of NIMH and later chief of its Office of Planning, Duhl notes that the Housing & Home Finance Agency's publication on September 7 includes suggestions for urban research, including Replication of the West End Urban Relocation and Mental Health Study.[159] He reports that the Space Cadets "did indicate to us that it was important for the Branch to consider further work in the area of poverty, lower socio-class culture, the emerging groups, and various aspects of community organization".[160] Duhl quotes from that publication:

> The West End urban relocation and mental health study has already had an important impact on the field of urban studies, pointing as it does to the social values that may be found in a community characterized by substandard housing, and the extended impact of the relocation experience on many people removed from such communities. . . . new types of relocation procedures . . . might include efforts to relocate the entire community, or as much of it as wished to go, in a single area of high vacancy, in order to reduce the damage of

breaking up the community completely; greater use of social services; attempts, through subsided middle-income and low-income housing, to rehouse as large a proportion of the relocated on the same site; close staging of demolition, to time it directly with the beginning of new building (the avoidance of the empty-lot syndrome and that bombed-out feeling), etc.

Duhl notes, "No comments are necessary".

Notes

1. White, Benjamin V. (son-in-law of Stanley Cobb and author of Cobb biography), interview by David G. Satin at the Francis A. Countway Library, 12/3/1979.
2. Lindemann, Erich, "4th Joint Meeting of Harvard Community Mental Health Units 1/18/1954". [box II A&B, folder Joint Meetings HSPH Commun. Health Projects 1954, Center for the History of Medicine, Francis A., Countway Library of Medicine, Boston, MA]
3. "Summary of the Discussion between Dr. John Knowles and Dr. Erich Lindemann on September 29, 1961". [folder "GEC Report by Dr. Lindemann for Dept. of Psychiatry—Dec. 6, 1961", Box IIIB1b box 1 of 2, Erich Lindemann Collection, Center for the History of Medicine, Francis A. Countway Library of Medicine, Boston, MA]
4. Caner, G. Coket, MD, of Boston wrote Lindemann that MGH was remiss in not having an ECT service and reported that Raymond Adams, MGH chief of neurological medicine, agreed; 2/1/1957. [folder "Misc. Correspondence C—1956–5", Box IIIA 1–3, Lindemann Collection, Center for the History of Medicine, Francis A. Countway Library of Medicine, Boston, MA]
5. [folder "Shock Therapy", Box IIIA 4 (P-S), Erich Lindemann Collection, Center for the History of Medicine, Francis A. Countway Library of Medicine, Boston, MA, document 1961–1963]
6. Berry, George Packer, memo to Jack Ewalt with copies to the Harvard University faculty, Talcott Parsons (chairperson of the Harvard Department of Sociology), Edwin B. Newman (director of the Harvard Psychological Laboratories), and David G. McClelland (Harvard professor of psychology). [folder "Correspondence 1963", Box IIIA 1–3, Lindemann Collection, Center for the History of Medicine, Francis A. Countway Library of Medicine, Boston, MA]
7. Berry, George Packer, letter to Erich Lindemann 2/12/1963, p. 1. Gans, Herbert, *The Urban Villagers* (New York: The Free Press of Glencoe, 1962). [folder "Correspondence 1963", Box IIIA 1–3, Lindemann Collection, Center for the History of Medicine, Francis A. Countway Library of Medicine, Boston, MA]
8. Between February 14, 1960, and May 25, 1961, there was a plan for a joint education program between the MGH Psychiatry Service and the Florence Heller School at Brandeis University in which both MGH social work fellows and Brandeis students interested in education in CMH would get credit for courses taken in each other's programs, and Heller doctoral students could write dissertations at MGH. [folder "Boston Social Service Exchange Inc.", Box IIIA 4 (A-E), Erich Lindemann Collection, Center for the History of Medicine, Francis A. Countway Library of Medicine, Boston, MA]

9. Morris, Laura, 11/19/1979, *ibid.*
10. Lindemann, Erich, letter to Niels Pörksen, 3/22/1973. [box XII 1 folder E107 Poerksen, Erich Lindemann Collection, Center for the History of Medicine, Francis A. Countway Library of Medicine, Boston, MA]
11. Caplan, Gerald letter to Lindemann from the Tavistock Institue of Human Relations in London, 7/6/1964. [folder "Correspondence 1964", Box IIIA 1–3, Lindemann Collection, Center for the History of Medicine, Francis A. Countway Library of Medicine, Boston, MA]
12. Medical School, Teaching Hospital and Social Responsibility, Second Institute on Medical Center Problems, Association of American Medical Colleges (Miami, FL 12/9/64); Panel Meeting, Task Force on Economic Growth and Opportunity, U.S. Chamber of Commerce (Washington, DC, 12/10/1964)
13. Knowles, John H., "The Medical Center and the Community Health Center", *Bulletin of the New York Academy of Medicine* Second Series, *40* no. 9: 713–742 (pp. 713–741) (9/1964). [copy found in file "J.H.K owles— Meidical Center + Community M.H. Center", Box XII #3, Lindemann Collection, Center for the History of Medicine, Francis A. Countway Library of Medicine, Harvard Medical School, Boston, MA]

The paper reads in part as follows:

Medicine . . . knows almost nothing of social as contrasted with biological well-being. Little attention is paid by the medical world to such causes of social disease as parental inadequacy, overcrowding, the oppressive threat of scientific war, poverty, inadequate educational opportunities, the nontherapeutic uses of leisure, the misuse of the mass media, or the suppression and persecution of minority groups. Yet, medicine today . . . has become inextricably a part of larger societal concerns. The obligatory interrelationship of social, mental and somatic dis-ease . . . demands a review of medicine's expanding role and suggests new functional departures. . . . Should medicine attempt to give comprehensive care and should it arrogate to itself the solution of the world's social dis-ease, thereby perhaps becoming a surrogate for the community's responsibility? . . . the "health center" which finds itself restricted to the treatment of established somatic disease by teams of specialists. There is no public health or *preventive* medicine discipline available. Most . . . have no social service and, at best, only poorly developed outpatient ambulatory clinics. There is not honest attempt to provide continuity of care or extension of services to the community and into the home. There is little coordination or communication with the other caring institutions of the community . . . Should it seize the opportunity to become the focal point for the community health care . . . chronic disease and mental illness, the two major health problems of the latter half of the 20th century. . . . medical schools ignore the social, economic and organizational issues surrounding them and when the teaching hospital has not yet extended its interest to the community. . . . Social and preventive psychiatry is effectively extending the interests of psychiatry . . . into the community. The psychiatrist interested in prevention attempts to intervene at strategic points in the social system of the community so as to prevent mental disease which results from a disruption or inadequacy of the social system. . . . His intervention may promote the social well-being of the community by altering inadequate social systems . . . and helping to provide the needed facilities and methods of coping with crisis and acute mental disease. He is interested in the improvement of the educational system, the elimination of poverty, the evolution of the legal system . . . the adequacy of recreational facilities, the upheaval of communities and their relocation . . . the proper use of the mass media . . . should work closely with and understand intimately the political and other power structures of the community—in order to obtain action and adaptive change . . . Social and behavioral science background is desirable for this role in addition to traditional psychiatric training.

(pp. 713–24)

The plan may sound grandiose. It is! It may also imply that improvement of social conditions will decrease mental disease. This is true . . . It may also imply that the psychiatrist should run the entire community. He should not, but should function as consultant . . . from Leonard Duhl of the National Institutes [*sic*] of Mental Health, in the recent book, *The Urban Condition.* "The psychiatrist must truly be a political personage in the best sense of the word. He must play a role in controlling the environment which [humankind] has created". . . . The function of the preventive psychiatrist is to influence communities and their social systems to improve themselves, utilizing the existing facilities or providing new facilities and services where necessary. He works with groups rather than individuals to strengthen the social system . . . other members of the medical profession who look upon studies in the social and behavioral sciences as "nonscientific", . . . the psychiatrist as social scientist is the only one trying to study and improve the situation from the field of medicine and the rest of medicine has let these responsibilities go by default. . . . Now that he [the psychiatrist] has launched into the urban setting and utilized the social and behavioral sciences, a natural extension of his individualized care . . . isn't he really in the best position to provide continuity of care and to understand all aspects of the patient's problem? . . . So why should not the psychiatrist become the general practitioner of the urban hospital and the medical school, displacing the department of medicine . . . develop a "community health center", transforming the present medical center into a positive force in the prevention of dis-ease and in the improved provision of comprehensive health services. . . . Hospital-based community health centers could be linked with each other to facilitate the regional planning of health facilities. Social and economic research would improve the possibilities of the prevention of disease, the value of public health and rehabilitation programs, and the provision of increasingly costly services. . . . By an expansion of its psychiatric and ambulatory clinic programs, it can play a broader role as a community health center and. . . . The perspective of the medical profession will enlarge, and, with the others [social agencies centralized in the health center] . . . help provide solutions to the ever increasing social and economic problems that beset the community. Medicine is a social as well as a biological science. Medical school facilities and those who inhabit the hospitals must recognize this balance and . . . function on this basis.

(p. 725–41)

14. Lindemann, Erich, "The What, Why and How of Mental Health", 11/1956, p. 15. [folder "Joseph Macy Jr. Foundation 11/56", Box IIIA7 1955–9 1 of 3, Erich Lindemann Collection, Center for the History of Medicine, Francis A. Countway Library of Medicine, Boston, MA]
15. Bragg, Robert, interview by David G. Satin at the Wellesley Human Relations Service, 7/13/1979. [Erich Lindemann Collection, David G. Satin, Newton, MA]

16. Lindemann correspondence with Walter Bauer, 1/15–4/5/1962. [folder "B Miscellaneous 1 of 2 file folders", Box IIIA 4 (A-E), Lindemann Collection, Center for the History of Medicine, Francis A. Countway Library of Medicine, Boston, MA]

17. "Summary of the Discussion between Dr. John Knowles and Dr. Erich Lindemann on September 29, 1961", p. 3. [folder "GEC Report by Dr. Lindemann for Dept. of Psychiatry—December 6, 1961", Box IIIB1b box 1 of 2, Erich Lindemann Collection, Center for the History of Medicine, Francis A. Countway Library of Medicine, Boston, MA]

18. "Summary of the Discussion between Dr. John Knowles and Dr. Erich Lindemann on September 29, 1961", p. 3. [folder "GEC Report by Dr. Lindemann for Dept. of Psychiatry—Dec. 6, 1961", Box IIIB1b box 1 of 2, Erich Lindemann Collection, Center for the History of Medicine, Francis A. Countway Library of Medicine, Boston, MA]

19. Cohen, Mandel, Curriculum Vitae, 10/28/1955. [folder "Cohen, Mandel, M.D.", Box IIIB1 e 2), A-E", Erich Lindemann Collection, Center for the History of Medicine, Francis A. Countway Library of Medicine, Boston, MA]

20. Adams, Raymond D. letter to Clark, Dean A., MGH general director, 10/28/1955. [folder "Cohen, Mandel, M.D.", Box IIIB1 e 2), A-E", Erich Lindemann Collection, Center for the History of Medicine, Francis A. Countway Library of Medicine, Boston, MA]

21. Adams, Raymond D. note to Lindemann, Erich, 10/28/1955. Further correspondence with Harry Solomon and Dean Clark continued the struggle about Cohen's appointment: see Solomon, Harry, letter to Lindemann, Erich, 11/10/1955; and Clark, Dean A., memo to Adams, Raymond, Barr, Joseph [MGH Chief of the Orthopedic Surgery Service], Bauer, Walter [MGH Chief of Medical Service], and Lindemann, Erich, 12/19/1955. [folder "Cohen, Mandel, M.D.", Box IIIB1 e 2), A-E", Erich Lindemann Collection, Center for the History of Medicine, Francis A. Countway Library of Medicine, Boston, MA]

22. Butler, Allan, MD, part of the Presidential Address, 66th Annual Meeting, American Pediatric Society, Buck Hill Falls, PA 5/9/1956; published as "Quo Vadis Pediatrics", *AMA Journal of the Diseases of Children* 92: 431–437 (p. 432) (11/1956). A handwritten note—presumably to Lindemann—stated, "These thoughts p. 432 might entertain you".

23. White, Benjamin V., *Stanley Cobb: A Builder of the Modern Neurosciences* (Boston, MA: The Francis A. Countway Library of Medicine, 1984) (references to manuscript form).

24. Annual Report of the Department of Psychiatry for 1957, p. 7. [folder "Annual Report 1957, Dept. Psychiatry—ALL Divisions", Box IIIB1b box 1 of 2, Erich Lindemann Collection, Center for the History of Medicine, Francis A. Countway Library of Medicine, Boston, MA]

25. Blom, Gaston E., MD, former director of the MGH Child Psychiatry Unit, then University of Colorado Medical Center, letter to Lindemann, Erich, 2/25/1959. [folder "Ad hoc Committee on Future of Pediatrics at MGH 3/31/59 (Butler) all mtg. material", Box IIIB1d, Erich Lindemann Collection, Center for the History of Medicine, Francis A. Countway Library of Medicine, Boston, MA]

26. Annual Report, Children's Medical Service—1957 [Alan Butler, MD], p. 4. [folder "Annual Report 1957, Dept. Psychiatry—All Divisions", Box IIIB1b box 1 of 2, Erich Lindemann Collection, Center for the History of Medicine, Francis A. Countway Library of Medicine, Boston, MA]

27. Annual Report: Child Psychiatry Unit of the Massachusetts General Hospital Department of Psychiatry, January1, 1957 through December 31, 1957,

p. 7. [folder "Annual Report 1957, Dept. Psychiatry—All Divisions", Box IIIB1b box 1 of 2, Erich Lindemann Collection, Center for the History of Medicine, Francis A. Countway Library of Medicine, Boston, MA]

28. Neurosurgical Service—Annual Report—1957, James C. White, p. 2. [folder "Annual Report 1957, Dept. Psychiatry—All Divisions", Box IIIB1b box 1 of 2, Erich Lindemann Collection, Center for the History of Medicine, Francis A. Countway Library of Medicine, Boston, MA]

29. ANNUAL REPORT, CHILDREN'S MEDICAL SERVICE—1957 [Alan Butler, MD], p. 4. [folder "Annual Report 1957, Dept. Psychiatry—ALL Divisions", Box IIIB1b box 1 of 2, Erich Lindemann Collection, Center for the History of Medicine, Francis A. Countway Library of Medicine, Boston, MA]

    Annual Report: Child Psychiatry Unit of the Massachusetts General Hospital Department of Psychiatry, January 1, 1957 through December 31, 1957, p. 2. [folder "Annual Report 1957, Dept. Psychiatry—ALL Divisions", Box IIIB1b box 1 of 2, Erich Lindemann Collection, Center for the History of Medicine, Francis A. Countway Library of Medicine, Boston, MA]

30. Talbot, Nathan B., MD, "Has Psychologic Malnutrition Taken the Place of Rickets and Scurvy in Contemporary Pediatric Practice?" Borden Award Address, 10/31/1962. [folder "Talbot—Psychiatric Malnutrition 1963", IIIB2 a+b (box 1 of 3), Erich Lindemann Collection, Center for the History of Medicine, Francis A. Countway Library of Medicine, Boston, MA]

31. Lindemann, Erich, letter to Talbot, Nathan, 3/12/1963. [folder "Talbot—Psychiatric Malnutrition 1963", IIIB2 a+b (box 1 of 3), Erich Lindemann Collection, Center for the History of Medicine, Francis A. Countway Library of Medicine, Boston, MA]

32. Waring, Peg, letter to Lindemann, Erich, and Elizabeth, 9/7/1971, p. 1. [Erich Lindemann Collection, Elizabeth Lindemann files—file #110a, Newton, MA]

33. Lindemann, Erich, with Duhl, Leonard, Seeley, John, and Lindemann, Elizabeth, interview at Lindemann's home in Palo Alto, CA by Leonard Duhl, 7/15/1074. [caddy4, tape8A,9B;7, Erich Lindemann Collection, Center for the History of Medicine, Francis A. Countway Library of Medicine, Boston, MA]

34. Waring, Peg, 9/7/1971, *ibid*.

35. Lindemann, Erich, "The Nature of Community Mental Health Education", keynote address presented to the National Assembly on Mental Health Education; Ithaca, New York; 09/11/1958, summary, pp. 1–2. [file #56; "Lindemann—The Mental Health Educator + The Community 1958", Box XII #3, Lindemann Collection, Center for the History of Medicine, Francis A. Countway Library of Medicine, Harvard Medical School, Boston, MA]

36. Reed, Allan W., letter to Lindemann, 11/8/1965. [folder "Correspondence 1965", Box IIIA 1–3, Lindemann Collection, Center for the History of Medicine, Francis A. Countway Library of Medicine, Boston, MA]

37. Letters from Paul E. Johnson to Lindemann, 6/1, 11/9/1956. [folder "Misc. Correspondence A,B—1956–57", Box IIIA 1–3, Lindemann Collection, Center for the History of Medicine, Francis A. Countway Library of Medicine, Boston, MA]

38. Greer, Ina, correspondence with Lindemann, Erich, 8/17/1956–2/25/1959. [folder "Misc G", Box IIIA 1–3, Lindemann Collection, Center for the History of Medicine, Francis A. Countway Library of Medicine, Boston, MA]. Participants included Paul Yacovlev (HMS neuropathologist); Avery Weisman, John Nemiah, and Clemens Benda (associated with the MGH Psychiatry Service); Parker, Burns, Thomas, Miller, Douglas, Ferre, Fletcher, and Miss Greer.

39. Huff, Richard H., Minister of the First Unitarian Church of New Bedford, Massachusetts, letter to Lindemann, 1/2/1958. [folder "Misc H", Box IIIA 1–3, Lindemann Collection, Center for the History of Medicine, Francis. A. Countway Library of Medicine, Boston, MA]

40. Lindemann correspondence with William Holden of Tufts University, 11/5/1960–2/3/1961. [folder "Misc H", Box IIIA 1–3, Lindemann Collection, Center for the History of Medicine, Francis. A. Countway Library of Medicine, Boston, MA]

41. Harvard Divinity School proposal to the NIMH, 1/3/1956; also letter from Horton to Lindemann 9/17/1956. [folder "Misc. Correspondence H,I,J 1956–57", Box IIIA 1–3, Lindemann Collection, Center for the History of Medicine, Francis A. Countway Library of Medicine, Boston, MA]

42. Hoffmann, Hans, letters to Lindemann, 6/17/1958 and 2/25/1959. [folder "Dr. Hans Hofmann—Harvard University Dept. of Theology", Box IIIA 1–3, Lindemann Collection, Center for the History of Medicine, Francis A. Countway Library of Medicine, Boston, MA]

43. Fiarblanks, Rolln J., professor of Pastoral Theology at the Episcopal Theological School, to Lindemann, 4/23/1958; Letter from Lindemann to George Packer Berry, dean of HMS, 6/19/1959. [folder "Dr. Hans Hofmann—Harvard University Dept. of Theology", Box IIIA 1–3, Lindemann Collection, Center for the History of Medicine, Francis A. Countway Library of Medicine, Boston, MA]

44. Hofmann, Hans (director of the University Project on Religion and Mental Health) to Lindemann, 2/1/1961. [folder "Dr. Hans Hofmann—Harvard University Dept. of Theology", Box IIIA 1–3, Lindemann Collection, Center for the History of Medicine, Francis A. Countway Library of Medicine, Boston, MA]

45. Miller, Samuel H. letter to Donald Klein, 6/27/1961. [folder "M", Box IIIA 1–3, Lindemann Collection, Center for the History of Medicine, Francis A. Countway Library of Medicine, Boston, MA]

46. Lindemann, Erich, 1960, *ibid.*, p. 64.

47. Lindemann, Erich, with Duhl, Leonard, and Seeley, John, interview at Lindemann's home in Palo Alto, CA by Leonard Duhl, 6/15,22/1974. [caddy 4, tape 3A, 4B;7, Erich Lindemann Collection, Center for the History of Medicine, Francis A. Countway Library of Medicine, Boston, MA]

48. *Curriculum vitæ* (selective): 1926–8 University of Rochester School of Medicine; 1928–31 New York University Graduate School Division of Biological Sciences—PhD; 1937–40 HMS—MD cum laude; 1931–7 New York University Instructor to Assistant. Professor in Biology; 1937–40 HSPH Instructor in Physiology,; 1942–3 MGH Psychiatry Residency, HMS Assistant in Psychiatry; 1943–55 Washington University Medical School Department of Neuropsychiatry and Medicine Instructor to Professor, Director of the Division of Psychosomatic Medicine; 1955 MGH Psychiatrist. [folder "Saslow, George", Box IIIB1e 2), S-Z", Erich Lindemann Collection, Center for the History of Medicine, Francis A. Countway Library of Medicine, Boston, MA]

49. Lindemann, Erich, 6/15,22/1974. *ibid.*

50. Lindemann, Elizabeth B., interviews in Wellesley and Boston, MA by David G. Satin, 6/27/1978–8/1979 [Erich Lindemann Collection, David G. Satin, Newton, MA]

She saw Saslow as having a poor sense of proportions and boundaries, reflected in his overindulged son, who failed in social relationships and education.

51. Saslow, George, handwritten letter to Lindemann, Erich, 2/17/1955, p. 1. [folder "Saslow—Early Letters", Box IIIB1e 2), S-Z", Erich Lindemann

Collection, Center for the History of Medicine, Francis A. Countway Library of Medicine, Boston, MA]

52. Rutstein, David D., letter to Saslow, George, 4/23/1954. [folder "Saslow—Early Letters", Box IIIB1e 2), S-Z", Erich Lindemann Collection, Center for the History of Medicine, Francis A. Countway Library of Medicine, Boston, MA]

53. "Additions to the department included George Saslow (professor of psychiatry, George Washington University, St. Louis) to develop the Out-Patient Department". "Annual Report for the Department of Psychiatry for the Year 1955 Statistical Summary from October 1, 1954–September 30, 1955". [folder "Annual Reports from Staff Members 1955", Box IIIB1b box 1 of 2, Erich Lindemann Collection, Center for the History of Medicine, Francis A. Countway Library of Medicine, Boston, MA]

> "Annual Report Hall Mercer Hospital Massachusetts General Hospital Division 1955–1956",
> > [folder "Hall-Mercer 1955", Box IIIB1b box 1 of 2,
> > Erich Lindemann Collection, Center for the History
> > of Medicine, Francis A. Countway Library of
> > Medicine, Boston, MA]

> "Dr. George Saslow . . . brings to us much experience . . . not only of those with psychiatric illness but also the many sick people whose illness is affected by social and emotional complications. Dr. Saslow and his group have established a resource in comprehensive medicine in the Medical Clinic, also vigorously participating in the overall planning of the program for ambulatory care".

54. Saslow, George, letter to Lindemann, Erich, 9/8/1954. He sought appointment as professor, salary of $15–16,000 plus a "cushion"" of $5000 yearly to be reduced by any amount he could earn in private practice, and a retirement fund increased from 5% to 10% of salary. [folder "Saslow, George", Box IIIB1e 2), S-Z", Erich Lindemann Collection, Center for the History of Medicine, Francis A. Countway Library of Medicine, Boston, MA]

55. Saslow, George, letter to Lindemann, Erich, 11/6/1954, p. 1. [folder "Saslow, George", Box IIIB1e 2), S-Z", Erich Lindemann Collection, Center for the History of Medicine, Francis A. Countway Library of Medicine, Boston, MA]

56. Lindemann, Erich, memo to Berry, George P., 1/11/1955. [folder "Saslow, George", Box IIIB1e 2), S-Z", Erich Lindemann Collection, Center for the History of Medicine, Francis A. Countway Library of Medicine, Boston, MA]

57. Lindemann, Erich, letter to Saslow, Dr. George, 11/10/1954, pp. 1–2. [folder "Saslow, George", Box IIIB1e 2), S-Z", Erich Lindemann Collection, Center for the History of Medicine, Francis A. Countway Library of Medicine, Boston, MA]

58. Saslow, George, letter to Lindemann, Erich, 5/9/1955. [folder "Saslow, George", Box IIIB1e 2), S-Z", Erich Lindemann Collection, Center for the History of Medicine, Francis A. Countway Library of Medicine, Boston, MA]

59. Matarazzo, Joseph D., PhD, assistant professor of medical psychology, Washington University School of Medicine, letter to Lindemann, Erich, 3/31/1955: "In reply to your letter of March 12, 1955 I accept with pleasure the stated appointment in your department. . . . Dr. Saslow and I would like to start our appointments in your department on July 1, 1955". [folder "Matarazzo, Joseph—staff", Box IIIB1e 2), F-Ma", Erich Lindemann Collection, Center

for the History of Medicine, Francis A. Countway Library of Medicine, Boston, MA]

60. Executive Committee of the Committee on Research: 6/24/1955 "Measurement of Human Interaction" $68,953 1/1–12/31/56; 5/13/1955 "Measurement of human interaction in relation to psychiatric diagnosis and therapy" to USPHS transfer grant from Wash U. to MGH for 7/1–12/31/55 $21,913. [box II A&B, folder Scientific Advisory Committee: MGH 1954, Center for the History of Medicine, Francis A. Countway Library of Medicine, Boston, MA]

61. Matarazzo, Joseph D., memo to Lindemann, Erich, with copies to Drs. Donald Klein, Ruth Matarazzo, Lovick Miller (director of MGH psychiatric resident education?), Pearl Rosenberg, George Talland, J.[ohn] M. von Felsinger (chief psychologist in the MGH Psychiatry Service), 8/3/1955:

> In following up our discussions at several of the last psychology division meetings, enclosed is a tentative outline for a course we might give to the psychiatric residents in our department . . . we have been advised by Erich to have him propose it to Lem White, who will see how it can best be integrated in the overall teaching program of our psychiatry department. I believe psychologists have a contribution they can make in the training of a psychiatric resident . . . we might want to think . . . where such a beginning course might fit in a broader, integrated series of courses comprising a 3 year period, which we as psychologists might want to develop for our residents of the future. another course . . . on the basis of the interests and experiences of our group, is one covering the broad area of social-cultural factors in illness.
>
> [folder "Matarazzo, Joseph—staff", Box IIIB1e 2),
> F-Ma", Erich Lindemann Collection, Center for the
> History of Medicine, Francis A. Countway Library
> of Medicine, Boston, MA]

62. Lindemann, Erich, 6/15,22/1974, *ibid*.

63. Matarazzo, Joseph D., letter to Lindemann, Erich, 12/12/1955, pp. 1–2:

> As you know, I have been for several years the chairman of the subcommittee on Psychology in Medical Education of the Education and Training Board of the American Psychological Association.
>
> In recognition of the growing national interest of medical educators in the role of the behavioral sciences in medical education, my committee has been asked . . . to make unofficial contact with the American Association of Medical Colleges. . . . If AAMC is interested in a multi-discipline study of the Behavioral Sciences in Medical Education, then the Board of Directors of APA will be asked to establish a formal psychology committee for this purpose. Anthropology, Sociology and Psychiatry (and possibly other groups) can be asked to appoint official committees. . . . Since Dean [of HMS George Packer] Berry is a prominent member of AAMC and since on many occasions he has expressed his interest in strengthening the contribution of the behavioral sciences in medical education. . . . I wonder if you could make an appointment for me (and yourself if you have the time) with him at his earliest convenience.
>
> [folder "Matarazzo, Joseph—staff", Box IIIB1e 2),
> F-Ma, Erich Lindemann Collection, Center for the
> History of Medicine, Francis A. Countway Library
> of Medicine, Boston, MA]

64. Lindemann, Erich, letter to Berry, George Packer, 3/1/1956:

> Dr. Dean Clark has been anxious to be helpful in salvaging for the hospital the services of Dr. Saslow who as you know is considering offers from elsewhere. I, myself, do not believe that a relationship can be worked out which is conducive to harmonious cooperation in developing our program. . . . I would be most grateful for your opinion about this statement and hope we can discuss this tomorrow.

Lindemann, Erich, letter to Clark, Dean A., 3/1/1956, pp. 1–2:

> As a result of your questions concerning Dr. Saslow's post in our Department I am writing you about the organization of the Department. . . . All of these men with executive responsibilities meet for a weekly policy meeting . . . and each . . . discusses personally with me details of the program. . . . In turn, I seek the counsel of various members of the group. . . . It was only natural to expect that Dr. Saslow with his large experience would gradually become more and more important in his influence on general policy and I was expecting with confidence that he would win the respect and trust of the members of the group. Unfortunately, Dr. Saslow's program has remained divorced from the rest of our activities and indeed has sometimes appeared as though it was tending to become a separate division of Psychiatry altogether. Dr. Saslow has not come to our Planning Meetings.
>
> To entrust to another person a larger amount of control of various activities in the Department can naturally be based only on the fullest confidence in this person's loyalty and in his basic wish to integrate his own special aims with those of the rest of the Department.

Lindemann, Erich, letter to Clark, Dean A., 3/5/1956, pp. 1–3:

> As a result of your questions concerning Dr. Saslow's post in our Department I am writing you. . . . As you may remember . . . I plan to base the Psychiatric Department firmly on four foundations: a. Psychodyamic psychiatry . . . b. Neuropsychiatric work. . . . c. Social and community psychiatry being based on experimental psychology, learning theory and social science. d. Developmental psychology. . . . The third area has been clearly the field in which Dr. Saslow has very considerable competence and in which his group is most experienced. In this area I hoped for a great deal of shared thinking and planning and indeed hoped that Dr. Saslow and I would make a major contribution.
>
> I do not believe that a representative of any of the four areas could properly be chosen to function as Associate Director for the whole Department. For over-all administration I prefer . . . the assistance of a younger administrative officer. . . . On the other hand the leaders of each of these sections will of course be much involved in over-all planning of those matters in which their field articulates with the other three areas. . . . The field which I have always discussed with Dr. Saslow . . . is that of the management of psychological and social components of medical illness as part of the development of a comprehensive program of ambulatory medical care. I consider Dr. Saslow's work in this area as of very great importance for the development of the program of the whole Department. He . . . has an entirely free hand in the development of the psychiatric component of medical care together with Dr. Stoeckle. . . . Dr. Saslow is also expected to become the central person for developing the psychiatric teaching for second year medical students. . . . It was only

natural to expect that Dr. Saslow . . . would gradually become more and more important in his influence on general policy and I was expecting with confidence that he would win the respect and trust of the members of the group. Unfortunately, Dr. Saslow's program has remained divorced from the rest of our activities and indeed has sometimes appeared as though it was tending to become a separate division of Psychiatry altogether. Dr. Saslow has not come to our Planning Meetings. To entrust to another person a larger amount of control of various activities in the Department can naturally be based only on the fullest confidence in this person's loyalty and in his basic wish to integrate his own special aims with those of the rest of the Department.

(pp. 1–3)

Lindemann, Erich, memo to Saslow, George, 7/27/1956:

In order to clarify your relation to the Department of Psychiatry, I am enumerating here your duties during the coming year. 1. You will continue and further develop the program in Comprehensive Medicine located in the Medical Clinic. Dr. Bauer, the Chief of the Medical Service, does not wish to have either the Medical House Officers . . . or 4th year medical students assigned to your Service. On the Psychiatric Staff I believe the Clinical and Research Fellows would benefit most from this program. . . . I would hope that you continue to participate on the Planning Committee for the new Ambulatory Program of the hospital that a proper place will be found for . . . the Comprehensive Medicine Program. . . . 2. You will develop the program for the Alcoholic Service and actually take charge of the program. . . . 3. You will continue your research program in the study of human interaction. . . . There has been some misunderstanding about the use of funds granted to the Department of Psychiatry in connection with the support of research activities. . . . 4. I expect that you and your group will continue to participate in our teaching grand rounds . . . I hope that you and your group will again participate in the second year teaching . . . the section work in connection with the Department of Medicine and by contributing to the lecture work. . . . You will be given Dr. Ludwig's office. . . . there is no further need for the participation of Dr. Ruth Matarazzo in the testing of psychiatric patients on the Ward. . . . it will not be necessary for her to have office space on B-7 [open psychiatric ward, MGH]. Since Dr. Joseph Matarazzo will be concerned with Alcoholic patients and Interaction Research only I expect that you will find office space for him. . . . So far as secretarial help is concerned we have been . . . provide you with a secretary . . . during this year. . . . It will be wise . . . to include in your own applications for support an item to cover this expense. Please let me know in writing whether these arrangements are satisfactory to you.

(pp. 1–2)

Lindemann, Erich, letter to Saslow, George, 7/28/1956:

In order to be sure that we understand each other about our relation to the Department of Psychiatry during the coming year I am enumerating here the essential points of your program as I see them. You will be known as the Director of our program in Comprehensive Medicine which is concerned with the psychological and social components and illness in general. . . . 1. You will continue and further develop; the program in Comprehensive Medicine located in the Medical Clinic . . . I expect that this work will arouse more and more interest on the part of the psychiatric staff. . . . So far as teaching in the Medical Service is concerned Dr. Walter Bauer [chief of med, MGH] does not wish as yet to have either the Medical House Officers . . . or the fourth year Medical Students assigned to your Service. I do hope as you continue your work with the Committee for the new Ambulatory Program of the hospital that a proper place will be found for the role of the Comprehensive Medicine Program. . . . 2. . . the development of the Alcoholic Service . . . is expected to show significant progress under your direction. . . . This program involves a closely integrated team work between Medicine, Neurology and Psychiatry. The work in the Alcohol Clinic may well become a model for good medical-psychiatric care. . . . 3. You will continue your <u>research program</u> in the Study of Human Interaction by which you are making a significant contribution to the quantitative study of human behavior. Your advice for the development of further sound research projects will be much appreciated. . . . I expect that you and your group will continue in our teaching <u>Grand Rounds</u>. . . . I also hope you will continue your Seminar on theoretical problems in comprehensive medicine. . . . I look forward to your participation in the second year teaching program. . . . In order to have the benefit of our participation in planning and in the development of the broader program of the Department and in order to ensure the integration of your work with the rest of our activities I believe it will be best for you and myself to continue to have weekly conferences and of course you will continue as an important member of our planning committee. I do hope that these arrangements provide a basis for fruitful work together. Please let me know in writing whether they are satisfactory.

(p. 2)

Lindemann, Erich, memo to Saslow, George, 7/28/1956:

In studying your application for renewal of your research project I notice that you have made no allowances for financing the considerable secretarial services which are engendered by the project . . . We are now supporting your secretary from funds related to another project which will be difficult to justify in the future. I, therefore, suggest that you include the request for secretarial services in your renewal application or apply the sums now considered for salary raises of professional personnel.

Saslow, George, memo to Lindemann, Erich, 8/7/1956:

I expect to carry out the assignments you have made as well as I can . . . You ask whether your definition of my relation to the Department of Psychiatry is satisfactory. I obtain no satisfaction from a definition which is a unilateral repudiation of 9/10ths of the basis of my agreeing to come here . . . described in the copy . . . of my letter to Dean [of HMS George Packer] Berry of May 12th.

[folder "Saslow, George", Box IIIB1e 2), S-Z",
Erich Lindemann Collection, Center for the History
of Medicine, Francis A. Countway Library of
Medicine, Boston, MA]

65. Weisman, Avery, quoted by Nemiah, John (another member of the psychiatry staff to whom Lindemann delegated major administrative responsibilities and thought might carry on his development of the department along social psychiatry lines but who had little sympathy with this perspective), author of the biographical sketch of Erich Lindemann in Castleman, Benjamin, MD, Crockett, David C., Sutton, S.B., *The Massachusetts General Hospital 1955–1980* (Boston, MA: Little Brown, 1983), p. 170.

66. Saslow, George, memo to Berry, George Packer, copy to Lindemann, Erich, 5/12/1956:

This letter is in response to your invitation to set down my conception of how I would function at the M.G.H., based upon the discussions with Erich before I came. . . . 1. Sharing with Erich systematic continuous examination of and decision on all major departmental polices regarding personnel, budget, promotions, duties assigned to personnel, etc.; policies · affecting relations with other hospital departments; policies involving the M.G.H. department's role in the medical school as a whole, in the university, and in the community.

As a result . . . I would be enabled to carry out Erich's desire that I act administratively for him in his absence . . . and on various important committees. . . . 2. Sharing with Erich in the first instance, and then with Alfred Stanton, possibly Gerald Caplan, possibly Eliz. Zetzel, Lem White and Avery Weisman, an attempt to create a type of psychiatric residency learning opportunity different from any in existence. . . . 3. Assuming official responsibility . . . for a unitary administration of all psychiatric ambulatory care at the M.G.H. . . . I expected to be in charge of the hospital consultation service. . . . 4. Participating at the policy-making level, with Erich, in the development of a more effective teaching program for staff . . . and medical students at the M.G.H., and for medical students in all-medical-school courses.

[folder "Saslow, George", Box IIIB1e 2), S-Z", Erich Lindemann Collection, Center for the History of Medicine, Francis A. Countway Library of Medicine, Boston, MA]

67. Solomon, Harry C., 6/22/1978, *ibid.*
68. Lindemann, Erich, letter to Saslow, George, 7/1//1956:

Dear George, At the end of your first year with the Psychiatric Service of the Massachusetts General Hospital, it has become clear that your original expectations with regard to the position have not been fulfilled. It appears that you had envisaged a role which would carry with it considerable autonomy with regard to executive action. Such a role is manifestly unsuitable to the conditions of collaborative teamwork under a single leader which, in my view, are essential to the proper functioning of a psychiatric service in a general hospital. Under these circumstances, it will be impossible for me to recommend to the University a renewal of your appointment when it expires in June, 1958. I deeply regret the failure of our joint efforts, carried on with mutual good will and earnestness, to find a basis for effective collaboration . . . and hope that you will find appropriate conditions elsewhere.

Lindemann, Erich, letter to Saslow, George, 9/14/1956:

I have been pondering your reply to my letter . . . You are quite correct . . . that your work with the Family Health Services is of great importance for our work in psychiatry and mental health . . . you state that your present activities represent only 10% of what you expected to do here. This clearly shows that with my best efforts I have not been able to create for you a role commensurate with your wishes. I hardly need to say how much I have been disappointed in turn because of your failure to relate more effectively to the other members of our group. It must be clear by now to both of us that the chances of developing a unified program in which you and I are closely involved with mutual understanding and communication and with a real joint purpose is not going to take place.

I do hope that you will be successful in finding another set-up. . . . In any case, there is no prospect that your appointment as Clinical Professor at Harvard Medical School in the Department of Psychiatry can be renewed at the end of your present tenure.

Lindemann, Erich, letter to Saslow, George, 10/18/1956:

I am writing to crystalize my understanding of our discussion concerning our present role in the Department of Psychiatry. We both agreed that our great efforts to find a satisfactory working relationship and to develop a unified program in which you and I are closely involved with mutual understanding and with a strong sense of joint purpose had not succeeded. We carefully discussed the possibility of working out this problem and felt that a solution was most unlikely. Since neither of us could conceive of any way of finding a new relationship we agreed that it would be unwise for you in terms of your own future career as a leader in psychiatry, and for me, as the person responsible for the welfare of the Harvard Medical School—Massachusetts General Hospital Department to continue working together in this situation. You indicated that in the near future you would let me know about the progress of your plans for developing your own program elsewhere. I cannot tell you how deeply I regret losing your potentially great contribution to our department.

Saslow, George, letter to Lindemann, Erich, copies to Berry, George P., and Clark, Dean A., 11/1/1956:

I am afraid I cannot agree that you have made any genuine efforts to find a satisfactory working relationship. . . . On August 7th, I wrote you that your redefinition of my departmental role . . . was a unilateral repudiation of the basis on which I agreed to come here. I have stated to you several times since that such repudiation would never be acceptable to me.

You have never discussed these issues seriously, although it is obvious that the breaking of commitments without mutual agreement destroys any working relationship.

[folder "Saslow, George", Box IIIB1e 2), S-Z",
Erich Lindemann Collection, Center for the
History of Medicine, Francis A. Countway Library
of Medicine, Boston, MA]

69. Lindemann, Erich, letter to Berry, George Packer, 4/22/1956:

I would like to inform you of the resignation of Dr. George Saslow from his position as Clinical Professor of Psychiatry effective June 30, 1957. Dr. Saslow now holds a three year appointment as Clinical Professor of which two years will have elapsed by that time.

Clark, Dean A., letter to Saslow, George, 4/11/1957:

This is to notify you officially that at the meeting of the Board of Trustees, held on April 5, 1957, it was voted to accept with regret your resignation from the position of Psychiatrist at this Hospital, effective June 30, 1957.

Saslow, George, memo to Lindemann, Erich, 4/25/1957:

Herewith I submit my resignation from the department of psychiatry at the Mass. General Hospital, to take effect on July 1, 1957. I have accepted the position of professor and head of the new full-time department of psychiatry at the University of Oregon Medical School.

Berry, George Packer, letter to Saslow, George, 4/30/1957:

> In writing to acknowledge the receipt of your letter of March 15, 1957, submitting your resignation from the Faculty of Medicine as of July 1, 1957, I take the occasion to offer my congratulations and best wishes to you as you are about to assume your important new post as Professor and chairperson of the new full-time Department of Psychiatry at the Medical School of the University of Oregon. . . . Climbing mountains is hard work—I hope some of the most arduous climbs are now matters of history.

Lindemann, Erich, letter to Clark, Dean A., 5/31/1957:

> In response to your memorandum concerning Dr. Saslow's travel expenses. . . . The present request of Dr. Saslow is based on an unwarranted assumption as so many previous requests in the past. I have not promised him money for his trip to Chicago. . . . I reminded Dr. Saslow, who was not planning to present a paper, in ample time before the meeting that no financial assistance to his trip to Chicago was available in our very much strained budget. As you know, the unfortunate way in which Dr. Saslow arranged for his time which he promised to devote to the Alcohol Clinic has brought about a very serious loss of funds on which I had counted. . . . I hope that you will understand that under these circumstances I will not further contribute to our financial problem by turning additional funds over to Dr. Saslow.
>
> Unfortunately, it is a sad truth that this man's presence here has done incalculable damage to our Department not only financially. I deeply regret that I was responsible for his coming and do appreciate your thoughtful concern and your helpful support during this difficult period.

Saslow, George, handwritten memo to Lindemann, Erich, 6/29/1957:

> Dear Erich, Since, unfortunately, your techniques of dealing with people destroy all ordinary social relations and procedures, this note will constitute my formal leave-taking. Yours truly, George Saslow.
> [folder "Saslow, George", Box IIIB1e 2), S-Z",
> Erich Lindemann Collection, Center for the History
> of Medicine, Francis A. Countway Library
> of Medicine, Boston, MA]

70. Newspaper clipping 1959: Reports a new hospital opened in 1956 with open ward psychiatric treatment theory and practice, and interaction chronograph research findings about subpopulations dealing with anxiety, smoking, etc. [folder "Saslow, George", Box IIIB1e 2), S-Z", Erich Lindemann Collection, Center for the History of Medicine, Francis A. Countway Library of Medicine, Boston, MA]

71. Matarazzo, Joseph D., PhD, letter to Lindemann, Erich, with copies to Berry, George P. (HMS Dean) and Clark Dean (MGH General Director), 3/25/1957:

> As you know from our several conversations during the past two months I have been offered, and have now formally accepted, a position as Professor of Medical Psychology at the University of Oregon Medical School. In view of this I wish you would accept my resignation as Associate Psychologist at the Massachusetts General Hospital and Research Associate in Psychology in the Harvard Medical School effective July 1, 1957.
> [folder "Matarazzo, Joseph—Staff", Box IIIB1e 2),
> F-Ma", Erich Lindemann Collection, Center for
> the History of Medicine, Francis A. Countway
> Library of Medicine, Boston, MA]

Matarazzo, Ruth, letter to Lindemann, Erich, 4/1/1957:

> I plan to accept the position [Assistant Professor of Medical Psychology, University of Oregon Medical School], and request that you accept my resignation from the Massachusetts General Hospital and Harvard Medical School, effective July 1, 1957.
> [folder "RUTH MATARAZZO", Box IIIB1e 2), F-Ma", Erich Lindemann Collection, Center for the History of Medicine, Francis A. Countway Library of Medicine, Boston, MA]

72. "Interview with Dr. Warren Vaughan May 9, 1957". [folder "Psychiatry Service—Misc. + Budgets", Box IIIB1c box 2 of 2, Erich Lindemann Collection, Center for the History of Medicine, Francis A. Countway Library of Medicine, Boston, MA]

73. "Suggestions for an Organizational Framework to Unite the Massachusetts General Hospital Psychiatric Service, The Mclean Hospital and The Bowdoin Square Mental Health Center". [folder "Psychiatry Service—Misc. + Budgets", Box IIIB1c box 2 of 2, Erich Lindemann Collection, Center for the History of Medicine, Francis A. Countway Library of Medicine, Boston, MA]

74. Morris, Laura B., "Material Pertinent for the Request to be Made to the Mass. Dept. of Mental Health for Support of the Mental Health Project at Mass. General Hospital", 6/1956. [envelope "Com. of Mass. 727 9542–5", IIIB2 b (box2 of 3), Erich Lindemann Collection, Center for the History of Medicine, Francis A. Countway Library of Medicine, Boston, MA]

75. Letters 1956–1958. [envelope "Com. of Mass. 727 9542–5", IIIB2 b (box2 of 3), Erich Lindemann Collection, Center for the History of Medicine, Francis A. Countway Library of Medicine, Boston, MA]

76. Hutchinson, Belenden R. letter to Lindemann, Elizabeth B., 9/29/1959. [folder "Hutchinson, B.R., MD; Director, Dept. of Mental Health Div. of Mental Hygiene, Com. of Mass.", Box IIIA 4 (F-H), Erich Lindemann Collection, Center for the History of Medicine, Francis A. Countway Library of Medicine, Boston, MA]

77. Kennedy, John F., "Message Regarding Mental Illness and Mental Retardation", p. 5. [folder "K Miscellaneous", Box IIIA 4 (I-Ma), Lindemann Collection, Center for the History of Medicine, Francis A. Countway Library of Medicine, Boston, MA]

78. Lindemann, Erich, letter to Hutchinson, Belenden H., 8/4/1961. [folder "Hutchinson, B.R., MD; director, Dept. of Mental Health Div. of Mental Hygiene, Com. of Mass.", Box IIIA 4 (F-H), Erich Lindemann Collection, Center for the History of Medicine, Francis A. Countway Library of Medicine, Boston, MA]

79. *Mental Hygiene News Bulletin*, 3–4/1960, p. 2; Hutchinson, Belenden R., letter to Lindemann, Erich, 5/27/1960. [folder "Hutchinson, B.R., MD; director, Dept. of Mental Health Div. of Mental Hygiene, Com. of Mass.", Box IIIA 4 (F-H), Erich Lindemann Collection, Center for the History of Medicine, Francis A. Countway Library of Medicine, Boston, MA]

80. "A Meeting of the General Executive Committee was held in the Trustees' Room, White Building, at 8:30 a.m. on Wednesday, December 6, 1961", pp. 3, 4. [folder "GEC Report by Dr. Lindemann for Dept. of Psychiatry—December 6, 1961", Box IIIB1b box 1 of 2, Erich Lindemann Collection, Center for the History of Medicine, Francis A. Countway Library of Medicine, Boston, MA]

81. Crockett, David C., letter to Lindemann, Erich, 7/11/1961. [folder "New Govt. Mental Health Center", Box IIIA 4 (Mb-O), Erich Lindemann

Collection, Center for the History of Medicine, Francis A. Countway Library of Medicine, Boston, MA]

82. Nemiah, John, letter to Crockett, David C. with copy to Lindemann, Erich, 1/24/1962 regarding meeting with Dr. James Dykens, Assistant Commissioner of Mental Health. [folder "New Govt. Mental Health Center", Box IIIA 4 (Mb-O), Erich Lindemann Collection, Center for the History of Medicine, Francis A. Countway Library of Medicine, Boston, MA]

83. Hutchinson, Belenden R. letter to Lindemann, Erich, 5/15/1962, p. 1. [folder "Hutchinson, B.R., MD; Director, Dept. of Mental Health Div. of Mental Hygiene, Com. of Mass.", Box IIIA 4 (F-H), Erich Lindemann Collection, Center for the History of Medicine, Francis A. Countway Library of Medicine, Boston, MA]

84. Includes Nemiah, John C. memo to Lindemann, Erich, "The Meeting with Dr. Harry Solomon on January 18, 1963 concerning Plans for the New Unit". [folder "New Govt. Mental Health Center", Box IIIA 4 (Mb-O), Erich Lindemann Collection, Center for the History of Medicine, Francis A. Countway Library of Medicine, Boston, MA]

85. Membership of the Advisory Committee would included Dr. James Dykens (assistant commissioner of mental health], Belenden Hutchinson (associate commissioner, Division of Mental Hygiene, DMH), Dr. John Knowles (general director, MGH), Dr. Ellsworth Neumann (associate director, MGH), Dean George Packer Berry (HMS) or alternate, Harriet Hardy (professor of industrial and preventive medicine, HMS and MGH), José Barchilon (candidate for director of the McLean Hospital), Dr. Drachman (neurologist, NIMH) or McHugh, Milton Greenblatt (at the time superintendent, Boston State Hospital or director of research at the MMHC)], Bernard Bandler (Massachusetts Memorial Hospital and professor and chairperson, Division of Psychiatry, Boston University School of Medicine), Dr. George Tarjan, Dr. Leonard Duhl, Prof. David McClelland (Harvard Department of Social Relations), Miss Eleanor Clark (social services, MGH), Miss Ruth Gilbert (Columbia University nursing department), Al Frechette (Massachusetts commissioner of public health] or alternate, Department of Education, Department of Welfare, Jack Ewalt [superintendent, MHC) or representative, NIMH, Dean Charles I. Schottland (Florence Heller School for Social Policy and Management, Brandeis University), an dedicated citizen, United Community Services, and Massachusetts Association for Mental Health.

   "Executive/Core Planning Group": Erich Lindemann, chairman (as potential superintendent of the CMHC), John Nemiah for development of clinical services, Gerald Caplan for development of community services, Gardner Quarton for development of research, Jason Aronson as executive secretary—with Ewalt, Bandler, and Dykens as coplanners.

   Committee on financial problems: DMH, MGH Comptroller, HMS Dean's office.

86. Massachusetts Medical Society, "Proceedings of the Council", 5/20/1963, pp. 12–14. [folder "New Govt. Mental Health Center", Box IIIA 4 (Mb-O), Erich Lindemann Collection, Center for the History of Medicine, Francis A. Countway Library of Medicine, Boston, MA]

87. Brickman, Henry G., Executive Director of the Massachusetts Hospital Association, memo to Neumann, Ellsworth, MD. chairperson of the Subcommittee on Welfare and Other Third Party Reimbursement and MGH Associate Director, 6/14/1963. [folder "New Govt. Mental Health Center", Box IIIA 4 (Mb-O), Erich Lindemann Collection, Center for the History of Medicine, Francis A. Countway Library of Medicine, Boston, MA]

88. Lindemann, Erich, memo to Solomon, Dr. Harry C., 6/15/1964. [HMS Dean's office files]
89. Lindemann, Erich, and Spivak, McGrath, 1965, *ibid.*
90. Lindemann, Erich, letter to Knowles, John H., 7/30/1962. [folder "Dr. John Knowles, Medical Director—MGH", Box IIIA 4 (I-Ma), Erich Lindemann Collection, Center for the History of Medicine, Francis A. Countway Library of Medicine, Boston, MA]
91. Lindemann, Erich, interview with two graduate students in sociology, 1965, p. 1. [folder "Stanford—Misc.", box IV 3 + 4 + 5, Erich Lindemann Collection, Center for the History of Medicine, Francis A., Countway Library of Medicine, Boston, MA]
92. Lindemann letter to Harvey H. Barten, 12/14/1964. [folder "B Miscellaneous 1 of 2 file folders", Box IIIA 4 (A-E), Lindemann Collection, Center for the History of Medicine, Francis A. Countway Library of Medicine, Boston, MA]
93. Lindemann, Erich, letter to Feldman, Raymond D., chief of the Training Branch, NIMH, 4/1/1963, p. 1. [folder "2/25–2/29/64—Training Institute Arden House, N.Y.C.", Box IIIA7 1964–1965 box 3 of 3, Erich Lindemann Collection, Center for the History of Medicine, Francis A. Countway Library of Medicine, Boston, MA]
94. Lindemann, Erich, memo to Solomon, Harry, 6/15/1964. [folder "Harry C. Solomon", Box IIIA 4 (P-S), Erich Lindemann Collection, Center for the History of Medicine, Francis A. Countway Library of Medicine, Boston, MA]
95. Lindemann, Erich, letter to Berry, George P., 12/19/1963.
96. Solomon, Harry and Lindemann, Erich exchange of letters 7/9,20/1964. [folder "Harry C. Solomon", Box IIIA 4 (P-S), Erich Lindemann Collection, Center for the History of Medicine, Francis A. Countway Library of Medicine, Boston, MA]
97. Lindemann, Erich, letter to Solomon, Harry, 12/14/1964. [folder "Harry C. Solomon", Box IIIA 4 (P-S), Erich Lindemann Collection, Center for the History of Medicine, Francis A. Countway Library of Medicine, Boston, MA]
98. Lindemann, Erich, letter to Solomon, Harry, 1/25/1965; minutes of meeting involving John Knowles, Erich Lindemann, Harry Solomon, James Dykens (Assistant Commissioner of the DMH), and John Nemiah, 6/14/1965; Solomon, Harrry letter to Lindemann, Erich, 12/21/1965. [folder "Harry C. Solomon", Box IIIA 4 (P-S), Erich Lindemann Collection, Center for the History of Medicine, Francis A. Countway Library of Medicine, Boston, MA]
99. Black, Herbert, "MGH, Harvard Will Staff State Mental Health to Be Built in Boston Government Center", *The Boston Herald*, Thursday, 3/7/1963, p. 32. [Erich Lindemann Collection, Elizabeth Lindemann files—file #110a, Newton, MA]
100. Black, Herbert, "Lowell Lecture VI Mass General Planning City Mental Health Tie-In", *The Boston Globe* Thursday, 3/7/1963, p. 4. [Erich Lindemann Collection, Elizabeth Lindemann files—file #110a, Newton, MA]
101. Erich Lindemann Collection, Elizabeth Lindemann files—file #110a, Newton, MA
102. Lindemann, Erich, letter to Solomon, Harry C., commissioner of the Massachusetts Department of Mental Health, 3/15/1962. [folder "G Miscellaneous", Box IIIA 4 (F-H), Lindemann Collection, Center for the History of Medicine, Francis A. Countway Library of Medicine, Boston, MA]

103. Solomon, Harry C. letter to Erich Lindemann 3/20/1962. [folder "Correspondence 1962", Box IIIA 1–3, Lindemann Collection, Center for the History of Medicine, Francis A. Countway Library of Medicine, Boston, MA]

104. Lindemann's memo record of a phone call from Berry, 10/1/1962. [folder "Dean George Packer Berry", Box IIIA 4 (A-E), Lindemann Collection, Center for the History of Medicine, Francis A. Countway Library of Medicine, Boston, MA]

105. Lindemann, Erich, letter to Berry, George Packer, 10/26/1964, pp. 1–2. [folder "Dean George Packer Berry", Box IIIA 4 (A-E), Lindemann Collection, Center for the History of Medicine, Francis A. Countway Library of Medicine, Boston, MA]

106. Morris, Laura, 11/19/1979, *ibid.*

107. Quarton, Gardner, Lindemann, Erich, Drachman, David, Dews, Peter B. correspondence 11/27/1962–4/12,1963, 12/3/1962, 3/18/1963. [folder "D Miscellaneous", Box IIIA 4 (A-E), Erich Lindemann Collection, Center for the History of Medicine, Francis A. Countway Library of Medicine, Boston, MA]

108. Farrell, Jean, letter to Lindemann, Erich, 1/28/1970. Speakers supporting the petition included Lucy Thoma (HRS), Lucy Carter, Matthew Dumont (NIMH), John von Felsinger (MGH), Marc Fried (West End Study—people remarked on his giving support despite the tension between him and Lindemann), Philip Kubzansky (West End Project, Boston University), Laura Morris (MGH), Louisa Howe (MGH, HSPH), Katherine Binderup, Fr. Moynihan (Mahoney—Boston College Department of Psychology), Dorothy Hickie (MGH), Peter Lucarelli, Shayna Gochberg (HRS), Tom Monahan (representing Dr. [Milton Greenblatt, commissioner of the Massachusetts Department of Mental Healt), and Armando Alfano (representing the Harbor Area Board). Mr. Ward from the HRS Board of Directors spoke, and State Senator Mario Umana read a list of supporters, including Senator Edward Kennedy—Thoma, Lucy letter to Lindemann, Erich, 1/26/1970. [Erich Lindemann Collection, Elizabeth Lindemann files—file #110a, Newton, MA]

109. Petition presented by Jean Farrell as introduced by State Senator Mario Umana in support of Senate bill#109, an act designating the mental health center presently being constructed in the Government Center, Boston as the Erich LIndemann Mental Health Center, 1/26/1970. [Erich Lindemann Collection, Elizabeth Lindemann files—file #110a, Newton, MA]

110. Klerman, Gerald, Welcoming remarks at the dedication of the ELMHC, 9/22/1972. [Erich Lindemann Collection, Elizabeth Lindemann files—file #110a, Newton, MA]

111. Erich Lindemann Collection, Elizabeth Lindemann files—file #110a, David G. Satin, Newton, MA

112. Program for the Dedication of the Erich Lindemann Mental Health Center, 9/22/1971. [Erich Lindemann Collection, Elizabeth Lindemann files—file #110a, David G. Satin, Newton, MA]

113. Klerman, Gerald L., letter to Lindemann, Erich, 8/20/1971. [Erich Lindemann Collection, Elizabeth Lindemann files—file #110a, David G. Satin, Newton, MA]

114. Klerman, Gerald L., letter to Lindemann, Erich, 10/4/1971. [Erich Lindemann Collection, Elizabeth Lindemann files—file #110a, David G. Satin, Newton, MA]

115. Leighton, Alexander, letter to Lindemann, Erich, 9/27/1971. [Erich Lindemann Collection, Elizabeth Lindemann files—file #110a, David G. Satin, Newton, MA]

116. Niles, Marion, letter to Lindemann, Erich, 10/1/1971, pp. 1–2. [Erich Lindemann Collection, Elizabeth Lindemann files—file #110a, David G. Satin, Newton, MA]

117. Waring, Peg, letter to Lindemann, Erich: and Elizabeth, 9/7/1971, p. 1. [Erich Lindemann Collection, Elizabeth Lindemann files—file #110a, David G. Satin, Newton, MA]

118. Leavell, Hugh R., letter to Lindemann, Erich, 9/6/1971. [Erich Lindemann Collection, Elizabeth Lindemann files—file #110a, David G. Satin, Newton, MA]

119. Lindemann, Erich, draft of a letter to Meadow, Henry, former associate dean of HMS, 1971. [Erich Lindemann Collection, Elizabeth Lindemann files—file #110a, David G. Satin, Newton, MA]

120. Lindemann, Erich, letter to Byler, John, executive director of The Grant Foundation, 9/16/1957. [folder "Grant Foundation-1957–58", IIIB2 b (box2 of 3), Erich Lindemann Collection, Center for the History of Medicine, Francis A. Countway Library of Medicine, Boston, MA]

121. Lindemann, Erich, letter to Byler, John, executive director of The Grant Foundation, 1/14/1958, p. 1. [folder "Grant Foundation-1957–58", IIIB2 b (box2 of 3), Erich Lindemann Collection, Center for the History of Medicine, Francis A. Countway Library of Medicine, Boston, MA]

122. Morris, Laura, "Minutes of Mental Health Service". [folder "State Department of Mental Health", "Mental Health Service—Nursery Schools", Box IIIB1a box 2 of 2, Erich Lindemann Collection, Center for the History of Medicine, Francis A. Countway Library of Medicine, Boston, MA]

123. Erich Lindemann Collection III A6 "NIMH". [Center for the History of Medicine, Francis A. Countway Library of Medicine, Harvard Medical School, Boston, MA

124. Proposed Plans for an Integrated Program of Service and Research in the Field of Community Mental Health 4/56 Submitted by the staff of the Mental Health Service Massachusetts General Hospital". [folder "Columbia-Washington Heights Community Mental Health Project", Box IIIA6 Da GAP, Erich Lindemann Collection, Center for the History of Medicine, Francis A. Countway Library of Medicine, Boston, MA]

125. "Relocation and Mental Health Adaptation Under Stress A. Summary of Research Project", undated. [envelope "Grant Foundation 1955–56", IIIB2 b (box2 of 3), Erich Lindemann Collection, Center for the History of Medicine, Francis A. Countway Library of Medicine, Boston, MA]

126. Persons Attending Advisory Committee Meeting for the West End February 12, 1959. [folder "Materials for—Sight [sic] Visit on Lindemann-Caplan Application", IIIB2 c (box1 of 2), Erich Lindemann Collection, Center for the History of Medicine, Francis A. Countway Library of Medicine, Boston, MA]

127. Morris, Laura memo to Lindemann, Erich, 10/2/1956. [folder "Columbia-Washington Heights Community Mental Health Project", Box IIIA6 Da GAP, Erich Lindemann Collection, Center for the History of Medicine, Francis A. Countway Library of Medicine, Boston, MA]

128. Lindemann, Erich, letter to Leonard Duhl, 9/30/1963 [folder "Leonard Duhl—NIMH Corr"., Box IIIA 4 (A-E), Erich Lindemann Collection, Center for the History of Medicine, Francis A. Countway Library of Medicine, Boston, MA]

129. 6/10/62 *Boston Globe* news article announcing that Lindemann was to address the Massachusetts Mental Health Center Auxiliary in a lecture titled "Mental Health and the Metropolis": "Dr. Erich Lindemann will

discuss the emotional reaction of families forced to find new homes because of slum clearance . . . and will particularly refer to families displaced by the West End housing project". [folder "Correspondence 1962", Box IIIA 1–3, Lindemann Collection, Center for the History of Medicine, Francis A.Countway Library of Medicine, Boston, MA]

130. folder "NIMH", Box III A6, Erich Lindemann Collection. [Center for the History of Medicine, Francis A. Countway Library of Medicine, Boston, MA]

131. Ryan, William, 12/14/1979, *ibid.*

132. Duhl, Leonard, MD, Department of Public Health, University of California—San Francisco and Department of Psychiatry, University of California—Berkeley; interviewed by telephone at the University of California—Berkeley by David G. Satin, 4/2/1979, 8/16/2007. [caddy 2, box 4, X, Lindemann Collection, Center for the History of Medicine, Francis A. Countway Library of Medicine, Boston, MA]

133. Gans was recommended by Duhl: Duhl, Leonard letter to Lindemann, Erich, 12/18/1956. [folder "Columbia-Washington Heights Community Mental Health Project", Box IIIA6 Da GAP, Erich Lindemann Collection, Center for the History of Medicine, Francis A. Countway Library of Medicine, Boston, MA]

134. Lindemann correspondence with Hugh Leavell of the HSPH (who was unavailable to attend this meeting), 5/4,6/1959. [folder "Misc L", Box IIIA 1–3, Lindemann Collection, Center for the History of Medicine, Francis A. Countway Library of Medicine, Boston, MA]

135. Lindemann, Erich, memo to Martin, Mr. Lawrence E., MGH, 12/2/1957. [folder "760–9544–2 West End Project (exchange [*sic*] no. for MGH)", IIIB2 b (box2 of 3), Erich Lindemann Collection, Center for the History of Medicine, Francis A. Countway Library of Medicine, Boston, MA]

> We have been awarded a new research grant, 'Relocation and Mental Health—Adaptation Under Stress', from the United States Public Health Service through Harvard Medical School. The grant became effective December 1, 1957 and has been awarded for a five year period.

136. Lindemann letter to Kane Simonian, 8/2/1957. [folder "Misc. Correspondence S—1956–7", Box IIIA 1–3, Lindemann Collection, Center for the History of Medicine, Francis A. Countway Library of Medicine, Boston, MA]

137. Spofford, William B., Jr. letter to Lindemann, 7/22/57. [folder "Misc. Correspondence S—1956–7", Box IIIA 1–3, Lindemann Collection, Center for the History of Medicine, Francis A. Countway Library of Medicine, Boston, MA]

138. Elling, Ray H., "To Strike a Balance", Ch. 2 in Elling, Ray H. and Sokolowska, Magdalena (eds.), *Medical Sociologists at Work* (New Brunswick, NJ: Transaction Books, 1978)

139. Hallman, Howard W. correspondence with Lindemann, 12/17/1958, 1/2/1959. [folder "Misc H", Box IIIA 1–3, Lindemann Collection, Center for the History of Medicine, Francis. A. Countway Library of Medicine, Boston, MA] Referred via John D. Stoeckle, MD, MGH.

140. Caplan, Gerald, associate professor of mental health at the HSPH, letter to Lindemann, 8/24/1959. [folder "M", Box IIIA 1–3, Lindemann Collection, Center for the History of Medicine, Francis A. Countway Library of Medicine, Boston, MA]

141. Lindemann letter to Kalman J. Mann, 9/4/1959. [folder "M", Box IIIA 1–3, Lindemann Collection, Center for the History of Medicine, Francis A. Countway Library of Medicine, Boston, MA]

142. Hargreaves, G. Ronald correspondence with Lindemann, 10/29/1957–5/9/1961. [folder "Misc H", Box IIIA 1–3, Lindemann Collection, Center for the History of Medicine, Francis. A. Countway Library of Medicine, Boston, MA]

143. Correspondence between Collins and Lindemann, 6/10,15/1957. [folder "Misc. Correspondence C—1956–5", Box IIIA 1–3, Lindemann Collection, Center for the History of Medicine, Francis A. Countway Library of Medicine, Boston, MA]

144. Fried earned his bachelor's degree and began psychology graduate studies at the City College of New York, completed his PhD at Harvard University, worked there as a research analyst, studies psychotherapy under Erich Lindemann and group psychotherapy under Elvin Semrad and was not chosen by Stanley Cobb to apply his experience with large-scale research methods to clinical data, though he was recommended by Clyde Kluckhohn (director of the Harvard Russian Research Center), Eugenia Hanfmann (Harvard Psychology Clinic and Brandeis University), Robert W. While (Harvard Department of Social Relations), and Elvin Semrad (Boston Psychopathic Hospital and Department of Social Relations). [folder "Old Applications C-F 1955", Box IIIB1 e 1), Erich Lindemann Collection, Center for the History of Medicine, Francis A. Countway Library of Medicine, Boston, MA]

145. Center for Community Studies memo 10/2/1956, folder "NIMH" *ibid.*

146. Morris, Laura, 11/19/1979, *ibid.*

147. Fried, Marc, interview by David G. Satin at Boston College, Newton, MA, 11/16/1979.

148. Morris, Laura, 11/19/1979, *ibid.*

149. Ryan, William, 12/14/1979, *ibid.*

150. Morris, Laura, 11/19/1979, *ibid.*

151. "Annual Report for the Department of Psychiatry for the Year 1955 Statistical Summary from October 1, 1954–September 30, 1955", p. 2. [folder "Annual Reports from Staff Members 1955", Box IIIB1b box 1 of 2, Erich Lindemann Collection, Center for the History of Medicine, Francis A. Countway Library of Medicine, Boston, MA]

152. Fried, Marc, and Rosenblith, Judith, memo to Lindemann, Erich, 1/9/1963. [folder "Allinsmith-Fried-Rosenblith Center for Studies in Human Development—1960", Box IIIB1a box 2 of 2, Erich Lindemann Collection, Center for the History of Medicine, Francis A. Countway Library of Medicine, Boston, MA]

153. Allinsmith, Wesley, and Klein, Donald, memos to Lindemann, Erich, 3/15/1961:

> Recommendations of successors as director of the Center for Studies in Human Development, include Judith Rosenblith [who was eventually appointed] vs. Donald Klein [Executive Director of HRS]; expand HRS role to cover coordination of the Center's projects including Dr. [Timothy] Leary's. Donald Klein interested—change his HRS role from Executive Director to consultant.

Klein, Donald memo to Lindemann, Erich:

> Addendum to Dr. Allinsmith's Memorandum to Dr. Lindemann from: Donald Klein. . . . One possibility, which I think warrants consideration, is that the "Little Red House" [Resident Physician's House, MGH] be the headquarters for the "Center for Mental Health Studies" of the MGH Department of Psychiatry. This would serve to consolidate such

activities as Parents Without Partners, the leadership training research Leary et al. are developing, the Woodland Community Project in Maine, and Mike's [von Felsinger] industrial work. I would be willing to coordinate such a center as I have the HRS to date. My position at HRS might then become that of a consultant.

154. Letter from Rosenblith, Judy F., to Lindemann, 3/4/1963. [folder "Correspondence 1963", Box IIIA 1–3, Lindemann Collection, Center for the History of Medicine, Francis A. Countway Library of Medicine, Boston, MA]
155. Lindemann, Erich, letter to Knowles, John H., 6/2/1964. [folder "Dr. John Knowles, Medical Director—MGH", Box IIIA 4 (I-Ma), Erich Lindemann Collection, Center for the History of Medicine, Francis A. Countway Library of Medicine, Boston, MA]
156. Lindemann, Erich, letter to Rosenblith Judith, 11/12/1964, p. 1:

> As you know, I have considered your contribution to this program as most important and was very much saddened by our inability to continue the program in human development [J.R. work in neonatal, child development & learning, incl cns on preschool screening & writing at HRS incl c EBL] because funds for further work were not forthcoming. It seems that Dr. [Nathan] Talbot [Chief of Ped, MGH] has made some very active advances to Dr. [Jerome] Kagan [HGSE] to work out his own pattern of collaboration between the Pediatrics Department and the Center for Human Development in the [Harvard] Graduate School of Education. I would be very pleased if some pattern of participation in the future program could be realized.
>
> [folder "Rosenblith, Dr. Judy", Box IIIB1e 2), F-Ma",
> Erich Lindemann Collection, Center for the History
> of Medicine, Francis A. Countway Library of
> Medicine, Boston, MA]

157. Publication of previously unpublished materials in the West End Study library include the following:

> Gans, Herbert J., *The Urban Villagers: Group and Class in the Life of Italian-Americans* (New York: The Free Press of Glencoe/The Macmillan Company, 1962)
> Fried, Marc, *The World of the Urban Working Class* (Cambridge, MA: Harvard University Press, 1974)
> Fried, Marc, *Grieving for a Lost Home: Psychological Costs of Relocation* (1966)
> Singer, Jerome and Opler, Marvin K., "Contrasting Patterns of Fantasy and Motility in Irish and Italian Schizophrenics", *Journal of Abnormal and Social Psychology* 53: 42–47 (1956)
> Opler Marvin K., "Cultural Anthropology and Social Psychiatry", *American Journal of Psychiatry* 113: 302–311 (1956)
> Bakst, Henry, Berg, Robert, Koster, Fred, and Raker, John, *The Worcester City Tornado: A Medical Study of the Disaster* (Washington, DC: Commission on Disaster Studies, Division of Anthropology and Psychology, National Academy of Sciences—National Research Council, 1/17/1955)
> White, Richard, "Mental Health and Housing" (manuscript)
> Poston, Richard W. (director of Department of Community Development, Division of Area Services, Southern Illinois University)—description of community development program in Cairo, Illinois for development of

better mental health via improving economy, services, etc. (manuscript, 10/5/1956)

Lindemann, Erich, notes on anthropology, psychiatry, mental and psychosomatic illness, conflict, and crisis

Gans, Herbert J. (research associate, University of Pennsylvania), proposal to John A. Clausen, NIMH, for a sociological/city planning study of a new community (Levittown, New Jersey) in terms of what makes for a desirable community relevant to mental health

"Housing and Welfare", *Journal of Housing* (National Association of Housing and Redevelopment Officials)—special issue re importance of housing in social welfare

"The Development, Content and Evaluation of the Group Mental Health Project with the Public Welfare Department of the City of Boston" (spring, 1956)—history of negotiations for a mental health consultation and training session with Welfare Department caseworkers

Morris, Frank W., Jr., chief of development in the State Housing Board, "Comments on Urban Redevelopment and Urban Renewal", giving a history and estimation of benefits of federally funded and state implemented urban renewal, including the New York Streets Project, West End Project, Mattapan (Massachusetts) Project, and the Demonstration Project (Metropolitan Housing Association of Greater Boston survey and study of the techniques of involving the community in urban renewal)

Mason, Helen A., MSW., "A Follow Up Study of Former Psychiatric Patients Who Lived in the West End of Boston". John Baldwin, MD consulted on the research design and analysis. General consultations were given by Peter E. Sifneos, MD, the director of the MGH Adult Psychiatry Clinic, and Laura Morris, community social worker in the MGH Mental Health Program. [folder "MASON, MISS HELEN MSW", Box IIIB1e 2), F-Ma", Erich Lindemann Collection, Center for the History of Medicine, Francis A. Countway Library of Medicine, Boston, MA]

Zola, Irving Kenneth, PhD, Harvard University Department of Social Relations, then 10/1962 MGH assistant sociologist, then 9/1963 Brandeis University assistant professor of sociology but continued his MGH appointment part time, "Socio-Cultural Factors in the Seeking of Medical Aid" (unpublished)

Stoekle, Joseph, MD, Zola, Irving Kenneth, PhD, and Davidson, Gerald E., MD, "On Going to See the Doctor, The Contributions of the Patient to the Decision to Seek Medical Aid", *Journal of Chronic Disease 16*: 975–989 (1963).

Fried, Marc: paper for Monday Luncheon of the Club of Male Social Work Executives, 10/27/1958

Sifneos, Peter E., "West End Seminars"

> [Erich Lindemann Collection, Center for the History of Medicine, Francis A. Countway Library of Medicine, Boston, MA]

158. Fried, Marc, PhD, Center for Community Studies, MGH and HMS, progress report to Duhl, Leonard J., 9/1963, p. 2. [folder "Leonard Duhl—NIMH Corr"., Box IIIA 4 (A-E), Lindemann Collection, Center for the History of Medicine, Francis A. Countway Library of Medicine, Boston, MA]

159. Memo from Duhl, Leonard J. to Erich Lindemann, 9/10/1962. [folder "Correspondence 1962", Box IIIA 1–3, Lindemann Collection, Center for the History of Medicine, Francis A. Countway Library of Medicine, Boston, MA]
160. Duhl, Leonard J. letter to Lindemann, Erich, 10/7/1963. [folder "Leonard Duhl—NIMH Corr"., Box IIIA 4 (A-E), Lindemann Collection, Center for the History of Medicine, Francis A. Countway Library of Medicine, Boston, MA]

8 Seeking a Place at Harvard for the Social Ideology

Teaching of Psychiatry in the Harvard Medical School

An important function of the MGH Department of Psychiatry according to Lindemann was teaching HMS medial students and psychiatric residents. Lindemann looked on this as another route to changing the face of medicine by influencing new physicians toward social and community medicine. And this was another theater of the struggle between CMH revolution and counterrevolution and the cycle of rise and eclipse of CMH.

Lindemann reviewed the history of Harvard's approach to psychology in the university and how this filtered down to the MGH:[1]

> In 1947, President Conant appointed a Commission to review the place of psychology in the University under the chairpersonship of Alan Gregg. The main concern then was to find a way of integrating in a complementary way the experimental approaches in psychology and the then budding social science contribution and social psychology, anthropology, and sociology itself. As most of you know, the recommendation of this Commission not to split the field into two competing and mutually, somewhat alien segments of university life was not heeded; and there followed shortly the Department of Social Relations as a group of investigators separate from the Laboratories of Experimental Psychology. It speaks well for the power of the Medical School to embrace simultaneously a wide range of concepts and issues that today we are trying to speak in a complementary way about both the experimental and social approaches to psychiatry.
>
> (p. 1)

> It was then that a period of [my] work in the Department of Social Relations followed by a period of studies at the School of Public Health helped us to capture for our purposes some of the significant concepts being developed at this time by Talcott Parsons and his co-workers as well as by Robert Merton and Theodore Newcomb.
>
> (p. 2)

This background had shaped Lindemann's formulation of mental health and illness:[2]

> Early clinical studies had shown us that an essential component of emotional crisis such as bereavement is the role transition which is engendered by the change in the social system. Adapting to the loss of an important other person required a redefinition and reorganization of a whole profile of roles, whether ascribed or acquired, whether shared or separate, whether complementary or autonomous to the roles played by the other person that was lost.

In 1955, near the beginning of Lindemann's tenure as a professor of psychiatry at Harvard University continued in its effort to develop psychology in its various forms throughout the university, as reflected in "The Summary of Staff + Activities related to Mental Health, 1955":[3]

7/26/55

MASSACHUSETTS GENERAL HOSPITAL . . . A mental health service is being established in the clinic which will be concerned with services and research in preventive psychiatry. A team of psychiatrists, psychologists, social workers, and social scientists will be organized for diagnosis and preventive intervention in crises which are known to produce stress. An investigative team will be concerned with the origins of social maladjustment and with the spectrum of reactions to emotional crises.

APPENDIX B. SUMMARY OF PRESENT STAFF AND ACTIVITIES RELATED TO MENTAL HEALTH

I. The Behavioral Sciences Dr. [Morton] Prince, in 1926, had established and financially supported the Harvard Psychological Clinic as a center for research activities in this field. After Dr. Prince's death, the leadership of the Clinic was taken over by Dr. Henry A. Murray who, though absent for considerable intervals from the university, remains the senior member of its staff. Explorations in Personality, 1938, by Murray and his staff, set forth the field of their research interests at this period. Dr. Robert W. White, author of The Abnormal Personality, is the other permanent member of the staff. In 1946 the Clinic was incorporated into the Laboratory of Social Relations as a research facility, and the teaching services of its staff have been taken over by the Department. After a few years' experience in the new organizational setting, the curriculum of the clinical psychology branch of the Department was drastically revised in the direction of placing more emphasis on research training in the field of personality and less on that of training practitioners of clinical psychology. . . .

With the recent appointment of David McClelland as Professor of Psychology, this field has been strengthened greatly.

(p. 1)

Talcott Parsons' sociological study of medical practice, social anthropologist William Caudill's study of the mental hospital. Graduate student dissertations: David Aberle and Kaspar Naegele at HRS; Ozzie Simmons at Boston State Hospital. Rich Solomon, associate professor of social psychology—experimental psychology. R[obert] F[ried] Bales, associate professor of social relations in small group research. In HGSE [Harvard Graduate School of Education] Laboratory of Human Development—John Whiting, director, long range study of child development including intercultural. Center of Field Studies director Prof. Cyril Sargent studies of school systems in various communities; Prof Neal Gross—societal role of school superintendent.

II. The Medical-Health Area The Department of Psychiatry in the Medical School is undergoing a through reorganization which has already greatly increased its potential".(p. 3) Dr. George Gardner, Clinical Professor of Child Psychiatry, Director of Psychiatric Services, Children's Medical Center, continues as Director of the Judge Baker Foundation which is made a part of Children's Medical Center. "Dr. Erich Lindemann, who worked very effectively in establishing a division on community mental health in the School of Public Health for a number of years, is now Professor of Psychiatry in the Medical School and Chief of the Psychiatric Service at the Massachusetts General Hospital, where the Professor of Medicine, Dr. Walter Bauer, has broad understanding of the importance of mental health and its somatic relations. Dr. George Saslow, also oriented to mental health, is now associated with Dr. Lindemann as Clinical Professor of Psychiatry. Dr. Alfred H. Stanton has been appointed Associate Professor of Psychiatry and Chief Psychiatrist at the McLean Hospital. All of these men have had close association with the behavioral sciences; both Dr. Gardner and Dr. Lindemann hold PhDs in psychology in addition to their medical training and both have held teaching appointments in the Department of Social Relations. Dr. Stanton has recently published (with Morris Schwartz, a sociologist) what is essentially a sociological study, The Mental Hospital . . . Following the appointment of Dr. Lindemann in the Medical School, Dr. Gerald Caplan took charge of the School of Public Health programs in mental health . . . Robert Reed, Associate Professor of Human Ecology and Biostatistics, trained in sociology and biostatistics, directs population studies in this area.

After the Department of Social Relations had very generously demonstrated the value of introducing behavioral science teaching in the School of Public Health, this was put on a firm basis by the full-time appointment of Benjamin Paul as Lecturer in Social Anthropology. In addition to collecting case studies of health problems viewed by behavioral scientists. . . . Dr. Paul, together with Ozzie Simmons (another social anthropologist with health experience), is conducting a community study of rehabilitation of patients discharged from mental hospitals. . . . The School of Public Health has close relationships with the Massachusetts Department of Public Health and with local health departments. . . . The Director of the Division of Health, Hospitals and Medical Care of United Community Services of Metropolitan Boston . . . is an enthusiastic member of the faculty.

(p. 5)

III. Interdisciplinary Collaboration . . . A striking example comes from the "Behavioral Sciences at Harvard", report by a Faculty Committee, June 1954, which reported research projects in the health area. . . . "At Harvard, anthropology, psychology, and sociology have had particularly close relations with the field of education, medicine and public health". . . . It is particularly noteworthy that early collaboration was quite spontaneous, representing the investigator with individual interests seeking out other individuals whose interests might throw new light on the problem being studies. A more comprehensive and balanced collaboration was suggested in the report on the "The Behavioral Sciences at Harvard", which said, "The administrative device of a coordinating committee, appointed by the president of Harvard through the appropriate deans, would seem to be the best procedure for assisting priorities in research grants and appointments which may involve relationships between a particular professional school and the relevant department in Arts and Sciences". (p. 475). Dean [George Packer] Berry of the Medical School proposed to President [of Harvard University Nathan] Pusey the formation of such a committee in the spring of 1955, saying that "Our thinking about these matters has been stimulated during the past five or six years by the increasing contacts between the groups working on both sides of the river [i.e. arts and sciences, and medicine]. It would help Harvard take advantage of the unparalleled opportunities here in the social sciences, including especially their role in medicine and public health.

The physician has a unique opportunity to open the door into the lives of individuals, families and communities. The social scientist, in walking through the door thus opened, can immediately capitalize on the, to him, otherwise unavailable areas for study. He can at the same time, furthermore, help the physician to understand better his activities as they relate to the individual in the family and community settings. All that the physician does will accordingly be enhanced. By pooling their talents and research techniques, the social scientist and the physician can accomplish as a team what neither can accomplish alone".

President Pusey appointed the Inter-Faculty Committee on the Behavioral Sciences in May 1955.

(pp. 6–7)

Members: Walter Bauer, Jackson professor of clinical medicine and head of the Department at MGH; George E. Gardner, clinical professor of psychiatry and director of the Psychiatry Services at the Children's Medical Center and lecturer on clinical psychology in the Department of Social Relations; Charles A. Janeway, Thomas Morgan Rotch professor of pediatrics and head of the Department at Children's Hospital; Hugh A. Leavell, professor of public health practice and head of the Department in HSPH (chairperson); Erich Lindemann, professor of psychiatry and head of the Department at MGH; Talcott Parson, professor of sociology and chairperson of the Department of Social Relations; Benjamin D. Paul, lecturer on social anthropology in HSPH; Samuel Stouffer, professor of sociology and director of the Laboratory of Social Relations; John W. Whiting, associate professor of education at the Harvard Graduate School of Education and lecturer on social anthropology and director of the Laboratory of Human Development; Henry C. Meadow, assistant (associate) dean of the Faculty of Medicine and Executive Secretary to the University Committee on Research and Development.

Lindemann from HMS and Hugh Leavell from HSPH quickly followed up on this Ford Foundation–sponsored university survey and planning project by negotiating for Ford Foundation funding for behavioral science senior faculty members and postgraduate fellows from their schools and Harvard nonmedical departments.[4] The HMS was unwilling to commit itself without permanent funding, while the HSPH was willing to participate in a pioneer program.

Lindemann saw this as introducing a broader adoption of his efforts in social psychiatry and its application in the health field:[5]

our original steering committee is active again at quite an "exalted" plane. Dr. [Nathan] Pusey, the new President of Harvard University has called together a standing committee for the further development of joint investigative and service efforts in the field of mental health. It combines psychiatrists, social scientists and experts in public health and medical practice. You will not be surprised to find that the group is essentially an enlarged steering committee as we first created it in relation to the Wellesley Project. . . . This group will plan new developments in the application of social science skills and know-how to problems not only in mental health but also to other problems in the health area. At the founding meeting it was made clear by Dr. Leavell . . . that the Wellesley Project had been the starting point of these significant developments.

This shift in medical and psychiatric ideology greatly influenced the MGH Psychiatry Service and supported Lindemann's efforts. It was reflected in the medical student curriculum in psychiatry.

Lindemann had been teaching psychiatry to first-year HMS students since Harry Solomon was in charge of this in 1942. Eugene Landis and his successor, George Wislocki, professors of physiology, each gave 10 hours for the early teaching of human behavior, response to stress, and symbol-using human organisms.[6] "The students must also learn to think of him [the person] as an individual living in a social context which contributes to or detracts from his well being" (p. 1). This approach was reaffirmed at the 1952 Ithaca Conference of medical school deans and psychiatrists, published by John Whitehorn. Lindemann recalled that[7]

I came back to the Medical School from the School of Public Health. . . . I was asked to come partly because it was desirable that the medical students, in the early stages of their development, as well as the residents in psychiatry, might be confronted with some of the areas of public health concerns. This has to do with the development in the Medical School in which the curative preoccupation of the young physician is expected to be altered to a "health" preoccupation of the mature physician. The medical man who "sells his" curative skills will become a responsible "health man" who feels by virtue of his knowledge and his skills, beholden to be the guardian of the health of a population.

The actual implementation of this program of bringing public health, and particularly "behavioral science public health", into the Medical School took place in the last two years. We no longer have a course in psychiatry in the first or second years of Medical School. We have instead a two-year course in <u>Growth and Development</u> which is jointly given by a faculty committee, in which the psychiatrist and mental health people are working together with the biostatistician of the Medical School from the Department of Preventive Medicine, with the people in Anatomy who are concerned with embryology and developmental anatomy, with the people in Child Psychiatry who are concerned with personality development, with the people from Social Science and Psychology who are studying personality structure, the life-cycle in terms of typical life crises, and the ways in which social organization and the institution of the family color the course of a given life-cycle, and affect the relative social well-being, in a population. The first year of this course deals with health issues, while the second year adds pathological issues to this type of consideration.

The negotiation with medicine, surgery, pediatrics, and neurology for time and coordination of teaching was hesitant and gradual.[8]

All psychiatry departments at HMS participated in this psychiatric education, with positive responses from students. Lindemann saw the psychiatry education as an aspect of a drive toward CMH in the Mental Health Service of the MGH Psychiatry Service:[9]

> The mental health program in the Harvard University Medical School came about when it was decided that medical students in the early stages of their development, as well as residents in psychiatry, should be confronted with . . . the concerns and methods of public health. . . . This resulted in a new educational emphasis, whereby the curative preoccupation of the budding physician would hopefully be expanded to a commitment to be the guardian of the health of a population and to be cognizant of mental health issues facing . . . that population. this program was greatly aided by Dr. Gerald Caplan at the Harvard School of Public Health. His appointment to the Medical School faculty and to the . . . Massachusetts General Hospital, and my continued faculty membership in Public Health insured close collaboration.
>
> At the residency in psychiatry . . . we formed a Mental Health Service within the [MGH] Department of Psychiatry. The major objective . . . Can health considerations be added to the medical objectives of the hospital in such a way that the medical staff member will view himself as a health officer?
>
> The psychiatrist . . . attempts to suggest that the relationship of the patient to the ward population and its caretakers is worthy of the joint attention . . . hope to interest the staff in the emotional well-being of the . . . patient population of the . . . ward . . . the mental health team seeks to study the emotional hazards as well as the supportive features of the ward experience . . . to help create the healthiest possible emotional environment . . . examine the ward "curriculum". Consultants broadened their focus to include . . . the mental health of the staff as well as the patients. [p. 4/230]. . . . The hospital itself is embedded in a larger community . . . its outpatients and by the . . . residential area which surrounds it. The Mental Health Service was concerned with both. . . [p. 10/236] . . . the flow of the patient population through this [medical outpatient] service . . . the West End program . . . gave access to the population surrounding the hospital. . . [p. 11/237] . . . a hospital mental health service . . . as part of the hospital community itself, it is often perceived as having vested interests of its own, including values which may clash with those of others and strivings for satisfactions and [p. 12/238] rewards. . . . Therefore, it moves toward . . . autonomous

activities . . . a secure base . . . the development of a coherent frame of reference" [p. 13/239].

More specifics were given about medical student teaching:[10]

The first and second year HMS course Growth and Development consists of biostatistics, anatomy, and the social sciences, including psychology, personality structure, responses to life stresses, and the structure and dynamics of the family, social institutions, and organizations (taught by . . . child and adult psychiatry, the biostatistician from the Department of Preventive Medicine . . . Anatomy concerned with embryology and developmental anatomy, and . . . psychologists and other social scientists). "The students, therefore, are encouraged to view matters of individual health and illness in relation to the ways in which groupings in the social environment color the pathway of a given life cycle and affect the relative physical, social, and emotional well-being of a population . . . student reaction is favorable, and the level of interest in broad cultural problems surprisingly high to those who had imagined that medical students, as a group, were primarily biologically oriented and basically disinterested in the social sciences". (However, this course proved to be too eclectic for several members of the sponsoring faculty committee and was replaced after several years by a course entitled The Study of Human Behavior. He complained about the paucity of psychiatry training in the internship year: "The part which psychiatry plays in such an internship in our hospital is rather small, only six weeks of the year's period are devoted to actual service on the psychiatric floor. The real opportunity is training in our area which comes at the end of the year's internship".)[11] Resident education under the Mental Health Service within Department of Psychiatry will be similar to past community work.

(pp. 2,3)

The first-year medical school course was described as follows:[12]

The contribution of the Department of Psychiatry is through a course entitled "Growth and Development". Eleven out of twenty-four lectures have been given by Drs. Gardner Quarton, Grete Bibring, and John Spiegel. In addition a Clinic was given in November illustrating psychological problems. This Clinic, under the direction of Dr. Erich Lindemann, proved exceptionally successful. . . . There is no question but that the cooperation between the Department o Psychiatry and the Departments of Anatomy, Physiology, and Biochemistry, have been particularly valuable.

The second-year medical school course was described as follows:

> Psychiatric instructors during the second semester will share two clinical sessions with the medical section instructors [John Nemiah-psychiatry and John Stoeckle-medicine] and two with the surgical section instructors. Each . . . is oriented 1) toward techniques of interviewing and observation of behavior as a means of obtaining psychological and social information that is relevant to the patient's illness; and 2) toward examining the nature of the relationship between doctor and patient.
>
> Seminars for the non-psychiatric instructors are being given . . . to present these instructors with the fundamental psychiatric concepts and operations, as a basis for the combined section teaching. c) Integrated Section Teaching. Dr. [Thomas] Dwyer has joined the committee on Gastro-intestinal Diseases. . . . it participates in the planning and teaching of this two week course. . . . It is hoped that in future years this type of integrated teaching with the other medical school departments will be increased.

Lindemann saw this HMS medical student teaching as part of a broad interdisciplinary, interfaculty approach to community mental health education generated from the MGH program:[13]

> Interfaculty relations outside the Medical School to other professional schools is maintained through membership of senior psychiatrists on planning and steering committees of these schools. In this way Dr. Lindemann is concerned with mental health teaching in the Divinity School. . . . Drs. [Alfred] Stanton [McLean Hospital] and [George] Gardner [Children's Hospital] are particularly interested in joint teaching with the Department of Social Relations and Dr. Lindemann has a close working relationship and cooperative program at the Harvard School of Public Health. . . . The teaching of psychiatry is discussed and planned by a committee of senior psychiatrists representing the seven cooperating hospital units in the Harvard orbit. It consists of Drs. Lindemann, [Gardner] Quarton and [John] Nemiah for the Massachusetts General Hospital; Dr. Grete Bibring for the Beth Israel Hospital; Drs. [Jack] Ewalt, [Elvin] Semrad and [Ives] Hendrick for the Massachusetts Mental Health Center; Dr. [George] Gardner for the Child Psychiatry Program; Dr. [Henry] Fox for the Peter Bent Brigham Hospital; Dr. Philip Solomon for the Boston City Hospital. . . . Dr. Quarton of the Massachusetts General Hospital is coordinating the first year teaching program. Dr. Nemiah of the Massachusetts General Hospital, the second year. Both of these programs have seen a new development in the last two years, becoming part of a teaching program in human growth and development

which provides the opportunity for much faculty interaction with other departments of the Medical School. The third year program is being coordinated by Dr. Elvin Semrad and is almost exclusively carried out at the Massachusetts Mental Health Center. The fourth year program. . . . the students are assigned to the various centers.

The graduate [residency] training program is essentially a function of the separate autonomous units and is being elaborated for special purposes by each unit. . . . The Massachusetts General Hospital has developed a program for training in community mental health open to psychiatrists, psychologists and social workers in close cooperation with the Harvard School of Public Health. . . . A beginning has been made for the development of a coordinated didactic graduate training program which is planned by a committee from all the units and has led to a central course in basic psychopathology, psychophysiology and social psychiatry . . . open now to all residents in the various units comprising one morning a week throughout the year.

(pp. 2–4)

Lindemann saw the teaching of medical students and psychiatric residents as extensions of the CMH perspective of his Mental Health Service in influencing the perspective of hospital staff:[14]

it was decided that medical students, . . . as well as residents in psychiatry, should be confronted with some of the areas of a public health concern. I also wished to seek the most suitable mental health orientation for a psychiatric team in a general hospital . . . part of a development in the Medical School of a new educational emphasis whereby the curative preoccupation of the budding physician . . . is expanded to a "man of health" beholden to be the guardian of the health of a population . . . cognizant of mental health issues facing large segments of that population . . . more particularly, "behavioral science public health". . . . A tangible expression of the altered orientation in the Medical School is the course in Growth and Development, which has incorporated some aspects of the previous offering in Psychiatry. . . . this two year course . . . brings together mental health specialists, the biostatistician from . . . Preventive Medicine, and those in Anatomy concerned with embryology and developmental anatomy . . . child psychiatrists focusing on personality development and . . . dynamic adult psychiatry concerned with the vicissitudes of the adult personality . . . psychologists and other social scientists . . . introduced the students to . . . personality structure and responses to typical stresses . . . the structure and dynamics of the family. . . [and] other institutions and social organizations. The students . . . view matters of individual health and illness in relation to the ways . . . groupings in the social environment color . . . a given life cycle and affect the relative physical, social, and emotional well-being of a population. . . [and] at the more advanced level of the residency in psychiatry. . . . <u>Can health considerations be added to the medical objectives of the hospital in such a way that the medical staff member will view himself as a health officer?</u> The psychiatrist member of the health team . . . suggest[s] that the relationship of the patient to the ward population and its caretakers is worthy of the joint attention of himself and the medical staff. . . . [He] hopes to interest the staff in the emotional well-being of the total patient population . . . including those who are allegedly mentally healthy as well as those with special needs in the personality sphere. . . . the mental health team seeks to study the emotional hazards as well as the supportive features of the ward experience . . . to help create the healthiest possible emotional environment. . . . Ward curricula . . . often rest largely on staff as vs. patient needs . . . our consultants have broadened their focus to include a concern for the mental health of the staff as well as the patients. . . . As the pattern of the Mental Health Service unfolds. . . . It continues to offer direct help with psychiatrically disturbed patients. . . . It [also] moves out increasingly into the flow of life in the hospital, relating . . . to significant segments of this community. . . . the hospital moves into focus as a community.

(pp. 1–5, 12)

Funding for long-term support of this manifestation of the CMH program was sought via a grant application to the Special Study Section, Division of Research Grants, National Institutes of Health. There was a broad range of support for this:[15]

Dr. Dean A. Clark, [Gen'l Dir] Mass. General Hospital, Dr. John Stoeckle, Medical Outpatient Department, (MGH), Professor Martin Meyerson, Center for Urban Studies, Harvard University, Dr. Robert Rapaport, McLean Hospital, Dr. Robert Reed, Harvard School of Public Health, Dr. Benjamin Paul, Harvard School of Public Health, Dr. Alex Inkeles, Professor of Sociology, Harvard University, Dr. John Whiting, Department of Social Relations, Harvard University, Dr. George P. Berry, Dean, HMS, Dean John C. Snyder, Harvard School of Public Health, Dr. Hugh R. Leavell, the Head of the Department of Public Health Practice, Harvard School of Public Health, Dr. Louisa Howe [HSPH], Dr. Rhona Rapoportl, Dr. Dean A. Clark, [General] Director, Massachusetts General Hospital, Dr. Harry C. Solomon, Commissioner of Mental Health, Massachusetts Department of Mental Health, Professor John W.M. Whiting, Director of the Laboratory of Human Development, Harvard University, Dr. Martha M. Eliot, Head, Department of Maternal and Child Health, Harvard School of Public Health, Dr. Robert W.

White, Department of Social Relations, Harvard University, Dr. Jack R. Ewalt, Medical Director, Massachusetts Mental Health Center, Dr. Martin Meyerson, Director of the Center for Urban Studies, Harvard University, Dr. Alex Inkeles, Professor of Sociology, Harvard University. . . . During the meeting . . . at the Massachusetts General Hospital, Dr. Gerald Caplan, Harvard School of Public Health, Dr. Donald Klein, HRS

Suggesting the shift of professional ideology and institutional policy, from 1960 psychiatry teaching was reduced in the revised Growth and Development course: "the result of a then prevailing opinion on the part of the medical faculty that integrated teaching of human biology was desirable and appropriate. This view is still held by a number of senior members particularly by Eugene Landis [HMS Professor of Physiology]". In response, Lindemann reiterated a social psychiatric view of comprehensive medical practice and the medical education to prepare for it:[16]

> During the last two decades there has been very considerable advance in the sciences which are basic for understanding and control of mental disease. . . . These have included the following: new insight into the structural aspects of the brain by application of ultra-microscopic methods; new understanding of the chemical processes in the Central Nervous System; and, most important, development in the understanding of the human personality. Personality is seen as the integration of organismic function for purposeful action, motivated by basic drives organized in terms of habituated adaptive patterns of behaviour, and co-ordinated with the actions of other organisms in patterns of role and status. This means that the social sciences relating to social structure and to group processes have become significant for the "mental" diseases as well as for certain forms of physical impairment. The very large field of psychological and emotional causation of illness in general, of unsuccessful treatment, for delayed recovery from surgery and of psychosomatic medicine—all this has become an important part of psychiatric research and service, and indeed of teaching.
>
> (p. 2)

> Simultaneously with this development [in medical education], there has been an impressive change in concepts and methods concerning the care of patients with severe mental illness.
>
> (p. 3)

> They are now seen (and often understood) as "persons in despair", and in the grip of an unsolvable predicament, or they are found to be in extreme panic because of frightful anticipation for the future. It is

true that they show misunderstandings and failure in judgement and that impaired brain conditions may aggravate their predicament; but it is also true that the life problems of many of them are so severe that many a doctor confronted with a similar problem would also break down. In other words, the new development in psychiatry has seen the ability to understand patients [as] troubled people who need emotional support and acceptance rather than persons to be segregated from their families and thrown together, perhaps locked up, with other people in equal despair . . . psychiatrist[s] have reacted to this new understanding by opening the doors of the hospital, and by giving patients much more freedom. They have also introduced a programme of intensive social service to tackle the unbearable situations at home which have often led to the patient's illness. They have invited the families to come into the hospital to keep up their contact with the patient and to remain aware that at any moment they may have to receive them back into the community. This [has] led to better communication between professional staff, the families and the community leaders. . . . They have learned to carry first aid into the families at times of emotional crises. They have carried programmes of education in mental health and in the prevention of mental breakdown forward into the community. As mental health workers they have been active with the school doctor and nurse in safe-guarding the mental health of school children. They have made common cause with the leaders in churches and religious organizations to help them understand psychological mechanisms and recognize early danger signals for mental break-downs. They have learned enough from these leaders about their religious values and traditions to respect them when they play a role in the mental conflict of the patient.

(p. 4)

Of necessity, this has opened a large area of joint effort between the physician and surgeon on the one side and the psychiatrist on the other. With greater mutual acquaintance there has come greater mutual confidence.

(p. 2)

Correspondingly, the psychiatrist has become an indispensable consultant and joint therapist in the care of many severe physical illnesses, such as ulcers of the stomach and asthma. . . . All this has meant close co-operation of medicine and psychiatry. The student will hear the psychological aspects of the illness discussed by the internists, will see the psychiatrist as a welcome consultant on medical and surgical rounds, will hear the psychiatrist's comments at staff meetings. . . . Only that which is in fact part of medical practice can be taught as part of medical education. . . . From the very first day the student is reminded that his new knowledge of anatomy and physiology as well as of biochemistry is ultimately to be put to the service of living human beings who have certain kinds of personalities, motivations and capacities, who develop and mature not only with their bones and endocrine glands but also with their mental capacities, who may be ruined in their growth not only by bad nutrition . . . but also by an overload of emotional problems at specially vulnerable periods of childhood development. Integrated courses on growth and development arranged by a joint committee composed of an anatomist, physiologist, pediatrician and psychiatrist have been the answer. A special kind of teaching exercise, linking techniques of physical diagnosis with proper interviewing techniques to ascertain the relative importance of emotional and social factors in every patient, has become an important part of the schedule of good medical teaching. Much of psychiatric teaching in this way becomes "implicit" rather than being labeled "psychiatry proper". These men have broadened the narrow fields of knowledge of old-fashioned psychiatric practice to include the latest developments in integrative neurophysiology, in personality theory and in social science, as well as interviewing techniques, psycho-analytic studies and the group-dynamic skills. If they are available as teachers, competent doctors will be trained who can carry out their community responsibility in curative and preventive psychiatry, and many will become so interested that they will want to specialize in this promising field of medicine.

(p. 3)

In 1961, he described the MGH teaching of psychiatry to medical students:[17] "In the Medical School the Psychiatric Service is responsible for the Psychiatric teaching in the 1st and 2nd year in Growth and Development, centered on personality development and the basic aspects of the social system of the growing individual". By 1962, Lindemann acknowledged a fundamental change:

However, there have been a series of new appointments to the Medical School faculty representing a different approach and different opinions stressing basic science studies at the level of small biological units and wishing to postpone references to integrated matters in the curriculum to a later stage in the student's development . . . As you know, I do not agree with their position and believe as do all the members of our senior faculty that our contribution to the first year should continue even though other parts of the program in Growth and Development will be taught from now on in different departments. . . . Peter Dews, Al Stanton and Frank Ervin are even now busy thinking of modifications for next year which would strengthen the interface with the biological sciences and reduce those segments of the teaching program in which the evidence presented may rest on clinical influence.

My hope would be that ultimately this course will be an introduction to the social and behavioral sciences in medicine and that as such it would continue to make an important contribution to the first year phase of the education of future physicians at Harvard.

(p. 2)

In 1962, the president of Harvard University, Nathan Pusey, appointed another ad hoc committee to review and plan the future of psychiatry at HMS. The tone had shifted from social toward basic science:[18]

In 1952, Mr. [James] Conant [President of Harvard University] appointed an ad hoc Committee to study how best to strengthen psychiatry at Harvard and to recommend a candidate for the professor of psychiatry to serve at the Massachusetts General Hospital. Dr. Erich Lindemann was proposed for this important position, the ad hoc Committee having recognized his great interest and ability in the areas of interaction of psychiatry and social science. As Head of the Department of Psychiatry at the M.G.H., Dr. Lindemann has served with distinction. . . . With the retirement of Dr. Harry C. Solomon [MMHC] and the mobilization of the Stanley Cobb Fund for the Development of Teaching and Research in Psychiatry at the Harvard Medical School, a new ad hoc Committee was appointed by Mr. [Nathan] Pusey [president, Harvard University] (in 1958) to study how best to strengthen psychiatry at Harvard and to propose a candidate to succeed Dr. Solomon as Professor of Psychiatry and Director of the Massachusetts Mental Health Center . . . and to nominate the first incumbent for the chair established in honor of Dr. Cobb. . . . The relationships of the Boston Psychoanalytic Institute to the Departments of Neurology and Psychiatry have been reviewed. . . . Early in their discussions, it became apparent to the ad hoc Committee that—in view of Harvard's present strong representation in the clinical areas of child and adult psychiatry. . . . the greatest contribution that the Cobb Professorship might provide within the Faculty of Medicine would be the implementation of a scientific area basic to clinical psychiatry. The Cobb Professor should preferably be located in the Longwood Quadrangle [the Harvard Medical School location] . . . might provide a resource for clinical psychiatry in a manner analogous to biochemistry, physiology or microbiology with respect to clinical medicine. . . . This seemed also to be especially appropriate because Dr. Cobb, in his own professional life and interests, dramatized so vividly this point of view. . . . Should he be selected from the field of neurophysiology, endocrinology, psychology, or the social sciences?. . . . It was repeatedly emphasized that a basic scientist working in such a highly specialized field of the chemistry or physiology of the nervous system would not . . . be the best choice. It was felt that the Cobb Professor, if a basic scientist, should be an individual whose basic studies extended into the behavior of the organism as a whole. . . . the ad hoc Committee reached a consensus that the outstanding candidate was already a tenured member of the Faculty of Medicine, namely Dr. Peter B. Dews, Associate Professor of Pharmacology. . . . He became deeply interested in the investigation of the influences of drugs on behavior . . . equip[ped] himself with the requisite factual and methodological knowledge in the relevant areas of psychology. Then he developed a laboratory for the study of the effects of drugs on behavior . . . nominate[d] for the Cobb Professorship a young man . . . to bring to the field of behavioral science and psychiatry . . . experience in medicine, physiology, pharmacology, mathematics, and psychology.

(pp. 1–8)

In response to this progressive shift, in 1962, Lindemann met with HMS Dean George Packer Berry, perhaps to test the medical school's direction and seek support: "I would like to get your reaction to my opinion and, indeed, to that of our Department about priorities in the development of the program in the behavioral and social sciences at the Medical School".[19] In 1964, Berry wrote to Lindemann: "As you know, various members of the faculty have been exploring the adequacies and inadequacies, depending on one's point of view, of our program for medical students having to do with sex".[20] This debate is reflected in a Curriculum Committee meeting:[21]

Debate over a shift, increase or decrease, hours assigned to psychiatry in the HMS first year education. "1. The course as given was not thought to be equivalent to the other basic sciences in presentation which it was felt placed the subject at a disadvantage. Finally, it was recommended that the Curriculum Committee make this course informal or voluntary for this academic year pending a decision. . . . Dr. [Jack R.] Ewalt [Bullard Professor of Psychiatry] felt . . . it seemed impossible to him to have a basic science year without touching on the sciences underlying understanding the emotions. He noted that . . . last year an attempt was made to introduce some Sociology and Neurophysiology. Dr. [Bernard D.] Davis [Professor of an endowed chair in Bacteriology and Immunology] remarked that . . . Biochemistry, Bacteriology etc. were subjects a student must know and understand before he goes into clinical work; however, he did not feel that Psychiatry was such a necessary part of the students' basic knowledge. Dr. Ewalt stated that students must know about human behavior before working with people.

Dr. Davis wondered if there was any evidence that students could do this any better after first year Psychiatry. Dr. [George W.] Nichols [Jr., associate dean for academic affairs, secretary of the Curriculum Committee, HMS] interjected that the majority of students felt that the material should be included in the first year, but did not like the way it was presented. . . . Dr. [Joseph. W.] Gardella [associate dean of Faculty for Student Affairs, HMS] felt that the pre-clinical state-ment was good but agreed that Psychiatry teaching was of immense value to the student. Dr. Kennedy pointed out that the course is what remains of a planned course on developmental biology and personality development. The students should be introduced to this material as soon as possible but it would be more beneficial if it was condensed into later years rather than having a large block during the basic science year".

(p. 3)

Debate over whether psychiatry time had previously been protected or made contingent on Biostatistics time assignment (Ewalt and David D. Rutstein, professor and chairperson of the Department of Preventive Medicine, HMS, supported psychiatry time, Kennedy opposed it). "Dr. [George W.] Thorn [HMS Professor of Medicine and Physician in Chief at the Peter Bent Brigham Hospital, and Com-mittee chairperson] felt that the Pre-Clinical Section did not have the right to make free time in the first semester, second year at the expense of Psychiatry when the Curriculum Committee had not agreed to reduce Psychiatry".

(p. 4)

Jack Ewalt, HMS senior psychiatrist, passed to Lindemann these changes in the teaching of psychiatry:[22]

I have the schedule . . . for the spring semester. . . . I notice that there are 8 lectures and 2 additional periods . . . or a total of 12 hours.

I have the distinct feeling that even this amount of time is in jeop-ardy and any expansion of it will be dependent on convincing the Curriculum Committee . . . that the material presented is really a basic science of behavior and not a study of the more total manifes-tations of behavior, that is, greater emphasis on the roles of neuro-physiology, anatomical structure and chemical procedures on man's behavior . . . more on conditioning, consciousness, arousal, memory, thinking functions, emotions and their control, with more hinting at social and psychoanalytic concepts . . . what we know about stress and the general bodily responses, without an attempt at this time to explain such phenomena as resistance, etc. . . . I would also ask if I could see copies of the information you send on to Dr. Nichols' office so I will be better prepared for the next meeting of the Curriculum Committee.

The Curriculum Committee further pursued this altered perspective:[23]

[T]he Curriculum Committee recognized the fact that the time formally assigned to the teaching of Psychiatry in the new curriculum represented a considerable reduction from that assigned to this department in the past. It felt however, that this change would be more than offset by collaborative exercises conducted by instructors in Psychiatry with instructors in Medicine and Surgery during which the emotional aspects complicating or arising from medical and surgical illness could be discussed. The usefulness of such exercises in bringing to the attention of students the importance of emotional factors in understanding somatic illness was commented upon by a number of committee members who had had personal experience with this type of teaching exercise.

Peter Sifneos, the MGH psychiatrist who coordinated the teaching of psychiatry in the HMS principal clinical year, reported that psychiatrists were in fact teaching the student groups alone, without being teamed with surgeons or internists.[24]

Lindemann suggested to Berry an agenda for their meeting on October 14, 1964:[25]

the teaching program of our Department in the first year continues to be attacked by Drs. Kennedy and Fawcett as unsuitable for the first year. I need your advice as to the best posture to take. This includes your opinion about the future of the behavioral and social science program at Harvard Medical School.

In this context, he also wanted to discuss the relationship of Harvard University and MGH in regard to the planned Government Center Mental Health Center. Following that meeting, Lindemann wrote a broad defense of the teaching of social psychiatry and not only addressed it to Berry but also gave copies to Dr. Thorn and Dr. Ewalt:[26] Lindemann appreciated Berry's discussion of the "controversy now existing in the Curriculum Committee concerning our first year teaching" (p. 1). He asked Berry to be at the Curriculum Committee meeting on November third:

The teaching of certain aspects of human behavior and of social context during the first year goes back more than twenty years supported by the keen interest of Drs. [George] Wislocki [HMS professor of anatomy], Eugene] Landis [professor of physiology], and [A. Baird]

Hastings [professor of biochemistry] who all were interested in the integrative aspects of human biology. Until 1954 Henry Fox [chief of psychiatry at the Peter Bent Brigham Hospital] and I shared this course. We were able to present to the students at least the rudiments of an organized approach to the study of human emotions and to the influences which impinge on the individual as part of a social system. When I became Professor, I understood the first and second year teaching to be my major assignment at the undergraduate level. I conceived of it as a cooperative program mobilizing the strength of the senior members of my department for a course in personality development and social organization. Drs. Wislocki and Landis helped us to gain an additional ten hours for more detailed discussion of personality development. We were happy when this course was integrated with certain other courses into a joint effort in the field of growth and development. Gardner Quarton [MGH psychiatry] with a large group of faculty members and in consultation with Drs. [A.] Clifford Barger [HMS professor of physiology] and Manfred Karnovsky [HMS professor of biochemistry and pharmacology] developed a course which reflected the consensus and strength of our department. We were naturally disappointed when new faculty appointments led to a change in prevailing opinion and to disintegration of the course in growth and development. This process of change went on without much discussion in the faculty at large. The appointment of Dr. Peter Dews [HMS researcher in psychobiology and pharmacology] promised to add great strength to the first year teaching but obviously some time was required before this could materialize. I, therefore, arranged for a committee reflecting our basic orientations, namely, that of social and dynamic psychiatry represented by Alfred Stanton; of biological psychiatry as represented by Frank Ervin; and the experimental psychology approach as represented by Peter Dews to arrive at a gradual modification of the first year course in order to articulate it with the expanding program of biological basic sciences at the medical school. . . [earlier draft: "We presented a course perceived the best of previous years but somewhat under the shadow of faculty awareness of the change in social climate" (p. 2).] Naturally, I have been much distressed by recent efforts of members of the Curriculum Committee to curtail the time of our course and to reduce it to one half its size. They buttressed these efforts with critical comments about our course and with the expression of doubts about its appropriateness for the first year. [earlier draft: "I have been surprised indeed that our course should be exposed to the danger of destruction by a shift in opinion of members of the curriculum committee" (p. 2).]. . . . [Preparations for] planning next year's course replacing multiple lectureships by continued presentation on the part of one lecturer and making an effort to align the presentation with laboratory evidence familiar to the students from their work in other departments. However, I would consider it a tragic development [in] this great medical school that a professor entrusted with the teaching of a given program can be subject to the short term fluctuations of faculty opinion which are inevitable in our fast growing faculty.

Lindemann's discouragement with the prevailing HMS ideology in regard to the teaching of psychiatry is reflected in his letter to George Thorn regarding the subsequent Curriculum Committee meeting on November 3, 1964, regarding the teaching of psychiatry to first-year medical students:[27]

> You will be interested in the enclosed copy of a letter to Dean Berry containing some comments on the development of our teaching in the first year. I doubt if it will be fruitful for me to appear and plead a cause which appears to have so little value to the members of the Committee.

This shift of dominance from social back to biological ideology at the MGH was reflected in the petition by MGH staff members of various departments (see more later). In part, it sought psychiatrists trained as physicians in medicine, neurology, and clinical neurophysiology and sought to "encourage the use of physical and chemical methods in the treatment of psychiatric illness". Perhaps another contribution to Lindemann's discouragement about his ability to influence this change and encouragement to seek early retirement was the impending retirement of HMS Dean George Packer Berry, who respected Lindemann and in some ways supported Lindemann's perspective.[28]

Lindemann described this arc of psychiatry teaching ideologies as follows:[29]

> many years ago the emphasis had been in the tradition of Cannon with the study of emotions. Later the emphasis was increased on the patient and on teachers as human beings, and there was the addition of a great number of detailed studies of personality development. More recently, because of various pressures within the school, there has been a decreased emphasis on clinical presentations and also a diminution in the number of hours available for psychiatry teaching. There has been a return to a more biological approach.

The Family Health Program of the Massachusetts General Hospital

One MGH social medicine program was the Family Medicine/Family Health/Home Care Program. It's struggle for legitimacy, acceptance, and a secure place in clinical care and medical education again reflected the coming and going of the era of social medicine.

Ida Cannon, who established the first medical social work program at MGH, remembered interest in social aspects of medicine dating years before:[30]

> I think too of the earlier efforts of Dr. Edsall, George Minot and George Reynolds and Howard Means, who for so many years so consistently taught social aspects of medicine in their clinics—but never really secured its adoption into the curriculum. . . . I remember him [Dr. Edsall] saying that his interest in the social side of medicine was largely due to his experience in district visiting in Philadelphia.

In 1947, an ad hoc committee on preventive medicine concluded that "There has been too little demonstration that personal, social and environmental factors influence the incidence of disease and may adversely affect the course of disease".[31] However, HMS Dean Berry convened a luncheon on home care,[32] and one was established shortly afterward. It had been built upon an MGH Children's Medical Service home visit program since 1945, one that was extended to bring comprehensive health care to 200 indigent children in the West End neighborhood, coordinated with public health and nursing agencies. This was extended to a Family Health Service without age limits, directed and staffed by MGH Children's Health, Medicine, and Psychiatry Services. Research on social factors in health and illness prevention was to be in collaboration with the HSPH, and it was expected to enrich the education in pediatrics and internal medicine regarding normal development and psychosomatic and socioeconomic environmental issues.[33]

It was recognized that there was an interest in some quarters at Harvard in social aspects of medicine:[34]

> It is excellent to have the interest and promised cooperation of some of the senior people from the Department of Social Relations [H.U.] and I suppose you have already been in touch with Professor Sears. As indicated by Dr. [Samuel] Stouffer [sociologist, director, Harvard Laboratory of Social Relations], his thinking should contribute a great deal along lines of research designs to explore emotional growth and development.

In June 1953, the philosophy of comprehensive family medicine and a structure of a Family Health Program was laid out by David Rutstein [HMS chairperson of the Department of Preventive Medicine],[35] the planning committee was made official,[36] and it began to meet.[37] Funding sources included the Hyams Fund,[38] the Rockefeller Foundation,[39] and "a letter from the New England Chapter, Arthritis and Rheumatism Foundation, expressing its interest in the Family Health Service and willingness to receive a request for part of its financial support".[40] The Family Health Service came into being:

> Starting December 14, 1953 a Family Health Service (FHS) will be inaugurated in this hospital to render medical care in the home and in the hospital to families who reside in the West End of Boston. At the start service will be provided to children up to the age of 16 years. Service to adults will be added at a later date (p. 1).[41]

Almost immediately there were doubts about the appropriateness and effectiveness of this education and resistance to adapting the regular curriculum to incorporate it rather than segregate it as a separate, elective specialty.[42] Whatever the reservations of some in medical administration and practice, this comprehensive, community medicine spoke to others— such as a third-year HMS student:[43]

> I feel that a truly major portion of medical education depends on seeing patients over a somewhat protracted period in their own home environments. . . . There are thus certainly three major advantages to be gained from such a teaching plan: first, a chance to see patients as full people living complicated lives, and the implications of this for their diseases; second, a chance to observe what the community actually thinks of medicine and what medicine is actually doing in the community; third, confrontation with the problem of what the place, duties, and potentialities of medicine really are in bringing something to people as they actually live their lives.

The HMS Dean appreciated this:[44]

> your thoughtful letter . . . explains better than I could why we have been working hard for two years to make possible at Harvard the sort of opportunity you discuss. . . . may I have your permission to duplicate your letter for the use of members of the committee working on family care programs with me?

The program was supported by the MGH and Rockefeller Foundation, and plans were made to incorporate the experience into the curriculum of medical students.[45] A Rockefeller Foundation grant was obtained for 1957–1959 (subsequently extended for another five years without additional funds) to fund an experiment in family health practice and education, with the MGH committing itself to fund the program after the grant period. Medical student educational goals were similar to those in CMH:[46]

> the network of human relations and the type of adaptive responses to these relations which the patients . . . develop. The four most important areas of inquiry . . . are
>
> 1. Those of personality development
>   . . .
> 2. The significance of role and station which the parents have in the social systems to which they belong
>   . . .
> 3. The kind of social interactions which are possible for a given individual in sickness or health due to his belonging to a group with inescapable influence over him
>   . . .
> 4. The area of value orientation, goals and desires for achievement . . . which differs from neighborhood to neighborhood and from ethnic group to ethnic group.
>
> (pp. 1–2)

There was no statistical evidence of effects on the students; those already interested in general practice, pediatrics, and psychiatry were most appreciative of the education, as opposed to those interested in surgery and other specialties.

After the grant funding plans were made to incorporate the service and education into ongoing MGH services,[47]

> B. Plans for the Program after the end of the Educational Experiment on June 30, 1959 1. Medical Care a. The Massachusetts General Hospital will keep space available and accept financial support of the Family Health Program in proportion to the service rendered to regional families. . . . b. The Well Child Conference in the Children's Medical Clinic should be continued. . . . d. Home Care services will be continued for families in the Program. 2. Teaching a. During the academic year 1959–60 the Program will participate with the 3rd year course in Medicine at the M.G.H. . . . responsible for a series of seminars . . . emphasizing the social, environmental and epidemiologic factors. . . . b. A 4th year elective course will be offered in "Family Medicine". c . . . house officers from the Children's Medical Service should be assigned several Program families . . . 3. Research After the end of the teaching experiment, the Program should be devoted primarily to research. There is at present an excellent opportunity to study the effects of displacements by the [West End] housing project.
>
> (pp. 1–2)

The program's Policy Committee worked on ways of continuing family/home health training by integrating it into conventional courses in clinical medicine, though it was hard to find adequate time for exposure to homes and environmental conditions.[48]

The HMS Curriculum Committee rejected the teaching proposal, students were no longer assigned to the Program, and the MGH pleaded inadequate funds for it,[49] though its general director

> reminded the Committee that at the time of the original Grant from the Rockefeller Foundation the Trustees of the . . . Hospital had agreed to accept financial responsibility for the Program at the termination of the Grant. He believed that the Hospital was obligated to live up to this commitment.
>
> (p. 2)

The clinical and teaching activities, affiliations, and staff commitment gradually dissipated.[50]

Ambulatory Clinics Committee of the Massachusetts General Hospital

Another manifestation of the social ideology subject to support and abandonment was the MGH Ambulatory Clinics Committee. It was appointment in August 1955, met December 1955–July 1957, and included the chiefs and some staff of all MGH services, including Lindemann and George Saslow from psychiatry, Physician Dana L. Farnsworth (chairperson), and Assistant Physician John D. Stoeckle (secretary).[51] Its purpose was to organize noninpatient medical care along modern lines, balance research and teaching with patient care, and slow the spiral of increasing costs of medical care. Lindemann brought the parallel values and goals of the MGH Mental Health Service:[52]

> your committee on the Massachusetts General Hospital as a community hospital. . . [parallels] the psychiatric approach to community problems is particularly auspicious because it does not meet with the same objections from the local doctors competition-wise. . . . We have not long ago been authorized by the hospital to create a mental health service which has had as its explicit aim to infiltrate the neighborhood of the hospital with preventive services. . . . I hope, as we did in Wellesley, to gradually get to know and to work with the various "care-taking professions" such as doctors, clergymen, educators, social agency workers and law enforcement workers. . . . The information which your committee is going to collect concerning on-going practices and desirable policies will be most welcome to us.

Its recommendations included the following:

1. A new building
2. Adequate offices, technical resources, and space
3. Allow addition of private offices and incorporate technical resources that can serve their patients
4. After approval of this report arrange immediate appointment with the building committee
5. Simplified administrative organization and patient processing
6. Admit patients independent of income—private payment if they can afford it
7. "That the possibility of developing prepayment plans for the treatment of illness without confinement to a hospital bed should be explored with Blue Cross-Blue Shield organizations as well as with private agencies" (pp. 3, 4).

The philosophy of community service is expressed in excerpts:
  Medicine in the Community

> It has gradually become evident that the hospital is an integral part of the community, whose function it is to recognize with broad perspective the health needs of the populace and to respond to those needs with appropriate action. In other words, the center of interest has shifted from whatever aspects of medicine seemed for the moment to be of prime importance, to the needs of the patient as he exists in his usual setting. . . . It does . . . call attention to the fact that medical knowledge in isolation is of less practical value to the community than when it is correlated with the rest of daily life. . . [the outpatient department] Beginning in 1821 as an adjunct to the main activity of the hospital and spontaneously offered . . . as a form of charity to such individuals as seemed in acute need.
>
> (pp. 4–5)

Wealth Not a Criterion

> the time has come for the hospital to abandon the policy of trying to differentiate between patients who can pay for hospital care and those who cannot, and to develop instead a policy of basing fees for health care on income. . . . Such a system would permit all patients to receive the same quality of care.
>
> (pp. 20–1)

What Was Rejected

1. Group practice with complete merging of private and clinic patients. This was thought to be unacceptable to a large proportion

of the present staff . . . and to involve too radical a change in the prevailing pattern of practice. It was comparable to a plan which had been studied and discarded in 1952.

(p. 22)

Who is Eligible?—Payment

The committee recommends that the Clinics of the Ambulatory Service accept as patients all individuals who apply for health care, regardless of their income level; that the quality of health care provided for all patients be the same, regardless of financial status.

(p. 23)

"Recently, points of view have changed, and many teachers feel that medical students should begin their professional training with direct clinical contacts. . . . They feel that such contacts introduce students more advantageously to the broad aspects of health care than do clinical experiences which are initiated at a later stage of training. Students who have from the beginning learned to observe and deal with the personal aspects of illness tend later to establish much more flexible therapeutic relationships with patients than do students who make their first clinical contacts after having acquired an intellectual armament with which to treat disease. . . . Before they can become physicians in the full sense of the term, medical students must undergo emotional as well as intellectual learning. This emotional learning is greatly facilitated by familiarity with the predicaments of patients as they come to the hospital"

(pp. 42–3)

An MGH surgeon did not see social issues as the hospital's business:[53]

I do think the report is perhaps more heavily weighted with expressions of a philosophy of comprehensive medical care and an exposition of economics and sociology than seems pertinent to the problems of the Committee.

An MGH administrator was concerned about competition and financing in the healthcare arena:[54]

One big question that is not answered in the Report is 'What is the community need for the M.G.H. Clinics?' . . . In view of the highly competitive health facilities situation in Boston, the expected change in the immediate neighborhood, the growth of prepayment plans . . . the need to have an agreed upon over all hospital plan.

The Ambulatory Clinics Committee also took account of the Family Health Service as another expedition into social medicine:

> the Program's administrative unit which includes: an internist and pediatrician, a public health nurse, social worker, administrative assistant, secretary, and medical and pediatric house officers . . . medical students assigned to the Program. . . . Space is also needed for combined epidemiological and laboratory research.
>
> (p. 60)

> 8. THE FAMILY HEALTH PROGRAM Since July 1954 the Family Health Program has selected . . . approximately 170 medically indigent families who live close to the Massachusetts General Hospital and who have traditionally come to this hospital for their medical care. The Program has agreed to provide complete medical care . . . including home care and preventive services, utilizing existing facilities within the hospital rather than establishing a separate . . . medical care unit.
>
> The Program was primarily established as an experiment in medical education, supported by the Rockefeller Foundation for the first five years. Each of the 15 third-year Medical School students is assigned to at least one Program family . . . He then takes supervised medical responsibility for this family during his last two years in the Medical School. This is the only opportunity for Harvard Medical School students to follow patients for more than a three month period.
>
> (p. 1)

The following year, the committee expressed interest in a public health scholar to address sick and recuperated patient, but it made no mention of social influences on illness, health maintenance, and illness prevention.[55]

In retrospect Lindemann recognized that the authority structure of the MGH restricted a CMH approach and that his "guru" role raised further barriers: "Lindemann weeps for the bleeding hearts of West Enders".[56]

Funding of Psychiatry at the Massachusetts General Hospital

Throughout his tenure, Lindemann sought funding for his network of community mental health programs from sources supportive of a social and community perspective.[57] A prime candidate was the William T. Grant Foundation, which had funded the HRS. The previously cited report indicates that it did contribute to the support of the Mental Health Service as a transfer of HRS work to the urban setting of MGH. In 1962, he wrote to thank them for a photograph of W.T. Grant and to note signs of support for this kind of work (perhaps more in other institutions than at the MGH):[58]

> We have just witnessed at an International meeting on Preventive Psychiatry in Holland how from the seeds which you helped to plant in Wellesley in 1948 there has grown a body of knowledge and a set of skills which make preventive work possible for many professional groups now engaged in clinical work and discouraged about the many therapeutic failures once disease and handicap are established.

Noting the Grant Foundation past support for HRS, the West End Project, and a small beginning working with patients and families in the MGH Emergency Ward and medical and surgical services, he proposed eight to ten years of support for programs at MGH and McLean Hospital:[59]

> Both units have solid facilities for neurobiological research. However, much significant growth is envisaged in the area of the <u>application of the social sciences to the study of behavior</u> and in the speedy <u>utilization of new knowledge to the actual care of the sick</u>. The leaders of both units also share a keen sense of responsibility for the detection of early signs of threatening future emotional disorders and for <u>preventive programs</u> which reach into the family, neighborhood and community institutions to safeguard the population by suitable methods of preventive intervention.

At this juncture, a bold new program in preventive psychiatry is envisaged, one that would involve operations in both units.

The program would include a laboratory of behavioral science at McLean Hospital; an MGH center of preventive psychiatry (studies of community background and predicaments leading to treatment in the Emergency Ward, outpatient department, inpatient service, and social agencies); the study of critical phases of human development; and the application of these studies to cross-cultural comparisons leading to the development of health services that recognize cultural factors promoting healthier lives. He included stipends for six preventive psychiatry trainees in clinical and social sciences and four fellows from India and other countries.[60] His plan extended to relations with other Harvard University units—especially divisions under Dr. Jack Ewalt [HMS psychiatry], the HDSR, the HSPH, and the HGSE, as well as an advisory committee from the World Health Organization and the World Federation of Mental Health. Following up on this proposal he reminded the Grant Foundation that "I undertook with the initial support of the Grant Foundation to carry mental health principles into a large metropolitan hospital while at the same time continuing the work in the

Wellesley Human Relations Service".[61] He requested major support for the stability of the mental health program at HSPH under Gerald Caplan and the interrelation of the MGH and HRS under Lindemann. He was optimistic about possibilities for the coordination of research and teaching in HRS, the Human Development Program at MGH (with the interest of Nathan Talbot, the new professor of pediatrics), and the James Jackson Putnam Center for early infant development.[62] Research methods and results could be taught to pediatric and psychiatry residents in conjunction with the HSPH. He pointed out that it was important to prepare the continuation of this social and community approach in light of his retirement coming up in three years, though he hoped for a successor, such as Dr. Anthony (St. Louis) or Dr. John Bowlby (London). In response, the foundation replied that its trustees agreed to continue funding projects and not endowment grants and therefore rejected the proposals.[63]

Lindemann was especially successful at winning grants from the federal NIMH. For instance, in 1959, he prepared extensive descriptions of plans and accomplishments in instituting public health, community, preventive, and interdisciplinary teaching and practice at MGH and Harvard University. They show his maintenance of his ideals and plans, even halfway through his tenure and after much resistance to converting MGH psychiatry to a force for converting MGH. Also his commitment to supporting health, preventing mental illness, and viewing people in a social context (see notes for his expositions).[64]

As part of the adaptation of HRS approaches to the MGH Lindemann applied to the NIMH for a grant for "An Exploration in Training of Psychologists for Community Mental Health", as well as those for psychiatry and social work.[65] His arguments for this grant are an exposition of his concepts of CMH as they had matured to this date. HRS under NIMH training grants experimented with including a public health/preventive and interdisciplinary approach to the core educations of psychology, psychiatry, and social work. He pointed out that the Institute on Education and Training for Psychological Contributions to Mental Health noted great opportunities for an expanded role for psychologists, leading to the incorporation of the HRS training program into the 1956 American Psychological Association report "Psychology and Mental Health". He highlighted the HRS program as inherently encouraging prevention, public health, the promotion of health, and the reduction of casualty rates. These applications for funding were focused on social psychiatry and CMH programs and training.[66]

Note that NIMH funding of CMH training programs for psychiatrists, psychologists, and social workers was credited to MGH as well as HRS. All this funding and these funding efforts quickly atrophied after Lindemann's retirement.

Psychiatry Research at the Massachusetts General Hospital

The Psychiatry Department initiated a spectrum of research projects and fielded proposals for expanded research and research resources and for integrating its research into other MGH disciplines and services.

Lindemann applied his social psychiatry perspective to his hopes and intentions for research in his department. He explained his reasoning:[67]

> 1. <u>The Field of Mental Health</u> Mental health as distinguished from physical health is a condition of personal, emotional and social well-being implying functioning at an optimal level for a given personality, a reasonable satisfaction of emotional needs (positive balance of frustration and gratification) and behavior which is both socially acceptable and productive. As in other fields of health this state is an ideal attained only by a segment of the population. There exists a biological gradient of health reaching from an optimum attained by few through various forms of common impairment in personality functioning, emotional balance and social integration to recognized forms of mental illness. . . . The biological gradient of disease means tracing an illness from the point of exposure to risk through latent forms, manifest symptoms, classical pictures and to fatal cases.
> 2. <u>Research</u> A pre-requisite for action is knowledge concerning causes of ill health and disease allocating the relative weight of contributing factors to host, agent and environment. The field of epidemiology is concerned with the diagnosis of disease as a mass phenomenon, namely, the distribution through a population of various stages of a given disease process and the investigation in the laboratory of the specific contributory aspects of host, agent and environment through the techniques of bacteriology and immunology. Behavioral science from this perspective can be used as a source of new methods and new concepts for the study of the social environment for the personality component of reactions of the host and for the details of host-environment interaction, namely the relationship of social system to personality structure and function. 3. <u>Service</u> Action for the control of disease and for the promotion of health deals with therapy for the sick, rehabilitation of those who cannot be treated successfully, discovery of early stages of the illness by case-finding methods, preventing more serious forms of disease process and finally by community-wide efforts to protect the population against the disease. In this last respect "the promotion of health" to the optimal level of functioning is considered as an unspecific effort in the prevention of illness but also is aimed at optimal development of potential resources (e.g., nutrition, education and recreation). In the field

of mental health this would lead to a keen interest in child-rearing methods, educational operations, job structure and preparation for the effects of the aging process.

The contribution which the behavioral sciences will make to the understanding of mental disease and to deviant behavior and to the promotion of good personality functioning, emotional balance and social integration should be expected to operate on all three levels of basic theory concerning social structure and personality integration with special reference to personality development and socialization but also with respect to those aspects of social systems such as primary groups, institutions and cultural orientations which may be relevant to mental health and mental illness.

(pp. 1–3)

He sought funding on the basis of social psychiatry research:[68]

UNDER THE DIRECTION OF THE PRESENT CHIEF OF PSYCHIATRY AT THE MASSACHUSETTS GENERAL HOSPITAL, THE RESEARCH PROGRAM HAS EXPANDED TO INCLUDE PROJECTS IN MENTAL HEALTH, COMMUNITY PSYCHIATRY, AND PREVENTIVE PSYCHIATRY. THESE HAVE BEEN CARRIED OUT IN COOPERATION WITH THE DEPARTMENT OF SOCIAL RELATIONS AT HARVARD UNIVERSITY, AND THE HUMAN RELATIONS SERVICE IN WELLESLEY, MASS., AND THE FAMILY GUIDANCE CENTER AT 20 WHITTIER STREET, BOSTON, MASS. . . . B. Research Program (a) Mental Health A major research interest is in the field of social psychiatry and human ecology . . . in addition to Dr. Lindemann, Dr. Gerald Caplan. . . . Dr. Peter Sifneos, Psychiatrist; Mrs. Laura Morris, M.A., Community Organization; Dr. A. Paul Hare, Social Psychologist; and Dr. Donald Klein, Clinical Psychologist. Drs. Sifneos, Gellert. . . . This group has four major objectives:

(1) Studies in the distribution of mental ill health in certain areas of metropolitan Boston, particularly in the so-called West End in the neighborhood of the M.G.H.
(2) The development of screening methods for the appraisal of personality and mental health in the patient population of the hospital and in the healthy population to which these patients give access.
(3) The systematic studies of interpersonal behavior in groups of patient and healthy individuals with respect to the assessment and development of social skills. . .
(4) The relationship of child rearing behavior of mothers of families in the neighborhood to the emotional development of

their healthy and their sick children. This study will be correlated with the Child Psychiatry Group and the Family Health Service"

Other research in Biochemistry, Human Physiology

"(d) Small Group Behavior Unit . . . research in group therapy, and for more systematic studies of the interaction of individuals in a small group setting".

(pp. 2–4, 6)

As noted, the recruitment of Alfred Stanton to direct the McLean Hospital was also intended to bring his social psychiatry interests to bolster that segment of the MGH psychiatry program. He was expected to bring social psychiatry to the MGH and Harvard University psychiatric research program:[69]

Research is . . . still very small in amount . . . and whose quality is exceedingly uneven. There do seem, however, to be significant breakthroughs in neurobiology, psychopharmacology, social psychiatry, and . . . psychotherapy and . . . psychological research. . . . Psychiatric research is still very weak however. Partly this can be attributed to the surprising but continuing opposition, not only to psychoanalysis but also even to psychology of any sort, which is still with us. . . . Harvard has also a rather thin research tradition in psychiatry which is now, fortunately, growing. . . . The reasons are . . . the senior persons are spread too thin, and with far too heavy administrative and service responsibilities. . . . Ultimately the School should look toward the installation of basic science courses in the behavioral sciences to prepare the student for his later medical work . . . analogous to the present preparation in biological sciences. . . . I am not using the term "basic" to indicate biological, neurological, or the like, but, for instance, studies of interviews, perception, and the like, which underlie not only psychiatry . . . but the practice of medicine itself. . . . Such a program should prepare the student for self-awareness, critical thinking in personal matters involving others, and research methods in the behavioral sciences.[70]

(pp. 2–4)

Anticipated Developments in the Department resulting from the Presence of a Research Professor. . . . There would develop a network of mutually facilitating groups located in our own Department and also in other parts of the University. To mention only a few: Dr. Robert [Jay] Lifton upon his return from Japan continuing his work on the effect of ideology and cultural transition on the patterning of psychopathology; Dr. Marc Fried, the co-ordinator of our inquiry concerning the effect of cultural variables on the adaptive behavior of families subjected to forced relocation; Dr. William Caudill in his future studies concerning the effect of the patterning of hospital administration upon the course of mental illness; and Dr. John Spiegel engaged with Dr. Florence Kluckhohn in studying the effect of different types of acculturation on the patterns of problem solving in families with different ethnic origin. All these would find a place for the exchange of ideas, for consultation and for companionship in the Center for Social Psychiatry which Dr. Stanton would develop. . . . the Research Center for Social Psychiatry . . . designating Dr. Stanton as Director of Clinical Research . . . consider the change of Dr. Stanton's Associate Professorship to a full Professorship . . . should the McLean facilities become for any reason inappropriate . . . the Massachusetts General Hospital facilities . . . can be arranged there.[71]

(pp. 18–21)

Large-scale funding was sought.[72] Lindemann also associated the search for expanded MGH space and resources with this social psychiatry research perspective:[73]

The chief aim of this unit [is] to lay the foundation for a preventive psychiatry of the future. The numerous illnesses which are wholly or in part based on psychological and emotional disturbances at present almost always reach the psychiatrist so late that long therapeutic efforts become necessary and even lengthy treatment may prove futile. It is argued that learning to find early danger signals in personality development when helpful intervention is still possible may be a far better way to the control of these illnesses. To make this possible, intensive research is needed on normal and faulty child development. We also need much more precise knowledge concerning the way in which networks of human relations, helpful or disturbing, develop for each growing individual. . . . we have to study the patterns of relatedness which exist between human beings in health and disease. It is now possible to study human interaction with precise methods in the laboratory. . . . It is hoped that on the floor adjacent to the new laboratory there will develop new facilities for the care of mentally and emotionally disturbed patients particularly those who develop their psychosis in the course of physical illness. The work of these laboratories together with the rich facilities of the Massachusetts General Hospital in bio-chemistry, metabolic studies and electro-physiology should do much to lift the veil of mystery which surrounds mental disease.

All this work presents a new chapter of intimate collaboration of psychiatrists with neurologists and internists, but the most important new step is the collaboration with scientists from the field of sociology and anthropology. Indeed some investigators like to describe this new field of endeavor as medical anthropology.

(pp. 1–2)

A selective array of research projects was suggested by clinical experience and rigorous study and analysis: the emotional health of the West End and its response to relocation, group consultation as a technique of preventive psychiatry, the study of unstable families and men who deserted their families and the effect on the deserted families, comparing multiproblem families with normal families, including as causes of justice-involved youth.

> The development of a center for more long range study of social behavior by assigning meaningful roles in a cooperative household to various individuals with psychoneurotic difficulties. This center would require development of special care-taking personnel and this would also necessitate the acquisition of a building in the neighborhood of the hospital. The other substantial request for support will be required for the child psychiatry unit. The emphasis will be [on] developing a set of screening methods to apply to a normal population and to children with various forms of illness in order to determine the range of adjustive potential of these children. The rapprochement of child psychiatry with the Roxbury Children's Center is envisaged in this respect.[74]

In refutation of complaints that Lindemann did not attend to financing the department, he continually planned for and sought support, including for research. In 1955, soon after his appointment, his plan "Needs for the Development of the Research Program in Psychiatry at the Massachusetts General Hospital"[75] sought the following:

1. Equip a research unit in the Medical Sciences Building, including social interaction and group behavior, experimental psychology, physiological aspects of emotional disturbance, and limited biochemical facilities.
2. Reorganize B-7 [the main psychiatric inpatient ward] as a joint medical-psychiatric service for the medical study of psychological reactions to severe social crises, such as bereavement.
3. Develop a center for the study of neuroses—observing, social skills, etc.
4. Engage personnel for the study of psychiatric rehabilitation, especially delayed recovery from accidents and surgery.
5. Investigate preventive psychiatry: "pathogenic effects which certain individuals have on other individuals without feeling sick".[76]

6. Study community programs regarding the pathogenic potential of critical periods in child development, including screening for early case finding in schools, baby clinics, and the community.
7. Study the effects of the social milieu on mental illness at McLean Hospital, by using social sciences, psychology, biochemistry, including a three-pronged attack on the problem of the metabolic concomitants of disordered behavior.

In 1962, he reviewed areas of research and their support needs:[77]

Future Objectives for Psychiatric Research

1. Provide long-range support for present senior investigators.
2. Develop suitable enlarged facilities for the care of patients with disorganized behavior, combined with research laboratories.
3. Jointly with McLean Hospital, extend these facilities to middle-income patients.
4. Provide acute psychiatric services based in the Emergency Ward and Over-Night Ward extending into the community (mobile teams).
5. Consolidate senior leadership for program in human development.
6. Further develop a center for the study of social processes within the hospital.

(See more later on regarding the development of a Social Science/Human Development Research Center.)

Lindemann sought research funding from various sources, especially the NIMH and W.T. Grant Foundation, which funded other aspects of his program.[78] When public policy and funding became available for preventive and social psychiatry, many academic institutions developed grant applications more or less in this field. As any grant writer does, Lindemann emphasized the strengths and accomplishments of his institutions, though also acknowledging complications and resistances.

The MGH[79] recognized that

> c) Community Mental Health. A major research activity of the department has continued to be the study of the relocation and mental health of the population of the Boston West End. . . . Dr. Elizabeth Gellert has been working on a project studying the reaction of children to illness and hospitalization,

as well as neuropsychological studies. The broad academic and community participation in this research is reflected in a memo from Dean A. Clark, MD, MGH general director; Erich Lindemann, PhD, M.D., chief of the MGH Psychiatric Service; Martin Meyerson, PhD, director of the Center for Urban Studies, Harvard University and Massachusetts

Institute of Technology; Bradford Washburn, director of the Museum of Science; Jane Dale, director of the Elizabeth Peabody House; and Laura B. Morris, community social worker in the MGH Department of Psychiatry.[80] It supported research in anticipation of new residents moving into the West End and recommended a larger meeting to think about institutions remaining in the West End to provide services; service overlaps and gaps to those likely to be tenants; their problems; "the elements which contribute to helping a community remain strong, creative and productive"; and the recommendation to "involve the residents in an active concern for the future welfare of their area".

Lindemann corresponded with Bernard Berelson, the director of the Behavioral Science Division of the Ford Foundation, including Lindemann's critique of a report from the Ford Foundation supported by Social Science Research Council.[81] Recommendations included training and recruitment to establish Institutes for Clinical Research in Therapeutic Process, Institutes for Research in Psychodynamics, Institutes for Research in Personality Development, Institutes for Research on Community and Social Aspects of Mental Health, and grants in aid for these purposes. Lindemann found these resources relevant to the MGH plans for research in the behavioral sciences and promised a careful response in August or September of 1954 from him, the HSPH, and the HRS. The Interfaculty Committee on the Behavioral Sciences approved a grant submission combining proposals by Lindemann and Fried Bayles, who were looking forward to William Caudill as a desirable program director.[82] Also, a "Rehabilitation Research Proposal, White 9", was prepared for the rehabilitation of those orthopedically disabled, with a focus on psychiatric, social, and community resource factors, and it suggested involving Joseph Stoeckle from the Medical Service and Gerald Davidson from the Psychiatry Service.[83] As part of planning for an MGH interservice research unit, the psychiatry researchers and projects at the time were listed:[84] "The first steps made possible by the new program for senior investigators in community mental health in the Massachusetts General Hospital orbit" (p. 1) Researchers included were Donald Klein, Paul Hare, Henrick Blum, Richard Poston, John Seeley, John Whiting, Timothy Leary (consultation visits), Wesley Allinsmith, Jason Aronson, Avery Weisman, Jerome Weinberger, and Louisa Howe. Projects included were Adaptive Responses in Families at the Advent of a Premature Baby (Family Guidance Center, HSPH), Adaptation to Entry into Public School (HRS), Adaptation of Families of Different Ethnic and Cultural Backgrounds to Urban Relocation (Center for Community Studies), and Adaptive Responses to Crises Leading to Acceptance of the "Patient Role" (MGH).

In social psychiatry, Dr. George Saslow and Dr. Joseph Matarazzo are continuing their quantitative measurement on social interaction in an interview setting. . . . As soon as we have facilities for the observation of groups of patients in interaction, such as are planned for the new research floor, we will put into effect a program of observations which has been planned by Dr. Paul Hare, a sociologist.[85]

In answer to a survey of research in medical school programs, the MGH Psychiatry services listed[86] "#18. principal research projects now being carried on":

- A. Relocation and Mental Health—Adaptation Under Stress (USPHS) $111,750 (Erich Lindemann, Marc Fried, Helen Herzan, Edw. Ryan, Peter Sifneos)
- B. Further Development and Research in Community Mental Health (USPHS) $74,750 (Erich Lindemann, Judith Rosenblith, Robert Bragg, Ralph Schwitzgebel, John Hill, Jason Aronson)
- C. Alcoholism Treatment and Initial Therapeutic Contact (USPHS) $68,527 (Erich Lindemann, Morris Chafetz, Howard Blane, Robert Bragg)
- D. Research on Information Processing in the Central Nervous System (Electronics Research Directorate, Air Force) $50,000 (Frank Ervin)
- E. Hall-Mercer Research Grant $32,535 (Erich Lindemann, Frank Ervin, Harry Olin, Peter Choras, John Nemiah, Jack Mendelson, Richmond Holder)
- F. Production of Alcohol Addiction in Experimental Animals (USPHS) $25,627 (Jack Mendelson, Nancy Mello)
- G. Death and the Denial of Death (Foundations Fund for Research in Psychiatry) $22,509 (Avery Weisman, Thomas Hackett).

In terms of Lindemann's research proposals, the MGH's response was both appreciative and hesitant. In the recommendations of its Scientific Advisory Committee on December 10–11, 1954, it observed the following:[87]

The Scientific Advisory Committee . . . is duly impressed . . . particularly with the free combination of disciplines in the attack on focal problems. In its desire to see this type of important service to the advance of medicine not only continued but further strengthened. . . . there has arisen a group of people not primarily a part of the affiliated educational institutions in the area, who are performing a valuable service in the furtherance of research. This group is making important contributions to new knowledge, is raising the stature of the MGH as an institution of learning, is providing an active program of interdisciplinary studies, and is enabling the Hospital to discharge better its responsibility for the care of patients. This function should be given recognition and its status be reaffirmed in the structure of the Hospital.

Reaction to Lindemann's detailed research agenda was more measured, the Committee needing to be introduced to the perspectives and practices of social psychiatry:[88]

> Mr. Ketchum [expressed] pleasure at efforts to draw McLean Hospital closer experimental association with MGH. [Joseph] Aub: [N] eurotic patients would be good subjects for biochemical study once the psychological disorder had been more clearly defined, that he, Dr. Aub, would think that the patients at the McLean Hospital with full-blown psychoses would be more appropriate material for biochemical study. Dr. Folch [Jordi Folch-Pi] wondered whether the intended study of patients in the presence of other members of their environment would not increase the complexity of the experiment by increasing the number of variables. Dr. Lindemann answered by pointing out that a study would be actually simplified because many manifestations of illness which would otherwise be concealed would be brought out in the presence of those who are important in the patient's life.

Dr. Churchill wished to know more clearly the boundaries of such a program, since Dr. Lindemann's presentation covered a good deal of ground. Dr. Lindemann pointed out that he had presented all the facets of the program and that he obviously will have to delineate a couple of areas in more detail for an application to the Ford Foundation. Dr. Berry agreed that a more specific formulation of one or more facets of the program should be undertaken and that these should be submitted to the Harvard Committee so that an integrated university program could gradually develop rather than a series of "splinter'" programs from various parts of the university.

The Harvard Committee then voted to encourage Dr. Lindemann to proceed in the formulation of his plans for one or more specific projects and to consult with others in the Hospital whose activities might be integrated with this application, the plan to be a part of the overall university plan in the behavioral sciences.

Note, however, that support was forthcoming: At the meeting on May 13, 1955, of the Executive Committee of the Committee on Research, Dr. Erich Lindemann's "Program of service and research in preventive psychiatry to be carried out by the Mental Health Service" was reviewed for transmission to the USPHS in the amount of $92,398 for the period July 1, 1955–June 30, 1956, with support requested for three years.[89]

Alexander Leighton, a major figure in social psychiatry, was, at that time, at the Psychiatric Clinic in Digby County, Nova Scotia, Canada, working on what became the Stirling County Study of mental health in the community context. He recruited Lindemann to write a chapter in an evolving book on that subject and asked for his critique of a report on the Deer Lake meeting for that purpose.[90] He also invited Lindemann to meetings to review the study and to comment on an article eventually published as "Studies in Social Psychiatry".[91]

In all, the Psychiatry Service accounted for 6%–15% of the research grants process by the MGH Committee on Research 1957–1962.[92]

Lindemann's social science approach was nontraditional in the MGH, including in terms of research. He tried to articulate it in the scientific terms familiar to the MGH:[93] He described CMH's concern with motivation; emotional reaction; and the antecedents, concomitants, and consequences of disease. While Cobb focused on anxiety, Lindemann's experience with the Coconut Grove fire focused him on grief and mourning as affecting the individual's visceral, psychological, and social integration, with a spectrum of responses, including mal-integration, beneficial integration as a model of crisis (change in the social situation), and reaction. (See John Gordon.)[94] Research in this area is not restricted to old conventions and nosology but instead seeks to quantify the significance of subjective states, social context, and cultural values in crisis.

> This philosophy is reflected in the establishment of mutually complementary research efforts in three laboratories: the Stanley Cobb Laboratory for the study of biological variables; the Center for the Study of Human Development for the investigation of personality variables; and the Center for Community Studies for investigations of social and cultural variables. In each of these centers we hope to get basic information which might buttress our clinical efforts to assist patients in adaptation to crises and in problem solving.
>
> (p. 2)

In support of this type of research, Lindemann suggested the appointment of at least three behavioral scientists to the MGH Scientific Advisory Committee, mentioning Roy Grinker, John Benjamin, Robert Merton, and John Romero.[95] Oliver Cope (who shared the psychosocial point of view and sat on the committee) replied that there were no vacancies on the committee in 1962 and would keep this suggestion on the list for the next year.[96]

Lindemann was recommended as the chief of the Psychiatry Service partly because of his interest and work in and with neurology, neurosurgery, endocrinology, biochemistry, and psychopharmacology.[97]

He looked toward enlarging this interservice collaboration from his enhanced position and suggested research laboratories shared by psychiatry, neurology, and neurosurgery, and a grant application was prepared for the Kennedy Foundation for this purpose.[98] In 1961, there was serious planning for a coordinated research unit to study the behavioral consequences of biological, psychological, and social factors. Lindemann wrote to William Sweet, MD, chief of the MGH Neurosurgery Service:[99]

> the development of a unit for clinical research in psychiatry . . . we are proposing a unit of twenty beds to provide the opportunities for studying disordered behavior in the great variety of clinical conditions which occur in a general hospital.
>
> The behavior disorder may be associated with endocrine or metabolic disturbances, drug effects or brain lesions but may also be arising in response to crises in the personal and social life situation. Among the latter will be of special interest the reaction to hospitalization, surgery and terminal illness.
>
> Many of these conditions are being studied now in collaboration with other departments in this hospital. The present investigations and the pertinent staff would provide the core of the proposed new unit. However, the unit would serve to integrate, expand and make more effective these efforts.
>
> (p. 1)

> Since most of these activities are concerned with the relations of behavioral processes to brain function the basic laboratories of experimental psychology, neurophysiology and biochemistry are of central importance to the new unit. . . . The unit would provide adequate facilities for the care of psychiatric patients. . . . Of particular importance would be rooms designed for the optimal care of surgical and medical patients with behavioral disturbances . . . would include special rooms for experimental psychological studies, electroencephalographic and other polygraphic studies, a small radio-isotope laboratory and a center for statistical mathematical processing . . . expanded to include . . . an enzyme laboratory and an enlarged unit for correlated studies on animal behavior. The Neurosurgical Department would work jointly with the Department of Psychiatry in the clinical program with respect to both spontaneous brain lesions and with respect to the results of surgical intervention. Both departments would expand the same joint work on animals. . . . A joint pharmacological laboratory would permit the evaluation of chemotherapeutic agents on brain function.
>
> (p. 2)

A rough draft of an NIMH proposal read as follows:

> A statement concerning the attitude of the Department of Psychiatry concerning a research center for clinical research in the behavioral sciences. . . . The study of disordered behavior is the primary concern of the Department of Psychiatry. . . . No matter how great the need is for such joint clinical studies, the responsibility for the care of the patients under investigation, the development of concepts and methods to deal with the behavioral aspects of the disorder and the integration of investigative work with the clinical situation of a given patient should be in the hands of the Department of Psychiatry. . . . It is important that an advisory committee be developed which reflects the attitudes and resources of the various departments of the hospital . . . neurosurgical . . . and multiple patterns of cooperative research with the various services and laboratories of the hospital.

The Committee on Psychiatric Research Institute would be composed of Erich Lindemann (psychiatry) as chairperson, William Sweet (neurosurgery); Gardner Quarton (psychiatry), Frank Ervin (psychiatry), George Talland (psychiatry), Raymond Kjellberg (neurosurgery), and Vernon Mark (neurosurgery).

A further memorandum on a Psychiatric Research Institute for the MGH argued for the advantages of a 60–80-bed clinical facility vs. a 20-research-bed unit. The following personnel were mentioned: on salary support for this purpose listed Gardner Quarton, George Talland, Jack Mendelson, Frank Ervin, Raymond Kjellberg, Vernon Mark, Sternbach, and Nancy Mello. Additional psychiatric personnel add other clinical medical disorders: Thomas Hackett, Avery Weisman (grief and depression), Peter Sifneos, and George Perrin.

Yet another iteration of the proposal of an expanded psychiatric clinical, research, and training unit follows:[100]

> Proposal of a new organization associated with the MGH, part of the Psychiatry Department of the hospital and Community Mental Health Services, a teaching unit of HMS. To be located in MGH: 3 floors of the Pathology Building and 11th floor and roof of the Baker Building. It will not replace the Child Psychiatry Unit (Burnham Building), psychosomatic and medical patients with acute psychiatric problems (Bulfinch Building wards 7 and 8), and Intake (Outpatient Building). It will include disturbed patients on the wards (private and research); neurotic patients on the wards, a social rehabilitation center, out-patient services (psychotherapy, social service, and alcoholism treatment), the CMHC (nursery school, consultation service, and research laboratories), research units (psychiatry, psychology, biochemistry, etc.), training (psychiatry, psychology, and social

science, CMH fellows, medical students, and social work students). Total resources include 21,546 square feet of space and 134 staff members and trainees.

Many of Lindemann's proposals for research in expanded fields of social psychiatry—bringing together related specialty services at the MGH and requesting enlarged resources—met an inhospitable reception and were not implemented. One can imagine the skeptical reputation that developed about his efforts. This reaction may have been partly because of the plans' expansiveness beyond traditional medicine. Partly, it may stem from the jealous separatism among the MGH departments—for which MGH was infamous. And partly, it may stem from traditional medicine's xenophobia about allowing the social sciences into the house of medicine. The following comments are relevant.

The conflict between biological and social science interests in research was recognized by Martin Deutsch, a physicist from the Massachusetts Institute of Technology:[101]

> Medical research . . . is developing in two quite different directions. In one direction lie all the fields related . . . to biochemistry . . . which investigate the mechanisms of biological processes. . . . On the other side there are the fields . . . linking up with the behavioral sciences and dealing with the total functional behavior of the organisms in all its aspects. Both fields deal of necessity not only with the pathological but also with the normal and it is this unavoidable aspect which must create a problem in an organization which has as its primary goal the dealing with the sick.
>
> I believe that I have sensed . . . a certain conflict or competition between these two broad directions of research. At present the emphasis is clearly on the . . . biochemical. I gather that this is a conscious and deliberate policy. I gather also, that there is an awareness of the probability that within the not too distant future this emphasis may shift gradually. . . . the great breakthrough will probably come, when, in a manner which we cannot yet foresee, a link is established between the two fields which really puts the integrated organisms into its proper perspective.

Unorthodoxy and new fields of research were encouraged in 1960 by René J. Dubos of the Rockefeller Institute in New York City, who was also a member of the MGH Scientific Advisory Committee:[102]

> during the oral presentations by Drs. Oliver Cope [MGH surgeon] and Walter Bauer [MGH Chief of the Medical Service] . . . Dr. Cope . . . in the patient whom he selected . . . the immunological factors and emotional disturbance were among the most influential

but also the most obscure determinants of clinical history. Later the same day, Dr. [Walter] Bauer expressed his concern with the increasing tendency to neglect the subtle and ill defined aspects of behavior and of emotional history, which are so important in patient care. I believe that you will agree with me that the study of immunological processes and of behavior could be strengthened at the MGH. . . . what impressed me while I was a member of the Harvard faculty was the extent to which the MGH differed from the rest of the school, thanks to the refreshingly large percentage of "odd" individuals on its staff. I hope a formula can be found to permit the MGH . . . to cultivate an experimental philosophy spiced with as much unorthodoxy as possible. If some of the members of the Executive Committee can find time to walk by the Arlington Street Church, they will see on one of the windows a statement by Kierkegaard which I find much to the point. "To venture causes anxiety, but not to adventure is to lose oneself".

(pp. 1–2)

Dr. Lindemann pointed out the significance of the difference of opinions and theoretical orientation which exists throughout the country between a great many neurologists on one side, and those psychiatrists who are concerned with personality development, personality functioning, and adaptive patterns of behavior. The Neurological Service has shown itself particularly intolerant of this form of psychiatric approach and has in the person of Mandel Cohen included among its staff a person who carries on psychiatric practice and psychiatric teaching of a nature which appears completely out-moded and inappropriate to many well-trained psychiatrists. The members of the Psychiatry Service have . . . not found a completely satisfactory mode of cooperating so far as the psychoneuroses and personality disorders are concerned. . . . In contrast to the relationship with the Neurological Service, there has been a very considerable degree of common effort and joint research with the Neurosurgical Department . . . concerned with the integrative functions of the nervous system and with the processes involved in adaptive failure.

(p. 3)

Stanley Cobb Laboratories for Research in Psychiatry

A major event for the MGH Psychiatry Service and opportunity for Lindemann to demonstrate his fealty to the traditions of that institution was the celebration on October 14–15, 1960, of the 25th anniversary of the founding of the department and simultaneous dedication of the Stanley Cobb Laboratories for Research in Psychiatry.[103] AlthoughE the laboratories paid tribute to the previous regime, it was assured that social and psychological psychiatry were vigorously represented.[104]

Another tie to the past was the renewed contact with Jacob Finesinger, former colleague in the MGH Psychiatry Service and erstwhile rival to succeed Cobb. An exchange of letters included sympathy for Finesinger's serious illness and his acceptance of an invitation to participate in the celebrations of the anniversaries of Cobb's professorship and of the founding of the department.[105] Lindemann contributed to the Sponsoring Committee for The Jacob E. Finesinger Memorial Library in The Psychiatric Institute of Baltimore.[106] Later, Cobb gave a lecture (on October 16, 1961) at the dedication of the Jacob E. Finesinger Reading Room at the University of Maryland School of Medicine.[107]

On October 14, 1960, Lindemann expressed greetings and chaired Session II addressing "A Look at the Future of Psychiatry". Topic titles included The Social Scientist, by John Seeley PhD, with comments by Leonard Duhl MD; The Biologist, by Francis O. Schmitt, PhD, with comments by Robert Grennell, PhD; The Psychiatric Investigator, by Gardner C. Quarton, MD; and closing remarks by Harold G. Wolff, MD. Session I addressed "Psychiatric Conceptions of Illness", with John C. Nemiah, MD, as chairperson. Topics titles included The Development of Mature Individuals, by John C. Whitehorn, MD, with discussion by Lucie Jessner, MD; The Psychodynamic Approach to Medical Illness, by Peter H. Knapp, MD, with discussion by Robert Cleghorn, MD; The Social Emphasis in Psychiatry, by Jurgen Ruesch, MD, with discussion by Alfred H. Stanton, MD. A luncheon meeting addressed "Social and Community Psychiatry": presiding was Alfred H. Stanton, MD, psychiatrist-in-chief of McLean Hospital and associate professor of psychiatry at HMS. The speaker was Stephen Fleck, MD, associate professor of psychiatry and public health at the Yale School of Medicine.

On October 15, 1960, one topic title was "Discussion of On-Going Research: The Stanley Cobb Research Laboratories". The introduction was given by Seymour S. Kety, MD. Reports were given by Frank R. Ervin, MD; George A. Talland, PhD; and Jack H. Mendelson, MD. The topic title "Social and Community Psychiatry" was introduced by Leonard J. Duhl, MD. Reports were given by Marc A. Fried, PhD; Donald C. Klein, PhD; and Wesley Allinsmith, PhD. The topic title "Clinical and Psychosomatic Problems" was introduced by George Engel, MD. Reports were given by Avery D. Weisman, MD; Thomas P. Hackett, MD; and Peter E. Sifneos, MD.

The Dedicatory Program was presided over by Mr. Phillips Ketchum, president of the MGH Corporation. The Speaker was Seymour S. Kety, MD, research director at NIMH and member of the Scientific Advisory Committee at MGH. Dinner was presided over by Carl A.L. Binger, MD, honorary physician at MGH. Speakers were Robert B. Livingston, MD, the director of basic research at NIMH, and Wilder Graves Penfield, MD, the director of the Montreal Neurological Institute.

Notes

1. Lindemann, Erich, "Social Psychiatry at the Harvard Medical School", Presented at the Harvard Medical School Faculty Meeting on 2/21/1964. [folder "2/21/64—Departmental Presentation to HMS Faculty", Box IIIA7 1964–1965 box 3 of 3, Erich Lindemann Collection, Center for the History of Medicine, Francis A. Countway Library of Medicine, Boston, MA]
2. Lindemann, Erich, 2/21/1964, *ibid.*, p. 2.
3. [folder "Summary of Staff + Activities related to Mental Health (at Harvard—Author unidentified) 1955?", Box IIIB1a box 1 of 2, Erich Lindemann Collection, Center for the History of Medicine, Francis A. Countway Library of Medicine, Boston, MA]
4. 2/10/55 Proposal for Stabilizing the Position of Behavioral Science at the Harvard School of Public Health and the Harvard Medical School:

   The recent Ford-sponsored Harvard Survey of the Behavioral Sciences found considerable social science ferment in the Schools of Public Health and Medicine. . . . A critical immediate need is to provide stable professional leadership within the health schools . . . by securing recognized positions within the Health Schools for senior behavioral scientists. . . . It is suggested that the University appoint a Standing Committee drawn from the faculties of the Schools of Medicine and Public Health and from the Faculty of Arts and Sciences, to be known as the Committee on Health and Human Behavior, would direct and supervise the activities of a full-time staff for a trial period of ten years. . . . The Staff . . . would consist of three senior behavioral scientists . . . from the fields of anthropology, psychology and sociology. They would hold appointments in appropriate departments on the Faculty of Medicine or . . . School of Public Health. . . . in one or more instances, they would also hold an appointment in a department of the Faculty of Arts and Sciences . . . fellowships . . . to advance understanding of human behavior in relation to health problems . . . cross-disciplinary training of young investigators and teachers from both fields.at least four annually . . . open to public health students, post-doctoral fellows in medicine, and graduate and post-doctoral students in the behavioral sciences . . . Budget for ten years . . . Total $825,500.

   (pp. 1–3)

   5/7/55 memo from H.[ugh] R. Levell [HSPH] to Members of the Inter-Faculty Committee on the Behavioral Sciences:

   Mr. [Dr. Bernard] Berelson [Ford Found.] . . . proposed recommending to his directors a project which would provide one position at $9000 and one at $12,000 for a seven year period . . . a total of $158.025 [*sic*]. . . . the Medical School was not prepared to undertake a program except on a firm basis. Since the School of Public Health already has a project under way. . . . H. R. L. informed Mr. Berelson that the Medical School did not feel that it could participate in the proposed 7 year program but that the School of Public Health would agree to do so if the Foundation were willing to entertain a separate proposal, on the seven year basis. . . . Berelson was willing to propose support for a program in the School of Public Health at a $10,000 level for a period of 7 years . . . for a total of $75,250.

(pp. 1–3)

[folder "HSPH Ford Foundation Applic 1955",
Box IIIC2 a+b, Erich Lindemann Collection, Center
for the History of Medicine, Francis A. Countway
Library of Medicine, Boston, MA]

5. Lindemann, Erich, letter to Galpin, Perrin C., executive director of The W.T. Grant Foundation, Inc., 4/15/1955, p. 2.
6. Lindemann, Erich, letter to Ewalt, Jack R., 4/24/1964. [folder "E Miscellaneous", Box IIIA 4 (A-E), Erich Lindemann Collection, Center for the History of Medicine, Francis A. Countway Library of Medicine, Boston, MA]
7. Lindemann, Erich, "The Training Program of the Massachusetts General HOSPITAL". [folder "Community Mental Health Program Harvard University _ Mass. Gen. Hosp. January 7, 1959—for Meeting in Washington, DC with Dr. Vestermark. [NIMH Manpower & Training Br]", Box IIIB1a box 2 of 2, Erich Lindemann Collection, Center for the History of Medicine, Francis A. Countway Library of Medicine, Boston, MA]
8. Folder "HMS 2nd Yr Teaching", Box IIIC2 a+b, Erich Lindemann Collection, Center for the History of Medicine, Francis A. Countway Library of Medicine, Boston, MA

Chapman, Earle M., letter to Stoeckle, John, 1/14/19:

You have asked why psychiatry is part of the medical course in the Second Year and when all this happened . . . In the nine years (1937–1945) . . . there was no time given for either lectures or teaching of Psychiatry in the Second Year Course in Medicine as directed by Dr. Henry Jackson . . . in 1947. . . . The Department of Surgery was invited to throw in its time to make this course a well-rounded experience . . . In the summer of 1950, Drs. [Stanley] Cobb [chief of psychiatry, MGH], [Harry] Solomon [director, Boston Psychopathic Hospital, chief of HMS psychiatry], [Oliver] Cope [surgeon, MGH] and [Mark] Altschule [internist ?McLean Hosp] held a conference and discussed the extension of psychiatric teaching into the Second Year. . . . Dr. [Joseph] Aub [MGH medicine], then chairperson of the Executive Committee of the Department of Medicine, stated in a letter of September 30, 1950, that they "felt that the teaching of psychiatry was the responsibility of the Department of Psychiatry rather than that of the Department of Medicine. But they decided that it would be a good idea to try it for a year or two and see whether it is worthwhile for Medicine and Surgery to give up" the time . . . in May of 1951. . . . A two week period (three sessions for each section) was given over to the consideration of patients in whom emotion played an important part in their disorder. . . . Dr. Altschule . . . recommended that at least two lectures on the signs, symptoms and pathologic physiology of the action of emotions should be given by the Department of Medicine. . . . this is being done for the first time in the 1957 lectures. In the 1951 report, Dr. Altshule also suggested that one session for each section should be held jointly with instructors in psychiatry . . . During 1952–53–54. . . under the direction of Dr. Sidney Burwell . . . the lectures in psychiatry were limited to six, and each section was given two sessions with one psychiatrist in medical and surgical sections. . . . In May of 1954, Sidney . . . indicated that this was a "hot potato". In 1955 the number of lectures in psychiatry was increased to twelve. . . . The same program of two sessions in psychiatry for sections in both medicine and surgery was maintained. . . . some of the older instructors at the M.G.H. relate how effective they considered George Saslow to have been last year. . . . in recent years, Surgery, Pediatics, Neurology and now Psychiatry have taken an active part in the instruction and so they must have their departmental interests satisfied. In the past two years it seems a considerable part of my job has been to coordinate the whole project and prevent interdepartmental conflicts. . . . Oliver Cope proposed to the Dean in 1954 that such a committee be reappointed and now the [Karnovsky] Committee has proposed the same idea. I agree.

(pp. 1–2)

Minutes of the Curriculum Committee for 1st and 2nd year H.MS Psychiatry (the sub-committee on curriculum of the Ad Hoc Committee), 5/3/1957:

Some decisions as to the second year curriculum were reached. . . . 1) To request an equivalent of 12 lectures [*sic*] hours on Clinical Psychopathology . . . 2) To request the number of section exercises in physical-psychological diagnosis to be increased to six.

9. Lindemann, Erich, "The Mental Health Service of the Massachusetts General Hospital: A Setting for Community Mental Health Training", a chapter based on an unpublished paper, about1956. [Box XII 2 folder "Mental Health Service + MGH: Setting for Community Mental Health Training", Erich Lindemann Collection, Center for the History of Medicine, Francis A. Countway Library of Medicine, Boston, MA]
10. Lindemann, Erich, "The Mental Health Service of the Massachusetts General Hospital: A Setting for Community Mental Health Training" (unpublished). [folder "Mental Health Services of MGH a Setting for Community MH", Box VII 2, Lindemann Collection, Center for the History of Medicine, Francis A. Countway Library of Medicine, Boston, MA]; edited in Lindemann, Erich, and Lindemann, Elizabeth (eds.), *Beyond Grief: Studies in Crisis Intervention* (New York: Jason Aronson, 1979), Ch. 9 "Community Mental Health Training at the Massachusetts General Hospital", pp. 155–166.
11. Lindemann letter to Albert Deutsch, MD, 1/11/1958. [folder "Misc D", Box IIIA 1–3, Lindemann Collection, Center for the History of Medicine, Francis A. Countway Library of Medicine, Boston, MA]
12. Annual Report of the Psychiatric Clinic for 1957. [folder "Annual Report 1957, Dept. Psychiatry—All Divisions", Box IIIB1b box 1 of 2, Erich Lindemann Collection, Center for the History of Medicine, Francis A. Countway Library of Medicine, Boston, MA]
13. Community Mental Health Program, Harvard University—Massachusetts General Hospital, 1/7/1959. [folder "Lindemann-Caplan Application Material—Sight [*sic*] VISIT", IIIB2 c (box1 of 2), Erich Lindemann Collection, Center for the History of Medicine, Francis A. Countway Library of Medicine, Boston, MA]
14. Lindemann, Erich, MD, "The Mental Health Service of the Massachusetts General Hospital: A Setting for Community Mental Health Training" [folder "Materials for—Sight [*sic*] Visit on Lindemann-Caplan Application", IIIB2 c (box1 of 2), Erich Lindemann Collection, Center for the History of Medicine, Francis A. Countway Library of Medicine, Boston, MA]
15. Lindemann, Erich, letters to members of the Advisory Committee for the West End Project, 6/1/1959; Caplan, Gerald, letter to Mrs. Olive R. Meader, Executive Secretary, Special Study Section, Division of Research Grants, National Institutes of Health, 6/2/59. [folder "Materials for—Sight [*sic*] visit

on Lindemann-Caplan Application", IIIB2 c (box1 of 2), Erich Lindemann Collection, Center for the History of Medicine, Francis A. Countway Library of Medicine, Boston, MA]

16. Lindemann, Erich, Dr. Erich Lindemann, Who Short-Term Consultant, Assignment Report on Teaching of Psychiatry in Medical Colleges, Who Project: India 158, 3/21/1960. [folder "Lindemann, Assignment Report—WHO Project—India 158", Box IIIA5 2), Erich Lindemann Collection, Center for the History of Medicine, Francis A. Countway Library of Medicine, Boston, MA]

17. "A Meeting of the General Executive Committee was held in the Trustees' Room, White Building, at 8:30 a.m. on Wednesday, December 6, 1961", p. 3. [folder "GEC Report by Dr. Lindemann for Dept. of Psychiatry—December 6, 1961", Box IIIB1b box 1 of 2, Erich Lindemann Collection, Center for the History of Medicine, Francis A. Countway Library of Medicine, Boston, MA]

18. "Strengthening Psychiatry at Harvard Summary of Steps Taken During the Past Decade—For the ad hoc Committee George W. Thorn, chairperson", 3/19/1962. [folder "HMS Faculty of Med. 1962", IIIC1 a, Erich Lindemann Collection, Center for the History of Medicine, Francis A. Countway Library of Medicine, Boston, MA] The committee included those supportive of and distant from social psychiatry:

Dr Eric G. Ball Professor of Biological Chemistry
Dr. George P. Berry Dean of the Faculty of Medicine and Professor of Bacteriology
Dr. Herrman L. Blumgart Professor of Medicine
Dr. Derek E. Denny-Brown James Jackson Putnam Professor of Neurology
Dr. Jack R. Ewalt Professor of Psychiatry
Dr. Otto Krayer Charles Wilder Professor of Pharmacology
Dr. Stephen W. Kuffler Professor of Neurophysiology and Neuropharmacology
Dr. Talcott Parsons Professor of Sociology
Dr. George W. Thorn (chairperson) Hersey Professor of the Theory and Practice of Physic

(p. 2)

19. Lindemann letter to Berry, 3/6/1962 regarding meeting 3/9/1962. [folder "Dean George Packer Berry", Box IIIA 4 (A-E), Lindemann Collection, Center for the History of Medicine, Francis A. Countway Library of Medicine, Boston, MA]

20. Berry memo to Lindemann, 2/24/1964. [folder "Dean George Packer Berry", Box IIIA 4 (A-E), Lindemann Collection, Center for the History of Medicine, Francis A. Countway Library of Medicine, Boston, MA]

21. [HMS] Curriculum Committee Minutes of the Meeting of September 24, 1964. [folder "Ewalt, Jack, M.D.", Box IIIA 4 (A-E), Erich Lindemann Collection, Center for the History of Medicine, Francis A. Countway Library of Medicine, Boston, MA]

22. Ewalt, Jack R. MD, letter to Lindemann, Erich, 9/25/1964. [folder "Course in Growth + Development—Harvard Med School 1964", Box IIIC2 a+b, Erich Lindemann Collection, Center for the History of Medicine, Francis A. Countway Library of Medicine, Boston, MA]

23. Nichols, George, Jr., MD, secretary of the Curriculum Committee and HMS associate dean for academic affairs, memo to chairmen of HMS clinical departments, 10/1/1964. [folder "HMS (Principal Clinical Year) 19644–65", Box IIIA 4 (F-H), Erich Lindemann Collection, Center for the History of Medicine, Francis A. Countway Library of Medicine, Boston, MA]

24. Sifneos, Peter memo to Lindemann, Erich, 10/13/1964. [folder "HMS (Principal Clinical Year) 1964–65", Box IIIA 4 (F-H), Erich Lindemann Collection, Center for the History of Medicine, Francis A. Countway Library of Medicine, Boston, MA]

25. Lindemann letter to Berry, 10/13/1964. [folder "Dean George Packer Berry", Box IIIA 4 (A-E), Lindemann Collection, Center for the History of Medicine, Francis A. Countway Library of Medicine, Boston, MA]

26. Letter from Lindemann to Berry, 10/26/1964, pp. 1–2. [folder "Dean George Packer Berry, Box IIIA 4 (A-E), Lindemann Collection, Center for the History of Medicine, Francis A. Countway Library of Medicine, Boston, MA]

27. Lindemann, Erich, letter to Thorn, George, 10/26/1964. [folder "T Miscellaneous", Box IIIA 4 (T-Z), Erich Lindemann Collection, Center for the History of Medicine, Francis A. Countway Library of Medicine, Boston, MA]

28. Berry, Geroge Packer, MD, letter to Hagen, Dr. Kristofer, medical advisor, Board of World Missions, Lutheran Church in America, 1/12/1965: "the time for my mandatory retirement from the deanship of the Faculty of Medicine at Harvard falls on June 30 next". [folder "Correspondence re India 1964–65", Box IIIA5 1), Erich Lindemann Collection, Center for the History of Medicine, Francis A. Countway Library of Medicine, Boston, MA]

29. "10/27–29/65 Summary of Departmental Retreat Asilomar—October 27–29, 1965 Transcription of Reporters' Summaries". [folder "Stanford Department of Psychiatry Planning 1965–66", box IV 3+4+5, Erich Lindemann Collection, Center for the History of Medicine, Francis A. Countway Library of Medicine, Boston, MA]

30. Cannon, Ida M., letter to Rutstein, Dr. David D. [HMS chairperson of the Department of Preventive Medicine], 7/28/1952, p. 2. [folder Family Health and Medical Care Program MGH ("Home Care") 1950–1953, Records of the Dean's Office, Harvard Medical School]

31. "Report of the ad hoc committee on Preventive Medicine", 2/19/1947, p. 2. Members were Walter Bauer, MD (MGH Chief of Medical Services), chairperson, Charles S. Davidson, MD [Boston City Hospital medicine] John F. Enders, PhD [HMS bacteriology], Henry M. Fox, MD [Peter Bent Brigham Hospital psychiatry], Charles A. Janeway, MD [Children's Hospital physician-in-chief), George R. Minot, MD [HMS]. [folder Family Health and Medical Care Program MGH ("Home Care") 1950–1953, Records of the Dean's Office, Harvard Medical School]

32. On 10/20/1952 Berry sent an invitation to a Home Care Luncheon on 10/27/1952. It was attended by Walter Bauer (MGH chief of medical services), Dean A. Clark (MGH General Director), Alan Butler (MGH chief of children's medicine), [Duncan] Reid (Boston Lying In Hospital physician-in-chief], [Charles] Janeway [Boston Children's Hospital physician-in-chief], David D. Rutstein (HMD chairperson of the Department of Preventive Medicine), Henry Meadow (HMS associate dean for finance), and George Packer Berry (HMS dean). Invited but declined: Stanley Cobb (MGH chief of the Psychiatry Service—has a cold), [Edward] Churchill (MGH chief of Surgical Services—out of town), and [Herrman] Blumgart (Beith Israel Hospital professor of medicine—out of town). [folder Family Health and Medical Care Program MGH ("Home Care") 1950–1953, Records of the Dean's Office, Harvard Medical School]

33. "Read by Leslie Corsa MGH Trustee's Room on the Establishment of an MGH Family Health Service for the West End", 2/23/1953. [folder Family Health and Medical Care Program MGH ("Home Care") 1950–1953, Records of the Dean's Office, Harvard Medical School]

34. Scoville, Milded C., executive associate at The Commonwealth Fund, letter to Berry, Dr. George P., HMS Dean, 1/18/1951. [folder Family Health and Medical Care Program MGH ("Home Care") 1950–1953, Records of the Dean's Office, Harvard Medical School]

35. "Family Health and Medical Care Program Notes by Dr. [David D.] Rutstein", 6/1/1953. [folder Family Health and Medical Care Program MGH ("Home Care") 1950–1953, Records of the Dean's Office, Harvard Medical School]:

> Comprehensive medical care is a continuous and integrated service for the promotion of health and the prevention and treatment of disease . . . and for making use of all needed community facilities; coordinating all with understanding of and in the best interests of the patient and his family . . . a statement approved last year by the Faculty entitled, "Plans for Improvement of Teaching Preventive Medicine". . . . it has become evident that the scope of such a program reaches beyond the confines of any one department . . . Explorations of potentialities at the MGH have indicated that they could provide the basis for a sound and broad program. To do so, substantial modifications must be made in the out-patient services of the Hospital and in the utilization and integration of community resources with those of the Hospital. This situation was brought to the attention of the Trustees of the MGH, who have given general approval. This reorganization would not only serve the proposed program but would better enable the Hospital to discharge its total out-patient responsibilities.
>
> Members of the Faculty heading the Departments of Medicine, Pediatrics and Psychiatry at the MGH, together with the Dean, the Director of the Hospital, and the Head of the Department of Preventive Medicine have met during the past year to define the scope of the proposed program and the role which each department could play. At this time it is agreed that a Family Health and Medical Care Program . . . should be implemented . . . it was agreed that the existing pediatric home care program should be continued. . . . This committee would . . . determine how best to modify it to serve a more general function. [p. 1] . . . it was further agreed that the following persons would serve as liaison members between the committee and the several departments: Medicine— Dr. Joseph Stokes II, Pediatrics—Dr. Frederic Blodgett and Dr. Leslie Corsa, Psychiatry—Dr. Peter Sifneos, Preventive Medicine—Miss Phyllis Walsh. It was agreed further that Mr. Michael White, Assistant Director of the Hospital, would serve as liaison with the Director of the MGH and that Dr. John Stoeckel, to whom reorganization of the out-patient department will be assigned, would co-ordinate his work with that of the committee.
>
> (pp. 1–2)

36. Berry, George Packer, MD Dean [HMS], letter to "Committee on Family Health and Medical Care Program", 6/1/1953. [folder Family Health and Medical Care Program MGH ("Home Care") 1950–1953, Records of the Dean's Office, Harvard Medical School]:

> During the past two years a group of those particularly interested in the potentialities for medical teaching of a Family Health and Medical Care Program have been meeting informally. . . . At the time of the last informal discussion at the Massachusetts General Hospital on April 27th, it

was decided that the time had come to formalize these discussions. I take the present opportunity to invite you to serve with the others listed below on a committee to report to the Administrative Board: Dr. Walter Bauer Dr. George Berry Dr. Allan Butler Dr. Dean Clark, Dr. Stanley Cobb, Mr. Henry Meadow Dr. David Rutstein, chairperson.

37. Minutes of Meeting of Committee on Family Health and Medical Care Program June 2, 1953, Trustees Room, Massachusetts General Hospital 10:00 am", 6/2/1953. [folder Family Health and Medical Care Program MGH ("Home Care") 1950–1953, Records of the Dean's Office, Harvard Medical School]:

> Dr. Corsa, the remainder of his income being supplied through the Whittier Street Field Training Unit under the auspices of the [Harvard] School of Public Health . . . Miss Phyllis Walsh, who is acting as liaison for Preventive Medicine . . . In the event that an unfavorable reply is received [reapplication for Hyams Fund funding], it was agreed that the Dean of the Medical School and the office of the General Director of the Hospital will guarantee the running expenses of the program for a period of six months. . . . The chairperson presented plans for immediate conferences with representatives of nursing and medical social work in the Hospital, and later in the autumn with representatives of community agencies including the Visiting nurse Association, Departments of Public Health and Public Welfare, the School Health Service, and appropriate voluntary health and welfare agencies.

38. "Family Health Service Program Tentative Procedure (Revised on basis of discussion of Committee 10/28/53". [folder Family Health and Medical Care Program MGH ("Home Care") 1950–1953, Records of the Dean's Office, Harvard Medical School]:

> A special grant has been made by the Hyams Fund, Fund No. 4855, in the amount of $27,300.00 to cover the cost of an experimental Family Health Serivce Program for the period July 1, 1953 to June 30, 1954. . . . Pediatrician, full-time (Dr. [Frederic] Blodgett) . . . Pediatrician, one-half time (Dr. L[eslie] Corsa) . . . Secretary to the Committee (Phyllis Worth Walsh) . . . Social Service Worker (1/2 time—Nov. 1) . . . Public Health Nurse (Part-time—1/2 time, Jan. 1). . . . A medical man, Dr. [Joseph] Stokes [III], is scheduled to replace Dr. Corsa on the budget on July 1, 1954.
>
> The Office of the Children's Medical Service has been designated as temporary admirative headquarters for the program.
>
> (pp. 1–2)

39. Rhind, Flora M., Secretary, The Rockefeller Foundation, letter to "Pusey, Dr. Nathan M., President, Harvard University", 6/29/1954. [folder Family Health and Medical Care Program MGH ("Home Care") 1954–1956, Records of the Dean's Office, Harvard Medical School]:

> I have the honor to inform you that at a meeting of the Executive Committee of The Rockefeller Foundation on June 29, 1954, action was taken providing up to $275,000 to Harvard University for research and teaching in a program of complete family medical care at the Massachusetts General Hospital. This fund is available during the five-year period beginning July 1, 1954.
>
> (p. 1)

40. "Committee on Family Health and Medical Care Program October 28, 1953 2 pm Tustees Room, Massachusetts General Hospital", 10/28/1953, p. 4. [folder Family Health and Medical Care Program MGH ("Home Care") 1950–1953, Records of the Dean's Office, Harvard Medical School]

41. Meenan, Miss, memo to OPD, 12/11/1953. [folder Family Health and Medical Care Program MGH ("Home Care") 1950–1953, Records of the Dean's Office, Harvard Medical School]

42. Folder Family Health and Medical Care Program MGH ("Home Care") 1957-, Records of the Dean's Office, Harvard Medical School

> "Memorandum Family Care Program at Massachusetts General Hospital Report of conversation with Dr. Joe Stokes, III, on June 22, 1959", 6/22/1959.
>
> It is under the management of an Advisory Committee, which includes Dr. David Rutstein, Dr. Dean Clark, Dr. Walter Bauer, Dr. Allan Butler, and Dr. Stokes, who serves as its director. . . . On the whole the students have not particularly enjoyed their experience in this program. The reasons for this have been . . . they resent the extra work assigned them, being called a voluntary course. Efforts have been made to see whether these students have a better knowledge of such aspects of medicine as socio-economic status, impingement of social and environmental factors on the treatment of disease, and so forth. . . . Although on the first year of trial there was some evidence that these students were better prepared for some of the exigencies of practice. . . . this difference could not be detected on the second year of trial.
>
> (p. 1)

Nichols George, Jr., MD, letter to Stokes, Dr. Joseph III, Massachusetts General Hospital, 7/23/1959:

> I had an opportunity . . . to discuss with Dr. Berry . . . your proposals concerning the third-year curriculum for next year. Fundamentally, neither he nor I are very enthusiastic about this scheme. . . . such an arrangement would mean rescheduling all the students who were interested . . . after the school year had started. . . . Secondly it is the custom to assign the transfer students to Medicine in the first trimester. . . . The final objection . . . and . . . the most important one, is that your scheme . . . means that a student would have all his third-year experience in a single hospital. . . . An alternative proposal . . . is that the Family Care Program be made a voluntary course for third-year students.
>
> (p. 1)

Stokes, Joseph III, MD, letter to Nichols, George, Jr., MD, Office of the Dean, Harvard Medical School, cc: Dr. George P. Berry, Dr. Evan Calkins, Dr. John D. Stoeckle [director of the MGH Medical Outpatient Department]", 8/18/1959:

> I would agree with you that this is not the year to try the experiment, but we are unhappy about your alternative proposal. . . . the Family Health Program should not continue as a separate and isolated teaching experience. . . . it should be possible to decide what part of this is important to incorporate in the conventional curriculum. . . . the core of the proposal was suggested by Evan Calkins as a method of strengthening the third year course in medicine and other third year clinical teaching at the M.G.H. . . . we should like to suggest the following: (1) The Department of Pediatrics should offer a third year course during at least

the second and third trimesters. (2). . . . Drs. Calkins, Stoeckle, Hamlin [surgery] and myself have an opportunity to meet with the appropriate sub-committee . . . to present our proposed experiment for the third year courses during 196–61.

(pp. 1–2)

43. Ehrlich, Fred, HMS III [third year HMS student) to Berry, George P., HMS Dean", 11/14/1953. [folder Family Health and Medical Care Program MGH ("Home Care") 1950–1953, Records of the Dean's Office, Harvard Medical School]

44. Berry, George Packer, letter to Ehrlich, Fred, 11/19/1953. [folder Family Health and Medical Care Program MGH ("Home Care") 1950–1953, Records of the Dean's Office, Harvard Medical School]

 Copies sent to Dr. [David] Rutstein [HMS chairperson of the Department of Preventive Medicine], Dr. [Walter] Bauer [MGH chief of Medical Services], Dr. [Allan] Butler [MGH chief of the Children's Medical Service], Dr. [Dean A.] Clark [MGH general director], Dr. [Stanley] Cobb [MGH chief of the Psychiatric Service], Mr. [Henry] Meadow [HMS associate dean for finance].

45. Berry, George Packer, MD, HMS Dean, letter to Bugher, Dr. John C., director for Medical Education and Public Health of The Rockefeller Foundation, 2/28/1959. [folder Family Health and Medical Care Program MGH ("Home Care") 1957-, Records of the Dean's Office, Harvard Medical School]

 The Policy Committee of the Family Health Program. . . [have come to] the conclusion that the experience already accumulated will provide the information necessary to select . . . parts to be incorporated in the permanent curriculum of the third- and fourth-year teaching of the School's Department of Medicine at the M.G.H. . . . it has also been agreed to bring the staff of the Family Health Program into the teaching of fourth-year medicine. Finally, with the approval of the School's Administrative Board, an elective one-month course in family medicine will be given at the M.G.H. by the staff of the Family Health Program . . . a sum of about $65,000 will remain from the Foundations original grant. . . . It has seemed . . . desirable to the Policy Committee . . . that these funds . . . and the funds contributed by the M.G.H. be used for the incorporation of the desirable parts of the Family Health Program into the permanent medical curriculum. During the past four years the M.G.H. has contributed each year approximately $6,000 directly . . . and $12,500 in addition for patient care. The M.G.H. Trustees have indicated their willingness to continue to support the program at this level, and to contribute in addition each year approximately $15,000 for four years".

(pp. 1–2)

46. "The Significance of the Family Care Program for the Education of Future Physicians", undated. [folder "Family Health Program", IIIB3 a-c, Erich Lindemann Collection, Center for the History of Medicine, Francis A. Countway Library of Medicine, Boston, MA]

47. "Family Health Program Policy Committee Meeting . . . January 29, 1959: "Proposed Changes in the Family Health Program after July 1, 1959". [folder "Family Health Program", IIIB3 a-c, Erich Lindemann Collection, Center for the History of Medicine, Francis A. Countway Library of Medicine, Boston, MA]

48. "Family Health Program Minutes of the Policy Committee Meeting April 16, 1959". [folder "Family Health Program", IIIB3 a-c, Erich Lindemann

Collection, Center for the History of Medicine, Francis A. Countway Library of Medicine, Boston, MA]:

> The Rockefeller Foundation Had Agreed to A Five Year Extension without Additional Funds. . . . So that the Program Could Apply the Experience Gained Over the First Five Years to a Teaching Program Closely Integrated with the Conventional Courses in Clinical Medicine. . . . Dr. Stokes reviewed . . . his plan for integrating the Family Health Program with the 3rd year course in Medicine at the Massachusetts General Hospital. . . . Dr. John Stoeckle [MGH chief of med. clinic] raised objections . . . to the limited time already available for the Medical Clinic instruction in 3rd year Medicine. He also believed that there would be insufficient opportunity for the students to visit the home and to investigate the environmental conditions. . . . Dr. [Walter] Bauer [MGH chief of medicine] agreed. . . . Dr. Bauer, Dr. Stoeckle, Dr. Stokes and Dr. Evan Calkins should . . . see if a better plan of instruction could be developed.
>
> (pp. 1–2)

49. "Family Health Program Minutes of the Policy Committee Meeting . . . September 16, 1960". [folder "Family Health Program", IIIB3 a-c, Erich Lindemann Collection, Center for the History of Medicine, Francis A. Countway Library of Medicine, Boston, MA]

> The proposal submitted to the Curriculum Committee had been turned down. . . . As a result . . . there had been no students assigned to the program last year. Dr. Rutstein stated his disappontment that Dr. Bauer and Dr. Stoeckle had not agreed to assign third year medical students to the Family Health Program. . . . Mr. Martin [Associate Director at MGH] then raised the question of the Massachusetts General's financial commitment to the Family Health Program. . . . the Hospital was currently running its largest deficits in history and that cuts would have to be made. . . . Mr. White and Miss Farrisey concurred with Mr. Martin.
>
> (p. 1)

50. "Family Health Program Meeting—March 29, 1961". [folder "Family Health Program", IIIB3 a-c, Erich Lindemann Collection, Center for the History of Medicine, Francis A. Countway Library of Medicine, Boston, MA]:

> ATTENDING: Drs. [Dean A.] Clark [Gen'l Dir, MGH], [Walter] Bauer [MGH Chief of Med], [Nathan] Talbot [MGH Chief of Ped], [Erich] Liindemann [MGH Chief of Psychiat], Abramson, [David A.] Rutstein [HMS Chmn of Prevent Med] (chairing), [Joseph] Stokes [Chief of Fam Med Prog], [John] Stoeckle [MGH Chief of Med Clinic], Federman, Richie; Misses [Ruth] Sleeper [MGH Dir Nsg], MacPherson, Farrisey [MGH Admin]. . . . The remaining $50,000.00 of Rockefeller Grant money shall be reserved to pay Professional Staff [sic] stipends . . . for part-time work. . . . the Grant residue will run for upwards of ten years. . . . The Harvard Medical School Program . . . will remain a voluntary one and will involve the Fourth-year men. . . . The Third-year Students will probably go to the Home Care Program at the Children's Medical Center. . . . The Medical Education Program at Massachusetts General Hospital . . . shall be geared primarily to individuals and families known to the Children's Medical Service and to Dr. Federman's small group of home care referrals. . . . The Medical School and the Family Health Program want to maintain a similar relationship as has [sic] with the Boston Lying-In Hospital. . . . The Hospital program was said by Dr. Clark to be one of his

continuing interests. . . . Family Health Program ought to be the continuing name of the Hospital Program . . . that the present patients . . . should be followed by the physicians who knew them best in The Clinics—but that the old Family Health Program connections would be discontinued.
(pp. 1–2)

51. Farnsworth, Dana L., chairperson, "Report of The Ambulatory Clinics Committee, Massachusetts General Hospital". [audio tape, Erich Lindemann Collection, Center for the History of Medicine, Francis A. Countway Library of Medicine, Boston, MA]

52. Lindemann, Erich, letter to Stoeckle, Joh D., MD (chief of the MGH Medical Outpatient Clinics), 8/12/1955.

53. Grillo, Hermes C., MD, MGH assistant in surgery, letter to Farnsworth, Dana, 5/22/1957. [audio tape, Erich Lindemann Collection, Center for the History of Medicine, Francis A. Countway Library of Medicine, Boston, MA]

54. Degan, Joseph W., assistant director, MGH, letter to Farnsworth, Dana L., chairperson, Ambulatory Clinics Committee, 5/28/1957. [audio tape, Erich Lindemann Collection, Center for the History of Medicine, Francis A. Countway Library of Medicine, Boston, MA]

55. "Report of the Scientific Advisory Committee of the Massachusetts General Hospital January 8 and 9, 1965", p. 2. [folder "MGH Scientific Advisory Committee—MGH 1962–65", Box IIIB1d, Erich Lindemann Collection, Center for the History of Medicine, Francis A. Countway Library of Medicine, Boston, MA]

56. Lindemann, Erich, 6/15,22/1974, *ibid.*

57. Among these were the following:

> (chart) "MGH HMS Psychiatric Service Administration Research: Etiological Studies on Crisis Theory. Studies on Social Child Development. Crisis of Relocation (Center for Community Studies (USPHS-$86,250)). Social Patterns in Schools (Wellesley Hum. Rel. Service (Hood Fdtn.-$8,000)). Mental Health Hazards in Gen. Hospital (MGH Wards & OPD (Hall Mercer Fund-$8,000)). Training: for Community Mental Health Specialists (About 1/3 of total staff support). in Community Mental Health Aspects of Psychiatry, Psychology Social Work & Social Science (About 2/3 of total)=$49,141".
>
> (chart) "Psychiatric Service Massachusetts General Hospital Harvard Medical School . . . TRAINING (MGH) . . . Community Mental Health Psychiatry $12,096* Psychology $18,090* Social Work $18,955* =$49,141 *funds received from the USPHS [United States Public Health Service]"
>
> > [folder "Community Mental Health Program Harvard University _ Mass. Gen. Hosp. January 7, 1959—for Meeting in Washington, DC with Dr. Vestermark [?NIMH Manpower & Trnging Br]", Box IIIB1a box 2 of 2, Erich Lindemann Collection, Center for the History of Medicine, Francis A. Countway Library of Medicine, Boston, MA]

58. Lindemann, Erich, letter to W.T. Grant, 10/30/1962, p. 2. [folder "Grant Foundation", Box IIIA 4 (F-H), Lindemann Collection, Center for the History of Medicine, Francis A. Countway Library of Medicine, Boston, MA]

59. Lindemann, Erich, "Memorandum in Connection with Discussion at the Office of the Grant Foundation of the Program in Psychiatry of the

Massachusetts General Hospital (McLean Hospital and the Psychiatric Service of the General Hospital)", 1962. [folder "Grant Foundation", Box IIIA 4 (F-H), Lindemann Collection, Center for the History of Medicine, Francis A. Countway Library of Medicine, Boston, MA]

60. Lindemann, Erich, "Memorandum" 1962, *ibid*.: MGH individuals he envisioned as contributing to this comprehensive program included Prof. John Seeley, Dr. Frederick Duhl (community psychiatry), Dr. Wesley Allinsmith (child personality development), and Dr. George Talland (intellectual decline with age). A service program would include Samuel Silverman, MD (adult psychiatry), Richmond Holder, MD (child psychiatry), Manon McGinnis (social work), John Stoeckle, MD (internist part time), and Robert Richie (pediatrics).

61. Lindemann, Erich, letter to Miss Adele W. Morrison, associate director and secretary of The W.T. Grant Foundation, 1/30/1963. [folder "Grant Foundation", Box IIIA 4 (F-H), Lindemann Collection, Center for the History of Medicine, Francis A. Countway Library of Medicine, Boston, MA]

62. In 1956, a training relationship between the Putnam Center and the MGH was recognized and authorized (correspondence between Samuel Kaplan, MD, Putnam Center Co-director; Erich Lindemann; and Dean Clark, MGH general director, 1/16–2/29/1956). Elizabeth A. Cobb, Stanley Cobb's wife, was listed on the Putnam Center's letterhead. (Rank, Beata, codirector of the Putnam Center, letter to Lindemann, Erich, 7/17/1956). [folder "James Jackson Putnam Center", Box IIIA 4 (I-Ma), Lindemann Collection, Center for the History of Medicine, Francis A. Countway Library of Medicine, Boston, MA]

63. Byler, John G., executive director of The Grant Foundation, letter to Lindemann, Erich, 2/6/1963. [folder "Grant Foundation", Box IIIA 4 (F-H), Lindemann Collection, Center for the History of Medicine, Francis A. Countway Library of Medicine, Boston, MA]

64. [folder "Community Mental Health Program Harvard University Mass. Gen. Hosp. January 7, 1959—for Meeting in Washington, DC with Dr. Vestermark [NIMH Manpower & Training Br]", Box IIIB1a box 2 of 2, Erich Lindemann Collection, Center for the History of Medicine, Francis A. Countway Library of Medicine, Boston, MA]

(undated) handwritten notes "Material for Washington" [* . . . * = circled in MS]:

A path for Research and Development in Cm. M. Health. A Cooperative program between Div. of M.H. H.S.P.H. and Psychiatric Service (Mental Health Service) MGH At the M.G.H. a Mental Health Service was created 1955 1. General service functions. to develop preventive measures in the field of Mental Illness and Health both inside the Hospital and in community areas adjacent to it. 2) teaching functions to provide for psychiatrists, psychologists and soc. workers early in their career teaching experiences which arouse their interest in Com wide programs of prevention and of promotion of mentally healthy living [MH promotion—presumptuous] to relate Mental Health operations closely to clinical content of the care of known casualties and provide teaching experiences on the faculty level for best communication to the clinical profession and clinical faculties in other medical areas. To extend mental health considerations to all aspects of medical care in the setting of a large mental hospital. 3) Research to provide ongoing research opportunities and field studies for cooperative enterprises between Mental Health workers and representatives of the psychological and social sciences. These studies are all part of a program to ascertain and classify the spectrum of maladaptive and well-adaptive responses to *crisis—situations* both inside and outside the hospital. The application and further development of the methods of mental health consultation in crisis situations particularly in the context of the social processes both in the hospital, but also in the schools and caretaking professions of open communities, particularly at middle class schools and a low class slum area. The evolution of consultative activities at the level of community and city planning both in the institutional contexts of special organizations of schools and churches, and also at the city- and regional level (such as relocation and urban renewal). This involves administrative and organizational issues. Cooperation now: S.P.H.: Caplanstaff member of MGH. In <u>service</u>: M.H. Cons. to nurses, but even more: joint planning of MGH activities in <u>teaching</u>: Field station at Whittier street, participation in seminars in <u>research</u>: coinvestigator of West End program. <u>MGH—E.L.</u> <u>Teaches</u> seminars at schools, review programs for division <u>development</u>, has many discussions concerning <u>research</u> What we need is a center for advanced studies. we are both too loaded with responsibilities have to suitably arrange for a network of diversified roles (like [] program) need representation in a new type of fields not now part of the regular university program in the health area. a) theory of community studies b) mental health aspects of community organization c) mental health epidemiology be primarily consultants to our group, to give it greater solidity, solidarity and effectiveness. The[y] would be also consultants to the S.P.H. group. They would be available to, and, indeed, attract consultees from many parts of the country. They could help to develop such efforts as mobile units to assist in disaster control. They could find an atmosphere of ongoing efforts and enthusiasm well suited for the further development of their own advanced work. <u>Composition of faculty</u>: headquarters MGH. ¶ <u>leaders</u> have also functions at the hospital ¶ <u>coleaders</u> are central persons in field stations ¶ equal presentation of service, research, and communication ¶ Composition of <u>student body</u>: ¶ first was very young ones, then some quite advanced ones. who liked the <u>particular</u> setting at a teaching hospital. ¶ Composition of research group—¶ a) the West end efforts ¶ b) the MGH efforts ¶ c) the Wellesley activities ¶ All of them miss top level guidance in the basic sciences which are the foundations for the efforts. (There is much consultation and an advisory committee (enumerated) ¶ but not a group of people unencumbered by a multitude of explicit administrative demands. ¶ They should be top experts and executive thinkers, contributing to and stimulating project development, but apart from their own research [EL second thoughts and recommendations by others to be guru rather than administrator/power-wielder] ¶ <u>Staff</u> ¶ In time we developed first a *service staff* ¶ a) in the hospital (community concerns) ¶ a) b) in Wellesley—relating it to central needs but giving it regional responsibilities rather than local ones only ¶ a) the West end ¶ b) a <u>teaching faculty</u> to reach ¶ young psychiatrists + psychologists + social workers + social scientists, to evolve a basic <u>dedicated program</u> and syllabus for C.M.H. ¶ to provide <u>field station</u> experience ¶ covering inter visitation, ¶ consult, ¶ com. organization ¶ research ¶ to give opportunity for supervised participation in M H work at all significant levels. ¶ to take this new orientation <u>along into the respective professions</u> or to use it as <u>first steps to advanced</u> work at S.P.H. ¶ d) evaluation of suitable community <u>practices</u> of mental disease control and health promotion ¶ e) The Mental Health aspects of Human development (child psych etc) ¶ Financial statements ¶ summary of present budgets ¶ our task force ¶ EL, —Sifneos + Laura—¶—v. Felsinger, Klein. ¶ Eleanor Clark + Bill Freeman ¶ <u>Teaching</u> ¶ combined efforts: ¶ v.

Felsinger—Sifneos —E. Clark. ¶ Research ¶ Mark Fried + Peg Ellens ¶ stress more—overall programs—¶ Overall program ¶ formal—historical accidents ¶ There is not duplication ¶ The program—¶ two aspects—¶ One basic philosophical standard ¶ which happens to be deployed in two places. One program not Public Mental Health ¶ Cmt Mental Health specialty ¶ a new specialty.

. . .

[re psychiat, med, surg residency]

Can health considerations be added to the medical considerations in such a way that a staff participant of a general hospital will view himself as a health officer? The trustees of the hospital allowed us to add to the Department of Psychiatry another section which was called the Mental Health Service of the Massachusetts General Hospital, and in this way the hospital became another field station for a health service. Now what are the functions of such a health service in a general hospital? . . . The public health man is concerned with a population. If a 'mental-health-man' comes onto a ward, he does not come like a psychiatrist who receives a given problem-patient identified as psychiatrically sick by another non-psychiatric physician for his investigation. He will rather be concerned with the total patient population of a medical or surgical ward, including those who are allegedly mentally healthy. He will be concerned with the hazards of the ward curriculum and ward experience for the emotional well-being of all the patients during their residence on the ward. He also will be interested in the mental health, not only of the patients, but also of the "care-taking personnel", and be interested in the interplay of social forces on the ward, because there are a good many doctors, nurses, and social workers who face difficult problems at the time of crises on the ward. The social process of a hospital ward context is likely to involve typical patterns of stress, by virtue of a series of professional groups having to live in proximity, having developed barriers to communication (which often are very dear to them because they are protective), and having very carefully guarded lines of hierarchy, organization, and line of command. The patient is at the mercy of this sort of system; he becomes a participant, and the less that is known about his emotional response to this order, the better it seems for medicine and surgery, but it only seems so. Now, the mental health officer is supposed to make these matters explicit. . . . Another example is in the area of rehabilitation: . . . These [patients] are now being treated . . . by the physical therapist, the orthopedic doctor, the nurse, and the social worker. These professions, working together with the same patient-load, find it difficult to operate with each other. . . . The mental health service set up (and there are fellows in training participating in this) a team consisting of a psychiatrist, a social anthropologist, and a psychologist, each asked to review the flow of social events on the rehabilitation ward, and it became quite clear that physical therapists, in terms of their status-self-perception, cannot work easily with the nurses, since they are now the major effective profession in this particular ward; they cannot defer to the nurse, who by hospital administration pattern, is in charge of the ward service. That creates many problems of status-clash, giving of orders, and cooperation and communication. It turns out that the mental health service can then ascertain, in the regular meetings which have been arranged with the various groups, what is actually going on, and help to achieve a new kind of self-perception of the professions within the hospital, so far as they affect their patients' health and so far as they might affect their own mental health with respect to happy and effective functioning. The third kind of example . . . is this: Rather than being concerned with just a <u>given</u> psychiatric patient who needs the ministrations of a skilled psychiatrist, the mental health service reviews what kind of flow or frequency of casualties occur form the various sections of the hospital community, with its institutions . . . a great many operations of the staff have a mental health hazard implication, it is possible to identify such hazards on a population-wide basis, and to try to achieve policy alterations in the institutions involved within the hospital context . . . by collaboration with the chief of the medical outpatient service, again we become concerned with the flow of a population through this service, in addition to medical checkup, to excluding physical disease, and to possibly referring some of the worst disturbed persons to psychiatrists. . . . Is there a social pattern, undesirable in many ways, which seems to be fostered by certain care-taking techniques on the sub-conscious level by the internist and surgeon, which might be made explicit, and which might be hindering the flow of the patients toward finding other care-taking resources within the community? . . . the so-called West End Program . . . is largely a training opportunity for individuals in the social sciences, as well as individuals in the medical sciences . . . with it is involved a number of social scientists, and it turns out that graduate students in social sciences from the Department of Social Relations at the [Harvard] University are increasingly interested in working with us in a learning role as well as in a giving role. Here they are being confronted with medical practice issues which might become significant sources for further developing and enriching their experimental and conceptual areas. Recently, a number of social science graduate students have come to the hospital to rub shoulders with us as receivers as well as givers. And the mental health team, just as in the school of public health, contains psychiatrists, psychologists, social workers, and social scientists who are closely working together in an interdisciplinary context and have plenty of opportunity during this year to learn about each other's professional identity, as well as to safeguard their own values in the clashing demands and fulfillments which they experience during this year.

(pp. 3–7)(undated) The Psychiatric Service of the Massachusetts General Hospital:

The teaching program is oriented toward training participants in research, teaching, and practice in four major areas: 1) dynamic psychiatry, 2) developmental psychiatry, 3) physiological aspects of behavior, and 4) social and community psychiatry. Specially qualified individuals are accepted for advanced training in Child Psychiatry (q.v.), in community psychiatry and mental health, and for special work in the psychiatric research laboratories.

(pp. 1–2)1/7/59 Community Mental Health Program Harvard University—Massachusetts General Hospital:

Some Comments on Harvard Psychiatry 1. Dr. Lindemann also represents the community mental health program at the Massachusetts General Hospital for which the Center for Community Studies in the West End and the Human Relations Service in Wellesley are field stations. . . . Interfaculty relations outside the Medical School to other professional schools is maintained through membership of senior psychiatrists on planning and steering committees of these schools. In this way Dr. Lindemann is concerned with mental health teaching in the Divinity School; . . . Drs. [Alfred] Stanton and [George] Gardner are particularly interested in joint teaching with the Department of Social Relations and Dr. Lindemann has a close working relationship and cooperative program at the Harvard School of Public Health. . . . The Massachusetts General Hospital has developed a program for training in community mental health open to psychiatrists, psychologists and social workers in close cooperation with the Harvard School of Public Health. . . . A beginning has been made for the development of a coordinated didactic graduate training program which is ploalned byu a committee from all the units and has led to a central course in basic psychopathology, psychophysiology and social psychiatry at the various levels. . . . This is necessitating cooperative efforts between the various research units concerned with related topics such as therapy, social psychiatry, developmental psychiatry, community psychiatry and neurophysiology and is expected to lead to seminars each constituted by a group of faculty members from several cooperating hospitals. A good beginning for this development has been made by a recent grant of fluid funds from the Foundations Fund. . . . OUTLINE OF INTRODUCTORY COMMENTS CONCERNING THE COMMUNITY MENTAL HEALTH PROGRAM AT THE MASSACHUSETTS GENERAL HOSPITAL. . . . The division of mental health at the Harvard School of Public Health had developed a program of teaching for students in public health comprising the essentials of psychopathology, personality study, and group dynamics. This type of program had been discussed at length at an NIMH sponsored conference in 1950. At this conference the need was expressed for further development of advanced training for future specialists in the area of Community Mental Health. Under Dr. [Gerald] Caplan's direction the mental health division of the school has developed precisely in this direction.

(pp. 1–2)

"However, there was an obvious need for bringing to younger psychiatrists, psychologists, social workers, and to the members of the care-taking professions in their formative years a certain amount of information about the possibilities of preventive work in the area of mental health. This was discussed vigorously at a conference called by the NIMH in the spring of 1954 and it was partly through the stimulation of this conference that the MGH service which already had established a Mental Health Unit, and started [a] program to bring to psychiatrists in the third or fourth year of their basic training, to psychologists in their first postdoctoral year, and to social workers after a period of professional experience following their MS, a program of studies in Community Mental Health which might stimulate some of these young people to make this new field the focus of their professional careers, but particularly to help many of these young members of the traditional care-taking professions to include a mental health orientation in their program of professional activities . . . stimulate interest in the potentialities of community-wide programs for the prevention of illness and for the promotion of mental health in contrast to remedial work in the individual cases". Multidisc faculty, "and permit infiltration of the other faculties of the hospital with a mental health orientation which would become a part of the system of medical care in a large metropolitan hospital. . . . We also need a theoretical frame of reference for the study of behavioral responses in a population which differed from the traditional nosological categories. We found this frame in the crisis theory and studied under various circumstances the spectrum of mal-adaptive and well-adaptive response to life situations demanding new solutions both in the motional and in the intellectual sphere. The practical application of the methods of Community Mental Health consultation in crisis situations inside the hospital as well as vis a vis the nonmedical care-taking professions in the community at different class levels also seemed desirable". Apply esp to city planning. At MGH svc or HRS enriched by W.E. proj. Fac assembled to develop syllabus, field stations in preventive intervention, mental health consultation, community organization and research. "Both the research and the training program would be tremendously strengthened if we could assemble a group of top experts in certain branches of the social sciences who have committed themselves to concerns with the application of their approach to the Community Mental Health filed". Cns, indep creativity & res., exch other dpets of university, "but particularly would lend stature to tour Community Mental Health Program as a source for consultation for other developing programs throughout this country".

(pp. 2–4)(course outline) Seminar in Community Mental Health Theory and Practice Erich Lindemann, MD, PhD, Wednesdays, 2:30–4:00 P.M. Medical conference Room—MGH [gives session dates, topics, speakers; section headings:] I. Background in Public Health and Social Science [5 sessions], II. Case Application [1 session], III Approaches to a Preventive Psychiatry [5 sessions], IV. Application of Crisis Theory in Mental Health Planning [3 sessions], V. Situational Appraisal and Preventive Intervention [2 sessions], [sic no numeral] Group Methods in Community Mental Health [1 session], VII. Mental Health Consultation [3 sessions], VIII. Mental Health Education [3 sessions], IX. The Epidemiology of Mental Health [2 sessions], X. The "Community" in Community Mental Health [7 sessions], XI. [no section title; session title] Role Development of the Mental Health Worker [1 session]

65. Draft of a grant application 8/17/1960. [folder "Misc L", Box IIIA 1–3, Lindemann Collection, Center for the History of Medicine, Francis A. Countway Library of Medicine, Boston, MA]

66. Draft of a grant application 8/17/1960, pp. 3–5. [folder "Misc L", Box IIIA 1–3, Lindemann Collection, Center for the History of Medicine, Francis A. Countway Library of Medicine, Boston, MA]
    See also "12/12/55 Application for Training Grant under National Mental Health Act". [folder "MGH Budget Preps 1964–65", Box IIIB1c box 2 of 2, Erich Lindemann Collection, Center for the History of Medicine, Francis A. Countway Library of Medicine, Boston, MA]:

    As our program develops we hope that psychiatrists in training in preventive psychiatry will rotate through these three services, namely: the Mental Health Unit of the Massachusetts General Hospital; the Mental Health Service at the Whittier Street Health Center; and the Wellesley Human Relations Service. This plan is already in operation for the training program in psychology. . . . A series of formal courses . . . for the psychologists in training were much appreciated by our psychiatric residents and have further stimulated their interest in mental health work . . . may form the basis for the program which is to include the psychiatric trainees. . . . The clinical phase . . . is designed to integrate clinical skills into the framework of a mental health orientation. . . . More than usual emphasis . . . is placed on consultation with professional colleagues for joint rehabilitation planning. Emphasis is placed on situational or social system analysis. . . . Home visits and interviews with relatives . . . are provided.

The impact of the immediate social environment is introduced by analysis of the patients' role in a delimited social system utilizing the ward and occupational therapy groups . . . fellows move increasingly into activities at field stations, where more complex community dynamics can be comprehended while special techniques are being learned. Combined field work and seminar training is provided in four areas: mental health consultation, preventive group methods, preventive clinical intervention at times of emotional crisis, and problems of community organization. . . . There is also in progress a series of seminars as follows: Preventive Intervention Dr. Erich Lindemann Consultation Dr. Donald Klein Group Practice Dr. Pearl Rosenberg Group Therapy and Practice Dr. Paul Hare . . . we should like to have Dr. George Saslow be able to spend about one-half of his time in this teaching program . . . with mental health practice inside the hospital community.

Dr. Peter Sifneos . . . is expected to spend one half of his time . . . concerned with the community outside the hospital.

Dr. Richmond Holder . . . is to be the medical director of the Wellesley Human Relations Service . . . supervisor of our trainees to be assigned there.

Dr. Erich Lindemann, himself, will give a considerable portion of his time and effort to this program.

Dr. Gerald Caplan of the Harvard School of Public Health and Dr. Alfred Stanton, recently appointed director of McLean Hospital will participate actively in the Planning Committee and supervision.

We believe that for the next year we would be ready to start the training program of three third year fellows in preventive psychiatry.

(pp. 6–9)

12/10/56 Application For Training Grant under National Mental Health Act [social work CMH training program]:

Sylvia Perry (prog dir), Marie McNabola, Laura Morris (all MSS), Barbara S. Morrison MSW. "The recent developments in the field of mental health and the social sciences has brought to the fore with renewed emphasis the deep originating goals of the field of social welfare: social reform and prevention. The findings in the field of the social sciences . . . have brought social work where the findings of other sciences need to be incorporated. . . . The goal of prevention and the efforts to study mental illness and mental health has brought with it the realization on the part of psychiatry, psychology, social work, sociology and anthropology that collaborative efforts on a multi-discipline basis may be one of the most productive methods of study and service. . . . The field of mental health . . . has stimulated the efforts of these disciplines to study human behavior within its social context as a unity, thus, hopefully, in time to affect features of community life that have a significant effect on individual health and growth. . . . The potential contribution of social work to these current developments rests with its long history of work and study in the area of the impact on individuals, groups, and communities of social institutions and stresses, and through the patterns of professional activity developed to influence adjustments in the social structures from which these stresses emanate. this pilot study was established to train social workers in community mental health.

(p. 6)

67. Lindemann, Erich, memo to Meadow, Mr. Henry C., HMS associate dean for finance and business and dean for planning and special projects 1978 until he retired in 1983] "Research in Mental Health", 7/11/1955, pp. 1–3. [folder "RESEARCH—1955", IIIB2 a+b (box1 of 3), Erich Lindemann Collection, Center for the History of Medicine, Francis A. Countway Library of Medicine, Boston, MA]

68. Application for Research Grant, Health Research Facilities Grant (NIH, PHS), 10/24/1958. [folder "Warren Building 6th Floor", IIIB2 c (box1 of 2), Erich Lindemann Collection, Center for the History of Medicine, Francis A. Countway Library of Medicine, Boston, MA]

69. [folder "Dr. Alfred Stanton—Application for Research Professorship. 1959–60", IIIB2 c (box1 of 2), Erich Lindemann Collection, Center for the History of Medicine, Francis A. Countway Library of Medicine, Boston, MA]

70. "Alfred H Stanton, MD Considerations Regarding the Development of Psychiatry at Harvard", 5/27/1958

71. "On-going research at the Massachusetts General Hospital can be Summarized under three headings, namely: Laboratory investigations. Studies in the community. Clinical studies at the adult and child level", revised 6/22/1960.

72. "Announcement of Grants for the Establishment of Full-time Research Positions in Departments of Psychiatry", 1/1960. Foundations Fund for Research in Psychiatry, 251 Edwards Street, New Haven, CT. "These grants are made possible by an award from the Ford Foundation for the support of training of investigators in the mental health field". (p. 2) [folder "Dr. Alfred Stanton—Application for Research Professorship. 1959–60", IIIB2 c (box1 of 2), Erich Lindemann Collection, Center for the History of Medicine, Francis A. Countway Library of Medicine, Boston, MA]

73. Some Comments on the New Psychiatric Unit in the Medical Science Building (undated) [folder "Warren Building 6th Floor", IIIB2 c (box 1 of 2), Erich Lindemann Collection, Center for the History of Medicine, Francis A. Countway Library of Medicine, Boston, MA]

74. "Psychiatry—MGH 1956–57", p. 2. [folder "Psychiatry Service—Misc. + Budgets", Box IIIB1c box 2 of 2, Erich Lindemann Collection, Center for the History of Medicine, Francis A. Countway Library of Medicine, Boston, MA]

75. 5/1955, Box II A&B, folder "Correspondence 1954", Lindemann Collection, Center for the History of Psychiatry, Francis A. Countway Library of Medicine, Boston, MA]

76. Lindemann, Erich, 5/1955, *ibid.*, p. 1.

77. "Future Objectives for Psychiatric Research", 1962. [folder "MGH Research in Psychiatry—1962", IIIB2 a+b (box1 of 3), Erich Lindemann Collection, Center for the History of Medicine, Francis A. Countway Library of Medicine, Boston, MA]

78. Lindemann, Erich, "Further Development and Research in Community Mental Health", ca. 1958:

Support is solicited for a ten-year program of research and development in community mental health to be carried out as a cooperative undertaking by the Community Mental Health Program of the Department of Psychiatry of the Massachusetts General Hospital and the Harvard

School of Public Health. It is proposed to assemble a core group of high level research workers who will be given long-term appointments and adequate technical assistance. They will be encouraged to plan and initiate a series of studies in the theory and practice of community mental health and preventive psychiatry. They will exercise [*sic*] a leadership role in the development of the specialist training program in the two units. In addition they will be available as consultants both for research projects in these and other Harvard Units as well as for pioneer community mental health programs in other parts of the country. . . . It is hoped that it will also bring the whole program into articulation with allied endeavors in the field of social science and psychiatric research and training at Harvard University in the Medical School, in the School of Public Health, in the School of Education and in the Department of Social Relations. . . . The various projects are bound together. by a common theoretical basis and research philosophy . . . placing emphasis on crises in individual, groups, and communities occasioned by certain of the inevitable hazards of human existence, as a focus for thinking about the etiology of mental disorders. . . . Studies . . . in designing methods of preventive intervention and environmental modification which may lead to a lowering of the incidence of mental disorders in a community. . . . the past and current research and demonstration projects . . . provide excellent [foundation].

[undated] 1. session of Mental Health Service Steering Committee [handwritten notes]:

Dr. Lindemann: Grant foundation funds available for one year exploratory period. Doubtful that future funds available from this source. Probable interest in NIMH in community factors which facilitate or impede optimal emotional development. Interest in such matters as housing arrangements, population movement, etc. May be facilitated by West End Housing Project planned for 5 years from now. Mrs. [Laura] Morris available as person skilled in macroscopic community survey. Miss [Elizabeth] Geller will attempt to develop approach to early child development through nursery school settings in hospital or adjacent community. . . . Dr. [Warren] Vaughn [Vaughan][Massachusetts DMH Division of Mental Hygiene]: . . . Stressed consultative as vs. clinical-treatment orientation and importance of local community involvement. Traced history of Dept. Ment. Hyg. contacts with Blossom St. [near MGH] health center, a city unit . . . Suggested desirability of 3 medical schools—all now interested in preventive psychiatry—linking more closely with Commonwealth. Commonwealth proposed that Harvard Med. School assume direction of a few adjacent units as center for training and research (on model of Boston Psychopathic Hosp.) in community mental health. Such arrangements now exist with Harv. Sch. Pub. Health re: Quincy unit and in Cambridge. Suggestion made to Dean [HMS, George Packer] Berry that Blossom St. unit be taken over by Harv. Med School (if MGH interested?). . . . Is West End a community or only a health district of some sort? . . . Dr. Lind[emann:] Access to west End area may facilitate study of distribution of psychosis, relationship to socio-economic factors, etc. Over-all attack may be implemented by use of differential coordinated study of specific problems at various centers. E.g., efficacy of parent discussion groups at different socio-economic levels. . . . Dr. Lind[emann]: MGH group eager to work out joint program with Commonwealth. John Whiting + Dean Clark [MGH General Director] (on West End Council) have been asked to participate. Someone from City Planning [MIT] considered. . . . Next meeting in early September.

(pp. 1–7)

Terminal Report on Project MH-03471–05 "Further Development and Research in Community Mental Health" by Erich Lindemann—1966: "The purpose of this program was to accelerate and enrich on-going research and service development by including certain senior men as long-term consultants and to test out new service operations. Particularly we were striving to introduce the patterns of community mental health work developed in Wellesley into the context of a metropolitan general hospital". Incr link & collab HSPH-MGH. "As this demonstration and investigative work was witnessed by other departments in the hospital it did much to kindle the enthusiasm and support of the general medical profession. The further development and integration between the teaching hospital and the medical school on one hand and the community at large has been made a central issue by the director of the Massachusetts General Hospital, Dr. John H. Knowles, and the new dean at Harvard Medical School, Dr. Robert Ebert. By the time of the end of this project the issue of prevention and community integration which was first formulated, elaborated and made real in the framework of psychiatry in community mental health has become a major pursuit in most of the services of the hospital and the medical school, particularly in Medicine, Pediatrics and Rehabilitation". Also tching & cons c India, Germany, Aberdeen Scotland, Taiwan; Int'l J. Psychiat/Jason Aaronson MD Also contin & core stability of HRS "presenting an example of successful community integration for a far flung set of coordinating and preventing services in the field of emotional disorders". List of projects & participants. "III Evaluation of Positive and Negative Outcomes of the Work: . . . We are satisfied with the rather striking change in the orientation of the administration of the Massachusetts General Hospital and of the new Dean at Harvard Medical School in the direction of serious considerations for the social component not only of psychiatry but all of medicine. . . . The development of a 'Walk-In' Service in the Emergency Ward of the hospital, the reorganization of psychiatric consultation as mental health consultation and the active participation of mental health personnel in the rehabilitation program in the Nursing Service as well as the School of Nursing resulted to a considerable extent from the initiative taken by various members of the project staff, particularly Drs. [Gerald] Caplan and Lindemann [note no mention of middle level staff— Avery Weisman/consultation, Morris Chafetz/EW; resented by them]. . . . We had hoped that perhaps one or the other of the consultants might be motivated to change his short-term presence into long-term participation, However, it was difficult for such a novel field as the social approach in psychiatry to secure high level positions which would have been necessary to attract these individuals. In this way, we rather lost Dr. [John] Seeley, Dr. [Henrik] Blum and Dr. [Wesley] Allinsmith. . . . Some of our investigators started their inquiry with us and then moved on to higher positions than we could offer or returned to their original base. In this way Dr. John Baldwin, Dr. James Kelley, and Dr. Donald Klein have continued their inquiries after leaving here".

(pp. 1–6)

Lindemann, Erich, letter to Sapir, Mr. Philip [NIMH], 8/1/1967:

When we started this we never dreamt of the rapid expansion of the nation-wide community mental health programs. All the more, we need thoughtful development of concepts and careful scrutiny of the routines which are being established in this field.

Memorandum in Connection with Discussion at the Office of the [William T.] Grant Foundation of the Program in Psychiatry of the Massachusetts General Hospital (McLean Hospital and the Psychiatric Service of the General Hospital), undated:

Harvard Programs in Mental Health I. Studies in the emerging concepts of mental health and illness, and in the determination of the occurrence and distribution of mental disorders. The Unitary Concept of health and disease [sic] ([John T.] Romano-Engle) [Univ. Rochester Schl of Med] Health and disease may be viewed as "phases of life, dependent at any time on the balance maintained by devices . . . intent on fulfilling needs and on adapting to and mastering stresses as they may arise form within the organism or from without". In this idiom "health represents the phase of successful adjustment, disease the phase of failure". This fundamental concept is applicable to society, personality, and culture as well as to the physiological aspect of the organism. One facet . . . focusses on the personality . . . i.e. his behavior treated as a system. . . . Mental disease or illness represents failure or impairment in the functioning of this behavior system. [APPENDIX A.]

[folder "Further Development + Res. in Community Mental Health—Sapir Report 1966", IIIB2 a+b (box1 of 3), Erich Lindemann Collection, Center for the History of Medicine, Francis A. Countway Library of Medicine, Boston, MA]

79. "Report on Research Activities for the Department of Psychiatry 1957", pp. 2–3. [folder "MGH Committee on Research 1957–59", Box IIIB1d, Erich Lindemann Collection, Center for the History of Medicine, Francis A. Countway Library of Medicine, Boston, MA]

80. "10/14/59 memo from Dean A. Clark, MD, Gen'l Dir. MGH, EL Chief Psychiat Svc MGH, Martin Meyerson PhD Dir Ctr for Urban Studies [?H.U.-MIT], Bradford Washburn Dir Mus of Sci, Jane Dale Dir Eliz Peabody Hse, Laura B. Morris Cmty S.W. Dept Psychiat MGH", p. 2. [folder "MGH Committee on Research 1957–59", Box IIIB1d, Erich Lindemann Collection, Center for the History of Medicine, Francis A. Countway Library of Medicine, Boston, MA]

81. Letter from Berelson, Bernard, 7/8/1954, and letter from Lindemann to Berelson, 7/24/1954. [box II A&B, folder "Correspondence 1954", Lindemann Collection, Center for the History of Psychiatry, Francis A. Countway Library of Medicine, Boston, MA]

82. 12/21/1955 Minutes of the Interfaculty Committee on the Behavioral Sciences (Dr. Hugh Leavell chairperson, Drs. George Gardner, Lindeman, Miller, Talcott Parson, Benjamin Paul, Samuel Stouffer, Whiting; HSPH Dean Snyder, Mr. Henry C. Meadow clerk). [folder "Lindemann Correspondence 1955", Box IIIA 1–3, Lindemann Collection, Center for the History of Medicine", Francis A. Countway Library of Medicine, Boston, MA]

83. [folder "Rehabilitation Research Proposal, White 9", Box IIIA 4 (P-S), Erich Lindemann Collection, Center for the History of Medicine, Francis A. Countway Library of Medicine, Boston, MA]

84. [folder "Sapir Grant Misc. Material", Box IIIA 4 (P-S), Erich Lindemann Collection, Center for the History of Medicine, Francis A., Countway Library of Medicine, Boston, MA]

85. Annual Report Hall-Mercer Hospital Massachusetts General Hospital Division 1955–1956: Essentially same as Annual Report for the Department of Psychiatry for the Year 1955 Statistical Summary from October 1, 1954-September 30, 1955, 5/19/1956. [folder "Annual Report—Psychiatric Service, MGH '55-'56 and 1959", Box IIIB1b box 1 of 2, Erich Lindemann Collection, Center for the History of Medicine, Francis A. Countway Library of Medicine, Boston, MA] Excerpts include:

86. Presurvey Questionnaire for Program Evaluation by the Liaison Committee on Medical Education Representing the Council on Medical Education and Hospitals of the American Medical Association and the Association of American Medical Colleges, 11/6/1962. [folder "Presurvey Questionnaire", Box IIIA 4 (P-S), Erich Lindemann Collection, Center for the History of Medicine, Francis A. Countway Library of Medicine, Boston, MA]

    Another list of the department's research projects included the following (* = CMH projects):

    *12/27/55 "A Proposed Study of the Reaction of Individuals to Hazardous Situations", Nemiah, John C., Sifneos, Peter E. MD

    *"A Research of Addiction in Experimentally formed Groups" (drug addict. to improve func in soc grps)

    "A Study of the Effect of Submaximal Doses of X-Ray on Human Learned Skill and Judgement", Nemiah, John C., Rosenblum

    9/21/54 applic, 5/1/55–10/31/57 funding "A Study of the Specificity of Current Psychological Factors Involved in the Production of Psychosomatic Disease in Patients, Each Suffering From Two Different Psychosomatic Illnesses", Nemiah, John C., MD, Bonner, Frances J., MD

    *6/2/58 "Twenty-four Hours on the Rehabilitation Ward", A. Paul Hare [sociologist], Dept. of Psychiatry, Mass. General Hospital: [sociol. anal. of ward soc struct & culture]

    *8/57 "Observations of a Psychiatric Ward for a 24 hour Period", Whelpton, Douglas M.

    * 11/18/57 "Twenty-four Hours on the Psychiatric Ward in a general hospital", Hare, A. Paul, Dept. of Psychiatry Mass. General Hospital, Division of Mental Health, Harvard School of Public Health

    *11/14/58 "The Dimensions of Social Interaction", Hare, A. Paul, ?Dept Soc Rel, H.U.

    *8/31/58 "Predicting Interactive Behavior" (NIMH grand applic.), Hare, A. Paul, Associate Sociologist, MGH

    *9/22/55 "Epidemiology of Mental Health", Hare, A. Paul, Dr. Hartigan

    *6/19–20/64 Workshop on Methods of Data Collection and Their Use in the Planning of Psychiatric Programs, Coordinator Duhl Frederick J.

    *"Simultaneous Recording of Bales and Chapple Interaction Measures During Initial Psychiatric Interviews", Hare, A. Paul, Waxler, Nancy (H.U.), Saslow, George, Matarazzo, Joseph (U.OR Med Schl)

    *"Socio-Cultural Factors in the Seeking of Medical Aid: Paths to the Doctor—An Analysis of Patient Decisions" (doctoral dissertation), Zola, Irving Kenneth, PhD

    "REDUCING THE EMOTIONAL STRESSES OF HOSPITALZATION FOR CHILDREN", Gellert, Elizabeth, EdD, Dept Psychiat, MGH

    [IIIB2 a+b (box1 of 3), Erich Lindemann Collection, Center for the History of Medicine, Francis A. Countway Library of Medicine, Boston, MA]

87. Scientific Advisory Committee of the Massachusetts General Hospital, "Recommendations of the Scientific Advisory Committee, Massachusetts General Hospital, December 10 and 11, 1954", p. 1. Committee members:

Herbert S. Gasser, MD; A. Baird Hastings, PhD; Colin M. MacLeod, MD; Paul A. Weiss, PhD; Lowell J. Reed, ScD (absent); and Linus Pauling, PhD (absent). [Box II A&B, folder Scientific Advisory Committee: MGH 1954, Center for the History of Medicine, Francis A. Countway Library of Medicine, Boston, MA]

88. Minutes of the Research Committee 17 May, pp. 2–3. Committee members: Drs. [Edward D.] Churchill, [Benjamin] Castleman, [Henry K.] Beecher, [George Packer] Berry, [Oliver] Cope, [Joseph] Aub, [Mahlon] Hoagland, Lindemann; Messers. [David] Crockett, [Phillips] Ketchum. Invited: Dr. Morton Schwartz. M Sahlon B. Hoagland, MD, executive secretary, Committee on Research. [Box II A&B, folder Scientific Advisory Committee: MGH 1954, Center for the History of Medicine, Francis A. Countway Library of Medicine, Boston, MA]

89. Executive Committee of the Committee on Research, Minutes 5/13/1955. [Box II A&B, folder Scientific Advisory Committee: MGH 1954, Center for the History of Medicine, Francis A. Countway Library of Medicine, Boston, MA]

90. Letter from Leighton, Alexander to Lindemann, 12/6/1954. [Box II A&B, folder "Correspondence 1954", Lindemann Collection, Center for the History of Psychiatry, Francis A. Countway Library of Medicine, Boston, MA]

91. (Social Science Research Council/Basic Books) Leighton, Alexander letter to Lindemann, 7/18,27–30/1955, 4/10/1956–6/20/1957. [folder "Misc. Correspondence K,L, 1956–7", Box IIIA 1–3, Lindemann Collection, Center for the History of Medicine, Francis A. Countway Library of Medicine, Boston, MA]

92. [folder "MGH Committee on Research 1957–59", "1958", "1960", Box IIIB1d, Erich Lindemann Collection, Center for the History of Medicine, Francis A. Countway Library of Medicine, Boston, MA]

93. Research in Psychiatry. [folder "MGH Committee on Research 1961", Box IIIB1d, Erich Lindemann Collection, Center for the History of Medicine, Francis A. Countway Library of Medicine, Boston, MA]

94. "Programs in Mental Health for Discussion by Interfaculty Committee on the Behavioral Sciences July 18, 1955", p. 1.

95. Lindemann, Erich, letters to Cope, Oliver, 3/2/1962 and 12/13/1963. [folder "MGH Scientific Advisory Committee—MGH 1962–65", Box IIIB1d, Erich Lindemann Collection, Center for the History of Medicine, Francis A. Countway Library of Medicine, Boston, MA]

96. Cope, Oliver, MD letter to Lindemann, Erich, 3/7/1962. [HorowitzBarbara 781–444–9369: manicky, sooner appt]

97. "Confidential Report of the Joint ad hoc Committee Appointed to Represent the Faculty of Medicine, the McLean Hospital and the Massachusetts General Hospital in seeking a Professor of Psychiatry. Recommendation of Dr. Eric [sic] Lindemann for appointment as Professor of Psychiatry (University Full-Time) and Psychiatrist-in-Chief at the Massachusetts General Hospital". (M.G.H. Lindemann File, 1954–1962, Associate Director Records ([David] Crockett) box 51), pp. 1–7. [Erich Lindemann Collection, Center for the History of Medicine, Countway Library of Medicine, Boston, MA]

98. Adams, Raymond D., chief of the MGH Neurology Service, letter to Lindemann, Erich, 8/21/1959, seeking to assure the space allocated to psychiatry. [folder "Kennedy Foundation", Box IIIA 4 (I-Ma), Lindemann Collection, Center for the History of Medicine, Francis A. Countway Library of Medicine, Boston, MA]

99. Lindemann, Erich, letter to William H. Sweet, MD, 1/3/1961. [folder "Sapir Grant Misc. Material", Box IIIA 4 (P-S), Erich Lindemann Collection, Center for the History of Medicine, Francis A., Countway Library of Medicine, Boston, MA]

100. Folder "MGH Institute of Mental Health", Box IIIB1a box 2 of 2, Erich Lindemann Collection, Center for the History of Medicine, Francis A. Countway Library of Medicine, Boston, MA.

101. Deutsch, Martin, letter to Wood, Dr. W. Barry, Jr. Department of Microbiology, Johns Hopkins University, 1/29/1962, p. 1. [folder "MGH Committee on Research 1962", Box IIIB1d, Erich Lindemann Collection, Center for the History of Medicine, Francis A. Countway Library of Medicine, Boston, MA]

102. René J. Dubos, The Rockefeller Institute, New York City letter to Mr. Francis C. Gray, chairperson, Board of Trustees, MGH, 6/17/1960, pp. 1–2. [folder "MGH Committee on Research 1960", Box IIIB1d, Erich Lindemann Collection, Center for the History of Medicine, Francis A. Countway Library of Medicine, Boston, MA]

103. "Report of the General Director to the Trustees of the Massachusetts General Hospital", "A Brief Review—1960, Massachusetts General Hospital", Standing Committees of the Staff: Medical Executive Committee:

> Two major research laboratories were opened this year . . . the Stanley Cobb Laboratories for Research in Psychiatry on October 14. Each of these laboratories was constructed with about fifty percent financial aid from the Federal Government.

(p. 4)
[folder "MGH Administration", Box IIIA 4 (Mb-O),
Erich Lindemann Collection, Center for the History
of Medicine, Francis A. Countway Library
of Medicine, Boston, MA]

104. Dedication of the Stanley Cobb Laboratories for Research in Psychiatry and the observance of the Twenty-Fifth Anniversary of the Psychiatry Service Massachusetts General Hospital, 10/14–5/1960. [folder "25th Anniversary Papers", Box IIIB1a box 2 of 2, Erich Lindemann Collection, Center for the History of Medicine, Francis A. Countway Library of Medicine, Boston, MA]

105. Correspondence between Lindemann and Finesinger, 5/28,8/5/1958. [folder "Misc F", Box IIIA 1–3, Lindemann Collection, Center for the History of Medicine, Francis A. Countway Library of Medicine, Boston, MA]

106. Guttmacher, Manfred, correspondence with Lindemann, 1/27,2/8/1960. The Committee included many luminaries: Franz Alexander, Kenneth Appel, Nathan Apter, Leo Bartemeier, Eugene B. Brody, Stanley Cobb, Albert Deutsch, Robert Felix, Jerome Frank, Sol Ginsberg, Maurice Greenhill, Roy Grinker, Manfred Guttmacher, M. Ralph Kaufman, Marion Kenworthy, Lawrence Kubie, David Levy, Ephraim T. Lisansky, Reginald Lourie, William Menninger, Talcott Parsons, Frederick, C. Redlich, John Rosen, Milton Rosenbaum, Jurgen Ruesch, Milton Sacks, George Saslow, John Spiegel, William Stone, and John Whitehorn. [folder "Misc G", Box IIIA 1–3, Lindemann Collection, Center for the History of Medicine, Francis A. Books Department, Countway Library of Medicine, Boston, MA]

107. Folder "Misc F", Box IIIA 1–3, Lindemann Collection, Center for the History of Medicine, Francis A. Countway Library of Medicine, Boston, MA.

9   Erich Lindemann's Activities at Harvard

Erich Lindemann's Span of Activities

In his new position of respect and influence, Lindemann was busy with psychiatry and mental health public health projects involving medical professionals, nonmedical health professionals, social scientists, and community residents.[1] His wife was aware of "Erich's mode of preaching the gospel (you know that his grandfather was an evangelist)".[2]

Clinical Psychiatry

- March 19–20, 1955: "Caring Concepts of Psychoanalytic Medicine", The Psychoanalytic Clinic for Training and Research, Columbia University: Erich Lindemann discussant of Child Development Interlocking Pathology in Family Relations, Treatment Centers of Children: Team Problems.
- August 27–September 1, 1955: Lindemann spoke as part of the American Psychological Association's Institute on Training of Psychological Contributions to Mental Health. He focused on bringing the HRS model of CMH to the education of psychologists:[3]

I am very happy to accept your kind invitation to participate in the Institute on training for psychological contributions to mental health which is to take place from August 27th to September 1st. As you probably know, during the last year I have become the Chief of Psychiatric Services at the Massachusetts General Hospital and Professor at the Harvard Medical School which is giving us an opportunity to introduce mental health practice and training for mental health practice to trainees both in psychiatry and psychology as well as adding a program for training of social scientists as future mental health workers. . . . we have worked out some ideas concerning psychologists as mental health workers in our Wellesley project which is now closely tied in to the overall program at the Massachusetts General Hospital.

- September 28, 1955: letter from Marc Fried requesting Lindemann letters of recommendation in applying to medical school after clinical psychology work.
- Lindemann scheduled a visit to the Allan Memorial Institute at McGill University, Montreal, Canada.[4]
- Lindemann corresponded with Morton M. Stern, MD, Psychiatric Division, Harrison S. Martland Medical Center of Newark City Hospital, about the survey of planned improvements in municipal hospitals undertaken by Jimmie C. Brocklman, MD.[5] Lindemann reported that the MGH Psychiatry Service addresses psychiatric problems via consultation, outpatient, and inpatient ward services and via research and teaching. Its emphasis is on psychotherapy and the treatment of psychosomatic and psychoneurotic cases. It needs twice as many as the 20 beds and ten beds for mental health patients and twice the resident staff.
- In 1956, Lindemann was contacted about MGH as a model for the expansion of psychiatry departments to meet expanded needs for psychiatric services and arranged a visit to MGH.[6]
- March 24–5, 1956: the American Psychosomatic Society meeting, Boston: March 24 2:30 PM Erich Lindemann, professor of psychiatry, HMS, psychiatrist-in-chief, MGH, Boston: "The Problem of Pluripersonal Illness".[7]
- April 17–21, 1956: Second European Conference on Psychosomatic Research, Amsterdam April 18, 1956, AM "The Philosophic and Psychiatric Basis of Psychosomatic Medicine" 11:00–11:25 AM Prof. Dr. E. Lindemann, professor of psychiatry, Boston, Massachusetts, US [only US participants].
- Lindemann committed himself to attend lectures and give an evening talk at Columbia University on May 21, 1956.[8]
- In 1956, Lindemann joined in a petition to the APA to establish a section on general hospital psychiatry.[9]
- In September 1956, Lindemann participated in a symposium, "Death and Behavior", at the annual meeting of the American Psychological Association in Chicago. He engaged in a long correspondence about writing chapter 1, "Psychological Aspects of Grief", for a book to be titled *The Psychology of Death and Dying*, to include such contributors as Herbert Marcuse. It is unclear whether he completed this chapter.[10]
- Lindemann wrote an addition to a *Disaster Manual for Nurses*, addressing psychological stress on nurses and how to prepare for and manage it.[11]
- In 1956 and 1957, Lindemann participated in planning two conferences on the convergence of viewpoints on the etiology of mental disease, leading to the publication of *Integrating the Approaches to Mental Disease* (New York: Paul B. Hoeber, Inc., 1957).[12]

- September 20, 1957: letter from Samuel Lazerow, assistant librarian for acquisitions, National Library of Medicine (formerly Armed Forces Medical Library) requesting an autographed photo for their portrait collection (more than 25,000 photos and prints of medical men in the past 400 years).[13] "It is our constant effort to enlarge this collection by securing portraits of contemporaries who have made significant contributions to the medical sciences".

- December 5, 1958: letter of invitation from Prof. Christian, Naturhistorisch-Medizinischer Verein zu Heidelberg to address the society in light of the report that Lindemann is traveling to Germany.[14] On April 24, 195,9 Lindemann wrote that he declined this visit but would keep the invitation in mind for future visits.

- From 1959 to 1971, Lindemann organized, led, and participated in the Lindauer Psychotherapie-Woche (Lindau Psychotherapy Week) in Germany. Once or twice a year, it organized workshops and lectures on psychotherapy for psychiatrists, general practitioners, youth and recreation workers, and other human service workers interested in the contribution of psychotherapy principles to their work. Lindemann tried to link Harvard University with European developments and universities (Freiburg, Heidelberg, Tübingen). The Lindau workshops developed a loyal cadre of professionals who grew professionally and personally through the educational activities and group process. December 4, 1958, and April 24, 1959, there was an exchange of correspondence between Prof. Dr. Ruffin, director of the psychiatry and neurology clinic, University of Freiburg, Germany, regarding Lindemann's presence at the Lindauer Psychotherapie-Woche at the beginning of May that led to an informal visit to the Freiburg clinic.[15]

- Lindemann worked with homemaker services as part of his concept of CMH as professional strengthening of community resources: C. Knight Aldrich of the University of Chicago asked for information on training personnel in CMH.[16] Frederick Duhl included them in a survey of community social agencies.[17] Lindemann corresponded with homemaker and home care programs—especially for people with mental illness—in the Boston area and spoke to them on May 29, 1962.[18]

- August 12, 59: letter from Prof. Dr. M.O. Anwary, Dean of the Faculty of Medicine, University of Kabul, Afghanistan (an HMS alumnus) requesting one-year to two-year internships or assistant residencies for one or two experienced doctors to learn academic medicine, clinical work, and teaching.

- April 12, 1960: letter from Nancy Morris, secretary, First Church: Thanks for talk to Senior Fellowship.[19]

- 1960: arranging to address the 79th Annual Convention of the National Funeral Directors Association in Denver.[20] He continued communication with this group.[21]

- October 1960: *Friends Bulletin* Friends Meeting at Cambridge, Young Friends Fellowship October 2, 1960, presentation "Patterns of Psychological Adaptation", Erich Lindemann, Head of the Department of Psychiatry at Massachusetts General Hospital.
- In 1960, Lindemann made an attempt to develop an academic exchange between the University of Aberdeen, Scotland and the MGH, since the professor at Aberdeen was interested in psychotherapy and public health mental health.
- In 1961, Lindemann addressed the Toronto Branch of the Ontario Division of the Canadian Mental Health Association with a workshop for ministers.[22]
- In 1961, Lindemann gave the talk "Stress Involved in the Grief Process" at the Ninth Annual Psychiatric Institute in New Jersey.[23]
- January 9, 1962: Harvard Medical Society, "Approaches to the Study of Human Behavior—Center for Community Studies and Stanley Cobb Laboratories for Research in Psychiatry": speakers included Marc Fried, George Talland, Jack Mendelson, and Frank Ervin; Lindemann moderator.
- February 3, 1962: letter from the senior class secretary and the Newton South High School thanking Lindemann for addressing an assembly on January 30, 1962. This was reported in the *Newton Graphic* in an article on February 8, 1962, about his talk on the future role of the behavioral sciences, and the need to look on aggressors with understanding rather than apprehension.
- On October 4, 1962, Lindemann agreed to serve on the Professional Advisory Committee to the Martha's Vineyard Guidance Center, stemming from his consultation with Milton Mazer, MD, center director, about clinical and research activities.[24]
- November 29, 1962: letter from R. Lomax Well, MD, chairperson of the Liaison Committee with the Clergy, Medical Society of the District of Columbia, thanking Lindemann for giving the Second Davidson Lecture on grief.
- In 1963 and 1964, Lindemann corresponded and attended meetings of members of Guidance Camps, Inc. (a mental health therapeutic program for children)—in 1963 the President was David C. Crockett, deputy to the general director of MGH; in 1964 the president was Richmond Holder, MD.[25]
- January 17, 1963: letter from Simon Donigear, editor of the journal *Pastoral Psychology*, appreciating Lindemann's agreement to join its Editorial Advisory Board.
- In March 1963, Lindemann was a discussant on a panel at the meeting of the American Orthopsychiatric Association addressing a paper by Albert C. Cain PhD, Staff Psychologist at the Children's Psychiatric Hospital of the University of Michigan: "Children's Disturbed Reactions to the Death of a Sibling".

- In 1963, Lindemann spoke to the Crystal Spring Rehabilitation Center, Department of Public Health and Welfare, County of San Mateo, California.[26]
- On March 11, 1964, Lindemann spoke at the Forest Hospital, Des. Plains, Illinois.[27]
- On April 10 and 12, 1964, Lindemann's articles on grief for the International Encyclopedia of the Social Sciences and The Encyclopedia of Mental Health.[28]
- April 12, 1963: letter from Edwin S. Schneidman, PhD, effusively praising Lindemann's speech at the dedication of the Suicide Prevention Center, Inc.: Lindemann was persuaded that suicide is a social and community psychiatry phenomenon—hoping that Lindemann might join for three to four months in early 1964. Later, Schneidman referred to a chapter on "Preventive Intervention in Community Health" by Lindemann to be published in the book *Essays in Self-Destruction*.[29]
- October 27, 1963: Program of the Fourth Emil A. Gutheil MD Memorial Conference of the Association for the Advancement of Psychotherapy Inc" "Psychotherapy with Adolescents". Lindemann lecture titled "Adolescent Behavior as a Community Concern".
- November 6, 1963: letter from Noah Gordon, editor, *Psychiatric Opinion*: Lindemann consented to serve on Consulting Board.
- On March 9, 1964, Lindemann participated in the conference of the Child Study Association of America.[30]
- On March 15, 1964, Lindemann visited and spoke at the Phoenix, Arizona Community Mental Health Program. (The endnotes include a summary of Lindemann's presentation of the theory and practice of CMH.)[31] On March 31, 1964, a letter to Lindemann from Robert E Lofgren, ACSW, acting director of the Division of Mental Health of the Arizona State Department of Health, thanking him for an inspirational contributions during his visit.
- March 20, 1964: letter from Sherry Stein ACSW to Lindemann with effusive appreciation of his visit and addresses at an open meeting and National Association of Social Workers workshop—noting a standing ovation, enthusiastic comments, and contributions greatly loved by all. On September 23, 1964, Lindemann led Group IV in the conference "The Role of the General Hospital in Psychiatric Treatment".[32]
- Lindemann was a cosigner of a letter to the Editor of *The Boston Globe* objecting to its parroting of William Sargent's July 1964 *Atlantic Monthly* diatribe against American psychoanalysis and psychotherapy.[33]
- Lindemann continued as an authority on grief and bereavement. On October 13, 1964, C.Q. Mattingly, editor of *Child and*

Family, requested permission to reprint Lindemann's May 1944 article "Symptomatology and Management of Acute Grief".[34] In 1965
he wrote a review of Berezin, Martin A., and Cath, Stanley: *Grief,
Loss and the Aging Process*.[35]

- Lindemann was a discussant on the panel "Teaching to Other Physicians", part of a symposium "Can Psychiatry Be Taught? A Reap-
praisal of the Goals and Techniques in the Teaching of Psychiatry",
October 30–31, 1964.[36]
- November 3, 1964: letter to Lindemann from Albert C. Cain, PhD,
regarding Lindemann acting as a resource participant (remarks and
then discussion) in the American Orthopsychiatric Association workshop on suicide prevention.
- Lindemann had lunch with Milton Rosenbaum, professor and chairperson of the Department of Psychiatry, Albert Einstein College of
Medicine and his staff.[37]
- Lindemann was consultant to the NIH Division of Research Grants
group developing methodology and theory regarding the evaluation
and analysis especially of interdisciplinary approaches.[38]
- On March 8, 1965, Lindemann was invited to speak at the Workshop on Mental Health to encourage physicians to respond to public
interest in mental and emotional problems:[39]

The American public is becoming increasingly aware of the importance of mental health. Demands are increasing for professional
attention to mental and emotional problems. It behooves the medical profession to continue its service and leadership in this important
aspect of human health, since several of the ancillary professions are
already indicating their eagerness to encroach on this field.

Lindemann begged off.
- Lindemann encouraged the wide variety of projects by department
members. Jason Aronson, MD, appreciated his five years of constant
encouragement toward the realization of the *International Journal
of Psychiatry*, which especially facilitated scholarly communication
between Soviet and US mental health professionals during the period
of political hostility.[40]
- As is the custom in academia, senior staff and faculty members were
asked to provide a premier level of care for their colleagues and colleagues' families.[41] When things went well, this earned Lindemann
personal gratitude and professional support. An interesting episode
in Lindemann's clinical practice even before he was appointed as
the chief was an episode in the care of the poet Sylvia Plath, whose
depression and temptation to suicide (eventually successful) are well
known.[42]

Public Health Mental Health

- Lindemann joined the Group for the Advancement of Psychiatry in June 1947[43] and continued throughout his tenure as professor of psychiatry, including on the Committee on Research in Psychiatry and the Social Sciences and the Committee on Preventive Psychiatry.[44],[45]
- On November 30, 1954, Lindemann addressed the annual meeting of the Family Service Bureau of Cincinnati about HRS.[46]
- February 9, 1955: letter from Seymour D. Vestermark, MD, acting director, NIMH regarding Lindemann's participation on a panel on "Problems of Recruitment and Training for Community Mental Health Programs" on February 16–18, 1955 at NIMH.
- March 3–7, 1955: correspondence from David A. Young, MD, and Dorothea C. Leighton, MD, regarding her paper "The Distribution of Psychiatric Symptoms in a Small Town"; Erich Lindemann was a discussant at the APA annual meeting in Atlantic City and discussed Thomas Rennie's paper.
- 5/19/55: letter from Perrin C. Galpin, executive director, The Grant Foundation, Inc. regarding a one-year grant to MGH to prepare a study of early case finding and intervention, training of nonpsychiatrist mental health workers. Lindemann was too modest in the final report of the accomplishments of the Wellesley project.
- June 20, 1955, and reappointment July 1, 1955–6, of Lindemann as a member of the Subcommittee on Stress, National Academic Sciences, National Research Council.
- August 23, 1955: letter and paper and then book *Studies in Social Psychiatry* from Alexander H. Leighton, MD (Psychiatric Clinic in Digby, Nova Scotia, Canada, and then moved to the Department of Sociology and Anthropology, Cornell University).[47] Lindemann to write a chapter on bereavement. "The present volume is based on the conviction of psychiatrists and social scientists that their respective disciplines have much to offer one another and may together build a more coherent understanding of human behavior. . . . The major emphasis throughout this series of studies is the assessment of social and cultural factors in their effect on individual health" (p. 1).
- Leighton offers definitions of social psychiatry:
  in the US,

  the development of preventive programs in the community, industrial psychiatry, group psychotherapy, forensic psychiatry, the participation of psychiatry in administrative medicine and the utilization of the social milieu in treatment as well as the study of social factors in the etiology and dynamics of mental illness . . . the relationship between forms of personality deviance and social and cultural systems, with the structure and functioning of treatment services as social institutions, and with the application of social science knowledge in developing and administering programs for the treatment or the prevention of mental illness.

(p. 3)

In England, it is "more concerned with the development of treatment services and less closely related to developments in social science" (p. 3).

- November 4, 1955: letter from David A. Hamburg, MD, associate director, Institute for Psychosomatic and Psychiatric Research and Training, Michael Reese Hospital, Chicago, asking for information about patient and family orientation to hospital and staff-to-patient ratios: "we have a great deal of respect for your organization and would benefit by learning something from your experience".
- In 1955, Lindemann corresponded with the Commonwealth Fund about his review of John Cumming and Elaine Cumming's book *Closed Ranks: An Experiment in Mental Health Education*, the study of the reaction of a small Saskatchewan town to the intensive promotion of mental health.[48] In 1956, they corresponded about several issues, including the funding of an HRS trainee, overseas visitors to Boston, and fellowships, including for Harley Shands and John Stoeckle (an MGH internist dedicated to community medicine and collaborator with Lindemann in community mental health).[49]
- From February 20 to March 6, 1956, Lindemann corresponded with John S. Crossman of McGraw-Hill publishers about his opinion of Thomas Rennie's three-volume work *Urban Mental Health*.
- March 6, 1956: letter from Ozzie G. Simmons regarding a lecture on social anthropology. Simmons was the director of the Community Health Project at the Whittier Street field station of HSPH. It also reported the approval of a one-year NIMH grant and expectations that they will apply for a four-year extension on July 1, 1957.[50]
- Lindemann participated in a roundtable discussion on "Opportunities in Community Psychiatry" at the May 1956 meeting of the American Psychiatric Association.[51]
- Lindemann participated in the conference "The Physical Environment as a Determinant of Mental Health", Washington, DC, on May 28–29, 1956 and October 11–12, 1956 and in May 1957.[52]
- Wallace W. Robbins, Minister of The First Unitarian Church in Worcester, Massachusetts, thanked Lindemann for addressing the Laymen's League on April 9, 1957, about the Wellesley Plan and for his interest in starting a similar plan in Worcester.[53]
- In 1957, Lindemann spoke on "Psychological Implications of Disaster" at the Institute in Disaster Nursing for Faculty Members of Basic School of Professional Nursing and at the Institute for Instructors of Basic Course in Disaster Nursing.[54]

- In 1958, Lindemann was elected to the Council of the Spring Lake Ranch (halfway house) in Cuttingsville, Vermont.[55]
- Also in 1958, Lindemann felt that academic burdens forced him to resign after serving several years on the Board of Trustees of the Hampshire Country School (governed by North Riding, Inc.).[56]
- Lindemann corresponded with Stephen Fleck, MD, of the Yale Psychiatric Institute (and future noted social psychiatrist) and Frederic C. Redlich, a professor and chairperson of the Department of Psychiatry at the Yale School of Medicine about Fleck's visit and lecture at MGH, and recommendation of his promotion to tenured associate professor.[57]
- In 1958, Lindemann was asked to write a review for the *New England Journal of Medicine* of Wilmer, Harry A. *et al*'s *Social Psychiatry in Action: A Therapeutic Community* (Springfield IL: Charles C. Thomas, 1958).[58]
- In 1959, Lindemann spoke about the West End Study at an Institute at the Hopedale (Massachusetts) Unitarian Parish.[59]
- March 3, 1959: 53rd annual conference of the Massachusetts Conference of Social Work (Hotel Somerset, Boston): leader of Institute D. "Principles and Applications of Preventive Psychiatry".[60]
- August 25, 1959: letter from Malcolm H. Merrill, director, and John C. Dement, chief of the Division of Community Health Services of the California Department of Public Health, requesting USPHS assistance for Lindemann as consultant in November 1959 to the Department regarding planning the development of a Mental Health Service and Institute for Educators program of Mental Health Education.[61]
- In 1959, R.C. Merecker, administrative assistant to the Community Services Branch of NIMH, looked to Lindemann for copies of "Community Mental Health—A Selected List of References" by James G. Kelly and Sidney Gelfand of the MGH Department of Psychiatry.
- In 1960, Lindemann became a member of the Executive Committee of the Massachusetts Committee on Children and Youth (formerly White House Conference on Children and Youth); on June 9, 1961, he resigned due to lack of time.[62]
- February 19, 1960: letter from Gerald Caplan to Lindemann in New Delhi, India (during his WHO consultation), reported that Caplan was busy with the International Preparatory Commission Meeting in regard to the 1962 Congress in Holland. He had suggested Lindemann as the main speaker on the topic of the influence of school, community, and family on the mental health of children as a matter of primary prevention.
- On June 7, 1960, Lindemann corresponded with John Harrington, MD, DPM, DPH, consultant in psychiatry and deputy medical director of the Uffculme Clinic in Birmingham, England, about his wish

to visit the US, including MGH, with special interests in social and industrial psychiatry.[63]

- In 1961, Lindemann addressed the National Convention of Parents Without Partners in New York City. The MGH provided consultation, group leadership in developing a group discussion program, the study of single parenthood, and training social scientists. In 1962, there were studies of the genesis, development, and benefits of self-help groups and of its members ("A Self-Help Organization Understands Itself", A study proposal for PWP (Boston Chapter) by its professional consultants from MGH: February, 1962"); and preparation of a guide for the Boston chapter.[64]

- A grant application was prepared for the NIMH on "Group Training in Community Mental Health" for July 1, 1961, to June 30, 1962, to address clinical-preventive intervention, group methods, and a survey of preventive practices.[65]

- In 1962, Lindemann participated in the discussion of the "New Challenges for the Mental Health Section" at a meeting of the Massachusetts Public Health Association.[66]

- On March 29, 1962, Thaddeus B. Clark, Minister at The First Unitarian Church, St. Louis, wrote to Lindemann referring to his remarks at the Institute on Preventive Psychiatry at Iowa City the previous year.[67]

- From May to June 1962, Lindemann wrote a letter to the Massachusetts state legislature in support of a bill to discontinue dumping refuse adjacent to the Columbia Point Housing Project, as "severe hazard to the self-respect of both parents and children . . . under conditions of social rejection and humiliation there is great likelihood of the development of increased delinquency and crime as well as other abnormal mental conditions in a population".[68]

- On June 16, 1962, Lindemann was a discussant at the annual meeting of the Massachusetts Society for Research in Psychiatry in conjunction with Northern New England District Branch of the American Psychiatric Association.[69]

- From November 1, 1962, to January 18, 1963: correspondence regarding Jan A.C. de Kock van Leeuwen, Head of the Department of Health Education at the Netherlands Institute for Preventive Medicine, Leiden, the Netherlands—teacher of psychiatric public health, including the social sciences.

- April 15, 1963: letter from Wallace H. Best, PhD, lecturer on public administration in the Department of Public Health Practice at HSPH thanking Lindemann for his participation in the New England Conference on Community Health Records Management in November 1962.

- In August 19–22, 1963, Lindemann was a conferee at the National Conference on Public Health Training.[70]

- In 1963, Lindemann and Gerald Caplan were called upon as consultants to Massachusetts Governor Endicott Peabody to help him defuse a muckraking assault on the state hospital system and mental health program and to redirect attention to plans for further improvement.[71]
- November 8 and December 12, 1963: correspondence among Leonard J. Duhl, MD, psychiatrist, Professional Services Branch, NIMH; Robert L. Leopold, MD, assistant professor of psychiatry, University of Pennsylvania; and Lindemann regarding Lindemann contributing the case study of the Wellesley project to a planned volume *A Casebook of Community Psychiatric Programs*, and it discussed the need for teaching materials for training psychiatric residents and others for community psychiatry practice.
- April 10, 1964: an invoice for $100 for a lecture on March 25, 1964, in the course "Education in Disadvantaged Areas".
- Between November 17, 1963 and January 4, 1964: correspondence between Lindemann and the American Orthopsychiatric Association about an abstract of Lindemann's paper "The Psychiatrist's Contribution to the Role of the Behavioral Sciences in Dealing with Community Change", given at the association's 42nd annual meeting. It portrayed psychiatrists as counselors in the community setting, bringing expertise on psychodynamics, human development, and the vicissitudes of the social context. Psychiatrists are sought after but only by invitation, and they are resented and suspected and can become pawns in power struggles. Staying neutral but acting as a catalyst for the adaptive solution of crises is hard and different from clinical practice. Their clinical insights are matched with other behavioral and social sciences.
- Lindemann studied the reactions to John F. Kennedy's assassination: Robert T. Bower, director of the Bureau of Social Science Research, Inc., Washington, DC, memo to those concerned with studies of Kennedy's assassination, based on informal committee meeting in Washington, DC, November 23, 1963, including Leonard Duhl, Erich Lindemann, Marc Fried, and Robert Leopold, University of Pennsylvania. There was a compilation of studies, including Marc Fried's study in schools in the Boston area, Mrs. Fried's study among patients at Children's Hospital, Boston; Robert Leopold and Erich Lindemann's survey of US psychoanalysts on reactions of patients (December 1964—handwritten note on December 21, 1964, letter from Fred Greenstein): "Erich wrote to Boston Psychoanalytic Society members, but very little of significance came back".
- Site visits included one on November 26, 1963, Department of Home and Family Life, Teachers College, Columbia University, Dr. Ernest Osborne "Preparation of Mental Health Educator-Consultants", and another on December 5, 1963, Psychiatric Day Center,

Baltimore City Health Department, Gertrude M. Gross, Dr. Matthew Tayback.

- December 1, 1963: Dietz, Jean "Mass. General Psychiatrist Analyzes Mrs. Kennedy's Reaction", *The Boston Sunday Globe* p. 44: The study refuses to intrude on Mrs. Kennedy's privacy but notes that people call on reserves in time of stress, need to withdraw to privacy to recharge after intense publicity, exhibit ceremonial behavior for the public, and seek good support and relationships, such as from children.

- Lindemann corresponded with and arranged visits from academics from other countries who were interested in social psychiatry[72] Dr. Bengt Berggren, Psykiatriska Kliniken, Södersjukhusset, Stockholm, Sweden (regarding research on psychiatric emergencies and a visit to/ study with Lindemann in Boston) and corresponded with Prof. N.I. Grashchenkov, Kotelnischeskaya Naberezhnaya, Moscow, USSR (regarding a shared interest in social medicine and arranged lectures on Russian medicine at HMS and HSPH—fall 1963).

- February 18, 1964: letter to Lindemann from James K. Allen, president of Dorchester House, Inc., and the Columbia Point Center (both in Boston) thanking him for an address on February 5, 1964, at the organizations' annual meeting, making CMH clear to laypeople.

- March 3, 1964: letter from Lindemann to Leonard Duhl at NIMH, sending a preliminary outline of a chapter on the Wellesley Program with a completed version promised in about three weeks. It also remarks on Duhl's four meetings on training in community psychiatrists, a draft of remarks at the GAP meeting, and looking forward to the meeting of the Space Cadets.

- On March 8, 1964, Lindemann spoke at the Child Study Association conference in New York City.[73]

- March 31, 1964: letter to Lindemann from Jimmie Holland, MD (former psychiatry fellow at MGH), program chairperson, School of Medicine, State University of New York at Buffalo regarding Lindemann giving the Fenton on November 5–6, 1964, and his appointment as a visiting professor to the Department of Psychiatry, to give workshops and meetings with trainees, the Law School, the Mental Health Association, etc.

- Lindemann gave the lecture "Mental Health Issues in Large City Complexes", emphasizing the need for preventive psychiatric treatment and referring to the West End Study, part of the Fenton Lecture Series (Department of Psychiatry, State University of New York at Buffalo) titled "Megalopolis: Urban Life and Urban Conditions". He was also a visiting lecturer in the Department of Psychiatry and participated in a university faculty panel discussion on "Mental Health Problems of Urban Society".[74]

- In April 1964, Lindemann collaborated with Raquel E. Cohen, MD, director of the North Suffolk Mental Health Association, on obtaining neurological consultation and recommended her appointment to the MGH for fuller collaboration and planning of CMH work.[75] (Cohen later was appointed superintendent of the ELMHC.)
- On June 30, 1964, Charlotte Trautwine (formerly Charlotte Richards, who worked for Stanley Cobb) thanked Lindemann for his talk to and cooperation with the Intercommunity Homemaker Service of Newton (Massachusetts).[76]
- In August 1964, Lindemann spoke at the First International Congress of Social Psychiatry and Psychotherapy (in London), where his paper received appreciation: William G. Hollister, MD, chief of the Community Research and Services Branch of NIMH, was enthusiastic,[77] and Alfred Solomon noted "your undisputed leadership as the foremost social psychiatrist of today".[78] He also was involved in planning for the 1967 conference in the Netherlands.[79]
- In 1964, Lindemann spoke in Berne, Switzerland, at the annual meeting of the World Federation for Mental Health.[80]
- In 1964, Lindemann was included in an American Psychiatric Association delegation to the World Federation for Mental Health.[81]
- In 1964, Lindemann participated in a Policy and Planning Board Meeting of the Agenda Committee, Training and Manpower Resources Branch, NIMH.[82]
- Lindemann was elected to a fellowship in the American Orthopsychiatric Association.[83]
- On November 9, 1964, Lindemann was the main speaker with a talk titled "The Concept of Community Mental Health" at the Work Conference in Graduate Education in Psychiatric-Mental Health Nursing at the Western Psychiatric Institute and Clinic in Pittsburgh during November 9–13, 1964.[84]
- On December 9, 1964, the director of publications of the Child Study Association of America wrote regarding Lindemann's speech at the organization's conference the previous spring.[85]
- Lindemann's interest in ever-broader conceptions and efforts in social and community psychiatry drew him to projects for International Conferences (Congresses, Associations) on/of social psychiatry.[86] He served, along with other distinguished figures, on the interim Working Committee and Executive Committee.[87] He served, along with other distinguished international figures, as a vice president of the First International Congress on Social Psychiatry in London, from August 17 to 22, 1964.[88] At that congress, Lindemann and John Seeley presented a talk titled "Basic Issues of Social Psychiatry". He was listed on the Organizing Committee for the Americas for a second International Congress of Social Psychiatry[89] in Amsterdam in 1967,

which could not be arranged. He was also included in the Provisional Organising Body for an International Association for Social Psychiatry.[90] He was interested in conferences bridging the East and the West and pointedly refused the US government's invitation to spy on Russian participants in the conference. He encouraged Jason Aronson in developing the *International Journal of Psychiatry*.

- On March 6, 1965, Lindemann accepted an invitation to sit at the head table and moderate a panel discussion on "Citizens' Role in Mental Health Centers" at a reception for Massachusetts governor John A. Volpe and William C. Menninger, MD.[91]

- On March 18, 1965, Lindemann spoke on crisis intervention and prevention as part of a workshop on suicide prevention at the American Orthopsychiatric Association's annual meeting.[92]

- In June 1965, Lindemann spoke in the session "Preventive Approaches in the Community", part of the "Rochester Conference on 'Emergent Approaches to Mental Health Problems'".[93]

- In September 1965, Lindemann accepted an invitation to join a committee planning a Mental Health Section in the American Public Health Association, still believing in a public health approach to mental health:[94]

I believe that it is possible to make now the beginnings of public health programs in the field of disordered behavior. Much research in health education is needed in this area. Public health personnel have many skills which are essential for this program. Their participation in research is vital if we ever want to learn to control mental disease. I am profoundly interested in the work of the new section and am applying for membership in the Association.

Administration

Lindemann also was involved in administrative duties as part of his chairpersonship:

- In a letter on May 15, 1962, Francis O. Schmitt, institute professor at Massachusetts Institute of Technology (MIT), acknowledged Lindemann as one of the original incorporators of the Neurosciences Research Foundation, Inc.[95]

- In 1962, Lindemann was involved in the search for a clinical director at McLean Hospital to allow Alfred H. Stanton, psychiatrist-in-chief, to focus on research. José Barchilon, MD, a psychoanalyst interested in the psychoanalytic treatment of schizophrenia, was considered but no agreement was reached.[96]

- In 1964–5, his last year as MGH chief of psychiatry, Lindemann was honored by being elected as chairperson of the hospital's General Executive Committee.[97]

- He sat on the ad hoc committee to select a successor to Robert H. Ebert as the Jackson professor of Clinical Medicine at HMS and the chief of the Medical Services at MGH (who later became HMS dean).[98]
- On October 15, 1965, Lindemann recommended that Dr. Jeanne Brand at NIMH provide grant funding to Jules Masserman and Walter Barton for the Fourth World Congress of Psychiatry in Madrid in September 1966.[99]

Social Action

Among the many activities reflected in Lindemann's correspondence,[100] some stand out as indicating his acting on his conviction that social and community psychiatry address social issues affecting mental health.

- He was a signer of "An Open Letter to President Kennedy" in *The New York Times* after the Bay of Pigs expedition. The letter disapproves of Castro and his communist dependence but argues that hostility with Cuba serves to strengthen it and recommends discontinuing any invasion of Cuba and instead working to detach Castro from the communist bloc diplomatically, resume trade, and address the social conditions feeding totalitarian nationalism. It was signed by Lindemann as the professor of psychiatry at HMS and faculty members of Harvard University, Brandeis University, Boston University, and the Massachusetts Institute of Technology (including Gordon Allport, Noam Chomsky, Giorgio de Santillana, Jacob Fine, Lillian Hellman [visiting lecturer in English at Harvard], Hans Hofmann, Timothy Leary, Salvador Luria, Boris Magasanik, Herbert Marcuse, Lewis Mumford, David Riesman, Jose Luis Sert, Harlow Shapley, John van Doren, Robert W. White, Norbert Wiener, and Edmund Wilson).
- As part of the Pinewoods Institute Silver Jubilee/25th Year, he spoke about social work's contributions to the New Frontier.[101]
- Lindemann received correspondence from Peace Research Institute (Donald N. Michael, Richard Krickus, Kenneth Boulding, Bernard Feld, Arthur Larson, Charles Osgood, Ithiel Pool, Richard Snyder, and Arthur I. Waskow), The Congress of Scientists On Survival (S.O.S.), The Institute for Arms Control and Peace Research, and Social Scientists for Peace.[102] In response to correspondence from the Federation of American Scientists, he asked Frank Ervin, "Frank, do you think this is a good alternative to SOS?"
- On February 18, 1962, the Peace Research Institute, Washington, DC (headed by former UN Ambassador James J. Wadsworth), issued a press release titled "Shelter Program Challenges U.S. Liberty and Security, Social Scientists Warn". It argued that shelter-centered civil defense encouraged hostility to negotiation with communists

and competition between elements of US society for shelter and that "troublesome personalities" might gain control of the program. Social science participants included Lindemann, Urie Bronfenbrenner, David Riesman (Harvard Department of Social Relations), Raymond Bauer, Morton Deutsch, Herbert Hyman, Stephen Withey, Donald N. Michael, and Arthur I. Waskow. He was a cosigner of a letter on June 8, 1962, titled "Shelter Program" to the editor of *Science* 136:910–1, the other cosigners being Raymond Bauer, Urie Bronfenbrenner, Morton Deutsch, Herbert Hyman, Donald Michael, David Riesman, Arthur Waskow, and Stephen Withey. The letter replied to a critique of a Peace Research Institute report and decried bomb shelters as producing a "shelter-centered society", amounting to regimentation and civil defense with adverse effects on disarmament. It advocated a social science study of the handling and consequences of civil defense.

- In 1962–1964, Lindemann was a member of the Ad Hoc Committee on Alternatives to War, chaired by Roy W. Menninger, MD.[103]
- Correspondence in 1962 with Robert Norton indicated that Lindemann subscribed to the Bulletin of the Atomic Scientists, undoubtedly regarding objections to nuclear weapons.[104]
- In a talk on December 11, 1963, Lindemann addressed the mental health relevance of social change and social policies, including marginalized and discriminated social groups:[105]

"a crisis is a set of circumstances requiring rapid change in personal behavior; it means new roles and new performances, and it means often painful adaptation to the abandonment of roles which were once fitting and proper and replacement by new untried and often uncomfortable types of roles" (p. 5). This may lead to well- or maladaptive responses. The chronic crisis of our time: "The critical aspects of our time are rather those arising in the very subtle American cultural patterns . . . namely, the greater tolerance of differences in people and with it desegregation in many walks of life. It further means the growing quest for responsible participation among those fellow citizens who have been disenfranchised or were considered as negligible. And, finally, the ever increasing acceleration of social change, be it by automation in industry, by creating a new frontier of progress through urban renewal, by the increasing rate of migration as exemplified by urbanization process, and the flight from the country into the city, from the metropolitan center to the suburb, and the ever-increasing rate of migration into foreign territory for business or cultural purposes—all this leads to a lasting sequence of minor crises of separation and role transition, which some individuals carry well but which are hazardous indeed for other individuals. Such minor crises are of great consequence for growth and development of the young generation. If no effort is made to include in our planning provision for healthful intervention, they may snowball into serious impairment of personality functioning. We need to prepare the young for a life of change without losing the capacity to develop sustained and meaningful interpersonal relationships and commitment to lasting causes and objectives. We have gradually come to learn that a certain amount of stability and coherence of the social structure is necessary for the development of a personal identity and a coherent personality system" (p. 14). Helpful are experiences of meaningful understanding and help (e.g., the Peace Corps), opportunity for responsible participation (e.g., alternatives to imposed urban relocation in Boston's West End); settlement houses evolving into multi-purpose centers with many human services; medical care more oriented to humane care, community participation and changed professional roles. Leaders need accurate information to attend to the consequences of their decisions, professional advice (form city planners and social scientists), and interdisciplinary collaboration and the involvement of human service professions.

- In July 1962, Lindemann accepted Sanford Gifford's invitation to become a sponsor of Physicians for Social Responsibility (PSR),[106] with a focus on the dangers of thermonuclear war, the pathogenesis of war, etc.[107] Bernard Lown welcomed Lindemann as a distinguished sponsor and enclosed a policy statement regarding the medical aspects of chemical, biological, and thermonuclear war, alternative approaches to conflict, and the use of atomic energy, the armament race and the nuclear threat.[108]

The Physicians for Social Responsibility Statement of Purpose read in part as follows:

1) that the armaments race and the continued testing of nuclear weapons increase the danger of war. 2) that planning by our own or any other government which tolerates the risk of nuclear war but promises an effective defense constitutes a vast and scientifically unsupportable gamble with human life. 3) that while the survival of some individuals may be possible no modern society can survive a full scale thermonuclear attack . . . prevention is the only effective therapy . . . explore a new area of preventive medicine, the prevention of thermonuclear war . . . provide for the medical community and the general public the scientific data on which political decisions must in part be based; to alert physicians to the dangerous implications of the arms race; to involve physicians in serious exploration of peaceful alternatives; and to develop support for programs promoting effective disarmament and peace.

The group held "Symposium: The Medical Consequences of Thermo-nuclear War", and published a summary in the *New England Journal of Medicine*, addressing the human and ecological effects of a thermonuclear attack.[109] Their conclusions were that the prevention of nuclear attack is the only feasible approach; protection and recovery are not feasible; and the bomb shelter program leads to false courage, fails to stem nuclear war, encourages a selfish and hostile mind set, and is demoralizing.

In a letter to Lindemann (as a PSR sponsor) on August 1, 1965, Shirley C. Fisk, MD, deputy assistant secretary (Health and Medical), assistant secretary of defense, contradicting a circular letter from Daniel Deykin, MD; Cavin Leeman, MD; and Bernard Lown, MD, decrying preparation and policy for using biological warfare (bubonic plague) in Vietnam.[110] In a response on August 23, 1965, Lindemann appreciated the reassurance regarding no proliferation of biological materials for destructive purposes and noted that it would have been helpful to receive a statement about studies of biological agents for destructive purposes. He reminded her that PSR believes in the free discussion and clarification of controversies—especially the abuse of biological findings—and that sponsors do not censor shared information but give moral support to members.

International Activities

Lindemann gave a summary of his many international consulting, advising, and teaching activities:[111]

> about the participation of the Department of Psychiatry in international health activities over the past five years . . . throughout my tenure I have been much interested in collaboration with departments in other countries and in extending our teaching efforts to such departments . . . tradition established by Dr. Stanley Cobb who exchanged a number of Residents and Fellows with the Maudsley Hospital in London . . . during the last five years was involved particularly with the Department of Psychiatry at the University of Aberdeen under Professor Millar and with the Department of Psychiatry at the University of Munich under Professor Ploog (Max Planck Institute for Psychiatric Research) . . . particularly concerned with neurophysiological research . . . under the supervision of Drs. Frank Ervin and Jack Mendelson, while the work with the Aberdeen group involved the staff of our community mental health program particularly Dr. Robert Bragg.
>
> Even before my becoming Professor I was . . . consultant to the World Health Organization having been appointed to one of their regular expert panels. I chaired a meeting on psychotropic drugs in Geneva and made a ninety-day study trip to India for the World Health Organization to report on opportunities for the development

of psychiatric teaching in ten of the outstanding medical schools of that country. I participated as one of the major invited reporters in the international meeting on child psychiatry in Holland in 1963 and was Vice President of the International Congress on Social Psychiatry in London in 1964. I have been a frequent referee for the National Institute of Mental Health in connection with decisions of support for international conferences and international research.

During the last year I was one of the four "generalist consultants" for an East-West meeting at the University of Hawaii arranged jointly by the World Health Organization and the National Institute of Mental Health. During the last five years I also was consultant and participant for an important teaching conference each spring in Germany involving the instruction in psychotherapy for German physicians. [Lindau Conference] . . . . successful effort to create an international journal of psychiatry for which Dr. Fritz Redlich and Dr. Carl Binger acted with me as a Planning Committee to advise Dr. Jason Aronson.

(pp. 1–2)

Miscellaneous

Any program administrator has to pay attention to and maintain many facets of their program as well as ancillary interests of their own.[112] Lindemann continued to teach the main course in psychoanalytic psychiatry at the Boston Psychoanalytic Institute and motivated many MGH psychiatry staff members to complete psychoanalytic training. He worked hard to maintain a friendship with the dean of HMS, George Packer Berry, who was excited by social psychiatry. He attempted to involve faculty members of the HDSR in helping him introduce social science concepts and scientists into the medical school and the MGH. He could not win Talcott Parsons over to commit to collaboration between the HDSR and the HMS, and Parsons did not want physicians teaching in the HDSR, but he joined Lindemann in teaching the social sciences to first-year HMS students. He used the HMS and MGH calendar of events to demonstrate issues that he shared with likeminded colleagues.

Lindemann also supported biological psychiatry activities in the department, though his focus was on social psychiatry. In 1956, he corresponded with Harold Persky, PhD, the director of biochemistry research in the Psychiatric Institute of Michael Reese Hospital.[113] Persky was looking for a job studying the biochemistry of endocrinology and metabolism in psychological stress and psychiatric illness. Lindemann was interested, met with Persky, and wrote of drawing up blueprints for a psychiatry research initiative in the Medical Science Building at MGH, to involve Gardner Quarton of his staff. On February 24, 1956, he introduced Kurt Goldstein's lecture "Cortical Lesions and Changes in Human

Personality".[114] With William H. Sweet, MD (MGH chief of neurosurgery), he worked toward developing a laboratory for tissue culture and study of the nervous system.[115] In 1956–1957, he was involved (including as research psychologist) in an ongoing project studying psychosurgery (including leucotomy and indwelling electrodes) for pain, movement disorders, psychoses, and severe psychoneuroses.[116]

The World Health Organization: Consultation to Improve Medical Education in India

A major consultation activity for Lindemann was his appointment to consult with medical schools in India to improve their psychiatry education of medical students. He noted that in 1946 the World Health Organization (WHO) had arranged for a British hospital psychiatrist to survey Indian hospitals.[117]

In 1959, the chief of the WHO Mental Health Section invited Lindemann to consult about the teaching of psychiatry in Indian medical schools.[118]

> Our Regional Office [for South East Asia] has asked us to provide a consultant who could advise a number of Indian medical schools as to the teaching of psychiatry. . . . It would give me great pleasure if this assignment interested you, as I feel that you would make a very good job of it.
>
> (Attached letter to the future consultant). . . . There has recently in India been an increase of interest in mental health and, as we expect, you know, the government have established an All-India Institute of Mental Health at Bangalore. However, in certain medical colleges there is apparently room for improvement in the teaching of those aspects of mental health which should be given to undergraduates and our purpose in seeking your help is to advise us on the best way in which WHO can assist with this problem.
>
> In consultation with the government some seven medical colleges have been selected and it is proposed that you should visit each of them, not with the idea of any formal teaching, but rather to examine and evaluate the teaching and practice already given in these institutions, to suggest how this might be improved, and to compile a report with recommendations for the use of this office in its future planning. . . . It appears that the time when India will have a sufficient coverage of trained psychiatrists so that their services will be available to the whole population is so far off as to be out of practical consideration. . . . We therefore think that a step in the right direction would be to improve and increase the knowledge of and familiarity of the undergraduate medical student with mental disorders so that he might at least be able to approach cases with more confidence

and skill. . . . We think that in a week or ten days at each medical college . . . you will be able to size up the position and to be of great assistance to the Principal and the relevant staff. Undoubtedly you will be asked to lead discussions on your subject with the faculty, and to give one or two lectures on such general points as the modern approach to mental health at each college you visit. . . . The colleges selected . . . to be visited are: 1. Medical College, Madras . . . 2. Medical College, Agra, 3. B.J. Medical College, Poona 4. Medical College, Nagpur 5. Osmania Medical College, Hyderabad . . . 6. Medical College, Bangalore . . . 7. Grand Medical College, Bombay.

Lindemann promptly responded positively: "Thank you very much for your letter concerning a possible assignment to India. I am very much interested in this assignment and believe I might make a worthwhile contribution to the particular problem which is involved", and thus, the formalities had been completed.[119]

Lindemann justified to Dean Berry this leave from HMS as broadening the perspective on social psychiatry and psychopathology:[120] The India consultation progresses his interest in "the effect which social system and cultural values have on mental health and disease" (p. 1) as in HRS, the West End Study, similar interests in The Harvard Department of Social Relations, Dr. Robert Lifton's study (research associate in MGH Department of Psychiatry) of attitudes and emotional responses of Chinese and Japanese recent arrivals, Dr. John Spiegel's study of problem-solving and pathology in Irish and Italian families, Dr. William Caudill's study of the influence of values on administration and psychotherapy in Japanese mental hospitals, and the MGH seminar "The Cultural Aspects of Psychodynamics" for social relations students, HMS students, and psychiatry residents. He adds,

One of the more important results of my inquiry might be a new classification of psychiatric disorders with greater emphasis on the social context to which they are related. . . . At the end of my tour I am expected to make a report to the World Health Organization to be used as part of the work of an Expert Committee dealing with psychiatric education for medical students in various regions of the world.

(p. 2)

He noted that WHO pays travel expenses, $700/month stipend (in comparison with his usual income of a monthly salary) plus about $900/month from consultations and private practice. He requested leave from HMS as of December 1, 1959, for three months.

Lindemann began early his outreach in India: A letter on December 11, 1959, from Dr. H.N. Bhatt, principal of the S.N. Medical College in

Agra, India, expressed his thanks for Lindemann's agreeing to inaugurate the Student Union of the College, with a tea to follow. He visited the following sites:[121] Medical Colleges at Bangalore (medical college and All-India Institute of Mental Health), Bombay, Poona (Army), Agra (S.N. Medical College), Hyderabad (Osmania Medical College and General Hospital and the Patancheru Health Unit, Niloufer Hospital for Women and Children), Secunderabad (KEM Hospital of Gandhi Medical College), Madras, Nagpur, and Delhi (All-India Institute of Medical Sciences).

In his correspondence with Gerald Caplan, Lindemann reported his excitement and the enjoyment of his experience in India from December 1959 to March 1960.[122] Leonard Duhl believed that this experience helped confirm Lindemann's shift of identification of the patient from the person to the community.[123] Although he believed that he had brought some structure to psychiatric education, he despaired bringing to India a pragmatic, scientific approach. He saw this work as part of his dedication to world peace and brotherhood, and one of his most valued possessions was his WHO passport.

Although he found that 15 of the 17 mental hospitals that he surveyed were bad, he recommended that hospital superintendents teach psychiatry (i.e. mental illness). The National Indian Institute of Mental Health, a 1200-bed hospital, had been developed to teach clinical cases and didactic material, leading to a diploma in psychological medicine, and its graduates were placed in other hospitals. Those interested in public health and community development were dissatisfied with the WHO's approach: The WHO had been encouraging advanced medical and surgical technology even though the medical system had no strong base. The WHO wanted to introduce US technical skills and chose Lindemann to bring them, because he had worked with medicine and surgery in regard to the psychiatric problems of their patients.

Lindemann was profoundly affected by his experience in India in regard to culture, ideology, and psychiatry practice and teaching. His report to the WHO reflects some of his experiences and conclusions, which resonated with his own ideas of preventive mental health, medical student education, and interdisciplinary collaboration:[124]

> Mental hospitals, as they are functioning at present, are entirely unsuitable for the teaching of undergraduate medical students, for the following reasons: The mental hospitals teach the student bad psychiatric practice, and make him callous, resentful, or guilty about what he sees. This is due to over-crowding, to poor organization, to lack of differentiation between diagnostic and therapeutic groups, inadequate staffing, staff dissatisfaction, [and] poor community liaison. They could be used only after very considerable and expensive reorganization and rebuilding. . . . the burdens of administrative and

purely custodial pressures impinging on the superintendent are not likely to allow for free energy to develop such a teaching service.

(p. 6)

. . .

Almost all the psychiatrists now in charge of mental hospital psychiatry are unqualified to teach medical psychiatry to undergraduates, unless they have additional training. . . . The skills in good administration and in co-operative work with other departments, acquaintance with current work in other medical fields and experience in effective psychotherapy are missing. . . . Mental hospitals are very useful for the students who have developed a secure footing in medical psychiatry to show the short comings of contemporary psychiatric hospital practice, and to underline the need for prevention and early treatment.

(p. 7)

He continued:[125]

Lindemann reviewed training at Dr. Narajan's mental hospital, including out-patient treatment when supportive family was available. "But the most important experience of the morning by far was the visit to the Health Center at SAMITHI, a demonstration and TR. program in rural preventive medicine. This was a really inspiring occasion. . . . The professor of prev. medicine was there himself, so was an assistant professor, a child and Mat. Health teacher and san. Engineer, and Health educator, a social worker, a P.H. nurse. We saw a class given in pictorial form, in form of a story to a group of most attractive and attentive looking young women, who were illiterate or were, at least preparing to deal with illiterate people. They are the Line-Workers in the village for family control . . . for sanitation, for nutrition, for contagious diseases, for health education, and they were very eager. . . . The med students come in their 3rd year one half day every week they take over the complete health care of one family, assess the initial state of sanitation, income, social intercourse and relations to the village, including its own health and social characteristics, then examine all the members of the family, including doing their own lab work, assemble a basic health record, visit them regularly at least once a month, which they continue through, the 4th year have special day at which the family comes to see them at the center. . . . The other time is taken up by studies in epidemiology, health education, and basic health measures, including knowledge how themselves to build a well and a latrine, and a smokeless stove. . . . The most important thing is that their records from prenatal to adult life allow for the scientific inspection of the natural history of disease and health in this area. Wouldn't it be wonderful, if similar studies could be done on urban populations and other populations all over the world? An important part of the whole program is the professor of pediatrics, who thoroughly believes in preventive programs. . . . It would be a pleasure to work with this group. I am not quite sure how much Dr. N. is involved".

(p. 2)

Lindemann tried to articulate the cultural and ideological insights in reports to various professional bodies:[126]

Indian juvenile delinquency may stem from objection to moral lapses in adults. For their sakes "it would be wise to mobilize for these youngsters . . . methods of self control which this youngster probably hasn't received because he didn't have the right guru around . . . the father, which often is a very remote person with whom the youngster has very little to do emotionally. In addition to this, the oldest brother who kicks him around a good deal, the oldest brother usually feels he is privileged to kick around his younger brother [possibly echoing Lindemann's early school and family experience]. . . . In addition to that it is a much kinder and friendly person in the cities . . . in the neighborhoods and in the villages, who is another incarnation of something, namely of the guru principle. He has a certain wisdom, he has dedication and he has the integrity which goes with . . . the kindly, guiding father for the young boy. We would probably look for the person in whom we would enjoy confidence [possibly reflecting Lindemann's maternal grandfather]. It would be very interesting to check at what point these people [gurus] enjoy universal confidence in neighborhoods are asked for . . . become something in between school which is existing only in its beginnings, and the family [reflecting Lindemann's CMH model of key community caregivers]. He is an auxiliary father. It is usually thought that the guru in some way has had not enough access to this child, or vice versa, if there is delinquency".

(p. 8)

Psychiatry can be viewed as two kinds of things. Psychiatry can be a medical specialty which like dermatology deals with a certain type of calamity or illness, disease. Psychiatry as we see it can also be a preoccupation with certain patterns of behavior which are unacceptable to the society in which we live [psychiatry as deviance control]. It can be relating to the emotional and motivational component in all illness [psychosomatics, grief]. I call this latter for now, since I came back from India, the infiltrating kind of psychiatry in contrast to the specialty of psychiatry.

(p. 13)

So I think that what is happening in India, which is very exciting to us, is that they would like to jump over the stage of development . . . which has taken 25 years, namely the inculcation of psycho-dynamics and the psycho-dynamic participation of the doctor-patient care and would like to jump right away to social science and with some psychiatric and psychological components for making our institutes useful. I don't know whether they are not right. I have been toying with the idea of doing just that. There is an institute in Bombay, the Tata Institute of Social Science, there are three deans, three hospitals, and three medical schools who are all interested in this to have a demonstration program which would be aligned with preventive medicine and would deal with issues of not motivation of single individuals, but motivation of groups of people for together looking after the welfare, emotional and physical, of the constituent members of these groups. That is the answer. If they did that together we might come out the richer.

(pp. 25–6)

Lindemann also saw the obstacles to mental health care inherent in Indian culture. This shed interesting light on the counterbalance between his spiritual values and his scientific values:[127]

the possibility of institutionalised neurosis . . . the fear to step on anybody's toes, Ayurvedic medicine. The lack of teamwork and cooperation . . . the religious blocks of even the psychiatrist, lack of distinction between scientific work and religion, their enjoyment of mystery, the wish to be fooled, the pleasure about magic, the masochistic adaptation, what was there for a long time must be good, the wish to hide, to colour, the orientation to art, the dislike of dissecting analysis, the disparagement of reason, the fear of decision making.

After his return from this consultation, Lindemann maintained his contact with Indian psychiatrists and was eager to promote educational exchanges with US psychiatric institutions, including the MGH. He initiated "a small group for a series of discussions about possibly cooperative work in psychiatry and mental health between professional persons from India and from this country. We are planning to have our first discussion on Wednesday, December 6, in my office . . . at the M.G.H".[128] This was meant to include MGH CMH fellows, Indian mental health professionals, people from HSPH, the Florence Heller

School for Social Policy and Management (Brandeis University), the WHO, HMS, MGH, and MGH psychiatry residents. The last seminar was held on May 23, 1962.

He arranged visits for Col. M.H. Shah in the US (with Paul Dudley White and the National Heart Institute; the Walter Reed Hospital; and time with Lindemann regarding the psychosomatic aspects of heart disease) and Canada as part of his planning for a clinic in Karachi, Pakistan.[129] Lindemann corresponded with Dr. L. Monteiro, dean of the T.N. Medical College in Bombay, about the placement of a neurology fellow and described the new neuropsychiatry laboratories under Gardner Quarton and Frank Ervin, which study the neurophysiology of the limbic system and the electrical and behavioral functions of the mammillary bodies.[130] He also discussed the experimental psychology laboratories' techniques for operant conditioning, with help from MIT regarding electrical studies. Lindemann was interested in developing collaboration between the T.N. Medical College, Bombay University, MGH, and possibly the WHO regarding medical teaching and research, especially in neuropsychiatry, social and cultural variables in the development of psychoneuroses, and the role of the physician in society and as the guardian of the mental health of a population. He referred to "our plans for facilitating significant publications with India".[131] However, he was not successful in interesting many US psychiatry faculty members in teaching in India.

Lindemann continued correspondence with the WHO about the results of his consultation:[132]

> As you remember, the principle aim is to do our part here at Harvard in contribution to the sort of development which was suggested in my report, namely a new emphasis in the teaching of undergraduate psychiatry on psychological and social factors in disease, on personality development and on community mental health. This should enable the young physician to develop psychological skills and to understand persons under stress and to work effectively with programs in preventive medicine and preventive psychiatry.
>
> (p. 1)

The plan includes

> the establishment of a demonstration project in psychiatric education to which Harvard would make a special contribution . . . I discussed with Dean George Berry the possibilities of our participation with an Indian university in undergraduate psychiatric teaching. Dean Berry expressed his wholehearted agreement.
>
> (p. 1–2)

He suggested that this be done on the department level rather than on an interuniversity level. Lindemann arranged grant-supported visits from senior psychiatrists from three Indian universities to HSPH and MGH to train in neuropsychiatry. He arranged an HMS postgraduate education program for senior Indian psychiatrists with a certificate acceptable to the Indian government. Possibly, Lindemann would return to India for five to six months in the fall of 1961 to work with one of the trained Indian psychiatrists to set up a planning group, which would develop an undergraduate psychiatry curriculum, including planning with the MGH Department of Psychiatry and an Indian department for an intercultural psychiatry research and teaching program.

Krapf responded with enthusiasm:

> I am immensely cheered by what you modestly call your 'progress note' of 6 June, but which in fact is rather more a programme. I think that the cross-exchange between India and Harvard is quite the pattern that we are looking for. What will now be necessary is to knit the WHO participation into our flying carpet,

including diplomatic overtures to the Indian government.[133] Shortly afterward, Krapf became concerned that these plans slowed and wondered whether the cause lay in India or in Harvard.[134]

However, the Rockefeller Foundation's interest in collaboration between MGH and India continued: The All-India Institute of Medical Sciences (AIIMS) wrote[135] that a complementary opportunity for research and teaching exited between the MGH and the AIIMS in New Delhi. Its purpose would be the exchange of top physician scientists, including an MGH person pursuing research at AIIMS for a four-month to 12-month tenure as well as a top physician teacher (usually a department chief) tenured for one month. Such a program would be funded by the Rockefeller Foundation (at $25,880 per year for five years), administered by MGH, with AIIMS providing a house, car, and staff.

Lindemann continued attached to his interest and contacts in India even years later. David Satyanand, one of Lindemann's contacts, wrote that "All of us are looking forward to your coming visit",[136] and there was an extended correspondence about attempts to arrange a visiting professorship for Lindemann.[137]

The HMS dean supported this continued involvement:[138]

> [Lindemann has a] great interest in India—he has visited the country on several occasions. Next year, he expects to spend some months at the All-India Institute of Medical Sciences in New Delhi as a counterpart professor of psychiatry, having been invited to inaugurate there a program in social psychiatry, a field in which Dr. Lindemann is

internationally recognized as a leader. To implement his program in New Delhi, Dr. Lindemann tells me that he expects to go to India for several visits during the next few years. His base of operations will be in Palo Alto, California, inasmuch as he has been appointed Consulting Professor of Social Psychiatry at Stanford University School of Medicine.

Berry recommended that visiting psychiatrists spend more than three months to get acculturated. The program needed subsidy. At Harvard, Jason Aronson, Theodore Dreier, and John Spiegel were interested in visiting India regarding cross-cultural issues. Hugh Leavell had made good on his plans for work in India, and from New Delhi, he looked forward to continued collaboration with Lindemann in public health mental health:[139]

> I was so delighted to have your letter telling of the possibility of your coming to New Delhi. . . . We certainly hope that you will decide to throw in your lot with us here, and promise you a warm welcome indeed. I suppose that it would not be the first time that other psychiatrists have had somewhat different ideas from yours! And we need more of your ideas here!

Morris Carstairs, too, welcomed Lindemann's continued interest and had some comments on the interchanges then under way:[140] "I learned with great pleasure that you were considering coming to India for one or more years to lend your support to the development of psychiatric teaching" (p. 1). He criticized Dr. David Satyanand, the department chairperson of the All-India Institute. In contrast, he was positive about the training institutes at Randu (Bhaskavan) and Bangalore (Surya) and recommended that Lindemann relocate there rather than AIIMS. Edinburgh University was sending six senior teachers per year for six years to Baroda to establish and maintain good standards of undergraduate teaching and clinical practice.

Lindemann contacted the Rockefeller Foundation about making this part of his retirement plans: "we developed a plan that I would come to New York for a discussion of the situation in India with respect to psychiatry and about my possible participation in the program in New Delhi".[141] Concrete plans were made though LeRoy Allen of the foundation, who was in India. Lindemann wrote,[142]

> I am still most enthusiastic about availing myself of the opportunity to work at the All-India Institute for Medical Sciences and to make myself useful in the development of a first class psychiatric department there. . . . [Regarding the international situation] it would be best to abandon the idea of a trip this winter and to think in terms of

a trip the late fall of 1966. . . . As I think I told you, I am retiring from my Harvard post within a few days. . . . What you told me about the new orientation of the Foundation in terms of the control of poverty, excessive growth of population and illiteracy is quite exciting and makes me even more interested in some form of future participation

Allen responded:[143]

> I recently have had very satisfactory conversations with both Professor K. L. Wig, director of the All-India Institute of Medical Sciences[,] and Professor Satyanand. Both desire that I proceed as rapidly as possible in making the necessary arrangements for your proposed visit. . . . Professor Wig and Satyanand and I hope it will . . . be possible for you to begin an assignment in New Delhi before the end of September 1966. . . . The Institute would like for you to continue through the academic year if this is feasible. This would be May 1967.

It is expected that arrangements would be made for you to live in the guest house on the institute campus. And Lindemann replied:[144] "I am pleased that the group still is interested in having me in spite of the delay and will make every effort to come in the fall of 1966".

These plans were undermined by the demands for his retirement transition from Harvard, post-retirement activities, and move to Stanford and by what later proved to be the early phase of his terminal illness. He wrote to Kirpal Singh:[145]

> My move to Stanford is to undertake the creation of a new solid base for my psychiatric work and teaching during my retirement period. As soon as I am solidly established in all probability I will think again seriously about my visit to India.

Many in India and at the Rockefeller Foundation were disappointed and held out hope for the future.[146] Lindemann did not give up hope either:[147] "So far as your plans and my plans are concerned, I am still very much interested myself in coming at a suitable time and would enjoy very much sharing in this program. Again with best wishes" (p. 2). (Lindemann was also drawn into some of the Indian academic rivalry, expressing general sympathy for Satya Nan's concern about rivalry from Kirpal Singh.)

In another complication the Rockefeller Foundation changed its priorities from medical education:[148]

> I was very sorry to learn about your illness and your inability to come to India as visiting professor of psychiatry at the All-India Institute of Medical Sciences. . . . In view of the Foundation's program

policy changes, which has shifted emphasis from the medical education field, I doubt very much that the Foundation would consider
sponsoring an alternate at this time. . . . Although an exception could
be made in your case, because of the earlier commitment, it would be
difficult to justify support for another person.

As will be documented later on, Lindemann's progressive illness foiled
several wishes and attempts to resume his work in India.

The World Health Organization: Chief of the Mental Health Section

As Lindemann's perspective on mental health broadened from the individual to the family to the community to the society, it naturally led him to an
interest in world mental health. In 1955, Ronald Hargreaves, then chief of
the WHO's Mental Health Section, encouraged Lindemann to become a
consultant from June to September 1955 to the WHO West Pacific Office,
which was organizing an Australian seminar, "Aspects of Child Health
Work", but Lindemann declined.[149] In the summer of 1955, Lindemann
received information about the WHO Mental Health Section and a notice
of a vacancy for the position of medical officer (psychiatry).[150] That fall,
John I. Armstrong, chief of Personnel Section at the WHO wrote to Lindemann: "The position of Chief of the Mental Health Section of this
Organization will shortly become vacant . . . It has been suggested to us
that you might be willing to allow yourself to be considered as a candidate
for this post".[151] This set Lindemann onto thinking about an opportunity
to expand his advocacy for CMH, and he replied that he was honored and
had to consider the loss of salary and tenure and the need to explore this
with HMS and Dr. Hargreaves, the outgoing chief.[152] He did present as his
credentials for this position Harvard's social psychiatry/CMH group that
his and his colleagues' appointments represented.[153]

Lindemann explored the opportunities and obstacles of the position.
He enlisted Robert H. Felix, founding director of the NIMH, as advisor
and sponsor,[154] and wrote him that "I have been asked rather urgently to
take the post as Chief of the Mental Health Section of the World Health
Organization which was vacated by Ronald Hargreaves".[155] He wrote
to Hargreaves:[156] "my whole value orientation both in terms of my philosophy with a strong concern about human problems which transcend
national boundaries and my religious orientation as Quaker make work
as a civil servant at the level of United Nations a most attractive prospect". Hugh Leavell sought to discourage Lindemann from taking a position as "a foundation man":

> you have shown the way to enormously stimulate and facilitate crea-
> tive thinking among various professional groups and broadening

horizons away from concerns with psychiatric practice and narrower problems of medical care to the total area of preventive psychiatry and positive mental health including its ethical implications.

(pp. 1–2)

Hargreaves responded that Leavell was right: The bureaucracy was extensively developed with diminished flexibility, and mental health was too low on the WHO hierarchy. Leavell saw Lindemann as important where he was:[157]

> I personally would be very sorry to see you leave your present post. I do not think you would now find the W.H.O. job as satisfying as the work you are already doing, and you would certainly find it a considerable financial sacrifice. . . . I do not want to discourage somebody who would, I think, be a magnificent person for the job for the sake of the Organization. On the other hand, I would not like to encourage a friend of mine to take the job under any misunderstanding of what it entailed. Perhaps, therefore, the best way of summarizing the situation is to say that I feel that if it were now the kind of job that you would enjoy as much as your present one I would not probably have left it.

He emphasized that "Your work with the Public Health School had an immense international impact".[158] Despite these warnings, Lindemann was attracted to this larger setting for CMH: "After having talked with you and later with Robert Felix I became quite enthusiastic about the possibility of doing a significant job in Geneva. I am planning to pay Dr. Peterson a visit during the third week in April".[159] He added,

> After much careful discussion and after rearrangement of my affairs at Harvard University I am now confident that I could free myself to begin work in Geneva by September 15th. I am, therefore, writing to say that I will be happy to have my name submitted for consideration for the post of Chief of the Mental Health Section.[160]

Ultimately, Lindemann was prevented from taking this position (perhaps fortunately) by the bureaucratic circumstances of which he had been warned:

> I wrote to Dr. Peterson that I was very much interested in the job of the Chief of the Mental Health Section of the World Health Organization. . . . However, I learned today that the post has been offered to Professor [Eduardo E.] Krapf of Argentina. I was naturally a little surprised after having made so much effort here to disengage myself to go to Geneva.[161]

Felix offered a soothing, balanced reaction:[162]

> My reaction to this appointment [of Dr. Krapf] was mixed, of course. I hated very much seeing you leave our present post, as I told you as frankly as I knew how when you were visiting me here. On the other hand, I am sorry that the decision was made as it was if you really wanted that job. In the long run, however, I really believe that your greatest contribution to the mental health field can be made in your present post.

Lindemann continued in other roles at the WHO. Peterson asked Lindemann to comment on a study of mental health problems in general hospitals that was being considered,[163] and on November 9, 1956, Lindemann responded with enthusiasm about

> an opportunity of further discussion with you on some of the problems which we mentioned last April. I am particularly happy to be able to talk with you personally on the very complicated problems of psychiatry and mental health work in general hospitals about which I have found it hard to send you a simple written statement.[164]

He added to this:

> I am also just now trying to formulate some statements in response to a letter from Dr. Krapf which may be useful for the work of the panel conference this coming December on "The Relation of the Mental Hospital to the Community".[165]

And he accepted the appointment to its Advisory Panel. In 1957, he chaired the WHO Study Group on tranquilizers and hallucinatory drugs. In addition, M.G. Candau, MD, director-general of the WHO wrote, "I have the pleasure, on behalf of the World Health Organization and after consultation with our Government, in inviting you to serve for a period of five years as a member of the WHO Expert Advisory Panel on Mental Health",[166] and Lindemann replied

> I was delighted to receive your invitation to serve for a period of five years as a member of the World Health Organization Expert Advisory Panel on Mental Health. I will be very glad to serve on this panel. As you know I am deeply convinced of the very great significance which the work of the Mental Health Section of the World Health Organization can have for the development of service and research in the field of psychiatry in various part of the world.[167]

In 1959, the WHO invited Lindemann to consult with psychiatrists and assistant psychiatric nurses in Ceylon, but Lindemann was uncertain, and the invitation was withdrawn.[168]

The Evolution of the Massachusetts General Hospital Psychiatry Service During Lindemann's Tenure as Chief

The evolution of the MGH Psychiatry Service during Lindemann's tenure reflects both his efforts in the supportive historical climate obtaining when he started and the changed historical forces that overtook him during the latter part of his tenure.

One source of information about the state and activities of the department is the department's annual reports by Lindemann to HMS dean George Packer Berry:[169]

1960–1

Budget 1960–1: Training in CMH psychiatry at $30,258, CMH, social work at $37,453, Relocation and Mental Health—Adaptation Under Stress (The West End Study) at $121,276 (the largest item), Further Development and Research in CMH at $60,000 (second largest item), and Psychiatry Training for General Practitioners at $11,800. In total, training cost $658,800.

1961–2

We are achieving gradually the transformation of our Department from a unit primarily concerned with neuroses and psychosomatic disorders to a model psychiatric unit in a general hospital which is prepared to deal with the whole spectrum of acute mental disorders on a short term basis, while at the same time we are strengthening the resources at the McLean Hospital for the rehabilitation and for the re-educative component of medical care. . . . mental illness and disordered behavior should not be segregated off as unique forms of pathology but should be viewed . . . just like any other forms of illness. We also believe that certain aspects of medical care which are predominantly designed for the re-motivation and re-education of patients such as connected with rehabilitation in the course of chronic illness and for retraining after injury or paralysis should be developed in close relationship to the rehabilitation and re-education of the mentally sick. . . . both an expansion of the Massachusetts General Hospital program and a revision of the psychiatric program at the McLean Hospital . . . are intimately interlocked with the development of the Massachusetts General Hospital from a predominantly curative institution to a resource for prevention, health education and community care. It is most gratifying that the Research Committee of the Massachusetts General Hospital believes that a major effort should be made in the near future in the area of the behavioral sciences as a natural and necessary counterpart to the development of large facilities in biochemistry and biophysics.

(p. 1)

. . .

We are happy to have the privilege of coordinating the behavioral science phase of the teaching in the first and second year of the Medical School. . . . Our studies on personality development and on human ecology under Judy Rosenblith and Marc Fried are continuing vigorously.

(p. 2)

Budget 1961–2: CMH psychiatry at $31,258, CMH, psychology at $8,160, CMH social work at $32067, psychiatry for general practitioners at $15,000, Relocation and Mental Health—Adaptation Under Stress at $95,224 (largest item), and Further Development and Research in CMH at $71,875 (3rd largest item). The budget had a total of $848,643.

1962–3

the present progress note . . . must mention a series of crises and challenges to our adaptive resources. It has not been easy to maintain the high morale of our senior staff in the face of events which convey to them a seeming lack of respect on the part of the rest of the faculty and failure to sympathize with our point of view. Let me mention the major "traumatic experiences". 1. The appointment of a non psychiatrist to the Stanley Cobb Professorship without sufficient opportunity for our group to participate in the evolution of this plan. 2. The creation of a Bullard Professorship for Psychiatry and its assignment to Jack Ewalt without any clarification of this change in the departmental balance. 3. The failure of the Committee on Promotions to accept the recommendations of the executive Committee of our Department for the advancement of Gardner Quarton and Marc Fried. . . . 4. The serious and completely unexpected complications which arose in the course of my efforts last spring to find a helpful solution for Dr. Stanton and the McLean Program. 5. The decline of Walter Bauer's helpful participation and his serious illness. These disturbing events were to some extent offset by your very kind visit to our laboratories., by the rich and productive collaboration between John Knowles and myself, and by the cooperative program with Nathan Talbot [chief of pediatrics at MGH]. There is, however, . . . a sense of dismay and uneasiness . . . concerning the way in which my partner, Jack Ewalt, has turned the relationship of the two departments of Psychiatry from a primarily cooperative one into a competitive one. This may be symbolic for the present trend in the Medical Division of the University toward a competitive structure of a diversity of highly individualistic investigators replacing a previous trend toward integrative, mutually supportive and harmonious programs of joint endeavors. . . . this discomfort is being felt not only by the psychiatric faculty . . . but is shared with such men as Eugene Landis [HMS professor of physiology], Cliff Barger [HMS professor of physiology], Eric Ball [HMS professor of biochemistry] and Oliver Cope [MGH surgery staff]. . . . We have mobilized our adaptive resources accordingly. . . . 1. Psychiatric participation in the first year teaching. As you know, Dr. Quarton's program has found strong supporters and also many critics among the faculty. The strong trend toward integration reflected in the course on Growth and Development disappeared and the present climate of faculty opinion is more in favor of focused teaching by the separate departments. . . . Dr. Quarton is again co-ordinating the program for this spring. However, I have advised him to accept an invitation to go to the Ford Center for Advanced Studies in Behavior at Palo Alto for the following academic year . . . I have then, after discussion with Jack Ewalt, asked Alfred Stanton representing social psychiatry and Frank Ervin representing the biologic aspects of psychiatry to join with Peter Dews in planning a program for the following year. . . . 5. Our research program is well underway . . . the work of the Center for Community Studies under Marc Fried is coming to a closure. One volume, The Urban Villagers, by Herb Gans has appeared recently . . . In the course of this year several volumes are expected to give the first basic description of a working class community with respect to attitudes concerning health, illness, aspirations and conduct control. This part of our work has aroused the interest of the staff at the Massachusetts General Hospital partly thanks to John Knowles' enthusiasm. On March 5th I will use my participation in the Lowelll lectures on the hospital and the community to describe some of our results. . . . 6. A long visit with Jose Barchilon which I had in New York showed clearly that his position at the McLean vis-a-vis Al Stanton would not appear secure enough to him as a basis for his further professional growth. We have, therefore, had to return to the idea of having a senior member of our own staff relieve Al of a large part of his clinical responsibilities to free him for his research. The person who we are now considering is Dr. Samuel Silverman, Assistant Clinical Professor of Psychiatry. . . . 7. The work of the Child Psychiatry Unit in close conjunction with the Department of Pediatrics is being reformulated to stress preventive services and inquiries concerning preventive opportunities in the community both with respect to pediatric disorders and with behavioral disturbances. . . . 8. There has been considerable progress in reaching an understanding with Harry Solomon concerning our role in the development of the new unit for community psychiatry at Bowdoin Square. As you know, Dr. Solomon does not like any exchange of written material. However, in a discussion between Dr. Solomon and his senior staff on the one side and Drs. Knowles, Neumann and myself on the other side we reached the following preliminary agreement. Dr. Solomon would look toward the Massachusetts General Hospital and particularly myself to bring together the staff of the new unit. Most of the individuals would have appointments from both the Massachusetts General Hospital and the Commonwealth. Certain senior staff members would be presented to you for possible appointments to the Medical School using the now existing channels for recommendations. We have reviewed architectural plans and are now working out a table of organization. We are assembling an advisory committee to help us interest the right kind of person in the development of a psychiatric program clearly based on general hospital principles. The new unit will serve a definite population with preventive, clinical and follow-up facilities and develop the closest possible cooperation with existing and new community agencies in the regions of health, education and welfare. Out of these considerations will come a blue print which I hope to present to you shortly in anticipation of your joining us in a meeting of the leaders of this program.

I am fully aware of the risk that the operations of a fairly large mental hospital not clearly part of our general hospital either in terms of spatial arrangements or in terms of administration may present pit falls for the realization of our own image of general hospital psychiatry and will be very grateful for your advice and counsel.

(pp. 1–4)

Budget 1962–3: Training CMH psychiatry at $33,818, CMH psychology at $8,640, CMH social work at $36,537, psychiatry for general practitioners at $43,200, Relocation and Mental Health—Adaptation Under Stress at $116,199, and Further Development and Research in CMH at $74,750. The budget had a total of $985,024.

1963–4

Core staff (George Talland, Frank Ervin, Jack Mendelson) have secure support. Gardner Quarton is at the Center for Advanced Studies in Palo Alto; if he returns he will receive support until the course for his career is clarified.

Budget 1963–4: USPHS training in CMH psychiatry at $32,778, psychology at $18,792, social work at $40,805, and psychiatry for general practitioners at $35,640; Relocation and Mental Health—Adaptation Under Stress at $111,401 (largest item); Further Research and Development in CMH at $83,520 (4th largest item); and initial contact of emotional crisis and the community at $60,000. The budget had a total of $1,171,136.

1964–5

"Since an ad hoc committee is already active in the search for my successor, I am not recommending at this time any changes in our budget". This shows an evolution from enthusiasm, optimism, and creativity through struggles with adversity to maintenance and resignation.

The overall budget for the Psychiatry Service had grown from $220,000 in 1954 to $1,360,000 in 1965. The funding for psychiatric research from the US Public Health Service had grown from $25,000 in 1954 to $624,00 in 1964–5 and from all other sources from $49,000 to about $250,000.[170] The following is a partial list of research project applications and awards:[171]

- Blom, Gaston E., Long, Robert T., Child Psychiatry Unit, Massachusetts General Hospital: "Study of Emotional Factors in Children with Rheumatoid Arthritis" (NIH—approved September 1, 1958–August 31, 1959 and extended to February 29, 1960)
- Chafetz, Morris E., MD: "Psycho-pharmacological Effects of Alcohol on the Chronic Alcoholic" (NIH—pending)
- Child Psychiatry Unit, Massachusetts General Hospital (Lamont, John) April 1959: "Application to Charles H. Hood Foundation" ("investigation of the effects upon child and family adjustment of different methods of clinic treatment, and of other case dispositions" [p. 1]).
- Clark, Eleanor, supervisor, Psychiatric Social Service, MGH: "Community Mental Health Training Program in Social Work" (NIH—July 1, 1959–June 30, 1960; awarded)
- Clark, Eleanor, Supervisor, Psychiatric Social Service, MGH: "Social Work—Community Mental Health" (NIH—July 1, 1960–June 30, 1961; awarded)
- Clark, Eleanor, Supervisor, Psychiatric Social Service, MGH: "The Training Program for Social Workers in Community Mental Health at the Massachusetts General Hospital" (NIH—July 1, 1958–June 30, 1959; awarded)
- Gellert, Elizabeth, EdD: "A Study of Children's Beliefs About Illness" (to Elizabeth McCormick Memorial Fund September 1, 1957–August 31, 1958)

- Hare, A. Paul: "Predicting Interactive Behavior" (NIH—July 1, 1957–June 30, 1958)
- Leiderman, P. Herbert, Instructor in Psychiatry, HMS: "Behavioral and Physiological Responses to Sensory Deprivation" (USAF)—approved
- Lindemann, Erich, Fried, Mark, PhD; Ryan, Edward J., PhD; Rapoport, Robert PhD: "Human Adaptation in Complex Situations" (NIH—submitted July 21, 1961; duration July 1, 1962–June 30, 1963)
- Lindemann, Erich, MD: "Graduate Training Program in Psychiatry (Community Mental Health)" (NIH—awarded July 1, 1957–June 30,19 58)
- Lindemann, Erich, MD: "Mental Health Graduate Training" (NIH—July 1, 1955–June 30, 1956; awarded)
- Lindemann, Erich, MD: "Mental Health Graduate Training" (NIH—July 1, 1956–June 30, 1957; awarded)
- Lindemann, Erich, MD: "Training Program in Preventive Psychiatry" (NIH—July 1, 1956–June 30, 1957)
- Miller, Lovick C., PhD: (to develop child psychology in the Child Psychiatry Unit, MGH) (NIH—July 1, 1957–June 30, 1958; not approved)
- Perry, Sylvia, Supervisor, Psychiatric Social Service, MGH; "USPH Training Grant for Social Workers in Community Mental Health" (NIH—July 1, 57–June 30, 58; awarded)
- Rapoport, Robert N., PhD: "Preventive Intervention in Family and Work Crises" (USPHS submitted November 1961 for September 1, 1962–August 31, 1963; rejected)
- Rutherford, Robert F. (director, Simmons College School of Social Work), Lindemann, Erich MD (chief of psychiatry, MGH): "A Survey Course for Advanced Practicing Social Workers in Community Mental Health, Theory and Practice" (Charles H. Hood Foundation application April 21, 1959)
- Shaw, Robert S. (Department of Surgery with participation of Talland, George, and Brazier, Mary; also neurology, neurosurgery, and biochemistry): "Study of Behavior and Performance" (United States Air Force: February 1, 1959–February 1, 1960)
- Talland, George A., PhD: "Research On the Adjustment To Hazardous Situations Through Group Action" (Ford Foundation—December 28, 1955 for July 1, 1956–June 30, 1961)

Toward the latter part of his tenure, Lindemann sketched the trajectory of the MGH Psychiatry Service:[172]

The MGH Service started in the fall of 1934 with Stanley Cobb and William Hermann, then joined by Jacob Finesinger and by Erich Lindemann in October 1935. It had ten beds in the Baker building, with two for acutely disturbed patients. The emphasis was on psychoneuroses and psychosomatic diseases as well as the short-term care of acute psychoses. In 1941, the service moved to the Bulfinch Building, occupying two-thirds of the third floor—17 beds for general psychiatry plus four beds for acute psychoses. Treatment focused on psychotherapy, psychiatric milieu therapy, occupational and recreational therapy, and day and night care. In 1937, under Lindemann's direction, an outpatient clinic was started for the treatment of psychoneuroses, psychosomatic illnesses referred from other clinics, the diagnosis of psychoses, and follow-up care of discharged ward patients. These were treated with intensive psychotherapy. Also in 1937, there was the subdivision of a clinic for child psychiatry. In 1948, under the direction of Lucy Jessner, this became an autonomous unit in collaboration with the MGH Department of Pediatrics. It treated psychosomatic and personality disorders as well as developmental crises. It cooperated with the James Jackson Putnam Children Center (for the treatment of infantile disturbances) and social agencies. Also in 1948, the Wellesley Human Relations Project/Service was founded for services in CMH, supported by the community and staffed by the MGH. Its goal was the prevention of mental illness via dealing with emotional and life crises, involving contacts with community resources such as physicians, clergy, social agencies, police, public schools, and the Town Planning and Zoning Board. Community work fed back to the MGH clinic: psychiatric care in the Emergency Ward doubled in five years, and the work of the Psychiatry Service as a whole increased tenfold. "Much of this change has been due to our orientation to emotional and developmental crises in contrast to concern with traditional diagnoses and psychiatry".[173] The service also developed a large psychiatric consultation service, including participation in patient management on medical, surgical, and specialty wards, and active work with emotional crises on the wards rather than waiting for referrals for consultation.

A history of Harvard medicine appreciated the perspectives and goals that Lindemann implemented in his tour of duty at the MGH:[174]

the Massachusetts General Hospital . . . expanded and reorganized program after Dr. Cobb's retirement. The choice fell on Erich Lindemann . . . had been actively working with psychotic patients . . . investigating the efficacy of . . . sodium amytal, in opening up the mental functions of depressed and schizophrenic patients. . . . The 'sodium amytal interview' is widely used in . . . narcosynthesis . . . amnesias and other hysterical reactions . . . a pioneer in the observation and study of reactions to loss and grief . . . the application of social science approaches to psychiatric problems . . . an essential component of an emotional crisis . . . is the change in the individual's social system . . . demands a redefinition and reorganization of the whole scheme of roles. . . . his interest in the sociological aspects of psychiatry developed throughout the thirty years he was associated with Harvard and the Massachusetts General Hospital. . . . In 1948 he was responsible for establishing the first community mental health center in the United States . . . to study community conditions that might lead to mental disaster in certain individuals. As director of the Wellesley Human Relations Service . . . he focused on preventive psychiatry and preservation of mental and emotional health . . . in clinical, consultative, and educational fields . . . support in unexpected life crises and guidance in ordinary daily situations . . . close working relationships with other professional individuals and groups. . . . the hope that public understanding of and interest in mental health objectives might occur . . . the Department of Psychiatry received substantial additional funds by designating part of its space as the Hall-Mercer Hospital . . . the West End Research Project, the first project of its kind in the United States. . . . A systematic appraisal of the social and psychological stress involved in relocation . . . to study . . . family life, community life, adaptation to stress, and the meaning of the physical environment. . . . significant was the fact that these families were being separated from a cluster of people upon whom they could depend.

The legacy of this social psychiatry interval in MGH psychiatry was the appointment as first successor chief of psychiatry of Leon Eisenberg, known for having participated in public health and preventive psychiatry.

The MGH, HMS, psychiatry, medicine, and society had changed its perspective and priorities from those when Lindemann's ideas and appointments were promoted enthusiastically. Ideology had shifted from social to biological; the wave of the future was becoming the wave of the past. There was much debate over this shift. An articulate critique of the change that was taking place also at the MGH and HMS was presented by Jurgen Ruesch, with supporting contributions from others. He was outspoken in his objection to the shift from clinical understanding and caring to large-scale biological research:[175]

The 20-fold increase in funds for medical research over the short span of 15 years has seriously disrupted the operations of medical schools, training centers, and hospitals. . . . The medical sciences will have to be separated from clinical medicine. Although the 2 fields are complementary to each other, they attract different kinds of people, require different kinds of organization, and are based on different philosophies. The disorganizing effect of increasing support for medical science can be mitigated by increasing support for clinical medicine and the education of physicians *"The primary aim of medicine is the care of the patient"*. *Thomas Sydenham*. The nationwide emphasis on science has interfered with the clinical tradition in both individual research and medical education. The question now arises, whether or not it is worth while to save the clinical tradition.

He found this to be stronger in Europe than in the US, including Vesalius, Harvey, Paré, Linde, Pinel, Jenner, Laennec, Auenbrugger, Morton, Lister, Freud, Pavlov, Minot, Fleming and in the observation of non-clinical living creatures in Aristotle, Linnaeus, Lamarck, Darwin, and the ethologists Lorenz, von Frisch, and Tinbergen.

> Clinical research employs only simple instruments, abstains from the elaborate control devices utilized in experimental laboratory research, and focuses on naturally existing conditions. Clinical measurements and observations lead to empirical generalizations which provide guideposts for future action. The development of therapeutic methods and the study of organisms in their natural habitats are the goals of most clinical pursuits. Consequently, the vast majority of effective surgical, medical, and psychiatric treatment methods have been developed by individuals or small groups; and all of this work may be subsumed under the heading "little science".

He saw the advance in technology moving medicine away from clinical observation and measurement toward design, hypotheses, theories, controlled variables, and precise measurements similar to the physical sciences and shifting toward equipment and large personnel rosters, leading to human organizations and research factories (as in pharmaceutical corporations, government, and university research institutes). This constitutes "big science", which has less influence on the treatment of the sick than does clinical science, leading to a decrease in interest in the medical profession, lower-quality students, unfilled residencies, foreign medical graduates filling nonacademic residencies, and an increase in the doctor–patient ratios because there are fewer doctors in clinical practice.

From Rutstein, David D. [HMS professor of preventive medicine] "Physicians for Americans: Two Medical Curricula", *Journal of Medical Education 36:12* (part 2), 129–138 (1961), "the medical schools of the United States pursue a policy favoring selection of applicants with scientific ability, curriculum emphasis on the preclinical sciences, appointment of residents with scientific ability, appointment of scientists rather than clinicians as heads of clinical departments, and appropriation of large funds for medical research while support of medical education is neglected" (Ruesch p. 111). Big science results in scientists and researchers outnumbering clinical faculty, and medical schools are diverted from teaching and community service to research.

From Kidd, C.V.: *American Universities and Federal Research* (Cambridge, Massachusetts: Harvard University Press, 1959), p. 272: physical research laboratories and social research via mammoth surveys are "converting university professors into administrators, housekeepers, and publicists".

From Weinberg, A.M. [director of the Oak Ridge National Laboratory]: "Impact of Large-Scale Science on United States" *Science 134:* 161–4 (1961): Big science absorbs capable scientists from the rest of the university. Major monuments of past ages (the Pyramids, Coliseum, cathedrals, Versailles) burdened economies and contributed to the decline of civilizations: "we must not allow ourselves, by short-sighted seeking after fragile monuments of Big Science, to be diverted from our real purpose, which is the enriching and broadening of human life" (Ruesch p. 112).

There were contradictions in the shift from social to biological medicine and psychiatry. Social and community factors in medicine shifted to concerns with the economics and administration of medicine. John Knowles, the new MGH general director, continued the call of the hospital to social consciousness and social service.[176]

In the case of the hospital, social action by the total institution becomes mandatory if effective solution of some of the social, political, and economic problems of medicine is to be found. A strong, institutional, social conscience leads to social action for the benefit of the community. As Titmuss has said (Titmuss, R.M., *Essays on the Welfare State* [New Haven: Yale University Press, 1959], p. 135), "progress in medical science in psychological theories and in the specialized division of medical skill has converted medicine from an individual intuitive enterprise into a social service" (p. 67).

The MGH and HMS staff shifted from social responsibility to adapting to socioeconomic factors in seeking opportunities and support for the institution, as reflected in their selection of Robert Ebert to succeed Walter Bauer as professor of medicine at the MGH:[177]

> Today, when no one but the insured can afford to be sick, and even the cost of ward care is scarcely less than for semi-private accommodation, the "social and organizational aspects" of medical service have become an urgent field of research by the Hospital's chiefs. This is understandably a traditional concern of the Massachusetts General Hospital, where two years after the opening of the Out-Patient Department, Dr. Richard C. Cabot in 1905 began the world's first medical social service and, less than a decade later, extended it with the help of Miss Ida M. Cannon to the ward patients. Today, to an ever-increasing degree, the hospital is looked upon as a center from which radiate the health services of the community.
>
> (p. 5)

Gerald Klerman is an example of one who shifted between these ideologies: He was a psychiatrist and trained psychoanalyst. He was a member of the psychiatry faculty at the Yale Medical School and also served as the director of the Connecticut community mental health center. (This will be discussed further in the chapter on examples of CMH programs.) He supported that center's activism in community movements to address poverty, the rights of the welfare population, and tenants' rights. Disapproval from university and local government resulted in his removal and transfer to a new job and attitude at the ELMHC:[178] "the wave of reform and progress associated with a period of economic growth in the 1950s and 1960s now gives way to the retrenchment and conservatism associated with recent economic depression and budgetary restriction" (p. 619). The fragments of past social and new biological ideology in his contradictory analysis of the mental health system give evidence of his (and others') struggle with the transition:[179]

> Today . . . we look to psychoactive drugs as therapeutic agents. . . . The success of these compounds has contributed greatly to the changes in the therapy of mental illness, to the restructuring of the mental health care system, and to the strengthening of a medical approach to mental illness. . . . However the necessity to go beyond (p. 619) the traditions of . . . the medical model. . . [to understand] the modes by which individuals and groups should regulate and control dependent and deviant behavior . . . require solutions that are social, ethical, and political . . . rather than scientific and professional.
>
> (p. 620)

> [W]idespread changes in public policy and the mental health care system have been determined to a great degree by recent advances in biological and psychosocial technologies. Accordingly, further progress toward deinstitutionalization and community treatment is likely to depend upon new technologies.
>
> (p. 629)

As he was leaving the MGH, Lindemann summed up his intentions and their implementation regarding the role of psychiatry at the MGH.[180] He expressed his abiding beliefs, enthusiasm, and evangelism for social psychiatry and the rueful recognition of the disparagement and rejection from his colleagues and profession. Significantly, he presented this to his last incoming group of psychiatric residents, showing his respect for colleagues of all ages (and disciplines) and hopes for the next generation. It is instructive to compare this with the hopes and plans in his manifestos upon assuming the chairpersonship:

> what is the essence of MGH-Harvard Psychiatry. I can express to you hopefully it is destined for survival in one form or another. . . . the various chiefs of service are extremely watchful vis-a-vis each other that each service remains excellent. . . . [MGH] is a

very visible place that is watched by many other places to be a model . . . and possibly also to find fault with it if one can because that makes a lot of people feel good. . . . One wants to be just a little better than one was yesterday . . . it is a stressful thing. At times one feels one hasn't done very well even though other people who don't know it so well think of it as excellent. One also . . . feels that the complexities of a huge institution like this and the obstacles to achievement are so big that one is out of breath and hasn't done very much. This is shared by almost all people . . . from the chiefs of service who are racing with each other and against themselves. . . . [The psychiatry department is] still concerned with the human factor in medicine, carrying the torch for the human factor in medicine against an awful lot of resistance on the part of our colleagues who think of illness and disease as primarily and perhaps exclusively a matter of organic disturbance. . . . we can be available throughout the hospital as confreres of the medical man, the surgeon, and other specialties . . . there developed the image of a department of psychiatry in a general hospital as participant caretakers of the patients.

(pp. 1–5)

. . .

Now the things which I believe we added to this during the last twelve years . . . were these. Surely, people have personality structures . . . of which we must be aware. But they also come to us almost always in consequence of a recent breakdown of functioning engendered by an overwhelming problem, predicament, or crisis. And . . . such overwhelming predicaments such as bereavement are not encountered by one person alone but there are always clusters, groups of people involved . . . and that there are different forms of mastery of their problems—one form being illness bringing the patient to the doctor and the other form being impairment of early capacities, or delinquency, or a variety of [p. 5] maladaptive patterns within the community. Therefore, the notion of the character of psychiatric attention changed from the individual to a group of people involved in a common problem. . . . Surely disordered states are . . . terribly important in terms of their remedies but they must be considered vis-a-vis other forms of states, not obviously disturbed, but possibly dangerous for other people. In this way one becomes interested in pathological structure, social structure, may they be committees in our hospital, may they be neighborhood groups, may they be families, may they be clusters of patients on your wards, and the whole problem of the study of social systems and their buttressing by appropriate social sciences. . . . In the area of service it leads to a choice of the kind of people whom one will choose for service.

In a general hospital we are quite likely to rather have a rapid flow of many people who you, in a quick way, want to serve with intervention in the life predicament rather than having a long term hospital where you can be involved in the reeducation of a few people. . . . Not all are sick enough to be excluded from society that they have to be for prolonged care in a specialized institution. . . . This is important but it does not constitute psychiatry—not modern psychiatry. Modern psychiatry means effective intervention in clusters of human beings concerned with the predicament which often is signaled by the disturbed state of one person who comes with an entrance ticket to an emergency ward or to a clinic, or to our ward, or to the medical ward. . . . Therefore, the acutely disordered state, including the participants' typical stress situations, their patterns of mastery and the physiological, psychological and social components of stress behavior have been the scene of this department. If you want to do that with a reference to excellence you have to find for each of the ingredients the basic issues involved. . . . You have to have adequate laboratories which deal with stress behavior. . . . What happens on the various levels of integration as a person faces a problem . . . you have to study memory . . . information storage . . . at the psychological level as George Talland does . . . at the physiological level as Frank Ervin does . . . at the chemical substrata . . . as is done with Francis Schmitt's group over at the Academy of Sciences in which Gardner Quarton is taking part. . . . Our department has also become known for studies on social context. . . . If you take social context seriously and are really willing to abide by your convictions that each patient arriving in your orbit of power is only a fragment of a disordered social system then your relationship to the participant in this social system is very much enhanced. You will become concerned with the family. . . . You will become concerned with the power structure to which the patient belongs, to those people who control his life. You will become concerned with institutional organization [in] which he is embedded. You will become concerned with city planning, the housing which he has, the prospects for advancement in his life situation, and so on, and, you will not only look common cause in the face and say—isn't it too bad—there you are. But you will decide to work out those psychological, sociological issues in the community which you can use as admonition vis-a-vis the power structure decision-makers in the community to tell them perhaps your next decision might be of such order that there will not be so many casualties, of a psychiatric kind anyway. And it will be at that point where our intervention of psychological disorders by social means comes about. This is a young field, a field very much attacked by others, a field considered by many as strange and paramedical for medical sciences, but a field which has tremendous enthusiasm in some other places and it has aroused enthusiasm with the head of this hospital [John Knowles]—so much that he feels that the future patterns of patient care and the future role of this hospital in the community must be that of a torch bearer in the crisis approach dealing not only with the casualties but dealing with the power structure, with the political structure, with the planning organization and some of you have seen . . . what kind of a sparking John Knowles has caused already. . . . But this is the direction in which we are set to go and let us hope that the march will go further in this direction. . . . By virtue of this orientation we are not anymore doing what we did some 12 years ago, namely . . . that we see a patient as an individual. But if a patient is now enmeshed in a social system, in this case the system of the ward, and those who are looking after him . . . then the psychiatrists' role cannot be along this way anymore . . . redefining the role of the psychiatrist as that of the participant-observer of the ward processes, the social nature, the social problems arising, and the way in which certain kinds of patients disturb certain people who look after them and often the reason for the disturbance is not just in the patient but in the doctor or the nurse or the social worker involved and then these people become just as much recipients of consultation as the patients themselves. . . . In some wards it works beautifully. There are bursts of enthusiasm and sometimes it falls flat and we have to collect some of our own casualties . . . because it is a difficult new thing to do but it has brought a framework to psychiatry which is—I like the words "medical anthropology" We like to see people who know something about human nature in terms of . . . the human context, social context and in terms of human organization. . . . We hope, of course, that all of you will be leaders in the field five, six, ten years from now and that all of you will carry the torch unless by then you have found this is obsolete and that you have developed a new kind of approach to care. If you can do that, all the more power to you.

(pp. 6–13)

Notes

1. [folder "Lindemann Correspondence 1955–65", Box IIIA 1–3, Lindemann Collection, Center for the History of Medicine, Francis A. Countway Library of Medicine, Boston, MA]
2. Lindemann, Elizabeth B., letter to Robert Evans, Director of the HRS, 1/4/1997. [folder "HRS 1989 ff", box Human Relations Service via Elizabeth Lindemann, Erich Lindemann Collection, Center for the History of Medicine, Francis A. Countway Library of Medicine, Boston, MA]
3. Lindemann, Erich, correspondence with Bruce V. Moore, Executive Officer, American Psychological Association Education and Training Board, 6/29, 7/26/1955. [folder "AMERICAN PSYCHOLOGICAL ASSOC.-1954—", Box IIIA6 2) A-M, Erich Lindemann Collection, Center for the History of Medicine, Francis A. Countway Library of Medicine, Boston, MA]

4. Cameron, Ewen, MD, letter to Lindemann, 1/4/1956. [folder "Misc. Correspondence C—1956–5", Box IIIA 1–3, Lindemann Collection, Center for the History of Medicine, Francis A. Countway Library of Medicine, Boston, MA]

5. Stern, Morton M., correspondence with Lindemann, 3/1,8/1956. [folder "Misc. Correspondence S—1956–7", Box IIIA 1–3, Lindemann Collection, Center for the History of Medicine, Francis A. Countway Library of Medicine, Boston, MA]

6. Correspondence between Lindemann and Kenneth E. Appel, MD, of the Functional Disease Service, Department of Psychiatry, Hospital of the University of Pennsylvania, and Dr. Paul Ecker of that university, 3/8–25/1956. [folder "Misc. Correspondence D, E,F 1956–57", Box IIIA 1–3, Lindemann Collection, Center for the History of Medicine, Francis A. Countway Library of Medicine, Boston, MA]

7. [folder "Correspondence 1956", Box IIIA 1–3, Lindemann Collection, Center for the History of Medicine, Francis A. Countway Library of Medicine, Boston, MA]

8. Lindemann letter to Gerald Caplan, 5/18/1956. [folder "Misc. Correspondence C—1956–5", Box IIIA 1–3, Lindemann Collection, Center for the History of Medicine, Francis A. Countway Library of Medicine, Boston, MA]

9. M. Ralph Kaufman, MD (The Mount Sinai Hospital) correspondence with Lindemann, 11/8,15/1956. Others signing were D. Ewen Cameron, A.E. Moll, William Malamud, Spafford Ackerly, John Romano, Harvey Tompkins, Roy R. Grinker, Robert Laidlaw, and John Cotton. [folder "Misc. Correspondence K,L, 1956–7", Box IIIA 1–3, Lindemann Collection, Center for the History of Medicine, Francis A. Countway Library of Medicine, Boston, MA]

10. Lindemann correspondence with Herman Feifel, 6/27/1956–10/15/1958. [folder "Herman Feifel, Re: Book—The Psychology of Death and Dying", Box IIIA 1–3, Lindemann Collection, Center for the History of Medicine, Francis A. Countway Library of Medicine, Boston, MA]

11. Lindemann letter and manuscript to Miss Helen G. Kearsley, assistant chief of the Medical Service for the Commonwealth of Massachusetts Civil Defense Agency, 1/24/1957. [folder "Misc. Correspondence C—1956–5", Box IIIA 1–3, Lindemann Collection, Center for the History of Medicine, Francis A. Countway Library of Medicine, Boston, MA]

12. Kruse, H.D., MD, executive secretary of the New York Academy of Medicine, correspondence with Lindemann, 8/20–11/1/1957. [folder "Misc. Correspondence K,L, 1956–7", Box IIIA 1–3, Lindemann Collection, Center for the History of Medicine, Francis A. Countway Library of Medicine, Boston, MA]

13. [folder "Correspondence 1957", Box IIIA 1–3, Lindemann Collection, Center for the History of Medicine, Francis A. Countway Library of Medicine, Boston, MA]

14. [folder "Correspondence 1958", Box IIIA 1–3, Lindemann Collection, Center for the History of Medicine, Francis A. Countway Library of Medicine, Boston, MA]

15. [folder "Correspondence 1959", Box IIIA 1–3, Lindemann Collection, Center for the History of Medicine, Francis A. Countway Library of Medicine, Boston, MA]

16. Aldrich, C. Knight., Department of Psychiatry, University of Chicago, chairperson of the Sub-Committee on Training of Professional Personnel for Consultation in Community Mental Health, letter to Lindemann, Erich, Dr. Harold C. Miles, Miss Mildred Mouw, and Mr. Edward J. Flynn, 8/25/1959.

[folder "Home-makers Service", Box IIIA 4 (F-H), Erich Lindemann Collection, Center for the History of Medicine, Francis A. Countway Library of Medicine, Boston, MA]

17. Duhl, Frederick, MGH Psychiatry Clinics, letter to Lindemann, Erich, 6/8/1962: Agenda for the 6/11/1962 meeting on the "Social Service Index"—a collection of information on services offered by social agencies. [folder "Home-makers Service", Box IIIA 4 (F-H), Erich Lindemann Collection, Center for the History of Medicine, Francis A. Countway Library of Medicine, Boston, MA]

18. Letters from homemaker and home care programs in Boston, 1962–1964. [folder "Home-makers Service", Box IIIA 4 (F-H), Erich Lindemann Collection, Center for the History of Medicine, Francis A. Countway Library of Medicine, Boston, MA]

19. [folder "Correspondence 1960", Box IIIA 1–3, Lindemann Collection, Center for the History of Medicine, Francis A. Countway Library of Medicine, Boston, MA]

20. DeGrace, George correspondence with Lindemann, 9/21,10/6/1960. [folder "Misc D", Box IIIA 1–3, Lindemann Collection, Center for the History of Medicine, Francis A. Countway Library of Medicine, Boston, MA]

21. Lindemann letter to Thomas Glidden, president of the National Funeral Directors Association referring to Lindemann's 1960 report to the Food and Drug Administration about studies of psychological help to the bereaved, 6/16/1961. [folder "Misc G", Box IIIA 1–3, Lindemann Collection, Center for the History of Medicine, Francis A. Books Department, Countway Library of Medicine, Boston, MA]

22. Laidlaw, R.G.N., PhD, letter to Lindemann, 10/2/1961. [folder "Misc D", Box IIIA 1–3, Lindemann Collection, Center for the History of Medicine, Francis A. Countway Library of Medicine, Boston, MA]

23. Barton, Walter E., MD, superintendent of the Boston State Hospital, letter to Lindemann, 11/8/1961. [folder "B Miscellaneous 1 of 2 file folders", Box IIIA 4 (A-E), Lindemann Collection, Center for the History of Medicine, Francis A. Countway Library of Medicine, Boston, MA]

24. Lindemann, Erich, letter to Avery, C. Stuart, President of Martha's Vineyard Community Services, Inc., 10/4/1962. [folder "M Miscellaneous", Box IIIA 4 (I-Ma), Lindemann Collection, Center for the History of Medicine, Francis A. Countway Library of Medicine, Boston, MA]

25. [folder "Guidance Camps, Inc.", Box IIIA 4 (F-H), Erich Lindemann Collection, Center for the History of Medicine, Francis A. Countway Library of Medicine, Boston, MA]

26. Nordby, Elinor H., Superintendent, Crystal Springs Rehabilitation Center, letter to Lindemann, Erich, 5/8/1963. [folder "N. Miscellaneous", Box IIIA 4 (Mb-O), Erich Lindemann Collection, Center for the History of Medicine, Francis A. Countway Library of Medicine, Boston, MA]

27. Handwritten note, 1/?19,1964. [folder "N. Miscellaneous", Box IIIA 4 (Mb-O), Erich Lindemann Collection, Center for the History of Medicine, Francis A. Countway Library of Medicine, Boston, MA]

28. Lindemann, Erich, article "Grief", in Deutsch, A. and Fishman, H. (eds.), *The Encyclopedia of Mental Health* (New York: Franklin Watts, 1963), vol. II, pp. 703–706

29. Schneidman, S., PhD, letter to Lindemann 12/30/1964. [folder "Correspondence 1964", Box IIIA 1–3, Lindemann Collection, Center for the History of Medicine, Francis A. Countway Library of Medicine, Boston, MA] Also letters from Schneidman to Lindemann in 1965 seeking this chapter: "The

book will not go to press without your contribution" (5/26/65). He noted other contributors: Henry Murray, Talott Parsons, Harvey Sacks, Edward Stainbrook, Norman Farberow, Norman Tabachnik, Avery Weisman, Gregory Bateson, Robert Litman, Lawrence Kubie, and Schneidman himself. The book was published by Jason Aronson. [folder "Correspondence 1964", Box IIIA 1–3, Lindemann Collection, Center for the History of Medicine, Francis A. Countway Library of Medicine, Boston, MA]

30. 3/2/1964 letter from Mrs. William E. Arnstein, Conference chairperson and A.D. Buchmueller, executive director, Child Study Association of America to Lindemann. [folder "Correspondence 1964", Box IIIA 1–3, Lindemann Collection, Center for the History of Medicine, Francis A. Countway Library of Medicine, Boston, MA]

31. [folder "S Miscellaneous", Box IIIA 4 (P-S), Erich Lindemann Collection, Center for the History of Medicine, Francis A. Countway Library of Medicine, Boston, MA] A summary of Lindemann's teaching CMH follows:

> "mental health" . . . is a value you might say, and we like people to be mentally healthy. It is also something quite different. Mental Health is a department of Public Health . . . some people are utopian enough and optimistic enough to think that perhaps we could do with some of the mental diseases what has been done with typhoid fever and malaria to get rid of them. If we want to do that we can't sit in the laboratory and look at test tubes, it is even not enough to go out in the swamps and chase down mosquitos. We have to look at people, and we have to look at people the way they live with each other and the way they affect each other and the way they are handicapped or hampered by the other people around them, because we have to assume that some aspects of human living are some of the factors leading to mental breakdown. There is a continuity between states of stress and unhappiness and actual breakdown. Now there is a third aspect of mental health which a lot of us get even more excited about, and that is the sort of thing which has to do with our way of life. We don't want people to just be there. We would like to have them the best kind of people they can be. There is some aspect of this that has to do with, we call it positive mental health. . . . A number of those people like to have a person live up to his best potential, and Mental Health therefore means to provide people with the resources to be their best selves.
>
> (p. 3–4)

> To the clinic, even the clinic of the Massachusetts General Hospital . . . you find people who come about ten years later than they should have, and by that time the original predicament which got them, it should have gotten them to a psychiatrist, has gotten them everywhere else but not to a psychiatrist. So finally you get to them, but then it is usually too late, and you analyze them for a couple of years, or your [sic] do psychotherapy for a long time, or you just get a little desperate and don't do anything, or do some shock treatment which doesn't do any good either. So there was air of a little helplessness and a little fed-upness, so I couldn't stand it any more [sic]. And that's the way we got to Wellesley.
>
> (p. 4)

> "It was called, not a clinic, because we didn't want to do too much clinical work, it was called Human Relations Service . . . we wanted to study human relations and their possibility of making people sick" (p. 5). Address broad range of indiv, fam, cmty crises. "There are lots of

people in a community who by virtue of their profession have the privilege and the duty to look after other people. We like to think of them as the care-takers, not the custodians of the mentally ill in institutions, but the people who look after other people [doctors, clergy, teachers, police officers, parole officers, social agencies, welfare agencies]. . . . It is quite possible by skillful consultation to help these persons, the caretakers, tremendously in their effectiveness of looking after other people in crisis and in counseling. . . . we call it . . . mental health consultation. We don't take on the client, but we consult about looking after the client" (p. 5). "If you have those people [participants in institutional systems] in trouble a good deal of the time, then the mental health consultant can come in as administrative consultant. He can review what we call the social system of the organization and the social processes going on between the various people . . . and see what goes on in the likelihood that all the people in it will be comfortable, or the very great likelihood that people must be uncomfortable in this system. . . . Then you can review this social system with your consultee and come to some conclusions how we might change this system to one a little more effectively in terms of avoiding casualties . . . there are forms of consultation dealing with the daily events which might be out of the level of organization rather than in face to face relationship to the given victim or casualty. . . . The fourth problem, and this for us is the really important one, we did all of the three first ones only for the last goal. That is—could we do research together. If we want to find out where our difficulties arise in the community which might lead to breakdown and find that out early in the life cycle . . . joint research with the citizens, and out of this grew then what we think now has been the most productive part of our community mental health work in Wellesley" (p. 6). Mothers of 1–5 year old discussion groups with professional facilitation to teach mothering; role transition—adaptive vs. maladaptive responses (e.g., in grief, marriage, 1st child, adolescent turmoil/delinquency, school entry, [leaving] high schl for more indep), geog & SES mapping of mental illness & study causes. MH wkrs need backing of gen'l hsp c MH div for leisurely study unrushed by clin svcs, soc. svc agencies, cmty ctr, child svcs.

32. Massachusetts Association for Mental Health, Massachusetts Medical Society, Massachusetts Department of Mental Health, Massachusetts Hospital Association, and American Psychiatric Association/Northern New England District Branch, "The Role of the General Hospital in Psychiatric Treatment". [folder "9/23/64—Mass. Assoc. for Mental Health; Conf—"The Role of the Gen. Hospital in Psychiatric Treatment", Box IIIA 4 (I-Ma), Lindemann Collection, Center for the History of Medicine, Francis A., Countway Library of Medicine, Boston, MA]

33. 7/8/1964 letter to the editor of *The Boston Globe* cosigned by Bernard Bandler (professor and chairperson, Division of Psychiatry, Boston University School of Medicine), Jack R. Ewalt (professor of psychiatry at HMS and past president of the American Psychiatric Association), Peter H. Knapp (research professor of psychiatry at the Boston University School of Medicine), Erich Lindemann (professor of psychiatry at HMS and chief of the Department of Psychiatry at MGH), James Mann (president of the Boston Psychoanalytic Society and Institute), Paul G. Myerson (professor and chairperson of the Department of Psychiatry at Tufts University School of Medicine), and a 8/6/1964 letter of support from Burness E. Moore, MD (chairperson of the Committee on Public Information of the American

Psychoanalytic Association). [folder "Correspondence 1964", Box IIIA 1–3, Lindemann Collection, Center for the History of Medicine, Francis A. Countway Library of Medicine, Boston, MA]

34. Mattingly, C.Q., letter to Lindemann, Erich, 10/13/11964. [folder "C Miscellaneous", Box IIIA 4 (A-E), Lindemann Collection, Center for the History of Medicine, Francis A. Countway Library of Medicine, Boston, MA]

35. Lindemann letter to Martin Berezin, 10/19/1965. [folder "Correspondence 1965", Box IIIA 1–3, Lindemann Collection, Center for the History of Medicine, Francis A. Countway Library of Medicine, Boston, MA]

36. Letter from John Vornberg, MD (chairperson of the Banquet Committee), 9/28/1964 and from Grete L. Bibring, MD (psychiatrist-in-chief), 12/5/1963, both at the Beth Israel Hospital, Boston. Participants included George Packer Berry (Dean of HMS), Douglas D. Bond, Lawrence S. Kubie, Milton Rosenbaum, Robert Knight, Rudolph Loewenstein, Max Gitelson, George L. Engel, Erik Erikson, Albert J. Solnit, and Charles Tidd (Beth Israel Hospital staff). In a letter dated 12/24/1963, Lindemann accepted. This led to a publication.

37. Lindemann letter to Milton Rosenbaum, 1/3/1965. [folder "Correspondence 1965", Box IIIA 1–3, Lindemann Collection, Center for the History of Medicine, Francis A. Countway Library of Medicine, Boston, MA]

38. Stuart Wright, PhD, Office of Research Analysis and Evaluation, to Lindemann 1/25/1965. [folder "Correspondence 1965", Box IIIA 1–3, Lindemann Collection, Center for the History of Medicine, Francis A. Countway Library of Medicine, Boston, MA]

39. Grobe, James L., MD, chairperson of the Committee on Mental Health of The American Academy of General Practice, letter to Erich Lindemann 3/8/1965, inviting him to the Third Regional Workshop on Mental Health in Boston. [folder "W Miscellaneous", Box IIIA 4 (T-Z), Erich Lindemann Collection, Center for the History of Medicine, Francis A. Countway Library of Medicine, Boston, MA]

40. 9/20/1965 letter from Jason Aronson to Lindemann. [folder "Correspondence 1965", Box IIIA 1–3, Lindemann Collection, Center for the History of Medicine, Francis A. Countway Library of Medicine, Boston, MA]

41. Nathaniel W. Faxon (former general director of the MGH) memo and check to Lindemann, thanking him and Dr. [Walter] Mann for care of Mrs. Mary Jane Faxon on the Psychiatry Ward, 7/10/1959. [folder "Misc F", Box IIIA 1–3, Lindemann Collection, Center for the History of Medicine, Francis A. Countway Library of Medicine, Boston, MA]

42. Elrod, Norman, personal communication to Satin, David, 11/19–25/2000 [folder "Research", Erich Lindemann Collection, David G. Satin, Newton, MA]. Boss, Medard and Red, Hans, *Sylvia Plath and Ruth Beuscher: Two Essays* (Zurich: Althea Publishing House, 2000)]:

Plath was depressed and talking of suicide; she received psychiatric treatment from I. Peter Thornton, MD, including electro-convulsive therapy (ECT) at Valley Head Hospital. When he left on vacation, Plath was covered by [Kenneth] Tillotson, MD, physician-in chief-at McLean Hospital. On August 24, 1953, Plath attempted suicide with an overdose of sleeping pills and was admitted for eight days to a private room at Newton-Wellesley Hospital. When Tillotson also went on vacation, the Unitarian minister, Rev. Wm. Brooks Rice, minister to Plath's mother, Mrs. Schober Plath, and also a CMH collaborator with Erich Lindemann, asked Lindemann to fill in. Olive Higgins Prouty, a successful author and friend of Plath's family, paid Lindemann's fee. On September 1, 1953, Lindemann evaluated Plath:

"Dr. Lindemann . . . told Mrs. Prouty 'that he believed Sylvia had no mental disease or psychosis but had suffered an adolescent nervous illness from which she should recover fully'. Dr. [Donald McPherson, Mrs. Prouty's psychiatrist, offering another opinion] thought that 'The symptoms suggest an acute schizophrenic episode in a highly endowed adolescent girl. . . . This is not at all a hopeless situation as many recover with or without treatment. The time factor is unpredictable and it is greatly to her advantage to have intelligent supervision. Insulin and shock therapy are often indicated and seem to be of real value in this kind of trouble'" (pp. 17–18). Plath was admitted to the MGH Psychiatry Service and became more depressed (attributed to association with more depressed patients). Lindemann recommended that she be transferred to McLean Hospital. Prouty, however, recommended Silver Hill Hospital in New Canaan, Connecticut, whose director, William Terhune, MD, had cured Prouty 25 years earlier. On September 14, 1953, Plath was admitted to McLean Hospital. (Elrod associated Plath to a borderline personality disorder.) At Prouty's request, Lindemann saw Plath approximately weekly, though reportedly did not influence her treatment. She was treated by Tiffany Barnhouse, MD (married name: Ruth Beuscher), two or three times per week, supervised by Paul Howard, MD (acting chief of staff); the treatment included insulin shock therapy. Lindemann recommended that Mrs. Prouty talk to Dr. Howard; she reported that he said that "Sylvia would 'recover completely in time.' There were 'no schizophrenic symptoms, no psychosis of any kind, and no fear the present neurosis. . . [would] develop into a more serious condition'" (p. 28) [i.e., he agreed with Lindemann].

Lindemann also provided care for Plath's mother. Olive Higgins Prouty thought his care was excellent and treasured this kind and understanding man.

43. Letter from Hugh T. Carmichael, MD, to Lindemann, 7/11/1947. [folder "GAP-1946–49"; Box IIA6 Da GAP, Erich Lindemann Collection]

44. [folder "Group for the Advancement of Psychiatry (GAP) 1956–57", Box IIIA6 Da GAP, folder "GAP-1946–49"; Box IIA6 Da GAP, folder "GAP-1953, 52, 51, 50", Box IIIA6 Da GAP; folder "Group for the Advancement of Psychiatry (GAP) 1956–57", Box IIIA6 Da GAP, Lindemann Collection, Center for the History of Medicine, Francis A. Countway Library of Medicine, Boston, MA]

45. In the 1950s, the active membership included also Dr. Ivan C. Berlien (Detroit), Dr. Gerald Caplan (HSPH), Dr. Leonard J. Duhl (NIMH), Dr. Stephen Fleck (Yale University), Dr. Edward C. Frank (Louisville), Dr. J.W. Gottlieb (Lafayette Clinic, Detroit), Dr. Maurice H. Greenhill (Psychiatry Institute, Jackson Memorial Hospital, Miami), Dr. Ernest M. Gruenberg (Milbank Memorial Fund, New York), Dr. Roger William Howell (The Lafayette Clinic, Detroit), Dr. Benjamin Jeffries (Detroit), Dr. Mary E. Mercer (Nyack New York), Dr. Lloyd J. Thompson (Winston-Salem, North Carolina). [folder "Misc. Correspondence G 1956–57", Box IIIA 1–3, Lindemann Collection, Center for the History of Medicine, Francis A. Countway Library of Medicine, Boston, MA]

46. Miriam H. Dettelbach, executive director of the Jewish Family Service Bureau of Cincinnati to Lindemann, 12/21/1954. [folder "Misc. Correspondence D, E,F 1956–57", Box IIIA 1–3, Lindemann Collection, Center for the History of Medicine, Francis A. Countway Library of Medicine, Boston, MA]

47. Leighton, Alexander H., letter, paper, and book *Studies in Social Psychiatry* to Erich Lindemann, 8/23/1955. [folder "Lindemann Correspondence 1955", Box IIIA 1–3, Lindemann Collection, Center for the History of Medicine, Francis A. Countway Library of Medicine, Boston, MA]

48. Lindemann correspondence with Roger A. Crane, Division of Publications of the Commonwealth Fund, 11/22/1955–2/29/1956. [folder "Commonwealth Fund", Box IIIA 1–3, Lindemann Collection, Center for the History of Medicine, Francis A. Countway Library of Medicine, Boston, MA]

49. Lindemann correspondence with Roerick Heffron, MD, medical associate of the Commonwealth Fund, 1956–1957. [folder "Commonwealth Fund", Box IIIA 1–3, Lindemann Collection, Center for the History of Medicine, Francis A. Countway Library of Medicine, Boston, MA]

50. [folder "Correspondence 1956", Box IIIA 1–3, Lindemann Collection, Center for the History of Medicine, Francis A. Countway Library of Medicine, Boston, MA]

51. Correspondence between Lindemann and Joseph Downing, MD, acting director of Community Mental Health Research of the New York State Department of Mental Hygiene, 9/16/1955–2/1/1956. [folder "Misc. Correspondence D, E,F 1956–57", Box IIIA 1–3, Lindemann Collection, Center for the History of Medicine, Francis A. Countway Library of Medicine, Boston, MA] Participants included Robert Hunt, assistant director of Local Mental Health Services, New York State Department of Mental Hygiene; Dr. Albert Glass, Graduate School of the Army Medical Center in Washington, DC; and Dr. Paul V. Lemkau, director of the New York City Community Mental Health Board.

52. Lindemann, Erich, and Calhoun, John B., PhD, Laboratory of Psychology, NIMH correspondence 9/25/1956, 1/24/1957. [folder "NIMH-Misc. Material 1956–1958", Box IIIA6 Da GAP, Erich Lindemann Collection, Center for the History of Medicine, Francis A. Countway Library of Medicine, Boston, MA]

53. Robbins, Wallace W. letters to Lindemann, 2/21,4/10/1957. [folder "Misc. Correspondence O,P,R—1956–7", Box IIIA 1–3, Lindemann Collection, Center for the History of Medicine, Francis A. Countway Library of Medicine, Boston, MA]

54. 4/27/1957 at the Boston college School of Nursing, sponsored by the Massachusetts League for Nursing and the Massachusetts Civil Defense Agency— chairperson Helen G. Kearsley, R.N., assistant chief of the Nursing Service at the Massachusetts Civil Defense Agency. 6/27/1957 at the United Community Services. [folder "Misc K", Box IIIA 1–3, Lindemann Collection, Center for the History of Medicine, Francis A. Countway Library of Medicine, Boston, MA]

55. Sarcka, Elizabeth Man (Mrs. Wayne A.) letter to Lindemann, 2/5/1958. [folder "Misc. Correspondence S—1956–7", Box IIIA 1–3, Lindemann Collection, Center for the History of Medicine, Francis A. Countway Library of Medicine, Boston, MA]

56. Lindemann correspondence 6/4–10/16/1958. [folder "Misc H", Box IIIA 1–3, Lindemann Collection, Center for the History of Medicine, Francis. A. Countway Library of Medicine, Boston, MA]

57. Correspondence 7/28/1958–3/13/1961. [folder "Misc F", Box IIIA 1–3, Lindemann Collection, Center for the History of Medicine, Francis A. Countway Library of Medicine, Boston, MA]

58. Correspondence between the Boston Medical Library and Lindemann, 12/8/1958. [folder "Misc. Correspondence A,B—1956–57", Box IIIA 1–3, Lindemann Collection, Center for the History of Medicine, Francis A. Countway Library of Medicine, Boston, MA]

59. Hammon, John K. letter to Lindemann, 1/5/1959. [folder "Misc H", Box IIIA 1–3, Lindemann Collection, Center for the History of Medicine, Francis. A. Countway Library of Medicine, Boston, MA]

60. Leader Erich Lindemann, Panel Eleanor Clark (chief psychiatric social worker), MGH, William Freeman, HRS, David A. Kaplan, HSPH.

61. [folder "Correspondence 1959", Box IIIA 1–3, Lindemann Collection, Center for the History of Medicine, Francis A. Countway Library of Medicine, Boston, MA]

62. Notice of Meeting of the Executive Committee, Massachusetts Committee on Children and Youth; Lindemann, Erich, letter to Eliot, Martha M., MD, chairperson of the Massachusetts Committee on Children and Youth, 6/9/1961. [folder "Mass Committee on Children & Youth (formerly White House Conf.)", Box IIIA 4 (I-Ma), Erich Lindemann Collection, Center for the History of Medicine, Francis A. Countway Library of Medicine, Boston, MA]

63. 6/7/1960. [folder "Misc H", Box IIIA 1–3, Lindemann Collection, Center for the History of Medicine, Francis. A. Countway Library of Medicine, Boston, MA]

64. [folder "Parents without Partners", Box IIIA 4 (P-S), Erich Lindemann Collection, Center for the History of Medicine, Francis A. Countway Library of Medicine, Boston, MA]

65. [folder "NIMH-Misc. Material 1956–1958", Box IIIA6 Da GAP, Lindemann Collection, Center for the History of Medicine, Francis A. Countway Library of Medicine, Boston, MA]

66. Calist, Luis J. P., DDS, MPhH, letter to Lindemann, Erich, 2/8/1962. [folder "Mass. P.H. Assoc.", Box IIIA 4 (Mb-O), Erich Lindemann Collection, Center for the History of Medicine, Francis A. Countway Library of Medicine, Boston, MA]

67. Clark, Thaddeus B. letter to Lindemann, Erich. [folder "C Miscellaneous", Box IIIA 4 (A-E), Lindemann Collection, Center for the History of Medicine, Francis A. Countway Library of Medicine, Boston, MA]

68. Lindemann, Erich, correspondence with McDonald, Anna, chairperson of the Dump Committee of the Columbia Point Improvement Association, 5/25–6/2/1962. [folder "M Miscellaneous", Box IIIA 4 (I-Ma), Lindemann Collection, Center for the History of Medicine, Francis A. Countway Library of Medicine, Boston, MA]

69. [folder "Mass. Soc. for Research in Psychiatry", Box IIIA 4 (Mb-O), Erich Lindemann Collection, Center for the History of Medicine, Francis A. Countway Library of Medicine, Boston, MA]

70. National Conference on Public Health Training, 8/19–22/1963. [folder "Nat'l. Conf. on P.H. Tr"., Box IIIA 4 (Mb-O), Erich Lindemann Collection, Center for the History of Medicine, Francis A. Countway Library of Medicine, Boston, MA] Other conferees included the following: Dr. Robert H. Hamlin, professor and head, Department of Public Health Practice, HSPH; Dr. Hugh R. Leavell, emeritus professor of Public Health Practice, HSPH, Committee on Mission of Public Health Training; Dr. Ernest L. Stebbins, dean, School of Hygiene and Public Health, The Johns Hopkins University; Dr. Ray E. Trussell., commissioner, New York City Department of Hospitals; and Dr. Leslie Silverman, director of the Radiology Hygiene Program, Harvard University.

71. Murphy, Margaret, in the governor's office, memos to Lindemann, 10/4/1963. [folder "B Miscellaneous 2 of 2 file folders", Box IIIA 4 (A-E), Lindemann Collection, Center for the History of Medicine, Francis A. Countway Library of Medicine, Boston, MA]

72. [folder "Correspondence—Europe 1960–65", Box IIIA5 1), Erich Lindemann Collection, Center for the History of Medicine, Francis A. Countway Library of Medicine, Boston, MA]

73. Lindemann's handwritten note, 1/19/1964. [folder "N. Miscellaneous", Box IIIA 4 (Mb-O), Erich Lindemann Collection, Center for the History of Medicine, Francis A. Countway Library of Medicine, Boston, MA]
74. Marvin letter to Lindemann, 11/6/1964. [folder "Correspondence 1964", Box IIIA 1–3, Lindemann Collection, Center for the History of Medicine, Francis A. Countway Library of Medicine, Boston, MA]
75. Lindemann, Erich, correspondence with Cohen, Raquel E., MD., 4/13–27/1964. [folder "N. Miscellaneous", Box IIIA 4 (Mb-O), Erich Lindemann Collection, Center for the History of Medicine, Francis A. Countway Library of Medicine, Boston, MA]
76. 6/30/1964 letter from Trautwine, Charlotte to Lindemann. [folder "Correspondence 1964", Box IIIA 1–3, Lindemann Collection, Center for the History of Medicine, Francis A. Countway Library of Medicine, Boston, MA]
77. Hollister, William G. letter to Lindemann 10/27/1964. [folder "Correspondence 1964", Box IIIA 1–3, Lindemann Collection, Center for the History of Medicine, Francis A. Countway Library of Medicine, Boston, MA]
78. 9/22/1964 letter from Alfred P. Solomon, MD, of Chicago to Lindemann. [folder "Correspondence 1964", Box IIIA 1–3, Lindemann Collection, Center for the History of Medicine, Francis A. Countway Library of Medicine, Boston, MA]
79. Correspondence between Rose Laub Coser, PhD (sociologist studying the psychiatric profession and its practice), and Lindemann, 9/2/1965. [folder "Correspondence 1965", Box IIIA 1–3, Lindemann Collection, Center for the History of Medicine, Francis A. Countway Library of Medicine, Boston, MA]
80. Letter from the director-general of the World Federation for Mental Health to Lindemann 9/17/1964. [folder "Correspondence 1964", Box IIIA 1–3, Lindemann Collection, Center for the History of Medicine, Francis A. Countway Library of Medicine, Boston, MA]
81. Lamkau, Paul V., delegation chairperson, letter to Blaine, Daniel, president of the American Psychiatric Association, 9/22/1964. The delegation to the meeting in Berne, Switzerland, on August 3–7, 1964, consisted of Lemkau, A.A. McLlean, A.P. Solomon, Erich Lindemann, Jurgen Ruesch, and Walter Barton. [folder "L Miscellaneous", Box IIIA 4 (I-Ma), Erich Lindemann Collection, Center for the History of Medicine, Francis A. Countway Library of Medicine, Boston, MA]
82. Raymond J. Balester, PhD, chairperson of the Agenda Committee for the Policy and Planning Board Meeting of the Training and Manpower Resource Branch of NIMH, to Lindemann, 10/13/1964. [folder "B Miscellaneous 1 of 2 file folders", Box IIIA 4 (A-E), Lindemann Collection, Center for the History of Medicine, Francis A. Countway Library of Medicine, Boston, MA]
83. Haddock, Benjamin H., Secretary to the Board of Directors of the American Orthopsychiatric Association, correspondence with Lindemann 10/26/1964, 3/26/1965. [folder "Amer. Orthopsychiatric Assoc.", Box IIIA 4 (A-E), Lindemann Collection, Center for the History of Medicine, Framcis A. Countway Library of Medicine, Boston, MA]
84. Letter to Lindemann. [folder "Correspondence 1964", Box IIIA 1–3, Lindemann Collection, Center for the History of Medicine, Francis A. Countway Library of Medicine, Boston, MA]
85. Cannon, Dolly N. letter to Lindemann, Erich. [folder "C Miscellaneous", Box IIIA 4 (A-E), Lindemann Collection, Center for the History of Medicine, Francis A. Countway Library of Medicine, Boston, MA]
86. Correspondence between Lindemann, Erich, and Ewalt, Jack, 1964: the minutes from 12/22/64 of a meeting regarding establishing an International

Association for Social Psychiatry, held at the Harvard Club of Boston, Commonwealth Avenue, Boston 12/22/1964. [folder "Ad Hoc Committee to explore possibilities for establishment of an International Assoc. for Social Psychiatry (1964) MGH", Box IIIB1d, Erich Lindemann Collection, Center for the History of Medicine, Francis A. Countway Library of Medicine, Boston, MA]. Those suggested and involved included Eliot Mischler (psychologist, MMHC), Robert Rapaport (Department of Sociology, Northeastern University), Dr. Daniel Levinson (social psychologist, MMHC), Dr. John Spiegel (social psychiatrist, Harvard University), Dr. Bernard Bandler (chairperson of the Division of Psychiatry, Massachusetts Memoria Hospital and Boston University School of Medicine), Dr. John Seeley (sociologist, Brandeis University), Dr. Milton Greenblatt (psychiatrist, superintendent, Boston State Hospital), Dr. Sol Levine (HSPH), J. de Arjuriaguerrra, MD, (University of Geneva); representatives from MGH (Jason Aronson, MD; Morris Chafetz, MD; Marc Fried, PhD); representatives from the HSPH (Gerald Caplan, MD; D. Hooper, MD; Belenden Hutcheson, MD). Those invited include Prof. Talcott Parsons (Department of Social Relations, Harvard University); Dr. Paul Myerson (chairperson, Department of Psychiatry, NEMC/Tufts Medical School—did not attend); Erich Lindemann; Louisa Howe (sociologist); Rose Coser (sociologist), Marc Fried, PhD; William Gray (psychiatrist); Alfred Stanton, MD (psychiatrist in chief, McLean Hospital); Robert Misch (psychologist MGH), Sam Silverman (NIMH); Johyn Siegel; Eliot Mischler; and Robt Bragg (psychiat MGH/HRS).

87. Bierer, Joshua, MD, letter to Lindemann, Erich, 4/12/1963:

> we are organising the First International Congress of Social Psychiatry to be held in London, in 1964. . . . I would like to suggest you honour us by joining the presidency of the Congress.

Lindemann, Erich, letter to Bierer, Joshua, 6/13/1963:

> I will be glad to accept your kind invitation to become one of the sponsors of this conference provided this would not involve a very large amount of organizational and editorial work.

Bierer letter to Lindemann 6/22/1963:

> Thank you very much for your kind letter of June 13 and for consenting to join the Asvisory [*sic*] Committee. . . . Being one of the pioneers in social psychiatry, I am sure the Committee would feel honored if you would agree to be a Vice President of the Congress.

Hollingsmith, Betty, general secretary, First International Congress of Social Psychiatry, letter to Lindemann, 9/9/1963:

> Dr. Bierer remembers that he received your answer in which you are kind enough to accept election as a Vice President of the Congress. . . . The Organizing Committee has further elected you as the Vice chairperson of the new International Association of Social Psychiatry: they hope you will accept this too.

Lindemann letter to Bierer, 2/7/1964:

> [if] you are still interested in having me serve as one of the Vice-Presidents of the coming Congress on Social Psychiatry. If this is correct, I will be pleased and honored to have my name added to the list. . . . I think you have had some conversations with Professor Jack Seeley about a possible symposium on Basic Concepts to which both he and I and a third social

scientist would contribute. If this is still possible, I would like to participate in this manner also.

Bierer letter to Lindemann, 2/25/1964:

Thank you very much . . . for accepting to serve as one of the Vice Presidents. I'm very happy to hear that you, Professor Jack Seeley and a third social scientist will contribute a paper. I would like very much to propose to the Programme Committee that your contribution should be one of the three or four fundamental opening speeches. . . . I've been asked to appear on Boston Television, will you kindly let me know if I may put your name forward to take part in this panel?.

Lindemann letter to Bierer, 3/26/1964:

If you would like me to make a contribution just the same [Seeley withdrew and was reinstated later], I would be very glad to work out a paper concerned with basic issues, in particular the patterns of collaboration between social scientists and psychiatrists both in the practical and in the research phase of programs in social psychiatry [regarding methods of collaboration in HRS and the West End Project].

[folder "Correspondence—Europe 1960–65", Box IIIA5 1), Erich Lindemann Collection, Center for the History of Medicine, Francis A. Countway Library of Medicine, Boston, MA]Also see the International Association for Social Psychiatry memo to Lindemann, Erich, 9/16/1964. Other members included John R. Seeley (USA and Canada, coordinator for USA, chairperson and secretary for the United Kingdom) and Maxwell Jones (chairperson). The Advisory Committee included, from the US, Sheldon Glueck, Paul Lemkau, Opler, N. Kline; from the UK, M. Carstairs, L. Trist, and R. Titmus; and from Nigeria, T. Lambo. [folder "International Congress for Social Psychiatry", Box IIIA 4 (I-Ma), Erich Lindemann Collection, Center for the History of Medicine, Francis A. Countway Library of Medicine, Boston, MA]

88. Congress Programme, 8/17–22/1964. The honorary president was Sir Julian Huxley. Vice presidents included Lindemann and Dr. F. Cloutier (director general, Work Federation for Mental Health), H. Eysenck (Maudsley Hospital, London), Erich Fromm (pioneer in social psychotherapy, Mexico), Sheldon Glueck (Harvard Law School), Maxwell Jones (Dingleton Hospital, Scotland), T. Lambo (University of Ibadan, Nigeria), Paul Lemkau (Johns Hopkins University), Margaret Meade (American Museum of Natural History, New York), Carl Rogers (Wisconsin Psychiatric Institute), Prof. W. Schulte (Universitäts-Nervenklinik, Tübingen, Germany), Carlos Sequin (Univeridad Nacional Mayor de San Marcos, Lima, Peru), P. Sivadon (Brussels University, Paris), Hans Strotzka (president, World Federation for Menta Health, Austria), and R. Titmus (London School of Economics, UK). First Congress chairperson was Dr. Joshua Bierer, vice chairperson Dr. Beric Wright. [folder "International Congress for Social Psychiatry", Box IIIA 4 (I-Ma) and Box IIIA6 2) A-M, Erich Lindemann Collection, Center for the History of Medicine, Francis A. Countway Library of Medicine, Boston, MA; and folder "Correspondence—Europe 1960–65", Box IIIA5 1), Erich Lindemann Collection, Center for the History of Medicine, Francis A. Countway Library of Medicine, Boston, MA]

89. Opler, Marvin K., professor of social psychiatry, Department of Psychiatry, State University of New York at Buffalo letter to Wright, Dr. H.B., Institute of the Director, London, 1/29/1965. [folder "International Journal of Psychiatry", Box IIIA 4 (I-Ma), Erich Lindemann Collection, Center for the History of Medicine, Francis A. Countway Library of Medicine, Boston, MA]

90. Other members were Eric L. Trist, Nevitt Sanford, H. Beric Wright, Maxwell Jones (chairperson), Jurgen Ruesch, and John Seeley (with Lindemann coordinator for the US). [folder "International Social Psychiatry Association", Box IIIA6 2) A-M, Lindemann Collection, Center for the History of Medicine, Countway Library of Medicine, Boston, MA] Efforts to develop such an association were frustrated by a lack of participation. Plans for another international meeting in Amsterdam also met with failure. See correspondence between Lindemann and Maxwell Jones, chairperson, International Association for Social Psychiatry (Provisional Organising Body) 12/7/1964–11/28/1966. [folder "Correspondence 1966 Misc", Box IV 1 + 2, Erich Lindemann Collection, Center for the History of Medicine, Countway Library of Medicine, Boston, MA]

91. Lindemann, Erich, letter to Jewell, Pliney, Jr., president of the Massachusetts Association for Mental Health, 3/30/1965. [folder "J Miscellaneous", Box IIIA 4 (I-Ma), Lindemann Collection, Center for the History of Medicine, Francis A. Countway Library of Medicine, Boston, MA]

92. Correspondence with Lindemann 2/24–3/12/1965. [folder "Correspondence 1965", Box IIIA 1–3, Lindemann Collection, Center for the History of Medicine, Francis A. Countway Library of Medicine, Boston, MA]

93. Letter from Emory Cowen, Elmer Gardner, Norman Harway, and Melin Zax, Departments of Psychiatry and Psychology, University of Rochester College of Arts and Science. This session included other prominent speakers and discussants, such as Frank Riessman, PhD (director of the Mental Health Aide program at Lincoln Hospital in the Bronx, New York, John Cumming, MD (director, Mental Health Research Unit, New York State Department of Mental Hygiene); Sheldon Roen, PhD (director of research, South Shore Mental Health Center); Robert Reiff; Richard Sanders; George Albee; Milton Greenblatt; Wilbert Lewis; George Donahue; Leon Eisenberg; Eli Bower; Ira Iscoe; Margaret Gildea; Herbt Zimiles; and William Morse.

94. Lindemann correspondence with the Committee for a Mental Health Section in the American Public Health Association, 9/1965. Members of the planning committee included many outstanding figures in mental health public health: John D. Porterfield (chairperson), Rema Lapouse (secretary), Leona Baumgartner, Lester Breslow, Dale C. Cameron, Leonard J. Duhl, Robert H. Felix, Ernest M. Gruenberg, Hugh R. Leavell, Paul V. Lemkau, Dorothy B. Nyswander, Thomas Parran, Benjamin Pasamanick, Mabel Ross, and Warrent T. Vaughan, Jr.—all MDs. [folder "MENTAL HEALTH SECTION-APHA", Box IIIA6 2) A-M, Erich Lindemann Collection, Center for the History of Medicine, Francis A. Countway Library of Medicine, Boston, MA]

95. Schmitt, Francis O., letter to Lindemann, Erich, 5/15/1962. [folder "Dr. Francis O. Schmitt, "Neurosciences Research Foundation, Inc.", Box IIIA 4 (P-S), Erich Lindemann Collection, Francis A. Countway Library of Medicine, Boston, MA]. Other incorporators were Henry R. Guild, Treasurer, MGH; Philips Ketchum, president, MGH Corporation; Ralph Lowell, member of the MIT Corporation and former president of the Board of Overseers of Harvard University; Francis O. Schmitt; Raymond Stevens, president of Arthur D. Little, Inc. (a prominent consulting firm); and Dr. William H. Sweet, chief of neurosurgery at MGH.

96. Barchilon José, MD, letter to Alfred H. Stanton, MD, psychiatrist in chief of McLean Hospital, 7/3/1962. Later Lindemann was involved in Onchiota Conferences, and Barchilon sat on the Program Committee: correspondence 12/6/1963, 3/17/1964. [folder "B Miscellaneous 1 of 2 file folders", Box IIIA 4 (A-E), Lindemann Collection, Center for the History of Medicine, Francis A. Countway Library of Medicine, Boston, MA]

97. Lindemann, Erich, letter to McNabola, Marie, 7/9/1964 [folder "M Miscellaneous", Box IIIA 4 (I-MA), Erich Lindemann Collection]; Lindemann, Erich, letter to Caplan, Gerald, 7/1/1964 [folder "Caplan, G. papers", Box IIIB1E 2), A-E", Erich Lindemann Collection], Lindemann, Erich, letter to Knolwes, John, 7/13/1964 [folder "Dr. John Knowles, Medical Director—MGH", Box IIIA 4 (I-Ma), Erich Lindemann Collection, Center for the History of Medicine, Francis A. Countway Library of Medicine, Boston, MA]

98. Knowles, John H., general director of the MGH, letter to George P. Berry, dean of HMS, 3/10/1965, nominating the ad hoc committee: Lindemann (as chief of the Psychiatry Service), Benjamin Castleman (chief of the Pathology Service), Paul Russell (chief of the Surgical Service), and Nathan Talbot (chief of the Children's Service), with Knowles ex officio. [folder "Correspondence 1965", Box IIIA 1–3, Lindemann Collection, Center for the History of Medicine, Francis A. Countway Library of Medicine, Boston, MA]

99. Lindemann, Erich, letter to Dr. Jeanne Brand. [folder "Correspondence 1965", Box IIIA 1–3, Lindemann Collection, Center for the History of Medicine, Francis A. Countway Library of Medicine, Boston, MA]

100. 5/14/61 *The Boston Sunday Globe* pp. 1, 20 quoted Lindemann's comment on dizziness and discomfort experienced on a new Metropolitan District Commission pedestrian bridge over Storrow Drive due to open sides and low rails. [folder "Correspondence 1961", Box IIIA 1–3, Lindemann Collection, Center for the History of Medicine, Francis A. Countway Library of Medicine, Boston, MA]

101. Lindemann, Erich, "In the Middle of the Hourglass: Will Time Begin or Run Out for Social Work on the New Frontier?" Keynote Speaker Erich Lindemann, MD, chief, Psychiatric Service, Massachusetts General Hospital, 7/28/61, Pinewoods Institute Silver Jubilee/25th year 7/27–30/61. [folder "Correspondence 1961", Box IIIA 1–3, Lindemann Collection, Center for the History of Medicine, Francis A. Countway Library of Medicine, Boston, MA]

102. [folder "Peace Research", Box IIIA 4 (P-S), Erich Lindemann Collection, Center for the History of Medicine, Francis A. Countway Library of Medicine, Boston, MA]

103. Menninger, Roy W., MD, letter to Lindemann, Erich, 5/28/1962. List of members: Roy W. Menninger, MD, chairperson (Topeka, Kansas); Jacob R. Fishman, MD (Department of Psychiatry, Howard University Medical College); Jerome Frank, MD (Phipps Clinic, Johns Hopkins Hospital); Lester Grinspoon, MD (MMHC); John Larson, MD (Springfield, Massachusetts); Erich Lindemann, MD (MGH); Jack Mendelson, MD (MGH); Hector Ritey, MD (New York City); and Frederic Solomon, MD (Phipps Clinic, Johns Hopkins Hospital). Also ditto'd newsletters 5/14/1963 and 4/20/1964. [folder "Meninger Foundation", Box IIIA 4 (Mb-O), Erich Lindemann Collection, Center for the History of Medicine, Francis A. Countway Library of Medicine, Boston, MA]

104. Lindemann correspondence with Robert Norton, Bulletin of the Atomic Scientists, 8/1962. [folder "B Miscellaneous 2 of 2 file folders", Box IIIA 4 (A-E), Lindemann Collection, Center for the History of Medicine, Francis A. Countway Library of Medicine, Boston, MA]

105. Lindemann, Erich, "Human Growth and Development in a World of Chronic Crisis", keynote talk at the Conference on Human Services, Harrisburg, PA, 12/11/1963. [folder "12/11/63—Conf. on Human Services, Harrisburg, Pa", Box IIIA7 1960–63 box 2 of 3, Erich Lindemann Collection,

Center for the History of Medicine, Francis A. Countway Library of Medicine, Boston, MA]

106. Lown, Bernard, chairperson, Physicians for Social Responsibility, letter to Lindemann, Erich 2/12/1965. [folder "L Miscellaneous", Box IIIA 4 (I-Ma), Erich Lindemann Collection, Center for the History of Medicine, Francis A. Countway Library of Medicine, Boston, MA] Other Sponsors were Joseph C. Aub, Benjamin Castleman, Brock Chisholm, Stanley Cobb, Bernard D. Davis, John T. Edsall, J. Russell Elkington, Sydney S. Gellis, Carl Menninger, John C. Rock, Albert Szent-Gyorgyi, and Maurice Visscher—all physicians, many affiliated with HMS. In 1964, the following physicians were added: Carl Binger, Leslie A. Falk, Howard Hiatt, and Louis Lasagna.

107. Gifford, Sanford, correspondence with Lindemann, Erich, 7/2–8/1/1962. [folder "Physicians for Social Responsibility", Box IIIA 4 (P-S), Erich Lindemann Collection, Center for the History of Medicine, Francis A. Countway Library of Medicine, Boston, MA]

108. Lown, Bernard, chairperson and member of the Executive Committee of Physicians for Social Responsibility, letter to Lindemann, Erich, 8/8/1962. [folder "Physicians for Social Responsibility", Box IIIA 4 (P-S), Erich Lindemann Collection, Center for the History of Medicine, Francis A. Countway Library of Medicine, Boston, MA]

109. Aronow, Saul; Avery, Nicholas; Coleman, Robert; Ervin, Frank R.; Geiger, Jack; Glazier, John B.; Leeman, Cavin; Leiderman, P. Herbert; Lown, Bernard; Mendelson, Jack H.; Nathan, David; Shohet, Stephen; and Side, Victor W.—MDs, *New England Journal of Medicine* 266: 1126–1155 (2/15/1962). [folder "Physicians for Social Responsibility", Box IIIA 4 (P-S), Erich Lindemann Collection, Center for the History of Medicine, Francis A. Countway Library of Medicine, Boston, MA]

110. [folder "Physicians for Social Responsibility", Box IIIA 4 (P-S), Erich Lindemann Collection, Center for the History of Medicine, Francis A. Countway Library of Medicine, Boston, MA]

111. Lindemann, Erich, letter to Nemiah, John C., acting chief of psychiatry, MGH, 9/30/1966, pp. 1–2. [folder "Correspondence—Europe—1967–69", Box IV 1 + 2, Erich Lindemann Collection, Center for the History of Medicine, Francis A. Countway Library of Medicine, Boston, MA]

112. Lindemann, Erich, with Duhl, Leonard, and Seeley, John, interview at Lindemann's home in Palo Alto, CA, by Leonard Duhl, 6/15,22/1974. [caddy 4, tape 3A, 4B;7, Erich Lindemann Collection, Center for the History of Medicine, Francis A. Countway Library of Medicine, Boston, MA]

113. Persky, Harold, correspondence with Lindemann, 1/24–9/10/1956. [folder "Misc. Correspondence O,P,R—1956–7", Box IIIA 1–3, Lindemann Collection, Center for the History of Medicine, Francis A. Countway Library of Medicine, Boston, MA]

114. Roth, David, Boston University School of Medicine student, correspondence with Lindemann, 1/29,2/1/1956. [folder "Misc. Correspondence O,P,R—1956–7", Box IIIA 1–3, Lindemann Collection, Center for the History of Medicine, Francis A. Countway Library of Medicine, Boston, MA]

115. Sweet, William H., letter to Dr. Michele Abercrombie, University College Department of Anatomy, London, indicating planning with Lindemann, 7/14/1958. [folder "Misc. Correspondence S—1956–7", Box IIIA 1–3, Lindemann Collection, Center for the History of Medicine, Francis A. Countway Library of Medicine, Boston, MA]

116. Correspondence including Frank Ervin, MD (psychiatrist); Stanley Cobb; James C. White (MGH Chief of Neurosurgery); Murray xonlconer (Guy's

Hospital Neurosurgical Unit); Joseph W. Grdella (HMS Committee on Student Fellowships); and Lindemann—7/17/1956–10/14/1957. They discuss patients from McLean Hospital and MGH, research projects, publishing reports, and students, to assist in the work. [folder "Misc. Correspondence T–Z—1956–7", Box IIIA 1–3, Lindemann Collection, Center for the History of Medicine, Francis A. Countway Library of Medicine, Boston, MA]

117. Lindemann, Erich, presentation before The Committee on Social and Physical Environment Variables as Determinants of Mental Health (Washington, DC: Department of Health, Education, and Welfare, 5/19/1960), unpublished. [Erich Lindemann Collection, Center for the History of Medicine, Francis A. Countway Library of Medicine, Harvard Medical School, Boston, MA]

118. Krapf, E.[duardo] E., letter to Lindemann, Erich, 5/14/1959. [folder "Correspondence-WHO 1959", Box IIIA5 1), Erich Lindemann Collection, Center for the History of Medicine, Francis A. Countway Library of Medicine, Boston, MA]

119. Krapf, E.[duardo] E., letter to Lindemann, Erich confirming the appointment, 6/15/1059; WHO formal offer of appointment for consultants of Lindemann, Erich, regarding three months appointment as Medical Consultant to India, 9/21/1959; Lindemann, Erich, letter to Brouland, J., WHO chief of personnel, 10/15/1959: "Enclosed please find the Letter of Acceptance and Oath of Office in connection with my appointment as medical consultant with the World Health Organization. I expect to present myself at your office in Geneva on December 1, 1959".

120. Lindemann, Erich, letter to Berry, George P., 10/29/1959. [folder "Correspondence-WHO 1959", Box IIIA5 1), Erich Lindemann Collection, Center for the History of Medicine, Francis A. Countway Library of Medicine, Boston, MA]

121. [folder "E.L. Notes on India Trip", Box IIIA5 2), Erich Lindemann Collection, Center for the History of Medicine, Francis A. Countway Library of Medicine, Boston, MA]

122. 2/19/1960 correspondence between Gerald Caplan and Erich Lindemann, *ibid.*

123. Duhl, Leonard, Department of Public Health, University of California–San Francisco; interviewed by telephone in University of California–Berkeley, California, by David G. Satin, 4/2/1979, 8/16/2007. [caddy 2, box 4, X, Lindemann Collection, Center for the History of Medicine, Francis A. Countway Library of Medicine, Boston, MA]

124. Lindemann, Erich, Dr. Erich Lindemann, WHO short-term consultant, Assignment Report on Teaching of Psychiatry in Medical Colleges, WHO Project: India 158, 3/21/1960, Introduction. [folder "Lindemann, Assignment Report—WHO Project—India 158", Box IIIA5 2), Erich Lindemann Collection, Center for the History of Medicine, Francis A. Countway Library of Medicine, Boston, MA]

125. Lindemann, Erich, "Comments on Monday A.M., 1/25/1960. [folder "E.L. Notes on India Trip", Box IIIA5 2), Erich Lindemann Collection, Center for the History of Medicine, Francis A. Countway Library of Medicine, Boston, MA]

126. [folder "Lindemann—Staff Conference Trip to India March 1960", Box IIIA5 2), Erich Lindemann Collection, Center for the History of Medicine, Francis A. Countway Library of Medicine, Boston, MA, p. 8] For Lindemann, the guru role is an important principle and someone with whom he identifies, as opposed to the power-hungry boss. This was his maternal

grandfather, whereas his father was distant, and he experienced sibling rivalry with his older brother. This metamorphosed into Lindemann's ideal of the mental health professional or community key caregiver and the principle of community psychiatry to identify and strengthen the community guru.

127. Lindemann, Erich, "Confidential report to Doctor Krapf (chief of the Mental Health Section of WHO). [folder "E.L. Notes on India Trip", Box IIIA5 2), Erich Lindemann Collection, Center for the History of Medicine, Francis A. Countway Library of Medicine, Boston, MA]

128. Lindemann, Erich, letter to invitees, 11/28/1961. [folder "India Seminar 1962 (Lect & Conf) Boston", Box IIIA7 1960–63 box 2 of 3, Erich Lindemann Collection, Center for the History of Psychiatry, Francis A. Countway Library of Medicine, Boston, MA]

129. Lindemann, Erich, correspondence with Col. M.H. Shah. [box II A&B, folder Shah, Col. M.H.; Lindemann Collection, Center for the History of Medicine, Francis A. Countway Library of Medicine, Boston, MA]

130. Lindemann letter to Dr. L. Monteiro, 3/17/1960. [folder "M", Box IIIA 1–3, Lindemann Collection, Center for the History of Medicine, Francis A. Countway Library of Medicine, Boston, MA]

131. Lindemann letter to Daniel Bailey, program director for scientific publications, National Library of Medicine, 1/7/1963, p. 1. [folder "B Miscellaneous 1 of 2 file folders", Box IIIA 4 (A-E), Lindemann Collection, Center for the History of Medicine, Francis A. Countway Library of Medicine, Boston, MA]

132. Lindemann, Erich, letter to Krapf, E.[duardo] E., 6/6/1960. [folder "Correspondence re India 1960–65", Box IIIA5 1), Erich Lindemann Collection, Center for the History of Medicine, Francis A. Countway Library of Medicine, Boston, MA]

133. Krapf, E.E. letter to Lindemann, Erich, 6/9/1960. [folder "Correspondence re India 1960–65", Box IIIA5 1), Erich Lindemann Collection, Center for the History of Medicine, Francis A. Countway Library of Medicine, Boston, MA]

134. Krapf, E.E. letter to Lindemann, Erich, 10/19/1960. [folder "Correspondence re India 1960–65", Box IIIA5 1), Erich Lindemann Collection, Center for the History of Medicine, Francis A. Countway Library of Medicine, Boston, MA]

135. Ramalingaswami, V., MD (All India Institute of Medical Sciences); Castleman, Benjamin, MD (MGH); and Stanbury, John B., MD (MGH), letter to Anderson, Dr. Richard (The Rockefeller Foundation, New York), 6/22/1964. [folder "Correspondence re India 1964–65", Box IIIA5 1), Erich Lindemann Collection, Center for the History of Medicine, Francis A. Countway Library of Medicine, Boston, MA]

136. Satyanand, David, professor of psychiatry, AIIM, New Delhi, India, letter to Lindemann, Erich, 1/4/1965, p. 1. [folder "Correspondence re India 1964–65", Box IIIA5 1), Erich Lindemann Collection, Center for the History of Medicine, Francis A. Countway Library of Medicine, Boston, MA]

137. Lindemann, Erich, letter to Satyanand, David (Department of Psychiatry, AIIMS, 2/7/1964:

> thank you . . . for your personal invitation . . . to come to New Delhi for a year as consultant to you and to the Rockefeller Foundation. This is a very challenging invitation, and if at all possible, I would like to work it out with you. There are some problems of timing. . . . From our conversations, it appears that you would like me to start January 1st,

1965. Would July 1st, 1965, be suitable also, or would that be too late in connection with your over-all program?

Lindemann, Erich, letter to Satyanand, David, 12/28/1964:

If . . . you still feel that a period of participation in your program of myself would be desirable I will seriously consider it for the late fall of next year.

Lindemann, Erich, letter to Satyanand, David, 9/13/1965:

We feel now that a visit with you this winter would not be opportune because of the war conditions demanding other commitments in your country. However, I still will be keenly interested in considering a later visit, perhaps starting in the later fall of 1966.

> [folder "Satyanand, D., M.D.", Box IIIA5 2),
> Erich Lindemann Collection, Center for the
> History of Medicine, Francis A. Countway
> Library of Medicine, Boston, MA]

138. Berry, George Packer letter to Hagen, Dr. Kristofer (Medical Advisor, Board of World Missions, Lutheran Church in America) with copies to Lindemann, Erich; Anderson, George (Rockefeller Foundation); Chacko, Rose (director, Institute of Mental Hygiene, Christian Medical College Hospital, Vellore, India); Aronson, Jason A. (instructor in psychiatry, MGH), Dreier, Theodore, Jr. (research fellow in psychiatry, McLean Hospital); and Spiegel, John P. (associate clinical professor of psychiatry, Department of Social Relations, Harvard University), 1/12/1965, p. 1. [folder "Correspondence re India 1964–65", Box IIIA5 1), Erich Lindemann Collection, Center for the History of Medicine, Francis A. Countway Library of Medicine, Boston, MA]

139. Leavell, Hugh R. letter to Lindemann, Erich, 1/2/1965. [folder "Correspondence re India 1964–65", Box IIIA5 1), Erich Lindemann Collection, Center for the History of Medicine, Francis A. Countway Library of Medicine, Boston, MA]

140. Carstairs, Morris, professor in the Department of Psychological Medicine, University of Edinburgh, Scotland, to Lindemann, Erich, 11/27,30/1966. [folder "Correspondence re India 1964–65", Box IIIA5 1), Erich Lindemann Collection, Center for the History of Medicine, Francis A. Countway Library of Medicine, Boston, MA]

141. Lindemann, Erich, letter to Maier, John, Rockefeller Foundation, New York City, 8/9/1965. [folder "Correspondence re India 1960–65", Box IIIA5 1), Erich Lindemann Collection, Center for the History of Medicine, Francis A. Countway Library of Medicine, Boston, MA]

142. Lindemann, Erich, letter to Allen, LeRoy R., MD, 9/29/1965. [folder "Correspondence re India 1960–65", Box IIIA5 1), Erich Lindemann Collection, Center for the History of Medicine, Francis A. Countway Library of Medicine, Boston, MA]

143. Allen, LeRoy R., letter to Lindemann, Erich, 12/14/1965. [folder "Correspondence re India 1960–65", Box IIIA5 1), Erich Lindemann Collection, Center for the History of Medicine, Francis A. Countway Library of Medicine, Boston, MA]

144. Lindemann, Erich, letter to Allen, LeRoy R., 1/3/1966. [folder "Correspondence re India 1960–65", Box IIIA5 1), Erich Lindemann Collection, Center for the History of Medicine, Francis A. Countway Library of Medicine, Boston, MA]

145. Lindemann, Erich, letter to Singh, Lt. Col. Kirpal, in Delhi, India, 6/22/1965. [folder "Correspondence re India 1964–65", Box IIIA5 1), Erich Lindemann Collection, Center for the History of Medicine, Francis A. Countway Library of Medicine, Boston, MA]

146. Singh, Lt. Col. Kirpal, letter to Lindemann, Erich, 6/10/1965: "I am disappointed to know that you will not be able to come to India for some time". David Satyanand, professor of psychiatry at the AIIMS, to Lindemann, Erich, 9/25/1965: "I was very happy indeed to receive your letter and that now you have taken official step to confirm your coming here. I am sorry that circumstances are such that it has to be postponed till end of 1966" (p. 1). (He also included complaints against Kirpal Singh as a cutthroat competitor for DSN's job and requested that Lindemann not support these efforts.). Surya, Dr. N.C., director of the AIIMH in Bangalore letter to Lindemann, Erich, 6/30/1965 kept the connection alive through the US visitors: "Perhaps Dr. Dreier would bring with him a more detailed impression of the situation [at the Institute]".

Waring, Peggy, letter to Lindemann, Erich, 7/9/1965:

> I thought you would be pleased to know that Dr. John Maier of the Rockefeller Foundation just called and wanted to chat with you about your plans for New Delhi. He said that he had heard from the people there who wanted you to come. He said he knows about your moving to Stanford and the settlement problem there so there is no talk of limitations of time. [folder "Correspondence re India 1964–65", Box IIIA5 1), Erich Lindemann Collection, Center for the History of Medicine, Francis A. Countway Library of Medicine, Boston, MA]

147. Lindemann, Erich, letter to Satyanand, David, 10/1/1965. [folder "Correspondence re India 1964–65", Box IIIA5 1), Erich Lindemann Collection, Center for the History of Medicine, Francis A. Countway Library of Medicine, Boston, MA]

148. Allen, LeRoy R. to Lindemann, Erich, 11/18/1966. [folder "Correspondence re India 1960–65", Box IIIA5 1), Erich Lindemann Collection, Center for the History of Medicine, Francis A. Countway Library of Medicine, Boston, MA]

149. Hargreaves, Ronald, Unisante, Geneva, Switzerland, letter to Lindemann, Erich, 1955. [folder "WHO Correspondence-1955–56", Box IIIA5 1), Erich Lindemann Collection, Center for the History of Medicine Francis A. Countway Library of Medicine, Boston, MA]

150. WHO Staff Regulations, JRRees speech about WHO MH Section, ≤7/6/55 Vacancy Notice for position of Medical Officer (psychiatry). [folder "WHO Correspondence-1955–56", Box IIIA5 1), Erich Lindemann Collection, Center for the History of Medicine Francis A. Countway Library of Medicine, Boston, MA]

151. Armstrong, John L., letter to Lindemann, Erich, 9/16/1955. [folder "WHO Correspondence-1955–56", Box IIIA5 1), Erich Lindemann Collection, Center for the History of Medicine Francis A. Countway Library of Medicine, Boston, MA]

152. Lindemann, Erich, letter to Armstrong, John I., 9/29/1955, pp. 1–2. [folder "WHO Correspondence-1955–56", Box IIIA5 1), Erich Lindemann Collection, Center for the History of Medicine Francis A. Countway Library of Medicine, Boston, MA]

> Harvard University created a special new Chair in Psychiatry with emphasis on the development of teaching and research in preventive and

social psychiatry to which I was elected as of July 1, 1954. Our new program of which the development of a mental health service in a general hospital setting is an important part is just beginning to take shape. Dr. Hugh Leavell, the Head of the Department of Public Health Practice at the Harvard School of Public Health; Dr. Dean Clark, the Director of the Massachusetts General Hospital; Dr. Gerald Caplan, who became my successor in the Division of Mental Health at the Harvard School of Public Health and Dr. Alfred Stanton, who took over the directorship of the McLean Hospital to further evolve research and practice in the social aspects of hospital psychiatry—these four men are working together with me in this development.

153. Lindemann, Erich, letter to Armstrong, John I., chief of the Personnel Section of WHO, 9/29/1955. [folder "WHO Correspondence-1955–56", Box IIIA5 1), Erich Lindemann Collection, Center for the History of Medicine Francis A. Countway Library of Medicine, Boston, MA]:

154. Lindemann, Erich, letter to Felix, Robert H., director of the NIMH, National Institutes of Health, Public Health Service, U.S. Department of Health, Education, and Welfare 3/2/1956. [folder "NIMH-Misc. Material 1956–1958", Box IIIA6 Da GAP, Erich Lindemann Collection, Center for the History of Medicine, Francis A. Countway Library of Medicine, Boston, MA]

155. Lindemann, Erich, letter to Felix, Robert, 2/17/1956. [folder "WHO Correspondence-1955–56", Box IIIA5 1), Erich Lindemann Collection, Center for the History of Medicine Francis A. Countway Library of Medicine, Boston, MA]

156. Lindemann, Erich, letter to Hargreaves, Ronald, Department of Psychiatry, Medical College, University of Leeds, Scotland (former chief of the Mental Health Section of the WHO), 10/19/1955, p. 1. [folder "WHO Correspondence-1955–56", Box IIIA5 1), Erich Lindemann Collection, Center for the History of Medicine Francis A. Countway Library of Medicine, Boston, MA]

157. Hargreaves, G.R., OBE, to Lindemann, Erich, 10/27/1955, pp. 1–2. [folder "WHO Correspondence-1955–56", Box IIIA5 1), Erich Lindemann Collection, Center for the History of Medicine Francis A. Countway Library of Medicine, Boston, MA]

158. Hargreaves, G.R., OBE, Department of Psychiatry, School of Medicine, University of Leeds, Scotland letter to Lindemann, Erich, 10/27/1955. [folder "WHO Correspondence-1955–56", Box IIIA5 1), Erich Lindemann Collection, Center for the History of Medicine Francis A. Countway Library of Medicine, Boston, MA]

159. Lindemann, Erich, letter to van Zyde Hyde, Dr. Henry, Department of State, UNE, 3/2/1956. [folder "WHO Correspondence-1955–56", Box IIIA5 1), Erich Lindemann Collection, Center for the History of Medicine Francis A. Countway Library of Medicine, Boston, MA]

160. Lindemann, Erich, letter to Armstrong, John I., at WHO, 3/12/1956. [folder "WHO Correspondence-1955–56", Box IIIA5 1), Erich Lindemann Collection, Center for the History of Medicine Francis A. Countway Library of Medicine, Boston, MA]

161. Lindemann, Erich, letter to Peterson, Jerome, chief of Health Services, WHO, 4/5/1956. [folder "WHO Correspondence-1955–56", Box IIIA5 1), Erich Lindemann Collection, Center for the History of Medicine Francis A. Countway Library of Medicine, Boston, MA]

162. Felix, Robert H. letter to Lindemann, Erich, 4/27/1956. [folder "WHO Correspondence-1955–56", Box IIIA5 1), Erich Lindemann Collection,

Center for the History of Medicine Francis A. Countway Library of Medicine, Boston, MA]

163. Peterson, Jerome S., MD, director of the Division of Organization of Public Health Services letter to Lindemann, Erich, 6/6/1956. [folder "WHO Correspondence-1955–56", Box IIIA5 1), Erich Lindemann Collection, Center for the History of Medicine Francis A. Countway Library of Medicine, Boston, MA]

164. Lindemann, Erich, letters to Peterson Jerome, 10/9,11/1956. [folder "WHO Correspondence-1955–56", Box IIIA5 1), Erich Lindemann Collection, Center for the History of Medicine Francis A. Countway Library of Medicine, Boston, MA]

165. Lindemann, Erich, letter to Peterson, Jerome, 11/2/1956. [folder "WHO Correspondence-1955–56", Box IIIA5 1), Erich Lindemann Collection, Center for the History of Medicine Francis A. Countway Library of Medicine, Boston, MA]

166. Candau, M.G., MD letter to Lindemann, Erich, 7/23/1956. [folder "WHO Correspondence-1955–56", Box IIIA5 1), Erich Lindemann Collection, Center for the History of Medicine Francis A. Countway Library of Medicine, Boston, MA]

167. Lindemann, Erich, letter to Candau, M.G., MD, 7/27/1956. [folder "WHO Correspondence-1955–56", Box IIIA5 1), Erich Lindemann Collection, Center for the History of Medicine Francis A. Countway Library of Medicine, Boston, MA]

168. Krapf, E.[duardo] E., chief of the Mental Health Section of WHO and Lindemann, Erich—correspondence 1/20–5/14/1959. [folder "Correspondence-WHO 1959", Box IIIA5 1), Erich Lindemann Collection, Center for the History of Medicine, Francis A. Countway Library of Medicine, Boston, MA]

169. [folder "Dean George Packer Berry", Box IIIA 4 (A-E), Lindemann Collection, Center for the History of Medicine, Francis A. Countway Library of Medicine, Boston, MA]

170. HMS Dean's Office files.

171. Research projects and applications, IIIB2 c (box1 of 2), Erich Lindemann Collection, Center for the History of Medicine, Francis A. Countway Library of Medicine, Boston, MA.

172. Lindemann correspondence with Walter E. Barton, MD, then president of the American Psychiatric Association, who was writing about the administrative organization of community psychiatry, 8/6,9/16/1963. [folder "Amer. Psychiatric Assoc.", Box IIIA 4 (A-E), Lindemann Collection, Center for the History of Medicine, Francis A. Countway Library of Medicine, Boston, MA]

173. Lindemann correspondence with Walter E. Barton, MD, then president of the American Psychiatric Association, who was writing about the administrative organization of community psychiatry, 8/6,9/16/1963; p. 2. [folder "Amer. Psychiatric Assoc.", Box IIIA 4 (A-E), Lindemann Collection, Center for the History of Medicine, Francis A. Countway Library of Medicine, Boston, MA]

174. Beecher, Henry K., and Altshuler, Mark D., *Medicine and Harvard, The First 300 Years* (Hanover, NH: The University Press of New England, 1977), pp. 401–402.

175. Ruesch, Jurgen, "Declining Clinical Tradition", *Journal of the American Medical Association 182* no. 2: 110–115 (10/13/1962).

176. Knowles, John H., MD, "The Social Conscience and the Primary Function of the Hospital Viewed in Historical Perspective", *The Pharos of Alpha*

Omega Alpha 26 no. 3: 67–74 (p. 67) (7/1963). [folder "Ad Hoc Committee on Dr. Ebert", Box IIIA 4 (A-E), Erich Lindemann Collection, Center for the History of Medicine, Francis A. Countway Library of Medicine, Boston, MA]

177. Joint Ad Hoc Committee Appointed to Examine the Posture of Medicine at the Massachusetts General Hospital and to Recommend a Successor to Dr. Walter Bauer; Nomination of Dr. Robert Higgins Ebert as Jackson Professor of Clinical Medicine (University Full-Time), p. 5. [folder "Ad Hoc Committee on Dr. Ebert", Box IIIA 4 (A-E), Erich Lindemann Collection, Center for the History of Medicine, Francis A. Countway Library of Medicine, Boston, MA]

178. Klerman, Gerald L., "Better But Not Well: Social and Ethical Issues in the Deinstitutionalization of the Mentally Ill", *Schizophrenia Bulletin* 3 no. 4: 617–631 (1977). [folder "History—Psychiatry, Medicine", David G. Satin files. Newton, MA]

179. Klerman, Gerald L., "Better But Not Well: Social and Ethical Issues in the Deinstitutionalization of the Mentally Ill", *Schizophrenia Bulletin* 3 no. 4: 617–631 (1977). [folder "History—Psychiatry, Medicine", David G. Satin files. Newton, MA]

180. [folder "The Role of Psychiatry at the M.G.H. July 1, 1965", IIIB3 a-c, Erich Lindemann Collection, Center for the History of Medicine, Francis A. Countway Library of Medicine, Boston, MA]

10 Responses to Erich Lindemann

Evaluations of and Reactions to Erich Lindemann

People and groups may be seen as entering social systems (including programs) with stores of potential for acceptance—their "acceptance capital"—based on past accomplishment, reputation, characteristics, etc. They can conserve and build this capital by staying within the tolerance of the social system, they may risk this capital by attempting to expand the social system, and they may diminish or lose this capital by exceeding the tolerance and adaptability of the social system.

John Knowles, Stanley Cobb, and Oliver Cope came from old Boston families; Lindemann came with a reputation and accomplishments in biological science research and psychosomatic clinical care. Cobb did this well by staying within the tolerance of MGH and professional society: being creative but proper. Cope did this within acceptable limits by challenging traditions politely. Knowles left the MGH when either that society or he were reaching the limits of their tolerance. Lindemann exceeded the MGH/HMS tolerance by deemphasizing biological medicine in favor of social medicine and valuing the social sciences and social scientists to the degree that made those committed to biological medicine and physicians uncomfortable, jealous, and critical. Did he do so because of a lack of understanding or sensitivity to the tolerances of the system, or did he do so out of dedication to his ideals and in defiance of the consequences?

Lloyd Etheredge constructed an interesting typology of leadership from his interest in those who determine foreign policy.[1] It may also be applied to psychiatry, and we may compare to other psychiatric leaders Lindemann's style in developing social and community and in this way shed light on reactions to him. Etheredge's model is as follows:

	Introvert	Extravert
High Dominance	Bloc Leaders	World Leaders
Low Dominance	Maintainers	Conciliators

- Bloc Leaders divide the world into preferred and rejected moral values, are stubborn, try to reshape the world into their visions, emphasize exclusion, use impersonal mechanisms, and are more likely to use force.
- World Leaders are more flexible and pragmatic; want to lead rather than contain; advocate change, cooperation, and advancement on many issues; emphasize inclusion; employ personal involvement and collaboration; and are more likely to use force.
- Maintainers advocate a holding action for the status quo, emphasize impersonal mechanisms, and are less likely to use force.
- Conciliators are egalitarian; hope to negotiate accommodations; are flexible, hopeful, and open to change; lack consistent and strong willpower; are peripheral and ineffectual; emphasize personal involvement and collaboration; and are less likely to use force.

Note the issues of goals, methods, and relationships. Bloc Leaders and World Leaders want to accomplish change. World Leaders and Conciliators seek collaboration and persuasion and use personal mechanisms. Although Bloc Leaders and World Leaders are said to be more likely to use force, observation teaches that it is persuasion and lack of collaboration are more likely. Erich Lindemann's goal was change in medicine and society toward caring and the avoidance of grief; considered himself a "guru" rather than a wielder of power (a teacher and example rather than an enforcer); and respected, encouraged, and incorporated people rather than labeling and compartmentalizing them. In Etheredge's terms, he had the goal and determination of the World Leader and the methods and relationship of the Conciliator. Perhaps this explains the admiration of those who shared his humanistic goals and methods and the disdain and resentment of those who wanted the relentless implementation of their own goals by their favored methods. Of course, his urging of change unsettled those invested in the status quo, as discussed earlier.

Conflicting attitudes toward CMH and social psychiatry in psychiatry, medicine, academia, and psychopolitics in macro were reflected in conflicting attitudes toward CMH and Lindemann in his department, hospital, medical school, and the state Department of Mental Health in micro. A major issue was the role that he played as chief and professor of psychiatry. His forte was as a "guru"—i.e., creative conceptualizer, integrator of ideas and approaches from many relevant sources, teacher, consultant, and supporter of others' efforts. William Ryan, community psychologist and advocate, thought that Lindemann taught by responding sensitively to student questions and subtly laying down a dense network of rich theory without overt structure.[2] If this is true, it is why he was revered and loved.

He was uncomfortable and arguably unsuited for the role of power broker and political infighter, as was reflected in the advice to avoid this role that he received when being considered for appointment as the chief of the MGH Psychiatry Service (see Chapter 6 and 7) and as chief of the WHO Mental Health Section. A review of his papers reveals recurrent instances of his withdrawal from and cancelation of participating in meetings, delays in answering letters and requests due to illness or lost correspondence, etc. His personality was beloved by some as warm, caring, and modest, while castigated by others as ineffective and disappointing:

> Much of Lindemann's troubles arose from his personality and from his ineffective . . . way of dealing with people. He was passive, afraid of combat, easily hurt, and quick to leave the scene, go home, and nurse his wounds. His word was not always good. His staff appointments were on an "acting" basis for too long . . . Couldn't make up his mind. Too soft and tender . . . Lindemann was a near disaster as an administrator. . . . for those who knew him, Lindemann's ineptness was fully as important in his life as his advocacy of any particular ideological position.[3]
>
> . . .
>
> I knew Erich Lindemann personally. . . . He was a "kind, gentle, profoundly caring man" with great breadth of interest in "all the medical sciences, social sciences, and humanities which shed light on the human condition". Equally he was . . . one who "promised more than he delivered, raised unrealistic expectations and left others to deal with problems of practical implementation". He chronically promised more and undertook more than he could accomplish, thus causing much difficulty for people trying to work with him. Managing his time was a major problem. these characteristics were the root of the different ways people reacted to him. Disagreement with his philosophy was secondary. people who agreed with this philosophy nevertheless became exasperated and annoyed.[4]

His wife acknowledged his store of unanswered or delayed correspondence.

In Francis Weld Peabody's perspective on the influential role of the chief of a clinic, previously referred to, he went on to comment on the place of the creative worker as administrator:[5]

> Even if he had great ability as an investigator he could not expect to accomplish much, as the multifarious demands on his time make it almost impossible to obtain the sense of leisure which thoughtful work requires. Indeed, I feel that if a man really has this rare gift, he ought not to be the head of a department of medicine lest his talent be wasted.

Another of his facets that was judged was his nontraditional social perspective. Even people close to him (such as his younger sister Gertrude)
accused him of losing his professional stability and going over to the radicals, not because of his advocacy but because of his actions (such as the
Lindau teaching). Elizabeth Lindemann thought this unjustified: He was
always a physician and healer, but unorthodox in his training in sociology and anthropology. He wanted to help individuals and communities
but also had an academic interest in studying them.

There is a striking similarity to the evaluation of John Gilbert Winant,
governor of New Hampshire, chairperson of board of the U.S. Social
Security Administration, and ambassador to Great Britain during World
War II:[6]

> By all accounts, he was a terrible administrator, the despair of his
> staff and the other (U.S. Social Security) board members for his ineffi-
> ciency and lateness. His desk was piled high with letters awaiting his
> signature, the room outside his office crammed with people waiting
> to see him; his filing system consisted of stuffing important papers in
> his pockets. But even Winant's severest critics acknowledged that he
> was an extraordinary leader, a visionary with the ability to inspire.
> "He was, beyond any shadow of a doubt, one of the great characters
> in American public life during the past twenty years", Frank Bane,
> Social Security's first executive director, declared. "Few people have
> made as significant an impression upon government as it should be,
> as did Governor Winant".

Professional background, medical and psychiatric ideology, personal
experience, and the personality of the critics are so intertwined in attitudes toward Lindemann that the reports of some individuals are presented as outstanding examples:

Members of the MGH Psychiatry Service

In Lindemann's department, there was much complaint that he did not
fight other departments and the administration effectively for budget,
staff appointments and promotions, space, etc. (Note that in 1960 salaries were as follows: professors made $14,400, instructors made $4,000–
$4,500, administrative assistants made $6000, and senior secretaries
made $4400.)[7] Jerome Weinberger, a psychoanalyst on the staff, was one
of those angry at Lindemann, accusing him of poor administration, bro-
ken promises, and seducing people with nice ideas but failing to support
them in implementing them.[8] Philip Gates, child psychiatrist and psychoanalyst at the MGH and James Jackson Putnam Children's Center, also
passed on criticisms of Lindemann as a poor administrator, who was

disorganized and who polarized people by giving the same assignment to two people and thus causing conflict.[9]

Jean Farrell

Jean Farrell was a former patient of Lindemann's, whom he then hired as secretary and administrative assistant at the Wellesley Human Relations Service, HSPH, and MGH 1955–1967.[10] (Perhaps this was an example of his replacement therapy, wherein a grief reaction is treated by the psychotherapist acting as a transitional replacement for a lost key member of the patient's social network.) In her experience, Lindemann was a private person. He had a delightful, though Germanic, sense of humor and liked to be called "the doctor".[11]

She thought Lindemann saw good in everyone, was kind, never wrote a bad report or reference, and always treated people as equals. With those who met with him, he kept notes on the feelings as well as the business addressed. If he saw someone who looked perturbed, he would stop and talk with them even if it made him late for his meeting. He would always have someone call with apologies for his lateness. He never spoke harshly of anyone, no matter how provoked he may have been. When prodded about his disliking someone, he would become evasive, and after being upset over a person or situation, he would become ill enough to stay home the day after. For example, after a discussion with Avery Weisman (a senior psychiatrist in the department) about a "hate letter" about Lindemann that Wiseman sent to the HMS dean, he was sick for two days. He could get angry: he would not yell but would test to see that a wall was solid and quiet and then pound it.

He inherited Dorothy Adams, his predecessor's secretary, whom he saw as a "blue blood" and felt too simple in comparison to work with her and asked Farrell to write his letters at home at night. He could not fire Adams and was rescued by Elizabeth Zetzel (a senior psychoanalyst in the department), who found a job for her at the Boston Psychoanalytic Institute.

Lindemann always worked with others and not alone. He offended some but tolerated enemies and seemed not to know who were his friends. Farrell could not understand why he employed people who hated him. Gardner Quarton, John Nemiah, and Peter Sifneos, hired by Cobb, were Lindemann's senior administrators. When Lindemann was absent at meetings, he appointed Nemiah or Quarton as temporary chief,[12] while Nemiah laughingly acknowledged that Farrell "ran the department". Quarton was especially devoted to Lindemann. Sifneos was angry and would voice tirades against him because Sifneos was never formally appointed director of the outpatient service, though he eulogized Lindemann in his absence ("the greatest man I have ever known"), and he refused to participate in the state legislature hearing to name the CMHC for Lindemann. Nemiah and Freddy Frankel (another senior department member) were supportive. Lindemann invited Gerald Caplan from Israel, who followed in his footsteps and took over his position at the HSPH.

MGH responses to Lindemann's perspective were varied. It was Farrell's impression that the MGH staff members did not learn much from Lindemann but were set in Cobb's approach to psychosomatic medicine. Eleanor Clark, eventually chief psychiatric social worker and later MGH chief of social work, considered CMH as setting up little MGHs in specific communities. Ellsworth Neumann, MGH associate director, who had experienced a wife with major mental illness and hospitalization at McLean Hospital, was friendly to Lindemann, as were John Knowles (MGH general director), Chester Jones (gastroenterologist with whom Lindemann had collaborated on studies of ulcerative colitis)[13], and Walter Bauer (rheumatologist and chief of medicine).

Lindemann was able to learn and teach: He was usually "uptight" before formal lectures to large gatherings. He had a hard time writing his talks in advance, agonized over the task, dictated directly to the typist, and needed approval—including asking his secretary's opinion. His "crutch" was a mammoth pile of books that he would carry to a conference but never used. If mandatory, he would prepare a lecture under stress, the day before. He needed personal interchange, and his tension dispelled as he started to speak. In response to his audience, he might depart entirely from his prepared outline. He would exult in giving a good talk. He had the ability to involve and interest others in his work. He would register for HMS courses to gain skills he thought important (e.g., biostatistics), sent Farrell to attend in his place, and never inquired about them. He was responsible for the HMS first-year and second-year courses in psychiatry and sent Farrell to report back on instructor performance.

Lindemann felt much more appreciated in other countries than at the MGH—somehow familiarity bred professional jealousy. He scheduled the annual Lindau Conference on the anniversary of his father's death. He was independent in his thought and action and accomplished what he set out to do. In clinical interviews, he could build a wall around himself and his patient without any attention to the observing audience. He had an informal and humble manner, but he imparted important teaching with exacting and rich information and gave the listener the feeling that the listener was the source of the insights. He spent time freely with trainees, who could never have enough of his teaching. He was involved, giving, and kind to patients on the MGH psychiatry wards and during the poliomyelitis epidemic in the 1950s, and he was known to visit the HRS on a Saturday to help the janitor dealing with problems with children.

Lindemann worked with caretakers in any community and was an early advocate of the importance of family physicians who knew the family backgrounds of illnesses and could prevent them. In psychiatrist–general practitioner sharing programs, they were grateful for the preventive mental health perspective. (See the Lindau Psychotherapie-Woche for his duplication of this work in Germany.)

As the administrative assistant who was involved in the functioning of the department, Farrell found Lindemann a good administrator: When he was appointed chief, he wrote a ten-year plan for the department, presumably sent to the general director, and reported on his accomplishments to directors, such as John Knowles. She observed that all intentions were fulfilled. He spent much time raising funds, and department funding increased from $300,00 to $1.5 million over his tenure. In fact, the MGH chief accountant thought that he was building an empire. He developed many programs, including CMH and the psychiatrist–general practitioner program, which died with his retirement. Weisman's Omega Project study of death was an offshoot of Lindemann's ideas about grief. He allowed others to develop their own ideas to their fullest abilities without his interference and gave advice when asked. His CMH interests did not overshadow other programs, but they were one of many department activities. He administered so kindly and said things so softly that people did not recognize that he had made decisions. (Perhaps this was another application of his talent for helping patients feel that they had resolved their problems.)

Lindemann retired one year before he had to do so, because he was afraid that he would be told to leave. Also, he was beset with his own children's adolescent problems and the beginning of the social rebellion period among hospital resident staff.

After Lindemann's retirement, Farrell held positions at the Douglas A. Thom Clinic, New England Deaconess Hospital, and New England Correctional Coordinating Council. Thereafter, she served on the Harbor Mental Health Area Board, Massachusetts Association for Mental Health, Health Planning Council of Greater Boston, and she was a volunteer at the MGH chaplain's office and main lobby.

In 1970, Farrell wrote and submitted to state Senator Umana (who represented the West End area encompassing the MGH and Bowdoin Square mental health center) a bill to name the center the Erich Lindemann Mental Health Center. She orchestrated the appearance of people to testify before the House Ways and Means Committee and was given a standing ovation by members of Hearing Committee for the best-prepared hearing. In 1972, she arranged a ceremony dedicating the ELMHC. After Lindemann's death in 1974, she arranged a memorial celebration. Finally, in 1975, she established the Lindemann Memorial Lecture Series and arranged its first nine lectures.

Pearl Rosenberg[14]

Pearl Rosenberg was a psychologist specializing in group process, who worked as a researcher and mental health consultant at the HRS and later moved with her husband and family to the University of Minnesota, where she became assistant dean at its medical school. Rosenberg had the following to say about Lindemann:

> His values and ethics were clear and uncompromising, and he lived by them instinctively. This struck me dramatically when he calmly announced that he would have to resign from the American Medical Association because the organization was planning to tax its members to fight Medicare. It was only later in the same day, during a casual conversation, that I discovered he always assumed a physician could not practice medicine in the United States if he were not a member of the AMA! . . . he was [not] a saint. He was hellion behind the wheel, shouting German imprecations at unhearing and unsuspecting motorists that impeded his way. He invariably missed appointments, and because he hated to say no, he made it almost impossible to find him when he felt he was going to be pinned down . . . no saint, but a very special man whom I both respected and adored.

John Nemiah

John Nemiah had trained at the MGH and was a junior member of the psychiatry staff when Lindemann was appointed chief. Nevertheless, Lindemann delegated to him major administrative responsibility for the routine management of the service—in charge of the inpatient wards and standing in for Lindemann when the latter was away. Nemiah was proper and polite and thus respected Lindemann for his position, but he never really understood or was interested in CMH. In fact, he appreciated Lindemann's allowing him to follow his own interests (psychoanalysis).[15] Nemiah's view of Lindemann was ambivalent, as was reflected in his appraisal:

> Lindemann was compassionate, so that people turned to him for help. He worked with psychiatrically ill members of MGH staff families, such as two schizophrenic children. With unrealistic optimism he made efforts to treat them at MGH (and also McLean Hospital), leading to tangled transference problems with their MGH staff relatives.

He believed that Lindemann was not close to anyone and observed that when hard decisions had to be made, he could not face them but reported in sick, went home to bed, and had much unanswered correspondence (behaviors also observed by Lindemann's wife). He was seen as never firm and sharp about his wishes, changed his mind, backed out of commitments, and made many promises without following through on them, thus leaving people "dangling and angry". He "just wasn't there as a leader". He could not stand up to the pressures of the hospital and its "hard-nosed, castrating bastards", such as Raymond Adams, chief of the Neuromedical (neurological) Service. In the face of conflict, hostility, and pressure, he would get sick or feel overwhelmed and ask others to take over, or he would go home. At times, he was depressed, anxious and confused. Nemiah reported that Lindemann carried a large briefcase of unanswered correspondence and had difficulty putting his ideas in writing—Gerald Caplan was his amanuensis. In psychoanalytic terms, Nemiah believed that a staff member who was an oral character wanting a strong daddy would have resented Lindemann, but Nemiah was a phallic character who did not mind the lack of leadership, went his own way, and presented proposals as Lindemann's ideas and thus got his sanction and freedom of action. In this role, Nemiah felt as close to Lindemann as anyone on the staff was. The psychiatry staff was ambivalent about Lindemann, who was lovable but gave no direction. Other MGH departments look on him as an odd, evanescent phenomenon.

Lindemann took a psychoanalytic approach but early on focused on external stress, including surgery and medical illness. In his social psychiatry studies in psychosomatic medicine, such as ulcerative colitis, he made brilliant contributions in collaboration with Chester Jones (gastroenterologist) and would have made major contributions if he had continued with clinical work. His study of the psychiatric casualties of the Coconut Grove nightclub fire led to his interest in social loss and the development of the HRS, which Nemiah saw as dealing with town politics. He was a consummate teacher and interviewer, but he would rarely practice these.

In a survey of remembrances of Lindemann, Nemiah reported the following:[16]

> Erich's interviewing of psychiatric patients . . . virtuoso performances. Erich's ability to enter empathetically into the patient's life and sorrows, to elicit rich and revealing clinical material as if no one else were resent, and to send the patient away heartened and uplifted by the encounter, was a unique experience. . . . Erich's absorbing interest in his community activities, which continued unabated after his appointment as professor and chief of psychiatry at the [Massachusetts General] Hospital, was sometimes distressing to those of us on the Staff whose primary concern was with the functioning of the hospital service proper. We often wished that he was more available to bring his remarkable clinical talents and his brilliance as a teacher to the everyday clinical problems that faced us. At the same time, he was always supportive and encouraging to each of us in the specific roles we played in the running of the psychiatric service, and his delegation of responsibly gave many of us an unparalleled opportunity for personal and professional growth. . . . Erich always

respected my interests and allowed me the freedom to pursue my idiosyncratic goals without the kind of interference that so often disrupts the professional fulfillment of younger members of an academic organization.

(pp. 533–4)

Lindemann was appointed chairperson of the MGH Department of Psychiatry on the basis of his scholarly accomplishments, good working relationships with MGH staff members, marvelous clinical skills, and having run the MGH psychiatry outpatient clinic. People believed that he was a good clinician, researcher, and administrator on the basis of his work before his appointment as chief. He delegated his responsibilities for psychiatry teaching in the first two years of HMS to Gardner Quarton and Nemiah, though he contributed some excellent lectures and clinics. He became uninterested in clinical programs and hospital psychiatry, which he delegated to the chiefs of the various psychiatry units, and followed his interests in the social sciences and the HRS, bringing "light-weight" staff members into the department. He strayed from psychiatry to fuzzy social science and CMH. His achievements at HRS were creative, including sensitive and effective administration. At MGH, he was unsuccessful at every social system he dealt with and was a terrible administrator.[17] He always tried to recruit staff into community work but did not insist. CMH ideas were implemented in the Emergency Ward and Alcoholism Clinic. At Nemiah's request, Lindemann brought Freddie Frankel from South Africa (a great humanitarian gesture given that Frankel was eager to leave), who worked with the DMH in helping Harry Solomon (commissioner) to develop outreach clinics, reorganized the MGH Emergency Ward along crisis intervention lines, and developed other clinical services. Lindemann brought in other good people who were not interested in CMH: George Talland regarding memory research, Frank Ervin regarding neuropsychology and psychosurgery, and Morris Chafetz in alcoholism. Alfred Stanton (psychiatrist-in-chief of McLean Hospitl) gave McLean real substance. In the realm of CMH, Lindemann was "always futzin' around out there with these vague ideas" and brought in nice but vague people like Paul Hare (a social psychologist), who conducted a 24-hour study of psychiatric inpatient ward activities, which was incomprehensible but the hit of the American Sociological Society meeting. Gerald Caplan implemented and popularized Lindemann's ideas.

He brought George Saslow in to shoulder the administration, but Saslow was nonanalytical and did not fit in. Also, the expectations of Saslow were not clarified: he expected to run the hospital services and left disappointed. This left an informal group of unit directors to carry administrative and clinical responsibilities: Peter Sifneos (originally appointed by Stanley Cobb) clinical programs, Nemiah medical programs, and Avery Weisman and Thomas Hackett consultation services.

They felt unappreciated and resented Lindemann's introduction of social scientists; Lindemann's favorite term of "cross-fertilization" was seen as a euphemism for "being screwed".

In all, Nemiah saw Lindemann as a founding father of community psychiatry with ideas, imagination, and sensitivity. His work on grief and the importance of loss in psychosomatic medicine were important and influential. He did not get adequate credit for this, because he did not publish his ideas and achievements and later "got off into worshipping sociologists".[18] The West End Study was a major force in changing urban redevelopment—rehabilitation rather than replacement. He was brilliant but troubled, with odd thinking, a need to be liked, and sensitivity to hurt. He was convincing about his ideas and one of the major people in American psychiatry.

Nemiah was chosen to write the official history of Lindemann and the Psychiatry Service in one of the periodic histories of the MGH. Importantly, someone who did not understand or sympathize with Lindemann and his quest was so chosen. This choice and Nemiah's perspective clearly demonstrate the ambivalence, discomfort, and lack of understanding by the psychiatry staff and the MGH of Lindemann's ideas of the relationship of social to psychological psychiatry and his goal of transforming psychiatry and medicine. Nemiah presents this articulately.[19]

Peter Sifneos

Peter Sifneos was a senior member of the MGH Psychiatry Service staff and eventually director of the psychiatry outpatient clinic. He was also part of the group that managed the daily tasks of the department.

He looked back on his years at MGH and HRS with Stanley Cobb and Erich Lindemann and an outstanding collection of service chiefs and visitors as the most stimulating and enjoyable of his life.[20] He found Lindemann creative and intellectually admirable, with original ideas (which Gerald Caplan adopted and elaborated on). A letter to Lindemann expressed effusive gratitude for his MGH Seminar on Existentialism—its warmth and clarity—and his affection for Lindemann as a teacher.[21] Sifneos judged that his contributions were in the areas of emotional equilibrium, expectable life crises, mobilization of adaptive and maladaptive defenses, the potential for deterioration or growth, and the identification of community caregivers who can intervene in crises and the practice of mental health consultation with them. These concepts became accepted as matters of course.

Sifneos thought Lindemann wanted the MGH chairpersonship in order to convert a traditional medical psychology department to community mental health. In turn, he was chosen because he was gifted in clinical, research, and social psychiatry. Sifneos doubted MGH's real interest in social medicine, having historically been confined to excellence in research, clinical care, and teaching. The general directors during Lindemann's tenure gave no real support to social medicine: Dean Clark was ineffectual, and John Knowles was interested but too busy. Also, other MGH departments wanted to reduce the power and presence of the Department of Psychiatry: his predecessor, Stanley Cobb, had been a towering figure, and Lindemann was expected to follow his social interests outside the hospital. Also, there were personal pressures from MGH staff members who had become strongly attached to and supportive of him: The chief of pediatrics had two schizophrenic daughters, and Lindemann treated the younger and the schizophrenic niece of a senior surgeon. Sifneos (and he remembers Cobb, too) thought Lindemann's clinical practice was poor.

Sifneos saw Lindemann abandoning psychoanalysis, clinical psychiatry, and good clinical judgment; devaluing psychological factors; and losing interest in the department's clinical treatment and teaching programs as he progressively turned toward his social interests. He was a poor administrator, failing to integrate the various elements of the department that were financed independently. He started good projects and then left them to develop on their own (research under Frank Ervin, the Acute Psychiatric Service under Morris Chafetz, the West End Study under Marc Fried); put them into poor hands (the HRS under Donald Klein); or undermined and frustrated their leaders (HRS under Robert Bragg and possibly research under Gardner Quarton).

Sifneos judged Lindemann to be ambivalent clinically and personally and unable to make prompt decisions. He was good at making contact and diagnosing and establishing relationships and programs, but he was disappointed by them and lost interest in carrying them through over the long term. He started projects (HRS, West End Study), tried to recruit people for these projects and agreed to appointments, and then turned the projects over to others. He was overcommitted and underinvested—for instance, leaving HRS for work at the MGH and the West End Study. He left the running of the clinical MGH Psychiatry Service to John Nemiah in inpatient service and residency training, Sifneos in the outpatient clinic and medical students, and Morris Chafetz and then Fred Frankel in the Acute Psychiatric Service. They appreciated his lack of interference but regretted and even resented the lack of his brilliant input. Sifneos remembers conflicts with Donald Klein, administrator of the HRS, whom Sifneos believed was disinterested in and hostile to clinical issues and psychiatrists and a poor choice as administrator.

Sifneos thought Lindemann retired two years early out of frustration and disappointment at having made no real impact on the MGH. He thought the suicide of a long-term patient also affected him. And frustration with Lindemann fueled a petition signed by members of the MGH staff asking that the new chief of psychiatry not be a psychoanalyst. At his retirement party, much to the outrage of the MGH psychiatrists who had managed the department, Lindemann acknowledged only John Seeley, who was not an MGH staff member. Sifneos thought that after Lindemann's retirement from the MGH, Lindemann sought a more flexible environment, acceptance, and the integration of clinical and social psychiatry in California.

Fred H. Frankel

Fred Frankel was a psychiatrist from The Union of South Africa. In 1950, he had one year of training at the MGH before returning to his country. Alarmed at the Sharpeville massacre, he wrote to Lindemann asking for a position so that he could move to the US. Lindemann cabled him offering him a job and travel funds but left it to Frankel and Charles Clay (MGH assistant director) to work out MGH sponsorship and licensing. Lindemann entrusted him with representing the MGH psychiatry service in negotiations with the DMH for collaborations in CMH/CMHC programs—perhaps another example of Lindemann's uncritical choice of collaborators in CMH.

However, Frankel was skeptical of CMH.[22] He observed that he came from a different, European culture which was more pragmatic, working through ideas to more-careful development. He saw the US as optimistic and overreacting to ideas, expecting that money can accomplish anything, which led to the decrease in psychiatric inpatient beds without providing alternative services and believing in the unproven concept of preventing mental illness. He saw Lindemann as a good clinician and a distinguished community psychiatrist addressing outreach clinical services and saw CMH as addressing preventive services and the use of community resources. There was insignificant understanding of the difference between these goals and the need to integrate them. It was instructive to recognize the relationship of political and social issues to mental health. However, in authoritarian countries such as communist countries, Nazi Germany, and South Africa, political orthodoxy could supersede professional competence, leading to a wariness about government involvement in professional affairs. In the US, there is no guarantee of the right kind of politics and politicians and their influence on mental health. He saw little evidence of the influence of social (as opposed to biological) factors on mental illness and saw CMHCs as little different from traditional mental hospitals. His ideal would be equal funding for inpatient and community follow-up programs.

Frankel saw in Action for Mental Health, the final report of the Joint Commission on Mental Illness and Health, an emphasis on saving money and denying the possibility of great changes in the mental health system—e.g., inexpensive indigenous workers replacing professionals. Lindemann's distinction between CMH and community psychiatry was lost.

In developing a CMHC associated with the MGH, the intention was to have two institutions with joint staff. The architectural plans were drawn without MGH input. Lindemann and DMH Commissioner Harry Solomon decided to appoint a junior staff member with joint appointments to report to both of them: DMH via Associate Commissioner James Dykens, MGH via Fred Frankel providing liaison between the MGH and DMH 1965–1968.

The DMH was keen to build a CMHC but vague about details: great change in mental health care, replacement of mental hospitals, selection of area board members to represent the community, and the role of the Massachusetts Association for Mental Health. For political reasons, the MGH general director, John Knowles, expressed support in principle and for cooperation with the DMH. The MGH Department of Psychiatry was excited about a new type of practice and access to resources and facilities. However, it was concerned about the ultimate purposes of the state and federal programs, beginning a program it would later have to withdraw from and leave responsibilities to others and (especially the Psychiatric Social Service Department) concerned about the quality of state mental health professionals and the consequences of becoming state employees. He found most psychiatry staff members uninterested and mistrustful, attached to hospital and medically based treatment, and tolerant of CMH only if it did not detract from hospital programs.

Frankel saw Lindemann's great contributions as the concepts of grief work and preventive intervention. He was a global dreamer who left it to others to implement his dreams. If smaller groups had researched and developed CMH ideas carefully over 20 years and politicians had not overextended them, the accomplishments would have been more solid and have avoided the disappointment of expectations with consequent hostility. It was not Lindemann's fault that effort and money were wasted on CMH.

Avery Weisman

Avery Weisman was a psychoanalyst and one of the senior members of the MGH Psychiatry Service. He began by appreciating Lindemann's contributions of the relevance of family and significant others to the diagnosis and treatment of such pathologies as grief and ulcerative colitis, as well as the appreciation of treatment by nonpsychiatrists, such as social workers, psychologists, and laypeople.[23] He was an excellent interviewer, capable of making quick assessments.

It was Weisman's interpretation that Lindemann was chosen as chief of the MGH Psychiatry Service and HMS professor of psychiatry as a compromise candidate: What was desired was not a psychoanalyst but someone eclectic who could work with many professions, so Lindemann was advanced from a mere clinical associate to professor and chairperson.

(Records indicate that Lindemann was a full psychiatrist at MGH from 1944 and at the time of his appointment as professor at HMS and chairperson at MGH was an associate professor of Mental Health at the Harvard School of Public Health 1950–1954 and an associate professor of Mental Health at Harvard College.)

Jacob Finesinger, the other bright young staff member, was much more charismatic, sought and secured disciples, and wanted the chairpersonship but was rejected. In contrast, Lindemann was self-effacing, insecure about his worth, a poor administrator, and did not want or know how to use and avoided power. He did not give promotions to or stand up for the department or its staff. He was ingratiating and took the side of outside, community mental health staff members. He was overcommitted, could not refuse invitations to projects, and so was never present. He did not appreciate the staff members who were doing the "scutwork" of the department, such as John Nemiah. At the MGH retirement dinner, he mentioned only Thomas (actually John) Seeley, who was a mere passing psychologist (actually sociologist). Lindemann acknowledged several times that he was not suited to administration[24] but found it hard to turn down the offer by Harvard. Weisman thought that the MGH staff did not want another psychiatry chairperson like Lindemann, because of him personally rather than because of hostility toward CMH. It was clear that Weisman hated Lindemann (Lindemann's administrative assistant, Jean Farrell, thought he was jealous), and upon his retirement, Weisman wrote a "hate letter" to HMS Dean Ebert recommending that no one like Lindemann be appointed again.[25] (Weisman did not mention his purported authorship of the petition against Lindemann's characteristics that was circulated among the MGH staff, though psychiatry staff members did not sign it.) The degree and persistence of his hostility and disdain raise questions about their source in Weisman. (See his contribution to the official history of the Psychiatry Service under Lindemann.[26])

Weisman was hard put to define CMH. He thought it grew because of the availability of federal money, leading people to give it lip service or gravitate toward it. When the money disappeared, people gravitated elsewhere without much lasting investment in CMH. Weisman claimed to feel no hostility toward Lindemann, and as he grew older, he recognized Lindemann's contributions to his practice of including family and significant others.

Thomas P. Hackett

Thomas Hackett's opinions stand out with special importance for two reasons: First, he is an example of the ambivalence about Lindemann both between and within individuals—outspoken criticism and resentment vs. warm appreciation of skills and caring. Second, Hackett was the department's preference, which eventually was reflected in the MGH and HMS choice, for a person who expressed its perspectives and gave it respite from work and struggle for nontraditional ideas—a comfortable homebody who would let the department carry on in peace rather than someone with alien ideas discomfiting the department with change.

Thomas Hackett was a junior staff member in the MGH Psychiatry Service under Lindemann and was the second person appointed to the chief position after him. As Avery Weisman's protégé, he apparently picked up Weisman's feelings and, just before he was appointed chief of psychiatry, to Jean Farrell's surprise, he said that he hated Lindemann.

Hackett came to the MGH for his psychiatric residency training because Stanley Cobb was its chief.[27] He was suspicious of Lindemann's friendliness and warmth to him, the staff, and patients (e.g., regarding patient suicide), saw it as calculated, and thought that Lindemann was really cold to them without remorse, was closed (including about his personal life), socially isolated, could not remember names, and grotesque and embarrassing in public. His attempts at being social were inept, as when at his reception for new psychiatric residents he made no preparation for swimming, included only one bottle of beer, and made the residents move a table. Hackett quoted Wiseman as observing that Lindemann "always tried to be one of the guys but failed". He was disappointing in that he made false promises and did not follow through with them—including failure to fulfill the promise of badly needed money for Hackett—and kept people waiting for hours. He remembers gently advising Lindemann not to make false promises, upon which Lindemann turned on him and was hostile and rejecting thereafter, would not talk, wrote nasty notes, gave him no pay raises or promotions despite good publication, and forbade Hackett to follow his interests in hypnotism (which was particularly hurtful). Lindemann could be critical in private meetings but forbade it in public and could not tolerate public conflict or criticism, and he was thus bad at dealing with the hurly-burly of practical politics where his authority was questioned and could not have dealt with inner-city communities. Hackett also remembers Lindemann overhearing Hackett's severe criticism and refusing to talk to him thereafter.

Hackett saw Lindemann's protégé, Gerald Caplan, as pretentious, absurd, egomaniacal, comical, inappropriate, and competitive through deferential with Lindemann. Ingrid Sondergaard, a Danish psychiatrist whom Lindemann brought, was nutty, overanalytical, and could not retain ideas. He saw Lindemann's appointment as chief of psychiatry as the MGH staff's (including Walter Bauer, chief of medicine) effort to downgrade psychiatry. They had no interest in social medicine, and Lindemann would have undermined it if they had. He focused on HRS, the West End Project, and his consultation with medical schools in India rather than the MGH, and Lindemann preferred to relate to community people and nonphysician professionals (psychologists, social workers, and social scientists) rather than psychiatrists and physicians.

Hackett recognized Lindemann's interest in human interaction, social science, collaboration, and the integration of ideas. He believed that Lindemann was uncomfortable with him because he thought that Lindemann saw him as a neurologist, though he felt welcomed by Lindemann to a (rare) salaried staff position. He could also say Lindemann was tolerant of other ideas (as when he defended George Murphy's anti-analytic approach). Lindemann was gracious publicly and in introductions; his exaggerated manners worked. He was generous financially and not devious. Hackett appreciated Lindemann's work with sodium amytal, the interaction chronograph, and psychosomatic medicine. He thought Lindemann was an excellent clinical interviewer, and he appreciated Lindemann's assigning Hackett to treat a Jesuit priest because of their shared religion and supervising him in that treatment. He appreciated Lindemann's technique of suggesting dreams as a way of reaching psychodynamics. He saw Lindemann as comfortable when Lindemann was in control of an audience: Lindemann could draw a magic circle and interact with them.

Lindemann, in his view, was a poor administrator, unable to hold onto and manage administrative power. He was seen as ambitious, an ivory tower teacher and thinker who found himself unexpectedly caught in US medicine's transition to a focus on managerial skills. He would have been better and happier as a clinician, researcher, and teacher. Hackett thought the MGH psychiatry residency program degenerated into a laughingstock with poor residents but good postgraduate fellows. He remembered the psychiatric consultation service inaugurated in 1956 as the first, largest, and best in the world and blamed Lindemann's indifference and lack of involvement (though he had worked with other services in the past, which had found him too analytical) for its failing to achieve its potential. (Hackett did not credit Lindemann's plan for the psychiatric consultation service as a vehicle for implementing mental health consultation with the MGH staff and structure.) Staff were not given academic or financial advancement—Nemiah held the rank of assistant professor, and Sifneos and Hackett instructor, though Hackett had published 38 papers and should have appealed to the HMS dean. Finances were poor because Lindemann did not take advantage of available funds (Hackett remembered the department budget as $500,000, compared with $8 million later under Hackett.) When Lindemann retired, department finances were found in great disorder, with deficits hidden by Lindemann's administrative assistant, Jean Farrell, which infuriated his successor, Leon Eisenberg.

In all, Hackett tried to appreciate Lindemann but did not trust and was not close to Lindemann. He saw no impact on MGH or the other clinical services by Lindemann because Lindemann was indifferent and did not participate in the hospital life. Staff on the other services found him too psychoanalytic, and it was Hackett and Weisman, with the aid of Quarton and Herman, who made good on the psychiatric consultation service that Lindemann had established.

Eleanor Clark

Eleanor Clark was an MGH psychiatric social worker, respected enough for her balanced perspective and administrative skill to rise to be chief psychiatric social worker and then chief of the MGH Department of Social Service.

She recognized Lindemann's expertise in clinical work and believed that his appointment as chief was justified on that basis.[28] A specific contribution was his change of treatment from long-term, psychoanalytically oriented psychotherapy under Stanley Cobb (despite his reputation for eclecticism) to short-term treatments and consultation with other MGH services.

She, too, remembered him as forgetful, inefficient, habitually appearing to agree with people and then disappointing, including not responding to people's needs for finances and promotions. She believed that through him, CMH got a bad reputation for not fulfilling its promises, for allowing novices to take on complex crisis intervention projects that required more than average skill, and for the catastrophes that resulted.

John M. von Felsinger

John "Mike" von Felsinger was a psychologist in the MGH Psychiatry Service, and when community mental health was abandoned there, he left to join the social psychology projects in the Department of Psychology at Boston College.

He saw Lindemann's principle contributions as being a brilliant interviewer and seminal thinker.[29] He did not politically build on his creativity, and others, such as Gerald Caplan, were given credit for ideas that were largely Lindemann's. He was not appreciated at MGH but was thought to have betrayed and abandoned psychiatry. When he retired, his work did not continue there, as von Felsinger had predicted.

People either loved or hated Lindemann. Von Felsinger thought this was a consequence of his knack for developing great self-esteem, confidence, and expectations in people, and those who were unable to live up to these goals projected their bitterness onto Lindemann: an example was Peter Sifneos, who turned against Lindemann.

James G. Kelly[30]

Kelly was a newly minted psychologist who came to the MGH Department of Psychiatry as a fellow in community mental health, absorbed the ethos, and participated in some research projects. He went on to become a premier advocate for community psychology in academia and in the American Psychological Association:

> Despite the overriding psychoanalytic orientation at Harvard and throughout Boston, Erich and Don Klein and their associates had established the first prototype of what in a few years would develop into community mental health centers and valiantly persisted with little in the way of resources, other than their band of energetic young mental health workers. The 1962–1963 Community Mental Health Centers Act was as much a tribute to Erich as it was to the National Mental Health Association and others who worked for its passage.

Gloria Liederman

As a CMH FELLOW at MGH in 1956, Dr. Lindemann prepared a research project on child school adjustment. Gloria found Lindemann supportive, open, and not intrusive in his supervision. Her impression was that the Department of Psychiatry staff was split between conservatives uninterested in CMH and those more sympathetic, though the department as a whole seemed open to hearing about it.

Stanley Cobb

Everyone liked Lindemann: He was gentle, sensitive, and patient with whoever he was talking to.[31] Stanley Cobb, chief when he came to the MGH, admired Lindemann's clinical and interview ability and came to appreciate Lindemann's social psychiatry approach.[32]

Cobb was interested in social psychiatry and may have been the one who recommended Lindemann for the Wellesley Human Relations Service project, which impressed Cobb when he visited. Cobb made no complaint about Lindemann's administrative ability (he had appointed him director of the MGH outpatient psychiatry clinic), had great confidence in him, admired his application to social and training issues, and made no criticism of his spreading himself too far. In contrast, there was resistance to psychoanalysis from Mandel Cohen (who held a fellowship in neurology under Cobb's supervision, and underwent a failed personal analysis with Hanns Sachs) and Raymond D. Adams (chief of the MGH Neurology Service), which Cobb tried to resolve.[33]

Cobb was very happy when Lindemann was appointed, though he preferred Gardner Quarton (a researcher who could not write) or John Nemiah (a clinician who could write). It was after his appointment that Cobb became disappointed at Lindemann's lack of organizational ability, including his recordkeeping. Cobb had been compulsive in this regard, and Cobb's secretary had a difficult time with Lindemann about this. In fact, Cobb went so far as to suggest to George Packer Berry, HMS dean, the reactivation of rotating department chairpersonships as a way out of Lindemann's misadministration.[34] Reportedly, Berry refused because of the difficulty of recruiting without tenure.[35] Cobb commented in general on the burdens of administration, perhaps revealing some of his own regrets as well as Lindemann's: "Both power and administrative duties are to my mind enemies of real scholarship".[36] Edward Churchill, MGH chief of surgery also noted that Harvard University had an 11-year tenure rule for department heads, to save them from themselves administratively.[37]

Laura Morris

Laura Morris was a community organization social worker who was a researcher at the Massachusetts Department of Welfare. Lindemann was interested in her background of contact with important business and government people and her understanding of the role of the settlement house as a pre-illness resource. (Note that Lindemann's wife was a social worker who worked in settlement houses.) After an illness, Lindemann invited her to attend an HRS staff meeting and hired her for 11 years as a major participant in the MGH Mental Health Service that Lindemann worked to establish. He also relied on her to explore and provide liaison with the West End community around the MGH. Later, she worked with William Ryan at the Massachusetts Committee on Children and Youth: they shared strong feelings about changing the direction of mental health.

Morris reported that she loved Lindemann like an uncle and learned much from him, those whom he attracted, and the opportunities he created.[38] In turn, she felt that he respected what she brought and looked forward to her new child.

Lindemann said that he was "not the world's greatest administrator", but this is not what Morris was looking for from Lindemann: he gave priority to people (unlike many good administrators), enabled exposure to big ideas and people with a sense of the future rather than the past, and was a teacher, visionary, and pioneer—these being much more important than administrative functions. He did not take on the mechanics and budgetary aspects of administration; hospital and grant funds allowed him to appoint others to these tasks. However, in crises, he took action, such as indulging and supporting a friend rather than letting him hang himself. He had the administrative and political requirements to become psychiatry chief and chairperson of psychiatry at MGH/HMS but used them sparingly. He was strong in bringing large federal teaching funds for new ideas. He had the courage to battle the MGH General Executive Committee when the general director, John Knowles, did not have strong relations with the staff, and Lindemann had the strength to change the psychiatry outpatient clinic. He was careful in how he timed decisions, though others thought that he was delaying and thought him weak.

Morris saw credentialled professionals throwing temper tantrums in his outer office and criticizing Lindemann because they did not have offices.

Lindemann was a complicated personality, appearing gentle and speaking simplistically but having deep meaning and bringing his listeners around to understanding the application of these ideas to the settings in question. He did not block intimacy and gave glimpses of his experiences and struggles. He could be hurt, sometimes seen as avoiding conflict, though he took action when conflict became unavoidable. Morris was not uncomfortable with him, because she felt a mutual liking and could help redirect staff jostling back to the task at hand. She believed that he was depressed when approaching retirement.

Lindemann was a man of ideas and taught others to absorb and apply them, though these ideas might get lost or others apply them—sometimes ineptly—without attribution to Lindemann, as happened in some of the HRS research projects. He created a learning environment in meetings with invited guests, where he would develop his ideas, such as in the NIMH Space Cadets and in the West End Project, with an impact on other participants who adopted and used them. He reached for new ideas, shared with people, and learned from Rabbi Gittleson and the sociologist Talcott Parsons that different frames of reference obscure commonalities. He admired Gerald Caplan's courage in action and chose without jealousy to do the talking and leave the writing to Caplan.

There was much rivalry and tension in the MGH Psychiatry Department. Lindemann playfully suggested the analogy of sibling relations to a papa. Alternatively, one could see Lindemann playing with his children and fostering an atmosphere of focus on himself because he wanted attention and to be liked. He was clear about his interests, such as replicating some collaborative leadership aspects of the Tavistock Clinic, which seemed like bad administration. He brought in a consultant in administration from Palo Alto, California (Henrik Blum), but his recommendations were not Lindemann's style. A contrasting style of administration was that of Edward Logue, director of the Boston Redevelopment Authority, who was superb at technical administration and had other staff to handle relations with people.

Morris thought that community mental health flowered when its time came. The availability of money, Lindemann's ideas, and his position as one of the few chairpersons of a department of psychiatry with these ideas in the US and in the world made it possible for him to set the stage for CMH.

Robert Bragg[39]

Bragg, administrator of the Wellesley Human Relations Service under Lindemann, saw Lindemann as a man of ideas and a conceptualizer, someone creative but disappointing in terms of implementing his ideas practically. He was wary of and sensitive to eventual failure and was reassured and warmed by the rapport he could develop with audiences and patients. His close relationship and frequent meetings with Gerald Caplan gradually cooled, as Caplan succeeded in publishing the ideas that had come from their collaboration, and Caplan grew to resent authority over him.

MGH Staff and Administration

Oliver Cope

Oliver Cope was a surgeon at the MGH, with a great interest in the psychosocial contributions to and consequences of illness.

He thought that Lindemann was selected as chairperson of the psychiatry department because Lindemann was extraordinary and creative and showed his teaching ability in an afternoon teaching clinic.[40] His interest in CMH and social medicine (especially in regard to alcoholism) was considered important by the search committee, which had strong ideas about who should be appointed

However, he did not think that Lindemann had much effect on MGH, whose medical and surgical services were uninterested. (Alan Butler, chief of the MGH Children's Medical Service, also wondered whether Lindemann had made any lasting impression on MGH.)[41] Nathan Talbot, chief of the Children's Medicine Service, had his own ideas about psychological medicine; had a good heart but incomplete understanding of psychological factors and was ineffectual at implementing a separate program of his own, which sometimes competed with that of the Psychiatry Service.[42]

Ellsworth Neumann[43]

Lindemann was well liked and offended almost no one except those who disliked all psychiatry—conservative physicians and surgeons and a chief of service whose sister had psychiatric treatment but died of myasthenia gravis, and this chief blamed psychiatry for not diagnosing this earlier. Neumann denied knowledge of objections to Lindemann and the petition against him. The Psychiatry Department was respected by nursing, social service, and most medicine; a minority of orthopedics; and a minority of surgery and neurosurgery, but all of neurology rejected it. Those who were politically conservative were against psychiatry, whereas political liberals were in favor. Chauvinistic surgeons were against any association with psychology, treated only by cutting out and thought liberals were taking medicine to ruin.

Neumann recognized that Lindemann explored nonphysical care of patients like psychiatric patients from a different point of view. Neumann advised him to offer help and was surprised at the positive response. He objected to neurological interest in lower brain implants as "mutilation". Stanton spoke out more openly than did Lindemann.

MGH General Director Dean Clark and MGH General Director John Knowles and trustees were generally interested in community medicine, as opposed to a strong staff bias toward physical aspects. The struggle was a matter of numbers of chiefs of service with strong personalities vs. a strong leader who could succeed with administrative support. Neumann was a strong supporter; the hospital administration had varied interest in psychiatry, aside from their own jobs. Neumann thought CMH has succeeded where it was tried and that the trend will stay with good advocates for the perspective that there is more to medicine than one-to-one relationships. Lindemann was successful before he became chief of psychiatry, such as with the HRS. At MGH, he never proposed large projects requiring heavy expenditures, and his projects within MGH were never resisted, including the West End Project, which was practically intramural and not extreme. It was applauded: everyone in the hospital worried about the West End residents, who included hospital employees and long-term patients, and it was seen as research rather than an extension of treatment

In discussions about the future direction of the hospital, Lindemann helped make the decision to remain MGH (a community hospital) rather than the Massachusetts Medical Center, though more of its patients come from outside the local community. Lindemann was elected chairperson of the MGH General Executive Committee because he would not be dictatorial, as some past chairpersons had been. After each committee meeting, Lindemann, Stanton, and Neumann had coffee to discuss Neumann's perception of hidden agendas and Lindemann's degree of success. Neumann's special interest is logic and emotion as well as personal bias openly or hidden behind intellectualization. Essential to his job satisfaction is his practice of therapeutic administration regarding the organization and participant individuals, feeling that it does more good than the treatment of individual patients. (People with these concerns usually have backgrounds of personal problems that have been talked out.) One of his most important and therapeutic tasks at MGH and his subsequent work at the Rockefeller Foundation is the reinterpretation of the parallels between opponents' aims and tenets: this applies to individuals as well as hospital services and departments.[44] Much has changed since Lindemann's time: No one is doing Neumann's job. MGH has brought in new business methods and people who do not respect department heads.

In evaluating Lindemann's contributions, Neumann thought that Lindemann emphasized psychiatry, how people feel, the importance of relationships, and seeing patients as people. Lindemann was a presence who did not demand agreement and gave fatherly approval. Many outside the psychiatry department appreciated Lindemann and psychiatry. He contrasted with his predecessor, who was a neurologist.

Neumann saw his own accomplishments as improved accounting, helping the hospital do well financially, giving respect to department heads, and providing information about the future so that people could adapt and craft solutions intellectually and then emotionally. His policy was to implement mandatory pay raises for staff or fire them. He sought to know and prepare for future government policy.

Neumann was a great admirer of Lindemann's and John Knowles's. Lindemann never demanded or complained of mistreatment. He recognized that psychiatry was viewed as a religion by those who felt like atheists. Although Knowles and Lindemann had the same ideals, Knowles was the opposite in temperament: he loved to confront, whereas Lindemann was too modest, nonconfronting, afraid of rejection, and careful in his speech. Upon Lindemann's appointment as chief, his relationship to his former peers changed, and this disturbed him, because he did not like giving orders, though he could be firm when driven to it and when it was required. He was not good at progressively moving people toward a goal and explaining their roles so that they were comfortable. He did not apply his clinical skills; he was raised in the German system of preemptive authority, which he could not adapt. His subordinates never complained of this, but of getting to see him, his dislike of answering phone calls (except from Neumann) until he knew what wanted, and his recurrent and chronic flu.

Lindemann was uncomfortable and not good as an administrator. He sacrificed thinking and research for the opportunity to move psychiatry in the direction he wanted. He was a good administrator if there was no conflict on issues; obedience was on the basis of love and admiration for him; and subordinates liked and loved him. But changing people and systems required the fighting, disharmony, and determination that he did not have. If there was an explosion or disagreement with him, he did not rush to quell it but instead got the flu and left his secretary as his protector.

Francis O. Schmitt

Francis Schmitt and his wife, Barbara, were attached to the MGH in that they were treated by its physicians.[45] Barbara Schmitt was referred to Lindemann as a sweet, nonfrightening psychiatrist who provided her with years of psychiatric therapy. As a therapist, he was painstaking and patient but could be ruthless (as in removing Barbara's mother from their house). Under his treatment, Barbara Schmitt went through crises but improved, and Lindemann rushed to support her when their medical student son died by suicide.

Schmitt was the only scientist on the MGH Board of Trustees. As a molecular neuroscientist, he shared intellectual stimulation with Lindemann, a behavioral scientist. Lindemann provided support and advice when Schmitt developed the Neuroscience Research Foundation and was a corporate member. They shared interests in creative developments in this field and consulted and supported one another.

Schmitt thought that at first Lindemann's department was thought to be well organized. He interacted with other departments, including helping Walter Bauer with personal problems. His ideas were abstract, so there was no evidence that he wanted to change the MGH. His influence was via teaching his own staff and students concepts of interpersonal and group dynamics. He was not neurologically based but a phenomenologist with a gut reaction to their interactions with people. These ideas need to be crystalized and articulated as sociological psychiatry. Lindemann was too academic and never produced a direct exposition of his ideas for the public.

Schmitt supported him out of friendship and admiration of his ideas, which were ahead of his time and at first refused to believe complaints by the general director and board. Later, Schmitt was convinced, though he sought to understand Lindemann as being too compassionate, hating being a boss and preferring to be a persuader, lacking programming of the staff and sensitive to criticism from the general directors, Dean Clark and John Knowles. Although he believed that he understood the interdisciplinary stimulation of ideas, he was a poor administrator. He was seen as a visionary, committed not to MGH but to HRS, lecturing in Germany and other places, personally involved in community projects (rather than sending subalterns), and wanting to run an unorthodox, top department along novel and far-reaching lines as a contribution to the field of psychiatry and medicine. Schmitt grieved that at one time, people became department chiefs to support their own ideas and programs, but department chiefs had redirected to getting funds for other people's programs.

In Schmitt's view there was never any thought of replacing Lindemann; it was he who wanted to retire early. On the eve of Lindemann's retirement, Lindemann had little impact; the MGH Board of Trustees was uninterested in the books, other materials, and outlines of ideas that he brought because of the preoccupation with staff and financial problems, even though the Surgical Service, too, had these problems. Schmitt wrote,

> Erich's heroic efforts to initiate a new way of dealing with mental health problems—through the family and the community. . . . Sic [transit] gloria mundi! Even within the MGH the greatness of his work was not recognized. I was at the Trustees' meeting at which he mustered all his persuasive powers—to no avail![46]

MGH was unaffected by him—new staff and chiefs never heard of him. Only some individuals were influenced by him, as Schmitt was. Lindemann was a loving, caring, gentle professional with a personal clinical approach. He was a clinician with good Christian concern and compassion, a first-rate intellect with a religious concern. It is hard for such individuals to be effective bosses. Note that Schmitt saw to it that Lindemann's papers were rescued from the MGH basement for preservation in the Francis A. Countway Library of Medicine.

Harvard Medical School and Harvard University

Gerald Caplan

As a colleague and as the director of the HMS Laboratory for Community Psychiatry, Caplan's view was that it was Lindemann's

> remarkable systematic grasp of multifactorial complexities that enabled him to clarify the essentials of a particular case or social situation and derive a constructive solution to the presenting problem. Erich was most successful in opening up paths that lots of others have since traveled, among them many who have not been as bashful in literary exposition [as he was] (pp. 1–2).[47]

George Packer Berry

George Packer Berry was the dean of the Harvard Medical School from 1949 to 1966. The interlocking relationship between the HMS and the MGH (and other HMS teaching hospitals)—though the hospitals were independent institutions, unlike in other medical schools—gave him some influence over MGH affairs and Lindemann.

He saw the MGH as long having had interest in social service, outreach, sharing its excellence with other hospitals, and other aspects of social medicine.[48] In this respect, he found Lindemann's ideas attractive. However, some faculty, including those involved in school consultation and forensic medicine, thought the Freudian approach was limited.

Berry thought Lindemann was appointed professor at HMS and chief of psychiatry at MGH because Berry—as well as Stanley Cobb (toward the end of his tenure), and Walter Bauer (MGH chief of medicine)—appreciated and shared his interest in expanding psychiatry and medicine beyond the molecular focus and the individual patient to dealing with social issues and the community. Additionally, Bauer, a member of the search committee, had a great interest in psychiatry: He had been psychoanalyzed by Helene Deutsch (Lindemann's training analyst), wanted the psychiatric viewpoint available to more people in medicine, and had been a strong supporter of Stanley Cobb as he built the MGH Psychiatry Service. Berry denied having heard of a contemporary national trend toward social medicine or President Harry Truman's advocacy, and he thought it unlikely that they would influence Harvard curriculum.

Berry thought that Harvard and its affiliated hospitals focused on molecular medicine. The social and home medical approach cannot demonstrate quantitative results as biochemistry can, but this does not mean that it contributed nothing. Lindemann contributed the dimension of the validity of a social experiment in psychiatry even if he did not change the course of psychiatry as a whole. Berry enjoyed the hour-long talks that Lindemann had with him two or three times a year to discuss his current activities. In comparison, he thought Gerald Caplan had difficulty getting his social psychiatry ideas across; some did not value his ideas, though they were worthwhile, and some did not like him personally.

Berry thought Lindemann had been a good choice and did a good job: Like other good leaders, Berry believed that Lindemann could accomplish more by quietly convincing people rather than by using an authoritarian approach. And Lindemann's creative ideas were beneficial, though he did not force them on people. He was strong, but did not want to lose the diversity in the department. Berry shared some concern that the HMS teaching of psychiatry, directed jointly by Lindemann and Grete Bibring of the Beth Israel Hospital, was uneven: Lindemann's teaching could be excellent but suffered when he had personal problems, and Bibring was thought to be too esoteric.[49]

Although Lindemann was not as good as an administrator, his ideas and contributions outweighed this deficit. He did not lack fortitude: There was the expected opposition to attempting change—"I think that is part and parcel of trying something new. After all, they crucified a man because he wanted to make something new". There was considerable turmoil at MGH during Lindemann's tenure: the general director, Dean Clark, was alcoholic and fired; department chairpersons (like Edward Churchill of Surgery) were old and inflexible, leading to isolation between departments; and Bauer died and was replaced by Alexander Leaf as chief of medicine with a narrower interest in molecular medicine.

Although Berry said that he did not know of the critical petition circulated upon Lindemann's retirement, he was not surprised: MGH had people of strong views who think they are the best and conflict with new ideas.

Jack R. Ewalt

Jack Ewalt was the HMS professor of psychiatry, director of the Joint Commission on Mental Illness and health, and DMH commissioner.[50]

> Erich, while rather shy, was a very warm and outgoing person with his friends and colleagues. . . . Erich had his eccentricity, which involved letters. Those of us who worked with him quickly learned that it did no good to write Erich a memo which went through the mail. Rumor had it that he never opened his mall and would not

permit his secretary to do so. I know from long experience that the only way to contact Erich was in person or by phone, where you always got a very prompt and cooperative response. Written missives disappeared into some void.

Ewalt found Lindeman kind, not hostile, and uncomfortable with hostility.[51] He thought of CMH as a well-intentioned movement with contributions by psychoanalytic, academic, and research people. He saw MGH as full of hostilities. Those especially hostile included Edward Churchill (chief of surgery) and Alan Butler (chief of the Children's Medical Service). He saw that those who also shared these interests in social medicine were not accepted at the hospital.

Outside Harvard University

Harry C. Solomon

Harry Solomon, as HMS professor of psychiatry and commissioner of the DMH, had a perspective on Lindemann of limited respect. He found Lindemann brilliant but not an administrator and found Lindemann unable to implement such ideas as community participation in action (despite Lindemann's involvement with the Wellesley community).[52] He believed that Lindemann had few friends and many opponents at MGH, including the psychiatrist-turned-neurologist Mandel Cohen. Solomon's policy was to tie all CMHCs to local hospitals. He saw Lindemann lacking the acceptance in his institution needed to be effective at getting MGH to fulfill its half-promises to provide space and in preparing the local community. Solomon took credit for helping Lindemann develop the local CMHC and arranged for the construction of the building. He sought what he thought would be better leadership for CMH at MGH, turning first to John Nemiah (chief of the psychiatric inpatient unit, a psychoanalyst with little understanding of or sympathy for CMH) and then Freddie Frankel (who was concerned with general clinical psychiatry and not the unconventional CMH). He found Raquel Cohen, a former psychiatric resident in Solomon's program, helpful locally: As executive director of the local CMH program for the North Suffolk Mental Health Association, she and her organization were active community partners with Lindemann and the MGH CMH program.

Bernard Bandler

Bernard Bandler was a psychoanalyst, professor of psychiatry and head of the Division of Psychiatry at the Boston University School of Medicine, and superintendent of the Solomon Carter Fuller Mental Health Center. Bandler believed that Lindemann maintained his identity as a

psychoanalyst and applied this background to his social and community psychiatry work.[53] He was unselfish and problem oriented. Bandler
thought Lindemann's innovations were not well understood or credited,
such as when Gerald Caplan—brilliant, visible, and prescient about
sources of support—took the limelight and may not have adequately
acknowledged Lindemann's contributions. Bandler traced Lindemann's
recruiting of Caplan and teaching Raquel as contributing to the perpetu-
ation of his programs. On the other side, he saw psychiatrists accusing Lindemann of having abandoned psychiatry and been taken over by
sociology; and in the psychoanalytic world, he heard people like Helene
(Lindemann's training analyst) and Felix Deutsch and the Boston Psychoanalytic Society criticize and make psychoanalytic interpretations of
Lindemann for having adulterated and abandoned psychoanalysis.

William Ryan

William Ryan was a psychologist and sociologist with a strong commitment to social justice, which he acted upon at the Connecticut community mental health center and Yale University, in mental health projects in
Boston, and in the social psychology department at Boston College.[54],[55]

He noted that Lindemann was criticized personally as being odd,
annoying, hard to get along and work with, a poor administrator and not
orderly and for messing things up by not carrying plans through, having
too much to psychoanalysis as the core of his work, and betraying psychoanalysis by admixing it with social sciences and social applications.
Ryan claimed never to have heard a rejection of his ideas.

Ryan found that Lindemann had great respect for others' integrity,
value, and autonomy. Lindemann was nurturing, supportive, and dis-
cerning of people's strengths. He was given to understanding and sharing openly, including with large groups. He showed different facets of
himself to different people; toward the end of his life, he became more
intimate and introspective.

Ryan thought Lindemann's contributions to mental health problems
stemmed from immediate events, a legacy of gestalt psychology, and
Kurt Lewin. He believed that supra-individual (e.g., community) events
needed consideration, though he had not worked out the theory for this.
He saw psychiatry related to both medicine and social science. He was a
conceptualizer rather than a bringer of ideas to workers in the field. His
thinking was intuitive rather than systematic. He never finished thinking—wanting more input—and never clearly articulated his ideas ver-
bally or in writing; his ideas were inherent in his recounted experiences.
Ryan summed up his judgment as follows:[56]

> how many persons . . . whose lives have been touched in similar ways
> by Erich—as friend, as mentor, as guide, and most important, as an

embodiment of how human a human being can become. . . . His contributions to the theory and practice of mental health are not . . . his crucial legacy. His message was broader; he . . . perceived . . . and [he] taught . . . the fundamental unity of mankind—that our bonds . . . are indivisible, to be bent and distorted only at our great peril. It . . . unifies his own work . . . not merely as a prodigally versatile genius . . . but as a[n] . . . observer and synthesizer of the . . . human condition. [He was] an advocate of peace and justice . . . between nations . . . within a community . . . between persons who are living . . . entwined with one another, and . . . in the heart of each individual.

Benson Snyder

Benson Snyder was the psychiatrist-in-chief at the Massachusetts Institute of Technology, a professor of psychiatry at HMS, and on the staff at MGH. Significant regarding his being considered a member of Lindemann's circle of supporters of social psychiatry was Snyder's book *The Hidden Curriculum* (1970), which is about the culture of MIT and how students cope with overload through selective neglect:[57]

> Snyder advocates the thesis that much of campus conflict and students' personal anxiety is caused by a mass of unstated academic and social norms, which thwart the students' ability to develop independently or think creatively. These obligations, unwritten yet inflexible, form what Snyder calls the hidden curriculum.[58]

Snyder shared Lindemann's strong concern for the values aspect of mental health. He thought Lindemann was motivated by a religious ideal of making things better for people on earth, based on some personal religious background.[59] He thought this was consistent with the Unitarian/Universalist Church in Wellesley, which, with some Roman Catholic interest, supported the HRS. He thought Lindemann appreciated the individual's values, categories, and frame of reference as well as reality issues. This contrasted with the bureaucratic development of CMH and HRS toward enhancing the individual's sense of competence and success via financial and ego gain. And he saw Gerald Caplan's mental health consultation model as manipulative, insulating the consultees from client data and subjecting and molding them to the consultant's categories, including denying real feelings about real problems.

Because Lindemann was not out to build an empire, he did not develop a political base. His effect was evanescent except in influencing individuals who respected him: Leonard Duhl, Benson Snyder, Robert Felix, Jeffrey Vickers, and Grete Bibring. In contrast, Gerald Caplan did develop political and recognition bases and packaged and disseminated Lindemann's ideas. The Space Cadets provided an arena in which to share ideas, a persisting communication network, and stimulation for project funding such as the West End Project.

John Seeley

John Seeley was a sociologist involved in many research projects in community organization and community mental health in the United States and Canada. Lindemann found in him shared ideals, warm mutual appreciation, and a validator of the ideas that Lindemann and his collaborators were developing. This comrade in arms in the battle for CMH saw Lindemann as so broad in his perspective that he made others uncomfortable in not being able to categorize him. He was not good at expounding his ideas and was reluctant to give them finality in writing. In a note to Lindemann dated October 1961 during a meeting of the Space Cadets, Seeley wrote, "Erich: I think the real truth is that you are a member in some sense of 'a heavenly city' in whose behalf you everywhere intervene. Why not see it so?, define the city?, rejoice in it?".[60]

Lindemann spoke but did not press his ideas; he made gentle, tentative suggestions, stemming from his clinical habit. He was uncertain in his self-esteem and regarding of others' acceptance of his position. His gentleness made him vulnerable to negative reactions, and ultimately, he was underestimated and inadequately remembered. Gerald Caplan gets more credit for expounding his ideas. Lindemann tended toward a paternal relationship with his intimates; in this, Seeley thought he was disappointed in Caplan, puzzled by Marc Fried's relative "sociologism", but was fondly understood by such as Herbert Gans, Leonard Duhl, Benson Snyder, and Seeley.

Leonard J. Duhl

Leonard Duhl, special assistant in several departments of the US federal government and later professor of psychiatry and urban planning in the University of California, was one of the people Lindemann was closest to in terms of ideology, perspective, and values. He was one of those in the extra-university national and international world whom Lindemann became closer to in sharing his ideas as he was alienated from his work world.

Duhl saw Lindemann as a secret mystic, hiding this until he discovered that Duhl, too, was interested. He knew much about Rudolf Steiner and German mysticism and about Goethe and his values expressed through *Faust*. He also had an unorthodox perspective on psychoanalysis. These contributed to his feeling odd and unique. He did not believe that he had a significant impact on the field of psychiatry, as opposed to helping individual patients, and looked for his immortality through having his ideas carried on by others rather than through public credit; Duhl had to demonstrate evidence that Lindemann was valued.

Duhl thought Lindemann's success was more through his influence on others and bearing witness to his beliefs through actions and identity rather than by reaching the top of hierarchies.[61] His knowledge of neurology, psychiatry, physiology, and psychoanalysis gave him the insight necessary to a higher level of understanding as well as the ability to deal with the real world. Without this grounding, one is mystical, unfocused, and ineffectual. Lindemann's progressive growth into "higher consciousness" made him poorly understood and appreciated by more-mundane minds, and he gradually lost the ability to return to dealing concretely and directly with mundane affairs.

Duhl saw the new ideal state with which Lindemann was concerned as beyond individuality, though individuality must be attained in order to progress to this interdependence. Lindemann creates a problem for those who have not attained this perspective. Some can appreciate him as a leader into this new state, while others may be unprepared and blame him for the changes that follow from his ideas. Understanding this state requires intuition rather than knowledge—Lindemann refers to "spirituality". Thus, he is drawn toward understanding and appreciative colleagues rather than to institutions (such as Harvard University). This perspective is one way of understanding the expansion of Lindemann's ideas and the strong reactions to him in both directions.

These evaluations of Lindemann vary between commentators and are mixed within individual commentators. Three factors about Lindemann seem to account for these variations: his theory and programs, his ideals, and his personality and relationships. Some admired and loved all three, seeing them as a consistent whole. Some were repelled by all three, seeing them as alien, undesirable, and uncomfortable. And some teetered between appreciating some and regretting others. Certainly, the strong reactions that he evoked speak to the strength of Lindemann's expression of his ideas and the impression that he made on his surroundings.

Henrik Blum Administrative Consultation

Henrik Blum had a unique opportunity to review Lindemann's professional and managerial function.[62] In 1948, he was a student at the HSPH, where he took Lindemann's course on mental health. While he was at first hesitant about Lindemann's appearance, he became captivated by him, including his ability to put a patient at ease with intimate conversation inside an amphitheater. Blum then developed a mental health program at the Contra Costa County, California Public Health Department, which was similar to HRS, though Blum claimed to be ignorant of HRS. (Yet the psychiatrist wife of Warren Vaughan [who also spent time at HSPH and MGH as a follower of Lindemann and then sought to implement his principles in the Massachusetts DMH] later directed the Contra Costa County mental health program and then the health department as a whole, and Erich Lindemann consulted with her department after his retirement from MGH and HMS.) In 1951, Leonard Duhl spent two years at the Contra Costa County department as a psychiatric resident and junior health officer. He brought news of others involved in CMH and later developed the Space Cadets, including both Lindemann and Blum.

In October 1959, Duhl arranged an invitation to Blum to return to MGH as a consultant, with the intention of offering him a professorship at HMS; teaching and administration functions at MGH, McLean Hospital, and HRS; and a working relationship with Gerald Caplan at HSPH. Lindemann wrote,[63]

> Your role here would be that of a resource person to whom many of us can turn with questions concerned with administrative problems in the mental health area. Not only do we have our three field programs in community mental health, we are also vitally concerned with making the best contribution to the development of a large hospital in the direction of becoming more and more of a Health Center. We are particularly interested in the possibility of designing a mental health maintenance program for the incoming population of middle class and upper middle class people which will be located in the relocation area around the hospital. . . . I have talked with Hugh Leavell [Professor of Public Health Practice, HSPH], . . . [who] will be happy to receive you at the department of Public Health Practice. . . . He also was very favorable in connection with any plans which we might have for long range developments in the future. At the hospital you will, of course, be a staff member in our mental health service pro tem.

After brief consideration, Blum and his wife decided not to accept this invitation and to move to Boston. Instead, he accepted Lindemann's request for consultation to ameliorate his problems by improving his administration.

Administration was a problem for Lindemann. He feared being a failure in his work, as his father was. Lydia Dawes remembered the following:[64]

> But he came to see me after he was made professor, and he sat there, and he said, "Gibbie, I wish I hadn't done it". He was just about crying. He said, "It's the wrong thing for me". I said, "Eric, I told you that, but your wife forced you into it, didn't she?" "Yes, she did" he said. And I said, "Now you've got to the pinnacle of power, get away from it". He said, "I'm going to be miserable"; he said, "I hate it" (p. 73), and he did hate it. He was never like he was after that, he was

always sort of . . . miserable and not full of life the way he was. He did his work, but it wasn't the way I knew him. Bouncing and full of all kinds of ideas, and wanting to try things out.

He tried to make the Psychiatry Department a warm family (his mother's contribution) and was uncomfortable with and avoided ambition and aggression in himself and others. He learned some of these skills in informal weekly sessions with Gerald Caplan. He was best respected as a teacher (the guru role he most identified with): a gifted interviewer who used multiple frames of reference and creativity. He championed the social sciences in the HMS, which was resisted by those threatened by the blurring of disciplinary boundaries. He was anxious as a national and international speaker but was charismatic and keyed into audience concerns and reactions.

Blum's analysis came from his human relations rather than administrative expertise. He saw Harvard University characteristically choosing Lindemann because it wanted the brightest, shiniest, best, smartest person to bring the most money without a clear programmatic goal. Lindemann had shown outstanding ideas, creative thinking, personal warmth, and appreciation by students. (Note that some supporters in the selection process knew and appreciated his interests.) He did the same with his subordinates, who believed that they were chosen as outstanding to follow their own interests, which they did without interference from Lindemann. Lindemann resented their failure to follow his interests and defer to him and became depressed at feeling that he was an inadequate administrator.

Lindemann was anxious at conflict, was indecisive, feared discussion, could not talk things over and resolve them, and let things drag on until they blew up. An example was his conflict with George Saslow, stemming from his inability to face Saslow's hard stance and style and his divergent direction. Lindemann could not definitively settle their different expectations about Saslow's taking over administrative authority, which lead to a major conflict. This contributed to his wish for administrative consultation, naively thinking that administrative techniques would solve his problems.

After his orthodox scientific accomplishments, Lindemann believed that it was time to let loose his unorthodox creativity. He wanted to change the HMS's/MGH's cold atmosphere to one better for staff and community. He was unhappy and felt like a failure because people did not pay attention and follow his views but followed their own tracks without caring about service and teaching. He was involved with residents in a firm but nonpunitive way, slowly redirected the department, bringing in Gerald Caplan with effective organization and writing, bringing visitors from around the world, and giving new meaning to psychiatry, and HRS inspired others—such as the state of California health department program. His talks were wildly popular, but when transcribed from recordings, they were ordinary. Lindemann blamed the recording equipment and continually bought new ones. Blum had to convince him that his success was because of the empathetic human context.

Lindemann was not a bad administrator, but rather, when he was appointed, he fit his organization and zeitgeist. In this way, organizations work beautifully under "incompetent" administrations. Federal money was easily available for new ideas like HRS, and inspired discussion of CMH programs in medical schools around the US (including Baylor and Pittsburgh). However, Lindemann allowed clerks to direct him, did not keep things tidy, failed to come to definitive understandings, and treated subordinates as patients without ultimatums. His style supported a good department: while "running a tight ship" is often equated with good administration, it would not have worked with his independent subordinates. Lynn Olson offered a similar understanding when writing of John Gilbert Winant, Governor of New Hampshire, chairperson of the Social Security Administration Board, and US ambassador to Great Britain during World War II:[65]

> By all accounts, he was a terrible administrator, the despair of his staff and the other (U.S. Social Security) board members for his inefficiency and lateness. His desk was piled high with letters awaiting his signature, the room outside his office crammed with people waiting to see him; his filing system consisted of stuffing important papers in his pockets. But even Winant's severest critics acknowledged that he was an extraordinary leader, a visionary with the ability to inspire. "He was, beyond any shadow of a doubt, one of the great characters in American public life during the past twenty years", declared Frank Bane, Social Security's first executive director. "Few people have made as significant an impression upon government as it should be, as did Governor Winant".

Many of the psychiatry staff members couldn't care less: They did not understand or value CMH, did not get their financial support from the department, had many interests, and were chosen for their psychiatric rather than CMH expertise. They deferred appropriately to their great chief but did their own things. He was criticized by those who wanted him to fight for them and praised by those who wanted to be left alone except for consultation as needed (which was Lindemann's style) and felt supported when he appreciated their accomplishments.

Blum found no hostility to Lindemann in the MGH administration: Dean Clark (the general director) was unorthodox in his thinking and sympathetic and supportive of Lindemann's letting people do their own things, and Ellsworth Neumann, the associate director, was supportive. At MGH, psychiatry and public health were held in low repute: "They seemed to not understand or think what he was doing was important, and he just really had move over to the community side totally". His support came more from the HSPH, whose students would not go to the MGH, because of the atmosphere, including the awful way that patients were treated. NIMH funded CMH in the amount of $1–$2 million per year, making Lindemann feel supported. Later in Lindemann's MGH career, national sentiment changed, including de-emphasizing social and mental health needs and those of disadvantaged populations. This made NIMH support less dependable and direct: A letter on April 29, 1964, from Robert H. Felix, MD, director of the NIMH, to Lindemann informed him of organizational changes: the Professional Services Branch (Leonard Duhl's appointment) was eliminated, and Duhl moved to the Planning Office in the Office of the Director. The Social Grants Review Committee was eliminated, and the NIMH contact person for Lindemann's projects was no longer Leonard Duhl but Dr. Thomas Gladwin, Consultant in the Social Science and Community Research and Services Branch (Duhl worked with him).[66]

Despite Lindemann's collaboration with the clergy, the Harvard Divinity School feared that he would be overwhelming and that they might lose some of their faculty members. When Blum arranged a meeting with some Divinity School professors and 30 mature students, Lindemann carried them away in their own field of thinking.

Lindemann's resistance to Blum's findings until a daylong review at the end of his consultation was consistent with his style of avoiding confrontation. He was confronted with the conclusion that his subordinates would not change unless he required their attendance at an administrative meeting at which they would have to accept a new set of expectations and goals or be fired. Lindemann acknowledged that he could not fire staff members and could not bring in a tough administrator to do so. Therefore, he had to accept staff's independent accomplishments and establish consistency in his beliefs, communications, and reactions to other's behavior and their functioning in a way that was comfortable for him. "The person has to learn to live within [their] own style". Blum was concerned that Elizabeth Lindemann hated him because of his findings about Lindemann; instead, they accomplished a long, friendly review of his recommendations, which brought Lindemann relief.

Later, Lindemann wrote supporting Blum's promotion to become the professor of public health at the University of California School of Public Health:[67] "Dr. Blum was a most helpful consultant and then lent me a hand in achieving a considerable reorganization of our administrative program".

The important lesson from Blum's administrative consultation with Lindemann is less a critique of Lindemann's performance than a generalizable commentary on the importance of personality in the development of programs and movements. This is not to say the individual makes the program or movement; historical environmental forces compose the tide. Individual personality is a semi-intractable factor that adds flavor to them and helps determine the outcome of the efforts of individuals as they operate in their social and historical contexts.

Notes

1. Etheredge, Lloyd S., *A World of Men: The Private Sources of American Foreign Policy* (Cambridge, MA: The MIT Press, 1978).
2. Ryan, William, interview by David G. Satin at Ryan's office in Boston College, Boston, MA, 12/14/1979. [Erich Lindemann Collection, David G. Satin, Newton, MA]
3. Anonymous review of paper Satin, David: "The Humanist as Revolutionary in Psychiatry: The Case of Erich Lindemann" submitted to *Archives of General Psychiatry*. [professional papers, David G. Satin, MD; Lindemann Collection, Center for the History of Medicine, Francis A. Francis A. Countway Library of Medicine, Harvard Medical School, Boston, MA]
4. Anonymous review of paper Satin, David: "The Humanist as Revolutionary in Psychiatry: The Case of Erich Lindemann", submitted to *Hospital and Community Psychiatry*. [professional papers, David G. Satin, MD; Lindemann Collection, Center for the History of Medicine, Francis A. Francis A. Countway Library of Medicine, Harvard Medical School, Boston, MA]
5. Peabody, Francis Weld, 1926, *ibid.*, quoted in 11/6/63 "Confidential Draft, Report of the Joint Ad Hoc Committee Appointed to Examine the Harvard-MGH Posture in Medicine and to Recommend a Successor to Dr. Walter Bauer as Jackson Professor of Clinical Medicine and Chief of Medical Services at the Massachusetts General Hospital", pp. 10–11. [folder "Correspondence 1963", Box IIIA 1–3, Lindemann Collection, Center for the History of Medicine, Francis A. Countway Library of Medicine, Boston, MA]
6. Olson, Lynn, *Citizens of London: The Americans Who Stood With Britain in Its Darkest, Finest Hour* (New York: Random House Trade Paperbacks, 2010), pp. 20–21.
7. [folder "Misc L", Box IIIA 1–3, Lindemann Collection, Center for the History of Medicine, Francis A. Countway Library of Medicine, Boston, MA]
8. Gifford, Sanford, "History of Boston and New England Psychoanalysis", interview at the Peter Bent Brigham Hospital, Boston, MA by David G. Satin, 3/29/1979. [Erich Lindemann Archive, David G. Satin, Newton, MA]
9. Gates, Philip, child psychiatrist and analyst at the MGH and James Jackson Putnam Children's Center, also passed on criticisms of Lindemann as a poor administrator, disorganized, and who polarized people by giving the same assignment to two and thus causing conflict. Interview by David G. Satin at the Social Security Administration office in Boston, MA, 3/1979. [Erich Lindemann Collection, David G. Satin, Newton, MA]
10. Farrell, Jean, 4/25/1981, *ibid.*
11. Farrell, Jean [Elizabeth Lindemann files—file #119, Erich Lindemann Collection, David G. Satin files, Newton, MA]
12. Lindemann, Erich, letters to Knowles, John H., 2/12,3/21/1963. [folder "Dr. John Knowles, Medical Director—MGH", Box IIIA 4 (I-Ma), Erich Lindemann Collection, Center for the History of Medicine, Francis A. Countway Library of Medicine, Boston, MA]
13. Chester M. Jones letter to Lindemann thanking him for a contribution to the MGH fund in Jones's name, with the handwritten note "And thanks

for many years of help and friendship", 10/28/1957. [folder "Misc. Correspondence H,I,J 1956–57", Box IIIA 1–3, Lindemann Collection, Center for the History of Medicine, Francis A. Countway Library of Medicine, Boston, MA]

14. Rosenberg Pearl, PhD, quoted in Kelly, James G., "In Honor of Erich Lindemann", *American Journal of Community Psychology* 12 no. 5: 511–536 (p. 534) (1984). [file #121, Box XII #2, Lindemann Collection, Center for the History of Medicine, Francis A. Countway Library of Medicine, Harvard Medical School, Boston, MA]

15. Nemiah, John C., interview by David G. Satin at Beth Israel Hospital 9/21/1978. [caddy 5, box 5, X, Lindemann Collection, Rare Books Department, Countway Library of Medicine, Boston, MA]

16. Nemiah, John C., psychiatrist-in-chief, Beth Israel Hospital; HMS professor of psychiatry, "In Honor of Erich Lindemann", *American Journal of Community Psychology* 12 no. 5: 511–536 (1984). [folder "Kelly, James G"., David G. Satin files, Newton, MA]

17. Those critical of Lindemann's administrative skills or ideological focus could quote psychiatry department members critical of his administrative function, as in White, Benjamin V., 1984, *ibid.*, Ch. 9, p. 35.

18. White, Benjamin V., *Stanley Cobb: A Builder of the Modern Neurosciences* (Boston, MA: The Francis A. Countway Library of Medicine, 1984) (references to manuscript form).

19. Nemiah, John C., "Erich Lindemann", in Ch. 18 "Psychiatry Service", in Castleman, Benjamin, Crockett and David C., Sutton, S.B. (eds.), *The Massachusetts General Hospital 1955–1980* (Boston, MA: Little Brown, 1983), pp. 168–175:

> But Lindemann's emphasis on the stress resulting from changes in human relationships had effects on his scientific thinking and activities that went far beyond the arena of the general hospital. . . . For this reason Lindemann directed his efforts away from the clinical activities of the hospital, and, with the help of a generous award from the Grant Foundation, he created the Wellesley Human Relations Service, the prototype of the modern community mental health center. Indeed, Lindemann may with justice be considered one of the prime movers and originators of the mental health movement that changed the face of American psychiatry during the 1960s and 1970s.
>
> By the time Lindemann was appointed chief of Psychiatry to succeed Stanley Cobb at the MGH he was already thoroughly entrenched in his work at the Wellesley Human Relations Service (the HRS), and it was perhaps that fact more than any other that determined the future course of the MGH Psychiatry Service for good and for ill. Established primarily as a clinical research and teaching unit, the service under Stanley Cobb had nonetheless developed a tradition of providing psychiatric care for the population who looked to the MGH for diagnosis and treatment. As Lindemann took over the reins, there was a strong potential for the development of the hospital-based service along these lines, as general hospital psychiatry and psychiatric residency training programs were strengthened throughout the country. . . . Although Lindemann's interests and research activities were already following a different direction, he recognized the need for strong leadership in the clinical area, and one of his earliest moves was the appointment of George Saslow as clinical director. According to Avery Weisman [psychiatry department staff member hostile to Lindemann]. . . . "In some respects he would have been an ideal complement for Lindemann, had the arrangement worked

out. When Saslow found that Lindemann encouraged him to make decisions and then would fail to support him on grounds that he was usurping authority, he went to the Dean, protested, made demands, and lost his case. After his departure Lindemann never filled the post of Clinical Director; instead he chose three comparatively junior staff men as his lieutenants—John Nemiah (inpatient), Peter Sifneos (outpatient), and Gardner Quarton (teaching) [actually research]. I was appointed to be in charge of consultation/liaison work on a very part-time basis. . . . That the department functioned with reasonable smoothness and productivity can be attributed to their inability to do a mediocre job". . . . After Saslow's departure the various clinical units continued to function under the guidance of the several unit chiefs who formed an informal but cooperative federation under the rather remote direction of Lindemann himself. Although this may have somewhat weakened the overall strength of psychiatry in the hospital. . . . it provided considerable autonomy to the unit chiefs . . . that enabled each to mature and grow professionally and academically. Lindemann added two important clinical units as a result of his concern for preventive and community psychiatry. An Alcoholism Clinic was created with the help of state funding under the leadership of Alfred Ludwig and later of Morris Chafetz when Ludwig moved to a similar position at the Peter Bent Brigham Hospital. Even more significant was the organizing of the Acute Psychiatric Service (APS). Lindemann recognized an opportunity to intervene early in emotional disorders during the initial crisis phase of the development of the illness, with a view to preventing the often chronic sequelae through prompt and intensive treatment of the patient during the acute stage of illness. When [Fred] Frankel, in the early sixties, turned his attention to the development of a state community mental health center, [Morris] Chafetz became the first formal head of the APS. The eventual acquisition of funds to build the Tilton Building contiguous to the Emergency Ward for the care of patients with alcohol problems provided the opportunity to create space specifically designated for . . . the APS, . . . a provider of cares for all kinds of psychiatric emergencies . . . that became a model for . . . the community mental health movement. . . . Even before the formal passing of the congressional CMHC act, Harry Solomon, then Commissioner of Mental Health of the Commonwealth of Massachusetts, had been setting up mental health centers within the state. High on his priority list was what eventually became the Lindemann Community [incorrect: not "Community"] Mental Health Center, a facility for which he and Lindemann had begun planning in the late 1950s. When Frankel arrived from South Africa, a part of his time was spent in the Department of Mental Health, not only assisting the Commissioner in creating outreach psychiatric clinics in the North End [of Boston, MA] but also helping to provide liaison and coordination between the MGH and the DMH in planning for the construction of the building to house the activities of the CMHC designated to fall under the direction of the MGH Department of Psychiatry. Shortly before Lindemann's retirement in 1967 [actually 1965], [John] Nemiah joined in the planning of this facility. . . . Finally, mention must be made of clinical activities that were carried out in the community under the active interest and direction of Lindemann himself. As a counterpart to the suburban setting of the Wellesley HRS, he also created an urban mental health clinic at Whittier Street [actually HSPH under Gerald Caplan], designed to provide help to a portion of Boston's inner-city disadvantaged population. [actually residential rather than clinical and focused on the working class rather than disadvantaged people]. In this endeavor he had the invaluable help of Gerald Caplan who, with Lindemann [limited degree of Lindemann's involvement], ultimately founded and headed the Laboratory for Community Psychiatry under the aegis of the Harvard School of Public Health [actually established only after the move to HMS]—a facility that rapidly developed an international reputation for the teaching and research carried out by its staff. [No mention of the MGH Mental Health Service.]

Despite the excellence of these various community activities, however, there was little contact between them and the hospital-based facilities. Lindemann's energies were largely focused on the former, and the latter . . . functioned relatively autonomously, neither segment of the overall clinical activities being fully aware of the nature of the work of the other. [True: hsp vs. mutual resistance.] . . . Lindemann's arrival as chief of Psychiatry coincided with a major expansion of psychiatric teaching at the Harvard Medical School. At that time there were two academic departments of psychiatry at Harvard, one based at the MGH, the other at the Boston Psychopathic Hospital (later the Massachusetts Mental Health Center) . . . responsibility for the first two years was assigned to the MGH. . . . the major innovation in the revised curriculum was the addition of a series of lectures in the first and second years. Under Lindemann's general direction, Gardner Quarton was responsible for the first-year lectures, which were devoted to a survey of behavioral science, and Nemiah for the lectures in psychopathology given throughout the second year. In addition Nemiah was charged with the administration of the psychiatric participation in the second-year Introduction to the Clinic course, which was taught at all of the general hospitals. . . . The MGH Department of Psychiatry also played a major role in providing month-long clinical clerkships to students in their fourth year. This general program continued in force until the first of the significant medical school revisions of the curriculum in the early seventies effectively dismantled the systematic teaching of psychiatry to medical students. . . . Like the clinical services, the research activities of the department were carried out in isolation from one another, leading to a relative lack of communication among three major groups of . . . clinical research, laboratory research, and the investigation of social and community processes.

In one sense, the whole of Lindemann's professional activities may be considered a form of research, for the Wellesley HRS was set up as an experimental project, and from the experiences gained there many basic principles of group process were discovered, later to be refined in the studies undertaken by the Laboratory of Community Psychiatry. . . . it was not until it was decided, as part of Boston's urban renewal plan, to destroy the West End and relocate its population that an opportunity was provided for a detailed scientific study of a population undergoing the crisis of a major transition. Accordingly, fortified by another large award from the Grant Foundation [actually NIMH funds were more direct], Lindemann gathered around him a team of social scientists, including Paul Hare and Marc Fried, to study the behavior of some 12,000 West End inhabitants before, during, and after the stress of losing their traditional homes and surroundings. Unfortunately, the findings from this study were never published in a detailed systematic monograph [true, though Gans "Grieving for a Lost Home" and Fried "The World of the Working Class" were published], but it became clear from the extensive investigations that the form of urban renewal to which the West End was subjected was a major psychologic trauma to many of the individuals who were forced to move. In this sense the project, a pioneering venture of its kind, provided significant guidelines for those responsible for later programs of urban renewal. . . . Most of the clinical research carried out during Lindemann's tenure was done without funding and accomplished through the systematic recording and analysis of data derived from observations made during the clinical activities [true: res funding increased greatly under EL]. . . . Lindemann was a brilliant clinician, observer, and theoretician, who despite his unique talents as a clinical psychiatrist turned his attention to group, community, and social processes. Here his genius for seeing familiar facts in a new light led him to develop original formulations and theories that provided the basis of what later became the Community Mental Health Movement. He had a peculiar knack for stimulating those who worked with him to amplify his basic observations and ideas, and for those who shared his interests in community process he was an inspiring leader. It is perhaps to be regretted that he abandoned his clinical concerns when he turned to more sociologic investigations, for this meant that, although chief of a clinical service, he did not provide the attention and leadership to the clinical arm of his department that were necessary to provide the cohesion and direction to make it a truly strong and effective organization. [EL used it as platform for humanistic reform of medicine.] Given what appears to be a fundamental incompatibility between the approaches of clinical and community psychiatry, perhaps this was inevitable, and certainly many of us, who were enabled to grow and to develop our own interests as members of the clinical hospital staff during his chairmanship, are grateful for the opportunities he afforded us.

(pp. 169–74)

20. Sifneos, Peter, interview by David G. Satin at the Department of Psychiatry, Beth Israel Hospital, 10/1/1978 and 11/10/1978. [caddy 6, Box 4, X, Lindemann Collection, Center for the History of Medicine, Countway Library of Medicine, Boston, MA]

21. Letter from Peter Sifneos to Lindemann, 4/21/1959. [folder "Correspondence 1959", Box IIIA 1–3, Lindemann Collection, Center for the History of Medicine, Francis A. Countway Library of Medicine, Boston, MA]

22. Frankel, Fred, interview by David G. Satin at the Department of Psychiatry, Beth Israel Hospital, Boston, MA, 11/24/1978. [box 4, X, Lindemann Collection, Rare Books Department, Countway Library of Medicine, Boston, MA]

23. Weisman, Avery, interview by David G. Satin on 6/16/1978. [caddy6, box 4, X, Erich Lindemann Collection, Center for the History of Medicine, Francis A. Countway Library of Medicine, Boston, MA]

24. For example, Lindemann, Erich, letter to Belien, Ivan C., chairperson of the GAP Committee on Preventive Psychiatry, 2/23/1955, soon after he accepted the position of chief of the MGH Psychiatry Service: "For a fellow like myself who is not exactly a born administrator the new job has not been an unmixed blessing". [folder "GROUP FOR THE ADVANCEMENT OF PSYCHIATRY (GAP) 1954—", Box IIIA6 Da GAP, Erich Lindemann Collection, Center for the History of Medicine, Francis A. Countway Library of Medicine, Boston, MA]

25. Farrell, Jean, interviews by David G. Satin at Farrell's apartment in Boston on 8/22/1978 and at the Countway Library of Medicine on 4/25/1981. [Erich Lindemann Collection, David G. Satin, Newton, MA]

26. "Sideline view of Erich Lindemann" by Avery Weisman, in "Erich Lindemann", in Ch. 18 "Psychiatry Service", in Castleman, Benjamin and

Crockett, David C., Sutton, S.B. (eds.), *The Massachusetts General Hospital 1955–1980* (Boston, MA: Little Brown, 1983), pp. 168–175:

> Everyone has a store of Lindemann anecdotes, most of which, I think, have their punchline in showing Erich as the forgetful savant, bewildered by everyday responsibilities, trying to be a good guy, but failing ludicrously.
>
> . . .
>
> Even after these many years, two questions are still alive: Why was Erich Lindemann chosen? Why did he accept? Those who really knew Erich came to see the man beneath the ruddy cheeks, piping voice, and Father Christmas image. He was capable of giving and taking away, of showing interest, and then forgetting all about it. Some of us even had an affection for this visionary, almost spiritual, even as he griped us by falling prey to those whom we considered opportunists. He was a spellbinder on the podium because he had a knack for simplifying complex issues with a colorful phrase or a dramatic formulation which everyone could understand. This gift had its drawbacks. For those who looked for simple answers, particularly colleagues who didn't want to be bothered with the metaphysical ideas promulgated by other psychiatrists. Erich's talent, eloquence, and eagerness for acceptance were an irresistible combination. Perhaps this contributed to his selection.
>
> Erich knew that he was not an administrator, that he was not by nature one to lead the troops, to battle it out, and to enjoy political frays. In later years he once told me that the offer had been too attractive; one did not turn down a Harvard professorship lightly. [vs. influential pulpit he sought] In my opinion, he never got over feeling like a foreigner, or a misfit. Consequently, he remained very sensitive, long-suffering, and quick to anger—at his friends. He tried to please everyone and, of course, failed. . . . I suppose it was discouraging to Erich through the years; I know that at the time of retirement, he became depressed, and wondered if he had accomplished anything at all.
>
> (p. 175)

27. Hackett, Thomas P., interview by David G. Satin at the MGH, 11/30/78. [Erich Lindemann Collection, David G. Satin, Newton, MA]

28. Clark, Eleanor, interview by David G. Satin, 7/14/1978. [caddy 1, Box 4, X, Lindemann Collection, Center for the History of Medicine, Francis A. Countway Library of Medicine, Boston, MA]

29. von Felsinger, John M., interviewed at 323 McGuinn Hall, Boston College, by David G. Satin, 9/8/1978. [caddy 2, Box 4, X, Lindemann Collection, Center for the History of Medicine, Francis A. Countway Library of Medicine, Boston, MA]

30. Kelly, James G., "In Honor of Erich Lindemann", *American Journal of Community Psychology* 12 no. 5: 511–536 (1984). [file #121, box XII #2, Lindemann Collection, Center for the History of Medicine, Francis A. Countway Library of Medicine, Harvard Medical School, Boston, MA]

31. Hall, Elizabeth Cobb, wife of Stanley Cobb, Lindemann's original chief and predecessor as chief of the MGH Psychiatry Service: telephone interview by David G. Satin, 6/6/1979. [caddy 3, box 4, X, Lindemann Collection, Center for the History of Medicine, Francis A. Countway Library of Medicine, Boston, MA]

32. Berry, George Packer, interview by David G. Satin by telephone to Berry's home in Princeton, NJ, 11/2/1979. [caddy 1, box 4, X, Lindemann Collection, Center for the History of Medicine, Francis A. Countway Library of Medicine, Boston, MA]

33. White, Benjamin V., 1984, *ibid.*
34. Cobb, Stanley, MGH Chief of Psychiatry *emeritus*: Correspondence with George Packer Berry, Dean of the Harvard Medical School, 1963. [Erich Lindemann Collection, Center for the History of Medicine, Francis A. Countway Library of Medicine, Boston, MA]
35. White, Benjamin V., 1984, *ibid.*
36. White, Benjamin V., 1984, *ibid.*, p. 8.
37. Berg, Robert L., MD, of the MGH associates—physicians with courtesy appointments at MGH: Letter to Dean A. Clark, MD, MGH general director. [folder "MGH 1956–6/61", Erich Lindemann Collection, Center for the History of Medicine, Francis A. Countway Library of Medicine, Boston, MA]
38. Morris, Laura, Interview by David G. Satin on 11/19/1979. [caddy 5, Box5, X, Erich Lindemann Collection, David G. Satin, Newton, MA]
39. Bragg, Robert, interview by David G. Satin at the Wellesley Human Relations Service, 7/13/1979. [Erich Lindemann Collection, David G. Satin, Newton, MA]
40. Cope, Oliver: interview by David G. Satin at the MGH, 11/21/1978. [Erich Lindemann Collection, David G. Satin, Newton, MA]
41. Butler, Alan interviewed by David G. Satin by telephone to his home on Cape Cod, Massachusetts, 12/8/1078. [Erich Lindemann Collection, David G. Satin, Newton, MA]
42. Barbour, Josephine, and Clark, Eleanor, MGH Social Service Department, letter to Knowles, John H., and from Knowles to Talbort, Nathan B. (chief of the MGH Children's Medical Service), 6/23, 4/1964: objection to and cancelation of the transfer of the Children's Social Service office to the Children's Medical Service.
43. Neumann, Ellsworth, interviewed by David G. Satin at his office in the Rockefeller Foundation, New York City, 4/27/1979. [caddy 5, box 5, X, Lindemann Collection, Center for the History of Medicine, Francis A. Countway Library of Medicine, Boston, MA]
44. Neumann, Ellsworth, interviewed by David G. Satin at his office in the Rockefeller Foundation, New York City, 4/27/1979. [caddy 5, box 5, X, Lindemann Collection, Center for the History of Medicine, Francis A. Countway Library of Medicine, Boston, MA]. He offered examples:

    > Groups and their leaders feel others don't listen to or understand their goals. The therapeutic administrator finds and points out common denominators for agreement, arranging for people to rectify relationships as if this was spontaneous. A leader may feel put upon by the strongest individuals (of any status) she faced, leading to breakdown and group anarchy. The task is to arrange mutuality of opportunity. For instance a head nurse must make decisions in 40 seconds thought it takes two minutes to develop a relationship. An administrative solution would be to develop a Department Clinical Administrator to relieve the head nurse of half to two-thirds of quick decisions, and leave her with patient-centered decisions. Mrs. Lawrence matched male and female dyads (a parental model), and gave head nurses offices independent of physicians.

45. Schmitt, Francis O., interview by David G. Satin at his home in Weston, MA, 11/30/1978, 4/3/79. [Erich Lindemann Collection, David G. Satin, Newton, MA]
46. Schmitt, Francis O. letter to David G. Satin 10/1/1982. [box XII 1 folder Satin-Bio of E.L., Erich Lindemann Collection, Center for the History of Medicine, Francis A. Countway Library of Medicine, Boston, MA]

47. Caplan, Gerald, letter to Lindemann, Elizabeth B., 6/1/1976. [box XII 2 folder "115a", Erich Lindemann Collection, Center for the History of Medicine, Francis A. Countway Library of Medicine, Boston, MA]

48. Berry, George Packer, 11/2/1979, *ibid.*

49. Berry, George Packer, "Memo on Conversation with Harry C. Solomon" [chairperson of the HMS Department of Psychiatry], conversation 5/29/1956, memo dated 5/30/1956. [folder "Neurology + Psychiatry 1956–65", drawer 6, George Packer Berry Archive, Center for the History of Medicine, Francis A. Countway Library of Medicine, Harvard Medical School, Boston, MA]

50. Ewalt, Jack R., Bullard professor of psychiatry, emeritus, HMS; Director mental health and behavioral sciences service, U.S. Veterans Administration (retired), "In Honor of Erich Lindemann", *American Journal of Community Psychology, 12* no. 5: 513–514 (p. 533) (1984).

51. Ewalt, Jack, 1/26/1979, *ibid.*

52. Solomon, Harry Ceasar, interview by David G. Satin at his home, 6/22/1978.

53. Bandler, Bernard, 8/11/1978, *ibid.*

54. Long, Tom, "William J. Ryan; Fought Bias against the Poor; 78", *The Boston Globe 261*no. 162: A32.

55. Ryan, William, 12/14/1979, *ibid.*

56. Ryan, William, Professor of Psychology, Boston College, "In Honor of Erich Lindemann", *American Journal of Community Psychology 12* no. 5: 511–536 (p. 353) (1984). [folder "Kelly, James G.", David G. Satin files, Newton, MA]

57. News Office, Massachusetts Institute of Technology, "Benson Rowell Snyder, former psychiatrist-in-chief at MIT, dies at 89", 9/5/2012.

58. Wikipedia, the free encyclopedia, http://en.wikipedia.org/wiki/The_Hidden_Curriculum_(book) (1/31/13).

59. Snyder, Benson R., interview by David G. Satin at The Division for Study and Research in Education at the Massachusetts Institute of Technology, 6/16/1978. [caddy6, Box 4, X, Erich Lindemann Collection, Center for the History of Medicine, Francis A. Countway Library of Medicine, Boston, MA]

60. Seeley, John note to Erich Lindemann, 10/1961. [folder "Correspondence 1961", Box IIIA 1–3, Lindemann Collection, Center for the History of Medicine, Francis A. Countway Library of Medicine, Boston, MA]

61. Duhl, Leonard J., recorded thoughts during an automobile trip, 6/22/1974. [Erich Lindemann Collection, David G. Satin, Newton, MA]

62. Blum, Henrik, interviewed by telephone by David G. Satin, 3/23/1979. [caddy 1, Box 4, X, Lindemann Collection, Center for the History of Medicine, Francis A. Countway Library of Medicine, Boston, MA]

63. Lindemann, Erich, letter to Blum, Dr. Henrick L., Health Department, Contra Costa County, CA, 7/15/1959, pp. 1–2. [folder "Blum, Dr. Henrik", Box IIIB1 e2), A-E", Erich Lindemann Collection, Center for the History of Medicine, Francis A. Countway Library of Medicine, Boston, MA]

64. Dawes, Lydia, MD—child analyst, Boston; former researcher, Human Relations Service of Wellesley: Interview 5/7/1973 by Gifford, Sanford, Librarian. Boston Psychoanalytic Society and Institute. [found int folder "Wellesley Human Relations Service", David G. Satin files, Newton, MA]

65. Olson, Lynn, 2010, *ibid.*, pp. 20–21

66. [folder "Correspondence 1964", Box IIIA 1–3, Lindemann Collection, Center for the History of Medicine, Francis A. Countway Library of Medicine, Boston, MA]

67. Lindemann, Erich, letter to Charles E. Smith, MD, dean, 8/3/1962, p. 1. [folder "Blum, Dr. Henrik", Box IIIB1 e2), A-E", Erich Lindemann Collection, Center for the History of Medicine, Francis A. Countway Library of Medicine, Boston, MA]

11 The Ending of the Lindemann Era at Harvard University

The Farewell Banquet

At the farewell banquet for Lindemann on September 25, 1965, one can find the reactions from academic, administrative, and professional practice viewpoints to his contributions, even allowing for the courtesies demanded on such an occasion.[1] It was a crucial event because it was later referred to as evidence of Lindemann's interests and accomplishments.

At the head table sat Erich Lindemann and Elizabeth Lindemann; Robert Ebert, MD (newly appointed dean of HMS), and his wife; Alfred Stanton, MD (psychiatrist-in-chief of McLean Hospital), and his wife, Harriet Stanton; Francis de Marneffe, MD (administrative director of McLean Hospital), and his wife; John Nemiah, MD (acting chief of the MGH Psychiatry Service), and his wife; Mr. John Lawrence (chairperson of the MGH and McLean Hospital Board of Trustees); and Ellsworth Neumann, MD (associate director of MGH). John Knowles, MD, MGH general director, was in Washington, DC, at the time.

Dr. Ebert spoke of the importance of the behavioral and social sciences in the next decade, and he said that Lindemann was the perfect person to work with on this.

Mr. Lawrence said in part the following:

> there is one point that I would like to mention, in my position as a layman trustee and businessman—and that is the tremendous contribution that I feel he has made in what is called Social Psychiatry. The one confusion that exists in the world of business, politics, every other kind of area that you can think of today, challenges the best minds to try to adjust people to the circumstances and the influences. . . . this is a tremendous field, and difficult and complicated as this whole distorted existence has been, in the last ten years, in the next ten years it is going to be extremely more so. Dr. Lindemann is well ahead of his time, we know. He has followed this pursuit with wisdom, with courage and with tremendous drive and vision.
>
> (pp. 11–12)

Dr. Stanton said in part the following:

> Erich has been a student of psycho-pharmacology; he has been a student of the crisis associated with grief; from this he developed, and became a student of, preventive intervention, as a public health worker in psychiatry. And out of this grew Social Psychiatry. . . . it is worth our while to pay attention to the dates in which Erich wrote his first works in these matters: Psychopharmacology was in the 30s, Grief was in the early 40s, Preventive Intervention in the early 50s. As a matter of fact, one of the difficulties we have in understanding Erich's contribution has been that he has been so insufferably far ahead of the rest of us. . . . many of the things that he has seen and advocated have been . . . more successful than made any sense. That is, procedures that he has advocated and developed have been rapidly grasped by a nation which needed them and placed into effect faster than permitted really their grasp. . . . Nor has there been anyone more consistent in saying that these various techniques need systematic exploration, study, appraisal, analysis . . . his initial insistence upon the importance of the social system as a stance from which one might view psychiatric disorders or other personality responses which appear to the unsophisticated to be psychiatric disorders. . . . I would like to nominate Erich as . . . a new kind of teacher. . . [described in] an account by the mathematician Polanyi on how to solve problems when he was trying to establish what he calls the heuristic method." Heuristic reasoning is reasoning not regarded as final and stripped, but as provisional and plausible only, whose purpose is to discover the solution of the present problem. We are often obliged to use heuristic reasoning. We shall attain complete certainty when we shall have attained the complete solution, but before attaining certainty, we must often be satisfied with a more or less plausible guess. We may need the provisional before the final. We need heuristic reasoning as we need scaffolding when we erect a building. Heuristic reasoning is good in itself. What is bad is to mix up heuristic reasoning with rigorous proof. What is worse is to sell heuristic reasoning for rigorous proof". That, Erich has exemplified for us.
>
> (pp. 14–18)

John Nemiah remembered meeting Lindemann in the 1940s when Nemiah was a first-year medical student and participating in research with the interaction chronograph. Then, as resident he was impressed by Lindemann as a "magician" in getting patients to vent their troubles before an audience and to leave feeling better. Under Lindemann the MGH Psychiatry Service increased its range of patient care, the residency program and obtaining accreditation as a three-year program, its participation in all years of medical school teaching, establishing the Stanley Cobb Laboratories for Research in Psychiatry, and developing a close relationship with the DMH such as through collaboration with the Danvers State Hospital and developing plans for working at the Bowdoin Square Mental Health Center. He brought experiences from the HSPH and HRS, including to the West End Project's social science research, joining and collaboration between the staffs of HRS and MGH, and wielding an insidious influence on staff ideas and practices. "I then realized at that point that I was beginning to look beyond the concern of the individual's own internal problem alone, and to see it in a broader social setting . . . slowly and gradually but steadily in all the areas and in all the services on which we deal with patients we have been applying Erich's ideas in practice, after making them our own. I think this is probably the most important thing, Erich, which you have given to us. . . . I am quite confident that in the months and the years ahead, we shall all continue to profit and benefit from your teaching".

(pp. 19–23)

He then read the inscription on the large silver bowl presented to Lindemann:
To Erich Lindemann, MD on the occasion of his retirement as Professor of Psychiatry at the Massachusetts General Hospital, with the deep appreciation and warm affection of the staff of the Psychiatric Service at the Massachusetts General Hospital and at the McLean Hospital. September 20, 1965.

Lindemann's response spoke to his hopes and doubts in his current situation:

"what Dr. Ebert said and what Mr. Lawrence said, and Al and John have said—this was something quite important for me, believe it or not. I was quite discouraged about this Department, and now I can think differently. So you see, being in the field of social psychiatry isn't always just fun" (p. 26). He referred to a picture from the *Saturday Evening Post* "where they were selling psychoanalysis for a quarter's worth at each corner. . . . This said something to me. Maybe they are right. Maybe there ought to be not analysis, but the equivalent of its services for a quarter for all to have. That was one of the starting points of the small modest preoccupation which I happen to have" (p. 27). He recalled Clyde Kluckhohn's (cultural anthropologist) study of waves of witchcraft among Navajo girls paralleling waves of pressure on Navajos from whites: "And then I thought, perhaps there is something, not quite a mental disease— not schizophrenic in a state hospital—perhaps there are some social attitudes and some orientations to your fellow man which can be very pernicious for them which might be a concern for psychiatrists" (pp. 27–8). He recalled an insight: "It doesn't really come from the laboratory—don't kid yourself—sure we are all biologists and we all love our doctors, and we are terribly proud of them, and the MGH has the most brilliant doctors in the world. But there is one form of knowledge to come from the systematic authority of the laboratories. There is another kind of insight and understanding which comes from simple insight at home which stems from person to person in the literature, in the stories which our writers tell, which go from person to person as they tell each other about their children. Over two decades, as we have seen, we have a change not in information but a change in attitude and values. Jack [Seeley] has called this the silent revolution" (p. 28). It applies to the alienation of citizens, desegregation, common experience and objectives with many more people than psychiatry thought to serve. It raises a new challenge for psychiatry to serve people from slums, not exactly our brethren, who demand to be heard. We need a right frame of values to deal with and accept them. "It can be done if we get not only laboratory information but the kind of inner value shift which makes it possible to meet the values of the people. That I began to call social psychiatry. And, I again thought about witchcraft, and began to think that perhaps there are certain social practices by which certain members of society influence in a pernicious and hazardous manner. I began to think that also in some power areas of society, there might be processes going on familiar to us as paranoia in individuals, but collectively paranoid in society in a much more dangerous way, in terms of us all. Then I thought, in our Department surely there were laboratories, but there were also perhaps within the <u>New England Journal</u> something about the A-bomb and something about hazardous aspects of biological warfare which might arise from that. I thought of that as a form of social psychiatry. What we see then is that beyond the clinic, there are waves of concern and waves of possible incidents which all are related to a deep understanding of the human condition. . . . Putting this together, and then taking a bit of a new perspective, one sees the psychiatrist as the doctor throughout the community and in the hospital, as at the Massachusetts General Hospital, in joint partnership with the other caretaking professions. In this partnership, he will look at his own mode of functioning in an entirely new way and will learn to share it with others rather than building barriers around his professional role. . . . [Dr. Ebert] knew that this might be a concern of the Medical School as such far transcending psychiatry, and I have the feeling that perhaps there is indeed a future and perhaps this is not an end. . . . So, all in all, there is room for hope on my part to see you again and to share some more exciting things at the MGH and at Harvard. So don't think you are rid of me yet!"

(pp. 28–31)

A contemporary seconding of Lindemann's campaign for a CMH perspective on mental health education and care was written by Jean Dietz, a journalist interested especially in mental health and social services. On October 3, 1965, she wrote about Lindemann's accomplishments, career development, and retirement (emphasis by Dietz):[2]

"I you are really willing to abide by your conviction that each patient arriving in your orbit of power is only a fragment of a disordered social system, your relationship to the participant in this social system is very much enhanced" Dr. Lindemann told M.G.H. residents. . . . This observation that the crises in peoples' lives are inseparable from the setting, whether home, school, or community, sounds mild enough, even obvious. **Strangely enough, the Lindemann view is still regarded in medical circles as highly controversial, and often attacked.** The M.G.H. department Dr. Lindemann first entered . . . was already accustomed to 'carrying the torch for the human factor' in medicine against resistance on the part of colleagues who even now "think of illness and disease as a matter of orderly disturbance". "Modern psychiatry means effective intervention in the clusters of human beings concerned with the predicament". This should lead the doctor to concern with the family." You will become concerned with the power structure to which the patient belongs, to those people who control his life. . . . **You will become concerned with city planning, the housing which he has, the prospect for advancement in his life situation.** You will not only look common cause in the face and say—isn't it too bad—there you are". This places the doctor's role squarely in the forefront of social responsibility. He may have to warn the powerful decision makers, Dr. Lindemann essays, "so perhaps the next decision may avoid so many casualties, of a psychiatric kind anyway". **The [West End] study forced the urban renewal people to take a new look at the way subsequent relocations were handled.** It was found the financial aspect of relocation was a relatively minor consideration of the uprooted families. . . . Far more significant . . . was being torn away from a cluster of people upon whom they could depend. . . . Better known among concrete achievements was establishment of the Wellesley Human Relations Center in 1948. . . . The first community mental health center in the United States is now a model for preventive care.

Lindemann was sent out with a mixture of whole-hearted understanding and appreciation and the formality of eulogy. He left with a more-honest-than-usual acknowledgment of the struggles and disappointments that he encountered and a (perhaps wishful) effort to see appreciation and continuation of his mission.

The Petition

There were ongoing criticisms and complaints from within the MGH. Some continued resentment of Lindemann's admitting the social sciences and scientists into the medical citadel, as in his farewell banquet talk, when he valued his shared interests with the sociologist John Seeley rather than appreciating the psychiatrists who managed the daily functions of the MGH department.[3] Lindemann was conscious of these hostilities to his program and himself (as Jean Dietz noted) and is said to have retired early for fear of more overt rejection.

A notorious expression of this hostility was a May 1965 petition from some MGH staff members to the ad hoc committee appointed to recommend his successor. It is worth presenting in its entirety:[4]

We, the undersigned, believing that this hospital should achieve and maintain a high level of excellence in the diagnosis and treatment of the mentally ill, are greatly concerned over the choice of a new Chief of Psychiatry at the M.G.H.

We have the following opinions:

(1) That acutely ill psychiatric patients should be cared for in a general hospital.
(2) That ill psychiatric patients with associated medical or surgical illnesses as well as patients with psychiatric symptoms secondary to nonpsychiatric illnesses must be cared for in a general hospital.
(3) That psychiatric leadership must be provided to:

    a) Re-establish in this hospital a spirit of inquiry free of dogma which will allow for enthusiastic investigation of all avenues of approach to the cause and cure of mental illness.

    b) Recruit psychiatrists with medical and neurological training, as well as psychiatric skills, who have an interest in the diagnosis and treatment of mental illness as it is seen in a large general hospital.

    c) Establish an environment in which intensive treatment and responsibility for the welfare of patients, rather than inquiries into the hypothetical cause or causes of psychiatric illness is made the paramount function of the Psychiatric Service.

    d) Encourage the use of physical and chemical methods in the treatment of psychiatric illness.

To accomplish these desiderata, we believe that Dr. Lindemann's successor should have the following qualifications:

(1) He should be trained as a physician, be well grounded in neurology and clinical neurophysiology, and be familiar with the progress being made in the behavioral sciences.
(2) He should have had a wide and varied experience with the treatment of acutely ill psychiatric patients.
(3) He should understand and be prepared to employ all forms of therapy in treating psychiatric disease.
(4) He should not be a member of, nor lend his support to, any school or cult of psychiatry which substitutes "faith" for the scientific method of diagnosing, treating and evaluating the results of treatment of mental illness.

We will be glad to further explain our views concerning the past, present and future of psychiatry at the M.G.H. to members of the ad hoc committee at their invitation.

[Those Who Have Signed the Letter—some on one version and not another]
OFFICERS OF THE GENERAL HOSPITAL

Honorary Physicians and Surgeons [retired]

F. Dennette Adams, MD
Arlie V. Bock, MD
Maurice Fremont-Smith, MD
Joseph Garland, MD
Chester M. Jones, MD [note he collaborated with Lindemann on ulcerative colitis]
Charles S. Kubik, MD
James H.[oward] Means, MD [former chief of the Medical Service]
Frances M. Rackeman, MD
Warren R. Sisson, MD
Henry R. Viets, MD
Paul D.[udley] White, MD [cardiology]

Board of Consultation

John A. Abbott., MD [medicine/neurology]	John Newell, MD
Theodore L. Badger, MD	Helen S. Pittman, MD
Edward B. Benedict, MD	Duncan E. Reid, MD
G. Colket Caner, MD	Howard B. Sprague, MD
Richard Chute, MD	Grantley W. Taylor, MD
Green Fitzhugh, MD	James H. Townsend, MD
E. Parker Hayden, MD	Vernon P. Williams, MD

GENERAL MEDICINE

Patricia Benedict, MD
Edward F. Bland, MD
D.W. Boardman, MD
Caesar Briefer, MD
John W. Cass, Jr., MD
Earle M. Chapman, MD
Milton H. Clifford, MD
James Currens, MD
Briant Decker, MD
William Franklin, MD
Harriet L. Hardy, MD

Reed Harwood, MD
John Homans, MD
Bernard M. Jacobson, MD
John W. Keller, MD
Jacob Lerman, MD
Walter W. Point, MD
Charles L. Short, MD
W[alter]. T. St. Goar, MD
Morton N. Swartz, MD
Arthur L. Watkins, MD
Conger Williams, MD

Neurology

Mandel E. Cohen, MD
Edwin M. Cole, MD
Pierre M. Dreyfus, MD
Peter R. Huttenlocher, MD
Hugo Moser, MD
Ernest H. Picard, MD

David C. Poskanzer, MD
Edward P. Richardson, M>D.
Robert S. Schwab, MD [EEG]
Henry deF. Webster, MD
Gerald F. Winkler, MD

Pediatrics

John P. Connelly, MD
Robert Ganz, MD
Richard B. Kearsley, MD

Dermatology

William R. Hill, MD

GENERAL SURGERY

W. Gerald Austen, MD
Marshall K. Bartlett, MD
Glenn E. Behringer, MD
John F. Burke, MD
Edwin L. Carter, MD
John G. Constable, MD
R. Clement Darling, MD
Gordon A. Donaldson, MD
Edward Hamlin, Jr., MD
John M. Head, MD

Charles E. Huggins, MD
Francis M. Ingersoll, MD
John B. McKittrick, MD
Charles G. Mixter, J., MD
Anthony P. Monaco, MD
George L. Nardi, MD
Edwin W. Salzman, MD
Claude E. Welch, MD
Frank Wheelock, MD

Anesthesia

Henrik H. Bendixen, MD
Phillips Hallowell, MD
Henning Pontoppidan, MD
Donald P. Todd, MD

Neurosurgery

H. Thomas Ballantine, Jr., MD
Hannibal Hamlin, MD
Raymond N. Kjellberg, MD
Jost J. Michelson, MD

Orthopedics

Otto L. Aufranc, MD
William C. Bostick, MD
Edwin F. Cave, MD
Drennan Lowell, MD
William R. MacAusland, Jr., MD

Eugene E. Record, MD
John A. Reidy, MD
Carter R. Rowe, MD
Morten Smith-Peterson, MD
William G. Stewart, Jr., MD

Urology

Sylvester B. Kelley, MD
Walter Kerr, MD
Wyland F. Leadbetter, MD [chief]

Guy W. Leadbetter, Jr., MD
Edward C. Parkhurst, MD

RADIOLOGY

Stanley L. Wyman, MD

Visiting Senior Surgeons

(E&E) [Massachusetts Eye and Ear Infirmary]
Charles H. Allman, MD
John Frasee, MD
John R. Richardson, MD

BLOOD BANK AND TRANSFUSION SERVICE

Morten Grove-Rasmussen, MD

Allan Friedlich, an MGH pediatric cardiologist, articulated more directly this anti-psychoanalytic complaint:[5]

> In common with many of my colleagues, I want to express great concern over the selection of the next Chief of Psychiatry. . . . in many

ways the discrepancy between the need for care and the furnishing of this care has been particularly wide in this field. . . . I would hope that the next Chief would not be so committed to the psychoanalytic school that he was not willing to encourage other avenues of approach, and not eager to establish some critical assessment of results not dependent on whether or not the patient's course substantiated preconceived notions of the mechanism of his disease. . . . it seems essential that the personnel come out more into the mainstream of hospital life, demonstrating actively their capability, interest, and responsibility. . . . I would hope that the new Chief would be an individual with very broad training and interests, willing to encourage approaches both research and therapeutic which were varied in their concept. . . . I hope he would be willing to exert effective leadership in developing the same objectives at the McLean Hospital and . . . free communication and effective co-operation between the staff of the Massachusetts General Hospital and the McLean Hospital.

Several issues are noteworthy:

1. Although this petition deals with Dr. Lindemann's successor, it was formulated and transmitted while he still occupied the positions of MGH chief of service and HMS professor and thus confronted him. The content clearly indicates the wish for the appointment of someone different from Dr. Lindemann, and thus, it is critical of him.
2. It seems unusual for the hospital staff as a whole to try to influence the appointment of a chief of service or a staff member.
3. The petition calls for psychiatry to engage in "enthusiastic investigation of all avenues of approach to the cause and cure of mental illness" but then wants "intensive treatment and responsibility for the welfare of patients, rather than inquiries into the hypothetical cause or causes of psychiatric illness is made the paramount function of the Psychiatric Service". This is a call for a Psychiatry Service that functions solely in the clinical care of patients. Every other medical service (as well as most nursing, social work, rehabilitation, and other services) in the MGH and every other medical school affiliated hospital is charged also with research and teaching. In fact, the joint HMS/MGH Ad Hoc Committee to examine medicine and appoint a new chief of the MGH medical service dated the modern period of medicine at the MGH to Dr. David Edsall's addition of research to clinical care and teaching as the functions of the medical staff.[6] The MGH Committee on Research concurred[7] with the emphatic

recommendations by the first Scientific Advisory Committee which met on December 12th and 13th, 1947—the Committee being comprised of Karl T. Compton, chairperson, Herbert S. Gasser, and Eugene M. Landis, Secretary. The following more specific recommendations were mentioned: #1. That an active program of research is not only desirable but essential if the hospital is to retain effectiveness and leadership in the treatment of patients. . . . 2. . . . That every effort should be made to extend the role of research at the Massachusetts General Hospital beyond its present scope. . . . 3. . . . That clinical investigation should always have the highest priority of importance in the research work of a hospital. . . . 4. That the Massachusetts General Hospital should continue its close association with the academic institutions of Boston but that this association should not inhibit the hospital from making additional independent full time or part time hospital appointments at any level, particularly with respect to the research staff. . . . 5. . . . That thought should be given to an extension of the present insufficient research facilities. . . . 7. That problems such as cancer or other chronic diseases which cut across conventional boundaries would be particularly appropriate for study within the organization of a general hospital. . . . Mr. Crockett stated that all of these recommendations have indeed been carried out and have wrought a tremendous influence on the development of research at the hospital.

Although the petition supports the transfer of psychiatric treatment from large psychiatric institutions to general hospitals, the relegation of the Psychiatry Service to nonacademic patient care sounds like the demotion by the other services that psychiatry feared.

4. In many places they call is for psychiatrists trained as physicians in medicine, neurology, and clinical neurophysiology, and to "encourage the use of physical and chemical methods in the treatment of psychiatric illness" (3.d). It contrasts this with several vague references to freedom from dogma, not belong to any school or cult, and not substitute faith for the scientific method. This seems a biological school's dogmatic rejection of psychoanalysis as a dogmatic school of thought.[8]

Thus, this represents a reproof to Lindemann personally, a rejection of social in favor of biological psychiatric ideology, the implied rejection of psychoanalysis as insubstantial, the exclusion of nonphysicians (such as social scientists), and the view of psychiatry as a clinical practice and not a scientific study.

Thomas Ballantine, a neurosurgeon (who had operated on patients thought to have psychosomatic problems) is credited with circulating the petition.[9] Importantly, there are no signatories from the Psychiatry Service, where there was a dissident faction strongly opposed to and resentful of social psychiatry and the inclusion of social sciences. It has been reported that, in fact, this petition originated in the Psychiatry Service, with the tactical decision that it appear to come from those with less theoretical bias in the field and also not as a rebellion of psychiatry staff members against their superior. It was suggested that Avery Weisman took a leadership role; in fact, he wrote to HMS Dean George Packer Berry offering his criticisms and ideas about Lindemann's successor. Jean Farrell, Lindemann's administrative assistant, remembers Lindemann's upset at an angry confrontation (very rare for Lindemann) with Weisman about this "hate letter".[10]

All in all, this petition was another indicator of the shift in ideology at the MGH, HMS, medicine, and society from social ideology/social responsibility to a biological ideology/individual responsibility. And it was an example of the reactionary form it could take in some quarters.

The Ending of Lindemann's Mission

As Lindemann neared the end of his tenure, MGH thought turned to the state and future of the MGH Psychiatry Service. Senior staff members were called upon to evaluate the contemporary and future directions of their programs. All acknowledged the influence of social and community psychiatry, and most credited Lindemann's leadership and influence:

John Nemiah, often seen as Lindemann's deputy for clinical and training, was practical:[11]

> 6. The new Mental Health Center in the Bowdoin Square area will enable us greatly to expand our service, training, and research activities. At the same time, it will pose many difficult problems for us as we attempt to incorporate these added facilities into our present organizational structure. I feel that it is essential for us to work out the administrative plans involving this new unit so that the center of gravity remains at the Massachusetts General Hospital.

John Lamont, director of the Child Psychiatry Unit, acknowledged community responsibility:[12]

> On the question of which, of these various directions, we should move in the future, I would have only these comments: (1) The trend towards a more responsible commitment to the community, in contrast to the socially isolated treatment of "optimal" cases (who would have done pretty well anyway) is already established beyond reverse, thanks in no small measure to your influence. This will go on anyway. . . . In the recent book put out by the Academy of Child Psychiatry and the APA, of the nine points they count in describing the "optimal" training center in child psychiatry, we fall short in only two: . . . in-patient facilities for disturbed children. Bowdoin Squire answers the latter.

Frank Ervin, researcher in neuropsychiatry, thoroughly endorsed the incorporation of the social sciences:[13]

> The first responsibility of a community general hospital is for the best possible patient care. It is on this base that teaching and research functions must rest (p. 1). . . . III. Research . . . Even less attention has been paid to the importance of environmental influences not uniquely individual, i.e. cultural patterns, social crises, group identity, etc., in determining behavior. It is in this area that Dr. Lindemann has been an important pioneer. While these are many facets to social psychiatry, in pragmatic application to the hospital, it would seem to be increasingly possible to predict aspects of an individual's behavior from information about his cultural, social, and economic background, independent of his unique intra-personal development. Extension of our knowledge in this area and its application to prevention of behavioral disorder, or its rapid control by appropriate social intervention, is most important if we are to deal meaningfully with the problems reflected in mental health statistics (p. 5). . . . Third, building on Dr. Lindemann's start, we must both increase our understanding of social psychiatric issues in our hospital population and the community from which it comes. This development calls for close collaboration with the [public health] program started by Dr. Sidel and careful delineation of the areas of appropriate concern for the two groups and their proper interface. In addition, it requires a senior staff member of superior competence as a social scientist. . . . Social and biological sciences in the past decade . . . have indicated routes to a systematic understanding of human behavior and the MGH should be in the forefront of this exciting period described in different context as a "race between the success of the behavioral sciences and nuclear physics" (p. 6–7). . . . It is necessary . . . that the clinical program within the [Massachusetts General] hospital have active and reciprocal links with McLean, the new Bowdoin Square Hospital, local guidance centers, etc. These relationships should provide a base for optimal planning for community needs. . . . For MGH, consideration of such a development . . . must take into account the geographic contiguity of the Bowdoin Square facility, state plans, and the staff relationships involved.

Jack Mendelson, a researcher in biological psychiatry, credited Lindemann with supporting this field:[14] He reviewed the research in his laboratory and commented:

> Under your leadership the Department of Psychiatry has developed and stressed a scholarly approach toward the study of human behavior. I sincerely hope that the future direction of the department will

continue to foster an eclectic program of teaching, investigation, and service.

The organizational chart for the MGH Department of Psychiatry in Lindemann's last full year of tenure illustrated the following:[15]

Psychiatric Services (in-patient, out-patient, etc.)
Psychiatry in Medical Care (pediatrics, medical outpatient, acute psychiatry service, rehabilitation, alcoholism)
Division of Community Services
West End Project, Mental Health Service—
Peter Sifneos MD, Laura Morris MSW, Gerald Caplan MD, part time consultation—Paul Hare PhD sociology, Michael von Felsinger PhD psychology;
Human Relations Service of Wellesley-
Robert Bragg MD, Robert Misch PhD, Helen Herzan MD, Alvin Simmons PhD M.Sc.Hyg.;
Mental Health Consultation to Professional Groups in: Hospitals, Community,
Government, and Other Countries
Erich Lindemann MD, Morris Chafetz MD, Robert Misch PhD

Lindemann looked back at it with more critical realism but still with (perhaps somewhat doubtful and plaintive) hope. He laid out his goals/ideals for MGH psychiatry as a case study for psychiatry in general but in the process gently acknowledged its conflict with other ideologies and hospital services and the stress and disappointment that this engendered. This summary came from his last address to incoming psychiatric residents:[16]

MGH

MGH-Harvard psychiatry "is destined for survival in one form or another" (p. 1). MGH suggests excellence, does not know what to do with mediocrity, which does not work. Chiefs of services are extremely watchful of one another that each service remains excellent; it is a very visible place watched by other places as a model "and possibly also to find fault with it if one can because that makes a lot of people feel good. Both things happen" (p. 1–2). This leads to self-competition, tension, and discomfort:

> At times one feels one hasn't done very well even though other people who don't know it so well think of it as excellent. One also, from time to time, no matter how much of an effort one makes, feels that the complexities of a huge institution like this and the

obstacles to achievement are so big that one is out of breath and hasn't done very much.

(p. 2)

Stanley Cobb started the department with the theme that one can't do psychiatry, especially in a general hospital, unless one has the notion of human beings as persons, not just a theory of personality. The mind is the highest level of total organism function, integrating mental function of the brain, and physical functions.

The department is even more active in nonpsychiatric inpatient service regions of the hospital and is

> still . . . carrying the torch for the human factor in medicine against an awful lot of resistance on the part of our colleagues who think of illness and disease as primarily and perhaps exclusively a matter of organic disturbance. . . . we can be available throughout the hospital as confreres of the medical man, the surgeon, and other specialties in terms of sharing with him his predicaments *vis-à-vis* the disorder facing him, because the patient . . . has always also a personality adaptive problem in mastering his illness and coming to terms with his impaired state. . . . There developed the image of a department of psychiatry in a general hospital as participant caretakers of the patients.

(p. 4–5)

Now the things which I believe we added to this during the last twelve years, more or less successfully, was this. Surely, people have personality structures. . . . But they also come to us almost always in consequence of a recent breakdown of functioning engendered by an overwhelming problem, predicament, or crisis. And out of this state grew another notion, namely, that such overwhelming predicaments such as bereavement are not encountered by one person alone but there are always clusters of people involved, groups of people involved, related to one another in one way or another, and there are different forms of mastery of their problem—one form being illness bringing the patient to the doctor and the other form being impairment of early capacities, or delinquency, or a variety of maladaptive patterns within the community. Therefore, . . . psychiatric attention changed from the individual to a group of people involved in a common problem. And those who succeed in mastering this problem are just as important . . . as those who fail. . . . In this way one becomes interested in pathological structure, social structure, may they be committees in our hospital, may they be neighborhood groups, may they be families, may they be clusters of patients on your wards, and the whole problem of the study of social systems and their buttressing by appropriate social sciences which is the center of the work that you know. . . . So we have arrived then now at a place where a context of biological sciences dealing with a mutual operation of several people involved in a common life basis who have to be meshed in some way to be the common platform on which the department of psychiatry operates as a service, as a teaching facility, as a research facility . . . this spread of orientation is crucial in maintaining one's excellence. . . . Not all [patients encountered] are sick enough to be excluded from society that they have to be for prolonged care in a specialized institution. This latter we cannot do here and it is terribly important that McLean for the wealthy and the State for the poor provide this specialized prolonged service. This is important but it does not constitute psychiatry—not modern psychiatry. Modern psychiatry means effective intervention in clusters of human beings concerned with the predicament which often is signaled by the disturbed state of one person who comes with an entrance ticket to an emergency ward or to a clinic, or to our ward, or to the medical ward for inspection and possible care. Therefore, the acutely disordered state, including the participants' typical stress situations, their patterns of mastery and the physiological, psychological and social components of stress behavior have been the scene of this department.

(pp. 5–7)

By virtue of this orientation we are not anymore doing what we did some 12 years ago. . . . a patient is now enmeshed in a social system, in this case the system of the ward and those who are looking after him, it is indeed bringing the fragments of a social system into this complex social system. . . . [This perspective] dramatically changed our consultation program in redefining the role of the psychiatrist as that of the participant-observer of the ward process, the social nature, the social problems arising, and the way in which certain kinds of patients disturb certain people who look after them and often the reason for the disturbance is not just in the patient but in the doctor or the nurse or the social worker involved and then these people become just as [much] recipients of consultation as the patients themselves. This is again a young field. In some wards it works beautifully. There are bursts of enthusiasm and sometimes it falls flat and we have to collect some of our own casualties in this project because it is a difficult new thing to do but it has brought a framework to psychiatry which is—I like the words "medical anthropology". We like to see people who know something about human nature . . . in terms of the human context, social context and in terms of human organization. If we have a fair amount of knowledge about these, then we can feel we are reasonable graduates of that odd system of psychiatry which operates as we have it today. We hope, of course, that all of you will hopefully carry the torch unless by then you have found this is obsolete and that you have developed a new kind of approach to care. If you can do that, all the more power to you.

(pp. 11–13)

Community Mental Health and Social Action

if you take social content seriously and are really willing to abide by your convictions that each patient arriving in your orbit of power is only a fragment of a disordered social system then your relationship to the participant in this social system is very much enhanced. You will become concerned with the family. . . . You will become concerned with the power structure to which the patient belongs, to those people who control his life. You will become concerned with institutional organization in which he is embedded. You will become concerned with city planning, the housing which he has, the prospects for advancement in his life situation, and so on, and you will not only look common cause in the face and say—isn't it too bad—there you are. But you will decide to work out those psychological, sociological issues in the community which you can use as admonition *vis-à-vis* the power structure decision-makers in the community to tell them perhaps your next decision might be of such order that there will not be so many casualties of a psychiatric kind anyway. And it will be at that point where our intervention of psychological disorders by social means comes about. This is a young field, a field very much attacked by others, a field considered by many as strange and paramedical for medical sciences, but a field which has tremendous enthusiasms in some other places and it has aroused enthusiasm with the head of this hospital—so much so that one feels that the future patterns of patient care and the future role of this hospital in the community must be that of a torch bearer in the crisis approach dealing not only with the casualties but dealing with the power structure, with the political structure, with the planning organization. . . . But this is the direction in which we are set to go and let us hope that the march will go further in this direction.

(pp. 10–11)

Lindemann recognized the realities of difficulties, struggles, and limitations as well as accomplishments. As usual, he tended to keep resentments and criticisms to himself to avoid open conflict—comments in a draft version did not appear in a presentation to the MGH General Executive Committee:[17]

The Psychiatric Service has developed from a small experimental unit for the study of neuroses and psychosomatic disorders into a larger organization . . . to take care of acute mental disturbances . . . to design special rehabilitation programs . . . and to have a systematic program of preventive work in the community.

We are still far short [of] this ideal. Instead of the necessary 70 beds, we have less [*sic*] than 20. . . and no facilities at all in the private pavilion.

The development of psychiatric techniques is very effective in some areas, such as personality appraisal, prognostication, and psychopharmacology, but it is still utterly inadequate in the area of social rehabilitation and in the control of the interpersonal factors of mental disease.

The integration of psychiatric services into the general hospital in this transition from a psychoneuroses unit to a mental disease unit has been difficult and has not been completely successful up to now. There are many complaints about us, and there are marked swings of opinion. There has been excessive admiration and expectations and discarding of our services [altogether]. Points of real advance are in the Emergency Ward, in the community services, in the development of a substantial research program . . . and in our liaison with the suitable parent departments at Harvard University. Points of real weakness are the preoccupation of the senior staff with academic and teaching problems to the detriment of direct services, the absence of any receptiveness [p. 1] for social science considerations among the medical staff, jurisdictional problems about areas of psychiatric participation, and finally certain difficulties in the integration of [a] variety of professional competences within the department itself.

Even in the face of changed dominant ideology and the imminent ending of his official appointments of influence at MGH and HMS, Lindemann hoped and worked for the implementation of his dearly held beliefs. In the last two years of his tenure, he championed the social sciences in medicine and championed community and health orientations. Former MGH general director Nathaniel Faxon gave his response to an article by William Sargent, a well-known critic of psychiatry and psychoanalysis: US psychiatry and especially professors and administrators were bound by Freudian theory, hoping that this diatribe distorted the situation and especially that the MGH was not "as obsessed with psychoanalysis as he states".[18] Lindemann rejoined with a defense of social and psychological psychiatry within an all-inclusive perspective:[19]

I fully agree with you that the picture he draws of the psychiatric teaching faculties in this country, in particular here at Harvard, is utterly distorted.

Sargent never understood Stanley Cobb and his point of view, according to which an integrated anomalistic approach to the study of human behavior is indicated. Such an approach combines observations and experiments at lower levels, for instance at the reflex level, with other observations which we make at the level of personality and social behavior in one coherent picture of human behavior. This has served us well in our clinical work.

A number of the members of our faculty have training in psychoanalysis, which enriches our work but does not limit it. It would be sad, indeed, if a restricted view of human behavior such as proposed by Sargent would become the dominant scientific approach in psychiatry. It would be equally harmful to clinical work and to research in the laboratory.

In answer to a survey of psychiatric inpatient units in general hospitals, MGH psychiatry reported the most frequent diagnoses as psychoneurosis and psychosomatic disorders; the most frequent treatment as individual psychotherapy; and the most therapeutic orientation as psychoanalytic.[20] The psychiatry staff was documented as follows:[21] There were 4273 MGH employees in total; 28 attending psychiatrists, nine visiting psychiatrists, and five consulting psychiatrists; 27 psychiatric residents; six psychologists; ten social workers; seven nurses; and 92 total psychiatry service staff.

Although he communicated with and appealed to people who were continuing in positions of influence (especially Robert L. Ebert, chief of medicine at the MGH and, later, dean of HMS), one must wonder receptive others were to his message.

- He looked to the integration of psychiatry and medicine in broad collaboration: "horizontal extension of the large functional units of the department with a functional division of labor between the chiefs rather than a regional division of labor. . . . This pattern which we are planning for Bowdoin Square might prove useful also for the whole organization of the three units—Massachusetts General Hospital, McLean Hospital and Bowdoin Square as one integrated enterprise".[22] Peter Sifneos outlined developing correlated teaching between medicine and psychiatry during a three-month medical clerkship of the principal clinical year involving medical students, medical house officers, and junior staff of both services.[23] Ebert participated in this joint teaching: He reported the success of his joint visit with Dr. Silverman on the psychiatry ward reported and wanting to review perpetuating "this kind of intimate association between psychiatry and medicine". Lindemann was eager to meet to continue its development.[24]
- Lindemann noted scattered evidence of interest in community medicine and especially respect for John Knowles in this field: He noted that Dr. Robert Glaser, professor of social medicine, was leaving Harvard to be the dean of Stanford Medical School and suggested

John H. Knowles, MD, MGH general director, to fill this academic post to develop leadership in the field of social medicine and administration at MGH, gathering social scientists, public health people, and MGH residents and staff. The appointment of Victor Sidel, MD to the Department of Medicine, focused on "applied social science, . . . was heralded into the hospital in a small way in the Department of Psychiatry[, and] is now widely recognized as a basic field in medical research and medical care"[25] (Burr letter). Knowles "has developed in a most impressive manner from a specialist in clinical medicine to an outstanding spokesman for the various aspects of social medicine and for the application of social science to clinical problems".

Far beyond the problems of hospital administration, he has become a competent leader as resource person for the solution of many problems of community organization, of the economics of medical care and of the social determinants of disease and rehabilitation . . . it is necessary to have a Department of Social and Community Medicine with significant guidance of a man like Dr. Knowles [in order to] become one of this hospital's major contributions to modern medicine (Lawrence letter).[26]

Ebert acknowledged these sentiments, though perhaps without specific commitment.[27]

- On the eve of Lindemann's retirement, he expected a flowering of community medicine dealing with the health of the community and Ebert's commitment to it.[28] Lindemann was happy with the meeting that morning:

I have great confidence now that at Harvard you will be able to do what probably no other university could do, namely, to revolutionize the whole concept of the practice of medicine as it is demanded by the emerging community problems. The medical profession can here feel secure enough with your leadership to remove some of the barriers which separate them from Education and Welfare to make possible a joint approach to the healthy growth of each citizen in his particular culture. I now believe that the terms Social Science in Medicine for the Research branch and Community Medicine for the practice branch of the new enterprise will be engaging labels and imply something of its organization.

In fact, the undoing of Lindemann's social and community psychiatry began in anticipation of his departure. Although he personally continued to champion CMH, professing optimism for its future, there was decreasing mention of these projects in the annual reports of the MGH

Psychiatry Service.[29] Perhaps this was because of Lindemann's absence on consultation and teaching projects, leaving the service administration to those more focused on traditional clinical service, research, and academic administration. Or it may reflect his discouragement about changing entrenched academic and professional vested interests at MGH and HMS (remember his discouragement about the reduction in HMS's teaching of psychiatry) and focusing more on more receptive outside bodies and programs, thereby validating comments that Lindemann shifted his investment away from his administrative responsibility to his department and toward outside interests.

The Psychiatry Service's annual report for 1964 recognized even more directly the impending passing of Lindemann and his CMH perspective rather than touting vigorous CMH programs. It presciently addressed the shift (back) to clinical care of people with mental illness in the absence of Lindemann's drive for CMH and his efforts to continue support of the CMH programs that he would leave behind:[30]

> The year just past was influenced by the impending departure of the Chief of this Service. Efforts were made to firm up the organization of each unit to make sure that adequate support will be available for the senior staff members during the next few years. . . [increase in service demands covered by trainees]. We have confidence that federal support will continue for this program though ultimately the hospital may have to come to terms with the fact that the psychiatric and human services which area component of the care of the sick will demand increasing attention both organizationally and financially.
>
> It also became important to integrate closely the various community services which have developed as part of our community mental health programs. They have been from the beginning a special concern of the present Chief and unified leadership must be provided for the future. They comprise: (1) the Wellesley Human Relations Service under Dr. Robert Bragg; (2) the Center for Community Studies concerned with problems of urban renewal under Dr. Marc Fried; (3) the community services in the alcoholism program under Dr. Morris Chafetz; (4) the community and settlement house program of the Psychiatric Clinic under Dr. Fred Duhl; and (5) the newly created Mental Health Telephone Information Center for Psychosocial Crises under Dr. Fred Frankel. They now work together in a "Division of Community Services" of the Department of Psychiatry. . . Social Work. . . . As the hospital fulfills more and more effectively its role as a community resource, attention to psychosocial crises and assistance in the use of community resources will be an ever growing obligation of the Department of Psychiatry.

There were contrasting signs regarding the future of CMH after Lindemann. Some suggested the continuation of a contracted form:[31] Robert Bragg, MD, from HRS—outside the MGH—inheriting the responsibility for integrating CMH into MGH (after Lindemann's frustrated efforts) and engaging with community social agencies; the Psychiatric Consultation Unit addressing ward staff working with emotionally ill rather than all patients; and the Child Psychiatry Unit recognizing the failure to collaborate with the Children's Medical Service and decreasing consultation with community agencies. Other signs suggested his own department feeling relieved at a beginning shift back from social systems and public health to treatment of people with mental illness:[32]

It was a great satisfaction and a stimulus to the whole staff to be a part of the reorientation of the Massachusetts General Hospital program in the direction of greater emphasis on patient care and on the use of social science approaches for the understanding of illness and recovery. . . . The detailed study of the emotional and social consequences of the relocation of the West End Population has come to its final stage and important new information is emerging concerning the style of life and typical emotional difficulties prevailing in a working class population.

Lindemann's last staff appointments sought institutional support for a group including a large proportion of CMH workers or those associated with CMH projects (see 1964 staff assignments):[33]

Aronson Jason A. (Assistant Psychiatrist)
Benda, Clemens E. (Assistant Psychiatrist)
Bragg R.L. (Assistant to Associate Psychiatrist, Instructor)
Caplan, Gerald (Psychiatrist)
Duhl Frederick (Assistant to Associate Psychiatrist, Instructor)
Dumont Matthew P. (Clinical Assistant in Psychiatry)
Finesinger Abraham L., MD (Assistant in Psychiatry)
Fried, Marc, PhD (Psychologist, Lecturer in Psychology)
Hagopian, Peter. B. (Clinical Associate in Psychiatry, Assistant.in Psychiatry)
Herzan Helen M. (Assistant Psychiatrist, Instructor)
Howe, Louisa P., PhD (Associate Sociologist)
Hutcheson Belendent, MD (Clinical Associate in Psychiatry)
Klein, Donald C., PhD (Associate Psychologist)
Lindemann, Erich, MD (Psych in Chief, Professor of Psychiatry)
Mazer, Milton, MD (Assistant Psychiatrist)
Rosenblith, Judith, PhD (Psychologist, Clinical Associate in Psychology)
Simmons, Alvin J., PhD (Assistant Psychologist)

Stanton Alfred J. (Psychiatrist, Associate Professor),
von Felsinger John, PhD (Psychologist)
Zola, Irving K., PhD (Assistant Sociologist)

Shards of CMH work continued the year after Lindemann's retirement in the form of Bragg's reaching out to outside agencies, Robert Misch's working with student nurses under stress, and Fred Frankel's liaisoning with planning organizations and setting up a school consultation program.[34] However, soon the continued appointment of people—mostly CMH workers—was questioned, whether for lack of enthusiasm for this perspective or because they had drifted away from the MGH—for reasons one might speculate about:[35] "Shouldn't you rescind or leave off the list people who are not connected with us at all? Like: . . . Alvin Simmons . . . John M. von Felsinger, Marc Fried, Judy Rosenblith . . . Gerald Caplan Fred Duhl . . . Edward Mason Milton Mazer B[elenden]. R. Hutcheson. Also JCN [John C. Nemiah] said to check Donald Klein [crossed off staff list] . . . Delete. . . [Matthew] Dumont . . . N[ancy] Mello".

Lindemann prepared for retirement from his major activities. In 1963, he requested leave to spend a month with David Hamburg at the new department of Psychiatry at Stanford University as well as lecturing in Germany and Sweden.[36] He was also asked to advise the Center for Advanced Study in the Behavioral Sciences at Stanford University about John Seeley's application for a year's participation.[37] In 1964, he notified John Knowles of his plan to retire on October 1, 1965. He also wrote to HMS Dean George Packer Berry to look for support in choosing a successor sympathetic to his program:[38]

> As we approach the second last year of my work at Harvard Medical School I would like to suggest strongly that an ad hoc committee to consider the present situation of psychiatry at the Massachusetts General Hospital and to search for my successor be appointed in the near future. . . . The development of our plans for considerable increase in facilities for psychiatric teaching and research . . . as part of the Government Center complex will have to be developed. . . . The new federal funds for the development of community mental health centers including facilities within general hospitals will make it possible to extend our facilities in the Massachusetts General Hospital proper to include considerable enrichment of our psychosomatic program and the care of acute emotional disturbances both in the private and in the general hospital sectors . . . Finally, and perhaps most of all, I would dearly wish to have the decision about the new leadership made while you, yourself are still Dean of the Medical School.

Future plans might include becoming visiting professor at the All-India Institute for Medical Sciences—the Rockefeller Foundation was interested in a one-year or two-year tenure.[39] He also had the opportunity to be a visiting professor without portfolio in the social psychiatry program at Stanford University, "which may continue as long as I wish and am able to make a contribution".[40] He decided to reject the position as superintendent of the Government Center mental health facility on the grounds that this should be an MGH staff member, to ensure close integration with the hospital, and reported his discussion with the commissioner of Mental Health about MGH psychiatry staff members to direct various aspects of the CMHC program (however realistic this might be both in terms of their commitment to CMH and the feasibility of such advance appointments).[41] He wrote John Knowles: "I am most happy that you believe during the terminal year of my work at the Massachusetts General Hospital I might make a meaningful contribution to the reorganization of medical care in the ambulatory program of the hospital".[42] In turn, Lindemann suggested Knowles as professor of social medicine in a department of social science, public welfare, and preventive medicine.[43] He also continued to advocate for psychiatry services at the MGH, reminding Knowles that several beds for acute psychiatry cases and 12 beds for general psychiatry in the Phillips/Baker Houses (the private care areas of the hospital) had been promised when he was first appointed, that his nature had been too gentle to fight for them, and that his successor would demand them.[44]

On June 15, 1965, Lindemann changed his status in the Group for the Advancement of Psychiatry from active to contributing,[45] to the disappointment of its secretary-treasurer, Malcolm J. Farrell, MD:

> It is with much regret that I learned that you wish to become a contributing member. You have made many contributions to GAP, but I realize that the time arrives when one must take stock of his activities. We are reluctantly changing our records accordingly.[46]

He resigned as an active member of the American Neurological Association and was pleased to be elevated to senior member.[47]

Lindemann resigned as MGH chief of the Psychiatry Services as of October 1, 1965,[48] and as HMS professor of psychiatry as of October 31, 1965.[49] A review of his influence on the department would include the following:

- During his chairpersonship, the department enlarged both internally and through affiliations: A federal Department of Health, Education, and Welfare inventory of the Department of Psychiatry at HMS and MGH included the Acute Psychiatric Service, Alcohol Clinic, Child Psychiatry Service, Consultation Service, Hall-Mercer Research Unit, In-Patient Service, Out-Patient Service, Private Psychiatric Service (consultation with other private services), and Wellesley Human

Relations Service—with a total of 41 full time and 55 part time staff, and 39 trainees.[50] Associated facilities included McLean Hospital, Danvers State Hospital, James Jackson Putnam Children's Center, the Psychiatry Service at the Veterans Administration Hospital in Boston, Eastern Middlesex Guidance Center (Reading, Massachusetts), Manchester Children's Aid Society (New Hampshire), and Cambridge Court Clinic.

- He enlarged Cobb's psychiatric consultation service, enriching it with social science (small group and crisis theories), and won the interest of nonpsychiatrists.

- He continued work in biological psychiatry in the Stanly Cobb Laboratories for Psychiatric Research and at the McLean Hospital.

- He raised awareness of social and preventive psychiatry as concerns for general hospitals and medicine in terms of social and community change and demands and awareness of settings such as the HRS, the West End of Boston, and the MGH itself as laboratories for research and foci of service.

- He recognized the hospital emergency ward as the recipient of life crises.

- He saw the alcoholism program as a focus for interest in social psychiatric etiology and treatment factors, rather than solely physiological processes and consequences.

- He increased the department's budget from $200,000 to $1,349,257. From 1954–5 to 1964–5, United States Public Health Service funds increased from $50,000 to $250,000, and all other funding increased from $25,000 to $250,000.[51] Of this, $406,386 (30%) went to CMH activities:[52] CMH psychiatrists received 47,498, CMH psychologists $23,792, CMH social workers $39,176; HRS $48,559; Soviet Psychiatry and Its Context (Jason Aronson) $15,498; Initial Contact, Emotional Crisis, and the Community (Morris Chafetz) $74,468; Alcoholism Treatment and Initial Therapeutic Contact (Chafetz) $8,500; Preventive Intervention in Alcohol-Related Conditions (Morris Chafetz) $74,895; Further Research and Development in Community Mental Health—carry over (Lindemann) $19,000; and Relocation and Mental Health—Adaptation Under Stress (the "West End Study"; Lindemann) $55,000.

- He maintained the affiliation between MGH and HSPH by being a consultant to the HSPH and including Gerald Caplan on the MGH Psychiatry Department's Policy Committee.

- He developed the MGH Mental Health Service as the vehicle for the continuation of research and clinical work relating mental illness and the human environment and the involvement of social scientists in mental health work. He addressed the West End urban renewal program as demonstrating the need for collaboration with community human services organizations in surveying available social and psychological resources and in planning to meet the mental health problems engendered by urban relocation.

Bernard Bandler thought that Lindemann recruited and taught Gerald Caplan and Raquel. Cohen of the HMS Laboratory for Community Psychiatry was a way of perpetuating his program.[53] Lindemann explained to HMS dean George Packer Berry that in light of the search for his successor, he was not recommending changes in the department budget for the next year.[54]

The Harvard University News Office for the Medical Area prepared this review of his tenure even as the MGH an HMS staff held contradictory opinions and "The Petition" was prepared:[55]

An experimental psychiatrist and psychologist, Dr. Erich Lindemann has pioneered studies on how people react to loss and grief and developed a highly original approach to the origin of mental disease in an American community.

Concentrating his research on the application of social science approaches to psychiatric problems, Dr. Lindemann has discovered that an essential component of emotional crises such as bereavement, is the transition which is engendered by the change in the social system. Adapting to the loss of an important other person requires a redefinition and reorganization of a whole profile of roles.

Although one of the first emotional crises studied by Dr. Lindemann was loss and/or grief, his interest in the sociological aspects of psychiatry has been keen throughout the 30 years he has been associated with Harvard and the Massachusetts General Hospital. . . . Dr. Lindemann was responsible for establishing the first community mental health center in the United States, the purpose of which was to study those community conditions conducive (p. 1) to mental breakdown. . . . Dr. Lindemann became head of the West End Research Project . . . a systematic appraisal of the social and psychological stresses involved in relocation.

There were various plans and proposals in what developed into preparation for his post-retirement professional career: Lindemann proposed a six-month sabbatical leave starting 1/1/1963, the first three months as visiting professor at Stanford University, leaving Gardner Quarton as acting chief at MGH.[56] His formal request read:[57] "10. My own original plans for a sabbatical leave had to be abandoned in the face of the many perplexing problems of the last few months. However, I would like to accept the invitation of Stanford University to be guest professor for a six weeks period beginning March 12th and follow this visit by several lectures in Germany and Scandinavia during May . . . and am asking for a leave of absence during that period in the same manner as was granted me for my sojourn to India". He later confirmed his month-long visit to Stanford,[58] including as Visiting professor at Stanford and "the rest being dedicated to completing a monograph on our work in community psychiatry"[59] On 12/3/1962 Lindemann received an appointment as Visiting Professor in the Department of Psychiatry and Behavioral Science for the spring quarter—3/12–4/30/1963.[60] In 1963 he corresponded with David Hamburg, chairperson of Psychiatry at Stanford, about visiting for a seminar on 3/19/1963,[61] a more extensive visit on 9/9/1964, and discussions about future more permanent participation in teaching and practice there (licensure, specific tasks, seminar topics, thesis supervision, and Elizabeth Lindemann's studies).[62] His explanation to HMS Dean Berry outlined a future career for himself:[63] "The purpose of my trip is to work with Professor David Hamburg at Stanford University on the development of a program of social psychiatry in Palo Alto and San Mateo County similar to the program we have developed at the Massachusetts General Hospital, in Wellesley, and in the West End of Boston. I also will have an opportunity to carefully study the operations of this relatively young Department of Psychiatry in connection with the possible development of the much expanded program of our own activities if the new psychiatry unit being planned with Dr. Harry Solomon is to become a reality. . . . I also hope that the period of relative freedom from administrative problems will make it possible for me to finish the book on our work in community psychiatry". He expressed his frank planning for his transition from HMS/MGH, stating that he must make decisions regarding the terminal phase of his administration at MGH:[64] The Rockefeller Foundation proposed that he help develop the psychiatry division of the All-India Institute of Medical Sciences in New Delhi in the fall of 1965.

There also was a proposal from Stanford to develop their social psychiatry resources in the next five to six years. The time spent at Stanford was filled with teaching, planning, and consultation in social and community psychiatry. One especially fruitful site was the San Mateo County Department of Public Health and Welfare, whose chief of the Consultation Service and then Mental Health Services Division was Clarice H. Haylett, MD, wife of Lindemann's supervisee and colleague Warren Vaughan. At MGH, Lindemann had hosted a visit from Howard Gurevitz, MD, assistant program chief, County of San Mateo, Department of Public Health and Welfare, who reported the following:

> Uppermost [in our plans], at this time, is the possibility of establishing a new multi-purpose mental health center providing services to the Northern part of San Mateo County. . . . all facilities, with the

exception of inpatient services, would be included. I have been designated to plan and develop this program. . . . a second aspect of my
trip is to . . . discuss with interested persons the possibility of working with the San Mateo County program . . . North County Mental
Health Center.[65]

Both Elizabeth and Erich Lindemann consulted to this program, and
it produced community mental health consultation programs and
publications.[66]

In 1965, Lindemann's post-retirement positions and activities developed apace: He confirmed being relieved of his HMS and MGH
appointments on October 1, 1965, and his appointment as professor of
psychiatry at the Institute and consulting professor in social psychiatry at
Stanford were confirmed.[67] His appointment as visiting professor at Stanford was acknowledged: "I am very pleased at the prospect . . . particularly because of the need to have someone with your clinical and social
viewpoint in the Department".[68] Herbert Liederman, director of Medical
Student Psychiatric Education at Stanford Medical School, asked Lindemann to discuss medical student education at HMS in a Stanford faculty retreat.[69] A psychiatric resident at Stanford expressed his interest in
working with Lindemann on transcultural psychiatry.[70] Charles Martell
Bryant, MD, of the Consultation Service, Department of Public Health
and Welfare, County of San Mateo, reminisced about "your comments at
the GAP meeting one year ago about the receptivity at Stanford to crises
theory and community mental health concepts".[71] Lindemann wrote in
support of the promotion of Thomas Gonda to the rank of professor
(later department chairperson) in the Stanford Medicals School's Department of Psychiatry, recommending him as strong in clinical teaching and
the administration of a complex program and supportive of the integrity
of basic research (though having done little himself) and in inpatient care
and teaching.[72]

In a parting exchange with Harvard University President Nathan
Pusey, Lindemann thanked him for his appreciation of Lindemann's
work.[73] Perhaps there was a touch of bitterness in Lindemann's memory
of "the intense anxiety at the height of intellectual and scientific struggles
which is so characteristic for work at Harvard" but also unquenched
determination in reporting his plan for further work at Stanford University and the All-India Institute of Medical Sciences in New Delhi and even
persistent hope for appreciation and inclusion at MGH:

> Fortunately I have the assurance of continued contact and exchange
> of ideas with [HMS] Dean [Robert H.] Ebert and with John Nemiah
> at the Massachusetts General Hospital, and thus will continue to
> have a sense of belonging and perhaps to make myself useful at suit-
> able occasions in my new role as emeritus professor.

Upon the appointment of an ad hoc committee to select his successor, he wrote to Leonard Duhl that he hoped Duhl would be a consultant in planning future developments at MGH and the Bowdoin Square mental health center. He noted that John Nemiah, Morris Chafetz, Jack Mendelson, and DMH participants appointed by Harry Solomon would be involved, and he was hopeful of continued involvement: "of course, I will be working closely with them until I leave my present post and will continue to be their consultant as much as they wish me to be afterwards".[74]

Lindemann planned to continue his interest and involvement in Indian psychiatry. In a letter to HMS Dean Berry, he mentioned his interest in visiting Indian medical centers: "If my plan to work in New Delhi part of next year becomes a reality".[75] He corresponded with Dr. John Maier of the Rockefeller Foundation about plans to work in India and with Prof. Satyanand about vising and involving Dr. Kirpal Sigh, who, he felt, was well trained in the social psychiatry approach to psychiatry and CMH.[76]

In light of the sometimes-harsh treatment of Lindemann leading to his retirement, it is relevant to note a letter that Stanley Cobb had sent to Lindemann about this phenomenon:

> P.S. I have a copy of the letter you wrote [HMS professor] Henry Viets. I want to congratulate you on the pleasant send-off you gave him for his retirement. In the past too many men have retired without receiving any kind words and I know that a number of them have resented it.[77]

At the end of Lindemann's tenure, he received recognition from within the MGH:

- Nathan B. Talbot, MD, professor of pediatrics at HMS and chief of the Children's Medical Service at MGH, sometimes had views of social factors in mental health that differed from Lindemann's. Talbot wrote, "Your pioneering work has resulted in establishment of models which will be of tremendous value to those of us who are striving to incorporate knowledge concerning the social aspects of health and disease into medicine".[78]
- John Knowles, MGH general director, recognized the hospital's obstacles to accomplishment in psychiatry:

> I am fully aware that the promise of adequate facilities which was made to you when you came here has never been fulfilled. . . . such facilities should exist and it has become a first order of business in my mind as we look for your successor. . . . We must stick with our plan to alter Warren-Baker 12 for the addition of single and double bed units.[79]

In a more personal vein, he went on:

> you have never failed to place the interests of the department and the hospital ahead of your own—and your many contributions to the advance of American psychiatry have brought honor and distinction to the M.G.H. As important to all of us have been your personal qualities of caring, compassion, good humor and integrity. Certainly the quality of your life has served as inspiration to your students and colleagues.[80]

- Robert H. Jones, MD, Coordinator of Rehabilitation at the MGH, wrote that

> Of all those with whom I have worked for the last six years, I feel I am more indebted to you than any other. Our discussions through the years have been a great interpretive significance and have led to some of my most basic concepts. Your support with Staff and Resident Fellow coverage of the floor has been unique and of more concrete assistance than from any-other quarter. . . . I look forward to my work at Rochester. . . . They even are attuned to your concepts of community mental health and are planning to make a community study of the mental health problem. . . . I wish you well in your retirement plans and sincerely hope that we see each other in the future.[81]

- Even some of his ambivalent department members paid their respects. For example, Fred H. Frankel, MD wrote,

> I have enjoyed immensely the opportunities I have had to sit and talk with you, and can only hope that some of the wisdom and vision so habitually yours will have been communicated to me . . . and hope, too, not to lose contact with you.[82]

- Frances C. Grady, RN, assistant director of the Bulfinch and Vincent Burnham (MGH) Nursing Department sent her good wishes on Lindemann's retirement: "we shall always be grateful to you for your personal interest and support. Your influence has made possible nursing care of the 'whole patient' ".[83]

Recognition came also from outside the MGH:

- HMS Dean Berry wrote to Quigg Newton, president of The Commonwealth Fund, lauding the accomplishments of the Field Training Program of HSPH at the Whittier Street Health Unit of the Boston City Health Department.[84] He appreciated the importance of CMH's pioneering activities in HMS in Dr. Lindemann's department through Lindemann and Gerald Caplan.

- Harvard University President Nathan Marsh Pusey wrote,

> I cannot let the bare vote recording your retirement pass into the chronicles of the University without sending a word of deep appreciation to you for your long and distinguished career. . . . surely your professional colleagues would insist that during your Harvard years you have become a world authority on community mental health, and one whose influence has been widely felt in shifting the emphasis of mental health services from institutional to community care. Further, you have made lasting contributions to the social welfare by your studies of bereavement and of the relationship of normal grieving to depressive illnesses.[85]

- Massachusetts Governor John Volpe thanked him for his service on the Advisory Council for the Massachusetts Mental Health Planning Program and requested that he remain in a standby position for further planning as occasions arise.[86]

The Search for a Successor

Lindemann wrote to HMS Dean George Packer Berry to ask him to initiate the search for his replacement to be involved in planning for the future of his department:[87]

> As we approach the second last year of my work at Harvard Medical School I would like to suggest strongly that an <u>ad hoc</u> committee to consider the present situation of psychiatry at the Massachusetts General Hospital and to search for my successor be appointed in the near future.
>
> This request is due to the following considerations: 1. our plans for considerable increase in facilities . . . as part of the Government Center complex will have to be developed to decision points. . . . By the beginning of the academic year 1965. . . a new professor ought to have an opportunity to participate in these decisions. 2. new federal funds for the development of community mental health centers including facilities within general hospitals. . . . Decisions will have to be made about the configuration and staffing of this new program and again the new professor will be much needed for the development of these plans. . . . 3. I am sure Dr. Robert Ebert would be happy to be able to plan soon in his new program together with a younger man . . . over a longer period of time. 4. Finally, and perhaps most of all, I would dearly wish to have the

decision about the new leadership made while you yourself are still Dean of the Medical School.

(pp. 1–2)

A few months later, Berry announced the formation of an ad hoc committee to select a new MGH chief of psychiatry and HMS professor of psychiatry:[88]

> the time has come to examine the posture of psychiatry at the MGH and to seek Dr. Lindemann's successor. . . . President [of Harvard University Nathan] Pusey has asked me . . . to appoint a joint ad hoc Committee to explore these matters for the Medical School and the MGH. . . . The membership . . . is given below. Dr. George Berry, Dr. Peter Dews [HMS senior psychiatrist], Dr. Jack Ewalt [senior psychiatrist of HMS-affiliated psychiatry departments], Dr. Manfred Karnovsky [HMS Physiology Department chairperson], Dr. Lawrence Kolb [Columbia University College of Physicians and Surgeons chairperson of the Psychiatry Department], Dr. Paul Russell [MGH surgeon], Dr. Nathan Talbot [MGH Chief of the Children's Medical Service], Dr. Robert Ebert [Chief of the MGH Medical Service], chairperson. Dr. John Knowles, General Director of the Massachusetts General Hospital, has been invited to sit with the ad hoc Committee . . . distinguished physicians be sought . . . from outside the Faculty of Medicine to serve as consultants.

In a letter on November 3, 1964, to Lindemann, Robert H. Ebert wanted to discuss problems in the further development of psychiatry at MGH, before the first meeting of the committee.

There were many rumors, suggestions, and candidates regarding Lindemann's successor. One list was as follows:[89]

Doug Bond (+ Helen Cannon Bond)
Geo Engel
John Romano
Ted Lidtz

Bernie Holland Emory (investigator)
Frazer Baylor
Bob Weiss Dartmouth

Brm[?] Bliss Utah
Robin [?Melvin] Sabshin Leston Havens
Lincoln Clark Utah. [former MGH Psychiatry staff] John Nemiah
Charles Rupp (Phila)

Murray ?Galnbsky

Shervert Frazier Texas at Baylor (younger by 10 yrs) Bond
Howard Rome—clinical strengths & good teacher
not an investigator

Millar in Aberdeen [professor of psychiatry, University of Aberdeen,
    Scotland]

Lindemann reviewed with Dean Berry the status and future of the department, and possible successors as chief:[90] He formally requested to be relieved of his position as of October 1, 1965, and requested the appointment of an ad hoc committee to select a successor:

> "I am profoundly grateful for the opportunity I have had to strengthen in some measure the program which Stanley Cobb had developed at the Massachusetts General Hospital and to make a modest contribution towards better appreciation of the psychosocial component of illness throughout the hospital . . . As you know, our department has had particularly cordial relationships here at the Massachusetts General Hospital with Drs. Knowles, Cope, Sweet, Talbot and, of course, Dr. Ebert is in a very special sense sharing our point of view and applying it on a larger scale than I ever dared hope" (p. 1). The leadership of the department could be given to senior members of the department—John Nemiah is a superb teacher and clinician, Frank Ervin is sound in laboratory neurophysiology and clinical work. "In addition, I still believe that Gardner Quarton is one of the best informed and most articulate men in the field of psychiatry theory in this country" (p. 1).

Because Berry asked for other recommendations, Lindemann mentioned Douglas Bond (Western Reserve Medical School), Morris Carstairs (Edinburgh), and Melvin Sabshin (Chicago). Lindemann reminded Berry that David Hamburg, chairperson of the Stanford Medical Center Department of Psychiatry and one of Lindemann's suggestions as his successor, knew the MGH department well[91] (in 1965, Hamburg visited the MGH to explore the Department of Psychiatry.[92]):

> the man most like me in outlook and interest and with a lot more administrative ability is David Hamburg in Stanford but he seems to be determined to stick to the program which he is developing with so much success on the West Coast.
>
> (p. 2)

He discussed this choice with Leonard Duhl, director of the Program Development Branch at NIMH. Lindemann urged support and status for child psychiatry and human development: "this area of psychiatric practice and research seems to me to be central to all the programs in community mental health which the federal government is fostering" (p. 2). In this area, Lindemann mentioned Wells Goodrich at NIMH and Elwin J. Anthony of St. Louis.

Dean Berry supported MGH Psychiatry Department member Gardner Quarton.[93] Lindemann noted that Quarton was at the Center for Advanced Studies in Palo Alto, California (created by Francis O. Schmitt), though he returned to the Boston area (MGH vs. Massachusetts Institute of Technology).[94] Lindemann hosted a lecture by Wells Goodrich, MD, chief of the Child Research Branch of NIMH, and suggested him to Ebert as a successor.[95] There were meetings introducing Douglas Bond to Robert Ebert (MGH chief of medicine), Kurt Isselbacher (chief of gastroenterology), Paul Russell (chief of surgery), Alfred Stanton (psychiatrist-in-chief at McLean Hospital), Francis DeMarneffe (clinical director at McLean Hospital), John H. Knowles (MGH general director), and Howard Hiatt (HMS professor of medicine and physician in chief at the Beth Israel Hospital, Boston), as well as James Dykens (Massachusetts Department of Mental Health), for a perspective on the planned community mental health center to be associated with the MGH.[96]

The search process was difficult and prolonged. Some thought that one contributing factor was the complex relationship of the Harvard Medical School to multiple autonomous teaching hospitals. Another suggestion was the fierce competition among departments at the MGH. Lindemann wrote to David Hamburg,

> You will not be surprised to hear that the ad hoc committee searching for my successor has not come to any conclusions. The negotiations with Douglas Bond seem to be still underway, possibly leading to a reorganization of the whole program here. In the meantime John Nemiah is going to be appointed acting chief of psychiatric service.[97]

Erich Lindemann's Personal Life

People often remember Lindemann's quaint manners and high-pitched voice.[98] Perhaps this contributed to his abiding insecure feeling that the MGH saw him as "that funny little man from Germany". Some used this to bolster their antipathy toward him and his ideas, and others saw the values and convictions behind this.[99]

Impressions of Lindemann as a person varied according to the reporter's degree of contact, sympathy with his ideas, and needs. Jack Ewalt, director of the Joint Commission on Mental Illness and Health, superintendent of the Massachusetts Mental Health Center, and commissioner of the Massachusetts Department of Mental Health,[100] found him warm and giving and a good spontaneous speaker but also shy, hypersensitive to slights and infringements on his territory, and avoidant of controversy (avoiding meetings to solve problems, leaving people angry). He found Lindemann a good administrator, assigning students and faculty to teach psychiatry in the first two years of Harvard Medical School, earning a good reputation for his education programs, and working well with funding from administration sources. He was a good spontaneous speaker—energetic and articulate—though not reliable in keeping commitments. However, he had a reputation for not opening and answering his mail and not allowing others to do so for him.

His wife, Elizabeth B. Lindemann, recognized that "The same sensitivity which allowed him to empathize with others made him vulnerable to hostility and rejection".[101] At times, she insisted that he was responsible and delayed only to think over difficult issues,[102] while at other times, she acknowledged that he carried unanswered mail around and resisted dealing with it. This required people to communicate with him by phone or over lunch.

Lindemann is also remembered as absenting himself from (especially troublesome) meetings with the excuse of ill health. He described recurrent lung problems (perhaps harking back to his siblings' tuberculosis):

> The condition of my chest, bronchiectasis, has gotten a lot worse since a recent cold and a gastro-intestinal infection on top of it which prevented me from attending the recent Macy Conference has put me into a pretty run-down condition. My doctor is very much against my undertaking any major exertions in the next month or so.[103]
>
> My recovery from pneumonitis, which struck me during the holiday period, is annoyingly slow, and my physician has insisted that I give up my plans to travel to Washington at this time.[104]

Lindemann's children felt somewhat left out of the close marital relationship, causing them both to idolize their parents as well as rebel against the disappointing relationship.[105] Lindemann hid his first marriage from his children, not wanting to be reminded of this embarrassing failure. His career limited his time with the children, though he was affectionate and loved to buy trinkets for the family. The struggle with the children's emotional and career problems were an ongoing concern for Lindemann and his wife: At home (as in his professional life), Lindemann did not like conflict and exhibited his rare anger at conflict within the family. His son, Jeffrey, rebelled against control and had an uncontrolled temper, causing Lindemann to cater to him and to participate in terrible battles between them. This cycle of mutually reinforcing aggravation grew: Lindemann found Jeffrey distasteful and showed no affection toward him, further aggravating Jeffrey's feelings of rejection and struggle with self-esteem. He felt unable to live up to his father's accomplishments and expectations and thus took a different career path (most recently theater lighting and building maintenance), further disappointing Lindemann's expectations of a professional upper-middle-class career and perpetuating Jeffrey's feelings of estrangement and failure. Brenda Lindemann more often lived up to Lindemann's expectations and so received more support from him. Her mother was more skeptical about her and waited for proof of achievement before giving appreciation. This left Brenda unsure and unsettled about career and life directions, though successful in caring careers—veterinary nursing, public health education, and tutoring.

Notes

1. Erich Lindemann Retirement Banquet, Anthony's Pier 4 Restaurant, Boston, MA, 9/20/1965. Elizabeth Lindemann files—file #108, Erich Lindemann Collection, David G. Satin, Newton, MA.
2. Dietz, Jean, "Illness, Family Go Together", *The Boston Sunday Globe* 10/3/65, p. A-73. [Elizabeth Lindemann files—file #108, Erich Lindemann Collection, David G. Satin, Newton, MA]
3. Seeley, John R. (chairperson of the Department of Sociology at Brandeis University and later at the Center for Advanced Study in the Behavioral Sciences at Stanford University) letters to Erich and Elizabeth Lindemann 5/14 and 11/5/1965, expressing his appreciation of Lindemann's tribute at his farewell banquet and Seeley's high regard for the Lindemanns. [folder "Correspondence 1965", Box IIIA 1–3, Lindemann Collection, Center for the History of Medicine, Francis A. Countway Library of Medicine, Boston, MA]
4. Petition to the *Ad Hoc* Committee to Recommend a Chief of the Psychiatry Service at the MGH. (?5/21–24/1965). [folders "Massachusetts General Hospital" and "Dean's Office Files", Erich Lindemann Collection, David G. Satin's files, Newton, MA]
5. Friedlich, Allan L., MD, letter to Ebert, Robert, MD (chairperson of the ad hoc committee to choose a successor chief of the Psychiatry Service), 4/13/1965. [Dean's Office files, HMS, Erich Lindemann Collection, Center for the History of Medicine, Francis A. Countway Library of Medicine, Boston, MA]
6. Joint Ad Hoc Committee Appointed to Examine the Posture of Medicine at the Massachusetts General Hospital and to Recommend a Successor to Dr. Walter Bauer; Nomination of Dr. Robert Higgins Ebert as Jackson professor of clinical medicine (University Full-Time) [folder "Ad Hoc Committee on Dr. Ebert", Box IIIA 4 (A-E), Erich Lindemann Collection, Center for the History of Medicine, Francis A. Countway Library of Medicine, Boston, MA]:

> The modern period of medicine at the Massachusetts General Hospital can be said to have begun in 1912 with the appointment of Dr. [David L.] Edsall as Jackson Professor [of Clinical Medicine] and Chief of one the two medical services. . . . Dr. Edsall desired to add to the long-established clinical and teaching skills of the medical staff a third activity, research, in order to bring the problems of patients to the laboratory and insight of science to the bedside.

...

> members of the Surgical Staff of the Massachusetts General Hospital, most of whom agree upon the importance of a primary clinical emphasis in the activities of the Medical Service under the leadership of a mature physician who will have already clearly demonstrated his own interest and ability in research.
>
> (pp. 3, 7)

7. "Minutes Committee on Research 17 December 1957", p. 2. [folder "MGH Committee on Research 1958", Box IIIB1d, Erich Lindemann Collection, Center for the History of Medicine, Francis A. Countway Library of Medicine, Boston, MA]

8. Gifford, Sanford, MD, "Psychoanalytic Emigrees at the MGH in the 1930s and 1940s", lecture at the MGH, 9/20/1983 [Erich Lindemann Collection, David G. Satin files, Newton, MA]; also see White, Benjamin V., *Stanley Cobb: A Builder of the Modern Neurosciences* (Boston, MA: The Francis A. Countway Library of Medicine, 1984) (references to manuscript form).

9. Gifford, Sanford, 9/20/1983, *ibid.*

10. Farrell, Jean, 4/25/1981, *ibid.*

11. Nemiah, John C., MD, "Current Activities and Ideas Concerning the Future of the Psychiatric Service", 11/23/1964, p. 4. [folder "Dr. Ebert Material Nov. 1964", Box IIIA 4 (A-E), Lindemann Collection, Center for the History of Medicine, Francis A. Countway Library of Medicine, Boston, MA]

12. Lamont, John, Letter to Erich Lindemann, 11/19/1964, p. 2. [folder "Dr. Ebert Material Nov. 1964", Box IIIA 4 (A-E), Lindemann Collection, Center for the History of Medicine, Francis A. Countway Library of Medicine, Boston, MA]

13. Ervin, Frank R., MD, "Considerations for Further Development of MGH Psychiatry Department", 10/4/1964. [folder "Dr. Ebert Material Nov. 1964", Box IIIA 4 (A-E), Lindemann Collection, Center for the History of Medicine, Francis A. Countway Library of Medicine, Boston, MA]

14. Mendelson, Jack H., MD, assistant professor of psychiatry, letter to Lindemann, Erich, 11/24/1064, p. 3. [folder "Dr. Ebert Material Nov. 1964", Box IIIA 4 (A-E), Lindemann Collection, Center for the History of Medicine, Francis A. Countway Library of Medicine, Boston, MA]

15. "MGH Dept. of Psychiatry Organization chart 1964–65". [folder "MGH Dept. of Psychiatry Organization chart 1964–65", Box IIIB1a box 1 of 2, Erich Lindemann Collection, Center for the History of Medicine, Francis A. Countway Library of Medicine, Boston, MA]

16. Lindemann, Erich, "The Role of Psychiatry at the M.G.H. 1965". [folder "The Role of Psychiatry at the M.G.H. 1965", Box VII 2, Lindemann Collection, Center for the History of Medicine, Francis A. Countway Library of Medicine, Boston, MA]

17. "G.E.C. Presentation—December 6th, 1961 Rough Draft", pp. 1, 2. [folder "GEC Report by Dr. Lindemann for Dept. of Psychiatry—Dec. 6, 1961", Box IIIB1b box 1 of 2, Erich Lindemann Collection, Center for the History of Medicine, Francis A. Countway Library of Medicine, Boston, MA]

18. Faxon, Nathaniel W., MD, letter to Lindemann, Erich, 6/30/1964. [folder "F Miscellaneous", Box IIIA 4 (F-H), Lindemann Collection, Center for the History of Medicine, Francis A. Countway Library of Medicine, Boston, MA]

19. Lindemann, Erich, letter to Faxon, Nathaniel W., 7/7/1964. [folder "F Miscellaneous", Box IIIA 4 (F-H), Lindemann Collection, Center for the History of Medicine, Francis A. Countway Library of Medicine, Boston, MA]

20. The Medical Care Research Center (St. Louis): "Survey on Psychiatric In-Patient Units in the General Hospital". [folder "M Miscellaneous", Box IIIA 4 (I-Ma), Lindemann Collection, Center for the History of Medicine, Francis A. Countway Library of Medicine, Boston, MA]

21. NIMH survey of psychiatry staff at non-psychiatric hospitals—the MGH, 5/?19/1965. [folder "NIMH", Box IIIA 4 (Mb-O), Erich Lindemann Collection, Center for the History of Medicine, Francis A. Countway Library of Medicine, Boston, MA]

22. Lindemann, Erich, memo to Ebert, Robert L., Chief of the Medical Service at MGH, 1/11/1965, p. 2. [folder "Ebert, Dr. Robert", Box IIIA 4 (A-E), Lindemann Collection, Center for the History of Medicine, Francis A. Countway Library of Medicine, Boston, MA]

23. Sifneos, Peter, memo to Ebert, Robert L., 11/23/1964. [folder "Ebert, Dr. Robert", Box IIIA 4 (A-E), Lindemann Collection, Center for the History of Medicine, Francis A. Countway Library of Medicine, Boston, MA]

24. Ebert, Robert L., and Lindemann, Erich, exchange of memos 4/30 and 5/25/1965. [[folder "Ebert, Dr. Robert", Box IIIA 4 (A-E), Lindemann Collection, Center for the History of Medicine, Francis A. Countway Library of Medicine, Boston, MA]

25. Lindemann, Erich, memo to Ebert, Robert L., 2/24/1965 and letters to Burr, Francis H., and Lawrence, John E. [MGH trustees]. [folder "Ebert, Dr. Robert", Box IIIA 4 (A-E), Lindemann Collection, Center for the History of Medicine, Francis A. Countway Library of Medicine, Boston, MA]

26. Lindemann, Erich, memo to Ebert, Robert L., 2/24/1965 and letters to Burr, Francis H. and Lawrence, John E. [MGH trustees]. [folder "Ebert, Dr. Robert", Box IIIA 4 (A-E), Lindemann Collection, Center for the History of Medicine, Francis A. Countway Library of Medicine, Boston, MA]

27. Ebert, Robert L., memo to Lindemann, Erich, 3/24/1965. [folder "Ebert, Dr. Robert", Box IIIA 4 (A-E), Lindemann Collection, Center for the History of Medicine, Francis A. Countway Library of Medicine, Boston, MA]

28. Lindemann, Erich, memo to Ebert, Robert L., by this time dean of HMS, 9/13/1965. [folder "Ebert, Dr. Robert", Box IIIA 4 (A-E), Lindemann Collection, Center for the History of Medicine, Francis A. Countway Library of Medicine, Boston, MA]

29. [box IIIB1b box 1 of 2, Erich Lindemann Collection, Center for the History of Medicine, Francis A. Countway Library of Medicine, Boston, MA]

30. The Annual Report of the Psychiatric Service for 1964, p. 1. [folder "Annual Report of the Psychiatric for 1964", Box IIIB1b box 1 of 2, Erich Lindemann Collection, Center for the History of Medicine, Francis A. Countway Library of Medicine, Boston, MA.]

31. [folder "Annual Report of Psychiatric Service 1965", Box IIIB1b box 1 of 2, Erich Lindemann Collection, Center for the History of Medicine, Francis A. Countway Library of Medicine, Boston, MA]

> The Annual Report of the Psychiatric Service for 1964: "3) Dr. Robert Bragg has become Director of the Community Psychiatry Unit and of the Wellesley Human Relations Service. It is anticipated that he will coordinate the community psychiatric research and training activities at the Massachusetts General Hospital and will draw them into closer collaboration with the work of the staff at the Wellesley Human Relations Service".
>
> (p. 2)

> "Psychiatric Consultation Unit (Dr. Avery Weisman, Director) . . . It is gradually becoming apparent that a major focus of concern must be on

the emotional environment of the patient as he lives in the hospital, and that a major function of the consulting resident is to work with the nurses and social workers assigned to his ward to help them in a consultative way with providing assistance to those patients with emotional needs".

(p. 6)

[Child Psychiatry Unit (Dr. John Lamont, Director)]. . . . During this period in which the Children's Medical Service has paid increasing attention to psychosocial factors in the patient population and has set up a Behavior Clinic, the role of the Child Psychiatry Unit in consulting with the pediatricians has been somewhat ambiguous, particularly in the minds of the pediatric residents. A policy of offering consultation and service when asked . . . has not been altogether satisfactory . . . and has had to leave many questions of policy unanswered.

Community Psychiatry (Dr. Robert L. Bragg, director) During the Fall Dr. Robert Bragg became Director of Community Psychiatry, thus marking an important step in the increasing commitment of the Psychiatric Service to the study, care and prevention of emotional disturbances in the community for which the Massachusetts General Hospital provides services. It will be the task of Dr. Bragg to work in close cooperation with the other units of the hospital concerned with community care and to coordinate the various community psychiatry oriented activities of the Psychiatry Service itself . . . survey the data collection processes . . . with a view to . . . adapting them for computer processing as a basis for epidemiological studies. Furthermore, with the collaboration of Dr. Fred Frankel, who is spending part of his time as an Assistant to the Commissioner of Mental Health, he has begun to develop a consultation program for social agencies in the town surrounding the hospital. These activities represent the beginning of programs, which, it is hoped will develop over the coming months as a strong but integral part of the total hospital orientation toward providing health facilities and services to the community.

(pp. 11–12)

32. Annual Report of the Psychiatric Service for the year 1963, p. 1. [folder "MGH Annual Report 1963", Box IIIB1b box 1 of 2, Erich Lindemann Collection, Center for the History of Medicine, Francis A. Countway Library of Medicine, Boston, MA]
33. [folder "Annual Report MGH Psych. Service 1964", Box IIIB1b box 1 of 2, Erich Lindemann Collection, Center for the History of Medicine, Francis A. Countway Library of Medicine, Boston, MA]

Massachusetts General Hospital Department of Psychiatry Administration (Erich Lindemann, MD): "MENTAL HEALTH PROGRAM West End Project P.[eter] Sifneos, MD, L.[aura] Morris, M.S.W., Community Mental Health Fellows. . . Mental Health Service G.[erald] Caplan, MD, P.[eter] Sifneos, MD, L.[aura] Morris, M.S.W. . . . Human Relations Service of Wellesley D.[onald] Klein, PhD, H.[elen] Herzan, MD, W.[illiam] Freeman, EdD, M.S.W., C.[lara] Mayo, PhD. . . . Mental Health Consultation to Professional Groups in: Hospitals, Community, Government, and Other Countries E.[rich] Lindemann, MD, G.[erald] Caplan, MD, M.[orris] Chafetz, MD, J.[ason] Aronson, MD

Educational Program Development Community Mental Health Training for Psychiatrists P.[eter] Sifneos, MD, F.[rederick] Duhl, MD, 4 Fellows. . . Psychologists D.[onald] Klein, PhD, C.[lara] Mayo, PhD, 1 Fellow. . . Social Workers W.[illiam] Freeman, EdD, M.S.W., L.[aura] Mlorris, M.S.W., 4 Fellows. . . Seminars on: . . . Social Psychiatry for Residents E.[rich] Lindemann, MD, Personality & Culture J.[ohn] Spiegel, MD.

Research and Development . . . Research in Community Psychiatry <u>Center</u> for Studies in Human Development J.[udith] Rosenblith, PhD, L. Lansky, PhD . . . <u>Center for Community Studies</u> M.[arc] Fried, PhD, E.[dward] Ryan, PhD

34. [folder "Annual Report of Psychiatric Service 10/1/65–9/30/66", Box IIIB1b box 1 of 2, Erich Lindemann Collection, Center for the History of Medicine, Francis A. Countway Library of Medicine, Boston, MA]

The Annual Report of the Psychiatric Service October 1, 1965–September 30, 1966: "7) A Community Psychiatry Unit has been formed within the framework of the Service, and first steps have been taken to try to coordinate the community functions of the Service with those of the rest of the hospital. "

[p. 1].

"7. Community Psychiatry Unit. . . . Dr. Robert L. Bragg . . . has continued his direction of the activities at the Human Relations Service of Wellesley and has made preliminary explorations with the John F. Kennedy Family Service Association in Charlestown and the North Suffolk Mental Hygiene Clinic in East Boston to work out a possible expansion of our training and field stations outside of the hospital. ¶The activities within the hospital were centered in four areas. 1) Dr. Robert Misch [PhD] has been seeing student nurses on a regular basis during stressful periods of transition in the course of their curriculum. 2) A walk-in service for student nurses was initiated . . . 3) A uniform record reporting system has been set up. . . . Department-wide use of the data form has been instituted. 4) Under the guidance of Dr. Fred Frankel, a school consultation program has been set up in the North End. The mental health unit has also been represented at various community group meetings including the professional advisory committee of the Massachusetts Association for Mental Health, the Committee on Psychiatric Needs for the Northeastern Region of Massachusetts, and the Government Mental Health Center Planning Group.

(p. 7)

35. Unsigned and undated, "MGH Appointments 1967–68". [folder "MGH Appointments 1967–68", Box IIIA 4 (Mb-O), Erich Lindemann Collection, Center for the History of Medicine, Francis A. Countway Library of Medicine, Boston, MA]

36. Lindemann, Erich, letter to Knowles, John H., 2/12/11963. [folder "Dr. John Knowles, Medical Director—MGH", Box IIIA 4 (I-Ma), Erich Lindemann Collection, Center for the History of Medicine, Francis A. Countway Library of Medicine, Boston, MA]

37. Lindemann, Erich, letter to Dr. Ralph Tyler, director of the Center, 12/31/1963:

I have known Professor [John, Brandeis Univ] Seeley for about fifteen years and am one of his great admirers. I believe that his profound insight concerning the nature of social processes and his remarkable capacity to make these insights articulate in verbal communication and in written form would promise that he would make a considerable contribution to the Center.

[folder "S Miscellaneous", Box IIIA 4 (P-S), Erich Lindemann Collection, Center for the History of Medicine, Francis A. Countway Library of Medicine, Boston, MA]

38. Lindemann, Erich, letter to Berry, George Packer, 6/122/1964, p. 1.

39. Lindemann, Erich, letter to Leavell, Hugh, 12/28/1964. [folder "L Miscellaneous", Box IIIA 4 (I-Ma), Erich Lindemann Collection, Center for the History of Medicine, Francis A. Countway Library of Medicine, Boston, MA]

40. Lindemann, Erich, letter to Knowles, John H., MGH general director, 10/26/1964. [folder "Dr. John Knowles, Medical Director—MGH", Box IIIA 4 (I-Ma), Lindemann Collection, Center for the History of Medicine, Francis A. Countway Library of Medicine, Boston, MA]; also Lindemann, Erich, 12/28/1964, *ibid.*, p. 2.

41. Lindemann letters to Knowles, 10/26/1964, *ibid.* and 8/2/1965. The people mentioned were Morris Chafetz for administration, John Nemiah for teaching, and Jack Mendelson for research, all to be appointed DMH assistant commissioners. He also appreciated Gardner Quarton (assisting Francis O. Schmitt in the program for the neurosciences) and Frank Ervin (coordinator of the Stanley Cobb Laboratories and a capable neurophysiologist, clinician, and teacher). This appears to be another example of Lindemann's wish for his associates to be committed to CMH, which was out of keeping with their real ideologies and interests.

42. Lindemann, Erich, 10/26/1964, *ibid.*

43. Burr, Francis H., chairperson of the MGH Board of Trustees, to Lindemann, Erich, 3/10/1965, indicating Burr's enthusiasm for the suggestion and offering to support it from behind the scenes. [folder "Dr. John Knowles, Medical Director—MGH", Box IIIA 4 (I-Ma), Erich Lindemann Collection, Center for the History of Medicine, Francis A. Countway Library of Medicine, Boston, MA]

44. Lindemann, Erich, draft of a letter to Knowles, John H., 3/2/1965. [folder "Dr. John Knowles, Medical Director—MGH", Box IIIA 4 (I-Ma), Erich Lindemann Collection, Center for the History of Medicine, Francis A. Countway Library of Medicine, Boston, MA]

45. Circular Letter No. 339 from the Group for the Advancement of Psychiatry. [folder "Group for the Advancement of Psychiatry (GAP) (folder#2)", Box IIIA 4 (F-H), Erich Lindemann Collection, Center for the History of Medicine, Francis A. Countway Library of Medicine, Boston, MA]

46. Farrell, Malcolm J., letter to Lindemann, Erich, 11/18/1964. [folder "Group for the Advancement of Psychiatry (GAP) (folder#1)", Box IIIA 4 (F-H), Lindemann Collection, Center for the History of Medicine, Francis A. Countway Library of Medicine, Boston, MA]

47. Correspondence between Lindemann and Melvin D. Yahr, MD, Secretary of the American Neurological Association, 6/14–25/1965. [folder "Amer. Neurological Assoc.", Box IIIA 4 (A-E), Lindemann Collection, Center for the History of Medicine, Francis A. Countway Library of Medicine, Boston, MA]

48. Meadow, Henry C., associate dean of the HMS letter to Lindemann 8/24/1965. [folder "Correspondence 1965", Box IIIA 1–3]; and Lindemann letter to John H. Knowles, MD, General Director, MGH, 8/6/65. [folder "Dr. John Knowles, Medical Director—MGH", Box IIIA 4 (I-Ma), file#86 Box XII#3, Lindemann Collection, Center for the History of Medicine, Francis A. Countway Library of Medicine, Boston, MA]

    "*Effective October 31, 1965*: Erich Lindemann as Professor of Psychiatry becoming Professor of Psychiatry, *Emeritus*". *Harvard University Gazette* 1/15/1966.

49. Documentation Elizabeth B. Lindemann folder 101 Box XII#3, Lindemann Collection, Center for the History of Medicine, Francis A. Countway Library of Medicine, Boston, MA.

50. Department of Health, Education, and Welfare, U.S. Public Health Service, Inventory of Psychiatric Facility—Department of Psychiatry Harvard Medical School and Massachusetts General Hospital. [folder "Inventory of Psych. Facility", Box IIIA 4 (I-Ma), Lindemann Collection, Center for the History of Medicine, Francis A., Countway Library of Medicine, Boston, MA]

A previous report of staff increase listed the following: psychiatrists, from five full time and six part time to 18 and 22; psychologists, from 1 part time to 12; social workers, from 3 to 12; and the addition of five social scientists. "Developments in the Activities of the Psychiatric Service (Draft—GEC Presentation)". [folder "GEC Report by Dr. Lindemann for Dept. of Psychiatry—Dec. 6, 1961", Box IIIB1b box 1 of 2, Erich Lindemann Collection, Center for the History of Medicine, Francis A. Countway Library of Medicine, Boston, MA]

51. "Psychiatric Research (Total including HMS)". [folder "Psychiatry Service—Misc. + Budgets", Box IIIB1c box 2 of 2, Erich Lindemann Collection, Center for the History of Medicine, Francis A. Countway Library of Medicine, Boston, MA]

52. "Psychiatry Department—Massachusetts General Hospital 1964–65 General Support". [folder "Psychiatry Service—Misc. + Budgets", Box IIIB1c box 2 of 2, Erich Lindemann Collection, Center for the History of Medicine, Francis A. Countway Library of Medicine, Boston, MA]

53. Bandler, Bernard, 11/16/1978, *ibid.*

54. Lindemann letter to Berry, 12/28/1964. [folder "Dean George Packer Berry", Box IIIA 4 (A-E), Lindemann Collection, Center for the History of Medicine, Francis A. Countway Library of Medicine, Boston, MA]

55. "Biographical Sketch" from the Harvard University News office for the Medical Area, 1/1965, p. 2.

56. Lindemann, Erich, letter to Hargreaves, G. Ronald, MD, the Nuffield professor of psychiatry at the University of Leeds, UK. [folder "H Miscellaneous", Box IIIA 4 (F-H), Erich Lindemann Collection, Center for the History of Medicine, Francis A. Countway Library of Medicine, Boston, MA]

57. Lindemann, progress report, 1/30/1963; p. 4. [folder "Dean George Packer Berry", Box IIIA 4 (A-E), Lindemann Collection, Center for the History of Medicine, Francis A. Countway Library of Medicine, Boston, MA]

58. Lindemann letter to Berry, 6/21/1963. [folder "Dean George Packer Berry", Box IIIA 4 (A-E), Lindemann Collection, Center for the History of Medicine, Francis A. Countway Library of Medicine, Boston, MA]

59. Lindemann letter to Berry, 3/6/1962. [folder "Dean George Packer Berry", Box IIIA 4 (A-E), Lindemann Collection, Center for the History of Medicine, Francis A. Countway Library of Medicine, Boston, MA]

60. Letter dated 12/3/1962 to Lindemann. [folder "Correspondence 1962", Box IIIA 1–3, Lindemann Collection, Center for the History of Medicine, Francis A. Countway Library of Medicine, Boston, MA]

61. Lindemann, Erich, letter to Hamburg, David, 3/1/1963. [folder "H Miscellaneous", Box IIIA 4 (F-H), Erich Lindemann Collection, Center for the History of Medicine, Francis A. Countway Library of Medicine, Boston, MA

62. Hamburg, David, MD letter to Lindemann, Erich, 8/24/1964, and Lindemann's notes and correspondence. [folder "H Miscellaneous", Box IIIA 4 (F-H), Erich Lindemann Collection, Center for the History of Medicine, Francis A. Countway Library of Medicine, Boston, MA]

63. Lindemann letter to Berry, 11/2/1963. [folder "Dean George Packer Berry", Box IIIA 4 (A-E), Lindemann Collection, Center for the History of Medicine, Francis A. Countway Library of Medicine, Boston, MA]

64. Lindemann letter to Berry, 10/13/1964. [folder "Dean George Packer Berry", Box IIIA 4 (A-E), Lindemann Collection, Center for the History of Medicine, Francis A. Countway Library of Medicine, Boston, MA]

65. Gurevitz, Howard, letter to Lindemann, Erich, 3/9/1964. [folder "G Miscellaneous", Box IIIA 4 (F-H), Lindemann Collection, Center for the History of Medicine, Francis A. Countway Library of Medicine, Boston, MA]

66. Kazanjian, Vad, Stei, Sherry, and Weinberg, William L., "An Introduction to Mental Health Consultation", *Public Health Monographs* no. 69 (1962). [folder "Kazanjian, Stein, Weinberg An Introd to M.H. Consultation", box Human Relations Service via Elizabeth Lindemann, Erich Lindemann Collection, Francis A. Countway Library of Medicine, Boston, MA]

67. Lindemann letter to Berry, 10/26/1964. [folder "Dean George Packer Berry", Box IIIA 4 (A-E), Lindemann Collection, Center for the History of Medicine, Francis A. Countway Library of Medicine, Boston, MA]

68. Liederman, Herbert, Department of Psychiatry, Stanford University School of Medicine, letter to Lindemann 1/19/1965. [folder "Correspondence 1965", Box IIIA 1–3, Lindemann Collection, Center for the History of Medicine, Francis A. Countway Library of Medicine, Boston, MA]

69. Liederman, Herbert T. letter to Lindemann, 8/16 and 19/1965. [folder "Correspondence 1965", Box IIIA 1–3, Lindemann Collection, Center for the History of Medicine, Francis A. Countway Library of Medicine, Boston, MA]

70. Balbaky, Yasin, MD exchange of letters with Lindemann 7/16,22/1965. [folder "Correspondence 1965", Box IIIA 1–3, Lindemann Collection, Center for the History of Medicine, Francis A. Countway Library of Medicine, Boston, MA]

71. Bryant, Charles Martell letter to Lindemann, 10/27/1964. [folder "B Miscellaneous 2 of 2 file folders", Box IIIA 4 (A-E), Lindemann Collection, Center for the History of Medicine, Francis A. Countway Library of Medicine, Boston, MA]

72. Lindemann correspondence with Prof. John P. Bunker, Department of Anesthesia at Stanford University Medical School, 3/26,4/2/1965. [folder "B Miscellaneous 2 of 2 file folders", Box IIIA 4 (A-E), Lindemann Collection, Center for the History of Medicine, Francis A. Countway Library of Medicine, Boston, MA]

73. Lindemann letter to Nathan Marsh Pusey, 12/15/1965. [folder "Correspondence 1965", Box IIIA 1–3, Lindemann Collection, Center for the History of Medicine, Francis A. Countway Library of Medicine, Boston, MA]

74. Lindemann, Erich, letter to Duhl, Leonard J., 11/7/1964. [folder "Leonard Duhl—NIMH Corr.", Box IIIA 4 (A-E), Lindemann Collection, Center for the History of Medicine, Francis A. Countway Library of Medicine, Boston, MA]

75. Lindemann letter to Berry, 12/21/1964, p. 1. [folder "Dean George Packer Berry", Box IIIA 4 (A-E), Lindemann Collection, Center for the History of Medicine, Francis A. Countway Library of Medicine, Boston, MA]

76. Lindemann letter to Dr. John Maier, 9/3/1965. [folder "Correspondence 1965", Box IIIA 1–3, Lindemann Collection, Center for the History of Medicine, Francis A. Countway Library of Medicine, Boston, MA]

77. Cobb, Stanley letter to Lindemann, 1950. [Box II A&B, folder 1950-Cobb; Lindemann Collection, Center for the History of Medicine, Francis A. Countway Library of Medicine, Boston, MA]

78. Talbot, Nathan B., letter to Lindemann, 1/7/1965. [folder "Correspondence 1965", Box IIIA 1–3, Lindemann Collection, Center for the History of Medicine, Francis A. Countway Library of Medicine, Boston, MA] In 6/12 and

15/1964, letters Lindemann wrote to Talbot: "As you know, I treasure our collaboration", and Talbot responded, "I should also like to take this opportunity to tell you how highly I value the collaborative association which we have developed over the years". [folder "Talbot, Dr. Nathan B"., Box IIIA 4 (T-Z), Erich Lindemann Collection, Center for the History of Medicine, Francis A. Countway Library of Medicine, Boston, MA]

79. Knowles, John H. memo to Lindemann 3/11/1965. [folder "Correspondence 1965", Box IIIA 1–3, Lindemann Collection, Center for the History of Medicine, Francis A. Countway Library of Medicine, Boston, MA]

80. Knowles, John H., MD, general director of the MGH letter to Lindemann. [folder "Correspondence 1965", Box IIIA 1–3, Lindemann Collection, Center for the History of Medicine, Francis A. Countway Library of Medicine, Boston, MA]

81. Jones, Robert H., MD, coordinator of rehabilitation, MGH, letter to Lindemann, Erich, 5/24/1965. [folder "J Miscellaneous", Box IIIA 4 (I-Ma), Lindemann Collection, Center for the History of Medicine, Francis A. Countway Library of Medicine, Boston, MA]

82. Frankel, Fred H. letter t Lindemann, 10/14/1965. [folder "Correspondence 1965", Box IIIA 1–3, Lindemann Collection, Center for the History of Medicine, Francis A. Countway Library of Medicine, Boston, MA]

83. Grady, Frances C., RN, letter to Lindemann, 9/24/1965. [folder "Correspondence 1965", Box IIIA 1–3, Lindemann Collection, Center for the History of Medicine, Francis A. Countway Library of Medicine, Boston, MA]

84. Berry letter to Newton, 12/21/1964. [folder "Dean George Packer Berry", Box IIIA 4 (A-E), Lindemann Collection, Center for the History of Medicine, Francis A. Countway Library of Medicine, Boston, MA]

85. Pusey, Nathan Marsh, letter to Lindemann, 11/3/1965. [folder "Correspondence 1965", Box IIIA 1–3, Lindemann Collection, Center for the History of Medicine, Francis A. Countway Library of Medicine, Boston, MA]

86. Volpe, John, letter to Lindemann, 10/8/1965. [folder "Correspondence 1965", Box IIIA 1–3, Lindemann Collection, Center for the History of Medicine, Francis A. Countway Library of Medicine, Boston, MA]

87. Lindemann, Erich, letter to Berry, George Packer, 6/12/1964. [Dean's Office, Harvard Medical School] Note the juxtaposition of Lindemann's conference with Harry Solomon: Lindemann directly planning for the MGH involvement in the new CMHC, his decision not to accept the position of superintendent of that facility, and his trust in Berry to support his hopes for the future of CMH at HMS and MGH.

88. Berry, George Packer, letter to Ebert, Robert, 10/29/1964. See also Knowles, John H., memo to Lindemann, Erich, 3/18/1965. [folder "Dean's Office, Harvard Medical School". See also folder "Dr. John Knowles, Medical Director—MGH", Box IIIA 4 (I-Ma), Erich Lindemann Collection, Center for the History of Medicine, Francis A. Countway Library of Medicine, Boston, MA] Note that in Knowles's memo Howard Ulfelder, MGH Urology Service, was included as a committee member.

89. Handwritten notes titled Larry Kolb (professor of psychiatry at Columbia College of Physicians and Surgeons). [Dean's Office, HMS]

90. Lindemann letter to Berry, 10/26/1964. [folder "Dean George Packer Berry", Box IIIA 4 (A-E), Lindemann Collection, Center for the History of Medicine, Francis A. Countway Library of Medicine, Boston, MA]

91. Lindemann letter to Berry, 4/9/1965. [folder "Dean George Packer Berry", Box IIIA 4 (A-E), Lindemann Collection, Center for the History of Medicine, Francis A. Countway Library of Medicine, Boston, MA]

92. Lindemann, Erich, memo to Ebert, Robert L., 4/9/1965. [folder "Ebert, Dr. Robert", Box IIIA 4 (A-E), Lindemann Collection, Center for the History of Medicine, Francis A. Countway Library of Medicine, Boston, MA]

93. Berry, George Packer, letter to Cobb, Stanley, 4/21/1965. [folder "Dean George Packer Berry", Box IIIA 4 (A-E), Lindemann Collection, Center for the History of Medicine, Francis A. Countway Library of Medicine, Boston, MA]

94. Lindemann letter to Berry, 1/22/1964. [folder "Dean George Packer Berry", Box IIIA 4 (A-E), Lindemann Collection, Center for the History of Medicine, Francis A. Countway Library of Medicine, Boston, MA]

95. Goodrich, Wells, letter to Lindemann, 9/21/1965. [folder "Correspondence 1965", Box IIIA 1–3, Lindemann Collection, Center for the History of Medicine, Francis A. Countway Library of Medicine, Boston, MA]

96. Lindemann correspondence with Bond and Ebert, 3/15,19/1965. [folder "B Miscellaneous 1 of 2 file folders", Box IIIA 4 (A-E), Lindemann Collection, Center for the History of Medicine, Francis A. Countway Library of Medicine, Boston, MA]

97. Lindemann, Erich, letter to David Hamburg at Stanford University Medical Center, 8/2/1965. [folder "Correspondence—David Hamburg", Box IV 1 + 2, Erich Lindemann Collection, Center for the History of Medicine, Countway Library of Medicine, Boston, MA]

98. White, Benjamin V. (son-in-law of Stanley Cobb and author of Cobb biography), interview by David G. Satin at the Francis A. Countway Library, 12/3/1979.

99. Seeley, John, note to Lindemann at the Space Cadets: "Erich: I think the real truth is that you are a member in some sense of 'a heavenly city' in whose behalf you everywhere intervene. Why not see it so? define the city? rejoice in it? Jack Seeley". [folder "Correspondence 1961", Box IIIA 1–3, Lindemann Collection, Center for the History of Medicine, Francis A. Countway Library of Medicine, Boston, MA]

100. Ewalt, Jack, 1/26/1979, *ibid.*

101. Lindemann, Elizabeth B., "In Honor of Erich Lindemann", *American Journal of Community Psychology* 12 no. 5: 513, 536 (1984) [folder "Kelly, James G"., David G. Satin files, Newton, MA]

102. Lindemann, Elizabeth B., 8/23 and 11/29/1998, *ibid.*

103. Lindemann, Erich, letter to Vestrmark, Seymour D., NIMH, 11/2/1956. [folder "NIMH-Misc. Material 1956–1958", Box IIIA6 Da GAP, Erich Lindemann Collection, Center for the History of Medicine, Francis A. Countway Library of Medicine, Boston, MA]

104. Lindemann, Erich, letter to Balester, Raymond J., PhD, chief, Pilot and Special Grants Section, Training Branch, NIMH, 1/14/1964. [folder "Jan. '64-Subcom on Pilot and Public Health Progs, Bethesda, MD-NIMH", Box IIIA6 Da GAP, Erich Lindemann Collection, Center for the History of Medicine, Francis A. Countway Library of Medicine, Boston, MA]

105. Lindemann, Brenda: Erich Lindemann's daughter and community health educator. Interviews 11/22/1978–10/1998, and later. Insights into Lindemann and his home life. [caddy 4, box 4, X, Lindemann Collection, Center for the History of Medicine, Francis A. Countway Library of Medicine, Boston, MA]

Conclusion

This period included the full flowering of CMH and social psychiatry and of the responses and counterreactions they engendered. This turning point in the cycle of psychiatric ideology is remarkably vivid and compressed in a relatively short period of time despite the major forces involved in federal and state government, contemporary social movements, professional bodies, and health institutions. The Boston area, Harvard University, Harvard Medical School, the Massachusetts General Hospital, and Erich Lindemann are exemplars of this process.

Many programs and organizations addressed social and community psychiatry as a major new force and perspective, encouraged by massive policy and financial support by federal and state governments. We are reminded that historical eras are not composed of homogenous ideologies, agents, and programs that result in clear interactions and outcomes. All is heterogeneous, including not only new departures but also the continuation of old structure, and active agents motivated by all variants of these, though some ideologies, programs, and agents may predominate and characterize the era. This was true of the era of social and community psychiatry: The history presented here records the heterogeneity in theory, goals, practices, and relationships in the social ideology, social psychiatry, and CMH. Harvard University and its elements adopted this zeitgeist as policy and implemented it through appointments—including that of Erich Lindemann. Lindemann saw this as the inevitable direction of history and the opportunity to realize his lifelong mission to change medicine into a social and community form.

Lindemann was clearly dedicated to a social ideology and to social and community psychiatry. He was consistent, indefatigable, and loyal to this cause despite the obstacles, disparagement, and rejections. This may well have stemmed from his early life experience of limitations and disfavor and from his maternal grandfather's gift of missionary zeal for fighting an unjust authority to win righteous change. The differences in reception and success in various portions of Lindemann's career were not due to changes in his belief and effort but rather due to changes in the contemporary ideology and consequential reactions of others and material support.

Social ideology and medical and psychiatric programs motivated by it were met with discomfort and skepticism in many quarters, and they galvanized disapproval and resistance in some. Conflict was sharp in the Joint Commission on Mental Illness and Health, academic institutions, the MGH, German universities such as Heidelberg and Tübingen, the great social policies such as the War on Poverty and The Great Society, and the civil rights and anti-Vietnam movements. There was much heterogeneity in theory, goals, practices, and relationships in the counterreaction too. The result was an intense struggle that limited the implementation of social and community psychiatry (and medicine and social policy). The consequences to those committed emotionally as well as intellectually to the social ideology and programs resulted in many cases of disappointment, disillusionment, and the abandonment of this belief—there were outstanding casualties. In the next chapters, we will observe the legacy of social and community ideas and programs.

At the end of this period, the dominant ideology had shifted from social to biological. The focus was on biological processes without emotional meaning; the individual without the complications of groups and populations; and avoiding the slings and arrows of social and political process. Often there was a vehement repudiation of the social ideology, programs motivated by it, and its adherents. Proponents of social and community psychiatry found themselves either stranded on inhospitable shoals or confined to islands of limited programs struggling for survival and adaptation to a changed climate of acceptance and resources.

The cycle of ideology had shifted to the next phase.

Photographs

Figure 1 Oliver Cope, MD, Massachusetts General Hospital Surgery, 1965 [courtesy Lindemann Estate]

Figure 2 Leonard J. Duhl, MD, National Institute of Mental Health [courtesy Lindemann Estate]

Figure 3 Erich Lindemann and Col. Kirpal Singh, Poona, India, 1960 [courtesy Lindemann Estate]

Figure 4 Erich Lindemann lecturing, Suicide Prevention Center, 1963 [courtesy Lindemann Estate]

Figure 5 Elizabeth B. Lindemann, MSW [courtesy Lindemann Estate]

Figure 6 Lindemann vacation home, Plainfield, VT [courtesy Lindemann Estate]

Figure 7 Lindemann retreat at Plainfield, VT [courtesy Lindemann Estate]

Figure 8 Erich Lindemann at the piano with sister Gertrud at Sister Margareta's home, 1956 [courtesy Lindemann Estate]

Appendix
Informants Interviewed

Interviewed by David G. Satin, MD

1. Adler, Gerald, chairperson, Psychiatry Department, Tufts Medical School, Boston, MA, 3/15,22/82
2. Almond, Richard and Barbara, Department of Psychiatry, Stanford Medical Center, Stanford University, Palo Alto, CA, 12/19/79
3. Astrachan, Boris, member, Department of Psychiatry, Yale University Medicine and Connecticut Mental Health Center, New, New Haven, CT, 7/22/82
4. Bandler, Bernard, chairperson, Division of Psychiatry, Boston University School of Medicine, MA, 8/11,11/16/78
5. Bandler, Louise, chief psychiatry social worker, Psychiatry Service, Massachusetts General Hospital, Boston, MA, 8/11/78
6. Batson, Ruth, director, Consultation and Education Service, Boston University Community Mental Health Center, Boston, MA, 1/5/79
7. Bernard, Viola, chief, Division of Community Mental Health, College of Physicians and Surgeons, Columbia University, New York, NY, 4/26/79
8. Berry, George Packer, emeritus dean, Harvard Medical School, Boston, MA, 11/2/79
9. Blum, Henrik, consultant to the Psychiatry Service, Massachusetts General Hospital, Boston, MA, 3/23/79
10. Board of Directors, Human Relations Service of Wellesley, Inc., Wellesley, MA, 3/18/82
11. Bragg, Robert, director, Human Relations Service of Wellesley, Wellesley, MA, 7/13/79
12. Brines, John K., board of directors member, Wellesley Human Relations Service, Wellesley, MA, 12/28/78
13. Butler, Allen, chief, Pediatrics Service, Massachusetts General Hospital and Professor of Pediatrics, Harvard Medical School, Boston, MA, 12/8/78
14. Caplan, Lee, social worker, Student Health Service, Stanford Medical Center, Stanford University, Palo Alto, CA, 12/79

15. Clark, Eleanor, former chief social worker, Psychiatry Service, Massachusetts General Hospital, Boston, MA, 7/14/78

16. Eulau, Cleo, chief social worker, Child Psychiatry Service, Department of Psychiatry, Stanford Medical Center, Stanford University, Palo Alto, CA, 12/19/79

17. Coffey, Hugh and Franchon, group trainer and researcher (respectively), Wellesley Human Relations Service, Wellesley, MA, 12/79

18. Cohen, Sanford I., chairperson, Division of Psychiatry, Boston University School of Medicine, Boston, MA, 12/1/78

19. Cope, Oliver, Surgical Service, Massachusetts General Hospital and Professor of Surgery, Harvard Medical School, Boston, MA, 11/21/78

20. Crockett, David, assistant to the general director, Massachusetts General Hospital, Boston, MA, 10/17/78

21. Daniels, David, Department of Psychiatry, Stanford Medical Center, Stanford University, Palo Alto, CA, 12/20/79

22. Dawes, Lydia, staff member, Wellesley Human Relations Service, Wellesley, MA, 6/5/79

23. Deutsch, Helene, training analyst, Boston Psychoanalytic Society and Institute, Boston, MA, 10/27/78

24. Dörner, Klaus, Leitender Arzt, Westfalisches Landeskrankenhaus, West Germany, 10/15/84

25. Dorosin, David, Department of Psychiatry, Stanford Medical Center, Stanford University, Palo Alto, CA, 12/17/79

26. Duffy, Mark, archivist, Episcopal Diocese of Massachusetts, 1/27/82

27. Duhl, Leonard, former special assistant and director, Special Committee on Social and Physical Environment Variables as Determinants of Mental Health, Office of Planning, National Institute of Mental Health, National Institutes of Health, US Public Health Service, Department of Health, Education and Welfare, Washington, DC, 6/22/74, 4/2,12/17/79, 8/16/07

28. Eisenberg, Leon, chief, Psychiatry Service, Massachusetts General Hospital, Boston, MA 11/27/78

29. Ewalt, Jack, director, Joint Commission on Mental Illness and Health and Commissioner of Mental Health, Commonwealth of Massachusetts, Boston, MA, 1/26/79

30. Farrell, Jean, administrative assistant to Erich Lindemann, Psychiatry Service, Massachusetts General Hospital, Boston, MA, 8/22/78

31. Frankel, Fred, Psychiatry Service, Massachusetts General Hospital, Boston, MA, 11/24/78

32. Fried, Marc, director, Center for Community Studies and Director, Institute of Human Sciences, Department of Psychology, Boston College, Newton, MA, 11/16/79

33. Gifford, George, Harvard Medical School, Boston, MA, 1/9/79

34. Gifford, Sanford, librarian, Boston Psychoanalytic Society, Department of Psychiatry, Peter Bent Brigham Hospital, Boston, MA 1/16,3/29/79

35. Glaser, Robert, medical student and associate dean, Harvard Medical School, Boston, MA and Dean, Stanford University, Palo Alto, CA, 12/18/79

36. Gonda, Thomas, chairperson, Department of Psychiatry, Stanford Medical Center, Stanford University, Palo Alto, CA, 12/17/79

37. Hackett, Thomas, chief of the Psychiatric Service, Massachusetts General Hospital, Boston, MA 11/30/78

38. Häfner, Heinz, director, Zentalinstitut Seelisches Gesundheit, Mannheim, West Germany, 10/26/84

39. Hall, Elizabeth Cobb, wife of Stanley Cobb, late chief of the Psychiatry Service, Massachusetts General Hospital, Boston, MA, 6/6/79

40. Hamberg, Beatrix, Department of Psychiatry, Stanford Medical Center, Stanford University, Palo Alto, CA, 1/26/79

41. Hamburg, David, chairperson, Stanford Medical Center, Department of Psychiatry, Stanford University, Palo Alto, CA, 1/26/79

42. Haylett, Clarice, public health officer, San Mateo County Health Department, San Mateo, CA, 12/17/79

43. Hilgard, Josephine, Department of Psychiatry, Stanford Medical Center, Stanford University, Palo Alto, CA, 12/18/79

44. Hoffmann, Ulrich, Aktien Psychisch Kranke, Bonn, West Germany, 10/22/8

45. Janzarik, Werner, professor, Psychiatrische Klinik, Universität Heidelberg, West Germany, 10/29/84

46. Katchadourian, Herant, Department of Psychiatry, Stanford Medical Center, Stanford University, Palo Alto, CA, 2/19/79

47. Kaufmann, Franz Xavier, professor of sociology, Universität Bielefeld, West Germany, 10/15/84

48. Kelly, James G., Psychiatry Service, Massachusetts General Hospital, Boston, MA, 4/29/83

49. Klein, Donald C., emeritus executive director, Wellesley Human Relations Service, Wellesley, MA 11/3/78

50. Klerman, Gerald, emeritus superintendent, Erich Lindemann Mental Health Center, Boston, MA, 1/26/79

51. Knapp, Peter, Division of Psychiatry, Boston University School of Medicine, Boston, MA, 6/12/81

52. Kraus, Alfred, Psychiatrische Klinik, Universität Heidelberg, West Germany, 10/29/84

53. Kulenkampff, Caspar, Aktien Psychisch Kranke, Bonn, West Germany, 10/22/84

54. Lazare, Aaron, director, In-Patient Unit and Day Hospital, Connecticut Mental Health Center, New Haven, CT and Psychiatry Service, Massachusetts General Hospital, Boston, MA, 1/20/81

55. Liederman, Gloria, Department of Psychiatry, Stanford Medical Center, Stanford University, Palo Alto, CA, 12/18/79

56. Liederman, Herbert, Psychiatry Service, Massachusetts General Hospital, Boston, MA and Department of Psychiatry, Stanford Medical Center, Stanford University, Palo Alto, CA, 12/18/79

57. Lindemann, Brenda, daughter of Erich Lindemann, 11/22/78

58. Lindemann, Elizabeth Brainerd, wife and colleague of Erich Lindemann and social worker, Wellesley Human Relations Service, Wellesley, MA and social work consultant, San Mateo County Health Department, CA, 12/7/77, 3,4/17,6/27,7/14,8/22,10/?,11/?,. 9/9/78, 8,10/4/79, 11/18/80,12/6/85, 8/14,23,11/29/98, 8/14/05, 8/22/06

59. Lindemann, Gertrude, sister of Erich Lindemann, 10/10,11/84, 5/1,2/88

60. Lindemann, Jeffery, son of Erich Lindemann, 10/4/79

61. Malamud, William I., Division of Psychiatry, Boston University School of Medicine, Boston, MA, 12/15/80, 2/2/81

62. Malamud, William, Sr., Iowa Psychopathic Hospital, Des Moines, IA, and chairperson, Division of Psychiatry, Boston University School of Medicine, Boston, MA, 10/25/79

63. Mayo, Clara, psychologist and researcher, Wellesley Human Relations Service, Wellesley, MA, 9/29/78

64. Meyn, M. Christa, minister, Ministerium Jugend-Familie-Gesundheit, Bonn, West Germany, 10/22/84

65. Morris, Laura, social worker, Mental Health Service, Psychiatry Service, Massachusetts General Hospital, Boston, MA 11/19/79

66. Mundt, Christoph, Psychiatrische Klinik, Universität Heidelberg, West Germany, 10/29/84

67. Myerson, Paul, chairperson, Department of Psychiatry, Tufts Medical School, Boston, MA, 6/19/81

68. Nemiah, John, staff member and acting chief, Psychiatry Service, Massachusetts General Hospital, Boston, MA, 9/21/78

69. Neumann, Ellsworth, associate director, Massachusetts General Hospital, Boston, MA, 4/27/79

70. Newman, Henry, Department of Psychology and Department of Social Relations, Harvard University, 1/20/79

71. Parker, Franklin, board of directors member, Wellesley Human Relations Service, Wellesley, MA, 11/17/78

72. Parsons, Talcott, chairperson, Department of Social Relations, Harvard University, Cambridge, MA, 6/29/78

73. Paul, Benjamin, anthropologist, Department of Social Relations, Harvard University and Harvard School of Public Health, Boston, MA, 12/18/79

74. Plog, Ursula, Department of Social Psychiatry, Freie Universität Berlin, West Germany, 10/11/84

75. Pörksen, Niels, Univesität Heiderlberg and Leitende Arzt, Fachbericht Psychiatrie, von Bodelschwinghsche Alstalten Bethel, Serepta und Nazareth, Bielefeld, West Germany 9/9/78, 10/3,13/84, 10/3/04

76. Randolph, Peter, superintendent, Bay Cove Mental Health Center, Boston, MA, 6/26/81

77. Reider, Norman, Psychiatry Department, Mount Zion Hospital. San Francisco, CA 7/86

78. Ryan, William, Connecticut Community Mental Health Center, New Haven, CT, 12/14/79

79. Schmidt, Wolfram, Psychiatrische Klinik, Universität Heidelberg, West Germany, 10/29/84

80. Schmitt, Francis O., trustee, Massachusetts General Hospital, Boston, MA, Director, Neurosciences Research Foundation, Massachusetts Institute of Technology, Cambridge, MA, 4/3/79

81. Schneider, Hartmut, Social Psychiatry Department, Zentralinstitut Seelisches Gesundheit, Mannheim, West Germany, 10/26/84

82. Seeley, John, Special Committee on Social and Physical Environment Variables as Determinants of Mental Health, Office of Planning, National Institute of Mental Health, National Institutes of Health, US Public Health Service, Department of Health, Education and Welfare, Washington, DC, 4/12/79

83. Shader, Richard, chairperson, Department of Psychiatry, Tufts Medical School, Boston, MA, 1/29/82

84. Shapiro, Leon, Department of Psychiatry, Tufts Medical School, Superintendent, Massachusetts Mental Health Center, Boston, MA, 6/11/81

85. Shore, Miles, superintendent, Bay Cove Mental Health Center, Boston, MA, 8/6/81

86. Siegel, Alberta, professor of psychology, Department of Psychiatry, Stanford Medical Center, Stanford University, Palo Alto, CA, 12/20/79

87. Sifneos, Peter, Psychiatry Service, Massachusetts General Hospital, Boston, MA, 10/13,11/10/78

88. Snyder, Benson, Massachusetts Institute of Technology, Cambridge, MA, 6/16/78

89. Solomon, Harry C., superintendent, Boston Psychopathic Hospital and Commissioner of Mental Health, Commonwealth of Massachusetts, Boston, MA, 6/22/78

90. Stoeckle, John D., chief of the Medical Outpatient Department, Massachusetts General Hospital, Boston, MA, 2/27/03

91. Stunkard, Albert J., chairperson, Department of Psychiatry, Stanford Medical Center, Stanford University, Palo Alto, CA, 2/15/84

92. Vaughan, Warren, Division of Mental Hygiene, Department of Mental Health, Commonwealth of Massachusetts, Boston, MA, 12/16/79

93. Von Baeyer, Walter Ritter, professor, Psychiatrische Klinik, Universität Heidelberg, West Germany, 10/30/84
94. Von Felsinger, John H., Psychiatry Service, Massachusetts General Hospital, Boston, MA and Department of Psychology, Boston College, Newton, MA, 9/8/78
95. Von Ferber, Christian, professor of sociology, Universität Düsseldorf, West Germany, 10/16/84
96. Wallace, John, board of directors member, Wellesley Human Relations Service, Wellesley, MA, 12/12/78
97. Wanta, Lorna Doone, executive assistant, Psychiatry Service, Massachusetts General Hospital, Boston, MA, 11/16/84
98. Webber, William, psychiatrist, Department of Psychiatry, Stanford Medical Center, Stanford University, Palo Alto, CA, 12/79
99. White, Benjamin, biographer of Stanley Cobb, late Chief, Psychiatric Service, Massachusetts General Hospital, Boston, MA 12/3/79
100. White, Robert W., Department of Social Relations, Harvard University, Cambridge, MA, 11/24/78

Interviewed by Leonard Duhl, MD

1. Lindemann, Erich, 6/8,22; 7/6,13; 8/6/74
2. Lindemann, Erich; Seeley, John, 7/15/74
3. Lindemann, Erich; Seeley, John; Lindemann, Elizabeth Lindemann, 6/15/74
4. Lindemann, Erich; Lindemann, Elizabeth Lindemann, 7/30/74
5. Duhl, Leonard, former special assistant and director, Special Committee on Social and Physical Environment Variables as Determinants of Mental Health, Office of Planning, National Institute of Mental Health, National Institutes of Health, US Public Health Service, Department of Health, Education and Welfare, Washington, DC, 6/6/74

Index

Note: Numbers in *italics* indicate a figure.